BLACKSTONE'S

CRIMINAL PRACTICE

BLACKSTONE'S

CRIMINAL PRACTICE

2012

SUPPLEMENT 1

GENERAL EDITORS

THE RIGHT HONOURABLE LORD JUSTICE HOOPER

DAVID ORMEROD

LAW COMMISSIONER, BARRISTER, BENCHER OF MIDDLE TEMPLE,
PROFESSOR OF CRIMINAL JUSTICE, QUEEN MARY,
UNIVERSITY OF LONDON

FOUNDING EDITOR

HHJ PETER MURPHY

CONSULTANT EDITOR

HHJ JOHN PHILLIPS CBE

CONTRIBUTORS

DUNCAN ATKINSON, ALEX BAILIN QC, DIANE BIRCH, ED CAPE,
ANAND DOOBAY, RUDI FORTSON QC, MICHAEL HIRST,
LAURA C. H. HOYANO, PETER HUNGERFORD-WELCH,
ADRIAN KEANE, ANDREW KEOGH, MICHAEL LEREGO QC,
RICHARD MCMAHON QC, VALSAMIS MITSILEGAS, TIM MOLONEY QC,
STEPHEN PARKINSON, DUNCAN PENNY, AMANDA PINTO QC,
EDWARD REES QC, HOWARD RIDDLE, HHJ PETER ROOK QC,
MAYA SIKAND, RICHARD D. TAYLOR,
MARK TOPPING, MARTIN WASIK CBE

OXFORD
UNIVERSITY PRESS

OXFORD
UNIVERSITY PRESS

Great Clarendon Street, Oxford OX2 6DP

Oxford University Press is a department of the University of Oxford.
It furthers the University's objective of excellence in research, scholarship,
and education by publishing worldwide in

Oxford New York

Auckland Cape Town Dar es Salaam Hong Kong Karachi
Kuala Lumpur Madrid Melbourne Mexico City Nairobi
New Delhi Shanghai Taipei Toronto

With offices in

Argentina Austria Brazil Chile Czech Republic France Greece
Guatemala Hungary Italy Japan Poland Portugal Singapore
South Korea Switzerland Thailand Turkey Ukraine Vietnam

Oxford is a registered trade mark of Oxford University Press
in the UK and in certain other countries

Published in the United States
by Oxford University Press Inc., New York

First published 2011

British Library Cataloguing in Publication Data
Data available

Typeset by Cenveo, Bangalore, India
Printed in Great Britain
on acid-free paper by
Ashford Colour Press Ltd,
Gosport, Hampshire

ISBN 978–0–19–969441–9

1 3 5 7 9 10 8 6 4 2

Introduction

This supplement is the first of three cumulative updating supplements to *Blackstone's Criminal Practice 2012*.

This supplement contains the complete text of the Criminal Procedure Rules 2011 and the Sentencing Guidelines as at 1st August 2011. David Ormerod is now the Criminal Law Commissioner for England and Wales, but nothing in this work should be taken as representing the views of the Law Commission unless expressly stated to do so.

Please visit the *Blackstone's Criminal Practice 2012* companion website at www.oup.com/blackstones/criminal for free online monthly updates, and an updated version of the Criminal Practice Rules 2011, taking in any amendments to the rules in the course of the practice year. You may also register to receive the *Blackstone's Criminal Practice Bulletin*, a free quarterly newsletter. If you have any queries, please contact blackstonescriminal@oup.com.

Contents

Table of Cases

Table of Statutes

Table of Statutory Instruments

Table of International Treaties and Conventions and other Legal Instruments

Table of European Legislation

Treaties

CRIMINAL PROCEDURE RULES 2011
(SI 2011 No. 1709)

Criminal Procedure Rules 2011 (SI 2011 No. 1709)

Part 1 The Overriding Objective

The overriding objective R-1

1.1 (1) The overriding objective of this new code is that criminal cases be dealt with justly.
(2) Dealing with a criminal case justly includes—
(a) acquitting the innocent and convicting the guilty;
(b) dealing with the prosecution and the defence fairly;
(c) recognising the rights of a defendant, particularly those under Article 6 of the European Convention on Human Rights;
(d) respecting the interests of witnesses, victims and jurors and keeping them informed of the progress of the case;
(e) dealing with the case efficiently and expeditiously;
(f) ensuring that appropriate information is available to the court when bail and sentence are considered; and
(g) dealing with the case in ways that take into account—
(i) the gravity of the offence alleged,
(ii) the complexity of what is in issue,
(iii) the severity of the consequences for the defendant and others affected, and
(iv) the needs of other cases.

The duty of the participants in a criminal case R-2

1.2 (1) Each participant, in the conduct of each case, must—
(a) prepare and conduct the case in accordance with the overriding objective;
(b) comply with these Rules, practice directions and directions made by the court; and
(c) at once inform the court and all parties of any significant failure (whether or not that participant is responsible for that failure) to take any procedural step required by these Rules, any practice direction or any direction of the court. A failure is significant if it might hinder the court in furthering the overriding objective.
(2) Anyone involved in any way with a criminal case is a participant in its conduct for the purposes of this rule.

The application by the court of the overriding objective R-3

1.3 The court must further the overriding objective in particular when—
(a) exercising any power given to it by legislation (including these Rules);
(b) applying any practice direction; or
(c) interpreting any rule or practice direction.

Part 2 Understanding and Applying the Rules

When the Rules apply R-4

2.1 (1) In general, the Criminal Procedure Rules apply—
(a) in all criminal cases in magistrates' courts and in the Crown Court; and
(b) in all cases in the criminal division of the Court of Appeal.
(2) If a rule applies only in one or two of those courts, the rule makes that clear.
(3) The Rules apply on and after 3rd October, 2011, but unless the court otherwise directs they do not affect a right or duty existing under The Criminal Procedure Rules 2010.

Definitions R-5

2.2 (1) In these Rules, unless the context makes it clear that something different is meant:
'business day' means any day except Saturday, Sunday, Christmas Day, Boxing Day, Good Friday, Easter Monday or a bank holiday;
'court' means a tribunal with jurisdiction over criminal cases. It includes a judge, recorder, District Judge (Magistrates' Courts), lay justice and, when exercising their judicial powers, the Registrar of Criminal Appeals, a justices' clerk or assistant clerk;
'court officer' means the appropriate member of the staff of a court;

'justices' legal adviser' means a justices' clerk or an assistant to a justices' clerk;
'live link' means an arrangement by which a person can see and hear, and be seen and heard by, the court when that person is not in court;
'Practice Direction' means the Lord Chief Justice's Consolidated Criminal Practice Direction, as amended, and 'Criminal Costs Practice Direction' means the Lord Chief Justice's Practice Direction (Costs in Criminal Proceedings), as amended;
'public interest ruling' means a ruling about whether it is in the public interest to disclose prosecution material under sections 3(6), 7A(8) or 8(5) of the Criminal Procedure and Investigations Act 1996; and
'Registrar' means the Registrar of Criminal Appeals or a court officer acting with the Registrar's authority.

(2) Definitions of some other expressions are in the rules in which they apply.

R-6 **References to Acts of Parliament and to Statutory Instruments**

2.3 In these Rules, where a rule refers to an Act of Parliament or to subordinate legislation by title and year, subsequent references to that Act or to that legislation in the rule are shortened: so, for example, after a reference to the Criminal Procedure and Investigations Act 1996 that Act is called 'the 1996 Act'; and after a reference to the Criminal Procedure and Investigations Act 1996 (Defence Disclosure Time Limits) Regulations 1997 those Regulations are called 'the 1997 Regulations'.

R-7 **The glossary**

2.4 The glossary at the end of the Rules is a guide to the meaning of certain legal expressions used in them.

R-8 **Representatives**

2.5 (1) Under these Rules, unless the context makes it clear that something different is meant, anything that a party may or must do may be done—
(a) by a legal representative on that party's behalf;
(b) by a person with the corporation's written authority, where that party is a corporation;
(c) with the help of a parent, guardian or other suitable supporting adult where that party is a defendant—
(i) who is under 18, or
(ii) whose understanding of what the case involves is limited.

(2) Anyone with a prosecutor's authority to do so may, on that prosecutor's behalf—
(a) serve on the magistrates' court officer, or present to a magistrates' court, an information under section 1 of the Magistrates' Courts Act 1980; or
(b) issue a written charge and requisition under section 29 of the Criminal Justice Act 2003.

Part 3 Case Management

R-9 **The scope of this Part**

3.1 This Part applies to the management of each case in a magistrates' court and in the Crown Court (including an appeal to the Crown Court) until the conclusion of that case.

R-10 **The duty of the court**

3.2 (1) The court must further the overriding objective by actively managing the case.

(2) Active case management includes—
(a) the early identification of the real issues;
(b) the early identification of the needs of witnesses;
(c) achieving certainty as to what must be done, by whom, and when, in particular by the early setting of a timetable for the progress of the case;
(d) monitoring the progress of the case and compliance with directions;
(e) ensuring that evidence, whether disputed or not, is presented in the shortest and clearest way;
(f) discouraging delay, dealing with as many aspects of the case as possible on the same occasion, and avoiding unnecessary hearings;
(g) encouraging the participants to co-operate in the progression of the case; and
(h) making use of technology.

(3) The court must actively manage the case by giving any direction appropriate to the needs of that case as early as possible.

The duty of the parties R-11

3.3 Each party must—
(a) actively assist the court in fulfilling its duty under rule 3.2, without or if necessary with a direction; and
(b) apply for a direction if needed to further the overriding objective.

Case progression officers and their duties R-12

3.4 (1) At the beginning of the case each party must, unless the court otherwise directs—
(a) nominate an individual responsible for progressing that case; and
(b) tell other parties and the court who he is and how to contact him.
(2) In fulfilling its duty under rule 3.2, the court must where appropriate—
(a) nominate a court officer responsible for progressing the case; and
(b) make sure the parties know who he is and how to contact him.
(3) In this Part a person nominated under this rule is called a case progression officer.
(4) A case progression officer must—
(a) monitor compliance with directions;
(b) make sure that the court is kept informed of events that may affect the progress of that case;
(c) make sure that he can be contacted promptly about the case during ordinary business hours;
(d) act promptly and reasonably in response to communications about the case; and
(e) if he will be unavailable, appoint a substitute to fulfil his duties and inform the other case progression officers.

The court's case management powers R-13

3.5 (1) In fulfilling its duty under rule 3.2 the court may give any direction and take any step actively to manage a case unless that direction or step would be inconsistent with legislation, including these Rules.
(2) In particular, the court may—
(a) nominate a judge, magistrate or justices' legal adviser to manage the case;
(b) give a direction on its own initiative or on application by a party;
(c) ask or allow a party to propose a direction;
(d) for the purpose of giving directions, receive applications and representations by letter, by telephone or by any other means of electronic communication, and conduct a hearing by such means;
(e) give a direction—
(i) at a hearing, in public or in private, or
(ii) without a hearing;
(f) fix, postpone, bring forward, extend or cancel a hearing;
(g) shorten or extend (even after it has expired) a time limit fixed by a direction;
(h) require that issues in the case should be determined separately, and decide in what order they will be determined; and
(i) specify the consequences of failing to comply with a direction.
(3) A magistrates' court may give a direction that will apply in the Crown Court if the case is to continue there.
(4) The Crown Court may give a direction that will apply in a magistrates' court if the case is to continue there.
(5) Any power to give a direction under this Part includes a power to vary or revoke that direction.
(6) If a party fails to comply with a rule or a direction, the court may—
(a) fix, postpone, bring forward, extend, cancel or adjourn a hearing;
(b) exercise its powers to make a costs order; and
(c) impose such other sanction as may be appropriate.

Application to vary a direction R-14

3.6 (1) A party may apply to vary a direction if—
(a) the court gave it without a hearing;
(b) the court gave it at a hearing in his absence; or
(c) circumstances have changed.
(2) A party who applies to vary a direction must—
(a) apply as soon as practicable after he becomes aware of the grounds for doing so; and
(b) give as much notice to the other parties as the nature and urgency of his application permits.

R-15 **Agreement to vary a time limit fixed by a direction**

3.7 (1) The parties may agree to vary a time limit fixed by a direction, but only if—
(a) the variation will not—
(i) affect the date of any hearing that has been fixed, or
(ii) significantly affect the progress of the case in any other way;
(b) the court has not prohibited variation by agreement; and
(c) the court's case progression officer is promptly informed.
(2) The court's case progression officer must refer the agreement to the court if he doubts the condition in paragraph (1)(a) is satisfied.

R-16 **Case preparation and progression**

3.8 (1) At every hearing, if a case cannot be concluded there and then the court must give directions so that it can be concluded at the next hearing or as soon as possible after that.
(2) At every hearing the court must, where relevant—
(a) if the defendant is absent, decide whether to proceed nonetheless;
(b) take the defendant's plea (unless already done) or if no plea can be taken then find out whether the defendant is likely to plead guilty or not guilty;
(c) set, follow or revise a timetable for the progress of the case, which may include a timetable for any hearing including the trial or (in the Crown Court) the appeal;
(d) in giving directions, ensure continuity in relation to the court and to the parties' representatives where that is appropriate and practicable; and
(e) where a direction has not been complied with, find out why, identify who was responsible, and take appropriate action.
(3) In order to prepare for a trial in the Crown Court, the court must conduct a plea and case management hearing unless the circumstances make that unnecessary.
(4) In order to prepare for the trial, the court must take every reasonable step to encourage and to facilitate the attendance of witnesses when they are needed.

R-17 **Readiness for trial or appeal**

3.9 (1) This rule applies to a party's preparation for trial or appeal, and in this rule and rule 3.10 trial includes any hearing at which evidence will be introduced.
(2) In fulfilling his duty under rule 3.3, each party must—
(a) comply with directions given by the court;
(b) take every reasonable step to make sure his witnesses will attend when they are needed;
(c) make appropriate arrangements to present any written or other material; and
(d) promptly inform the court and the other parties of anything that may—
(i) affect the date or duration of the trial or appeal, or
(ii) significantly affect the progress of the case in any other way.
(3) The court may require a party to give a certificate of readiness.

R-18 **Conduct of a trial or an appeal**

3.10 In order to manage the trial or an appeal, the court—
(a) must establish, with the active assistance of the parties, what are the disputed issues;
(b) must consider setting a timetable that—
(i) takes account of those issues and any timetable proposed by a party, and
(ii) may limit the duration of any stage of the hearing;
(c) may require a party to identify—
(i) which witnesses that party wants to give evidence in person,
(ii) the order in which that party wants those witnesses to give their evidence,
(iii) whether that party requires an order compelling the attendance of a witness,
(iv) what arrangements are desirable to facilitate the giving of evidence by a witness,
(v) what arrangements are desirable to facilitate the participation of any other person, including the defendant,
(vi) what written evidence that party intends to introduce,
(vii) what other material, if any, that person intends to make available to the court in the presentation of the case,
(viii) whether that party intends to raise any point of law that could affect the conduct of the trial or appeal, and
(d) may limit—
(i) the examination, cross-examination or re-examination of a witness, and

(ii) the duration of any stage of the hearing.

Case management forms and records R-19

3.11 (1) The case management forms set out in the Practice Direction must be used, and where there is no form then no specific formality is required.

(2) The court must make available to the parties a record of directions given.

(3) Where a person is entitled or required to attend a hearing, the court officer must give as much notice as reasonably practicable to—

(a) that person; and

(b) that person's custodian (if any).

PART 4 SERVICE OF DOCUMENTS

When this Part applies R-20

4.1 The rules in this Part apply to the service of every document in a case to which these Rules apply, subject to any special rules in other legislation (including other Parts of these Rules) or in the Practice Direction.

Methods of service R-21

4.2 (1) A document may be served by any of the methods described in rules 4.3 to 4.6 (subject to rule 4.7), or in rule 4.8.

(2) Where a document may be served by electronic means, the general rule is that the person serving it will use that method.

Service by handing over a document R-22

4.3 (1) A document may be served on—

(a) an individual by handing it to him or her;

(b) a corporation by handing it to a person holding a senior position in that corporation;

(c) an individual or corporation who is legally represented in the case by handing it to that representative;

(d) the prosecution by handing it to the prosecutor or to the prosecution representative;

(e) the court officer by handing it to a court officer with authority to accept it at the relevant court office; and

(f) the Registrar of Criminal Appeals by handing it to a court officer with authority to accept it at the Criminal Appeal Office.

(2) If an individual is under 18, a copy of a document served under paragraph (1)(a) must be handed to his or her parent, or another appropriate adult, unless no such person is readily available.

Service by leaving or posting a document R-23

4.4 (1) A document may be served by leaving it at the appropriate address for service under this rule or by sending it to that address by first class post or by the equivalent of first class post.

(2) The address for service under this rule on—

(a) an individual is an address where it is reasonably believed that he or she will receive it;

(b) a corporation is its principal office, and if there is no readily identifiable principal office then any place where it carries on its activities or business;

(c) an individual or corporation who is legally represented in the case is that representative's office;

(d) the prosecution is the prosecutor's office;

(e) the court officer is the relevant court office; and

(f) the Registrar of Criminal Appeals is the Criminal Appeal Office, Royal Courts of Justice, Strand, London WC2A 2LL.

Service through a document exchange R-24

4.5 A document may be served by document exchange (DX) where—

(a) the person to be served—

(i) has given a DX box number, and

(ii) has not refused to accept service by DX; or

(b) the person to be served is legally represented in the case and the representative has given a DX box number.

R-25 Service by electronic means

4.6 (1) A document may be served by electronic means where—
(a) the person to be served—
(i) has given an electronic address, and
(ii) has not refused to accept service by that method; or
(b) the person to be served is legally represented in the case and the representative has given an electronic address.
(2) Where a document is served under this rule the person serving it need not provide a paper copy as well.

R-26 Documents that must be served by specified methods

4.7 (1) The documents listed in paragraph (2) may be served—
(a) on an individual, only under rule 4.3(1)(a) (handing over) or rule 4.4(1) and (2)(a) (leaving or posting); and
(b) on a corporation only under rule 4.3(1)(b) (handing over) or rule 4.4(1) and (2)(b) (leaving or posting)
(2) Those documents are—
(a) a summons, requisition or witness summons;
(b) notice of an order under section 25 of the Road Traffic Offenders Act 1988;
(c) a notice of registration under section 71(6) of that Act;
(d) notice of a hearing to review the postponement of the issue of a warrant of detention or imprisonment under section 77(6) of the Magistrates' Courts Act 1980;
(e) notice under section 86 of that Act of a revised date to attend a means inquiry;
(f) any notice or document served under part 19 (bail in magistrates' courts and the Crown Court);
(g) notice under rule 37.15 of when and where an adjourned hearing will resume;
(h) notice under rule 42.5(3) of an application to vary or discharge a compensation order;
(i) notice under rule 42.10(2) of the location of the sentencing or enforcing court;
(j) a collection notice, or notice requiring payment, served under rule 52.2(a).
(3) An application or written statement, and notice, under rule 62.9 alleging contempt of court may be served—
(a) on an individual, only under rule 4.3(1)(a) (by handing it to him or her);
(b) on a corporation, only under rule 4.3(1)(b) (by handing it to a person holding a senior position in that corporation).

R-27 Service by person in custody

4.8 (1) A person in custody may serve a document by handing it to the custodian addressed to the person to be served.
(2) The custodian must—
(a) endorse it with the time and date of receipt;
(b) record its receipt; and
(c) forward it promptly to the addressee.

R-28 Service by another method

4.9 (1) The court may allow service of a document by a method—
(a) other than those described in rules 4.3 to 4.6 and in rule 4.8.
(b) other than one specified by rule 4.7, where that rule applies.
(2) An order allowing service by another method must specify—
(a) the method to be used; and
(b) the date on which the document will be served.

R-29 Date of service

4.10 (1) A document served under rule 4.3 or rule 4.8 is served on the day it is handed over.
(2) Unless something different is shown, a document served on a person by any other method is served—
(a) in the case of a document left at an address, on the next business day after the day on which it was left;
(b) in the case of a document sent by first class post or by the equivalent of first class post, on the second business day after the day on which it was posted or despatched;
(c) in the case of a document served by document exchange, on the second business day after the day on which it was left at the addressee's DX or at a correspondent DX;

(d) in the case of a document transmitted by electronic means, on the next business day after it was transmitted; and
(e) in any case, on the day on which the addressee responds to it if that is earlier.

(3) Unless something different is shown, a document produced by a court computer system is to be taken as having been sent by first class post or by the equivalent of first class post to the addressee on the business day after the day on which it was produced.

(4) Where a document is served on or by the court officer, 'business day' does not include a day on which the court office is closed.

Proof of service R-30

4.11 The person who serves a document may prove that by signing a certificate explaining how and when it was served.

Court's power to give directions about service R-31

4.12 (1) The court may specify the time as well as the date by which a document must be—
(a) served under rule 4.3 or rule 4.8; or
(b) transmitted by electronic means, if it is served under rule 4.6.

(2) The court may treat a document as served if the addressee responds to it even if it was not served in accordance with the rules in this Part.

PART 5 FORMS AND COURT RECORDS

Section 1: forms

Forms R-32

5.1 The forms set out in the Practice Direction and in the Criminal Costs Practice Direction shall be used as appropriate in connection with the rules to which they apply.

Forms in Welsh R-33

5.2 (1) Any Welsh language form set out in the Practice Direction, or in the Criminal Costs Practice Direction, is for use in connection with proceedings in courts in Wales.

(2) Both a Welsh form and an English form may be contained in the same document.

(3) Where only a Welsh form, or only the corresponding English form, is served—
(a) the following words in Welsh and English must be added:
'Darperir y ddogfen hon yn Gymraeg / Saesneg os bydd arnoch ei heisiau. Dylech wneud cais yn ddi-oed i (swyddog y llys) (rhodder yma'r cyfeiriad)
This document will be provided in Welsh / English if you require it. You should apply immediately to (the court officer) (address)'; and
(b) the court officer, or the person who served the form, must, on request, supply the corresponding form in the other language to the person served.

Signature of forms R-34

5.3 (1) This rule applies where a form provides for its signature.

(2) Unless other legislation otherwise requires, or the court otherwise directs, signature may be by any written or electronic authentication of the form by, or with the authority of, the signatory.

Section 2: court records

Duty to make records R-35

5.4 For each case, as appropriate, the court officer must record, by such means as the Lord Chancellor directs—
(a) each charge or indictment against the defendant;
(b) the defendant's plea to each charge or count;
(c) each acquittal, conviction, sentence, determination, direction or order;
(d) each decision about bail;
(e) the power exercised where the court commits or adjourns the case to another court—
(i) for sentence, or
(ii) for the defendant to be dealt with for breach of a community order, a deferred sentence, a conditional discharge, or a suspended sentence of imprisonment, imposed by that other court;

(f) the court's reasons for a decision, where legislation requires those reasons to be recorded;
(g) any appeal;
(h) each party's presence or absence at each hearing;
(i) any consent that legislation requires before the court can proceed with the case, or proceed to a decision;
(j) in a magistrates' court—
  (i) any indication of sentence given in connection with the allocation of a case for trial, and
  (ii) the registration of a fixed penalty notice for enforcement as a fine, and any related endorsement on a driving licence;
(k) in the Crown Court, any request for assistance or other communication about the case received from a juror; and
(l) the identity of—
  (i) the prosecutor,
  (ii) the defendant,
  (iii) any other applicant to whom these Rules apply,
  (iv) the parties' legal representatives, if any, and
  (v) the judge, magistrate or magistrates, justices' legal adviser or other person who made each recorded decision.

(2) Such records must include—
(a) each party's and representative's address, including any electronic address and telephone number available;
(b) the defendant's date of birth, if available; and
(c) the date of each event and decision recorded.

R-36 Recording and transcription of proceedings in the Crown Court

5.5 (1) Where someone may appeal to the Court of Appeal, the court officer must—
(a) arrange for the recording of the proceedings in the Crown Court, unless the court otherwise directs; and
(b) arrange for the transcription of such a recording if—
  (i) the Registrar wants such a transcript, or
  (ii) anyone else wants such a transcript (but that is subject to the restrictions in paragraph (2)).

(2) Unless the court otherwise directs, a person who transcribes a recording of proceedings under such arrangements—
(a) must not supply anyone other than the Registrar with a transcript of a recording of—
  (i) a hearing in private, or
  (ii) information to which reporting restrictions apply;
(b) subject to that, must supply any person with any transcript for which that person asks—
  (i) in accordance with the transcription arrangements made by the court officer, and
  (ii) on payment by that person of any fee prescribed.

(3) A party who wants to hear a recording of proceedings must—
(a) apply—
  (i) in writing to the Registrar, if an appeal notice has been served where Part 65 applies (Appeal to the Court of Appeal: general rules), or
  (ii) orally or in writing to the Crown Court officer;
(b) explain the reasons for the request; and
(c) pay any fee prescribed.

(4) If the Crown Court or the Registrar so directs, the Crown Court officer must allow that party to hear a recording of—
(a) a hearing in public;
(b) a hearing in private, if the applicant was present at that hearing.

R-37 Custody of case materials

5.6 Unless the court otherwise directs, in respect of each case the court officer may—
(a) keep any evidence, application, representation or other material served by the parties; or
(b) arrange for the whole or any part to be kept by some other appropriate person, subject to—
  (i) any condition imposed by the court, and
  (ii) the rules in Part 63 (Appeal to the Crown Court) and Part 65 (Appeal to the Court of Appeal: general rules) about keeping exhibits pending any appeal.

Supply to a party of information or documents from records or case materials R-38

5.7 (1) This rule applies where a party wants information, or a copy of a document, from records or case materials kept by the court officer (for example, in case of loss, or to establish what is retained).

(2) Such a party must—

(a) apply to the court officer;

(b) specify the information or document required; and

(c) pay any fee prescribed.

(3) The application—

(a) may be made orally, giving no reasons, if paragraph (4) requires the court officer to supply the information or document requested;

(b) must be in writing, unless the court otherwise permits, and must explain for what purpose the information is required, in any other case.

(4) The court officer must supply to the applicant party—

(a) a copy of any document served by, or on, that party (but not of any document not so served);

(b) by word of mouth, or in writing, as requested—

(i) information that was received from that party in the first place,

(ii) information about any direction or order directed to that party, or made on an application by that party, or at a hearing in public,

(iii) information about the outcome of the case.

(5) If the court so permits, the court officer may supply to the applicant party, by word of mouth or in writing, as requested, information that paragraph (4) does not require the court officer to supply.

Supply to the public, including reporters, of information about a case R-38A

5.8 (1) This rule applies where a member of the public, including a reporter, wants information about a case from the court officer.

(2) Such a person must—

(a) apply to the court officer;

(b) specify the information requested; and

(c) pay any fee prescribed.

(3) The application—

(a) may be made orally, giving no reasons, if paragraph (4) requires the court officer to supply the information requested;

(b) must be in writing, unless the court otherwise permits, and must explain for what purpose the information is required, in any other case.

(4) The court officer must supply to the applicant—

(a) any information listed in paragraph (6), if—

(i) the information is available to the court officer,

(ii) the supply of the information is not prohibited by a reporting restriction, and

(iii) the trial has not yet concluded, or the verdict was not more than 6 months ago; and

(b) details of any reporting or access restriction ordered by the court.

(5) The court officer will supply that information—

(a) by word of mouth; or

(b) by such other arrangements as the Lord Chancellor directs.

(6) The information that paragraph (4) requires the court officer to supply is—

(a) the date of any hearing in public, unless any party has yet to be notified of that date;

(b) each alleged offence and any plea entered;

(c) the court's decision at any hearing in public, including any decision about—

(i) bail, or

(ii) the committal, sending or transfer of the case to another court;

(d) whether the case is under appeal;

(e) the outcome of any trial and any appeal; and

(f) the identity of—

(i) the prosecutor,

(ii) the defendant,

(iii) the parties' representatives, including their addresses, and

(iv) the judge, magistrate or magistrates, or justices' legal adviser by whom a decision at a hearing in public was made.

(7) If the court so directs, the court officer will—
(a) supply to the applicant, by word of mouth, other information about the case; or
(b) allow the applicant to inspect or copy a document, or part of a document, containing information about the case.
(8) The court may determine an application to which paragraph (7) applies—
(a) at a hearing, in public or in private; or
(b) without a hearing.

R-38B Supply of written certificate or extract from records

5.9 (1) This rule applies where legislation—
(a) allows a certificate of conviction or acquittal, or an extract from records kept by the court officer, to be introduced in evidence in criminal proceedings; or
(b) requires such a certificate or extract to be supplied by the court officer to a specified person for a specified purpose.
(2) A person who wants such a certificate or extract must—
(a) apply in writing to the court officer;
(b) specify the certificate or extract required;
(c) explain under what legislation and for what purpose it is required; and
(d) pay any fee prescribed.
(3) If the application satisfies the requirements of that legislation, the court officer must supply the certificate or extract requested—
(a) to a party;
(b) unless the court otherwise directs, to any other applicant.

Part 6 Investigation Orders

Section 1: understanding and applying this Part

R-39 When this Part applies

6.1 (1) Sections 2 and 3 of this Part apply where, for the purposes of a terrorist investigation—
(a) a Circuit judge can make, vary or discharge—
(i) an order for the production of, or for giving access to, material, or for a statement of its location, under paragraphs 5 and 10 of Schedule 5 to the Terrorism Act 2000,
(ii) an explanation order, under paragraphs 10 and 13 of Schedule 5 to the 2000 Act,
(iii) a customer information order, under paragraphs 1 and 4 of Schedule 6 to the 2000 Act;
(b) a Circuit judge can make, and the Crown Court can vary or discharge, an account monitoring order, under paragraphs 2 and 4 of Schedule 6A to the 2000 Act.
(2) Sections 2 and 4 of this Part apply where, for the purposes of a confiscation investigation or a money laundering investigation, a Crown Court judge can make, and the Crown Court can vary or discharge—
(a) a production order, under sections 345 and 351 of the Proceeds of Crime Act 2002;
(b) an order to grant entry, under sections 347 and 351 of the 2002 Act;
(c) a disclosure order, under sections 357 and 362 of the 2002 Act;
(d) a customer information order, under sections 363 and 369 of the 2002 Act;
(e) an account monitoring order, under sections 370 and 375 of the 2002 Act.

R-40 Meaning of 'court', 'applicant' and 'respondent'

6.2 In this Part—
(a) a reference to the 'court' includes a reference to any judge who can exercise a power to which this Part applies;
(b) 'applicant' means any person who can apply for an order to which this Part applies; and
(c) 'respondent' means a person against whom such an order is sought or made.

Section 2: general rules

R-41 Exercise of court's powers

6.3 (1) The court must determine an application for an order—
(a) at a hearing (which will be in private unless the court otherwise directs); and
(b) in the applicant's presence.

(2) The court must not determine such an application in the absence of the respondent or any other person affected, unless—
(a) the absentee has had at least 2 business days in which to make representations; or
(b) the court is satisfied that—
(i) the applicant cannot identify or contact the absentee,
(ii) it would prejudice the investigation if the absentee were present, or
(iii) it would prejudice the investigation to adjourn or postpone the application so as to allow the absentee to attend.

(3) The court may determine an application to vary or discharge an order—
(a) at a hearing (which will be in private unless the court otherwise directs), or without a hearing; and
(b) in the absence of—
(i) the applicant,
(ii) the respondent,
(iii) any other person affected by the order.

Court's power to vary requirements under this Part R-42

6.4 (1) The court may—
(a) shorten or extend (even after it has expired) a time limit under this Part;
(b) dispense with a requirement for service under this Part (even after service was required); and
(c) consider an application made orally instead of in writing.

(2) A person who wants an extension of time must—
(a) apply when serving the application for which it is needed; and
(b) explain the delay.

Custody of documents R-43

6.5 Unless the court otherwise directs, the court officer may—
(a) keep a written application; or
(b) arrange for the whole or any part to be kept by some other appropriate person, subject to any conditions that the court may impose.

Section 3: orders under the Terrorism Act 2000

Application for an order under the Terrorism Act 2000 R-44

6.6 (1) This rule applies where an applicant wants the court to make one of the orders listed in rule 6.1(1).

(2) The applicant must—
(a) apply in writing;
(b) serve the application on—
(i) the court officer, and
(ii) the respondent (unless the court otherwise directs);
(c) identify the respondent;
(d) give the information required by whichever of rules 6.7 to 6.10 applies; and
(e) serve any order made on the respondent.

Content of application for a production etc. order R-45

6.7 As well as complying with rule 6.6, an applicant who wants the court to make an order for the production of, or access to, material, or for a statement of its location, must—
(a) describe that material;
(b) explain why the applicant thinks the material is—
(i) in the respondent's possession, custody or power, or
(ii) likely to be so within 28 days of the order;
(c) explain how the material constitutes or contains excluded material or special procedure material;
(d) confirm that none of the material is expected to be subject to legal privilege;
(e) explain why the material is likely to be of substantial value to the investigation;
(f) explain why it is in the public interest for the material to be produced, or for the applicant to be given access to it, having regard to—
(i) the benefit likely to accrue to the investigation if it is obtained, and
(ii) the circumstances in which the respondent has the material, or is expected to have it; and
(g) propose—
(i) the terms of the order, and
(ii) the period within which it should take effect.

R-46 **Content of application for an explanation order**

6.8 As well as complying with rule 6.6, an applicant who wants the court to make an explanation order must—

(a) identify the material that the applicant wants the respondent to explain;
(b) confirm that the explanation is not expected to infringe legal privilege; and
(c) propose—
  (i) the terms of the order, and
  (ii) the period within which it should take effect, if 7 days from the date of the order would not be appropriate.

R-47 **Content of application for a customer information order**

6.9 As well as complying with rule 6.6, an applicant who wants the court to make a customer information order must—

(a) explain why it is desirable for the purposes of the investigation to trace property said to be terrorist property within the meaning of the Terrorism Act 2000;
(b) explain why the order will enhance the effectiveness of the investigation; and
(c) propose the terms of the order.

R-48 **Content of application for an account monitoring order**

6.10 As well as complying with rule 6.6, an applicant who wants the court to make an account monitoring order must—

(a) specify—
  (i) the information sought,
  (ii) the period during which the applicant wants the respondent to provide that information (to a maximum of 90 days), and
  (iii) where, when and in what manner the applicant wants the respondent to provide that information;
(b) explain why it is desirable for the purposes of the investigation to trace property said to be terrorist property within the meaning of the Terrorism Act 2000;
(c) explain why the order will enhance the effectiveness of the investigation; and
(d) propose the terms of the order.

R-49 **Application to vary or discharge an order**

6.11 (1) This rule applies where one of the following wants the court to vary or discharge an order listed in rule 6.1(1)—

(a) an applicant;
(b) the respondent; or
(c) a person affected by the order.

(2) That applicant, respondent or person affected must—

(a) apply in writing as soon as practicable after becoming aware of the grounds for doing so;
(b) serve the application on—
  (i) the court officer, and
  (ii) the respondent, applicant, or any person known to be affected, as applicable;
(c) explain why it is appropriate for the order to be varied or discharged;
(d) propose the terms of any variation; and
(e) ask for a hearing, if one is wanted, and explain why it is needed.

R-50 **Application containing information withheld from a respondent or other person**

6.12 (1) This rule applies where—

(a) an applicant serves on a respondent or other person an application for one of the orders listed in rule 6.1(1), or for the variation or discharge of such an order; and
(b) the application includes information that the applicant thinks ought not be revealed to that recipient.

(2) The applicant must—

(a) omit that information from the part of the application that is served on the respondent or other person;
(b) mark the other part, to show that it is only for the court; and
(c) in that other part, explain why the applicant has withheld it.

(3) A hearing of an application to which this rule applies may take place, wholly or in part, in the absence of the respondent and any other person.
(4) At a hearing of an application to which this rule applies—
(a) the general rule is that the court will receive, in the following sequence—
(i) representations first by the applicant and then by the respondent and any other person, in the presence of them all, and then
(ii) further representations by the applicant, in the others' absence; but
(b) the court may direct other arrangements for the hearing.

Application to punish for contempt of court R-51

6.13 (1) This rule applies where a person is accused of disobeying—
(a) a production etc. order made under paragraph 5 of Schedule 5 to the Terrorism Act 2000;
(b) an explanation order made under paragraph 13 of that Schedule; or
(c) an account monitoring order made under paragraph 2 of Schedule 6A to that Act.
(2) An applicant who wants the court to exercise its power to punish that person for contempt of court must comply with the rules in Part 62 (Contempt of court).

Section 4: orders under the Proceeds of Crime Act 2002

Application for an order under the Proceeds of Crime Act 2002 R-52

6.14 (1) This rule applies where an applicant wants the court to make one of the orders listed in rule 6.1(2).
(2) The applicant must—
(a) apply in writing;
(b) serve the application on—
(i) the court officer, and
(ii) the respondent (unless the court otherwise directs);
(c) identify—
(i) the respondent, and
(ii) the person the subject of the confiscation or money laundering investigation;
(d) explain why the applicant thinks the person under investigation has—
(i) benefited from criminal conduct, in the case of a confiscation investigation, or
(ii) committed a money laundering offence, in the case of a money laundering investigation;
(e) give the additional information required by whichever of rules 6.15 to 6.19 applies; and
(f) serve any order made on each respondent.

Content of application for a production order R-53

6.15 As well as complying with rule 6.14, an applicant who wants the court to make an order for the production of, or access to, material, must—
(a) describe that material;
(b) explain why the applicant thinks the material is in the respondent's possession or control;
(c) confirm that none of the material is—
(i) expected to be subject to legal privilege, or
(ii) excluded material;
(d) explain why the material is likely to be of substantial value to the investigation;
(e) explain why it is in the public interest for the material to be produced, or for the applicant to be given access to it, having regard to—
(i) the benefit likely to accrue to the investigation if it is obtained, and
(ii) the circumstances in which the respondent has the material; and
(f) propose—
(i) the terms of the order, and
(ii) the period within which it should take effect, if 7 days from the date of the order would not be appropriate.

Content of application for an order to grant entry R-54

6.16 An applicant who wants the court to make an order to grant entry must—
(a) specify the premises to which entry is sought;
(b) explain why the order is needed; and
(c) propose the terms of the order.

R-55 Content of application for a disclosure order

6.17 As well as complying with rule 6.14, an applicant who wants the court to make a disclosure order must—
- (a) describe in general terms the information that the applicant wants the respondent to provide;
- (b) confirm that none of the information is—
  - (i) expected to be subject to legal privilege, or
  - (ii) excluded material;
- (c) explain why the information is likely to be of substantial value to the investigation;
- (d) explain why it is in the public interest for the information to be provided, having regard to the benefit likely to accrue to the investigation if it is obtained; and
- (e) propose the terms of the order.

R-56 Content of application for a customer information order

6.18 As well as complying with rule 6.14, an applicant who wants the court to make a customer information order must—
- (a) explain why customer information about the person under investigation is likely to be of substantial value to that investigation;
- (b) explain why it is in the public interest for the information to be provided, having regard to the benefit likely to accrue to the investigation if it is obtained; and
- (c) propose the terms of the order.

R-57 Content of application for an account monitoring order

6.19 As well as complying with rule 6.14, an applicant who wants the court to make an account monitoring order for the provision of account information must—
- (a) specify—
  - (i) the information sought,
  - (ii) the period during which the applicant wants the respondent to provide that information (to a maximum of 90 days), and
  - (iii) when and in what manner the applicant wants the respondent to provide that information;
- (b) explain why the information is likely to be of substantial value to the investigation;
- (c) explain why it is in the public interest for the information to be provided, having regard to the benefit likely to accrue to the investigation if it is obtained; and
- (d) propose the terms of the order.

R-58 Application to vary or discharge an order

6.20 (1) This rule applies where one of the following wants the court to vary or discharge an order listed in rule 6.1(2)—
- (a) an applicant;
- (b) the respondent; or
- (c) a person affected by the order.

(2) That applicant, respondent or person affected must—
- (a) apply in writing as soon as practicable after becoming aware of the grounds for doing so;
- (b) serve the application on—
  - (i) the court officer, and
  - (ii) the respondent, applicant, or any person known to be affected, as applicable;
- (c) explain why it is appropriate for the order to be varied or discharged;
- (d) propose the terms of any variation; and
- (e) ask for a hearing, if one is wanted, and explain why it is needed.

R-59 Application containing information withheld from a respondent or other person

6.21 (1) This rule applies where—
- (a) an applicant serves on a respondent or other person an application for one of the orders listed in rule 6.1(2), or for the variation or discharge of such an order; and
- (b) the application includes information that the applicant thinks ought not be revealed to that recipient.

(2) The applicant must—
- (a) omit that information from the part of the application that is served on the respondent or other person;
- (b) mark the other part, to show that it is only for the court; and
- (c) in that other part, explain why the applicant has withheld it.

(3) A hearing of an application to which this rule applies may take place, wholly or in part, in the absence of the respondent and any other person.
(4) At a hearing of an application to which this rule applies—
(a) the general rule is that the court will receive, in the following sequence—
(i) representations first by the applicant and then by the respondent and any other person, in the presence of them all, and then
(ii) further representations by the applicant, in the others' absence; but
(b) the court may direct other arrangements for the hearing.

Application to punish for contempt of court R-60

6.22 (1) This rule applies where a person is accused of disobeying—
(a) a production order made under section 345 of the Proceeds of Crime Act 2002; or
(b) an account monitoring order made under section 370 of that Act.
(2) An applicant who wants the court to exercise its power to punish that person for contempt of court must comply with the rules in Part 62 (contempt of court).

Section 5: orders under the Coroners and Justice Act 2009

Exercise of court's powers R-61

6.23 (1) The court may determine an application for an investigation anonymity order, and any appeal against the refusal of such an order—
(a) at a hearing (which will be in private unless the court otherwise directs); or
(b) without a hearing.
(2) The court must determine an application to discharge an investigation anonymity order, and any appeal against the decision on such an application—
(a) at a hearing (which will be in private unless the court otherwise directs); and
(b) in the presence of the person specified in the order, unless—
(i) that person applied for the discharge of the order,
(ii) that person has had an opportunity to make representations, or
(iii) the court is satisfied that it is not reasonably practicable to communicate with that person.
(3) The court may consider an application or an appeal made orally instead of in writing.

Application for an investigation anonymity order R-62

6.24 (1) This rule applies where an applicant wants a magistrates' court to make an investigation anonymity order.
(2) The applicant must—
(a) apply in writing;
(b) serve the application on the court officer;
(c) identify the person to be specified in the order, unless—
(i) the applicant wants the court to determine the application at a hearing, or
(ii) the court otherwise directs;
(d) explain how the proposed order meets the conditions prescribed by section 78 of the Coroners and Justice Act 2009;
(e) say if the applicant intends to appeal should the court refuse the order;
(f) attach any material on which the applicant relies; and
(g) propose the terms of the order.
(3) At any hearing of the application, the applicant must—
(a) identify to the court the person to be specified in the order, unless—
(i) the applicant has done so already, or
(ii) the court otherwise directs; and
(b) unless the applicant has done so already, inform the court if the applicant intends to appeal should the court refuse the order.

Application to discharge an investigation anonymity order R-63

6.25 (1) This rule applies where one of the following wants a magistrates' court to discharge an investigation anonymity order—
(a) an applicant; or
(b) the person specified in the order.
(2) That applicant or the specified person must—
(a) apply in writing as soon as practicable after becoming aware of the grounds for doing so;

(b) serve the application on—
(i) the court officer, and as applicable
(ii) the applicant for the order, and
(iii) the specified person;
(c) explain—
(i) what material circumstances have changed since the order was made, or since any previous application was made to discharge it, and
(ii) why it is appropriate for the order to be discharged; and
(d) attach—
(i) a copy of the order, and
(ii) any material on which the applicant relies.
(3) A party must inform the court if that party intends to appeal should the court discharge the order.

R-64 Appeal

6.26 (1) This rule applies where one of the following ('the appellant') wants to appeal to the Crown Court—
(a) the applicant for an investigation anonymity order, where a magistrates' court has refused to make the order;
(b) a party to an application to discharge such an order, where a magistrates' court has decided that application.
(2) The appellant must—
(a) serve on the Crown Court officer a copy of the application to the magistrates' court; and
(b) where the appeal concerns a discharge decision, notify each other party, not more that 21 days after the decision against which the appellant wants to appeal.
(3) The Crown Court must hear the appeal without justices of the peace.

Part 7 Starting a Prosecution in a Magistrates' Court

R-65 When this Part applies

7.1 (1) This part applies in a magistrates' court where—
(a) a prosecutor wants the court to issue a summons or warrant under section 1 of the Magistrates' Courts Act 1980;
(b) a public prosecutor—
(i) wants the court to issue a warrant under section 1 of the Magistrates' Courts Act 1980, or
(ii) issues a written charge and requisition under section 29 of the Criminal Justice Act 2003; or
(c) a person who is in custody is charged with an offence.
(2) In this Part, 'public prosecutor' means one of those public prosecutors listed in section 29 of the Criminal Justice Act 2003.

R-66 Information and written charge

7.2 (1) A prosecutor who wants the court to issue a summons must—
(a) serve an information in writing on the court officer; or
(b) unless other legislation prohibits this, present an information orally to the court, with a written record of the allegation that it contains.
(2) A prosecutor who wants the court to issue a warrant must—
(a) serve on the court officer—
(i) an information in writing, or
(ii) a copy of a written charge that has been issued; or
(b) present to the court either of those documents.
(3) A public prosecutor who issues a written charge must notify the court officer immediately.
(4) A single document may contain—
(a) more than one information; or
(b) more than one written charge.

(5) Where an offence can be tried only in a magistrates' court, then unless other legislation otherwise provides—
(a) a prosecutor must serve an information on the court officer or present it to the court; or
(b) a public prosecutor must issue a written charge, not more than 6 months after the offence alleged.
(6) Where an offence can be tried in the Crown Court then—
(a) a prosecutor must serve an information on the court officer or present it to the court; or
(b) a public prosecutor must issue a written charge, within any time limit that applies to that offence.

Allegation of offence in information or charge R-67

7.3 (1) An allegation of an offence in an information or charge must contain—
(a) a statement of the offence that—
(i) describes the offence in ordinary language, and
(ii) identifies any legislation that creates it; and
(b) such particulars of the conduct constituting the commission of the offence as to make clear what the prosecutor alleges against the defendant.
(2) More than one incident of the commission of the offence may be included in the allegation if those incidents taken together amount to a course of conduct having regard to the time, place or purpose of commission.

Summons, warrant and requisition R-68

7.4 (1) The court may issue or withdraw a summons or warrant—
(a) without giving the parties an opportunity to make representations; and
(b) without a hearing, or at a hearing in public or in private.
(2) A summons, warrant or requisition may be issued in respect of more than one offence.
(3) A summons or requisition must—
(a) contain notice of when and where the defendant is required to attend the court;
(b) specify each offence in respect of which it is issued; and
(c) in the case of a summons, identify—
(i) the court that issued it, unless that is otherwise recorded by the court officer,
(ii) the court office for the court that issued it; and
(d) in the case of a requisition, identify the person under whose authority it is issued.
(4) A summons may be contained in the same document as an information.
(5) A requisition may be contained in the same document as a written charge.
(6) Where the court issues a summons—
(a) the prosecutor must—
(i) serve it on the defendant, and
(ii) notify the court officer; or
(b) the court officer must—
(i) serve it on the defendant, and
(ii) notify the prosecutor.
(7) Where a public prosecutor issues a requisition that prosecutor must—
(a) serve on the defendant—
(i) the requisition, and
(ii) the written charge; and
(b) serve a copy of each on the court officer.
(8) Unless it would be inconsistent with other legislation, a replacement summons or requisition may be issued without a fresh information or written charge where the one replaced—
(a) was served by leaving or posting it under rule 4.7 (documents that must be served only by handing them over, leaving or posting them); but
(b) is shown not to have been received by the addressee.
(9) A summons or requisition issued to a defendant under 18 may require that defendant's parent or guardian to attend the court with the defendant, or a separate summons or requisition may be issued for that purpose.

Part 8 Discontinuing a Prosecution

R-69 **When this Part applies**

8.1 (1) This Part applies where—

(a) the Director of Public Prosecutions, or the Director of Revenue and Customs Prosecutions, can discontinue a case in a magistrates' court, under section 23 of the Prosecution of Offences Act 1985;

(b) the Director of Public Prosecutions, or another public prosecutor, can discontinue a case sent for trial in the Crown Court, under section 23A of the Prosecution of Offences Act 1985.

(2) In this Part, 'prosecutor' means one of those authorities.

R-70 **Discontinuing a case**

8.2 (1) A prosecutor exercising a power to which this Part applies must serve notice on—

(a) the court officer;

(b) the defendant; and

(c) any custodian of the defendant.

(2) Such a notice must—

(a) identify—

(i) the defendant and each offence to which the notice relates,

(ii) the person serving the notice, and

(iii) the power that that person is exercising;

(b) explain—

(i) in the copy of the notice served on the court officer, the reasons for discontinuing the case,

(ii) that the notice brings the case to an end,

(iii) if the defendant is in custody for any offence to which the notice relates, that the defendant must be released from that custody, and

(iv) if the notice is under section 23 of the 1985 Act, that the defendant has a right to require the case to continue.

(3) Where the defendant is on bail, the court officer must notify—

(a) any surety; and

(b) any person responsible for monitoring or securing the defendant's compliance with a condition of bail.

R-71 **Defendant's notice to continue**

8.3 (1) This rule applies where a prosecutor serves a notice to discontinue under section 23 of the 1985 Act.

(2) A defendant who wants the case to continue must serve notice—

(a) on the court officer; and

(b) not more than 35 days after service of the notice to discontinue.

(3) If the defendant serves such a notice, the court officer must—

(a) notify the prosecutor; and

(b) refer the case to the court.

R-72

Part 9

[There are no rules in this part.]

Part 10 Committal for Trial

R-73 **Restrictions on reports of committal proceedings**

10.1 (1) Except in a case where evidence is, with the consent of the accused, to be tendered in his absence under section 4(4)(b) of the Magistrates' Courts Act 1980 (absence caused by ill health), a magistrates' court acting as examining justices shall before admitting any evidence explain to the accused the restrictions on reports of committal proceedings imposed by section 8 of that Act and inform him of his right to apply to the court for an order removing those restrictions.

(2) Where a magistrates' court has made an order under section 8(2) of the 1980 Act removing restrictions on the reports of committal proceedings, such order shall be entered in the register.

(3) Where the court adjourns any such proceedings to another day, the court shall, at the beginning of any adjourned hearing, state that the order has been made.

Committal for trial without consideration of the evidence R-74

10.2 (1) This rule applies to committal proceedings where the accused has a solicitor acting for him in the case and where the court has been informed that all the evidence falls within section 5A(2) of the Magistrates' Courts Act 1980.

(2) A magistrates' court inquiring into an offence in committal proceedings to which this rule applies shall cause the charge to be written down, if this has not already been done, and read to the accused and shall then ascertain whether he wishes to submit that there is insufficient evidence to put him on trial by jury for the offence with which he is charged.

(3) If the court is satisfied that the accused or, as the case may be, each of the accused does not wish to make such a submission as is referred to in paragraph (2) it shall, after receiving any written evidence falling within section 5A(3) of the 1980 Act, determine whether or not to commit the accused for trial without consideration of the evidence, and where it determines not to so commit the accused it shall proceed in accordance with rule 10.3.

Consideration of evidence at committal proceedings R-75

10.3 (1) This rule does not apply to committal proceedings where under section 6(2) of the Magistrates' Courts Act of 1980 a magistrates' court commits a person for trial without consideration of the evidence.

(2) A magistrates' court inquiring into an offence as examining justices, having ascertained—

(a) that the accused has no legal representative acting for him in the case; or

(b) that the accused's legal representative has requested the court to consider a submission that there is insufficient evidence to put the accused on trial by jury for the offence with which he is charged, as the case may be,

shall permit the prosecutor to make an opening address to the court, if he so wishes, before any evidence is tendered.

(3) After such opening address, if any, the court shall cause evidence to be tendered in accordance with sections 5B(4), 5C(4), 5D(5) and 5E(3) of the 1980 Act, that is to say by being read out aloud, except where the court otherwise directs or to the extent that it directs that an oral account be given of any of the evidence.

(4) The court may view any exhibits produced before the court and may take possession of them.

(5) After the evidence has been tendered the court shall hear any submission which the accused may wish to make as to whether there is sufficient evidence to put him on trial by jury for any indictable offence.

(6) The court shall permit the prosecutor to make a submission—

(a) in reply to any submission made by the accused in pursuance of paragraph (5); or

(b) where the accused has not made any such submission but the court is nevertheless minded not to commit him for trial.

(7) After hearing any submission made in pursuance of paragraph (5) or (6) the court shall, unless it decides not to commit the accused for trial, cause the charge to be written down, if this has not already been done, and, if the accused is not represented by counsel or a solicitor, shall read the charge to him and explain it in ordinary language.

Objection to committal statements being read at trial R-76

10.4 (1) This rule applies where—

(a) a written statement is admitted as evidence in committal proceedings;

(b) under Schedule 2 to the Criminal Procedure and Investigations Act 1996, the statement may be introduced in evidence at trial; and

(c) a party wants to object to that.

(2) Such a party must serve notice of objection—

(a) on each other party and on the Crown Court officer;

(b) not more than 14 days after the defendant is committed for trial.

(3) A prosecutor who introduces a written statement in committal proceedings must serve with it on the defendant a notice—

(a) of the right to object, and of the time limit; and

(b) that if the defendant does not object, the prosecutor may decide not to call the witness to give evidence in person at trial, but to rely on the written statement instead.

(4) The magistrates' court that commits the defendant for trial must remind the defendant of that right to object.

(5) The Crown Court may extend the time limit under this rule, even after it has expired.

R-77 **Material to be sent to court of trial**

10.5 (1) As soon as practicable after the committal of any person for trial, and in any case within 4 days from the date of his committal (not counting Saturdays, Sundays, Good Friday, Christmas Day or Bank Holidays), the magistrates' court officer shall, subject to the provisions of section 7 of the Prosecution of Offences Act 1985 (which relates to the sending of documents and things to the Director of Public Prosecutions), send to the Crown Court officer—

(a) the information, if it is in writing;

(b)

(i) the evidence tendered in accordance with section 5A of the Magistrates' Courts Act 1980 and, where any of that evidence consists of a copy of a deposition or documentary exhibit which is in the possession of the court, any such deposition or documentary exhibit, and

(ii) a certificate to the effect that that evidence was so tendered;

(c) any notification by the prosecutor under section 5D(2) of the 1980 Act;

(d) a copy of the record made in pursuance of section 5 of the Bail Act 1976 relating to the grant or withholding of bail in respect of the accused on the occasion of the committal;

(e) any recognizance entered into by any person as surety for the accused together with a statement of any enlargement thereof under section 129(4) of the 1980 Act;

(f) a list of the exhibits produced in evidence before the justices or treated as so produced;

(g) such of the exhibits referred to in paragraph (1)(f) as have been retained by the justices;

(h) the names and addresses of any interpreters engaged for the defendant for the purposes of the committal proceedings, together with any telephone numbers at which they can be readily contacted, and details of the languages or dialects in connection with which they have been so engaged;

(i) if the committal was under section 6(2) of the 1980 Act (committal for trial without consideration of the evidence), a statement to that effect;

(j) if the magistrates' court has made an order under section 8(2) of the 1980 Act (removal of restrictions on reports of committal proceedings), a statement to that effect;

(k) the certificate of the examining justices as to the costs of the prosecution under the Costs in Criminal Cases (General) Regulations 1986;

(l) if any person under the age of 18 is concerned in the committal proceedings, a statement whether the magistrates' court has given a direction under section 39 of the Children and Young Persons Act 1933 (prohibition of publication of certain matter in newspapers);

(m) a copy of any representation order previously made in the case;

(n) a copy of any application for a representation order previously made in the case which has been refused; and

(o) any documents relating to an appeal by the prosecution against the granting of bail.

(2) The period of 4 days specified in paragraph (1) may be extended in relation to any committal for so long as the Crown Court officer directs, having regard to the length of any document mentioned in that paragraph or any other relevant circumstances.

Part 11 Transfer for Trial of Serious Fraud Cases or Cases Involving Children

R-78 **Interpretation of this part**

11.1 (1) In this Part:

'notice of transfer' means a notice referred to in section 4(1) of the Criminal Justice Act 1987 or section 53(1) of the Criminal Justice Act 1991.

(2) Where this Part requires a document to be given or sent, or a notice to be communicated in writing, it may, with the consent of the addressee, be sent by electronic communication.

(3) Electronic communication means a communication transmitted (whether from one person to another, from one device to another or from a person to a device or vice versa)—
(a) by means of an electronic communications network (within the meaning of the Communications Act 2003); or
(b) by other means but while in an electronic form.

Transfer on bail R-79

11.2 (1) Where a person in respect of whom notice of transfer has been given—
(a) is granted bail under section 5(3) or (7A) of the Criminal Justice Act 1987 by the magistrates' court to which notice of transfer was given; or
(b) is granted bail under paragraph 2(1) or (7) of Schedule 6 to the Criminal Justice Act 1991 by the magistrates' court to which notice of transfer was given,
the magistrates' court officer shall give notice thereof in writing to the governor of the prison or remand centre to which the said person would have been committed by that court if he had been committed in custody for trial.
(2) Where notice of transfer is given under section 4(1) of the 1987 Act in respect of a corporation the magistrates' court officer shall give notice thereof to the governor of the prison to which would be committed a male over 21 committed by that court in custody for trial.

Notice where person removed to hospital R-80

11.3 Where a transfer direction has been given by the Secretary of State under section 47 or 48 of the Mental Health Act 1983 in respect of a person remanded in custody by a magistrates' court and, before the direction ceases to have effect, notice of transfer is given in respect of that person, the magistrates' court officer shall give notice thereof in writing—
(a) to the governor of the prison to which that person would have been committed by that court if he had been committed in custody for trial; and
(b) to the managers of the hospital where he is detained.

Variation of arrangements for bail R-81

11.4 (1) A person who intends to make an application to a magistrates' court under section 3(8) of the Bail Act 1976 as that subsection has effect under section 3(8A) of that Act shall give notice thereof in writing to the magistrates' court officer, and to the designated authority or the defendant, as the case may be, and to any sureties concerned.
(2) Where, on an application referred to in paragraph (1), a magistrates' court varies or imposes any conditions of bail, the magistrates' court officer shall send to the Crown Court officer a copy of the record made in pursuance of section 5 of the 1976 Act relating to such variation or imposition of conditions.

Documents to be sent to the Crown Court R-82

11.5 As soon as practicable after a magistrates' court to which notice of transfer has been given has discharged the functions reserved to it under section 4(1) of the Criminal Justice Act 1987 or section 53(3) of the Criminal Justice Act 1991, the magistrates' court officer shall send to the Crown Court officer—
(a) a list of the names, addresses and occupations of the witnesses;
(b) a copy of the record made in pursuance of section 5 of the Bail Act 1976 relating to the grant of withholding of bail in respect of the accused;
(c) any recognizance entered into by any person as surety for the accused together with a statement of any enlargement thereof;
(d) a copy of any representation order previously made in the case; and
(e) a copy of any application for a representation order previously made in the case which has been refused.

Part 12 Sending for Trial

Documents to be sent to the Crown Court R-83

12.1 (1) As soon as practicable after any person is sent for trial (pursuant to section 51 of the Crime and Disorder Act 1998), and in any event within 4 days from the date on which he is sent (not counting Saturdays, Sundays, Good Friday, Christmas Day or Bank Holidays), the magistrates' court officer shall, subject to section 7 of the Prosecution of Offences Act 1985 (which relates to the sending of documents and things to the Director of Public Prosecutions), send to the Crown Court officer—

(a) the information, if it is in writing;
(b) the notice required by section 51(7) of the 1998 Act;
(c) a copy of the record made in pursuance of section 5 of the Bail Act 1976 relating to the granting or withholding of bail in respect of the accused on the occasion of the sending;
(d) any recognizance entered into by any person as surety for the accused together with any enlargement thereof under section 129(4) of the Magistrates' Courts Act 1980;
(e) the names and addresses of any interpreters engaged for the defendant for the purposes of the appearance in the magistrates' court, together with any telephone numbers at which they can be readily contacted, and details of the languages or dialects in connection with which they have been so engaged;
(f) if any person under the age of 18 is concerned in the proceedings, a statement whether the magistrates' court has given a direction under section 39 of the Children and Young Persons Act 1933 (prohibition of publication of certain matter in newspapers);
(g) a copy of any representation order previously made in the case;
(h) a copy of any application for a representation order previously made in the case which has been refused; and
(i) any documents relating to an appeal by the prosecution against the granting of bail.

(2) The period of 4 days specified in paragraph (1) may be extended in relation to any sending for trial for so long as the Crown Court officer directs, having regard to any relevant circumstances.

R-84 **Time for first appearance of accused sent for trial**

12.2 A Crown Court officer to whom notice has been given under section 51(7) of the Crime and Disorder Act 1998, shall list the first Crown Court appearance of the person to whom the notice relates in accordance with any directions given by the magistrates' court.

Part 13 Dismissal of Charges Transferred or Sent to the Crown Court

R-85 **Interpretation of this Part**

13.1 In this Part:

'notice of transfer' means a notice referred to in section 4(1) of the Criminal Justice Act 1987 or section 53(1) of the Criminal Justice Act 1991; and

'the prosecution' means the authority by or on behalf of whom notice of transfer was given under the 1987 or 1991 Acts, or the authority by or on behalf of whom documents were served under paragraph 1 of Schedule 3 to the Crime and Disorder Act 1998.

R-86 **Written notice of oral application for dismissal**

13.2 (1) Where notice of transfer has been given under the Criminal Justice Act 1987 or the Criminal Justice Act 1991, or a person has been sent for trial under the Crime and Disorder Act 1998, and the person concerned proposes to apply orally—

(a) under section 6(1) of the 1987 Act;
(b) under paragraph 5(1) of Schedule 6 to the 1991 Act; or
(c) under paragraph 2(1) of Schedule 3 to the 1998 Act

for any charge in the case to be dismissed, he shall give notice of his intention in writing to the Crown Court officer at the place specified by the notice of transfer under the 1987 or 1991 Acts or the notice given under section 51(7) of the 1998 Act as the proposed place of trial. Notice of intention to make an application under the 1987 or 1991 Acts shall be in the form set out in the Practice Direction.

(2) Notice of intention to make an application shall be given—

(a) in the case of an application to dismiss charges transferred under the 1987 Act, not later than 28 days after the day on which notice of transfer was given;
(b) in the case of an application to dismiss charges transferred under the 1991 Act, not later than 14 days after the day on which notice of transfer was given; and
(c) in the case of an application to dismiss charges sent under the 1998 Act, not later than 14 days after the day on which the documents were served under paragraph 1 of Schedule 3 to that Act,

and a copy of the notice shall be given at the same time to the prosecution and to any person to whom the notice of transfer relates or with whom the applicant for dismissal is jointly charged.

(3) The time for giving notice may be extended, either before or after it expires, by the Crown Court, on an application made in accordance with paragraph (4).

(4) An application for an extension of time for giving notice shall be made in writing to the Crown Court officer, and a copy thereof shall be given at the same time to the prosecution and to any other person to whom the notice of transfer relates or with whom the applicant for dismissal is jointly charged. Such an application made in proceedings under the 1987 or 1991 Acts shall be in the form set out in the Practice Direction.

(5) The Crown Court officer shall give notice in the form set out in the Practice Direction of the judge's decision on an application under paragraph (3)—
(a) to the applicant for dismissal;
(b) to the prosecution; and
(c) to any other person to whom the notice of transfer relates or with whom the applicant for dismissal is jointly charged.

(6) A notice of intention to make an application under section 6(1) of the 1987 Act, paragraph 5(1) of Schedule 6 to the 1991 Act or paragraph 2(1) of Schedule 3 to the 1998 Act shall be accompanied by a copy of any material on which the applicant relies and shall—
(a) specify the charge or charges to which it relates;
(b) state whether the leave of the judge is sought under section 6(3) of the 1987 Act, paragraph 5(4) of Schedule 6 to the 1991 Act or paragraph 2(4) of Schedule 3 to the 1998 Act to adduce oral evidence on the application, indicating what witnesses it is proposed to call at the hearing; and
(c) in the case of a transfer under the 1991 Act, confirm in relation to each such witness that he is not a child to whom paragraph 5(5) of Schedule 6 to that Act applies.

(7) Where leave is sought from the judge for oral evidence to be given on an application, notice of his decision, indicating what witnesses are to be called if leave is granted, shall be given in writing by the Crown Court officer to the applicant for dismissal, the prosecution and to any other person to whom the notice of transfer relates or with whom the applicant for dismissal is jointly charged. Notice of a decision in proceedings under the 1987 or 1991 Acts shall be in the form set out in the Practice Direction.

(8) Where an application for dismissal under section 6(1) of the 1987 Act, paragraph 5(1) of Schedule 6 to the 1991 Act or paragraph 2(1) of Schedule 3 to the 1998 Act is to be made orally, the Crown Court officer shall list the application for hearing before a judge of the Crown Court and the prosecution shall be given the opportunity to be represented at the hearing.

Written application for dismissal R-87

13.3 (1) Application may be made for dismissal under section 6(1) of the Criminal Justice Act 1987, paragraph 5(1) of Schedule 6 to the Criminal Justice Act 1991 or paragraph 2(1) of Schedule 3 to the Crime and Disorder Act 1998 without an oral hearing. Such an application shall be in writing, and in proceedings under the 1987 or 1991 Acts shall be in the form set out in the Practice Direction.

(2) The application shall be sent to the Crown Court officer and shall be accompanied by a copy of any statement or other document, and identify any article, on which the applicant for dismissal relies.

(3) A copy of the application and of any accompanying documents shall be given at the same time to the prosecution and to any other person to whom the notice of transfer relates or with whom the applicant for dismissal is jointly charged.

(4) A written application for dismissal shall be made—
(a) not later than 28 days after the day on which notice of transfer was given under the 1987 Act;
(b) not later than 14 days after the day on which notice of transfer was given under the 1991 Act; or
(c) not later than 14 days after the day on which documents required by paragraph 1 of Schedule 3 to the 1998 Act were served

unless the time for making the application is extended, either before or after it expires, by the Crown Court; and rule 13.2(4) and (5) shall apply for the purposes of this paragraph as if references therein to giving notice of intention to make an oral application were references to making a written application under this rule.

Prosecution reply R-88

13.4 (1) Not later than seven days from the date of service of notice of intention to apply orally for the dismissal of any charge contained in a notice of transfer or based on documents served under paragraph 1 of Schedule 3 to the Crime and Disorder Act 1998, the prosecution may apply to the Crown Court under section 6(3) of the Criminal Justice Act 1987, paragraph 5(4) of Schedule 6 to the Criminal Justice Act 1991 or paragraph 2(4) of Schedule 3 to the 1998 Act for leave to adduce oral evidence at the hearing of the application, indicating what witnesses it is proposed to call.

(2) Not later than seven days from the date of receiving a copy of an application for dismissal under rule 13.3, the prosecution may apply to the Crown Court for an oral hearing of the application.

(3) An application under paragraph (1) or (2) shall be served on the Crown Court officer in writing and, in the case of an application under paragraph (2), shall state whether the leave of the judge is sought to adduce oral evidence and, if so, shall indicate what witnesses it is proposed to call. Where leave is sought to adduce oral evidence under paragraph 5(4) of Schedule 6 to the 1991 Act, the application should confirm in relation to each such witness that he is not a child to whom paragraph 5(5) of that Schedule applies. Such an application in proceedings under the 1987 or 1991 Acts shall be in the form set out in the Practice Direction.

(4) Notice of the judge's determination upon an application under paragraph (1) or (2), indicating what witnesses (if any) are to be called shall be served in writing by the Crown Court officer on the prosecution, on the applicant for dismissal and on any other party to whom the notice of transfer relates or with whom the applicant for dismissal is jointly charged. Such a notice in proceedings under the 1987 or 1991 Acts shall be in the form set out in the Practice Direction.

(5) Where, having received the material specified in rule 13.2 or, as the case may be, rule 13.3, the prosecution proposes to adduce in reply thereto any written comments or any further evidence, the prosecution shall serve any such comments, copies of the statements or other documents outlining the evidence of any proposed witnesses, copies of any further documents and, in the case of an application to dismiss charges transferred under the 1991 Act, copies of any video recordings which it is proposed to tender in evidence, on the Crown Court officer not later than 14 days from the date of receiving the said material, and shall at the same time serve copies thereof on the applicant for dismissal and any other person to whom the notice of transfer relates or with whom the applicant is jointly charged. In the case of a defendant acting in person, copies of video recordings need not be served but shall be made available for viewing by him.

(6) The time for—
(a) making an application under paragraph (1) or (2) above; or
(b) serving any material on the Crown Court officer under paragraph (5) above
may be extended, either before or after it expires, by the Crown Court, on an application made in accordance with paragraph (7) below.

(7) An application for an extension of time under paragraph (6) above shall be made in writing and shall be served on the Crown Court officer, and a copy thereof shall be served at the same time on to the applicant for dismissal and on any other person to whom the notice of transfer relates or with whom the applicant for dismissal is jointly charged. Such an application in proceedings under the 1987 or 1991 Acts shall be in the form set out in the Practice Direction.

R-89 Determination of applications for dismissal

13.5 (1) A judge may grant leave for a witness to give oral evidence on an application for dismissal notwithstanding that notice of intention to call the witness has not been given in accordance with the foregoing provisions of this Part.

(2) Where an application for dismissal is determined otherwise than at an oral hearing, the Crown Court officer shall as soon as practicable, send to all the parties to the case written notice of the outcome of the application. Such a notice in proceedings under the 1987 and 1991 Acts shall be in the form set out in the Practice Direction.

Part 14 The Indictment

R-90 Service and signature of indictment

14.1 (1) The prosecutor must serve a draft indictment on the Crown Court officer not more than 28 days after—
(a) service on the defendant and on the Crown Court officer of copies of the documents containing the evidence on which the charge or charges are based, in a case where the defendant is sent for trial;
(b) a High Court judge gives permission to serve a draft indictment;

(c) the Court of Appeal orders a retrial; or
(d) the committal or transfer of the defendant for trial.
(2) The Crown Court may extend the time limit, even after it has expired.
(3) Unless the Crown Court otherwise directs, the court officer must—
(a) sign, and add the date of receipt on, the indictment; and
(b) serve a copy of the indictment on all parties.

Form and content of indictment R-91

14.2 (1) An indictment must be in one of the forms set out in the Practice Direction and must contain, in a paragraph called a 'count'—
(a) a statement of the offence charged that—
(i) describes the offence in ordinary language, and
(ii) identifies any legislation that creates it; and
(b) such particulars of the conduct constituting the commission of the offence as to make clear what the prosecutor alleges against the defendant.
(2) More than one incident of the commission of the offence may be included in a count if those incidents taken together amount to a course of conduct having regard to the time, place or purpose of commission.
(3) An indictment may contain more than one count if all the offences charged—
(a) are founded on the same facts; or
(b) form or are a part of a series of offences of the same or a similar character.
(4) The counts must be numbered consecutively.
(5) An indictment may contain—
(a) any count charging substantially the same offence as one—
(i) specified in the notice of the offence or offences for which the defendant was sent for trial,
(ii) on which the defendant was committed for trial, or
(iii) specified in the notice of transfer given by the prosecutor; and
(b) any other count based on the prosecution evidence already served which the Crown Court may try.

PART 15 PREPARATORY HEARINGS IN THE CROWN COURT

When this Part applies R-92

15.1 (1) This Part applies where the Crown Court—
(a) can order a preparatory hearing, under—
(i) section 7 of the Criminal Justice Act 1987 (cases of serious or complex fraud), or
(ii) section 29 of the Criminal Procedure and Investigations Act 1996 (other complex, serious or lengthy cases);
(b) must order such a hearing, to determine an application for a trial without a jury, under—
(i) section 44 of the Criminal Justice Act 2003 (danger of jury tampering), or
(ii) section 17 of the Domestic Violence, Crime and Victims Act 2004 (trial of sample counts by jury, and others by judge alone);
(c) must order such a hearing, under section 29 of the 1996 Act, where section 29(1B) or (1C) applies (cases in which a terrorism offence is charged, or other serious cases with a terrorist connection).

Exercise of court's powers R-93

15.2 The court may decide whether to order a preparatory hearing—
(a) on an application or on its own initiative;
(b) at a hearing, in public or in private, or without a hearing;
(c) in a party's absence, if that party—
(i) applied for the order, or
(ii) has had at least 14 days in which to make representations.

Application for preparatory hearing R-94

15.3 (1) A party who wants the court to order a preparatory hearing must—
(a) apply in writing—
(i) as soon as reasonably practicable, and in any event
(ii) not more than 14 days after the defendant pleads not guilty;

(b) serve the application on—
(i) the court officer, and
(ii) each other party.
(2) The applicant must—
(a) if relevant, explain what legislation requires the court to order a preparatory hearing;
(b) otherwise, explain—
(i) what makes the case complex or serious, or makes the trial likely to be long,
(ii) why a substantial benefit will accrue from a preparatory hearing, and
(iii) why the court's ordinary powers of case management are not adequate.
(3) A prosecutor who wants the court to order a trial without a jury must explain—
(a) where the prosecutor alleges a danger of jury tampering—
(i) what evidence there is of a real and present danger that jury tampering would take place,
(ii) what steps, if any, reasonably might be taken to prevent jury tampering, and
(iii) why, notwithstanding such steps, the likelihood of jury tampering is so substantial as to make it necessary in the interests of justice to order such a trial; or
(b) where the prosecutor proposes trial without a jury on some counts on the indictment—
(i) why a trial by jury involving all the counts would be impracticable,
(ii) how the counts proposed for jury trial can be regarded as samples of the others, and
(iii) why it would be in the interests of justice to order such a trial.

R-95 Application containing information withheld from a defendant

15.4 (1) This rule applies where—
(a) the prosecutor applies for an order for a trial without a jury because of a danger of jury tampering; and
(b) the application includes information that the prosecutor thinks ought not be revealed to a defendant.
(2) The prosecutor must—
(a) omit that information from the part of the application that is served on that defendant;
(b) mark the other part to show that, unless the court otherwise directs, it is only for the court; and
(c) in that other part, explain why the prosecutor has withheld that information from that defendant.
(3) The hearing of an application to which this rule applies—
(a) must be in private, unless the court otherwise directs; and
(b) if the court so directs, may be, wholly or in part, in the absence of a defendant from whom information has been withheld.
(4) At the hearing of an application to which this rule applies—
(a) the general rule is that the court will receive, in the following sequence—
(i) representations first by the prosecutor and then by each defendant, in all the parties' presence, and then
(ii) further representations by the prosecutor, in the absence of a defendant from whom information has been withheld; but
(b) the court may direct other arrangements for the hearing.
(5) Where, on an application to which this rule applies, the court orders a trial without a jury—
(a) the general rule is that the trial will be before a judge other than the judge who made the order; but
(b) the court may direct other arrangements.

R-96 Representations in response

15.5 (1) This rule applies where a party wants to make representations about—
(a) an application for a preparatory hearing;
(b) an application for a trial without a jury.
(2) Such a party must—
(a) serve the representations on—
(i) the court officer, and
(ii) each other party;
(b) do so not more than 14 days after service of the application;
(c) ask for a hearing, if that party wants one, and explain why it is needed.

(3) Where representations include information that the person making them thinks ought not be revealed to another party, that person must—
(a) omit that information from the representations served on that other party;
(b) mark the information to show that, unless the court otherwise directs, it is only for the court; and
(c) with that information include an explanation of why it has been withheld from that other party.
(4) Representations against an application for an order must explain why the conditions for making it are not met.

Commencement of preparatory hearing R-96A

15.6 At the beginning of a preparatory hearing, the court must—
(a) announce that it is such a hearing; and
(b) take the defendant's plea (unless already done).

Court's power to vary requirements R-96B

15.7 (1) The court may—
(a) shorten or extend (even after it has expired) a time limit under this Part; and
(b) allow an application or representations to be made orally.
(2) A person who wants an extension of time must—
(a) apply when serving the application or representations for which it is needed; and
(b) explain the delay.

Part 16 Reporting, Etc. Restrictions

Section 1: general rules

When this Part applies R-97

16.1 (1) This Part applies where the court can—
(a) impose a restriction on—
(i) reporting what takes place at a public hearing, or
(ii) public access to what otherwise would be a public hearing;
(b) vary or remove a reporting or access restriction that is imposed by legislation;
(c) withhold information from the public during a public hearing;
(d) order a trial in private;
(e) allow there to take place during a hearing—
(i) sound recording, or
(ii) communication by electronic means.
(2) This Part does not apply to arrangements required by legislation, or directed by the court, in connection with—
(a) sound recording during a hearing, or the transcription of such a recording; or
(b) measures to assist a witness or defendant to give evidence.

Exercise of court's powers to which this Part applies R-98

16.2 (1) When exercising a power to which this Part applies, as well as furthering the overriding objective, in accordance with rule 1.3, the court must have regard to the importance of—
(a) dealing with criminal cases in public; and
(b) allowing a public hearing to be reported to the public.
(2) The court may determine an application under this Part—
(a) at a hearing, in public or in private; or
(b) without a hearing.
(3) But the court must not exercise a power to which this Part applies unless each party and any other person directly affected—
(a) is present; or
(b) has had an opportunity—
(i) to attend, or
(ii) to make representations.

R-99 Court's power to vary requirements under this Part

16.3 (1) The court may—
(a) shorten or extend (even after it has expired) a time limit under this Part;
(b) require an application to be made in writing instead of orally;
(c) consider an application or representations made orally instead of in writing;
(d) dispense with a requirement to—
(i) give notice, or
(ii) serve a written application.
(2) Someone who wants an extension of time must—
(a) apply when making the application or representations for which it is needed; and
(b) explain the delay.

Section 2: reporting and access restrictions

R-100 Reporting and access restrictions

16.4 (1) This rule applies where the court can—
(a) impose a restriction on—
(i) reporting what takes place at a public hearing, or
(ii) public access to what otherwise would be a public hearing;
(b) withhold information from the public during a public hearing.
(2) The court may do so—
(a) on application by a party; or
(b) on its own initiative.
(3) A party who wants the court to do so must—
(a) apply as soon as reasonably practicable;
(b) notify—
(i) each other party, and
(ii) such other person (if any) as the court directs;
(c) specify the proposed terms of the order, and for how long it should last;
(d) explain—
(i) what power the court has to make the order, and
(ii) why an order in the terms proposed is necessary;
(e) where the application is for a reporting direction in respect of a witness under section 46 of the Youth Justice and Criminal Evidence Act 1999, explain—
(i) how the witness is eligible for assistance, and
(ii) why a reporting direction would be likely to improve the quality of the witness' evidence, or the level of co-operation the witness gives the applicant in connection with the preparation of the applicant's case.

R-101 Varying or removing restrictions

16.5 (1) This rule applies where the court can vary or remove a reporting or access restriction.
(2) The court may do so—
(a) on application by a party or person directly affected; or
(b) on its own initiative.
(3) A party or person who wants the court to do so must—
(a) apply as soon as reasonably practicable;
(b) notify—
(i) each other party, and
(ii) such other person (if any) as the court directs;
(c) specify the restriction;
(d) explain, as appropriate, why it should be varied or removed.

R-102 Trial in private

16.6 (1) This rule applies where the court can order a trial in private.
(2) A party who wants the court to do so must—
(a) apply in writing not less than 5 business days before the trial is due to begin; and
(b) serve the application on—
(i) the court officer, and
(ii) each other party.

(3) The applicant must explain—
(a) the reasons for the application;
(b) how much of the trial the applicant proposes should be in private; and
(c) why no measures other than trial in private will suffice, such as—
(i) reporting restrictions,
(ii) an admission of facts,
(iii) the introduction of hearsay evidence,
(iv) a direction for a special measure under section 19 of the Youth Justice and Criminal Evidence Act 1999,
(v) a witness anonymity order under section 86 of the Coroners and Justice Act 2009, or
(vi) arrangements for the protection of a witness.
(4) Where the application includes information that the applicant thinks ought not be revealed to another party, the applicant must—
(a) omit that information from the part of the application that is served on that other party;
(b) mark the other part to show that, unless the court otherwise directs, it is only for the court; and
(c) in that other part, explain why the applicant has withheld that information from that other party.
(5) The court officer must at once—
(a) display notice of the application somewhere prominent in the vicinity of the courtroom; and
(b) give notice of the application to reporters by such other arrangements as the Lord Chancellor directs.
(6) The application must be determined at a hearing which—
(a) will be in private, unless the court otherwise directs;
(b) if the court so directs, may be, wholly or in part, in the absence of a party from whom information has been withheld; and
(c) in the Crown Court, must be after the defendant is arraigned but before the jury is sworn.
(7) At the hearing of the application—
(a) the general rule is that the court will receive, in the following sequence—
(i) representations first by the applicant and then by each other party, in all the parties' presence, and then
(ii) further representations by the applicant, in the absence of a party from whom information has been withheld; but
(b) the court may direct other arrangements for the hearing.
(8) The court must not hear a trial in private until—
(a) the business day after the day on which it orders such a trial, or
(b) the disposal of any appeal against, or review of, any such order, if later.

Representations in response **R-103**

16.7 (1) This rule applies where a party, or person directly affected, wants to make representations about an application.
(2) Such a party or person must—
(a) serve the representations on—
(i) the court officer,
(ii) the applicant,
(iii) each other party, and
(iv) such other person (if any) as the court directs;
(b) do so as soon as reasonably practicable after notice of the application; and
(c) ask for a hearing, if that party or person wants one, and explain why it is needed.
(3) Representations must—
(a) explain the reasons for any objection;
(b) specify any alternative terms proposed.

Order about restriction or trial in private **R-104**

16.8 (1) This rule applies where the court—
(a) orders, varies or removes a reporting or access restriction; or
(b) orders a trial in private.

(2) The court officer must—
(a) record the court's reasons for the decision; and
(b) as soon as reasonably practicable, arrange for notice of the decision to be—
(i) displayed somewhere prominent in the vicinity of the courtroom, and
(ii) communicated to reporters by such other arrangements as the Lord Chancellor directs.

Sound recording and electronic communication

R-105 **Sound recording and electronic communication**

16.9 (1) This rule applies where the court can give permission to—
(a) bring into a hearing for use, or use during a hearing, a device for—
(i) recording sound, or
(ii) communicating by electronic means; or
(b) publish a sound recording made during a hearing.
(2) The court may give such permission—
(a) on application; or
(b) on its own initiative.
(3) A person who wants the court to give such permission must—
(a) apply as soon as reasonably practicable;
(b) notify—
(i) each party, and
(ii) such other person (if any) as the court directs; and
(c) explain why the court should permit the use or publication proposed.
(4) As a condition of the applicant using such a device, the court may direct arrangements to minimise the risk of its use—
(a) contravening a reporting restriction;
(b) disrupting the hearing; or
(c) compromising the fairness of the hearing, for example by affecting—
(i) the evidence to be given by a witness, or
(ii) the verdict of a jury.
(5) Such a direction may require that the device is used only—
(a) in a specified part of the courtroom;
(b) for a specified purpose;
(c) for a purpose connected with the applicant's activity as a member of a specified group, for example representatives of news-gathering or reporting organisations;
(d) at a specified time, or in a specified way.

R-106–7 **Forfeiture of unauthorised sound recording**

16.10 (1) This rule applies where someone without the court's permission—
(a) uses a device for recording sound during a hearing; or
(b) publishes a sound recording made during a hearing.
(2) The court may exercise its power to forfeit the device or recording—
(a) on application by a party, or on its own initiative;
(b) provisionally, despite rule 16.2(3), to allow time for representations.
(3) A party who wants the court to forfeit a device or recording must—
(a) apply as soon as reasonably practicable;
(b) notify—
(i) as appropriate, the person who used the device, or who published the recording, and
(ii) each other party; and
(c) explain why the court should exercise that power.

PART 17 EXTRADITION

R-108 **Refusal to make an order of committal**

17.1 (1) Where a magistrates' court refuses to make an order of committal in relation to a person in respect of the offence or, as the case may be, any of the offences to which the authority to proceed relates and the state, country or colony seeking the surrender of that person immediately informs the court that it intends to make an application to the court to state a case for the opinion of the High Court, if the magistrates' court makes an order in accordance with section 10(2) of the Extradition Act 1989 releasing that person on bail, the court officer shall forthwith send a copy of that order to the Administrative Court Office.

(2) Where a magistrates' court refuses to make an order of committal in relation to a person in respect of the offence or, as the case may be, any of the offences to which the authority to proceed relates and the state, country or colony seeking his surrender wishes to apply to the court to state a case for the opinion of the High Court under section 10(1) of the 1989 Act, such application must be made to the magistrates' court within the period of 21 days following the day on which the court refuses to make the order of committal unless the court grants a longer period within which the application is to be made.

(3) Such an application shall be made in writing and shall identify the question or questions of law on which the opinion of the High Court is sought.

(4) Within 21 days after receipt of an application to state a case under section 10(1) of the 1989 Act, the magistrates' court officer shall send a draft case to the solicitor for the state, country or colony and to the person whose surrender is sought or his solicitor and shall allow each party 21 days within which to make representations thereon; within 21 days after the latest day on which such representations may be made the court of committal shall, after considering any such representations and making such adjustments, if any, to the draft case as it thinks fit, state and sign the case which the court officer shall forthwith send to the solicitor for the state, country or colony.

Notice of waiver R-109

17.2 (1) A notice given under section 14 of, or paragraph 9 of Schedule 1 to, the Extradition Act 1989 (notice of waiver under the simplified procedure) shall be in the form set out in the Practice Direction or a form to the like effect.

(2) Such a notice shall be signed in the presence of the Senior District Judge (Chief Magistrate) or another District Judge (Magistrates' Courts) designated by him for the purposes of the Act, a justice of the peace or a justices' clerk.

(3) Any such notice given by a person in custody shall be delivered to the Governor of the prison in whose custody he is.

(4) If a person on bail gives such notice he shall deliver it to, or send it by post in a registered letter or by recorded delivery service addressed to, the Secretary of State for the Home Department, c/o Extradition Section, Home Office, 5th Floor, Fry Building, 2 Marsham Street, London SW1P 4DF.

Notice of consent R-110

17.3 (1) A person arrested in pursuance of a warrant under section 8 of or paragraph 5 of Schedule 1 to the Extradition Act 1989 may at any time consent to his return; and where such consent is given in accordance with the following provisions of this rule, the Senior District Judge (Chief Magistrate) or another District Judge (Magistrates' Courts) designated by him for the purposes of the Act may order the committal for return of that person in accordance with section 14(2) of that Act or, as the case may be, paragraph 9(2) of Schedule 1 to the Act.

(2) A notice of consent for the purposes of this rule shall be given in the form set out in the Practice Direction and shall be signed in the presence of the Senior District Judge (Chief Magistrate) or another District Judge (Magistrates' Courts) designated by him for the purposes of the 1989 Act.

Notice of consent (parties to 1995 Convention) R-111

17.4 (1) This rule applies as between the United Kingdom and states other than the Republic of Ireland that are parties to the Convention drawn up on the basis of Article 31 of the Treaty on European Union on Simplified Extradition Procedures between the Member States of the European Union, in relation to which section 14A of the Extradition Act 1989 applies by virtue of section 34A and Schedule 1A of that Act.

(2) Notice of consent for the purposes of section 14A(3) of the 1989 Act shall be given in the form set out in the Practice Direction and shall be signed in the presence of the Senior District Judge (Chief Magistrate) or another District Judge (Magistrates' Courts) designated by him for the purposes of that Act.

(3) A Senior District Judge (Chief Magistrate) or another District Judge (Magistrates' Courts) designated by him for the purposes of the Act may order the committal for return of a person if he gives consent under section 14A of the 1989 Act in accordance with paragraph (2) above before he is committed under section 9 of that Act.

R-112 Consent to early removal to Republic of Ireland

17.5 (1) A notice given under section 3(1)(a) of the Backing of Warrants (Republic of Ireland) Act 1965 (consent to surrender earlier than is otherwise permitted) shall be signed in the presence of a justice of the peace or a justices' clerk.

(2) Any such notice given by a person in custody shall be delivered to the Governor of the prison in whose custody he is.

(3) If a person on bail gives such notice, he shall deliver it to, or send it by post in a registered letter or by recorded delivery service addressed to, the police officer in charge of the police station specified in his recognizance.

(4) Any such notice shall be attached to the warrant ordering the surrender of that person.

R-113 Bail pending removal to Republic of Ireland

17.6 (1) The person taking the recognizance of a person remanded on bail under section 2(1) or 4(3) of the Backing of Warrants (Republic of Ireland) Act 1965 shall furnish a copy of the recognizance to the police officer in charge of the police station specified in the recognizance.

(2) The court officer for a magistrates' court which ordered a person to be surrendered and remanded him on bail shall deliver to, or send by post in a registered letter or by recorded delivery service addressed to, the police officer in charge of the police station specified in the recognizance the warrant ordering the person to be surrendered.

(3) The court officer for a magistrates' court which refused to order a person to be delivered under section 2 of the 1965 Act but made an order in accordance with section 2A(2) of that Act releasing that person on bail, upon the chief officer of police immediately informing the court that he intended to make an application to the court to state a case for the opinion of the High Court, shall forthwith send a copy of that order to the Administrative Court Office.

R-114 Delivery of warrant issued in Republic of Ireland

17.7 (1) The court officer for a magistrates' court which ordered a person to be surrendered under section 2(1) of the Backing of Warrants (Republic of Ireland) Act 1965 shall deliver to, or send by post in a registered letter or by recorded delivery service addressed to—

(a) if he is remanded in custody under section 5(1)(a) of the 1965 Act, the prison Governor to whose custody he is committed;

(b) if he is remanded on bail under section 5(1)(b) of the 1965 Act, the police officer in charge of the police station specified in the recognizance; or

(c) if he is committed to the custody of a constable pending the taking from him of a recognizance under section 5(1) of the 1965 Act, the police officer in charge of the police station specified in the warrant of commitment,

the warrant of arrest issued by a judicial authority in the Republic of Ireland and endorsed in accordance with section 1 of the 1965 Act.

(2) The Governor or police officer to whom the said warrant of arrest is delivered or sent shall arrange for it to be given to the member of the police force of the Republic into whose custody the person is delivered when the person is so delivered.

R-115 Verification of warrant etc. issued in Republic of Ireland

17.8 (1) A document purporting to be a warrant issued by a judicial authority in the Republic of Ireland shall, for the purposes of section 7(a) of the Backing of Warrants (Republic of Ireland) Act 1965, be verified by a certificate purporting to be signed by a judicial authority, a clerk of a court or a member of the police force of the Republic and certifying that the document is a warrant and is issued by a judge or justice of a court or a peace commissioner.

(2) A document purporting to be a copy of a summons issued by a judicial authority in the Republic shall, for the purposes of section 7(a) of the 1965 Act, be verified by a certificate purporting to be signed by a judicial authority, a clerk of a court or a member of the police force of the Republic and certifying that the document is a true copy of such a summons.

(3) A deposition purporting to have been made in the Republic, or affidavit or written statement purporting to have been sworn therein, shall, for the purposes of section 7(c) of the 1965 Act, be verified by a certificate purporting to be signed by the person before whom it was sworn and certifying that it was so sworn.

R-116 Application to state a case where court declines to order removal to Republic of Ireland

17.9 (1) Where a magistrates' court refuses to make an order in relation to a person under section 2 of the Backing of Warrants (Republic of Ireland) Act 1965, any application to the court under section 2A(1) of that Act to state a case for the opinion of the High Court on any question of law arising in the proceedings must be made to the court by the chief officer of police within the period of 21 days following the day on which the order was refused, unless the court grants a longer period within which the application is to be made.

(2) Such an application shall be made in writing and shall identify the question or questions of law on which the opinion of the High Court is sought.

Draft case where court declines to order removal to Republic of Ireland **R-117**

17.10 Within 21 days after receipt of an application to state a case under section 2A(1) of the Backing of Warrants (Republic of Ireland) Act 1965, the magistrates' court officer shall send a draft case to the applicant or his solicitor and to the person to whom the warrant relates or his solicitor and shall allow each party 21 days within which to make representations thereon; within 21 days after the latest day on which such representations may be made the court shall, after considering such representations and making such adjustments, if any, to the draft case as it thinks fit, state and sign the case which the court officer shall forthwith send to the applicant or his solicitor.

Forms for proceedings for removal to Republic of Ireland **R-118**

17.11 Where a requirement is imposed by the Backing of Warrants (Republic of Ireland) Act 1965 for the use of a form, and an appropriate form is contained in the Practice Direction, that form shall be used.

Part 18 Warrants for Arrest, Detention or Imprisonment

When this Part applies **R-119**

18.1 (1) This Part applies where the court can issue a warrant for arrest, detention or imprisonment.

(2) In this Part, 'defendant' means anyone against whom such a warrant is issued.

Terms of a warrant for arrest **R-120**

18.2 A warrant for arrest must require the person(s) to whom it is directed to arrest the defendant and—

(a) bring the defendant to a court—
  (i) specified in the warrant, or
  (ii) required or allowed by law; or

(b) release the defendant on bail (with conditions or without) to attend court at a date, time and place—
  (i) specified in the warrant, or
  (ii) to be notified by the court.

Terms of a warrant for detention or imprisonment **R-121**

18.3 (1) A warrant for detention or imprisonment must—

(a) require the person(s) to whom it is directed to—
  (i) arrest the defendant,
  (ii) take the defendant to any place specified in the warrant, and
  (iii) deliver the defendant to the custodian of that place; and

(b) require that custodian to keep the defendant in custody, as ordered by the court, until in accordance with the law—
  (i) the defendant is delivered to the appropriate court or place, or
  (ii) the defendant is released.

(2) Where a magistrates' court remands a defendant to police detention under section 128(7) or section 136 of the Magistrates' Courts Act 1980, or to customs detention under section 152 of the Criminal Justice Act 1988, the warrant it issues must—

(a) be directed, as appropriate, to—
  (i) a constable, or
  (ii) an officer of Her Majesty's Revenue and Customs; and

(b) require that constable or officer to keep the defendant in custody—
  (i) for a period (not exceeding the maximum permissible) specified in the warrant, or
  (ii) until in accordance with the law the defendant is delivered to the appropriate court or place.

R-122 Information to be included in a warrant

18.4 (1) A warrant must identify—
(a) the person(s) to whom it is directed;
(b) the defendant against whom it was issued;
(c) the reason for its issue;
(d) the court that issued it, unless that is otherwise recorded by the court officer; and
(e) the court office for the court that issued it.
(2) A warrant for detention or imprisonment must contain a record of any decision by the court under—
(a) section 23 of the Children and Young Persons Act 1969 (remand to local authority accommodation);
(b) section 80 of the Magistrates' Courts Act 1980 (application of money found on defaulter to satisfy sum adjudged); or
(c) section 82(1) or (4) of the 1980 Act (conditions for issue of a warrant).
(3) A warrant that contains an error is not invalid, as long as—
(a) it was issued in respect of a lawful decision by the court; and
(b) it contains enough information to identify that decision.

R-123 Execution of a warrant

18.5 (1) A warrant may be executed—
(a) by any person to whom it is directed; or
(b) if the warrant was issued by a magistrates' court, by anyone authorised to do so by section 125 (warrants), 125A (civilian enforcement officers) or 125B (execution by approved enforcement agency) of the Magistrates' Courts Act 1980.
(2) The person who executes a warrant must—
(a) explain, in terms the defendant can understand, what the warrant requires, and why;
(b) show the defendant the warrant, if that person has it; and
(c) if the defendant asks—
(i) arrange for the defendant to see the warrant, if that person does not have it, and
(ii) show the defendant any written statement of that person's authority required by section 125A or 125B of the 1980 Act.
(3) The person who executes a warrant of arrest that requires the defendant to be released on bail must—
(a) make a record of—
(i) the defendant's name,
(ii) the reason for the arrest,
(iii) the defendant's release on bail, and
(iv) when and where the warrant requires the defendant to attend court; and
(b) serve the record on—
(i) the defendant, and
(ii) the court officer.
(4) The person who executes a warrant of detention or imprisonment must—
(a) take the defendant—
(i) to any place specified in the warrant, or
(ii) if that is not immediately practicable, to any other place at which the defendant may be lawfully detained (and the warrant then has effect as if it specified that place);
(b) obtain a receipt from the custodian; and
(c) notify the court officer that the defendant has been taken to that place.

R-124 Warrants that cease to have effect on payment

18.6 (1) This rule applies to a warrant issued by a magistrates' court under any of the following provisions of the Magistrates' Courts Act 1980—
(a) section 76 (enforcement of sums adjudged to be paid);
(b) section 83 (process for securing attendance of offender);
(c) section 86 (power of magistrates' court to fix day for appearance of offender at means inquiry, etc.);
(d) section 136 (committal to custody overnight at police station for non-payment of sum adjudged by conviction).

(2) The warrant no longer has effect if—
(a) the sum in respect of which the warrant was issued is paid to the person executing it;
(b) that sum is offered to, but refused by, that person; or
(c) that person is shown a receipt for that sum given by—
(i) the court officer, or
(ii) the authority to which that sum is due.

Warrant issued when the court office is closed R-125

18.7 (1) This rule applies where the court issues a warrant when the court office is closed.
(2) The applicant for the warrant must, not more than 72 hours later, serve on the court officer—
(a) a copy of the warrant; and
(b) any written material that was submitted to the court.

Part 19 Bail in Magistrates' Courts and the Crown Court

Application to a magistrates' court to vary conditions of bail R-126

19.1 (1) An application under section 43B(1) of the Magistrates' Courts Act of 1980 or section 47(1E) of the Police and Criminal Evidence Act 1984, to vary conditions of police bail shall—
(a) be made in writing;
(b) contain a statement of the grounds upon which it is made;
(c) specify the offence with which the applicant was charged before his release on bail;
(d) where the applicant has been bailed following charge, specify the offence with which he was charged and, in any other case, specify the offence under investigation;
(e) specify the name and address of any surety provided by the applicant before his release on bail to secure his surrender to custody; and
(f) specify the address at which the applicant would reside, if the court imposed a condition of residence.
(2) Any such application shall be sent to the court officer for—
(a) the magistrates' court appointed by the custody officer as the court before which the applicant has a duty to appear; or
(b) if no such court has been appointed, a magistrates' court acting for the local justice area in which the police station at which the applicant was granted bail or at which the conditions of his bail were varied, as the case may be, is situated.
(3) The court officer to whom an application is sent under paragraph (2) above shall serve not less than 24 hours' notice in writing of the date, time and place fixed for the hearing of the application on—
(a) the applicant;
(b) the prosecutor or, if the applicant has not been charged, the chief officer of police or other investigator, together with a copy of the application; and
(c) any surety in connection with bail in criminal proceedings granted to, or the conditions of which were varied by a custody officer in relation to, the applicant.
(4) The time fixed for the hearing shall be not later than 72 hours after receipt of the application. In reckoning for the purposes of this paragraph any period of 72 hours, no account shall be taken of Christmas Day, Boxing Day, Good Friday, any bank holiday, or any Saturday or Sunday.
(5) A party who wants a magistrates' court to vary or to impose conditions of bail under section 3(8) of the Bail Act 1976, must—
(a) serve notice, not less than 24 hours before the hearing at which that party intends to apply, on—
(i) the court officer, and
(ii) he other party; and
(b) in that notice—
(i) specify the variation or conditions proposed, and
(ii) explain the reasons.
(6) If the magistrates' court hearing an application under section 43B(1) of the 1980 Act or section 47(1E) of the 1984 Act discharges or enlarges any recognizance entered into by any surety or increases or reduces the amount in which that person is bound, the court officer shall forthwith give notice thereof to the applicant and to any such surety.

(7) The court may—
(a) vary or waive a time limit under paragraph (3) or (5) of this rule; and
(b) allow a notice to be—
(i) in a different form to one set out in the Practice Direction, or
(ii) given orally.

R-127 Application to a magistrates' court to reconsider grant of police bail

19.2 (1) The appropriate court for the purposes of section 5B of the Bail Act 1976 in relation to the decision of a constable to grant bail shall be—
(a) the magistrates' court appointed by the custody officer as the court before which the person to whom bail was granted has a duty to appear; or
(b) if no such court has been appointed, a magistrates' court acting for the local justice area in which the police station at which bail was granted is situated.

(2) An application under section 5B(1) of the 1976 Act shall—
(a) be made in writing;
(b) contain a statement of the grounds on which it is made;
(c) specify the offence which the proceedings in which bail was granted were connected with, or for;
(d) specify the decision to be reconsidered (including any conditions of bail which have been imposed and why they have been imposed);
(e) specify the name and address of any surety provided by the person to whom the application relates to secure his surrender to custody; and
(f) contain a notice of the powers available to the court under section 5B of the 1976 Act.

(3) The court officer to whom an application is sent under paragraph (2) above shall serve notice in writing of the date, time and place fixed for the hearing of the application on—
(a) the prosecutor who made the application;
(b) the person to whom bail was granted, together with a copy of the application; and
(c) any surety specified in the application

(4) The time fixed for the hearing shall be not later than 72 hours after receipt of the application. In reckoning for the purpose of this paragraph any period of 72 hours, no account shall be taken of Christmas Day, Good Friday, any bank holiday or any Sunday.

(5) At the hearing of an application under section 5B of the 1976 Act the court shall consider any representations made by the person affected (whether in writing or orally) before taking any decision under that section with respect to him; and, where the person affected does not appear before the court, the court shall not take such a decision unless it is proved to the satisfaction of the court, on oath or in the manner set out by rule 4.11, that the notice required to be given under paragraph (3) of this rule was served on him before the hearing.

(6) Where the court proceeds in the absence of the person affected in accordance with paragraph (6)—
(a) if the decision of the court is to vary the conditions of bail or impose conditions in respect of bail which has been granted unconditionally, the court officer shall notify the person affected;
(b) if the decision of the court is to withhold bail, the order of the court under section 5B(5)(b) of the 1976 Act (surrender to custody) shall be signed by the justice issuing it or state his name and be authenticated by the signature of the clerk of the court.

R-128 Notice of change of time for appearance before magistrates' court

19.3 Where—
(a) a person has been granted bail under the Police and Criminal Evidence Act 1984 subject to a duty to appear before a magistrates' court and the court before which he is to appear appoints a later time at which he is to appear; or
(b) a magistrates' court further remands a person on bail under section 129 of the Magistrates' Courts Act 1980 in his absence,

it shall give him and his sureties, if any, notice thereof.

R-129 Directions by a magistrates' court as to security, etc

19.4 Where a magistrates' court, under section 3(5) or (6) of the Bail Act 1976, imposes any requirement to be complied with before a person's release on bail, the court may give directions as to the manner in which and the person or persons before whom the requirement may be complied with.

Requirements to be complied with before release on bail granted by a magistrates' court R-130

19.5 (1) Where a magistrates' court has fixed the amount in which a person (including any surety) is to be bound by a recognizance, the recognizance may be entered into—

(a) in the case of a surety where the accused is in a prison or other place of detention, before the governor or keeper of the prison or place as well as before the persons mentioned in section 8(4)(a) of the Bail Act 1976;

(b) in any other case, before a justice of the peace, a justices' clerk, a magistrates' court officer, a police officer who either is of the rank of inspector or above or is in charge of a police station or, if the person to be bound is in a prison or other place of detention, before the governor or keeper of the prison or place; or

(c) where a person other than a police officer is authorised under section 125A or 125B of the Magistrates' Courts Act 1980 to execute a warrant of arrest providing for a recognizance to be entered into by the person arrested (but not by any other person), before the person executing the warrant.

(2) The court officer for a magistrates' court which has fixed the amount in which a person (including any surety) is to be bound by a recognizance or, under section 3(5), (6) or (6A) of the 1976 Act imposed any requirement to be complied with before a person's release on bail or any condition of bail shall issue a certificate showing the amount and conditions, if any, of the recognizance, or as the case may be, containing a statement of the requirement or condition of bail; and a person authorised to take the recognizance or do anything in relation to the compliance with such requirement or condition of bail shall not be required to take or do it without production of such a certificate as aforesaid.

(3) If any person proposed as a surety for a person committed to custody by a magistrates' court produces to the governor or keeper of the prison or other place of detention in which the person so committed is detained a certificate to the effect that he is acceptable as a surety, signed by any of the justices composing the court or the clerk of the court and signed in the margin by the person proposed as surety, the governor or keeper shall take the recognizance of the person so proposed.

(4) Where the recognizance of any person committed to custody by a magistrates' court or of any surety of such a person is taken by any person other than the court which committed the first-mentioned person to custody, the person taking the recognizance shall send it to the court officer for that court:

Provided that, in the case of a surety, if the person committed has been committed to the Crown Court for trial or under any of the enactments mentioned in rule 43.1(1), the person taking the recognizance shall send it to the Crown Court officer.

Notice to governor of prison, etc, where release from custody is ordered by a magistrates' court R-131

19.6 Where a magistrates' court has, with a view to the release on bail of a person in custody, fixed the amount in which he or any surety of such a person shall be bound or, under section 3(5), (6) or (6A) of the Bail Act 1976, imposed any requirement to be complied with before his release or any condition of bail—

(a) the magistrates' court officer shall give notice thereof to the governor or keeper of the prison or place where that person is detained by sending him such a certificate as is mentioned in rule 19.5(2); and

(b) any person authorised to take the recognizance of a surety or do anything in relation to the compliance with such requirement shall, on taking or doing it, send notice thereof by post to the said governor or keeper and, in the case of a recognizance of a surety, shall give a copy of the notice to the surety.

Release when notice received by governor of prison that recognizances have been taken or requirements complied with R-132

19.7 Where a magistrates' court has, with a view to the release on bail of a person in custody, fixed the amount in which he or any surety of such a person shall be bound or, under section 3(5) or (6) of the Bail Act 1976, imposed any requirement to be complied with before his release and given notice thereof in accordance with this Part to the governor or keeper of the prison or place where that person is detained, the governor or keeper shall, when satisfied that the recognizances of all sureties required have been taken and that all such requirements have been complied with, and unless he is in custody for some other cause, release him.

R-133 Notice from a magistrates' court of enlargement of recognizances

19.8 (1) If a magistrates' court before which any person is bound by a recognizance to appear enlarges the recognizance to a later time under section 129 of the Magistrates' Courts Act 1980 in his absence, it shall give him and his sureties, if any, notice thereof.

(2) If a magistrates' court, under section 129(4) of the 1980 Act, enlarges the recognizance of a surety for a person committed for trial on bail, it shall give the surety notice thereof.

R-134 Further remand by a youth court

19.9 Where a child or young person has been remanded, and the period of remand is extended in his absence in accordance with section 48 of the Children and Young Persons Act 1933, notice shall be given to him and his sureties (if any) of the date at which he will be required to appear before the court.

R-135 Notes of argument in magistrates' court bail hearings

19.10 Where a magistrates' court hears full argument as to bail, the clerk of the court shall take a note of that argument.

R-136 Bail records to be entered in register of magistrates' court

19.11 Any record required by section 5 of the Bail Act 1976 to be made by a magistrates' court (together with any note of reasons required by section 5(4) to be included and the particulars set out in any certificate granted under section 5(6A)) shall be made by way of an entry in the register.

R-137 Notification of bail decision by magistrate after arrest while on bail

19.12 Where a person who has been released on bail and is under a duty to surrender into the custody of a court is brought under section 7(4)(a) of the Bail Act 1976 before a justice of the peace, the justice shall cause a copy of the record made in pursuance of section 5 of that Act relating to his decision under section 7(5) of that Act in respect of that person to be sent to the court officer for that court: Provided that this rule shall not apply where the court is a magistrates' court acting for the same local justice area as that for which the justice acts.

R-138 Transfer of remand hearings

19.13 (1) Where a magistrates' court, under section 130(1) of the Magistrates' Courts Act 1980, orders that an accused who has been remanded in custody be brought up for any subsequent remands before an alternate magistrates' court, the court officer for the first-mentioned court shall, as soon as practicable after the making of the order and in any case within 2 days thereafter (not counting Sundays, Good Friday, Christmas Day or bank holidays), send to the court officer for the alternate court—

(a) a statement indicating the offence or offences charged;
(b) a copy of the record made by the first-mentioned court in pursuance of section 5 of the Bail Act 1976 relating to the withholding of bail in respect of the accused when he was last remanded in custody;
(c) a copy of any representation order previously made in the same case;
(d) a copy of any application for a representation order;
(e) if the first-mentioned court has made an order under section 8(2) of the 1980 Act (removal of restrictions on reports of committal proceedings), a statement to that effect.
(f) a statement indicating whether or not the accused has a solicitor acting for him in the case and has consented to the hearing and determination in his absence of any application for his remand on an adjournment of the case under sections 5, 10(1) and 18(4) of the 1980 Act together with a statement indicating whether or not that consent has been withdrawn;
(g) a statement indicating the occasions, if any, on which the accused has been remanded under section 128(3A) of the 1980 Act without being brought before the first-mentioned court; and
(h) if the first-mentioned court remands the accused under section 128A of the 1980 Act on the occasion upon which it makes the order under section 130(1) of that Act, a statement indicating the date set under section 128A(2) of that Act.

(2) Where the first-mentioned court is satisfied as mentioned in section 128(3A) of the 1980 Act, paragraph (1) shall have effect as if for the words 'an accused who has been remanded in custody be brought up for any subsequent remands before' there were substituted the words 'applications for any subsequent remands of the accused be made to'.

(3) The court officer for an alternate magistrates' court before which an accused who has been remanded in custody is brought up for any subsequent remands in pursuance of an order made as aforesaid shall, as soon as practicable after the order ceases to be in force and in any case within 2 days thereafter (not counting Sundays, Good Friday, Christmas Day or bank holidays), send to the court officer for the magistrates' court which made the order—
(a) a copy of the record made by the alternate court in pursuance of section 5 of the 1976 Act relating to the grant or withholding of bail in respect of the accused when he was last remanded in custody or on bail;
(b) a copy of any representation order made by the alternate court;
(c) a copy of any application for a representation order made to the alternate court;
(d) if the alternate court has made an order under section 8(2) of the 1980 Act (removal of restrictions on reports of committal proceedings), a statement to that effect;
(e) a statement indicating whether or not the accused has a solicitor acting for him in the case and has consented to the hearing and determination in his absence of any application for his remand on an adjournment of the case under sections 5, 10(1) and 18(4) of the 1980 Act together with a statement indicating whether or not that consent has been withdrawn; and
(f) a statement indicating the occasions, if any, on which the accused has been remanded by the alternate court under section 128(3A) of the 1980 Act without being brought before that court.

(4) Where the alternate court is satisfied as mentioned in section 128(3A) of the 1980 Act paragraph (2) above shall have effect as if for the words 'an accused who has been remanded in custody is brought up for any subsequent remands' there shall be substituted the words 'applications for the further remand of the accused are to be made'.

Notice of further remand in certain cases **R-139**

19.14 Where a transfer direction has been given by the Secretary of State under section 47 of the Mental Health Act 1983 in respect of a person remanded in custody by a magistrates' court and the direction has not ceased to have effect, the court officer shall give notice in writing to the managers of the hospital where he is detained of any further remand under section 128 of the Magistrates' Courts Act 1980.

Cessation of transfer direction **R-140**

19.15 Where a magistrates' court directs, under section 52(5) of the Mental Health Act 1983, that a transfer direction given by the Secretary of State under section 48 of that Act in respect of a person remanded in custody by a magistrates' court shall cease to have effect, the court officer shall give notice in writing of the court's direction to the managers of the hospital specified in the Secretary of State's direction and, where the period of remand has not expired or the person has been committed to the Crown Court for trial or to be otherwise dealt with, to the Governor of the prison to which persons of the sex of that person are committed by the court if remanded in custody or committed in custody for trial.

Lodging an appeal against a grant of bail by a magistrates' court **R-141**

19.16 (1) Where the prosecution wishes to exercise the right of appeal, under section 1 of the Bail (Amendment) Act 1993, to a judge of the Crown Court against a decision to grant bail, the oral notice of appeal must be given to the justices' clerk and to the person concerned, at the conclusion of the proceedings in which such bail was granted and before the release of the person concerned.

(2) When oral notice of appeal is given, the justices' clerk shall announce in open court the time at which such notice was given.

(3) A record of the prosecution's decision to appeal and the time the oral notice of appeal was given shall be made in the register and shall contain the particulars set out.

(4) Where an oral notice of appeal has been given the court shall remand the person concerned in custody by a warrant of commitment.

(5) On receipt of the written notice of appeal required by section 1(5) of the 1993 Act, the court shall remand the person concerned in custody by a warrant of commitment, until the appeal is determined or otherwise disposed of.

(6) A record of the receipt of the written notice of appeal shall be made in the same manner as that of the oral notice of appeal under paragraph (3).

(7) If, having given oral notice of appeal, the prosecution fails to serve a written notice of appeal within the two hour period referred to in section 1(5) of the 1993 Act the justices' clerk shall, as soon as practicable, by way of written notice (served by a court officer) to the persons in

whose custody the person concerned is, direct the release of the person concerned on bail as granted by the magistrates' court and subject to any conditions which it imposed.

(8) If the prosecution serves notice of abandonment of appeal on a court officer, the justices' clerk shall, forthwith, by way of written notice (served by the court officer) to the governor of the prison where the person concerned is being held, or the person responsible for any other establishment where such a person is being held, direct his release on bail as granted by the magistrates' court and subject to any conditions which it imposed.

(9) A court officer shall record the prosecution's failure to serve a written notice of appeal, or its service of a notice of abandonments.

(10) Where a written notice of appeal has been served on a magistrates' court officer, he shall provide as soon as practicable to a Crown Court officer a copy of that written notice, together with—
(a) the notes of argument made by the court officer for the court under rule 19.10; and
(b) a note of the date, or dates, when the person concerned is next due to appear in the magistrates' court, whether he is released on bail or remanded in custody by the Crown Court.

(11) References in this rule to 'the person concerned' are references to such a person within the meaning of section 1 of the 1993 Act.

R-142 Crown Court procedure on appeal against grant of bail by a magistrates' court

19.17 (1) This rule shall apply where the prosecution appeals under section 1 of the Bail (Amendment) Act 1993 against a decision of a magistrates' court granting bail and in this rule 'the person concerned' has the same meaning as in that Act.

(2) The written notice of appeal required by section 1(5) of the 1993 Act shall be in the form set out in the Practice Direction and shall be served on—
(a) the magistrates' court officer; and
(b) the person concerned.

(3) The Crown Court officer shall enter the appeal and give notice of the time and place of the hearing to—
(a) the prosecution;
(b) the person concerned or his legal representative; and
(c) the magistrates' court officer.

(4) The person concerned shall be entitled to be present at the hearing of the appeal.

(5) Where a person concerned has not been able to instruct a solicitor to represent him at the appeal, he may give notice to the Crown Court requesting that the Official Solicitor shall represent him at the appeal, and the court may, if it thinks fit, assign the Official Solicitor to act for the person concerned accordingly.

(6) At any time after the service of written notice of appeal under paragraph (2), the prosecution may abandon the appeal by giving notice in writing in the form set out in the Practice Direction.

(7) The notice of abandonment required by the preceding paragraph shall be served on—
(a) the person concerned or his legal representative;
(b) the magistrates' court officer; and
(c) the Crown Court officer.

(8) Any record required by section 5 of the Bail Act 1976 (together with any note of reasons required by subsection (4) of that section to be included) shall be made by way of an entry in the file relating to the case in question and the record shall include the following particulars, namely—
(a) the effect of the decision;
(b) a statement of any condition imposed in respect of bail, indicating whether it is to be complied with before or after release on bail; and
(c) where bail is withheld, a statement of the relevant exception to the right to bail (as provided in Schedule 1 to the 1976 Act) on which the decision is based.

(9) The Crown Court officer shall, as soon as practicable after the hearing of the appeal, give notice of the decision and of the matters required by the preceding paragraph to be recorded to—
(a) the person concerned or his legal representative;
(b) the prosecution;
(c) the police;
(d) the magistrates' officer; and
(e) the governor of the prison or person responsible for the establishment where the person concerned is being held.

(10) Where the judge hearing the appeal grants bail to the person concerned, the provisions of rule 19.18(9) (informing the Court of any earlier application for bail) and rule 19.22 (conditions

attached to bail granted by the Crown Court) shall apply as if that person had applied to the Crown Court for bail.

(11) The notices required by paragraphs (3), (5), (7) and (9) of this rule may be served under rule 4.6 (service by fax, e-mail or other electronic means) and the notice required by paragraph (3) may be given by telephone.

(12) The Crown Court may hear an appeal to which this rule applies in public or in private.

Application or appeal to the Crown Court relating to bail **R-143**

19.18 (1) This rule applies where—

(a) an application to the Crown Court relating to bail is made otherwise than during the hearing of proceedings in the Crown Court;

(b) a defendant appeals under section 16 of the Criminal Justice Act 2003.

(2) Subject to paragraph (7) below, notice in writing of intention to make such an application to the Crown Court shall, at least 24 hours before it is made, be given to the prosecutor and if the prosecution is being carried on by the Crown Prosecution Service, to the appropriate Crown Prosecutor or, if the application is to be made by the prosecutor or a constable under section 3(8) of the Bail Act 1976, to the person to whom bail was granted.

(3) On receiving notice under paragraph (2), the prosecutor or appropriate Crown Public Prosecutor or, as the case may be, the person to whom bail was granted shall—

(a) notify the Crown Court officer and the applicant that he wishes to be represented at the hearing of the application;

(b) notify the Crown Court officer and the applicant that he does not oppose the application; or

(c) give to the Crown Court officer, for the consideration of the Crown Court, a written statement of his reasons for opposing the application, at the same time sending a copy of the statement to the applicant.

(4) A notice under paragraph (2) shall be in the form set out in the Practice Direction or a form to the like effect, and the applicant shall give a copy of the notice to the Crown Court officer.

(5) Except in the case of an application made by the prosecutor or a constable under section 3(8) of the 1976 Act, the applicant shall not be entitled to be present on the hearing of his application unless the Crown Court gives him leave to be present.

(6) Where a person who is in custody or has been released on bail desires to make an application relating to bail and has not been able to instruct a solicitor to apply on his behalf under the preceding paragraphs of this rule, he may give notice in writing to the Crown Court of his desire to make an application relating to bail, requesting that the Official Solicitor shall act for him in the application, and the Court may, if it thinks fit, assign the Official Solicitor to act for the applicant accordingly.

(7) Where the Official Solicitor has been so assigned the Crown Court may, if it thinks fit, dispense with the requirements of paragraph (2) and deal with the application in a summary manner.

(8) Any record required by section 5 of the 1976 Act (together with any note of reasons required by section 5(4) to be included) shall be made by way of an entry in the file relating to the case in question and the record shall include the following particulars, namely—

(a) the effect of the decision;

(b) a statement of any condition imposed in respect of bail, indicating whether it is to be complied with before or after release on bail;

(c) where conditions of bail are varied, a statement of the conditions as varied; and

(d) where bail is withheld, a statement of the relevant exception to the right to bail (as provided in Schedule 1 to the 1976 Act) on which the decision is based.

(9) Every person who makes an application to the Crown Court relating to bail shall inform the Court of any earlier application to the High Court or the Crown Court relating to bail in the course of the same proceedings.

(10) The Crown Court may hear an application or appeal to which this rule applies in public or in private.

Notice to governor of prison of committal on bail **R-144**

19.19 (1) Where the accused is committed or sent for trial on bail, a magistrates' court officer shall give notice thereof in writing to the governor of the prison to which persons of the sex of the person committed or sent are committed or sent by that court if committed or sent in custody for trial and also, if the person committed or sent is under 21, to the governor of the remand centre to which he would have been committed or sent if the court had refused him bail.

(2) Where a corporation is committed or sent for trial, a magistrates' court officer shall give notice thereof to the governor of the prison to which would be committed or sent a man committed or sent by that court in custody for trial.

R-145 **Notices on committal of person subject to transfer direction**

19.20 Where a transfer direction has been given by the Secretary of State under section 48 of the Mental Health Act 1983 in respect of a person remanded in custody by a magistrates' court and, before the direction ceases to have effect, that person is committed or sent for trial, a magistrates' court officer shall give notice—

(a) to the governor of the prison to which persons of the sex of that person are committed or sent by that court if committed or sent in custody for trial; and
(b) to the managers of the hospital where he is detained.

R-146 **Variation of arrangements for bail on committal to the Crown Court**

19.21 Where a magistrates' court has committed or sent a person on bail to the Crown Court for trial or under any of the enactments mentioned in rule 43.1(1) and subsequently varies any conditions of the bail or imposes any conditions in respect of the bail, the magistrates' court officer shall send to the Crown Court officer a copy of the record made in pursuance of section 5 of the Bail Act 1976 relating to such variation or imposition of conditions.

R-147 **Conditions attached to bail granted by the Crown Court**

19.22 (1) Where the Crown Court grants bail, the recognizance of any surety required as a condition of bail may be entered into before an officer of the Crown Court or, where the person who has been granted bail is in a prison or other place of detention, before the governor or keeper of the prison or place as well as before the persons specified in section 8(4) of the Bail Act 1976.

(2) Where the Crown Court under section 3(5) or (6) of the 1976 Act imposes a requirement to be complied with before a person's release on bail, the Court may give directions as to the manner in which and the person or persons before whom the requirement may be complied with.

(3) A person who, in pursuance of an order made by the Crown Court for the grant of bail, proposes to enter into a recognizance or give security must, unless the Crown Court otherwise directs, give notice to the prosecutor at least 24 hours before he enters into the recognizance or gives security as aforesaid.

(4) Where, in pursuance of an order of the Crown Court, a recognizance is entered into or any requirement imposed under section 3(5) or (6) of the 1976 Act is complied with (being a requirement to be complied with before a person's release on bail) before any person, it shall be his duty to cause the recognizance or, as the case may be, a statement of the requirement to be transmitted forthwith to the court officer; and a copy of the recognizance or statement shall at the same time be sent to the governor or keeper of the prison or other place of detention in which the person named in the order is detained, unless the recognizance was entered into or the requirement was complied with before such governor or keeper.

(5) Where, in pursuance of section 3(5) of the 1976 Act, security has been given in respect of a person granted bail with a duty to surrender to the custody of the Crown Court and either—

(a) that person surrenders to the custody of the Court; or
(b) that person having failed to surrender to the custody of the Court, the Court decides not to order the forfeiture of the security,

the court officer shall as soon as practicable give notice of the surrender to custody or, as the case may be, of the decision not to forfeit the security to the person before whom the security was given.

R-148 **Estreat of recognizances in respect of person bailed to appear before the Crown Court**

19.23 (1) Where a recognizance has been entered into in respect of a person granted bail to appear before the Crown Court and it appears to the Court that a default has been made in performing the conditions of the recognizance, other than by failing to appear before the Court in accordance with any such condition, the Court may order the recognizance to be estreated.

(2) Where the Crown Court is to consider making an order under paragraph (1) for a recognizance to be estreated, the court officer shall give notice to that effect to the person by whom the recognizance was entered into indicating the time and place at which the matter will be considered; and no such order shall be made before the expiry of 7 days after the notice required by this paragraph has been given.

Forfeiture of recognizances in respect of person bailed to appear before the Crown Court R-149

19.24 (1) Where a recognizance is conditioned for the appearance of an accused before the Crown Court and the accused fails to appear in accordance with the condition, the Court shall declare the recognizance to be forfeited.

(2) Where the Crown Court declares a recognizance to be forfeited under paragraph (1), the court officer shall issue a summons to the person by whom the recognizance was entered into requiring him to appear before the Court at a time and place specified in the summons to show cause why the Court should not order the recognizance to be estreated.

(3) At the time specified in the summons the Court may proceed in the absence of the person by whom the recognizance was entered into if it is satisfied that he has been served with the summons.

Grant of bail subject to a condition of residence R-150

19.25 (1) The defendant must notify the prosecutor of the address at which the defendant would reside if released on bail with a condition of residence–

(a) as soon as practicable after the institution of proceedings, unless already done; and

(b) as soon as practicable after any change of that address.

(2) The prosecutor must help the court to assess the suitability of an address proposed as a condition of residence.

Grant of bail subject to electronic monitoring requirements R-151

19.26 (1) This rule applies where the court imposes electronic monitoring requirements (where available) as a condition of bail.

(2) The court officer must—

(a) inform the person responsible for the monitoring ('the monitor') of—

(i) the defendant's name, and telephone number (if available),

(ii) the offence or offences with which the defendant is charged,

(iii) details of the place at which the defendant's presence must be monitored,

(iv) the period or periods during which the defendant's presence at that place must be monitored, and

(v) if fixed, the date on which the defendant must surrender to custody;

(b) inform the defendant and, where the defendant is under 16, an appropriate adult, of the monitor's name, and the means by which the monitor may be contacted; and

(c) notify the monitor of any subsequent—

(i) variation or termination of the electronic monitoring requirements, or

(ii) fixing or variation of the date on which the defendant must surrender to custody.

Grant of bail subject to accommodation or support requirements R-152

19.27 (1) This rule applies where the court imposes as a condition of bail a requirement (where available) that the defendant must—

(a) reside in accommodation provided for that purpose by, or on behalf of, a public authority;

(b) receive bail support provided by, or on behalf of, a public authority.

(2) The court officer must—

(a) inform the person responsible for the provision of any such accommodation or support ('the service provider') of—

(i) the defendant's name, and telephone number (if available),

(ii) the offence or offences with which the defendant is charged,

(iii) details of the requirement,

(iv) any other bail condition, and

(v) if fixed, the date on which the defendant must surrender to custody;

(b) inform the defendant and, where the defendant is under 16, an appropriate adult, of—

(i) the service provider's name, and the means by which the service provider may be contacted, and

(ii) the address of any accommodation in which the defendant must reside; and

(c) notify the service provider of any subsequent—

(i) variation or termination of the requirement,

(ii) variation or termination of any other bail condition, and

(iii) fixing or variation of the date on which the defendant must surrender to custody.

PART 20 CUSTODY TIME LIMITS

R-153 Appeal to the Crown Court against a decision of a magistrates' court in respect of a custody time limit

20.1 (1) This rule applies—
(a) to any appeal brought by an accused, under section 22(7) of the Prosecution of Offences Act 1985, against a decision of a magistrates' court to extend, or further extend, a custody time limit imposed by regulations made under section 22(1) of the 1985 Act; and
(b) to any appeal brought by the prosecution, under section 22(8) of the 1985 Act, against a decision of a magistrates' court to refuse to extend, or further extend, such a time limit.
(2) An appeal to which this rule applies shall be commenced by the appellant's giving notice in writing of appeal—
(a) to the court officer for the magistrates' court which took the decision;
(b) if the appeal is brought by the accused, to the prosecutor and, if the prosecution is to be carried on by the Crown Prosecution Service, to the appropriate Crown Prosecutor;
(c) if the appeal is brought by the prosecution, to the accused; and
(d) to the Crown Court officer.
(3) The notice of an appeal to which this rule applies shall state the date on which the custody time limit applicable to the case is due to expire and, if the appeal is brought by the accused under section 22(7) of the 1985 Act, the date on which the custody time limit would have expired had the court decided not to extend or further extend that time limit.
(4) On receiving notice of an appeal to which this rule applies, the Crown Court officer shall enter the appeal and give notice of the time and place of the hearing to—
(a) the appellant;
(b) the other party to the appeal; and
(c) the court officer for the magistrates' court which took the decision.
(5) Without prejudice to the power of the Crown Court to give leave for an appeal to be abandoned, an appellant may abandon an appeal to which this rule applies by giving notice in writing to any person to whom notice of the appeal was required to be given by paragraph (2) of this rule not later than the third day preceding the day fixed for the hearing of the appeal: Provided that, for the purpose of determining whether notice was properly given in accordance with this paragraph, there shall be disregarded any Saturday and Sunday and any day which is specified to be a bank holiday in England and Wales under section 1(1) of the Banking and Financial Dealings Act 1971.

R-153A Hearing of application or appeal to the Crown

20.2 The court may hear in public or in private—
(a) an application under section 22(3) of the 1985 Act to extend a custody time limit;
(b) an appeal to which rule 20.1 applies.

PART 21 INITIAL DETAILS OF THE PROSECUTION CASE

R-154 When this Part applies

21.1 (1) This Part applies in a magistrates' court, where the offence is one that can be tried in a magistrates' court.
(2) The court may direct that, for a specified period, this Part will not apply—
(a) to any case in that court; or
(b) to any specified category of case.

R-155 Providing initial details of the prosecution case

21.2 The prosecutor must provide initial details of the prosecution case by—
(a) serving those details on the court officer; and
(b) making those details available to the defendant,
at, or before, the beginning of the day of the first hearing.

R-156 Content of initial details

21.3 Initial details of the prosecution case must include—
(a) a summary of the evidence on which that case will be based; or
(b) any statement, document or extract setting out facts or other matters on which that case will be based; or

(c) any combination of such a summary, statement, document or extract; and
(d) the defendant's previous convictions.

Part 22 Disclosure

When this Part applies R-157

22.1 This Part applies—
(a) in a magistrates' court and in the Crown Court;
(b) where Parts I and II of the Criminal Procedure and Investigations Act 1996 apply.

Prosecution disclosure R-158

22.2 (1) This rule applies in the Crown Court where, under section 3 of the Criminal Procedure and Investigations Act 1996, the prosecutor—
(a) discloses prosecution material to the defendant; or
(b) serves on the defendant a written statement that there is no such material to disclose.
(2) The prosecutor must at the same time so inform the court officer.

Prosecutor's application for public interest ruling R-159

22.3 (1) This rule applies where—
(a) without a court order, the prosecutor would have to disclose material; and
(b) the prosecutor wants the court to decide whether it would be in the public interest to disclose it.
(2) The prosecutor must—
(a) apply in writing for such a decision; and
(b) serve the application on—
(i) the court officer,
(ii) any person who the prosecutor thinks would be directly affected by disclosure of the material, and
(iii) the defendant, but only to the extent that serving it on the defendant would not disclose what the prosecutor thinks ought not be disclosed.
(3) The application must—
(a) describe the material, and explain why the prosecutor thinks that—
(i) it is material that the prosecutor would have to disclose,
(ii) it would not be in the public interest to disclose that material, and
(iii) no measure such as the prosecutor's admission of any fact, or disclosure by summary, extract or edited copy, adequately would protect both the public interest and the defendant's right to a fair trial;
(b) omit from any part of the application that is served on the defendant anything that would disclose what the prosecutor thinks ought not be disclosed (in which case, paragraph (4) of this rule applies); and
(c) explain why, if no part of the application is served on the defendant.
(4) Where the prosecutor serves only part of the application on the defendant, the prosecutor must—
(a) mark the other part, to show that it is only for the court; and
(b) in that other part, explain why the prosecutor has withheld it from the defendant.
(5) Unless already done, the court may direct the prosecutor to serve an application on—
(a) the defendant;
(b) any other person who the court considers would be directly affected by the disclosure of the material.
(6) The court must determine the application at a hearing which—
(a) will be in private, unless the court otherwise directs; and
(b) if the court so directs, may take place, wholly or in part, in the defendant's absence.
(7) At a hearing at which the defendant is present—
(a) the general rule is that the court will receive, in the following sequence—
(i) representations first by the prosecutor and any other person served with the application, and then by the defendant, in the presence of them all, and then
(ii) further representations by the prosecutor and any such other person in the defendant's absence; but
(b) the court may direct other arrangements for the hearing.

(8) The court may only determine the application if satisfied that it has been able to take adequate account of—
(a) such rights of confidentiality as apply to the material; and
(b) the defendant's right to a fair trial.
(9) Unless the court otherwise directs, the court officer—
(a) must not give notice to anyone other than the prosecutor—
(i) of the hearing of an application under this rule, unless the prosecutor served the application on that person, or
(ii) of the court's decision on the application;
(b) may—
(i) keep a written application or representations, or
(ii) arrange for the whole or any part to be kept by some other appropriate person, subject to any conditions that the court may impose.

R-160 Defence disclosure

22.4 (1) This rule applies where—
(a) under section 5 or 6 of the Criminal Procedure and Investigations Act 1996, the defendant gives a defence statement;
(b) under section 6C of the 1996 Act, the defendant gives a defence witness notice.
(2) The defendant must serve such a statement or notice on—
(a) the court officer; and
(b) the prosecutor.

R-161 Defendant's application for prosecution disclosure

22.5 (1) This rule applies where the defendant—
(a) has served a defence statement given under the Criminal Procedure and Investigations Act 1996; and
(b) wants the court to require the prosecutor to disclose material.
(2) The defendant must serve an application on—
(a) the court officer; and
(b) the prosecutor.
(3) The application must—
(a) describe the material that the defendant wants the prosecutor to disclose;
(b) explain why the defendant thinks there is reasonable cause to believe that—
(i) the prosecutor has that material, and
(ii) it is material that the Criminal Procedure and Investigations Act 1996 requires the prosecutor to disclose; and
(c) ask for a hearing, if the defendant wants one, and explain why it is needed.
(4) The court may determine an application under this rule—
(a) at a hearing, in public or in private; or
(b) without a hearing.
(5) The court must not require the prosecutor to disclose material unless the prosecutor—
(a) is present; or
(b) has had at least 14 days in which to make representations.

R-162 Review of public interest ruling

22.6 (1) This rule applies where the court has ordered that it is not in the public interest to disclose material that the prosecutor otherwise would have to disclose, and—
(a) the defendant wants the court to review that decision; or
(b) the Crown Court reviews that decision on its own initiative.
(2) Where the defendant wants the court to review that decision, the defendant must—
(a) serve an application on—
(i) the court officer, and
(ii) the prosecutor; and
(b) in the application—
(i) describe the material that the defendant wants the prosecutor to disclose, and
(ii) explain why the defendant thinks it is no longer in the public interest for the prosecutor not to disclose it.
(3) The prosecutor must serve any such application on any person who the prosecutor thinks would be directly affected if that material were disclosed.

(4) The prosecutor, and any such person, must serve any representations on—
(a) the court officer; and
(b) the defendant, unless to do so would in effect reveal something that either thinks ought not be disclosed.
(5) The court may direct—
(a) the prosecutor to serve any such application on any person who the court considers would be directly affected if that material were disclosed;
(b) the prosecutor and any such person to serve any representations on the defendant.
(6) The court must review a decision to which this rule applies at a hearing which—
(a) will be in private, unless the court otherwise directs; and
(b) if the court so directs, may take place, wholly or in part, in the defendant's absence.
(7) At a hearing at which the defendant is present—
(a) the general rule is that the court will receive, in the following sequence—
(i) representations first by the defendant, and then by the prosecutor and any other person served with the application, in the presence of them all, and then
(ii) further representations by the prosecutor and any such other person in the defendant's absence; but
(b) the court may direct other arrangements for the hearing.
(8) The court may only conclude a review if satisfied that it has been able to take adequate account of—
(a) such rights of confidentiality as apply to the material; and
(b) the defendant's right to a fair trial.

Defendant's application to use disclosed material **R-163**

22.7 (1) This rule applies where a defendant wants the court's permission to use disclosed prosecution material—
(a) otherwise than in connection with the case in which it was disclosed; or
(b) beyond the extent to which it was displayed or communicated publicly at a hearing.
(2) The defendant must serve an application on—
(a) the court officer; and
(b) the prosecutor.
(3) The application must—
(a) specify what the defendant wants to use or disclose; and
(b) explain why.
(4) The court may determine an application under this rule—
(a) at a hearing, in public or in private; or
(b) without a hearing.
(5) The court must not permit the use of such material unless—
(a) the prosecutor has had at least 28 days in which to make representations; and
(b) the court is satisfied that it has been able to take adequate account of any rights of confidentiality that may apply to the material.

Unauthorised use of disclosed material **R-164**

22.8 (1) This rule applies where a person is accused of using disclosed prosecution material in contravention of section 17 of the Criminal Procedure and Investigations Act 1996.
(2) A party who wants the court to exercise its power to punish that person for contempt of court must comply with the rules in Part 62 (Contempt of court).
(3) The court must not exercise its power to forfeit material used in contempt of court unless—
(a) the prosecutor; and
(b) any other person directly affected by the disclosure of the material, is present, or has had at least 14 days in which to make representations.

Court's power to vary requirements under this Part **R-165**

22.9 The court may—
(a) shorten or extend (even after it has expired) a time limit under this Part;
(b) allow a defence statement, or a defence witness notice, to be in a different written form to one set out in the Practice Direction, as long as it contains what the Criminal Procedure and Investigations Act 1996 requires;
(c) allow an application under this Part to be in a different form to one set out in the Practice Direction, or to be presented orally; and

(d) specify the period within which—
  (i) any application under this Part must be made, or
  (ii) any material must be disclosed, on an application to which rule 22.5 applies (defendant's application for prosecution disclosure).

Part 23

[There are no rules in this part.]

Part 24

[There are no rules in this part.]

Part 25

[There are no rules in this part.]

Part 26

[There are no rules in this part.]

Part 27 Witness Statements

R-166 When this Part applies

27.1 This Part applies where a party wants to introduce a written statement in evidence under section 9 of the Criminal Justice Act 1967.

R-167 Content of written statement

27.2 (1) The statement must contain—
  (a) at the beginning—
    (i) the witness' name, and
    (ii) the witness' age, if under 18;
  (b) a declaration by the witness that—
    (i) it is true to the best of the witness' knowledge and belief, and
    (ii) the witness knows that if it is introduced in evidence, then it would be an offence wilfully to have stated in it anything that the witness knew to be false or did not believe to be true;
  (c) if the witness cannot read the statement, a signed declaration by someone else that that person read it to the witness; and
  (d) the witness' signature.

R-168 Reference to exhibit

27.3 Where the statement refers to a document or object as an exhibit—
  (a) the statement must contain such a description of that exhibit as to identify it clearly; and
  (b) the exhibit must be labelled or marked correspondingly, and the label or mark signed by the maker of the statement.

R-169 Written statement in evidence

27.4 (1) A party who wants to introduce in evidence a written statement must—
  (a) before the hearing at which that party wants to do so, serve a copy of the statement on—
    (i) the court officer, and
    (ii) each other party; and
  (b) at or before that hearing, serve the statement itself on the court officer.

(2) If that party relies on only part of the statement, that party must mark the copy in such a way as to make that clear.
(3) A prosecutor must serve on a defendant, with the copy of the statement, a notice—
(a) of the right within 7 days of service to object to the introduction of the statement in evidence instead of the witness giving evidence in person; and
(b) that if the defendant does not object in time, the court—
(i) can nonetheless require the witness to give evidence in person, but
(ii) may decide not to do so.
(4) The court may exercise its power to require the witness to give evidence in person—
(a) on application by any party; or
(b) on its own initiative.
(5) A party entitled to receive a copy of a statement may waive that entitlement by so informing—
(a) the party who would have served it; and
(b) the court.

Part 28 Witness Summonses, Warrants and Orders

When this Part applies R-170

28.1 (1) This Part applies in magistrates' courts and in the Crown Court where—
(a) a party wants the court to issue a witness summons, warrant or order under—
(i) section 97 of the Magistrates' Courts Act 1980,
(ii) section 2 of the Criminal Procedure (Attendance of Witnesses) Act 1965, or
(iii) section 7 of the Bankers' Books Evidence Act 1879;
(b) the court considers the issue of such a summons, warrant or order on its own initiative as if a party had applied; or
(c) one of those listed in rule 28.7 wants the court to withdraw such a summons, warrant or order.
(2) A reference to a 'witness' in this Part is a reference to a person to whom such a summons, warrant or order is directed.

Issue etc. of summons, warrant or order with or without a hearing R-171

28.2 (1) The court may issue or withdraw a witness summons, warrant or order with or without a hearing.
(2) A hearing under this Part must be in private unless the court otherwise directs.

Application for summons, warrant or order: general rules R-172

28.3 (1) A party who wants the court to issue a witness summons, warrant or order must apply as soon as practicable after becoming aware of the grounds for doing so.
(2) The party applying must—
(a) identify the proposed witness;
(b) explain—
(i) what evidence the proposed witness can give or produce,
(ii) why it is likely to be material evidence, and
(iii) why it would be in the interests of justice to issue a summons, order or warrant as appropriate.
(3) The application may be made orally unless—
(a) rule 28.5 applies; or
(b) the court otherwise directs.

Written application: form and service R-173

28.4 (1) An application in writing under rule 28.3 must be in the form set out in the Practice Direction, containing the same declaration of truth as a witness statement.
(2) The party applying must serve the application—
(a) in every case, on the court officer and as directed by the court; and
(b) as required by rule 28.5, if that rule applies.

Application for summons to produce a document, etc.: special rules R-174

28.5 (1) This rule applies to an application under rule 28.3 for a witness summons requiring the proposed witness—
(a) to produce in evidence a document or thing; or

(b) to give evidence about information apparently held in confidence, that relates to another person.

(2) The application must be in writing in the form required by rule 28.4.

(3) The party applying must serve the application—

(a) on the proposed witness, unless the court otherwise directs; and

(b) on one or more of the following, if the court so directs—

(i) a person to whom the proposed evidence relates,

(ii) another party.

(4) The court must not issue a witness summons where this rule applies unless—

(a) everyone served with the application has had at least 14 days in which to make representations, including representations about whether there should be a hearing of the application before the summons is issued; and

(b) the court is satisfied that it has been able to take adequate account of the duties and rights, including rights of confidentiality, of the proposed witness and of any person to whom the proposed evidence relates.

(5) This rule does not apply to an application for an order to produce in evidence a copy of an entry in a banker's book.

R-175 Application for summons to produce a document, etc.: court's assessment of relevance and confidentiality

28.6 (1) This rule applies where a person served with an application for a witness summons requiring the proposed witness to produce in evidence a document or thing objects to its production on the ground that—

(a) it is not likely to be material evidence; or

(b) even if it is likely to be material evidence, the duties or rights, including rights of confidentiality, of the proposed witness or of any person to whom the document or thing relates outweigh the reasons for issuing a summons.

(2) The court may require the proposed witness to make the document or thing available for the objection to be assessed.

(3) The court may invite—

(a) the proposed witness or any representative of the proposed witness; or

(b) a person to whom the document or thing relates or any representative of such a person, to help the court assess the objection.

R-176 Application to withdraw a summons, warrant or order

28.7 (1) The court may withdraw a witness summons, warrant or order if one of the following applies for it to be withdrawn—

(a) the party who applied for it, on the ground that it no longer is needed;

(b) the witness, on the grounds that—

(i) he was not aware of any application for it, and

(ii) he cannot give or produce evidence likely to be material evidence, or

(iii) even if he can, his duties or rights, including rights of confidentiality, or those of any person to whom the evidence relates outweigh the reasons for the issue of the summons, warrant or order; or

(c) any person to whom the proposed evidence relates, on the grounds that—

(i) he was not aware of any application for it, and

(ii) that evidence is not likely to be material evidence, or

(iii) even if it is, his duties or rights, including rights of confidentiality, or those of the witness outweigh the reasons for the issue of the summons, warrant or order.

(2) A person applying under the rule must—

(a) apply in writing as soon as practicable after becoming aware of the grounds for doing so, explaining why he wants the summons, warrant or order to be withdrawn; and

(b) serve the application on the court officer and as appropriate on—

(i) the witness,

(ii) the party who applied for the summons, warrant or order, and

(iii) any other person who he knows was served with the application for the summons, warrant or order.

(3) Rule 28.6 applies to an application under this rule that concerns a document or thing to be produced in evidence.

Court's power to vary requirements under this Part R-177

28.8 (1) The court may—
(a) shorten or extend (even after it has expired) a time limit under this Part; and
(b) where a rule or direction requires an application under this Part to be in writing, allow that application to be made orally instead.
(2) Someone who wants the court to allow an application to be made orally under paragraph (1)(b) of this rule must—
(a) give as much notice as the urgency of his application permits to those on whom he would otherwise have served an application in writing; and
(b) in doing so explain the reasons for the application and for wanting the court to consider it orally.

Part 29 Measures to Assist a Witness or Defendant to Give Evidence

Section 1: understanding and applying this Part

When this Part applies R-178

29.1 This Part applies—
(a) where the court can give a direction (a 'special measures direction'), under section 19 of the Youth Justice and Criminal Evidence Act 1999, on an application or on its own initiative, for any of the following measures—
(i) preventing a witness from seeing the defendant (section 23 of the 1999 Act),
(ii) allowing a witness to give evidence by live link (section 24 of the 1999 Act),
(iii) hearing a witness' evidence in private (section 25 of the 1999 Act),
(iv) dispensing with the wearing of wigs and gowns (section 26 of the 1999 Act),
(v) admitting video recorded evidence (sections 27 and 28 of the 1999 Act),
(vi) questioning a witness through an intermediary (section 29 of the 1999 Act),
(vii) using a device to help a witness communicate (section 30 of the 1999 Act);
(b) where the court can vary or discharge such a direction, under section 20 of the 1999 Act;
(c) where the court can give, vary or discharge a direction (a 'defendant's evidence direction') for a defendant to give evidence—
(i) by live link, under section 33A of the 1999 Act, or
(ii) through an intermediary, under sections 33BA and 33BB of the 1999 Act;
(d) where the court can—
(i) make a witness anonymity order, under section 86 of the Coroners and Justice Act 2009, or
(ii) vary or discharge such an order, under section 91, 92 or 93 of the 2009 Act;
(e) where the court can give or discharge a direction (a 'live link direction'), on an application or on its own initiative, for a witness to give evidence by live link under—
(i) section 32 of the Criminal Justice Act 1988, or
(ii) sections 51 and 52 of the Criminal Justice Act 2003;
(f) where the court can exercise any other power it has to give, vary or discharge a direction for a measure to help a witness give evidence.

Meaning of 'witness' R-179

29.2 In this Part, 'witness' means anyone (other than a defendant) for whose benefit an application, direction or order is made.

Section 2: general rules

Making an application for a direction or order R-180

29.3 A party who wants the court to exercise its power to give or make a direction or order must—
(a) apply in writing as soon as reasonably practicable, and in any event not more than—
(i) 28 days after the defendant pleads not guilty, in a magistrates' court, or
(ii) 14 days after the defendant pleads not guilty in the Crown Court; and
(b) serve the application on—
(i) the court officer, and
(ii) each other party.

R-181 **Decisions and reasons**

29.4 (1) A party who wants to introduce the evidence of a witness who is the subject of an application, direction or order must—
(a) inform the witness of the court's decision as soon as reasonably practicable; and
(b) explain to the witness the arrangements that as a result will be made for him or her to give evidence.
(2) The court must announce, at a hearing in public before the witness gives evidence, the reasons for a decision—
(a) to give, make, vary or discharge a direction or order; or
(b) to refuse to do so.

R-182 **Court's power to vary requirements under this Part**

29.5 (1) The court may—
(a) shorten or extend (even after it has expired) a time limit under this Part; and
(b) allow an application or representations to be made in a different form to one set out in the Practice Direction, or to be made orally.
(2) A person who wants an extension of time must—
(a) apply when serving the application or representations for which it is needed; and
(b) explain the delay.

R-183 **Custody of documents**

29.6 Unless the court otherwise directs, the court officer may—
(a) keep a written application or representations; or
(b) arrange for the whole or any part to be kept by some other appropriate person, subject to any conditions that the court may impose.

R-184 **Declaration by intermediary**

29.7 (1) This rule applies where—
(a) a video recorded interview with a witness is conducted through an intermediary;
(b) the court directs the examination of a witness or defendant through an intermediary.
(2) An intermediary must make a declaration—
(a) before such an interview begins;
(b) before the examination begins (even if such an interview with the witness was conducted through the same intermediary).
(3) The declaration must be in these terms—
'I solemnly, sincerely and truly declare [*or* I swear by Almighty God] that I will well and faithfully communicate questions and answers and make true explanation of all matters and things as shall be required of me according to the best of my skill and understanding.'

Section 3: special measures directions

R-185 **Exercise of court's powers**

29.8 The court may decide whether to give, vary or discharge a special measures direction—
(a) at a hearing, in public or in private, or without a hearing;
(b) in a party's absence, if that party—
(i) applied for the direction, variation or discharge, or
(ii) has had at least 14 days in which to make representations.

R-186 **Special measures direction for a young witness**

29.9 (1) This rule applies where, under section 21 or section 22 of the Youth Justice and Criminal Evidence Act 1999, the primary rule requires the court to give a direction for a special measure to assist a child witness or a qualifying witness—
(a) on an application, if one is made; or
(b) on the court's own initiative, in any other case.
(2) A party who wants to introduce the evidence of such a witness must as soon as reasonably practicable—
(a) notify the court that the witness is eligible for assistance;
(b) provide the court with any information that the court may need to assess the witness' views, if the witness does not want the primary rule to apply; and
(c) serve any video recorded evidence on—
(i) the court officer, and
(ii) each other party.

Content of application for a special measures direction R-187

29.10 An applicant for a special measures direction must—
- (a) explain how the witness is eligible for assistance;
- (b) explain why special measures would be likely to improve the quality of the witness' evidence;
- (c) propose the measure or measures that in the applicant's opinion would be likely to maximise so far as practicable the quality of that evidence;
- (d) report any views that the witness has expressed about—
  - (i) his or her eligibility for assistance,
  - (ii) the likelihood that special measures would improve the quality of his or her evidence, and
  - (iii) the measure or measures proposed by the applicant;
- (e) in a case in which a child witness or a qualifying witness does not want the primary rule to apply, provide any information that the court may need to assess the witness' views;
- (f) in a case in which the applicant proposes that the witness should give evidence by live link—
  - (i) identify someone to accompany the witness while the witness gives evidence,
  - (ii) name that person, if possible, and
  - (iii) explain why that person would be an appropriate companion for the witness, including the witness' own views;
- (g) in a case in which the applicant proposes the admission of video recorded evidence, identify—
  - (i) the date and duration of the recording,
  - (ii) which part the applicant wants the court to admit as evidence, if the applicant does not want the court to admit all of it;
- (h) attach any other material on which the applicant relies; and
- (i) if the applicant wants a hearing, ask for one, and explain why it is needed.

Application to vary or discharge a special measures direction R-188

29.11 (1) A party who wants the court to vary or discharge a special measures direction must—
- (a) apply in writing, as soon as reasonably practicable after becoming aware of the grounds for doing so; and
- (b) serve the application on—
  - (i) the court officer, and
  - (ii) each other party.

(2) The applicant must—
- (a) explain what material circumstances have changed since the direction was given (or last varied, if applicable);
- (b) explain why the direction should be varied or discharged; and
- (c) ask for a hearing, if the applicant wants one, and explain why it is needed.

Application containing information withheld from another party R-189

29.12 (1) This rule applies where—
- (a) an applicant serves an application for a special measures direction, or for its variation or discharge; and
- (b) the application includes information that the applicant thinks ought not be revealed to another party.

(2) The applicant must—
- (a) omit that information from the part of the application that is served on that other party;
- (b) mark the other part to show that, unless the court otherwise directs, it is only for the court; and
- (c) in that other part, explain why the applicant has withheld that information from that other party.

(3) Any hearing of an application to which this rule applies—
- (a) must be in private, unless the court otherwise directs; and
- (b) if the court so directs, may be, wholly or in part, in the absence of a party from whom information has been withheld.

(4) At any hearing of an application to which this rule applies—
- (a) the general rule is that the court will receive, in the following sequence—
  - (i) representations first by the applicant and then by each other party, in all the parties' presence, and then
  - (ii) further representations by the applicant, in the absence of a party from whom information has been withheld; but
- (b) the court may direct other arrangements for the hearing.

R-190 **Representations in response**

29.13 (1) This rule applies where a party wants to make representations about—
(a) an application for a special measures direction;
(b) an application for the variation or discharge of such a direction; or
(c) a direction, variation or discharge that the court proposes on its own initiative.
(2) Such a party must—
(a) serve the representations on—
(i) the court officer, and
(ii) each other party;
(b) do so not more than 14 days after, as applicable—
(i) service of the application, or
(ii) notice of the direction, variation or discharge that the court proposes; and
(c) ask for a hearing, if that party wants one, and explain why it is needed.
(3) Where representations include information that the person making them thinks ought not be revealed to another party, that person must—
(a) omit that information from the representations served on that other party;
(b) mark the information to show that, unless the court otherwise directs, it is only for the court; and
(c) with that information include an explanation of why it has been withheld from that other party.
(4) Representations against a special measures direction must explain, as appropriate—
(a) why the witness is not eligible for assistance; or
(b) if the witness is eligible for assistance, why—
(i) no special measure would be likely to improve the quality of the witness' evidence,
(ii) the proposed measure or measures would not be likely to maximise so far as practicable the quality of the witness' evidence, or
(iii) the proposed measure or measures might tend to inhibit the effective testing of that evidence;
(c) in a case in which the admission of video recorded evidence is proposed, why it would not be in the interests of justice for the recording, or part of it, to be admitted as evidence.
(5) Representations against the variation or discharge of a special measures direction must explain why it should not be varied or discharged.

Section 4: defendant's evidence directions

R-191 **Exercise of court's powers**

29.14 The court may decide whether to give, vary or discharge a defendant's evidence direction—
(a) at a hearing, in public or in private, or without a hearing;
(b) in a party's absence, if that party—
(i) applied for the direction, variation or discharge, or
(ii) has had at least 14 days in which to make representations.

R-192 **Content of application for a defendant's evidence direction**

29.15 An applicant for a defendant's evidence direction must—
(a) explain how the proposed direction meets the conditions prescribed by the Youth Justice and Criminal Evidence Act 1999;
(b) in a case in which the applicant proposes that the defendant give evidence by live link—
(i) identify a person to accompany the defendant while the defendant gives evidence, and
(ii) explain why that person is appropriate;
(c) ask for a hearing, if the applicant wants one, and explain why it is needed.

R-193 **Application to vary or discharge a defendant's evidence direction**

29.16 (1) A party who wants the court to vary or discharge a defendant's evidence direction must—
(a) apply in writing, as soon as reasonably practicable after becoming aware of the grounds for doing so; and
(b) serve the application on—
(i) the court officer, and
(ii) each other party.
(2) The applicant must—
(a) on an application to discharge a live link direction, explain why it is in the interests of justice to do so;

(b) on an application to discharge a direction for an intermediary, explain why it is no longer necessary in order to ensure that the defendant receives a fair trial;
(c) on an application to vary a direction for an intermediary, explain why it is necessary for the direction to be varied in order to ensure that the defendant receives a fair trial; and
(d) ask for a hearing, if the applicant wants one, and explain why it is needed.

Representations in response R-194

29.17 (1) This rule applies where a party wants to make representations about—
(a) an application for a defendant's evidence direction;
(b) an application for the variation or discharge of such a direction; or
(c) a direction, variation or discharge that the court proposes on its own initiative.
(2) Such a party must—
(a) serve the representations on—
(i) the court officer, and
(ii) each other party;
(b) do so not more than 14 days after, as applicable—
(i) service of the application, or
(ii) notice of the direction, variation or discharge that the court proposes; and
(c) ask for a hearing, if that party wants one, and explain why it is needed.
(3) Representations against a direction, variation or discharge must explain why the conditions prescribed by the Youth Justice and Criminal Evidence Act 1999 are not met.

Section 5: witness anonymity orders

Exercise of court's powers R-195

29.18 (1) The court may decide whether to make, vary or discharge a witness anonymity order—
(a) at a hearing (which will be in private, unless the court otherwise directs), or without a hearing (unless any party asks for one);
(b) in the absence of a defendant.
(2) The court must not exercise its power to make, vary or discharge a witness anonymity order, or to refuse to do so—
(a) before or during the trial, unless each party has had an opportunity to make representations;
(b) on an appeal by the defendant to which applies Part 63 (appeal to the Crown Court) or Part 68 (appeal to the Court of Appeal about conviction or sentence), unless in each party's case—
(i) that party has had an opportunity to make representations, or
(ii) the appeal court is satisfied that it is not reasonably practicable to communicate with that party;
(c) after the trial and any such appeal are over, unless in the case of each party and the witness—
(i) each has had an opportunity to make representations, or
(ii) the court is satisfied that it is not reasonably practicable to communicate with that party or witness.

Content and conduct of application for a witness anonymity order R-196

29.19 (1) An applicant for a witness anonymity order must—
(a) include in the application nothing that might reveal the witness' identity;
(b) describe the measures proposed by the applicant;
(c) explain how the proposed order meets the conditions prescribed by section 88 of the Coroners and Justice Act 2009;
(d) explain why no measures other than those proposed will suffice, such as—
(i) an admission of the facts that would be proved by the witness,
(ii) an order restricting public access to the trial,
(iii) reporting restrictions, in particular under section 46 of the Youth Justice and Criminal Evidence Act 1999 or under section 39 of the Children and Young Persons Act 1933,
(iv) a direction for a special measure under section 19 of the Youth Justice and Criminal Evidence Act 1999,
(v) introduction of the witness' written statement as hearsay evidence, under section 116 of the Criminal Justice Act 2003, or
(vi) arrangements for the protection of the witness;

(e) attach to the application—
  (i) a witness statement setting out the proposed evidence, edited in such a way as not to reveal the witness' identity,
  (ii) where the prosecutor is the applicant, any further prosecution evidence to be served, and any further prosecution material to be disclosed under the Criminal Procedure and Investigations Act 1996, similarly edited, and
  (iii) any defence statement that has been served, or as much information as may be available to the applicant that gives particulars of the defence; and
(f) ask for a hearing, if the applicant wants one.

(2) At any hearing of the application, the applicant must—
(a) identify the witness to the court, unless at the prosecutor's request the court otherwise directs; and
(b) present to the court, unless it otherwise directs—
  (i) the unedited witness statement from which the edited version has been prepared,
  (ii) where the prosecutor is the applicant, the unedited version of any further prosecution evidence or material from which an edited version has been prepared, and
  (iii) such further material as the applicant relies on to establish that the proposed order meets the conditions prescribed by section 88 of the 2009 Act.

(3) At any such hearing—
(a) the general rule is that the court will receive, in the following sequence—
  (i) representations first by the applicant and then by each other party, in all the parties' presence, and then
  (ii) information withheld from a defendant, and further representations by the applicant, in the absence of any (or any other) defendant; but
(b) the court may direct other arrangements for the hearing.

(4) Before the witness gives evidence, the applicant must identify the witness to the court—
(a) if not already done;
(b) without revealing the witness' identity to any other party or person; and
(c) unless at the prosecutor's request the court otherwise directs.

R-197 Duty of court officer to notify the Director of Public Prosecutions

29.20 The court officer must notify the Director of Public Prosecutions of an application, unless the prosecutor is, or acts on behalf of, a public authority.

R-198 Application to vary or discharge a witness anonymity order

29.21 (1) A party who wants the court to vary or discharge a witness anonymity order, or a witness who wants the court to do so when the case is over, must—
(a) apply in writing, as soon as reasonably practicable after becoming aware of the grounds for doing so; and
(b) serve the application on—
  (i) the court officer, and
  (ii) each other party.

(2) The applicant must—
(a) explain what material circumstances have changed since the order was made (or last varied, if applicable);
(b) explain why the order should be varied or discharged, taking account of the conditions for making an order; and
(c) ask for a hearing, if the applicant wants one.

(3) Where an application includes information that the applicant thinks might reveal the witness' identity, the applicant must—
(a) omit that information from the application that is served on a defendant;
(b) mark the information to show that it is only for the court and the prosecutor (if the prosecutor is not the applicant); and
(c) with that information include an explanation of why it has been withheld.

(4) Where a party applies to vary or discharge a witness anonymity order after the trial and any appeal are over, the party who introduced the witness' evidence must serve the application on the witness.

Representations in response R-199

29.22 (1) This rule applies where a party or, where the case is over, a witness, wants to make representations about—
(a) an application for a witness anonymity order;
(b) an application for the variation or discharge of such an order; or
(c) a variation or discharge that the court proposes on its own initiative.
(2) Such a party or witness must—
(a) serve the representations on—
(i) the court officer, and
(ii) each other party;
(b) do so not more than 14 days after, as applicable—
(i) service of the application, or
(ii) notice of the variation or discharge that the court proposes; and
(c) ask for a hearing, if that party or witness wants one.
(3) Where representations include information that the person making them thinks might reveal the witness' identity, that person must—
(a) omit that information from the representations served on a defendant;
(b) mark the information to show that it is only for the court (and for the prosecutor, if relevant); and
(c) with that information include an explanation of why it has been withheld.
(4) Representations against a witness anonymity order must explain why the conditions for making the order are not met.
(5) Representations against the variation or discharge of such an order must explain why it would not be appropriate to vary or discharge it, taking account of the conditions for making an order.
(6) A prosecutor's representations in response to an application by a defendant must include all information available to the prosecutor that is relevant to the conditions and considerations specified by sections 88 and 89 of the Coroners and Justice Act 2009.

Section 6: live link directions

Exercise of court's powers R-200

29.23 The court may decide whether to give, vary or discharge a live link direction—
(a) at a hearing, in public or in private, or without a hearing;
(b) in a party's absence, if that party—
(i) applied for the direction, variation or discharge, or
(ii) has had at least 14 days in which to make representations.

Content of application for a live link direction R-201

29.24 An applicant for a live link direction must—
(a) unless the court otherwise directs, identify the place from which the witness will give evidence;
(b) if that place is in the United Kingdom, explain why it would be in the interests of the efficient or effective administration of justice for the witness to give evidence by live link;
(c) if the applicant wants the witness to be accompanied by another person while giving evidence—
(i) name that person, if possible, and
(ii) explain why it is appropriate for the witness to be accompanied;
(d) ask for a hearing, if the applicant wants one, and explain why it is needed.

Application to discharge a live link direction R-202

29.25 (1) A party who wants the court to discharge a live link direction must—
(a) apply in writing, as soon as reasonably practicable after becoming aware of the grounds for doing so; and
(b) serve the application on—
(i) the court officer, and
(ii) each other party.

(2) The applicant must—
(a) explain what material circumstances have changed since the direction was given;
(b) explain why it is in the interests of justice to discharge the direction; and
(c) ask for a hearing, if the applicant wants one, and explain why it is needed.

R-203 Representations in response

29.26 (1) This rule applies where a party wants to make representations about—
(a) an application for a live link direction;
(b) an application for the discharge of such a direction; or
(c) a direction or discharge that the court proposes on its own initiative.
(2) Such a party must—
(a) serve the representations on—
(i) the court officer, and
(ii) each other party;
(b) do so not more than 14 days after, as applicable—
(i) service of the application, or
(ii) notice of the direction or discharge that the court proposes; and
(c) ask for a hearing, if that party wants one, and explain why it is needed.
(3) Representations against a direction or discharge must explain, as applicable, why the conditions prescribed by the Criminal Justice Act 1988 or the Criminal Justice Act 2003 are not met.

Part 30

[There are no rules in this part]

Part 31 Restriction on Cross-Examination by a Defendant Acting in Person

R-204 Restrictions on cross-examination of witness

31.1 (1) This rule and rules 31.2 and 31.3 apply where an accused is prevented from cross-examining a witness in person by virtue of section 34, 35 or 36 of the Youth Justice and Criminal Evidence Act 1999.
(2) The court shall explain to the accused as early in the proceedings as is reasonably practicable that he—
(a) is prevented from cross-examining a witness in person; and
(b) should arrange for a legal representative to act for him for the purpose of cross-examining the witness.
(3) The accused shall notify the court officer within 7 days of the court giving its explanation, or within such other period as the court may in any particular case allow, of the action, if any, he has taken.
(4) Where he has arranged for a legal representative to act for him, the notification shall include details of the name and address of the representative.
(5) The notification shall be in writing.
(6) The court officer shall notify all other parties to the proceedings of the name and address of the person, if any, appointed to act for the accused.
(7) Where the court gives its explanation under paragraph (2) to the accused either within 7 days of the day set for the commencement of any hearing at which a witness in respect of whom a prohibition under section 34, 35 or 36 of the 1999 Act applies may be cross-examined or after such a hearing has commenced, the period of 7 days shall be reduced in accordance with any directions issued by the court.
(8) Where at the end of the period of 7 days or such other period as the court has allowed, the court has received no notification from the accused it may grant the accused an extension of time, whether on its own motion or on the application of the accused.
(9) Before granting an extension of time, the court may hold a hearing at which all parties to the proceedings may attend and be heard.
(10) Any extension of time shall be of such period as the court considers appropriate in the circumstances of the case.

(11) The decision of the court as to whether to grant the accused an extension of time shall be notified to all parties to the proceedings by the court officer.

Appointment of legal representative by the court R-205

31.2 (1) Where the court decides, in accordance with section 38(4) of the Youth Justice and Criminal Evidence Act 1999, to appoint a qualified legal representative, the court officer shall notify all parties to the proceedings of the name and address of the representative.

(2) An appointment made by the court under section 38(4) of the 1999 Act shall, except to such extent as the court may in any particular case determine, terminate at the conclusion of the cross-examination of the witness or witnesses in respect of whom a prohibition under section 34, 35 or 36 of the 1999 Act applies.

Appointment arranged by the accused R-206

31.3 (1) The accused may arrange for the qualified legal representative, appointed by the court under section 38(4) of the Youth Justice and Criminal Evidence Act 1999, to be appointed to act for him for the purpose of cross-examining any witness in respect of whom a prohibition under section 34, 35 or 36 of the 1999 Act applies.

(2) Where such an appointment is made—

(a) both the accused and the qualified legal representative appointed shall notify the court of the appointment; and

(b) the qualified legal representative shall, from the time of his appointment, act for the accused as though the arrangement had been made under section 38(2)(a) of the 1999 Act and shall cease to be the representative of the court under section 38(4).

(3) Where the court receives notification of the appointment either from the qualified legal representative or from the accused but not from both, the court shall investigate whether the appointment has been made, and if it concludes that the appointment has not been made, paragraph (2)(b) shall not apply.

(4) An accused may, notwithstanding an appointment by the court under section 38(4) of the 1999 Act, arrange for a legal representative to act for him for the purpose of cross-examining any witness in respect of whom a prohibition under section 34, 35 or 36 of the 1999 Act applies.

(5) Where the accused arranges for, or informs the court of his intention to arrange for, a legal representative to act for him, he shall notify the court, within such period as the court may allow, of the name and address of any person appointed to act for him.

(6) Where the court is notified within the time allowed that such an appointment has been made, any qualified legal representative appointed by the court in accordance with section 38(4) of the 1999 Act shall be discharged.

(7) The court officer shall, as soon as reasonably practicable after the court receives notification of an appointment under this rule or, where paragraph (3) applies, after the court is satisfied that the appointment has been made, notify all the parties to the proceedings—

(a) that the appointment has been made;

(b) where paragraph (4) applies, of the name and address of the person appointed; and

(c) that the person appointed by the court under section 38(4) of the 1999 Act has been discharged or has ceased to act for the court.

Prohibition on cross-examination of witness R-207

31.4 (1) An application by the prosecutor for the court to give a direction under section 36 of the Youth Justice and Criminal Evidence Act 1999 in relation to any witness must be sent to the court officer and at the same time a copy thereof must be sent by the applicant to every other party to the proceedings.

(2) In his application the prosecutor must state why, in his opinion—

(a) the evidence given by the witness is likely to be diminished if cross-examination is undertaken by the accused in person;

(b) the evidence would be improved if a direction were given under section 36(2) of the 1999 Act; and

(c) it would not be contrary to the interests of justice to give such a direction.

(3) On receipt of the application the court officer must refer it—

(a) if the trial has started, to the court of trial; or

(b) if the trial has not started when the application is received—

(i) to the judge or court designated to conduct the trial, or

(ii) if no judge or court has been designated for that purpose, to such judge or court designated for the purposes of hearing that application.

(4) Where a copy of the application is received by a party to the proceedings more than 14 days before the date set for the trial to begin, that party may make observations in writing on the application to the court officer, but any such observations must be made within 14 days of the receipt of the application and be copied to the other parties to the proceedings.

(5) A party to whom an application is sent in accordance with paragraph (1) who wishes to oppose the application must give his reasons for doing so to the court officer and the other parties to the proceedings.

(6) Those reasons must be notified—

(a) within 14 days of the date the application was served on him, if that date is more than 14 days before the date set for the trial to begin;

(b) if the trial has begun, in accordance with any directions issued by the court; or

(c) if neither paragraph (6)(a) nor (b) applies, before the date set for the trial to begin.

(7) Where the application made in accordance with paragraph (1) is made before the date set for the trial to begin and—

(a) is not contested by any party to the proceedings, the court may determine the application without a hearing;

(b) is contested by a party to the proceedings, the court must direct a hearing of the application.

(8) Where the application is made after the trial has begun—

(a) the application may be made orally; and

(b) the court may give such directions as it considers appropriate to deal with the application.

(9) Where a hearing of the application is to take place, the court officer shall notify each party to the proceedings of the time and place of the hearing.

(10) A party notified in accordance with paragraph (9) may be present at the hearing and be heard.

(11) The court officer must, as soon as possible after the determination of an application made in accordance with paragraph (1), give notice of the decision and the reasons for it to all the parties to the proceedings.

(12) A person making an oral application under paragraph (8)(a) must—

(a) give reasons why the application was not made before the trial commenced; and

(b) provide the court with the information set out in paragraph (2).

Part 32 International Co-operation

R-208 **Notice required to accompany process served outside the United Kingdom and translations**

32.1 (1) The notice which by virtue of section 3(4)(b) of the Crime (International Co-operation) Act 2003 (general requirements for service of process) must accompany any process served outside the United Kingdom must give the information specified in paragraphs (2) and (4) below.

(2) The notice must—

(a) state that the person required by the process to appear as a party or attend as a witness can obtain information about his rights in connection therewith from the relevant authority; and

(b) give the particulars specified in paragraph (4) about that authority.

(3) The relevant authority where the process is served—

(a) at the request of the prosecuting authority, is that authority; or

(b) at the request of the defendant or the prosecutor in the case of a private prosecution, is the court by which the process is served.

(4) The particulars referred to in paragraph (2) are—

(a) the name and address of the relevant authority, together with its telephone and fax numbers and e-mail address; and

(b) the name of a person at the relevant authority who can provide the information referred to in paragraph (2)(a), together with his telephone and fax numbers and e-mail address.

(5) The justices' clerk or Crown Court officer must send, together with any process served outside the United Kingdom—

(a) any translation which is provided under section 3(3)(b) of the 2003 Act; and

(b) any translation of the information required to be given by this rule which is provided to him.

(6) In this rule 'process' has the same meaning as in section 51(3) of the 2003 Act.

Proof of service outside the United Kingdom R-209

32.2 (1) A statement in a certificate given by or on behalf of the Secretary of State—

(a) that process has been served on any person under section 4(1) of the Crime (International Co-operation) Act 2003 (service of process otherwise than by post);

(b) of the manner in which service was effected; and

(c) of the date on which process was served;

shall be admissible as evidence of any facts so stated.

(2) In this rule 'process' has the same meaning as in section 51(3) of the 2003 Act.

Supply of copy of notice of request for assistance abroad R-210

32.3 Where a request for assistance under section 7 of the Crime (International Co-operation) Act 2003 is made by a justice of the peace or a judge exercising the jurisdiction of the Crown Court and is sent in accordance with section 8(1) of the 2003 Act, the justices' clerk or the Crown Court officer shall send a copy of the letter of request to the Secretary of State as soon as practicable after the request has been made.

Persons entitled to appear and take part in proceedings before a nominated court, and exclusion of public R-211

32.4 A court nominated under section 15(1) of the Crime (International Co-operation) Act 2003 (nominating a court to receive evidence) may—

(a) determine who may appear or take part in the proceedings under Schedule 1 to the 2003 Act before the court and whether a party to the proceedings is entitled to be legally represented; and

(b) direct that the public be excluded from those proceedings if it thinks it necessary to do so in the interests of justice.

Record of proceedings to receive evidence before a nominated court R-212

32.5 (1) Where a court is nominated under section 15(1) of the Crime (International Co-operation) Act 2003 the justices' clerk or Crown Court officer shall enter in an overseas record—

(a) details of the request in respect of which the notice under section 15(1) of the 2003 Act was given;

(b) the date on which, and place at which, the proceedings under Schedule 1 to the 2003 Act in respect of that request took place;

(c) the name of any witness who gave evidence at the proceedings in question;

(d) the name of any person who took part in the proceedings as a legal representative or an interpreter;

(e) whether a witness was required to give evidence on oath or (by virtue of section 5 of the Oaths Act 1978) after making a solemn affirmation; and

(f) whether the opportunity to cross-examine any witness was refused.

(2) When the court gives the evidence received by it under paragraph 6(1) of Schedule 1 to the 2003 Act to the court or authority that made the request or to the territorial authority for forwarding to the court or authority that made the request, the justices' clerk or Crown Court officer shall send to the court, authority or territorial authority (as the case may be) a copy of an extract of so much of the overseas record as relates to the proceedings in respect of that request.

Interpreter for the purposes of proceedings involving a television or telephone link R-213

32.6 (1) This rule applies where a court is nominated under section 30(3) (hearing witnesses in the UK through television links) or section 31(4) (hearing witnesses in the UK by telephone) of the Crime (International Co-operation) Act 2003.

(2) Where it appears to the justices' clerk or the Crown Court officer that the witness to be heard in the proceedings under Part 1 or 2 of Schedule 2 to the 2003 Act ('the relevant proceedings') is likely to give evidence in a language other than English, he shall make arrangements for an interpreter to be present at the proceedings to translate what is said into English.

(3) Where it appears to the justices' clerk or the Crown Court officer that the witness to be heard in the relevant proceedings is likely to give evidence in a language other than that in which the proceedings of the court referred to in section 30(1) or, as the case may be, 31(1) of the 2003 Act ('the external court') will be conducted, he shall make arrangements for an interpreter to be present at the relevant proceedings to translate what is said into the language in which the proceedings of the external court will be conducted.

(4) Where the evidence in the relevant proceedings is either given in a language other than English or is not translated into English by an interpreter, the court shall adjourn the proceedings until such time as an interpreter can be present to provide a translation into English.

(5) Where a court in Wales understands Welsh—
(a) paragraph (2) does not apply where it appears to the justices' clerk or Crown Court officer that the witness in question is likely to give evidence in Welsh;
(b) paragraph (4) does not apply where the evidence is given in Welsh; and
(c) any translation which is provided pursuant to paragraph (2) or (4) may be into Welsh instead of English.

R-214 Record of television link hearing before a nominated court

32.7 (1) This rule applies where a court is nominated under section 30(3) of the Crime (International Co-operation) Act 2003.

(2) The justices' clerk or Crown Court officer shall enter in an overseas record—
(a) details of the request in respect of which the notice under section 30(3) of the 2003 Act was given;
(b) the date on which, and place at which, the proceedings under Part 1 of Schedule 2 to that Act in respect of that request took place;
(c) the technical conditions, such as the type of equipment used, under which the proceedings took place;
(d) the name of the witness who gave evidence;
(e) the name of any person who took part in the proceedings as a legal representative or an interpreter; and
(f) the language in which the evidence was given.

(3) As soon as practicable after the proceedings under Part 1 of Schedule 2 to the 2003 Act took place, the justices' clerk or Crown Court officer shall send to the external authority that made the request a copy of an extract of so much of the overseas record as relates to the proceedings in respect of that request.

R-215 Record of telephone link hearing before a nominated court

32.8 (1) This rule applies where a court is nominated under section 31(4) of the Crime (International Co-operation) Act 2003.

(2) The justices' clerk or Crown Court officer shall enter in an overseas record—
(a) details of the request in respect of which the notice under section 31(4) of the 2003 Act was given;
(b) the date, time and place at which the proceedings under Part 2 of Schedule 2 to the 2003 Act took place;
(c) the name of the witness who gave evidence;
(d) the name of any interpreter who acted at the proceedings; and
(e) the language in which the evidence was given.

R-216 Overseas record

32.9 (1) The overseas records of a magistrates' court shall be part of the register (within the meaning of section 150(1) of the Magistrates' Courts Act 1980).

(2) The overseas records of any court shall not be open to inspection by any person except—
(a) as authorised by the Secretary of State; or
(b) with the leave of the court.

R-217 Overseas freezing orders

32.10 (1) This rule applies where a court is nominated under section 21(1) of the Crime (International Co-operation) Act 2003 to give effect to an overseas freezing order.

(2) Where the Secretary of State serves a copy of such an order on the court officer—
(a) the general rule is that the court will consider the order no later than the next business day;
(b) exceptionally, the court may consider the order later than that, but not more than 5 business days after service.

(3) The court must not consider the order unless—
(a) it is satisfied that the chief officer of police for the area in which the evidence is situated has had notice of the order; and
(b) that chief officer of police has had an opportunity to make representations, at a hearing if that officer wants.

(4) The court may consider the order—
(a) without a hearing; or
(b) at a hearing, in public or in private.

Part 33 Expert Evidence

Reference to expert R-218

33.1 A reference to an 'expert' in this Part is a reference to a person who is required to give or prepare expert evidence for the purpose of criminal proceedings, including evidence required to determine fitness to plead or for the purpose of sentencing.

Expert's duty to the court R-219

33.2 (1) An expert must help the court to achieve the overriding objective by giving objective, unbiased opinion on matters within his expertise.
(2) This duty overrides any obligation to the person from whom he receives instructions or by whom he is paid.
(3) This duty includes an obligation to inform all parties and the court if the expert's opinion changes from that contained in a report served as evidence or given in a statement.

Content of expert's report R-220

33.3 (1) An expert's report must—
(a) give details of the expert's qualifications, relevant experience and accreditation;
(b) give details of any literature or other information which the expert has relied on in making the report;
(c) contain a statement setting out the substance of all facts given to the expert which are material to the opinions expressed in the report or upon which those opinions are based;
(d) make clear which of the facts stated in the report are within the expert's own knowledge;
(e) say who carried out any examination, measurement, test or experiment which the expert has used for the report and—
(i) give the qualifications, relevant experience and accreditation of that person,
(ii) say whether or not the examination, measurement, test or experiment was carried out under the expert's supervision, and
(iii) summarise the findings on which the expert relies;
(f) where there is a range of opinion on the matters dealt with in the report—
(i) summarise the range of opinion, and
(ii) give reasons for his own opinion;
(g) if the expert is not able to give his opinion without qualification, state the qualification;
(h) contain a summary of the conclusions reached;
(i) contain a statement that the expert understands his duty to the court, and has complied and will continue to comply with that duty; and
(j) contain the same declaration of truth as a witness statement.
(2) Only sub-paragraphs (i) and (j) of rule 33.3(1) apply to a summary by an expert of his conclusions served in advance of that expert's report.

Service of expert evidence R-221

33.4 (1) A party who wants to introduce expert evidence must—
(a) serve it on—
(i) the court officer, and
(ii) each other party;
(b) serve it—
(i) as soon as practicable, and in any event
(ii) with any application in support of which that party relies on that evidence; and
(c) if another party so requires, give that party a copy of, or a reasonable opportunity to inspect—
(i) a record of any examination, measurement, test or experiment on which the expert's findings and opinion are based, or that were carried out in the course of reaching those findings and opinion, and
(ii) anything on which any such examination, measurement, test or experiment was carried out.

(2) A party may not introduce expert evidence if that party has not complied with this rule, unless—
(a) every other party agrees; or
(b) the court gives permission.

R-222 Expert to be informed of service of report

33.5 A party who serves on another party or on the court a report by an expert must, at once, inform that expert of that fact.

R-223 Pre-hearing discussion of expert evidence

33.6 (1) This rule applies where more than one party wants to introduce expert evidence.
(2) The court may direct the experts to—
(a) discuss the expert issues in the proceedings; and
(b) prepare a statement for the court of the matters on which they agree and disagree, giving their reasons.
(3) Except for that statement, the content of that discussion must not be referred to without the court's permission.

R-224 Failure to comply with directions

[The former r. 33.7 was not reproduced in the new part 33 having effect from 5 October 2009.]

R-225 Court's power to direct that evidence is to be given by a single joint expert

33.7 (1) Where more than one defendant wants to introduce expert evidence on an issue at trial, the court may direct that the evidence on that issue is to be given by one expert only.
(2) Where the co-defendants cannot agree who should be the expert, the court may—
(a) select the expert from a list prepared or identified by them; or
(b) direct that the expert be selected in another way.

R-226 Instructions to a single joint expert

33.8 (1) Where the court gives a direction under rule 33.7 for a single joint expert to be used, each of the co-defendants may give instructions to the expert.
(2) When a co-defendant gives instructions to the expert he must, at the same time, send a copy of the instructions to the other co-defendant(s).
(3) The court may give directions about—
(a) the payment of the expert's fees and expenses; and
(b) any examination, measurement, test or experiment which the expert wishes to carry out.
(4) The court may, before an expert is instructed, limit the amount that can be paid by way of fees and expenses to the expert.
(5) Unless the court otherwise directs, the instructing co-defendants are jointly and severally liable for the payment of the expert's fees and expenses.

R-227 Court's power to vary requirements under this Part

33.9 (1) The court may—
(a) extend (even after it has expired) a time limit under this Part;
(b) allow the introduction of expert evidence which omits a detail required by this Part.
(2) A party who wants an extension of time must—
(a) apply when serving the expert evidence for which it is required; and
(b) explain the delay.

Part 34 Hearsay Evidence

R-228 When this Part applies

34.1 This Part applies—
(a) in a magistrates' court and in the Crown Court;
(b) where a party wants to introduce hearsay evidence, within the meaning of section 114 of the Criminal Justice Act 2003.

Notice to introduce hearsay evidence R-229

34.2 (1) This rule applies where a party wants to introduce hearsay evidence for admission under any of the following sections of the Criminal Justice Act 2003—
(a) section 114(1)(d) (evidence admissible in the interests of justice);
(b) section 116 (evidence where a witness is unavailable);
(c) section 121 (multiple hearsay).
(2) That party must—
(a) serve notice on—
(i) the court officer, and
(ii) each other party;
(b) in the notice—
(i) identify the evidence that is hearsay,
(ii) set out any facts on which that party relies to make the evidence admissible,
(iii) explain how that party will prove those facts if another party disputes them, and
(iv) explain why the evidence is admissible; and
(c) attach to the notice any statement or other document containing the evidence that has not already been served.
(3) A prosecutor who wants to introduce such evidence must serve the notice not more than—
(a) 28 days after the defendant pleads not guilty, in a magistrates' court; or
(b) 14 days after the defendant pleads not guilty, in the Crown Court.
(4) A defendant who wants to introduce such evidence must serve the notice as soon as reasonably practicable.
(5) A party entitled to receive a notice under this rule may waive that entitlement by so informing—
(a) the party who would have served it; and
(b) the court.

Opposing the introduction of hearsay evidence R-230

34.3 (1) This rule applies where a party objects to the introduction of hearsay evidence.
(2) That party must—
(a) apply to the court to determine the objection;
(b) serve the application on—
(i) the court officer, and
(ii) each other party;
(c) serve the application as soon as reasonably practicable, and in any event not more than 14 days after—
(i) service of notice to introduce the evidence under rule 34.2,
(ii) service of the evidence to which that party objects, if no notice is required by that rule, or
(iii) the defendant pleads not guilty whichever of those events happens last; and
(d) in the application, explain—
(i) which, if any, facts set out in a notice under rule 34.2 that party disputes,
(ii) why the evidence is not admissible,
(iii) any other objection to the application.
(3) The court—
(a) may determine an application—
(i) at a hearing, in public or in private, or
(ii) without a hearing;
(b) must not determine the application unless the party who served the notice—
(i) is present, or
(ii) has had a reasonable opportunity to respond;
(c) may adjourn the application; and
(d) may discharge or vary a determination where it can do so under—
(i) section 8B of the Magistrates' Courts Act 1980 (ruling at pre-trial hearing in a magistrates' court), or
(ii) section 9 of the Criminal Justice Act 1987, or section 31 or 40 of the Criminal Procedure and Investigations Act 1996 (ruling at preparatory or other pre-trial hearing in the Crown Court).

R-231 Unopposed hearsay evidence

34.4 (1) This rule applies where—
(a) a party has served notice to introduce hearsay evidence under rule 34.2; and
(b) no other party has applied to the court to determine an objection to the introduction of the evidence.
(2) The court will treat the evidence as if it were admissible by agreement.

R-232 Court's power to vary requirements under this Part

34.5 (1) The court may—
(a) shorten or extend (even after it has expired) a time limit under this Part;
(b) allow an application or notice to be given in a different form to one set out in the Practice Direction, or to be made or given orally; or
(c) dispense with the requirement for notice to introduce hearsay evidence.
(2) A party who wants an extension of time must—
(a) apply when serving the application or notice for which it is needed; and
(b) explain the delay.

Part 35 Evidence of Bad Character

R-233 When this Part applies

35.1 This Part applies—
(a) in a magistrates' court and in the Crown Court;
(b) where a party wants to introduce evidence of bad character, within the meaning of section 98 of the Criminal Justice Act 2003.

R-234 Content of application or notice

35.2 (1) A party who wants to introduce evidence of bad character must—
(a) make an application under rule 35.3, where it is evidence of a non-defendant's bad character;
(b) give notice under rule 35.4, where it is evidence of a defendant's bad character.
(2) An application or notice must—
(a) set out the facts of the misconduct on which that party relies,
(b) explain how that party will prove those facts (whether by certificate of conviction, other official record, or other evidence), if another party disputes them, and
(c) explain why the evidence is admissible.

R-235 Application to introduce evidence of a non-defendant's bad character

35.3 (1) This rule applies where a party wants to introduce evidence of the bad character of a person other than the defendant.
(2) That party must serve an application to do so on—
(a) the court officer; and
(b) each other party.
(3) The applicant must serve the application—
(a) as soon as reasonably practicable; and in any event
(b) not more than 14 days after the prosecutor discloses material on which the application is based (if the prosecutor is not the applicant).
(4) A party who objects to the introduction of the evidence must—
(a) serve notice on—
(i) the court officer, and
(ii) each other party not more than 14 days after service of the application; and
(b) in the notice explain, as applicable—
(i) which, if any, facts of the misconduct set out in the application that party disputes,
(ii) what, if any, facts of the misconduct that party admits instead,
(iii) why the evidence is not admissible, and
(iv) any other objection to the application.
(5) The court—
(a) may determine an application—
(i) at a hearing, in public or in private, or
(ii) without a hearing;

(b) must not determine the application unless each party other than the applicant—
  (i) is present, or
  (ii) has had at least 14 days in which to serve a notice of objection;
(c) may adjourn the application; and
(d) may discharge or vary a determination where it can do so under—
  (i) section 8B of the Magistrates' Courts Act 1980 (ruling at pre-trial hearing in a magistrates' court), or
  (ii) section 9 of the Criminal Justice Act 1987, or section 31 or 40 of the Criminal Procedure and Investigations Act 1996 (ruling at preparatory or other pre-trial hearing in the Crown Court).

Notice to introduce evidence of a defendant's bad character **R-236**

35.4 (1) This rule applies where a party wants to introduce evidence of a defendant's bad character.
(2) That party must serve notice on—
  (a) the court officer; and
  (b) each other party.
(3) A prosecutor who wants to introduce such evidence must serve the notice not more than—
  (a) 28 days after the defendant pleads not guilty, in a magistrates' court; or
  (b) 14 days after the defendant pleads not guilty, in the Crown Court.
(4) A co-defendant who wants to introduce such evidence must serve the notice—
  (a) as soon as reasonably practicable; and in any event
  (b) not more than 14 days after the prosecutor discloses material on which the notice is based.
(5) A party who objects to the introduction of the evidence must—
  (a) apply to the court to determine the objection;
  (b) serve the application on—
    (i) the court officer, and
    (ii) each other party not more than 14 days after service of the notice; and
  (c) in the application explain, as applicable—
    (i) which, if any, facts of the misconduct set out in the notice that party disputes,
    (ii) what, if any, facts of the misconduct that party admits instead,
    (iii) why the evidence is not admissible,
    (iv) why it would be unfair to admit the evidence, and
    (v) any other objection to the notice.
(6) The court—
  (a) may determine an application—
    (i) at a hearing, in public or in private, or
    (ii) without a hearing;
  (b) must not determine the application unless the party who served the notice—
    (i) is present, or
    (ii) has had a reasonable opportunity to respond;
  (c) may adjourn the application; and
  (d) may discharge or vary a determination where it can do so under—
    (i) section 8B of the Magistrates' Courts Act 1980 (ruling at pre-trial hearing in a magistrates' court), or
    (ii) section 9 of the Criminal Justice Act 1987, or section 31 or 40 of the Criminal Procedure and Investigations Act 1996 (ruling at preparatory or other pre-trial hearing in the Crown Court).
(7) A party entitled to receive a notice may waive that entitlement by so informing—
  (a) the party who would have served it; and
  (b) the court.

Reasons for decisions **R-237**

35.5 The court must announce at a hearing in public (but in the absence of the jury, if there is one) the reasons for a decision—
(a) to admit evidence as evidence of bad character, or to refuse to do so; or
(b) to direct an acquittal or a retrial under section 107 of the Criminal Justice Act 2003.

R-238 **Court's power to vary requirements under this Part**

35.6 (1) The court may—
(a) shorten or extend (even after it has expired) a time limit under this Part;
(b) allow an application or notice to be in a different form to one set out in the Practice Direction, or to be made or given orally;
(c) dispense with a requirement for notice to introduce evidence of a defendant's bad character.
(2) A party who wants an extension of time must—
(a) apply when serving the application or notice for which it is needed; and
(b) explain the delay.

Part 36 Evidence of a Complainant's Previous Sexual Behaviour

R-239 **When this Part applies**

36.1 This Part applies in magistrates' courts and in the Crown Court where a defendant wants to—
(a) introduce evidence; or
(b) cross-examine a witness about a complainant's sexual behaviour despite the prohibition in section 41 of the Youth Justice and Criminal Evidence Act 1999.

R-240 **Application for permission to introduce evidence or cross-examine**

36.2 The defendant must apply for permission to do so—
(a) in writing; and
(b) not more than 28 days after the prosecutor has complied or purported to comply with section 3 of the Criminal Procedure and Investigations Act 1996 (disclosure by prosecutor).

R-241 **Content of application**

36.3 The application must—
(a) identify the issue to which the defendant says the complainant's sexual behaviour is relevant;
(b) give particulars of—
(i) any evidence that the defendant wants to introduce, and
(ii) any questions that the defendant wants to ask;
(c) identify the exception to the prohibition in section 41 of the Youth Justice and Criminal Evidence Act 1999 on which the defendant relies; and
(d) give the name and date of birth of any witness whose evidence about the complainant's sexual behaviour the defendant wants to introduce.

R-242 **Service of application**

36.4 The defendant must serve the application on the court officer and all other parties.

R-243 **Reply to application**

36.5 A party who wants to make representations about an application under rule 36.2 must—
(a) do so in writing not more than 14 days after receiving it; and
(b) serve those representations on the court officer and all other parties.

R-244 **Application for special measures**

36.6 If the court allows an application under rule 36.2 then—
(a) a party may apply not more than 14 days later for a special measures direction or for the variation of an existing special measures direction; and
(b) the court may shorten the time for opposing that application.

R-245 **Court's power to vary requirements under this Part**

36.7 The court may shorten or extend (even after it has expired) a time limit under this Part.

Part 37 Trial and Sentence in a Magistrates' Court

R-246 **When this Part applies**

37.1 (1) This Part applies in a magistrates' court where—
(a) the court tries a case; or
(b) the defendant pleads guilty.

(2) Where the defendant is under 18, in this Part—
(a) a reference to convicting the defendant includes a reference to finding the defendant guilty of an offence; and
(b) a reference to sentence includes a reference to an order made on a finding of guilt.

General rules R-247

37.2 (1) Where this Part applies—
(a) the general rule is that the hearing must be in public; but
(b) the court may exercise any power it has to—
(i) impose reporting restrictions,
(ii) withhold information from the public, or
(iii) order a hearing in private; and
(c) unless the court otherwise directs, only the following may attend a hearing in a youth court—
(i) the parties and their legal representatives,
(ii) a defendant's parents, guardian or other supporting adult,
(iii) a witness,
(iv) anyone else directly concerned in the case, and
(v) a representative of a news-gathering or reporting organisation.
(2) Unless already done, the justices' legal adviser or the court must—
(a) read the allegation of the offence to the defendant;
(b) explain, in terms the defendant can understand (with help, if necessary)—
(i) the allegation, and
(ii) what the procedure at the hearing will be;
(c) ask whether the defendant has been advised about the potential effect on sentence of a guilty plea;
(d) ask whether the defendant pleads guilty or not guilty; and
(e) take the defendant's plea.
(3) The court may adjourn the hearing—
(a) at any stage, to the same or to another magistrates' court; or
(b) to a youth court, where the court is not itself a youth court and the defendant is under 18.

Procedure on plea of not guilty R-248

37.3 (1) This rule applies—
(a) if the defendant has—
(i) entered a plea of not guilty, or
(ii) not entered a plea; or
(b) if, in either case, it appears to the court that there may be grounds for making a hospital order without convicting the defendant.
(2) If a not guilty plea was taken on a previous occasion, the justices' legal adviser or the court must ask the defendant to confirm that plea.
(3) In the following sequence—
(a) the prosecutor may summarise the prosecution case, identifying the relevant law and facts;
(b) the prosecutor must introduce the evidence on which the prosecution case relies;
(c) at the conclusion of the prosecution case, on the defendant's application or on its own initiative, the court—
(i) may acquit on the ground that the prosecution evidence is insufficient for any reasonable court properly to convict, but
(ii) must not do so unless the prosecutor has had an opportunity to make representations;
(d) the justices' legal adviser or the court must explain, in terms the defendant can understand (with help, if necessary)—
(i) the right to give evidence, and
(ii) the potential effect of not doing so at all, or of refusing to answer a question while doing so;
(e) the defendant may introduce evidence;
(f) a party may introduce further evidence if it is then admissible (for example, because it is in rebuttal of evidence already introduced);

(g) the prosecutor may make final representations in support of the prosecution case, where—
(i) the defendant is represented by a legal representative, or
(ii) whether represented or not, the defendant has introduced evidence other than his or her own; and
(h) the defendant may make final representations in support of the defence case.
(4) Where a party wants to introduce evidence or make representations after that party's opportunity to do so under paragraph (3), the court—
(a) may refuse to receive any such evidence or representations; and
(b) must not receive any such evidence or representations after it has announced its verdict.
(5) If the court—
(a) convicts the defendant; or
(b) makes a hospital order instead of doing so,
it must give sufficient reasons to explain its decision.
(6) If the court acquits the defendant, it may—
(a) give an explanation of its decision; and
(b) exercise any power it has to make—
(i) a civil behaviour order,
(ii) a costs order.

R-249 **Evidence of a witness in person**

37.4 (1) This rule applies where a party wants to introduce evidence by calling a witness to give that evidence in person.
(2) Unless the court otherwise directs—
(a) a witness waiting to give evidence must not wait inside the courtroom, unless that witness is—
(i) a party, or
(ii) an expert witness;
(b) a witness who gives evidence in the courtroom must do so from the place provided for that purpose; and
(c) a witness' address must not be announced unless it is relevant to an issue in the case.
(3) Unless other legislation otherwise provides, before giving evidence a witness must take an oath or affirm.
(4) In the following sequence—
(a) the party who calls a witness must ask questions in examination-in-chief;
(b) every other party may ask questions in cross-examination;
(c) the party who called the witness may ask questions in re-examination;
(d) at any time while giving evidence, a witness may refer to a record of that witness' recollection of events, if other legislation so permits;
(e) the party who calls a witness, in examination-in-chief may ask that witness to adopt all or part of such a record as part of that witness' evidence, but only if—
(i) the parties agree, and
(ii) the court so permits;
(f) if the witness adopts any part of such a record—
(i) that part must be read aloud, or
(ii) with the court's permission, its contents may be summarised aloud.
(5) The justices' legal adviser or the court may—
(a) ask a witness questions; and in particular
(b) where the defendant is not represented, ask any question necessary in the defendant's interests.

R-250 **Evidence by written statement**

37.5 (1) This rule applies where a party introduces in evidence the written statement of a witness.
(2) The party introducing the statement must read or summarise aloud those parts that are relevant to the issues in the case.

R-251 **Evidence by admission**

37.6 (1) This rule applies where—
(a) a party introduces in evidence a fact admitted by another party; or
(b) parties jointly admit a fact.

(2) Unless the court otherwise directs, a written record must be made of the admission.

Procedure on plea of guilty R-252

37.7 (1) This rule applies if—
(a) the defendant pleads guilty; and
(b) the court is satisfied that the plea represents a clear acknowledgement of guilt.
(2) The court may convict the defendant without receiving evidence.

Written guilty plea: special rules R-253

37.8 (1) This rule applies where—
(a) the offence alleged—
(i) can be tried only in a magistrates' court, and
(ii) is not one specified under section 12(1)(a) of the Magistrates' Courts Act 1980;
(b) the defendant is at least 16 years old;
(c) the prosecutor has served on the defendant—
(i) the summons or requisition,
(ii) the material on which the prosecutor relies to set out the facts of the offence and to provide information relevant to sentence,
(iii) a notice that the procedure set out in this rule applies, and
(iv) a notice for the defendant's use if the defendant wants to plead guilty without attending court; and
(d) the prosecutor has served on the court officer—
(i) copies of those documents, and
(ii) a certificate of service of those documents on the defendant.
(2) A defendant who wants to plead guilty without attending court must, before the hearing date specified in the summons or requisition—
(a) serve a notice of guilty plea on the court officer; and
(b) include with that notice any representations that the defendant wants the court to consider on that date.
(3) A defendant who wants to withdraw such a notice must notify the court officer in writing before the hearing date.
(4) The court may accept such a guilty plea on the hearing date, and if it does so must take account only of—
(a) the material served by the prosecutor on the defendant under this rule; and
(b) any representations by the defendant.
(5) With the defendant's agreement, the court may deal with the case in the same way as under paragraph (4) where the defendant—
(a) is present; and
(b) has served a notice of guilty plea under paragraph (2); or
(c) pleads guilty there and then.

Application to withdraw a guilty plea R-254

37.9 (1) This rule applies where the defendant wants to withdraw a guilty plea.
(2) The defendant must apply to do so—
(a) as soon as practicable after becoming aware of the reasons for doing so; and
(b) before sentence.
(3) Unless the court otherwise directs, the application must be in writing and the defendant must serve it on—
(a) the court officer; and
(b) the prosecutor.
(4) The application must—
(a) explain why it would be unjust not to allow the defendant to withdraw the guilty plea;
(b) identify—
(i) any witness that the defendant wants to call, and
(ii) any other proposed evidence; and
(c) say whether the defendant waives legal professional privilege, giving any relevant name and date.

R-255 **Procedure if the court convicts**

37.10 (1) This rule applies if the court convicts the defendant.

(2) The court—

(a) may exercise its power to require—

(i) a statement of the defendant's financial circumstances,

(ii) a pre-sentence report; and

(b) may (and in some circumstances must) remit the defendant to a youth court for sentence where—

(i) the defendant is under 18, and

(ii) the convicting court is not itself a youth court.

(3) The prosecutor must—

(a) summarise the prosecution case, if the sentencing court has not heard evidence;

(b) identify any offence to be taken into consideration in sentencing;

(c) provide information relevant to sentence; and

(d) where it is likely to assist the court, identify any other matter relevant to sentence, including—

(i) aggravating and mitigating factors,

(ii) the legislation applicable, and

(iii) any sentencing guidelines or guideline cases.

(4) The defendant must provide information relevant to sentence, including details of financial circumstances.

(5) Where the defendant pleads guilty but wants to be sentenced on a different basis to that disclosed by the prosecution case—

(a) the defendant must set out that basis in writing, identifying what is in dispute;

(b) the court may invite the parties to make representations about whether the dispute is material to sentence; and

(c) if the court decides that it is a material dispute, the court will—

(i) invite such further representations or evidence as it may require, and

(ii) decide the dispute.

(6) Where the court has power to order the endorsement of the defendant's driving licence, or power to order the disqualification of the defendant from holding or obtaining one—

(a) if other legislation so permits, a defendant who wants the court not to exercise that power must introduce the evidence or information on which the defendant relies;

(b) the prosecutor may introduce evidence; and

(c) the parties may make representations about that evidence or information.

(7) Before the court passes sentence—

(a) the court must—

(i) give the defendant an opportunity to make representations and introduce evidence relevant to sentence, and

(ii) where the defendant is under 18, give the defendant's parents, guardian or other supporting adult, if present, such an opportunity as well; and

(b) the justices' legal adviser or the court must elicit any further information relevant to sentence that the court may require.

(8) If the court requires more information, it may exercise its power to adjourn the hearing for not more than—

(a) 3 weeks at a time, if the defendant will be in custody; or

(b) 4 weeks at a time.

(9) When the court has taken into account all the evidence, information and any report available, the general rule is that the court will—

(a) pass sentence there and then;

(b) explain the sentence, the reasons for it, and its effect, in terms the defendant can understand (with help, if necessary); and

(c) consider exercising any power it has to make a costs or other order.

(10) Despite the general rule—

(a) the court must adjourn the hearing if—

(i) the case started with a summons or requisition, and the defendant is absent, and

(ii) the court considers passing a custodial sentence, or

(iii) the court considers imposing a disqualification (unless it has already adjourned the hearing to give the defendant an opportunity to attend);

(b) the court may exercise any power it has to—
(i) commit the defendant to the Crown Court for sentence (and in some cases it must do so), or
(ii) defer sentence for up to 6 months.

Procedure where a party is absent R-256

37.11 (1) This rule—
(a) applies where a party is absent; but
(b) does not apply where the defendant has served a notice of guilty plea under rule 37.8 (written guilty plea: special rules).
(2) Where the prosecutor is absent, the court may—
(a) if it has received evidence, deal with the case as if the prosecutor were present; and
(b) in any other case—
(i) enquire into the reasons for the prosecutor's absence, and
(ii) if satisfied there is no good reason, exercise its power to dismiss the allegation.
(3) Where the defendant is absent—
(a) the general rule is that the court will proceed as if the defendant—
(i) were present, and
(ii) had pleaded not guilty (unless a plea already has been taken)
and the court must give reasons if it does not do so; but
(b) the general rule does not apply if the defendant is under 18;
(c) the general rule is subject to the court being satisfied that—
(i) any summons or requisition was served on the defendant a reasonable time before the hearing, or
(ii) in a case in which the hearing has been adjourned, the defendant had reasonable notice of where and when it would resume;
(d) the general rule is subject also to rule 37.10(10)(a) (restrictions on passing sentence in the defendant's absence); and
(e) the hearing must be treated as if it had not taken place at all if—
(i) the case started with a summons or requisition,
(ii) the defendant makes a statutory declaration of not having found out about the case until after the hearing began, and
(iii) the defendant serves that declaration on the court officer not more than 21 days after the date of finding out about the case, unless the court extends that time limit.
(4) Where the defendant is absent, the court—
(a) must exercise its power to issue a warrant for the defendant's arrest, if it passes a custodial sentence; and
(b) may exercise its power to do so in any other case, if it does not apply the general rule in paragraph (3)(a) of this rule about proceeding in the defendant's absence.

Provision of documents for the court R-257

37.12 (1) This rule applies where a party—
(a) introduces in evidence any document; or
(b) relies on any other document in the presentation of that party's case.
(2) Unless the court otherwise directs, that party must supply sufficient copies of such a document for—
(a) each other party;
(b) the court; and
(c) the justices' legal adviser.

Place of trial R-258

37.13 (1) Unless the court otherwise directs, the hearing must take place in a courtroom provided by the Lord Chancellor.
(2) Where the hearing takes place in Wales—
(a) any party or witness may use the Welsh language; and
(b) if practicable, at least one member of the court must be Welsh-speaking.

Duty of justices' legal adviser R-259

37.14 (1) A justices' legal adviser must attend, unless the court—
(a) includes a District Judge (Magistrates' Courts); and
(b) otherwise directs.

(2) A justices' legal adviser must—
  (a) give the court legal advice; and
  (b) if necessary, attend the members of the court outside the courtroom to give such advice; but
  (c) inform the parties of any such advice given outside the courtroom.
(3) A justices' legal adviser must—
  (a) assist an unrepresented defendant;
  (b) assist the court by—
    (i) making a note of the substance of any oral evidence or representations, to help the court recall that information,
    (ii) if the court rules inadmissible part of a written statement introduced in evidence, marking that statement in such a way as to make that clear,
    (iii) ensuring that an adequate record is kept of the court's decisions and the reasons for them, and
    (iv) making any announcement, other than of the verdict or sentence.
(4) Where the defendant has served a notice of guilty plea to which rule 37.8 (written guilty plea: special rules) applies, a justices' legal adviser must read aloud to the court—
  (a) the material on which the prosecutor relies to set out the facts of the offence and to provide information relevant to sentence (or summarise any written statement included in that material, if the court so directs); and
  (b) any written representations by the defendant.

R-260 **Duty of court officer**

37.15 The court officer must—
  (a) serve on each party notice of where and when an adjourned hearing will resume, unless—
    (i) the party was present when that was arranged, or
    (ii) the defendant has served a notice of guilty plea to which rule 37.8 applies, and the adjournment is for not more than 4 weeks;
  (b) if the reason for the adjournment was to postpone sentence, include that reason in any such notice to the defendant;
  (c) unless the court otherwise directs, make available to the parties any written report to which rule 37.10 applies;
  (d) where the court has ordered a defendant to provide information under section 25 of the Road Traffic Offenders Act 1988, serve on the defendant notice of that order unless the defendant was present when it was made;
  (e) serve on the prosecutor—
    (i) any notice of guilty plea to which rule 37.8 applies, and
    (ii) any declaration served under rule 37.11(3)(e) that the defendant did not know about the case;
  (f) record in the magistrates' court register the court's reasons for not proceeding in the defendant's absence where rule 37.11(3)(a) applies; and
  (g) give the court such other assistance as it requires.

Part 38

[There are no rules in this part]

Part 39 Trial on Indictment

R-261 **Time limits for beginning of trials**

39.1 The periods set out for the purposes of section 77(2)(a) and (b) of the Senior Courts Act 1981 shall be 14 days and 8 weeks respectively and accordingly the trial of a person committed by a magistrates' court—
  (a) shall not begin until the expiration of 14 days beginning with the date of his committal, except with his consent and the consent of the prosecution; and
  (b) shall, unless the Crown Court has otherwise ordered, begin not later than the expiration of 8 weeks beginning with the date of his committal.

Appeal against refusal to excuse from jury service or to defer attendance R-262

39.2 (1) A person summoned under the Juries Act 1974 for jury service may appeal in accordance with the provisions of this rule against any refusal of the appropriate court officer to excuse him under section 9(2), or to defer his attendance under section 9A(1), of that Act.
(2) Subject to paragraph (3), an appeal under this rule shall be heard by the Crown Court.
(3) Where the appellant is summoned under the 1974 Act to attend before the High Court in Greater London the appeal shall be heard by a judge of the High Court and where the appellant is summoned under that Act to attend before the High Court outside Greater London or before a county court and the appeal has not been decided by the Crown Court before the day on which the appellant is required by the summons to attend, the appeal shall be heard by the court before which he is summoned to attend.
(4) An appeal under this rule shall be commenced by the appellant's giving notice of appeal to the appropriate court officer of the Crown Court or the High Court in Greater London, as the case may be, and such notice shall be in writing and shall specify the matters upon which the appellant relies as providing good reason why he should be excused from attending in pursuance of the summons or why his attendance should be deferred.
(5) The court shall not dismiss an appeal under this rule unless the appellant has been given an opportunity of making representations.
(6) Where an appeal under this rule is decided in the absence of the appellant, the appropriate court officer of the Crown Court or the High Court in Greater London, as the case may be, shall notify him of the decision without delay.

Application to change a plea of guilty R-263

39.3 (1) The defendant must apply as soon as practicable after becoming aware of the grounds for making an application to change a plea of guilty, and may only do so before the final disposal of the case, by sentence or otherwise.
(2) Unless the court otherwise directs, the application must be in writing and it must—
(a) set out the reasons why it would be unjust for the guilty plea to remain unchanged;
(b) indicate what, if any, evidence the defendant wishes to call;
(c) identify any proposed witness; and
(d) indicate whether legal professional privilege is waived, specifying any material name and date.
(3) The defendant must serve the written application on—
(a) the court officer; and
(b) the prosecutor.

Part 40 Tainted Acquittals

Time of certification R-264

40.1 Where a person is convicted of an offence as referred to in section 54(1)(b) of the Criminal Procedure and Investigations Act 1996 and it appears to the court before which the conviction has taken place that the provisions of section 54(2) are satisfied, the court shall make the certification referred to in section 54(2) at any time following conviction but no later than—
(a) immediately after the court sentences or otherwise deals with that person in respect of the offence; or
(b) where the court, being a magistrates' court, commits that person to the Crown Court, or remits him to another magistrates' court, to be dealt with in respect of the offence, immediately after he is so committed or remitted, as the case may be; or
(c) where that person is a child or young person and the court, being the Crown Court, remits him to a youth court to be dealt with in respect of the offence, immediately after he is so remitted.

Form of certification in the Crown Court R-265

40.2 A certification referred to in section 54(2) of the Criminal Procedure and Investigations Act 1996 by the Crown Court shall be drawn up in the form set out in the Practice Direction.

Service of a copy of the certification R-266

40.3 Where a magistrates' court or the Crown Court makes a certification as referred to in section 54(2) of the Criminal Procedure and Investigations Act 1996, the court officer shall, as soon as practicable after the drawing up of the form, serve a copy on the acquitted person referred to in the certification, on the prosecutor in the proceedings which led to the acquittal, and, where the acquittal has taken place before a court other than, or at a different place to, the court where the certification has been made, on—

(a) the clerk of the magistrates' court before which the acquittal has taken place; or
(b) the Crown Court officer at the place where the acquittal has taken place.

R-267 **Entry in register or records in relation to the conviction which occasioned certification**

40.4 A clerk of a magistrates' court or an officer of a Crown Court which has made a certification under section 54(2) of the Criminal Procedure and Investigations Act 1996 shall enter in the register or records, in relation to the conviction which occasioned the certification, a note of the fact that certification has been made, the date of certification, the name of the acquitted person referred to in the certification, a description of the offence of which the acquitted person has been acquitted, the date of the acquittal, and the name of the court before which the acquittal has taken place.

R-268 **Entry in the register or records in relation to the acquittal**

40.5 The court officer of the court before which an acquittal has taken place shall, as soon as practicable after receipt of a copy of a form recording a certification under section 54(2) of the Criminal Procedure and Investigations Act 1996 relating to the acquittal, enter in the register or records a note that the certification has been made, the date of the certification, the name of the court which has made the certification, the name of the person whose conviction occasioned the making of the certification, and a description of the offence of which that person has been convicted. Where the certification has been made by the same court as the court before which the acquittal has occurred, sitting at the same place, the entry shall be made as soon as practicable after the making of the certification. In the case of an acquittal before a magistrates' court the entry in the register shall be signed by the clerk of the court.

R-269 **Display of copy certification form**

40.6 (1) Where a court makes a certification as referred to in section 54(2) of the Criminal Procedure and Investigations Act 1996, the court officer shall, as soon as practicable after the drawing up of the form, display a copy of that form at a prominent place within court premises to which place the public has access.

(2) Where an acquittal has taken place before a court other than, or at a different place to, the court which has made the certification under section 54(2) of the 1996 Act in relation to the acquittal, the court officer at the court where the acquittal has taken place shall, as soon as practicable after receipt of a copy of the form recording the certification, display a copy of it at a prominent place within court premises to which place the public has access.

(3) The copy of the form referred to in paragraph (1), or the copy referred to in paragraph (2), shall continue to be displayed as referred to, respectively, in those paragraphs at least until the expiry of 28 days from, in the case of paragraph (1), the day on which the certification was made, or, in the case of paragraph (2), the day on which the copy form was received at the court.

R-270 **Entry in the register or records in relation to decision of High Court**

40.7 (1) The court officer at the court where an acquittal has taken place shall, on receipt from the Administrative Court Office of notice of an order made under section 54(3) of the Criminal Procedure and Investigations Act 1996 quashing the acquittal, or of a decision not to make such an order, enter in the register or records, in relation to the acquittal, a note of the fact that the acquittal has been quashed by the said order, or that a decision has been made not to make such an order, as the case may be.

(2) The court officer of the court which has made a certification under section 54(2) of the 1996 Act shall, on receipt from the Administrative Court Office of notice of an order made under section 54(3) of that Act quashing the acquittal referred to in the certification, or of a decision not to make such an order, enter in the register or records, in relation to the conviction which occasioned the certification, a note that the acquittal has been quashed by the said order, or that a decision has been made not to make such an order, as the case may be.

(3) The entries in the register of a magistrates' court referred to, respectively, in paragraphs (1) and (2) above shall be signed by the magistrates' court officer.

Display of copy of notice received from High Court R-271

40.8 (1) Where the court officer of a court which has made a certification under section 54(2) of the Criminal Procedure and Investigations Act 1996 or before which an acquittal has occurred to which such a certification refers, receives from the Administrative Court Office notice of an order quashing the acquittal concerned, or notice of a decision not to make such an order, he shall, as soon as practicable after receiving the notice, display a copy of it at a prominent place within court premises to which place the public has access.

(2) The copy notice referred to in paragraph (1) shall continue to be displayed as referred to in that paragraph at least until the expiry of 28 days from the day on which the notice was received at the court.

Part 41 Retrial Following Acquittal for Serious Offence

Interpretation R-272

41.1 In this Part:

'business day' means any day other than a Saturday, Sunday, Christmas Day, Good Friday or a bank holiday under the Banking and Financial Dealings Act 1971, in England and Wales; and

'section 76 application' means an application made by a prosecutor under section 76(1) or (2) of the Criminal Justice Act 2003.

Notice of a section 76 application R-273

41.2 (1) A prosecutor who wants to make a section 76 application must serve notice of that application in the form set out in the Practice Direction on the Registrar and the acquitted person.

(2) That notice shall, where practicable, be accompanied by—

(a) relevant witness statements which are relied upon as forming new and compelling evidence of guilt of the acquitted person as well as any relevant witness statements from the original trial;

(b) any unused statements which might reasonably be considered capable of undermining the section 76 application or of assisting an acquitted person's application to oppose that application under rule 41.3;

(c) a copy of the indictment and paper exhibits from the original trial;

(d) copies of the transcript of the summing up and any other relevant transcripts from the original trial; and

(e) any other documents relied upon to support the section 76 application.

(3) The prosecutor must, as soon as practicable after service of that notice on the acquitted person, file with the Registrar a witness statement or certificate of service which exhibits a copy of that notice.

Response of the acquitted person R-274

41.3 (1) An acquitted person who wants to oppose a section 76 application must serve a response in the form set out in the Practice Direction on the Registrar and the prosecutor which—

(a) indicates if he is also seeking an order under section 80(6) of the Criminal Justice Act 2003 for—

(i) the production of any document, exhibit or other thing, or

(ii) a witness to attend for examination and to be examined before the Court of Appeal; and

(b) exhibits any relevant documents.

(2) The acquitted person must serve that response not more than 28 days after receiving notice under rule 41.2.

(3) The Court of Appeal may extend the period for service under paragraph (2), either before or after that period expires.

Examination of witnesses or evidence by the Court of Appeal R-275

41.4 (1) Prior to the hearing of a section 76 application, a party may apply to the Court of Appeal for an order under section 80(6) of the Criminal Justice Act 2003 for—

(a) the production of any document, exhibit or other thing; or

(b) a witness to attend for examination and to be examined before the Court of Appeal.

(2) An application under paragraph (1) must be in the form set out in the Practice Direction and must be sent to the Registrar and a copy sent to each party to the section 76 application.

(3) An application must set out the reasons why the order was not sought from the Court when—

(a) the notice was served on the Registrar under rule 41.2, if the application is made by the prosecutor; or

(b) the response was served on the Registrar under rule 41.3, if the application is made by the acquitted person.

(4) An application must be made at least 14 days before the day of the hearing of the section 76 application.

(5) If the Court of Appeal makes an order under section 80(6) of the 2003 Act on its own motion or on application from the prosecutor, it must serve notice and reasons for that order on all parties to the section 76 application.

R-276 Bail or custody hearings in the Crown Court

41.5 (1) Rules 19.18, 19.22 and 19.23 shall apply where a person is to appear or be brought before the Crown Court pursuant to sections 88 or 89 of the Criminal Justice Act 2003 (with the modification as set out in paragraph (2)), as if they were applications under rule 19.18(1).

(2) Substitute the following for Rule 19.18:
'Where a person is to appear or be brought before the Crown Court pursuant to sections 88 or 89 of the Criminal Justice Act 2003, the prosecutor must serve notice of the need for such a hearing on the court officer.'

(3) Where a person is to appear or be brought before the Crown Court pursuant to sections 88 or 89 of the 2003 Act the Crown Court may order that the person shall be released from custody on entering into a recognizance, with or without sureties, or giving other security before—

(a) the Crown Court officer; or

(b) any other person authorised by virtue of section 119(1) of the Magistrates' Courts Act 1980 to take a recognizance where a magistrates' court having power to take the recognizance has, instead of taking it, fixed the amount in which the principal and his sureties, if any, are to be bound.

(4) The court officer shall forward to the Registrar a copy of any record made in pursuance of section 5(1) of the Bail Act 1976.

R-277 Further provisions regarding bail and custody in the Crown Court

41.6 (1) The prosecutor may only apply to extend or further extend the relevant period before it expires and that application must be served on the Crown Court officer and the acquitted person.

(2) A prosecutor's application for a summons or a warrant under section 89(3)(a) or (b) of the Criminal Justice Act 2003 must be served on the court officer and the acquitted person.

R-278 Bail or custody orders in the Court of Appeal

41.7 Rules 68.8 and 68.9 shall apply to bail or custody orders made in the Court of Appeal under section 90 of the Criminal Justice Act 2003 as if they were orders made pursuant to an application under rule 68.7.

R-279 Application for restrictions on publication

41.8 (1) An application by the Director of Public Prosecutions, under section 82 of the Criminal Justice Act 2003, for restrictions on publication must be in the form set out in the Practice Direction and be served on the Registrar and the acquitted person.

(2) If notice of a section 76 application has not been given and the Director of Public Prosecution has indicated that there are reasons why the acquitted person should not be notified of the application for restrictions on publication, the Court of Appeal may order that service on the acquitted person is not to be effected until notice of a section 76 application is served on that person.

(3) If the Court of Appeal makes an order for restrictions on publication of its own motion or on application of the Director of Public Prosecutions, the Registrar must serve notice and reasons for that order on all parties, unless paragraph (2) applies.

R-280 Variation or revocation of restrictions on publication

41.9 (1) A party who wants to vary or revoke an order for restrictions on publication, under section 82(7) of the Criminal Justice Act 2003, may apply to the Court of Appeal in writing at any time after that order was made.

(2) A copy of the application to vary or revoke shall be sent to all parties to the section 76 application unless paragraph (3) applies.

(3) If the application to vary or revoke is made by the Director of Public Prosecutions and—

(a) the notice of a section 76 application has not been given under rule 41.2; and

(b) the Director of Public Prosecutions has indicated that there are reasons why the acquitted person should not be notified of an application for restrictions on publication, the Court of Appeal may order that service on the acquitted person is not to be effected until notice of a section 76 application is served on that person.

(4) If the Court of Appeal varies or revokes an order for restrictions on publication of its own motion or on application, it must serve notice and reasons for that order on all parties, unless paragraph (3) applies.

Powers exercisable by a single judge of the Court of Appeal **R-281**

41.10 (1) The following powers under the Criminal Justice Act 2003 and under this Part may be exercised by a single judge in the same manner as they may be exercised by the Court of Appeal and subject to the same provisions, namely to—

(a) order the production of any document, exhibit or thing under section 80(6)(a) of the 2003 Act;

(b) order any witness who would be a compellable witness in proceedings pursuant to an order or declaration made on the application to attend for examination and be examined before the Court of Appeal under section 80(6)(b) of the 2003 Act;

(c) extend the time for service under rule 41.3(2); and

(d) delay the requirement of service on the acquitted person of an application for restrictions on publication under rules 41.8(2) and 41.9(3).

(2) A single judge may, for the purposes of exercising any of the powers specified in paragraph (1), sit in such place as he appoints and may sit otherwise than in open court.

(3) Where a single judge exercises one of the powers set out in paragraph (1), the Registrar must serve notice of the single judge's decision on all parties to the section 76 application.

Powers exercisable by the Registrar **R-282**

41.11 (1) The Registrar may require the Crown Court at the place of original trial to provide the Court of Appeal with any assistance or information which it may require for the purposes of exercising its jurisdiction under Part 10 of the Criminal Justice Act 2003 or this Part.

(2) The following powers may be exercised by the Registrar in the same manner as the Court of Appeal and subject to the same provisions

(a) order the production of any document, exhibit or thing under section 80(6)(a) of the 2003 Act;

(b) order any witness who would be a compellable witness in proceedings pursuant to an order or declaration made on the application to attend for examination and be examined before the Court of Appeal under section 80(6)(b) of the 2003 Act; and

(c) extend the time for service under rule 41.3(2).

(3) Where the Registrar exercises one of the powers set out in paragraph (2) the Registrar must serve notice of that decision on all parties to the section 76 application.

(4) Where the Registrar has refused an application to exercise any of the powers referred to in paragraph (2), the party making the application may have it determined by a single judge by serving a renewal in the form set out in the Practice Direction within 14 days of the day on which notice of the Registrar's decision is served on the party making the application, unless that period is extended by the Court of Appeal.

Determination by full court **R-283**

41.12 (1) Where a single judge has refused an application to exercise any of the powers referred to in rule 41.10, the applicant may have that application determined by the Court of Appeal by serving a notice of renewal in the form set out in the Practice Direction.

(2) A notice under paragraph (1) must be served on the Registrar within 14 days of the day on which notice of the single judge's decision is served on the party making the application, unless that period is extended by the Court of Appeal.

(3) If a notice under paragraph (1) is not served on the Registrar within the period specified in paragraph (2) or such extended period as the Court of Appeal has allowed, the application shall be treating as having been refused by the Court of Appeal.

R-284 **Notice of the determination of the application**

41.13 (1) The Court of Appeal may give its determination of the section 76 application at the conclusion of the hearing.

(2) If determination is reserved, the Registrar shall as soon as practicable, serve notice of the determination on the parties to the section 76 application.

(3) If the Court of Appeal orders under section 77 of the Criminal Justice Act 2003 that a retrial take place, the Registrar must as soon as practicable, serve notice on the Crown Court officer at the appropriate place of retrial.

R-285 **Notice of application to set aside order for retrial**

41.14 (1) If an acquitted person has not been arraigned before the end of 2 months after the date of an order under section 77 of the Criminal Justice Act 2003 he may apply in the form set out in the Practice Direction to the Court of Appeal to set aside the order.

(2) An application under paragraph (1) must be served on the Registrar and the prosecutor.

R-286 **Leave to arraign**

41.15 (1) If the acquitted person has not been arraigned before the end of 2 months after the date of an order under section 77 of the Criminal Justice Act 2003, the prosecutor may apply in the form set out in the Practice Direction to the Court of Appeal for leave to arraign.

(2) An application under paragraph (1) must be served on the Registrar and the acquitted person.

R-287 **Abandonment of the application**

41.16 (1) A section 76 application may be abandoned by the prosecutor before the hearing of that application by serving a notice in the form set out in the Practice Direction on the Registrar and the acquitted person.

(2) The Registrar must, as soon as practicable, after receiving a notice under paragraph (1) send a copy of it endorsed with the date of receipt to the prosecutor and acquitted person.

Part 42 Sentencing Procedures in Special Cases

R-288 **Reasons for deciding not to follow a guideline or make an order**

42.1 (1) This rule applies where the court decides—
- (a) not to follow a relevant sentencing guideline;
- (b) not to make, where it could—
  - (i) a reparation order (unless it passes a custodial or community sentence),
  - (ii) a compensation order, or
  - (iii) a travel restriction order;
- (c) not to order, where it could—
  - (i) that a suspended sentence of imprisonment is to take effect,
  - (ii) the endorsement of the defendant's driving record, or
  - (iii) the defendant's disqualification from driving, for the usual minimum period or at all.

(2) The court must explain why it has not done so, when it explains the sentence that it has passed.

R-289 **Requirements of community sentence, etc.**

42.2 (1) This rule applies where the court—
- (a) imposes a requirement in connection with—
  - (i) a community sentence,
  - (ii) a youth rehabilitation order, or
  - (iii) a suspended sentence of imprisonment; or
- (b) orders the defendant to attend meetings with a supervisor.

(2) The court officer must—
- (a) notify the defendant and, where the defendant is under 14, an appropriate adult, of—
  - (i) the requirement or requirements imposed, and
  - (ii) the name of the responsible officer or supervisor, and the means by which that person may be contacted; and
- (b) notify the responsible officer or supervisor, and, where the defendant is under 14, the appropriate qualifying officer (if that is not the responsible officer), of—
  - (i) the defendant's name, address and telephone number (if available),
  - (ii) the offence or offences of which the defendant was convicted, and
  - (iii) the requirement or requirements imposed.

(3) If the court imposes an electronic monitoring requirement, the monitor of which is not the responsible officer, the court officer must—
(a) notify the defendant and, where the defendant is under 16, an appropriate adult, of the monitor's name, and the means by which the monitor may be contacted; and
(b) notify the monitor of—
(i) the defendant's name, address and telephone number (if available),
(ii) the offence or offences of which the defendant was convicted,
(iii) the place or places at which the defendant's presence must be monitored,
(iv) the period or periods during which the defendant's presence there must be monitored, and
(v) the responsible officer's name, and the means by which that officer may be contacted.

Notification requirements **R-290**

42.3 (1) This rule applies where, on a conviction, sentence or order, legislation requires the defendant—
(a) to notify information to the police; or
(b) to be included in a barred list.
(2) The court must tell the defendant that notification requirements apply, and under what legislation.

Variation of sentence **R-291**

42.4 (1) This rule—
(a) applies where a magistrates' court or the Crown Court can vary or rescind a sentence or order; and
(b) authorises the Crown Court, in addition to its other powers, to do so within the period of 56 days beginning with another defendant's acquittal or sentencing where—
(i) defendants are tried separately in the Crown Court on the same or related facts alleged in one or more indictments, and
(ii) one is sentenced before another is acquitted or sentenced.
(2) The court may exercise its power—
(a) on application by a party; or
(b) on its own initiative.
(3) A party who wants the court to exercise that power must—
(a) apply in writing as soon as reasonably practicable after—
(i) the sentence or order that that party wants the court to vary or rescind, or
(ii) where paragraph (1)(b) applies, the other defendant's acquittal or sentencing;
(b) serve the application on—
(i) the court officer, and
(ii) each other party; and
(c) in the application—
(i) explain why the sentence should be varied or rescinded,
(ii) specify the variation that the applicant proposes, and
(iii) if the application is late, explain why.
(4) The court must not exercise its power in the defendant's absence unless—
(a) the court makes a variation proposed by the defendant; or
(b) the defendant has had an opportunity to make representations at a hearing (whether or not the defendant in fact attends).
(5) The court may—
(a) extend (even after it has expired) the time limit under paragraph (3), unless the court's power to vary or rescind the sentence cannot be exercised; and
(b) allow an application to be made orally.

Application to vary or discharge a compensation order **R-292**

42.5 (1) This rule applies where a magistrates' court can vary or discharge a compensation order on application by the defendant.
(2) A defendant who wants the court to exercise that power must—
(a) apply in writing as soon as practicable after becoming aware of the grounds for doing so;
(b) serve the application on the magistrates' court officer;
(c) where the compensation order was made in the Crown Court, serve a copy of the application on the Crown Court officer; and

(d) in the application, specify the compensation order that the defendant wants the court to vary or discharge and explain (as applicable)—
   (i) what civil court finding shows that the injury, loss or damage was less than it had appeared to be when the order was made,
   (ii) in what circumstances the person for whose benefit the order was made has recovered the property for the loss of which it was made,
   (iii) why a confiscation order makes the defendant now unable to pay compensation in full, or
   (iv) in what circumstances the defendant's means have been reduced substantially and unexpectedly, and why they seem unlikely to increase for a considerable period.

(3) The court officer must serve a copy of the application on the person for whose benefit the compensation order was made.

(4) The court must not vary or discharge the compensation order unless—
   (a) the defendant, and the person for whose benefit it was made, each has had an opportunity to make representations at a hearing (whether or not either in fact attends); and
   (b) where the order was made in the Crown Court, the Crown Court has notified its consent.

R-293 Application to remove, revoke or suspend a disqualification or restriction

42.6 (1) This rule applies where, on application by the defendant, the court can remove, revoke or suspend a disqualification or restriction included in a sentence (except a disqualification from driving).

(2) A defendant who wants the court to exercise such a power must—
   (a) apply in writing, no earlier than the date on which the court can exercise the power;
   (b) serve the application on the court officer; and
   (c) in the application—
      (i) specify the disqualification or restriction, and
      (ii) explain why the defendant wants the court to remove, revoke or suspend it.

(3) The court officer must serve a copy of the application on the chief officer of police for the local justice area.

R-294 Application for a restitution order by the victim of a theft

42.7 (1) This rule applies where, on application by the victim of a theft, the court can order a defendant to give that person goods obtained with the proceeds of goods stolen in that theft.

(2) A person who wants the court to exercise that power if the defendant is convicted must—
   (a) apply in writing as soon as practicable (without waiting for the verdict);
   (b) serve the application on the court officer; and
   (c) in the application—
      (i) identify the goods, and
      (ii) explain why the applicant is entitled to them.

(3) The court officer must serve a copy of the application on each party.

(4) The court must not determine the application unless the applicant and each party has had an opportunity to make representations at a hearing (whether or not each in fact attends).

(5) The court may—
   (a) extend (even after it has expired) the time limit under paragraph (2); and
   (b) allow an application to be made orally.

R-295 Requests for medical reports, etc.

42.8 (1) This rule applies where the court—
   (a) requests a medical examination of the defendant and a report; or
   (b) requires information about the arrangements that could be made for the defendant where the court is considering—
      (i) a hospital order, or
      (ii) a guardianship order.

(2) Unless the court otherwise directs, the court officer must, as soon as practicable, serve on each person from whom a report or information is sought a note that—
   (a) specifies the power exercised by the court;
   (b) explains why the court seeks a report or information from that person; and
   (c) sets out or summarises any relevant information available to the court.

Information to be supplied on admission to hospital or guardianship R-296

42.9 (1) This rule applies where the court—
(a) orders the defendant's detention and treatment in hospital; or
(b) makes a guardianship order.
(2) Unless the court otherwise directs, the court officer must, as soon as practicable, serve on (as applicable) the hospital or the guardian—
(a) a record of the court's order;
(b) such information as the court has received that appears likely to assist in treating or otherwise dealing with the defendant, including information about—
(i) the defendant's mental condition,
(ii) the defendant's other circumstances, and
(iii) the circumstances of the offence.

Information to be supplied on committal for sentence, etc. R-297

42.10 (1) This rule applies where a magistrates' court or the Crown Court convicts the defendant and—
(a) commits or adjourns the case to another court—
(i) for sentence, or
(ii) for the defendant to be dealt with for breach of a deferred sentence, a conditional discharge, or a suspended sentence of imprisonment, imposed by that other court;
(b) deals with a deferred sentence, a conditional discharge, or a suspended sentence of imprisonment, imposed by another court; or
(c) makes an order that another court is, or may be, required to enforce.
(2) Unless the convicting court otherwise directs, the court officer must, as soon as practicable—
(a) where paragraph (1)(a) applies, arrange the transmission from the convicting to the other court of relevant copy court records and other relevant documents, including any—
(i) certificate of conviction,
(ii) magistrates' court register entry,
(iii) record relating to bail,
(iv) note of evidence,
(v) statement or other document introduced in evidence,
(vi) medical or other report,
(vii) representation order or application for such order, and
(viii) interim driving disqualification;
(b) where paragraph (1)(b) or (c) applies, arrange—
(i) the transmission from the convicting to the other court of notice of the convicting court's order, and
(ii) the recording of that order at the other court;
(c) in every case, notify the defendant and, where the defendant is under 14, an appropriate adult, of the location of the other court.

Part 43

[There are no rules in this part.]

Part 44 Breach, Revocation and Amendment of Community and Other Orders

When this Part applies R-298

44.1 This Part applies where—
(a) the person responsible for a defendant's compliance with an order to which applies—
(i) Schedule 3, 5, 7 or 8 to the Powers of Criminal Courts (Sentencing) Act 2000,
(ii) Schedule 8 or 12 to the Criminal Justice Act 2003,
(iii) Schedule 2 to the Criminal Justice and Immigration Act 2008,
(iv) or the Schedule to the Street Offences Act 1959
wants the court to deal with that defendant for failure to comply;

(b) one of the following wants the court to exercise any power it has to revoke or amend such an order—
(i) the responsible officer or supervisor,
(ii) the defendant, or
(iii) where the legislation allows, a person affected by the order; or
(c) the court considers exercising on its own initiative any power it has to revoke or amend such an order.

R-299 **Application by responsible officer or supervisor**

44.2 (1) This rule applies where—
(a) the responsible officer wants the court to—
(i) deal with a defendant for failure to comply with an order to which this Part applies, or
(ii) revoke or amend such an order; or
(b) the court considers exercising on its own initiative any power it has to—
(i) revoke or amend such an order, and
(ii) summon the defendant to attend for that purpose.
(2) Rules 7.2 to 7.4, which deal, among other things, with starting a prosecution in a magistrates' court by information and summons, apply—
(a) as if—
(i) a reference in those rules to an allegation of an offence included a reference to an allegation of failure to comply with an order to which this Part applies, and
(ii) a reference to the prosecutor included a reference to the responsible officer or supervisor; and
(b) with the necessary consequential modifications.

R-300 **Application by defendant or person affected**

44.3 (1) This rule applies where—
(a) the defendant wants the court to exercise any power it has to revoke or amend an order to which this Part applies; or
(b) where the legislation allows, a person affected by such an order wants the court to exercise any such power.
(2) That defendant, or person affected, must—
(a) apply in writing, explaining why the order should be revoked or amended; and
(b) serve the application on—
(i) the court officer,
(ii) the responsible officer or supervisor, and
(iii) as appropriate, the defendant or the person affected.

R-301 **Procedure on application by responsible officer or supervisor**

44.4 (1) Except for rule 37.8, the rules in Part 37, which deal with the procedure at a trial in a magistrates' court, apply—
(a) as if—
(i) a reference in those rules to an allegation of an offence included a reference to an allegation of failure to comply with an order to which this Part applies,
(ii) a reference to the court's verdict included a reference to the court's decision to revoke or amend such an order, or to exercise any other power it has to deal with the defendant, and
(iii) a reference to the court's sentence included a reference to the exercise of any such power; and
(b) with the necessary consequential modifications.
(2) The court officer must serve on each party any order revoking or amending an order to which this Part applies.

Part 45

[There are no rules in this part]

Part 46

[There are no rules in this part.]

Part 47

[There are no rules in this part.]

Part 48

[There are no rules in this part.]

Part 49

[There are no rules in this part.]

Part 50 Civil Behaviour Orders after Verdict or Finding

When this Part applies R-302

50.1 (1) This Part applies in magistrates' courts and in the Crown Court where the court could decide to make, vary or revoke a civil order—
(a) under a power that the court can exercise after reaching a verdict or making a finding, and
(b) that requires someone to do, or not do, something.
(2) A reference to a 'behaviour order' in this Part is a reference to any such order.
(3) A reference to 'hearsay evidence' in this Part is a reference to evidence consisting of hearsay within the meaning of section 1(2) of the Civil Evidence Act 1995.

Behaviour orders: general rules R-303

50.2 (1) The court must not make a behaviour order unless the person to whom it is directed has had an opportunity—
(a) to consider what order is proposed and why; and
(b) to make representations at a hearing (whether or not that person in fact attends).
(2) That restriction does not apply to making an interim behaviour order, but such an order has no effect unless the person to whom it is directed—
(a) is present when it is made; or
(b) is handed a document recording the order not more than 7 days after it is made.
(3) Where the court decides not to make, where it could—
(a) a football banning order;
(b) a parenting order, after a person under 16 is convicted of disobeying an anti-social behaviour order; or
(c) a drinking banning order,
the court must announce, at a hearing in public, the reasons for its decision.

Application for behaviour order: special rules R-304

50.3 (1) This rule applies where a prosecutor wants the court to make—
(a) an anti-social behaviour order; or
(b) a serious crime prevention order,
if the defendant is convicted.
(2) The prosecutor must serve a notice of intention to apply for such an order on—
(a) the court officer;
(b) the defendant against whom the prosecutor wants the court to make the order; and
(c) any person on whom the order would be likely to have a significant adverse effect, as soon as practicable (without waiting for the verdict).
(3) The notice must be in the form set out in the Practice Direction and must—
(a) summarise the relevant facts;
(b) identify the evidence on which the prosecutor relies in support;
(c) attach any written statement that the prosecutor has not already served; and
(d) specify the order that the prosecutor wants the court to make.
(4) The defendant must then—
(a) serve written notice of any evidence on which the defendant relies on—
(i) the court officer, and
(ii) the prosecutor, as soon as practicable (without waiting for the verdict); and

(b) in the notice, identify that evidence and attach any written statement that has not already been served.

(5) This rule does not apply to an application for an interim anti-social behaviour order.

R-305 Evidence to assist the court: special rules

50.4 (1) This rule applies where the court indicates that it may make on its own initiative—

(a) a football banning order;

(b) a restraining order;

(c) an anti-social behaviour order; or

(d) a drinking banning order.

(2) A party who wants the court to take account of any particular evidence before making that decision must—

(a) serve notice in writing on—

(i) the court officer, and

(ii) every other party, as soon as practicable (without waiting for the verdict); and

(b) in that notice identify that evidence and attach any written statement that has not already been served.

R-306 Application to vary or revoke behaviour order

50.5 (1) The court may vary or revoke a behaviour order if—

(a) the legislation under which it is made allows the court to do so; and

(b) one of the following applies—

(i) the prosecutor,

(ii) the person to whom the order is directed,

(iii) any other person mentioned in the order,

(iv) the relevant authority or responsible officer,

(v) the relevant Chief Officer of Police, or

(vi) the Director of Public Prosecutions.

(2) A person applying under this rule must—

(a) apply in writing as soon as practicable after becoming aware of the grounds for doing so, explaining—

(i) what material circumstances have changed since the order was made, and

(ii) why the order should be varied or revoked as a result;

(b) serve the application on—

(i) the court officer,

(ii) as appropriate, the prosecutor or defendant,

(iii) any other person listed in paragraph (1)(b), if the court so directs.

(3) A party who wants the court to take account of any particular evidence before making its decision must, as soon as practicable—

(a) serve notice in writing on—

(i) the court officer,

(ii) as appropriate, the prosecutor or defendant, and

(iii) as appropriate, anyone listed in paragraph (1)(b) on whom the court directed the application to be served; and

(b) in that notice identify the evidence and attach any written statement that has not already been served.

(4) The court may decide an application under this rule with or without a hearing.

(5) But the court must not—

(a) dismiss an application under this rule unless the applicant has had an opportunity to make representations at a hearing (whether or not the applicant in fact attends); or

(b) allow an application under this rule unless everyone required to be served, by this rule or by the court, has had at least 14 days in which to make representations, including representations about whether there should be a hearing.

(6) The court officer must—

(a) serve the application on any person, if the court so directs; and

(b) give notice of any hearing to—

(i) the applicant, and

(ii) any person required to be served, by this rule or by the court.

Notice of hearsay evidence R-307

50.6 (1) A party who wants to introduce hearsay evidence must—
(a) serve notice in writing on—
(i) the court officer, and
(ii) every other party directly affected; and
(b) in that notice—
(i) explain that it is a notice of hearsay evidence,
(ii) identify that evidence,
(iii) identify the person who made the statement which is hearsay, or explain why if that person is not identified, and
(iv) explain why that person will not be called to give oral evidence.
(2) A party may serve one notice under this rule in respect of more than one statement and more than one witness.

Cross-examination of maker of hearsay statement R-308

50.7 (1) This rule applies where a party wants the court's permission to cross-examine a person who made a statement which another party wants to introduce as hearsay.
(2) The party who wants to cross-examine that person must—
(a) apply in writing, with reasons, not more than 7 days after service of the notice of *hearsay* evidence; and
(b) serve the application on—
(i) the court officer,
(ii) the party who served the hearsay evidence notice, and
(iii) every party on whom the hearsay evidence notice was served.
(3) The court may decide an application under this rule with or without a hearing.
(4) But the court must not—
(a) dismiss an application under this rule unless the applicant has had an opportunity to make representations at a hearing (whether or not the applicant in fact attends); or
(b) allow an application under this rule unless everyone served with the application has had at least 7 days in which to make representations, including representations about whether there should be a hearing.

Credibility and consistency of maker of hearsay statement R-309

50.8 (1) This rule applies where a party wants to challenge the credibility or consistency of a person who made a statement which another party wants to introduce as hearsay.
(2) The party who wants to challenge the credibility or consistency of that person must—
(a) serve a written notice of intention to do so on—
(i) the court officer, and
(ii) the party who served the notice of hearsay evidence
not more than 7 days after service of that hearsay evidence notice; and
(b) in the notice, identify any statement or other material on which that party relies.
(3) The party who served the hearsay notice—
(a) may call that person to give oral evidence instead; and
(b) if so, must serve a notice of intention to do so on—
(i) the court officer, and
(ii) every party on whom he served the hearsay notice
not more than 7 days after service of the notice under paragraph (2).

Court's power to vary requirements under this Part R-310

50.9 The court may—
(a) shorten a time limit or extend it (even after it has expired);
(b) allow a notice or application to be given in a different form, or presented orally.

Part 51

[There are no rules in this part.]

Part 52 Enforcement of Fines and Other Orders for Payment

R-311 When this Part applies

52.1 (1) This Part applies where a magistrates' court can enforce payment of—
(a) a fine, or a sum that legislation requires the court to treat as a fine; or
(b) any other sum that a court has ordered to be paid—
(i) on a conviction, or
(ii) on the forfeiture of a surety.
(2) Rules 52.7 to 52.9 apply where the court, or a fines officer, issues a warrant that requires someone to—
(a) take control of goods or money belonging to the defendant;
(b) remove and sell any such goods; and
(c) pay any such money, and any proceeds of such a sale, to the court officer towards payment of a sum to which this Part applies.
(3) In this Part—
(a) 'defendant' means anyone liable to pay a sum to which this Part applies;
(b) 'payment terms' means by when, and by what (if any) instalments, such a sum must be paid.

R-312 Exercise of court's powers

52.2 The court must not exercise its enforcement powers unless—
(a) the court officer has served on the defendant any collection order or other notice of—
(i) the obligation to pay,
(ii) the payment terms, and
(iii) how and where the defendant must pay; and
(b) the defendant has failed to comply with the payment terms.

R-313 Duty to give receipt

52.3 (1) This rule applies where the defendant makes a payment to—
(a) the court officer specified in an order or notice served under rule 52.2;
(b) another court officer;
(c) any—
(i) custodian of the defendant,
(ii) supervisor appointed to encourage the defendant to pay, or
(iii) responsible officer appointed under a community sentence or a suspended sentence of imprisonment; or
(d) a person executing a warrant to which rule 18.6 (warrants for arrest, detention or imprisonment that cease to have effect on payment) or this Part applies.
(2) The person receiving the payment must—
(a) give the defendant a receipt; and
(b) as soon as practicable transmit the payment to the court officer specified in an order or notice served under rule 52.2, if the recipient is not that court officer.

R-314 Appeal against decision of fines officer

52.4 (1) This rule applies where—
(a) a collection order is in force;
(b) a fines officer makes a decision under one of these paragraphs of Schedule 5 to the Courts Act 2003—
(i) paragraph 22 (Application to fines officer for variation of order or attachment of earnings order, etc.),
(ii) paragraph 31 (Application to fines officer for variation of reserve terms), or
(iii) paragraph 37 (Functions of fines officer in relation to defaulters: referral or further steps notice); and
(c) the defendant wants to appeal against that decision.
(2) Unless the court otherwise directs, the defendant must—
(a) appeal in writing not more than 10 business days after the decision;
(b) serve the appeal on the court officer; and
(c) in the appeal—
(i) explain why a different decision should be made, and
(ii) specify the decision that the defendant proposes.

(3) Where the court determines an appeal—
(a) the general rule is that it will do so at a hearing; but
(b) it may do so without a hearing.

Application to reduce a fine or vary payment terms R-315

52.5 (1) This rule applies where—
(a) no collection order is in force; and
(b) the defendant wants the court to—
(i) reduce the amount of a fine, or
(ii) vary payment terms.
(2) Unless the court otherwise directs, the defendant must—
(a) apply in writing;
(b) serve the application on the court officer; and
(c) in the application, explain—
(i) what relevant circumstances have not yet been considered by the court, and
(ii) why the fine should be reduced, or the payment terms varied.

Claim to avoid fine after penalty notice R-316

52.6 (1) This rule applies where—
(a) a chief officer of police serves on the magistrates' court officer a certificate registering, for enforcement as a fine, a sum payable by a defendant after failure to comply with a penalty notice; and
(b) the court or a fines officer enforces the fine.
(2) A defendant who claims not to be the person to whom the penalty notice was issued must, unless the court otherwise directs—
(a) make that claim in writing; and
(b) serve it on the court officer.
(3) The court officer must—
(a) notify the chief officer of police by whom the certificate was registered; and
(b) refer the case to the court.
(4) Where such a claim is made—
(a) the general rule is that the court will adjourn the enforcement for 28 days and fix a hearing; but
(b) the court may make a different order.
(5) At any such hearing, the chief officer of police must introduce any evidence to contradict the defendant's claim.

Information to be included in a warrant to take goods, etc. R-317

52.7 (1) A warrant must identify—
(a) the person(s) to whom it is directed;
(b) the defendant against whom it was issued;
(c) the sum for which it was issued and the reason that sum is owed;
(d) the court or fines officer who issued it, unless that is otherwise recorded by the court officer; and
(e) the court office for the court or fines officer who issued it.
(2) A person to whom a warrant is directed must record on it the date and time at which it is received.
(3) A warrant that contains an error is not invalid, as long as—
(a) it was issued in respect of a lawful decision by the court or fines officer; and
(b) it contains enough information to identify that decision.

Execution of a warrant to take goods, etc. R-318

52.8 (1) A warrant may be executed by—
(a) any person to whom it is directed; or
(b) anyone authorised to do so by section 125 (warrants), 125A (civilian enforcement officers) or 125B (execution by approved enforcement agency) of the Magistrates' Courts Act 1980.
(2) The person who executes a warrant must—
(a) explain, in terms the defendant can understand—
(i) the order or decision that the warrant was issued to enforce,
(ii) the sum for which the warrant was issued, and
(iii) any extra sum payable in connection with the execution of the warrant;

(b) show the defendant the warrant, if that person has it;
(c) if the defendant asks—
(i) arrange for the defendant to see the warrant, if that person does not have it, and
(ii) show the defendant any written statement of that person's authority required by section 125A or 125B of the 1980 Act; and
(d) clearly mark any goods that are taken under the warrant, unless that person removes those goods at once.
(3) These goods must not be taken under the warrant—
(a) clothes or bedding used by the defendant or by anyone living with the defendant;
(b) tools, books, vehicles or other equipment that the defendant needs to use in the defendant's employment, business or vocation, unless the defendant is a corporation.
(4) Unless the court otherwise directs, or the defendant otherwise agrees, if the person who executes the warrant takes household goods they must not be removed until the day of sale.
(5) The warrant no longer has effect if—
(a) there is paid to the person executing it the sum for which it was issued and any extra sum payable in connection with its execution;
(b) those sums are offered to, but refused by, that person; or
(c) that person—
(i) is shown a receipt given under rule 52.3 for the sum for which the warrant was issued, and
(ii) is paid any extra sum payable in connection with its execution.

R-319 **Sale of goods taken under a warrant**

52.9 (1) Unless the court otherwise directs or the defendant otherwise agrees, goods taken under a warrant must be sold—
(a) at public auction; and
(b) as soon as reasonably practicable after the expiry of 5 business days from the date of execution of the warrant.
(2) After a sale, the person who executed the warrant must, as soon as reasonably practicable—
(a) collect the proceeds of sale;
(b) deduct any sum payable in connection with the execution of the warrant;
(c) pay the court officer specified in an order or notice served under rule 52.2 the sum for which the warrant was issued;
(d) pay any balance remaining to the defendant; and
(e) deliver an account of those deductions and payments to the court officer.

R-319A **Financial penalties imposed in other European Union member States**

52.10 (1) This rule applies where the Lord Chancellor gives the court officer a request to enforce a financial penalty imposed in another European Union member State.
(2) The court officer must serve on the defendant—
(a) notice of the request for enforcement, and of its effect;
(b) a copy of—
(i) the certificate requesting enforcement, and
(ii) the decision requiring payment to which that certificate relates; and
(c) notice that the procedure set out in this rule applies.
(3) A defendant who wants the court to refuse enforcement must—
(a) serve notice of objection on the court officer;
(b) unless the court otherwise directs, serve that notice not more than 14 days after service of notice of the request; and
(c) in the notice of objection—
(i) identify each ground for refusal on which the defendant relies,
(ii) summarise any relevant facts not already included in the certificate and decision served with the notice of the request, and
(iii) identify any other document that the defendant thinks the court will need to determine the request (and serve any such document with the notice).
(4) The court—
(a) may determine a request for enforcement—
(i) at a hearing, which will be in public unless the court otherwise directs, or
(ii) without a hearing; but

(b) must not allow enforcement unless the defendant has had at least 14 days in which to serve notice of objection.

(5) Paragraphs (2) and (3) do not apply if, on receipt of the request, the court decides that a ground for refusal applies.

(6) The court officer must serve on the Lord Chancellor notice of the court's decision.

Part 53

[There are no rules in this part.]

Part 54

[There are no rules in this part.]

Part 55 Road Traffic Penalties

Application to remove a disqualification from driving R-320

55.1 (1) This rule applies where, on application by the defendant, the court can remove a disqualification from driving.

(2) A defendant who wants the court to exercise that power must—

(a) apply in writing, no earlier than the date on which the court can exercise the power;

(b) serve the application on the court officer; and

(c) in the application—

(i) specify the disqualification that the defendant wants the court to remove, and

(ii) explain why.

(3) The court officer must serve a copy of the application on the chief officer of police for the local justice area

Information to be supplied on order for endorsement of driving record, etc. R-321

55.2 (1) This rule applies where the court—

(a) convicts the defendant of an offence involving obligatory endorsement, and orders there to be endorsed on the defendant's driving record and on any counterpart licence—

(i) particulars of the conviction,

(ii) particulars of any disqualification from driving that the court imposes, and

(iii) the penalty points to be attributed to the offence;

(b) disqualifies the defendant from driving for any other offence; or

(c) suspends or removes a disqualification from driving.

(2) The court officer must, as soon as practicable, serve on the Secretary of State notice that includes details of—

(a) where paragraph (1)(a) applies—

(i) the local justice area in which the court is acting,

(ii) the dates of conviction and sentence,

(iii) the offence, and the date on which it was committed,

(iv) the sentence, and

(v) the date of birth, and sex, of the defendant, where those details are available;

(b) where paragraph (1)(b) applies—

(i) the date and period of the disqualification,

(ii) the power exercised by the court;

(c) where paragraph (1)(c) applies—

(i) the date and period of the disqualification,

(ii) the date and terms of the order for its suspension or removal,

(iii) the power exercised by the court, and

(iv) where the court suspends the disqualification pending appeal, the court to which the defendant has appealed.

R-322 Statutory declaration to avoid fine after fixed penalty notice

55.3 (1) This rule applies where—
(a) a chief officer of police, or the Secretary of State, serves on the magistrates' court officer a certificate registering, for enforcement as a fine, a sum payable by a defendant after failure to comply with a fixed penalty notice;
(b) the court officer notifies the defendant of the registration; and
(c) the defendant makes a statutory declaration with the effect that—
(i) the fixed penalty notice, or any associated notice sent to the defendant as owner of the vehicle concerned, and
(ii) the registration and any enforcement proceedings become void.

(2) The defendant must serve that statutory declaration not more than 21 days after service of notice of the registration, unless the court extends that time limit.

(3) The court officer must—
(a) serve a copy of the statutory declaration on the person by whom the certificate was registered,
(b) cancel any endorsement on the defendant's driving record and on any counterpart licence, and
(c) notify the Secretary of State of any such cancellation.

R-323 Application for declaration about a course or programme certificate decision

55.4 (1) This rule applies where the court can declare unjustified—
(a) a course provider's failure or refusal to give a certificate of the defendant's satisfactory completion of an approved course; or
(b) a programme provider's giving of a certificate of the defendant's failure fully to participate in an approved programme.

(2) A defendant who wants the court to exercise that power must—
(a) apply in writing, not more than 28 days after—
(i) the date by which the defendant was required to complete the course, or
(ii) the giving of the certificate of failure fully to participate in the programme;
(b) serve the application on the court officer; and
(c) in the application, specify the course or programme and explain (as applicable)—
(i) that the course provider has failed to give a certificate,
(ii) where the course provider has refused to give a certificate, why the defendant disagrees with the reasons for that decision, or
(iii) where the programme provider has given a certificate, why the defendant disagrees with the reasons for that decision.

(3) The court officer must serve a copy of the application on the course or programme provider.

(4) The court must not determine the application unless the defendant, and the course or programme provider, each has had an opportunity to make representations at a hearing (whether or not either in fact attends).

R-324 Appeal against recognition of foreign driving disqualification

55.5 (1) This rule applies where—
(a) a minister gives a disqualification notice under section 57 of the Crime (International Co-operation) Act 2003(159); and
(b) the person to whom it is given wants to appeal under section 59 of the Act to a magistrates' court.

(2) That person ('the appellant') must serve an appeal notice on—
(a) the court officer, at a magistrates' court in the local justice area in which the appellant lives; and
(b) the minister, at the address given in the disqualification notice.

(3) The appellant must serve the appeal notice within the period for which section 59 of the 2003 Act provides.

(4) The appeal notice must—
(a) attach a copy of the disqualification notice;
(b) explain which of the conditions in section 56 of the 2003 Act is not met, and why section 57 of the Act therefore does not apply; and
(c) include any application to suspend the disqualification, under section 60 of the Act.

(5) The minister may serve a respondent's notice, and must do so if—
(a) the minister wants to make representations to the court; or
(b) the court so directs.

(6) The minister must—
(a) unless the court otherwise directs, serve any such respondent's notice not more than 14 days after—
(i) the appellant serves the appeal notice, or
(ii) a direction to do so;
(b) in any such respondent's notice—
(i) identify the grounds of opposition on which the minister relies,
(ii) summarise any relevant facts not already included in the disqualification and appeal notices, and
(iii) identify any other document that the minister thinks the court will need to decide the appeal (and serve any such document with the notice).
(7) Where the court determines an appeal—
(a) the general rule is that it will do so at a hearing (which will be in public, unless the court otherwise directs); but
(b) it may do so without a hearing.
(8) The court officer must serve on the minister—
(a) notice of the outcome of the appeal; and
(b) notice of any suspension of the disqualification; and
(c) the appellant's driving licence, if surrendered to the court officer.

Part 56 Confiscation Proceedings under the Criminal Justice Act 1988 and the Drug Trafficking Act 1994

Statements etc., relevant to making confiscation orders R-325

56.1 (1) Where a prosecutor or defendant—
(a) tenders to a magistrates' court any statement or other document under section 73 of the Criminal Justice Act 1988 in any proceedings in respect of an offence listed in Schedule 4 to that Act; or
(b) tenders to the Crown Court any statement or other document under section 11 of the Drug Trafficking Act 1994 or section 73 of the 1988 Act in any proceedings in respect of a drug trafficking offence or in respect of an offence to which Part VI of the 1988 Act applies,

he must serve a copy as soon as practicable on the defendant or the prosecutor, as the case may be.

(2) Any statement tendered by the prosecutor to the magistrates' court under section 73 of the 1988 Act or to the Crown Court under section 11(1) of the 1994 Act or section 73(1A) of the 1988 Act shall include the following particulars—
(a) the name of the defendant;
(b) the name of the person by whom the statement is made and the date on which it was made;
(c) where the statement is not tendered immediately after the defendant has been convicted, the date on which and the place where the relevant conviction occurred; and
(d) such information known to the prosecutor as is relevant to the determination as to whether or not the defendant has benefited from drug trafficking or relevant criminal conduct and to the assessment of the value of his proceeds of drug trafficking or, as the case may be, benefit from relevant criminal conduct.
(3) Where, in accordance with section 11(7) of the 1994 Act or section 73(1C) of the 1988 Act, the defendant indicates the extent to which he accepts any allegation contained within the prosecutor's statement, if he indicates the same in writing to the prosecutor, he must serve a copy of that reply on the court officer.
(4) Expressions used in this rule shall have the same meanings as in the 1994 Act or, where appropriate, the 1988 Act.

Postponed determinations R-326

56.2 (1) Where an application is made by the defendant or the prosecutor—
(a) to a magistrates' court under section 72A(5)(a) of the Criminal Justice Act 1988 asking the court to exercise its powers under section 72A(4) of that Act; or
(b) to the Crown Court under section 3(5)(a) of the Drug Trafficking Act 1994 asking the Court to exercise its powers under section 3(4) of that Act, or under section 72A(5)(a)

of the 1988 Act asking the court to exercise its powers under section 72A(4) of the 1988 Act,

the application must be made in writing and a copy must be served on the prosecutor or the defendant, as the case may be.

(2) A party served with a copy of an application under paragraph (1) shall, within 28 days of the date of service, notify the applicant and the court officer, in writing, whether or not he proposes to oppose the application, giving his reasons for any opposition.

(3) After the expiry of the period referred to in paragraph (2), the court shall determine whether an application under paragraph (1) is to be dealt with—

(a) without a hearing; or

(b) at a hearing at which the parties may be represented.

R-327 **Confiscation orders—revised assessments**

56.3 (1) Where the prosecutor makes an application under section 13, 14 or 15 of the Drug Trafficking Act 1994 or section 74A, 74B or 74C of the Criminal Justice Act 1988, the application must be in writing and a copy must be served on the defendant.

(2) The application must include the following particulars—

(a) the name of the defendant;

(b) the date on which and the place where any relevant conviction occurred;

(c) the date on which and the place where any relevant confiscation order was made or, as the case may be, varied;

(d) the grounds on which the application is made; and

(e) an indication of the evidence available to support the application.

R-328 **Application to the Crown Court to discharge or vary order to make material available**

56.4 (1) Where an order under section 93H of the Criminal Justice Act 1988 (order to make material available) or section 55 of the Drug Trafficking Act 1994 (order to make material available) has been made by the Crown Court, any person affected by it may apply in writing to the court officer for the order to be discharged or varied, and on hearing such an application a circuit judge may discharge the order or make such variations to it as he thinks fit.

(2) Subject to paragraph (3), where a person proposes to make an application under paragraph (1) for the discharge or variation of an order, he shall give a copy of the application, not later than 48 hours before the making of the application—

(a) to a constable at the police station specified in the order; or

(b) to the office of the appropriate officer who made the application, as specified in the order,

in either case together with a notice indicating the time and place at which the application for discharge or variation is to be made.

(3) A circuit judge may direct that paragraph (2) need not be complied with if he is satisfied that the person making the application has good reason to seek a discharge or variation of the order as soon as possible and it is not practicable to comply with that paragraph.

(4) In this rule:

'constable' includes a person commissioned by the Commissioners for Her Majesty's Revenue and Customs;

'police station' includes a place for the time being occupied by Her Majesty's Revenue and Customs.

R-329 **Application to the Crown Court for increase in term of imprisonment in default of payment**

56.5 (1) This rule applies to applications made, or that have effect as made, to the Crown Court under section 10 of the Drug Trafficking Act 1994 and section 75A of the Criminal Justice Act 1988 (interest on sums unpaid under confiscation orders).

(2) Notice of an application to which this rule applies to increase the term of imprisonment or detention fixed in default of payment of a confiscation order by a person ('the defendant') shall be made by the prosecutor in writing to the court officer.

(3) A notice under paragraph (2) shall—

(a) state the name and address of the defendant;

(b) specify the grounds for the application;

(c) give details of the enforcement measures taken, if any; and

(d) include a copy of the confiscation order.

(4) On receiving a notice under paragraph (2), the court officer shall—
(a) forthwith send to the defendant and the magistrates' court required to enforce payment of the confiscation order under section 140(1) of the Powers of Criminal Courts (Sentencing) Act 2000, a copy of the said notice; and
(b) notify in writing the applicant and the defendant of the date, time and place appointed for the hearing of the application.

(5) Where the Crown Court makes an order pursuant to an application mentioned in paragraph (1) above, the court officer shall send forthwith a copy of the order—
(a) to the applicant;
(b) to the defendant;
(c) where the defendant is at the time of the making of the order in custody, to the person having custody of him; and
(d) to the magistrates' court mentioned in paragraph (4)(a).

Drug trafficking—compensation on acquittal in the Crown Court **R-330**

56.6 Where a Crown Court cancels a confiscation order under section 22(2) of the Drug Trafficking Act 1994, the court officer shall serve notice to that effect on the High Court and on the magistrates' court which has responsibility for enforcing the order.

Part 57 Proceeds of Crime Act 2002: Rules Applicable to all Proceedings

Interpretation **R-331**

57.1 In this Part and in Parts 58, 59, 60 and 61:
'business day' means any day other than a Saturday, Sunday, Christmas Day or Good Friday, or a bank holiday under the Banking and Financial Dealings Act 1971, in England and Wales;
'document' means anything in which information of any description is recorded;
'hearsay evidence' means evidence consisting of hearsay within the meaning of section 1(2) of the Civil Evidence Act 1995;
'restraint proceedings' means proceedings under sections 42 and 58(2) and (3) of the Proceeds of Crime Act 2002;
'receivership proceedings' means proceedings under sections 48, 49, 50, 51, 54(4), 59(2) and (3), 62 and 63 of the 2002 Act;
'witness statement' means a written statement signed by a person which contains the evidence, and only that evidence, which that person would be allowed to give orally; and
words and expressions used have the same meaning as in Part 2 of the 2002 Act.

Calculation of time **R-332**

57.2 (1) This rule shows how to calculate any period of time for doing any act which is specified by this Part and Parts 58, 59, 60 and 61 for the purposes of any proceedings under Part 2 of the Proceeds of Crime Act 2002 or by an order of the Crown Court in restraint proceedings or receivership proceedings.
(2) A period of time expressed as a number of days shall be computed as clear days.
(3) In this rule 'clear days' means that in computing the number of days—
(a) the day on which the period begins; and
(b) if the end of the period is defined by reference to an event, the day on which that event occurs are not included.
(4) Where the specified period is five days or less and includes a day which is not a business day that day does not count.

Court office closed **R-333**

57.3 When the period specified by this Part or Parts 58, 59, 60 and 61, or by an order of the Crown Court under Part 2 of the Proceeds of Crime Act 2002, for doing any act at the court office falls on a day on which the office is closed, that act shall be in time if done on the next day on which the court office is open.

Application for registration of Scottish or Northern Ireland Order **R-334**

57.4 (1) This rule applies to an application for registration of an order under article 6 of the Proceeds of Crime Act 2002 (Enforcement in different parts of the United Kingdom) Order 2002.
(2) The application may be made without notice.

(3) The application must be in writing and may be supported by a witness statement which must—
(a) exhibit the order or a certified copy of the order; and
(b) to the best of the witness's ability, give full details of the realisable property located in England and Wales in respect of which the order was made and specify the person holding that realisable property.
(4) If the court registers the order, the applicant must serve notice of the registration on—
(a) any person who holds realisable property to which the order applies; and
(b) any other person whom the applicant knows to be affected by the order.
(5) The permission of the Crown Court under rule 57.13 is not required to serve the notice outside England and Wales.

R-335 Application to vary or set aside registration

57.5 (1) An application to vary or set aside registration of an order under article 6 of the Proceeds of Crime Act 2002 (Enforcement in different parts of the United Kingdom) Order 2002 may be made to the Crown Court by—
(a) any person who holds realisable property to which the order applies; and
(b) any other person affected by the order.
(2) The application must be in writing and may be supported by a witness statement.
(3) The application and any witness statement must be lodged with the Crown Court.
(4) The application must be served on the person who applied for registration at least seven days before the date fixed by the court for hearing the application, unless the Crown Court specifies a shorter period.
(5) No property in England and Wales may be realised in pursuance of the order before the Crown Court has decided the application.

R-336 Register of orders

57.6 (1) The Crown Court must keep, under the direction of the Lord Chancellor, a register of the orders registered under article 6 of the Proceeds of Crime Act 2002 (Enforcement in different parts of the United Kingdom) Order 2002.
(2) The register must include details of any variation or setting aside of a registration under rule 57.5 and of any execution issued on a registered order.
(3) If the person who applied for registration of an order which is subsequently registered notifies the Crown Court that the court which made the order has varied or discharged the order, details of the variation or discharge, as the case may be, must be entered in the register.

R-337 Statements of truth

57.7 (1) Any witness statement required to be served by this Part or by Parts 58, 59, 60 or 61 must be verified by a statement of truth contained in the witness statement.
(2) A statement of truth is a declaration by the person making the witness statement to the effect that the witness statement is true to the best of his knowledge and belief and that he made the statement knowing that, if it were tendered in evidence, he would be liable to prosecution if he wilfully stated in it anything which he knew to be false or did not believe to be true.
(3) The statement of truth must be signed by the person making the witness statement.
(4) If the person making the witness statement fails to verify the witness statement by a statement of truth, the Crown Court may direct that it shall not be admissible as evidence.

R-338 Use of witness statements for other purposes

57.8 (1) Except as provided by this rule, a witness statement served in proceedings under Part 2 of the Proceeds of Crime Act 2002 may be used only for the purpose of the proceedings in which it is served.
(2) Paragraph (1) does not apply if and to the extent that—
(a) the witness gives consent in writing to some other use of it;
(b) the Crown Court gives permission for some other use; or
(c) the witness statement has been put in evidence at a hearing held in public.

R-339 Expert evidence

57.9 (1) A party to proceedings under Part 2 of the Proceeds of Crime Act 2002 who wishes to adduce expert evidence (whether of fact or opinion) in the proceedings must, as soon as practicable—
(a) serve on the other parties a statement in writing of any finding or opinion which he proposes to adduce by way of such evidence; and

(b) serve on any party who requests it in writing, a copy of (or if it appears to the party proposing to adduce the evidence to be more practicable, a reasonable opportunity to examine)—
 (i) the record of any observation, test, calculation or other procedure on which the finding or opinion is based, and
 (ii) any document or other thing or substance in respect of which the observation, test, calculation or other procedure mentioned in paragraph (1)(b)(i) has been carried out.
(c) A party may serve notice in writing waiving his right to be served with any of the matters mentioned in paragraph (1) and, in particular, may agree that the statement mentioned in paragraph (1)(a) may be given to him orally and not served in writing.
(d) If a party who wishes to adduce expert evidence in proceedings under Part 2 of the 2002 Act fails to comply with this rule he may not adduce that evidence in those proceedings without the leave of the court, except where rule 57.10 applies.

Exceptions to procedure for expert evidence R-340

57.10 (1) If a party has reasonable grounds for believing that the disclosure of any evidence in compliance with rule 57.9 might lead to the intimidation, or attempted intimidation, of any person on whose evidence he intends to rely in the proceedings, or otherwise to the course of justice being interfered with, he shall not be obliged to comply with those requirements in relation to that evidence, unless the Crown Court orders otherwise.
(2) Where, in accordance with paragraph (1), a party considers that he is not obliged to comply with the requirements imposed by rule 57.9 with regard to any evidence in relation to any other party, he must serve notice in writing on that party stating—
 (a) that the evidence is being withheld; and
 (b) the reasons for withholding the evidence.

Service of documents R-341

57.11 (1) Part 4 and rule 32.1 (notice required to accompany process served outside the United Kingdom and translations) shall not apply in restraint proceedings and receivership proceedings.
(2) Where this Part or Parts 58, 59, 60 or 61 requires service of a document, then, unless the Crown Court directs otherwise, the document may be served by any of the following methods—
 (a) in all cases, by delivering the document personally to the party to be served;
 (b) if no solicitor is acting for the party to be served by delivering the document at, or by sending it by first class post to, his residence or his last-known residence; or
 (c) if a solicitor is acting for the party to be served—
  (i) by delivering the document at, or sending it by first class post to, the solicitor's business address, or
  (ii) where the solicitor's business address includes a numbered box at a document exchange, by leaving the document at that document exchange or at a document exchange which transmits documents on every business day to that document exchange, or
  (iii) if the solicitor has indicated that he is willing to accept service by facsimile transmission, by sending a legible copy of the document by facsimile transmission to the solicitor's office.
(3) A document shall, unless the contrary is proved, be deemed to have been served—
 (a) in the case of service by first class post, on the second business day after posting;
 (b) in the case of service in accordance with paragraph (2)(c)(ii), on the second business day after the day on which it is left at the document exchange; and
 (c) in the case of service in accordance with paragraph (2)(c)(iii), where it is transmitted on a business day before 4 p.m., on that day and in any other case, on the next business day.
(4) An order made in restraint proceedings or receivership proceedings may be enforced against the defendant or any other person affected by it notwithstanding that service of a copy of the order has not been effected in accordance with this rule if the Crown Court is satisfied that the person had notice of the order by being present when the order was made.

Service by an alternative method R-342

57.12 (1) Where it appears to the Crown Court that there is a good reason to authorise service by a method not otherwise permitted by rule 57.11, the court may make an order permitting service by an alternative method.
(2) An application for an order permitting service by an alternative method—
 (a) must be supported by evidence; and
 (b) may be made without notice.

(3) An order permitting service by an alternative method must specify—
(a) the method of service; and
(b) the date when the document will be deemed to be served.

R-343 **Service outside the jurisdiction**

57.13 (1) Where this Part requires a document to be served on someone who is outside England and Wales, it may be served outside England and Wales with the permission of the Crown Court.
(2) Where a document is to be served outside England and Wales it may be served by any method permitted by the law of the country in which it is to be served.
(3) Nothing in this rule or in any court order shall authorise or require any person to do anything in the country where the document is to be served which is against the law of that country.
(4) Where this Part requires a document to be served a certain period of time before the date of a hearing and the recipient does not appear at the hearing, the hearing must not take place unless the Crown Court is satisfied that the document has been duly served.

R-344 **Certificates of service**

57.14 (1) Where this Part requires that the applicant for an order in restraint proceedings or receivership proceedings serve a document on another person, the applicant must lodge a certificate of service with the Crown Court within seven days of service of the document.
(2) The certificate must state—
(a) the method of service;
(b) the date of service; and
(c) if the document is served under rule 57.12, such other information as the court may require when making the order permitting service by an alternative method.
(3) Where a document is to be served by the Crown Court in restraint proceedings and receivership proceedings and the court is unable to serve it, the court must send a notice of non-service stating the method attempted to the party who requested service.

R-345 **External requests and orders**

57.15 (1) The rules in this Part and in Parts 59 to 61 and 71 to 73 apply with the necessary modifications to proceedings under the Proceeds of Crime Act 2002 (External Requests and Orders) Order 2005 in the same way that they apply to corresponding proceedings under Part 2 of the Proceeds of Crime Act 2002.
(2) This table shows how provisions of the 2005 Order correspond with provisions of the 2002 Act.

Article of the Proceeds of Crime Act 2002 (External Requests and Orders) Order 2005	*Section of the Proceeds of Crime Act 2002*
8	41
9	42
10	43
11	44
15	48
16	49
17	58
23	31
27	50
28	51
41	62
42	63
44	65
45	66

Part 58 Proceeds of Crime Act 2002: Rules Applicable only to Confiscation Proceedings

Statements in connection with confiscation orders R-346

58.1 (1) When the prosecutor or the Director is required, under section 16 of the Proceeds of Crime Act 2002, to give a statement to the Crown Court, the prosecutor or the Director, as the case may be, must also, as soon as practicable, serve a copy of the statement on the defendant.

(2) Any statement given to the Crown Court by the prosecutor under section 16 of the 2002 Act must, in addition to the information required by the 2002 Act, include the following information—

(a) the name of the defendant;

(b) the name of the person by whom the statement is made and the date on which it is made; and

(c) where the statement is not given to the Crown Court immediately after the defendant has been convicted, the date on which and the place where the relevant conviction occurred.

(3) Where, under section 17 of the 2002 Act, the Crown Court orders the defendant to indicate the extent to which he accepts each allegation in a statement given by the prosecutor, the defendant must indicate this in writing to the prosecutor and must give a copy to the Crown Court.

(4) Where the Crown Court orders the defendant to give to it any information under section 18 of the 2002 Act, the defendant must provide the information in writing and must, as soon as practicable, serve a copy of it on the prosecutor.

Postponement of confiscation proceedings R-347

58.2 The Crown Court may grant a postponement under section 14(1)(b) of the Proceeds of Crime Act 2002 without a hearing.

Application for reconsideration R-348

58.3 (1) This rule applies where the prosecutor makes an application under section 19, 20 or 21 of the Proceeds of Crime Act 2002.

(2) The application must be in writing and give details of—

(a) the name of the defendant;

(b) the date on which and the place where any relevant conviction occurred;

(c) the date on which and the place where any relevant confiscation order was made or varied;

(d) the grounds for the application; and

(e) an indication of the evidence available to support the application.

(3) The application must be lodged with the Crown Court.

(4) The application must be served on the defendant at least seven days before the date fixed by the court for hearing the application, unless the Crown Court specifies a shorter period.

Application for new calculation of available amount R-349

58.4 (1) This rule applies where the prosecutor or a receiver makes an application under section 22 of the Proceeds of Crime Act 2002 for a new calculation of the available amount.

(2) The application must be in writing and may be supported by a witness statement.

(3) The application and any witness statement must be lodged with the Crown Court.

(4) The application and any witness statement must be served on—

(a) the defendant;

(b) the receiver, if the prosecutor is making the application and a receiver has been appointed under section 50 of the 2002 Act; and

(c) the prosecutor, if the receiver is making the application,

at least seven days before the date fixed by the court for hearing the application, unless the Crown Court specifies a shorter period.

Variation of confiscation order due to inadequacy of available amount R-350

58.5 (1) This rule applies where the defendant or a receiver makes an application under section 23 of the Proceeds of Crime Act 2002 for the variation of a confiscation order.

(2) The application must be in writing and may be supported by a witness statement.

(3) The application and any witness statement must be lodged with the Crown Court.

(4) The application and any witness statement must be served on—

(a) the prosecutor;

(b) the defendant, if the receiver is making the application; and

(c) the receiver, if the defendant is making the application and a receiver has been appointed under section 50 of the 2002 Act,

at least seven days before the date fixed by the court for hearing the application, unless the Crown Court specifies a shorter period.

R-351 Application by magistrates' court officer to discharge confiscation order

58.6 (1) This rule applies where a magistrates' court officer makes an application under section 24 or 25 of the Proceeds of Crime Act 2002 for the discharge of a confiscation order.

(2) The application must be in writing and give details of—
(a) the confiscation order;
(b) the amount outstanding under the order; and
(c) the grounds for the application.

(3) The application must be served on—
(a) the defendant;
(b) the prosecutor; and
(c) any receiver appointed under section 50 of the 2002 Act.

(4) The Crown Court may determine the application without a hearing unless a person listed in paragraph (3) indicates, within seven days after the application was served on him, that he would like to make representations.

(5) If the Crown Court makes an order discharging the confiscation order, the court must, at once, send a copy of the order to—
(a) the magistrates' court officer who applied for the order;
(b) the defendant;
(c) the prosecutor; and
(d) any receiver appointed under section 50 of the 2002 Act.

R-352 Application for variation of confiscation order made against an absconder

58.7 (1) This rule applies where the defendant makes an application under section 29 of the Proceeds of Crime Act 2002 for the variation of a confiscation order made against an absconder.

(2) The application must be in writing and supported by a witness statement which must give details of—
(a) the confiscation order made against an absconder under section 6 of the 2002 Act as applied by section 28 of the 2002 Act;
(b) the circumstances in which the defendant ceased to be an absconder;
(c) the defendant's conviction of the offence or offences concerned; and
(d) the reason why he believes the amount required to be paid under the confiscation order was too large.

(3) The application and witness statement must be lodged with the Crown Court.

(4) The application and witness statement must be served on the prosecutor at least seven days before the date fixed by the court for hearing the application, unless the Crown Court specifies a shorter period.

R-353 Application for discharge of confiscation order made against an absconder

58.8 (1) This rule applies if the defendant makes an application under section 30 of the Proceeds of Crime Act 2002 for the discharge of a confiscation order.

(2) The application must be in writing and supported by a witness statement which must give details of—
(a) the confiscation order made under section 28 of the 2002 Act;
(b) the date on which the defendant ceased to be an absconder;
(c) the acquittal of the defendant if he has been acquitted of the offence concerned; and
(d) if the defendant has not been acquitted of the offence concerned—
(i) the date on which the defendant ceased to be an absconder,
(ii) the date on which the proceedings taken against the defendant were instituted and a summary of steps taken in the proceedings since then, and
(iii) any indication given by the prosecutor that he does not intend to proceed against the defendant.

(3) The application and witness statement must be lodged with the Crown Court.

(4) The application and witness statement must be served on the prosecutor at least seven days before the date fixed by the court for hearing the application, unless the Crown Court specifies a shorter period.

(5) If the Crown Court orders the discharge of the confiscation order, the court must serve notice on the magistrates' court responsible for enforcing the order.

Application for increase in term of imprisonment in default **R-354**

58.9 (1) This rule applies where the prosecutor makes an application under section 39(5) of the Proceeds of Crime Act 2002 to increase the term of imprisonment in default of payment of a confiscation order.

(2) The application must be made in writing and give details of—
(a) the name and address of the defendant;
(b) the confiscation order;
(c) the grounds for the application; and
(d) the enforcement measures taken, if any.

(3) On receipt of the application, the court must—
(a) at once, send to the defendant and the magistrates' court responsible for enforcing the order, a copy of the application; and
(b) fix a time, date and place for the hearing and notify the applicant and the defendant of that time, date and place.

(4) If the Crown Court makes an order increasing the term of imprisonment in default, the court must, at once, send a copy of the order to—
(a) the applicant;
(b) the defendant;
(c) where the defendant is in custody at the time of the making of the order, the person having custody of the defendant; and
(d) the magistrates' court responsible for enforcing the order.

Compensation—general **R-355**

58.10 (1) This rule applies to an application for compensation under section 72 of the Proceeds of Crime Act 2002.

(2) The application must be in writing and may be supported by a witness statement.

(3) The application and any witness statement must be lodged with the Crown Court.

(4) The application and any witness statement must be served on—
(a) the person alleged to be in default; and
(b) the person or authority by whom the compensation would be payable under section 72(9) or 302(7A) of the 2002 Act (or if the compensation is payable out of a police fund under section 72(9)(a) or 302(7A), the chief officer of the police force concerned),

at least seven days before the date fixed by the court for hearing the application, unless the Crown Court directs otherwise.

Compensation—confiscation order made against absconder **R-356**

58.11 (1) This rule applies to an application for compensation under section 73 of the Proceeds of Crime Act 2002.

(2) The application must be in writing and supported by a witness statement which must give details of—
(a) the confiscation order made under section 28 of the 2002 Act;
(b) the variation or discharge of the confiscation order under section 29 or 30 of the 2002 Act;
(c) the realisable property to which the application relates; and
(d) the loss suffered by the applicant as result of the confiscation order.

(3) The application and witness statement must be lodged with the Crown Court.

(4) The application and witness statement must be served on the prosecutor at least seven days before the date fixed by the court for hearing the application, unless the Crown Court specifies a shorter period.

Payment of money in bank or building society account in satisfaction of confiscation order **R-357**

58.12 (1) An order under section 67 of the Proceeds of Crime Act 2002 requiring a bank or building society to pay money to a magistrates' court officer ('a payment order') shall—
(a) be directed to the bank or building society in respect of which the payment order is made;
(b) name the person against whom the confiscation order has been made;
(c) state the amount which remains to be paid under the confiscation order;
(d) state the name and address of the branch at which the account in which the money ordered to be paid is held and the sort code of that branch, if the sort code is known;

(e) state the name in which the account in which the money ordered to be paid is held and the account number of that account, if the account number is known;
(f) state the amount which the bank or building society is required to pay to the court officer under the payment order;
(g) give the name and address of the court officer to whom payment is to be made; and
(h) require the bank or building society to make payment within a period of seven days beginning on the day on which the payment order is made, unless it appears to the court that a longer or shorter period would be appropriate in the particular circumstances.

(2) The payment order shall be served on the bank or building society in respect of which it is made by leaving it at, or sending it by first class post to, the principal office of the bank or building society.

(3) A payment order which is served by first class post shall, unless the contrary is proved, be deemed to have been served on the second business day after posting.

(4) In this rule 'confiscation order' has the meaning given to it by section 88(6) of the Proceeds of Crime Act 2002.

Part 59 Proceeds of Crime Act 2002: Rules Applicable only to Restraint Proceedings

R-358 Application for restraint order or ancillary order

59.1 (1) This rule applies where the prosecutor, or an accredited financial investigator, makes an application for a restraint order under section 42 of the Proceeds of Crime Act 2002 for—
(a) a restraint order, under section 41(1) of the 2002 Act; or
(b) an ancillary order, under section 41(7) of that Act, for the purpose of ensuring that a restraint order is effective.

(2) The application may be made without notice if the application is urgent or if there are reasonable grounds for believing that giving notice would cause the dissipation of realisable property which is the subject of the application.

(3) An application for a restraint order must be in writing and supported by a witness statement which must—
(a) give the grounds for the application;
(b) to the best of the witness's ability, give full details of the realisable property in respect of which the applicant is seeking the order and specify the person holding that realisable property;
(c) include the proposed terms of the order.

(4) An application for an ancillary order must be in writing and supported by a witness statement which must—
(a) give the grounds for, and details of, the application;
(b) include, if appropriate—
(i) any request for an order for disclosure of documents to which rule 61.9 applies (rules applicable to restraint and receivership proceedings: disclosure and inspection of documents),
(ii) the identity of any person whom the applicant wants the court to examine about the extent or whereabouts of realisable property,
(iii) a list of the main questions that the applicant wants to ask any such person, and
(iv) a list of any documents to which the applicant wants to refer such a person; and
(c) include the proposed terms of the order.

(5) An application for a restraint order and an application for an ancillary order may (but need not) be made at the same time and contained in the same documents.

(6) An application by an accredited financial investigator must include a statement that, under section 68 of the 2002 Act, the applicant has authority to apply.

R-359 Restraint and ancillary orders

59.2 (1) The Crown Court may make a restraint order subject to exceptions, including, but not limited to, exceptions for reasonable living expenses and reasonable legal expenses, and for the purpose of enabling any person to carry on any trade, business or occupation.

(2) But the Crown Court must not make an exception for legal expenses where this is prohibited by section 41(4) of the Proceeds of Crime Act 2002.

(3) An exception to a restraint order may be made subject to conditions.
(4) The Crown Court must not require the applicant for a restraint order to give any undertaking relating to damages sustained as a result of the restraint order by a person who is prohibited from dealing with realisable property by the restraint order.
(5) The Crown Court may require the applicant for a restraint order to give an undertaking to pay the reasonable expenses of any person, other than a person who is prohibited from dealing with realisable property by the restraint order, which are incurred in complying with the restraint order.
(6) An order must include a statement that disobedience of the order, either by a person to whom the order is addressed, or by another person, may be contempt of court and the order must include details of the possible consequences of being held in contempt of court.
(7) Unless the Crown Court otherwise directs, an order made without notice has effect until the court makes an order varying or discharging it.
(8) The applicant for an order must—
(a) serve copies of the order and of the witness statement made in support of the application on the defendant and any person who is prohibited by the order from dealing with realisable property; and
(b) notify any person whom the applicant knows to be affected by the order of its terms.

Application for discharge or variation of restraint or ancillary order by a person affected by the order **R-360**

59.3 (1) This rule applies where a person affected by a restraint order makes an application to the Crown Court under section 42(3) of the Proceeds of Crime Act 2002 to discharge or vary the restraint order or any ancillary order made under section 41(7) of the Act.
(2) The application must be in writing and may be supported by a witness statement.
(3) The application and any witness statement must be lodged with the Crown Court.
(4) The application and any witness statement must be served on the person who applied for the restraint order and any person who is prohibited from dealing with realisable property by the restraint order (if he is not the person making the application) at least two days before the date fixed by the court for hearing the application, unless the Crown Court specifies a shorter period.

Application for variation of restraint or ancillary order by the person who applied for the order **R-361**

59.4 (1) This rule applies where the applicant for a restraint order makes an application under section 42(3) of the Proceeds of Crime Act 2002 to the Crown Court to vary the restraint order or any ancillary order made under section 41(7) of the 2002 Act (including where the court has already made a restraint order and the applicant is seeking to vary the order in order to restrain further realisable property).
(2) The application may be made without notice if the application is urgent or if there are reasonable grounds for believing that giving notice would cause the dissipation of realisable property which is the subject of the application.
(3) The application must be in writing and must be supported by a witness statement which must—
(a) give the grounds for the application;
(b) where the application is for the inclusion of further realisable property in a restraint order give full details, to the best of the witness's ability, of the realisable property in respect of which the applicant is seeking the order and specify the person holding that realisable property;
(c) where the application is to vary an ancillary order, include, if appropriate—
(i) any request for an order for disclosure of documents to which rule 61.9 applies (rules applicable to restraint and receivership proceedings: disclosure and inspection of documents),
(ii) the identity of any person whom the applicant wants the court to examine about the extent or whereabouts of realisable property,
(iii) a list of the main questions that the applicant wants to ask any such person, and
(iv) a list of any documents to which the applicant wants to refer such a person; and
(d) include the proposed terms of the variation.
(4) An application by an accredited financial investigator must include a statement that, under section 68 of the 2002 Act, the applicant has authority to apply.
(5) The application and witness statement must be lodged with the Crown Court.

(6) Except where, under paragraph (2), notice of the application is not required to be served, the application and witness statement must be served on any person who is prohibited from dealing with realisable property by the restraint order at least 2 days before the date fixed by the court for hearing the application, unless the Crown Court specifies a shorter period.

(7) If the court makes an order for the variation of a restraint or ancillary order, the applicant must serve copies of the order and of the witness statement made in support of the application on—
- (a) the defendant;
- (b) any person who is prohibited from dealing with realisable property by the restraint order (whether before or after the variation); and
- (c) any other person whom the applicant knows to be affected by the order.

R-362 Application for discharge of restraint or ancillary order by the person who applied for the order

59.5 (1) This rule applies where the applicant for a restraint order makes an application under section 42(3) of the Proceeds of Crime Act 2002 to discharge the order or any ancillary order made under section 41(7) of the 2002 Act.

(2) The application may be made without notice.

(3) The application must be in writing and must state the grounds for the application.

(4) If the court makes an order for the discharge of a restraint order, the applicant must serve copies of the order on—
- (a) the defendant;
- (b) any person who is prohibited from dealing with realisable property by the restraint order (whether before or after the discharge); and
- (c) any other person whom the applicant knows to be affected by the order.

R-363 Application to punish for contempt of court

59.6 (1) This rule applies where a person is accused of disobeying—
- (a) a restraint order; or
- (b) an ancillary order made for the purpose of ensuring that a restraint order is effective.

(2) An applicant who wants the Crown Court to exercise its power to punish that person for contempt of court must comply with the rules in Part 62 (Contempt of court).

Part 60 Proceeds of Crime Act 2002: Rules Applicable only to Receivership Proceedings

R-364 Application for appointment of a management or an enforcement receiver

60.1 (1) This rule applies to an application for the appointment of a management receiver under section 48(1) of the Proceeds of Crime Act 2002 and an application for the appointment of an enforcement receiver under section 50(1) of the 2002 Act.

(2) The application may be made without notice if—
- (a) the application is joined with an application for a restraint order under rule 59.1;
- (b) the application is urgent; or
- (c) there are reasonable grounds for believing that giving notice would cause the dissipation of realisable property which is the subject of the application.

(3) The application must be in writing and must be supported by a witness statement which must—
- (a) give the grounds for the application;
- (b) give full details of the proposed receiver;
- (c) to the best of the witness's ability, give full details of the realisable property in respect of which the applicant is seeking the order and specify the person holding that realisable property;
- (d) where the application is made by an accredited financial investigator, include a statement that, under section 68 of the 2002 Act, the applicant has authority to apply; and
- (e) if the proposed receiver is not a person falling within section 55(8) of the 2002 Act and the applicant is asking the court to allow the receiver to act—
  - (i) without giving security, or
  - (ii) before he has given security or satisfied the court that he has security in place,

  explain the reasons why that is necessary.

(4) Where the application is for the appointment of an enforcement receiver, the applicant must provide the Crown Court with a copy of the confiscation order made against the defendant.
(5) The application and witness statement must be lodged with the Crown Court.
(6) Except where, under paragraph (2), notice of the application is not required to be served, the application and witness statement must be lodged with the Crown Court and served on—
(a) the defendant;
(b) any person who holds realisable property to which the application relates; and
(c) any other person whom the applicant knows to be affected by the application,
at least seven days before the date fixed by the court for hearing the application, unless the Crown Court specifies a shorter period.
(7) If the court makes an order for the appointment of a receiver, the applicant must serve copies of the order and of the witness statement made in support of the application on—
(a) the defendant;
(b) any person who holds realisable property to which the order applies; and
(c) any other person whom the applicant knows to be affected by the order.

Application for conferral of powers on a management receiver or an enforcement receiver **R-365**

60.2 (1) This rule applies to an application for the conferral of powers on a management receiver under section 49(1) of the Proceeds of Crime Act 2002 or an enforcement receiver under section 51(1) of the 2002 Act.
(2) The application may be made without notice if the application is to give the receiver power to take possession of property and—
(a) the application is joined with an application for a restraint order under rule 59.1;
(b) the application is urgent; or
(c) there are reasonable grounds for believing that giving notice would cause the dissipation of the property which is the subject of the application.
(3) The application must be made in writing and supported by a witness statement which must—
(a) give the grounds for the application;
(b) give full details of the realisable property in respect of which the applicant is seeking the order and specify the person holding that realisable property; and
(c) where the application is made by an accredited financial investigator, include a statement that, under section 68 of the 2002 Act, the applicant has authority to apply
(d) where the application is for power to start, carry on or defend legal proceedings in respect of the property, explain—
(i) what proceedings are concerned, in what court, and
(ii) what powers the receiver will ask that court to exercise.
(4) Where the application is for the conferral of powers on an enforcement receiver or Director's receiver, the applicant must provide the Crown Court with a copy of the confiscation order made against the defendant.
(5) The application and witness statement must be lodged with the Crown Court.
(6) Except where, under paragraph (2), notice of the application is not required to be served, the application and witness statement must be served on—
(a) the defendant;
(b) any person who holds realisable property in respect of which a receiver has been appointed or in respect of which an application for a receiver has been made;
(c) any other person whom the applicant knows to be affected by the application; and
(d) the receiver (if one has already been appointed), at least seven days before the date fixed by the court for hearing the application, unless the Crown Court specifies a shorter period.
(7) If the court makes an order for the conferral of powers on a receiver, the applicant must serve copies of the order on—
(a) the defendant;
(b) any person who holds realisable property in respect of which the receiver has been appointed; and
(c) any other person whom the applicant knows to be affected by the order.

Applications for discharge or variation of receivership orders, and applications for other orders **R-366**

60.3 (1) This rule applies to applications under section 62(3) of the Proceeds of Crime Act 2002 for orders (by persons affected by the action of receivers) and applications under section 63(1) of the 2002 Act for the discharge or variation of orders relating to receivers.
(2) The application must be made in writing and lodged with the Crown Court.

(3) The application must be served on the following persons (except where they are the person making the application)—
(a) the person who applied for appointment of the receiver;
(b) the defendant;
(c) any person who holds realisable property in respect of which the receiver has been appointed;
(d) the receiver; and
(e) any other person whom the applicant knows to be affected by the application, at least seven days before the date fixed by the court for hearing the application, unless the Crown Court specifies a shorter period.

(4) If the court makes an order for the discharge or variation of an order relating to a receiver under section 63(2) of the 2002 Act, the applicant must serve copies of the order on any persons whom he knows to be affected by the order.

R-367 Sums in the hands of receivers

60.4 (1) This rule applies where the amount payable under a confiscation order has been fully paid and any sums remain in the hands of an enforcement receiver or Director's receiver.
(2) The receiver must make an application to the Crown Court for directions as to the distribution of the sums in his hands.
(3) The application and any evidence which the receiver intends to rely on in support of the application must be served on—
(a) the defendant; and
(b) any other person who held (or holds) interests in any property realised by the receiver,
at least seven days before the date fixed by the court for hearing the application, unless the Crown Court specifies a shorter period.
(4) If any of the provisions listed in paragraph (5) (provisions as to the vesting of funds in a trustee in bankruptcy) apply, then the Crown Court must make a declaration to that effect.
(5) These are the provisions—
(a) section 31B of the Bankruptcy (Scotland) Act 1985;
(b) section 306B of the Insolvency Act 1986; and
(c) article 279B of the Insolvency (Northern Ireland) Order 1989.

R-368 Security

60.5 (1) This rule applies where the Crown Court appoints a receiver under section 48, 50 or 52 of the Proceeds of Crime Act 2002 and the receiver is not a person falling within section 55(8) of the 2002 Act (and it is immaterial whether the receiver is a permanent or temporary member of staff or on secondment).
(2) The Crown Court may direct that before the receiver begins to act, or within a specified time, he must either—
(a) give such security as the Crown Court may determine; or
(b) file with the Crown Court and serve on all parties to any receivership proceedings evidence that he already has in force sufficient security,
to cover his liability for his acts and omissions as a receiver.
(3) The Crown Court may terminate the appointment of a receiver if he fails to—
(a) give the security; or
(b) satisfy the court as to the security he has in force, by the date specified.

R-369 Remuneration

60.6 (1) This rule applies where the Crown Court appoints a receiver under section 48, 50 or 52 of the Proceeds of Crime Act 2002 and the receiver is not a person falling within section 55(8) of the 2002 Act (and it is immaterial whether the receiver is a permanent or temporary member or he is on secondment from elsewhere).
(2) The receiver may only charge for his services if the Crown Court—
(a) so directs; and
(b) specifies the basis on which the receiver is to be remunerated.
(3) Unless the Crown Court orders otherwise, in determining the remuneration of the receiver, the Crown Court shall award such sum as is reasonable and proportionate in all the circumstances and which takes into account—
(a) the time properly given by him and his staff to the receivership;
(b) the complexity of the receivership;

(c) any responsibility of an exceptional kind or degree which falls on the receiver in consequence of the receivership;
(d) the effectiveness with which the receiver appears to be carrying out, or to have carried out, his duties; and
(e) the value and nature of the subject matter of the receivership.

(4) The Crown Court may refer the determination of a receiver's remuneration to be ascertained by the taxing authority of the Crown Court and rules 76.11 to 76.14 shall have effect as if the taxing authority was ascertaining costs.
(5) A receiver appointed under section 48 of the 2002 Act is to receive his remuneration by realising property in respect of which he is appointed, in accordance with section 49(2)(d) of the 2002 Act.
(6) A receiver appointed under section 50 of the 2002 Act is to receive his remuneration by applying to the magistrates' court officer for payment under section 55(4)(b) of the 2002 Act.
(7) A receiver appointed under section 52 of the 2002 Act is to receive his remuneration by applying to the Director for payment under section 57(4)(b) of the 2002 Act.

Accounts **R-370**

60.7 (1) The Crown Court may order a receiver appointed under section 48, 50 or 52 of the Proceeds of Crime Act 2002 to prepare and serve accounts.
(2) A party to receivership proceedings served with such accounts may apply for an order permitting him to inspect any document in the possession of the receiver relevant to those accounts.
(3) Any party to receivership proceedings may, within 14 days of being served with the accounts, serve notice on the receiver—
(a) specifying any item in the accounts to which he objects;
(b) giving the reason for such objection; and
(c) requiring the receiver within 14 days of receipt of the notice, either—
(i) to notify all the parties who were served with the accounts that he accepts the objection, or
(ii) if he does not accept the objection, to apply for an examination of the accounts in relation to the contested item.

(4) When the receiver applies for the examination of the accounts he must at the same time lodge with the Crown Court—
(a) the accounts; and
(b) a copy of the notice served on him under this section of the rule.

(5) If the receiver fails to comply with paragraph (3)(c) of this rule, any party to receivership proceedings may apply to the Crown Court for an examination of the accounts in relation to the contested item.
(6) At the conclusion of its examination of the accounts the court will certify the result.

Non-compliance by receiver **R-371**

60.8 (1) If a receiver appointed under section 48, 50 or 52 of the Proceeds of Crime Act 2002 fails to comply with any rule, practice direction or direction of the Crown Court, the Crown Court may order him to attend a hearing to explain his non-compliance.
(2) At the hearing, the Crown Court may make any order it considers appropriate, including—
(a) terminating the appointment of the receiver;
(b) reducing the receiver's remuneration or disallowing it altogether; and
(c) ordering the receiver to pay the costs of any party.

Part 61 Proceeds of Crime Act 2002: Rules Applicable to Restraint and Receivership Proceedings

Distress and forfeiture **R-372**

61.1 (1) This rule applies to applications under sections 58(2) and (3) and 59(2) and (3) of the Proceeds of Crime Act 2002 for leave of the Crown Court to levy distress against property or exercise a right of forfeiture by peaceable re-entry in relation to a tenancy, in circumstances where the property or tenancy is the subject of a restraint order or a receiver has been appointed in respect of the property or tenancy.
(2) The application must be made in writing to the Crown Court.

(3) The application must be served on—
(a) the person who applied for the restraint order or the order appointing the receiver; and
(b) any receiver appointed in respect of the property or tenancy,
at least seven days before the date fixed by the court for hearing the application, unless the Crown Court specifies a shorter period.

R-373 **Joining of applications**

61.2 An application for the appointment of a management receiver or enforcement receiver under rule 60.1 may be joined with—
(a) an application for a restraint order under rule 59.1; and
(b) an application for the conferral of powers on the receiver under rule 60.2.

R-374 **Applications to be dealt with in writing**

61.3 Applications in restraint proceedings and receivership proceedings are to be dealt with without a hearing, unless the Crown Court orders otherwise.

R-375 **Business in chambers**

61.4 Restraint proceedings and receivership proceedings may be heard in chambers.

R-376 **Power of court to control evidence**

61.5 (1) When hearing restraint proceedings and receivership proceedings, the Crown Court may control the evidence by giving directions as to—
(a) the issues on which it requires evidence;
(b) the nature of the evidence which it requires to decide those issues; and
(c) the way in which the evidence is to be placed before the court.
(2) The court may use its power under this rule to exclude evidence that would otherwise be admissible.
(3) The court may limit cross-examination in restraint proceedings and receivership proceedings.

R-377 **Evidence of witnesses**

61.6 (1) The general rule is that, unless the Crown Court orders otherwise, any fact which needs to be proved in restraint proceedings or receivership proceedings by the evidence of a witness is to be proved by their evidence in writing.
(2) Where evidence is to be given in writing under this rule, any party may apply to the Crown Court for permission to cross-examine the person giving the evidence.
(3) If the Crown Court gives permission under paragraph (2) but the person in question does not attend as required by the order, his evidence may not be used unless the court gives permission.

R-378 **Witness summons**

61.7 (1) Any party to restraint proceedings or receivership proceedings may apply to the Crown Court to issue a witness summons requiring a witness to—
(a) attend court to give evidence; or
(b) produce documents to the court.
(2) Rule 28.3 applies to an application under this rule as it applies to an application under section 2 of the Criminal Procedure (Attendance of Witnesses) Act 1965.

R-379 **Hearsay evidence**

61.8 Section 2(1) of the Civil Evidence Act 1995 (duty to give notice of intention to rely on hearsay evidence) does not apply to evidence in restraint proceedings and receivership proceedings.

R-380 **Disclosure and inspection of documents**

61.9 (1) This rule applies where, in the course of restraint proceedings or receivership proceedings, an issue arises as to whether property is realisable property.
(2) The Crown Court may make an order for disclosure of documents.
(3) Part 31 of the Civil Procedure Rules 1998 as amended from time to time shall have effect as if the proceedings were proceedings in the High Court.

R-381 **Court documents**

61.10 (1) Any order which the Crown Court issues in restraint proceedings or receivership proceedings must—
(a) state the name and judicial title of the person who made it;

(b) bear the date on which it is made; and
(c) be sealed by the Crown Court.
(2) The Crown Court may place the seal on the order—
(a) by hand; or
(b) by printing a facsimile of the seal on the order whether electronically or otherwise.
(3) A document purporting to bear the court's seal shall be admissible in evidence without further proof.

Consent orders R-382

61.11 (1) This rule applies where all the parties to restraint proceedings or receivership proceedings agree the terms in which an order should be made.
(2) Any party may apply for a judgment or order in the terms agreed.
(3) The Crown Court may deal with an application under paragraph (2) without a hearing.
(4) Where this rule applies—
(a) the order which is agreed by the parties must be drawn up in the terms agreed;
(b) it must be expressed as being 'By Consent'; and
(c) it must be signed by the legal representative acting for each of the parties to whom the order relates or by the party if he is a litigant in person.
(5) Where an application is made under this rule, then the requirements of any other rule as to the procedure for making an application do not apply.

Slips and omissions R-383

61.12 (1) The Crown Court may at any time correct an accidental slip or omission in an order made in restraint proceedings or receivership proceedings.
(2) A party may apply for a correction without notice.

Supply of documents from court records R-384

61.13 (1) No document relating to restraint proceedings or receivership proceedings may be supplied from the records of the Crown Court for any person to inspect or copy unless the Crown Court grants permission.
(2) An application for permission under paragraph (1) must be made on notice to the parties to the proceedings.

Disclosure of documents in criminal proceedings R-385

61.14 (1) This rule applies where—
(a) proceedings for an offence have been started in the Crown Court and the defendant has not been either convicted or acquitted on all counts; and
(b) an application for a restraint order under section 42(1) of the Proceeds of Crime Act 2002 has been made.
(2) The judge presiding at the proceedings for the offence may be supplied from the records of the Crown Court with documents relating to restraint proceedings and any receivership proceedings.
(3) Such documents must not otherwise be disclosed in the proceedings for the offence.

Preparation of documents R-386

61.15 (1) Every order in restraint proceedings or receivership proceedings will be drawn up by the Crown Court unless—
(a) the Crown Court orders a party to draw it up;
(b) a party, with the permission of the Crown Court, agrees to draw it up; or
(c) the order is made by consent under rule 61.10.
(2) The Crown Court may direct that—
(a) an order drawn up by a party must be checked by the Crown Court before it is sealed; or
(b) before an order is drawn up by the Crown Court, the parties must lodge an agreed statement of its terms.
(3) Where an order is to be drawn up by a party—
(a) he must lodge it with the Crown Court no later than seven days after the date on which the court ordered or permitted him to draw it up so that it can be sealed by the Crown Court; and
(b) if he fails to lodge it within that period, any other party may draw it up and lodge it.
(4) Nothing in this rule shall require the Crown Court to accept a document which is illegible, has not been duly authorised, or is unsatisfactory for some other similar reason.

R-387 **Change of solicitor**

61.16 (1) This rule applies where—
(a) a party for whom a solicitor is acting in restraint proceedings or receivership proceedings wants to change his solicitor;
(b) a party, after having represented himself in such proceedings, appoints a solicitor to act on his behalf (except where the solicitor is appointed only to act as an advocate for a hearing); or
(c) a party, after having been represented by a solicitor in such proceedings, intends to act in person.
(2) Where this rule applies, the party or his solicitor (where one is acting) must—
(a) lodge notice of the change at the Crown Court; and
(b) serve notice of the change on every other party and, where paragraph (1)(a) or (c) applies, on the former solicitor.
(3) The notice lodged at the Crown Court must state that notice has been served as required by paragraph (2)(b).
(4) Subject to paragraph (5), where a party has changed his solicitor or intends to act in person, the former solicitor will be considered to be the party's solicitor unless and until—
(a) notice is served in accordance with paragraph (2); or
(b) the Crown Court makes an order under rule 61.17 and the order is served as required by paragraph (3) of that rule.
(5) Where the certificate of a LSC funded client is revoked or discharged—
(a) the solicitor who acted for that person will cease to be the solicitor acting in the proceedings as soon as his retainer is determined under regulation 4 of the Community Legal Service (Costs) Regulations 2000; and
(b) if that person wishes to continue, where he appoints a solicitor to act on his behalf paragraph (2) will apply as if he had previously represented himself in the proceedings.
(6) 'Certificate' in paragraph (5) means a certificate issued under the Funding Code (approved under section 9 of the Access to Justice Act 1999) and 'LSC funded client' means an individual who receives services funded by the Legal Services Commission as part of the Community Legal Service within the meaning of Part I of the 1999 Act.

R-388 **Application by solicitor for declaration that solicitor has ceased to act**

61.17 (1) A solicitor may apply to the Crown Court for an order declaring that he has ceased to be the solicitor acting for a party to restraint proceedings or receivership proceedings.
(2) Where an application is made under this rule—
(a) notice of the application must be given to the party for whom the solicitor is acting, unless the Crown Court directs otherwise; and
(b) the application must be supported by evidence.
(3) Where the Crown Court makes an order that a solicitor has ceased to act, the solicitor must serve a copy of the order on every party to the proceedings.

R-389 **Application by other party for declaration that solicitor has ceased to act**

61.18 (1) Where—
(a) a solicitor who has acted for a party to restraint proceedings or receivership proceedings—
(i) has died,
(ii) has become bankrupt,
(iii) has ceased to practise, or
(iv) cannot be found, and
(b) the party has not given notice of a change of solicitor or notice of intention to act in person as required by rule 61.16,

any other party may apply to the Crown Court for an order declaring that the solicitor has ceased to be the solicitor acting for the other party in the proceedings.
(2) Where an application is made under this rule, notice of the application must be given to the party to whose solicitor the application relates unless the Crown Court directs otherwise.
(3) Where the Crown Court makes an order under this rule, the applicant must serve a copy of the order on every other party to the proceedings.

R-390 **Order for costs**

61.19 (1) This rule applies where the Crown Court is deciding whether to make an order for costs in restraint proceedings or receivership proceedings.

(2) The court has discretion as to—
  (a) whether costs are payable by one party to another;
  (b) the amount of those costs; and
  (c) when they are to be paid.
(3) If the court decides to make an order about costs—
  (a) the general rule is that the unsuccessful party will be ordered to pay the costs of the successful party; but
  (b) the court may make a different order.
(4) In deciding what order (if any) to make about costs, the court must have regard to all of the circumstances, including—
  (a) the conduct of all the parties; and
  (b) whether a party has succeeded on part of an application, even if he has not been wholly successful.
(5) The orders which the court may make include an order that a party must pay—
  (a) a proportion of another party's costs;
  (b) a stated amount in respect of another party's costs;
  (c) costs from or until a certain date only;
  (d) costs incurred before proceedings have begun;
  (e) costs relating to particular steps taken in the proceedings;
  (f) costs relating only to a distinct part of the proceedings; and
  (g) interest on costs from or until a certain date, including a date before the making of an order.
(6) Where the court would otherwise consider making an order under paragraph (5)(f), it must instead, if practicable, make an order under paragraph (5)(a) or (c).
(7) Where the court has ordered a party to pay costs, it may order an amount to be paid on account before the costs are assessed.

Assessment of costs R-391

61.20 (1) Where the Crown Court has made an order for costs in restraint proceedings or receivership proceedings it may either—
  (a) make an assessment of the costs itself; or
  (b) order assessment of the costs under rule 76.11.
(2) In either case, the Crown Court or the assessing authority, as the case may be, must—
  (a) only allow costs which are proportionate to the matters in issue; and
  (b) resolve any doubt which it may have as to whether the costs were reasonably incurred or reasonable and proportionate in favour of the paying party.
(3) The Crown Court or the assessing authority, as the case may be, is to have regard to all the circumstances in deciding whether costs were proportionately or reasonably incurred or proportionate and reasonable in amount.
(4) In particular, the Crown Court or the assessing authority must give effect to any orders which have already been made.
(5) The Crown Court or the assessing authority must also have regard to—
  (a) the conduct of all the parties, including in particular, conduct before, as well as during, the proceedings;
  (b) the amount or value of the property involved;
  (c) the importance of the matter to all the parties;
  (d) the particular complexity of the matter or the difficulty or novelty of the questions raised;
  (e) the skill, effort, specialised knowledge and responsibility involved;
  (f) the time spent on the application; and
  (g) the place where and the circumstances in which work or any part of it was done.

Time for complying with an order for costs R-392

61.21 (1) A party to restraint proceedings or receivership proceedings must comply with an order for the payment of costs within 14 days of—
  (a) the date of the order if it states the amount of those costs;
  (b) if the amount of those costs is decided later under rule 76.11, the date of the assessing authority's decision; or
  (c) in either case, such later date as the Crown Court may specify.

R-393 Application of costs rules

61.22 Rules 61.19, 61.20 and 61.21 do not apply to the assessment of costs in proceedings to the extent that section 11 of the Access to Justice Act 1999 applies and provisions made under that Act make different provision.

Part 62 Contempt of Court

Section 1: general rules

R-394 When this Part applies

62.1 (1) This Part applies where the court can deal with a person for conduct—
(a) in contempt of court; or
(b) in contravention of the legislation to which rules 62.5 and 62.9 refer.
(2) In this Part, 'respondent' means any such accused person.

R-395 Exercise of court's power to deal with contempt of court

62.2 (1) The court must determine at a hearing—
(a) an enquiry under rule 62.8;
(b) an allegation under rule 62.9.
(2) The court must not proceed in the respondent's absence unless—
(a) the respondent's behaviour makes it impracticable to proceed otherwise; or
(b) the respondent has had at least 14 days' notice of the hearing, or was present when it was arranged.
(3) If the court hears part of an enquiry or allegation in private, it must announce at a hearing in public—
(a) the respondent's name;
(b) in general terms, the nature of any conduct that the respondent admits, or the court finds proved; and
(c) any punishment imposed.

R-396 Notice of suspension of imprisonment by Court of Appeal or Crown Court

62.3 (1) This rule applies where—
(a) the Court of Appeal or the Crown Court suspends an order of imprisonment for contempt of court; and
(b) the respondent is absent when the court does so.
(2) The respondent must be served with notice of the terms of the court's order—
(a) by any applicant under rule 62.9; or
(b) by the court officer, in any other case.

R-397 Application to discharge an order for imprisonment

62.4 (1) This rule applies where the court can discharge an order for a respondent's imprisonment for contempt of court.
(2) A respondent who wants the court to discharge such an order must—
(a) apply in writing, unless the court otherwise directs, and serve any written application on—
(i) the court officer, and
(ii) any applicant under rule 62.9 on whose application the respondent was imprisoned;
(b) in the application—
(i) explain why it is appropriate for the order for imprisonment to be discharged, and
(ii) give details of any appeal, and its outcome; and
(c) ask for a hearing, if the respondent wants one.

Section 2: contempt of court by obstruction, disruption, etc.

R-398 Initial procedure on obstruction, disruption etc.

62.5 (1) This rule applies where the court observes, or someone reports to the court—
(a) in the Court of Appeal or the Crown Court, obstructive, disruptive, insulting or intimidating conduct, in the courtroom or in its vicinity, or otherwise immediately affecting the proceedings;

(b) in the Crown Court, a contravention of—
(i) section 3 of the Criminal Procedure (Attendance of Witnesses) Act 1965 (disobeying a witness summons);
(ii) section 20 of the Juries Act 1974 (disobeying a jury summons);
(iii) section 8 of the Contempt of Court Act 1981 (obtaining details of a jury's deliberations, etc.);
(c) in a magistrates' court, a contravention of—
(i) section 97(4) of the Magistrates' Courts Act 1980 (refusing to give evidence), or
(ii) section 12 of the Contempt of Court Act 1981 (insulting or interrupting the court, etc.);
(d) a contravention of section 9 of the Contempt of Court Act 1981 (without the court's permission, recording the proceedings, etc.);
(e) any other conduct with which the court can deal as, or as if it were, a criminal contempt of court, except failure to surrender to bail under section 6 of the Bail Act 1976.
(2) Unless the respondent's behaviour makes it impracticable to do so, the court must—
(a) explain, in terms the respondent can understand (with help, if necessary)—
(i) the conduct that is in question,
(ii) that the court can impose imprisonment, or a fine, or both, for such conduct,
(iii) (where relevant) that the court has power to order the respondent's immediate temporary detention, if in the court's opinion that is required,
(iv) that the respondent may explain the conduct,
(v) that the respondent may apologise, if he or she so wishes, and that this may persuade the court to take no further action, and
(vi) that the respondent may take legal advice; and
(b) allow the respondent a reasonable opportunity to reflect, take advice, explain and, if he or she so wishes, apologise.
(3) The court may then—
(a) take no further action in respect of that conduct;
(b) enquire into the conduct there and then; or
(c) postpone that enquiry (if a magistrates' court, only until later the same day).

Review after temporary detention R-399

62.6 (1) This rule applies in a case in which the court has ordered the respondent's immediate temporary detention for conduct to which rule 62.5 applies.
(2) The court must review the case—
(a) if a magistrates' court, later the same day;
(b) in the Court of Appeal or the Crown Court, no later than the next business day.
(3) On the review, the court must—
(a) unless the respondent is absent, repeat the explanations required by rule 62.5(2)(a); and
(b) allow the respondent a reasonable opportunity to reflect, take advice, explain and, if he or she so wishes, apologise.
(4) The court may then—
(a) take no further action in respect of the conduct;
(b) if a magistrates' court, enquire into the conduct there and then; or
(c) if the Court of Appeal or the Crown Court—
(i) enquire into the conduct there and then, or
(ii) postpone the enquiry, and order the respondent's release from such detention in the meantime.

Postponement of enquiry R-400

62.7 (1) This rule applies where the Court of Appeal or the Crown Court postpones the enquiry.
(2) The court must arrange for the preparation of a written statement containing such particulars of the conduct in question as to make clear what the respondent appears to have done.
(3) The court officer must serve on the respondent—
(a) that written statement;
(b) notice of where and when the postponed enquiry will take place; and
(c) a notice that—
(i) reminds the respondent that the court can impose imprisonment, or a fine, or both, for contempt of court, and
(ii) warns the respondent that the court may pursue the postponed enquiry in the respondent's absence, if the respondent does not attend.

R-401 Procedure on enquiry

62.8 (1) At an enquiry, the court must—
(a) ensure that the respondent understands (with help, if necessary) what is alleged, if the enquiry has been postponed from a previous occasion;
(b) explain what the procedure at the enquiry will be; and
(c) ask whether the respondent admits the conduct in question.
(2) If the respondent admits the conduct, the court need not receive evidence.
(3) If the respondent does not admit the conduct, the court will receive—
(a) any statement served under rule 62.7;
(b) any other evidence of the conduct;
(c) any evidence introduced by the respondent; and
(d) any representations by the respondent about the conduct.
(4) If the respondent admits the conduct, or the court finds it proved, the court must—
(a) before imposing any punishment for contempt of court, give the respondent an opportunity to make representations relevant to punishment;
(b) explain, in terms the respondent can understand (with help, if necessary)—
(i) the reasons for its decision, including its findings of fact, and
(ii) the punishment it imposes, and its effect; and
(c) if a magistrates' court, arrange for the preparation of a written record of those findings.
(5) The court that conducts an enquiry—
(a) need not include the same member or members as the court that observed the conduct; but
(b) may do so, unless that would be unfair to the respondent.

Section 3: contempt of court by failure to comply with court order

R-402 Initial procedure on failure to comply with court order, etc.

62.9 (1) This rule applies where—
(a) a party, or other person directly affected, alleges—
(i) in the Crown Court, a failure to comply with an order to which rule 6.13 or 6.22 (certain investigation orders), or rule 59.6 (a restraint order), applies,
(ii) in the Court of Appeal or the Crown Court, any other conduct with which that court can deal as a civil contempt of court, or
(iii) in the Crown Court or a magistrates' court, unauthorised use of disclosed prosecution material under section 17 of the Criminal Procedure and Investigations Act 1996;
(b) the court deals on its own initiative with conduct to which paragraph (1)(a) applies.
(2) Such a party or person must—
(a) apply in writing and serve the application on the court officer; and
(b) serve on the respondent—
(i) the application, and
(ii) notice of where and when the court will consider the allegation (not less than 14 days after service).
(3) The application must—
(a) identify the respondent;
(b) explain that it is an application for the respondent to be dealt with for contempt of court;
(c) contain such particulars of the conduct in question as to make clear what is alleged against the respondent; and
(d) include a notice warning the respondent that the court—
(i) can impose imprisonment, or a fine, or both, for contempt of court, and
(ii) may deal with the application in the respondent's absence, if the respondent does not attend the hearing.
(4) A court which acts on its own initiative under paragraph (1)(b) must—
(a) arrange for the preparation of a written statement containing the same information as an application; and
(b) arrange for the service on the respondent of—
(i) that written statement, and
(ii) notice of where and when the court will consider the allegation (not less than 14 days after service).

Procedure on hearing R-403

62.10 (1) At the hearing of an allegation under rule 62.9, the court must—
(a) ensure that the respondent understands (with help, if necessary) what is alleged;
(b) explain what the procedure at the hearing will be; and
(c) ask whether the respondent admits the conduct in question.
(2) If the respondent admits the conduct, the court need not receive evidence.
(3) If the respondent does not admit the conduct, the court will receive—
(a) the application or written statement served under rule 62.9;
(b) any other evidence of the conduct;
(c) any evidence introduced by the respondent; and
(d) any representations by the respondent about the conduct.
(4) If the respondent admits the conduct, or the court finds it proved, the court must—
(a) before imposing any punishment for contempt of court, give the respondent an opportunity to make representations relevant to punishment;
(b) explain, in terms the respondent can understand (with help, if necessary)—
(i) the reasons for its decision, including its findings of fact, and
(ii) the punishment it imposes, and its effect; and
(c) in a magistrates' court, arrange for the preparation of a written record of those findings.

Introduction of written witness statement or other hearsay R-404

62.11 (1) Where rule 62.9 applies, an applicant or respondent who wants to introduce in evidence the written statement of a witness, or other hearsay, must—
(a) serve a copy of the statement, or notice of other hearsay, on—
(i) the court officer, and
(ii) the other party; and
(b) serve the copy or notice—
(i) when serving the application under rule 62.9, in the case of an applicant, or
(ii) not more than 7 days after service of that application or of the court's written statement, in the case of the respondent.
(2) Such service is notice of that party's intention to introduce in evidence that written witness statement, or other hearsay, unless that party otherwise indicates when serving it.
(3) A party entitled to receive such notice may waive that entitlement.

Content of written witness statement R-405

62.12 (1) This rule applies to a written witness statement served under rule 62.11.
(2) Such a written witness statement must contain a declaration by the person making it that it is true to the best of that person's knowledge and belief.

Content of notice of other hearsay R-405A

62.13 (1) This rule applies to a notice of hearsay, other than a written witness statement, served under rule 62.6.
(2) Such a notice must—
(a) set out the evidence, or attach the document that contains it; and
(b) identify the person who made the statement that is hearsay.

Cross-examination of maker of written witness statement or other hearsay R-405B

62.14 (1) This rule applies where a party wants the court's permission to cross-examine a person who made a statement which another person wants to introduce as hearsay.
(2) The party who wants to cross-examine that person must—
(a) apply in writing, with reasons; and
(b) serve the application on—
(i) the court officer, and
(ii) the party who served the hearsay.
(3) A respondent who wants to cross-examine such a person must apply to do so not more than 7 days after service of the hearsay by the applicant.
(4) An applicant who wants to cross-examine such a person must apply to do so not more than 3 days after service of the hearsay by the respondent.
(5) The court—
(a) may decide an application under this rule without a hearing; but
(b) must not dismiss such an application unless the person making it has had an opportunity to make representations at a hearing.

R-405C Credibility and consistency of maker of written witness statement or other hearsay

62.15 (1) This rule applies where a party wants to challenge the credibility or consistency of a person who made a statement which another party wants to introduce as hearsay.

(2) The party who wants to challenge the credibility or consistency of that person must—

(a) serve a written notice of intention to do so on—

(i) the court officer, and

(ii) the party who served the hearsay; and

(b) in it, identify any statement or other material on which that party relies.

(3) A respondent who wants to challenge such a person's credibility or consistency must serve such a notice not more than 7 days after service of the hearsay by the applicant.

(4) An applicant who wants to challenge such a person's credibility or consistency must serve such a notice not more than 3 days after service of the hearsay by the respondent.

(5) The party who served the hearsay—

(a) may call that person to give oral evidence instead; and

(b) if so, must serve a notice of intention to do so on—

(i) the court officer, and

(ii) the other party

as soon as practicable after service of the notice under paragraph (2).

R-405D Magistrates' courts' powers to adjourn

62.16 (1) This rule applies where a magistrates' court deals with unauthorised disclosure of prosecution material under sections 17 and 18 of the Criminal Procedure and Investigations Act 1996.

(2) The sections of the Magistrates' Courts Act 1980 listed in paragraph (3) apply as if in those sections—

(a) 'complaint' and 'summons' each referred to an application or written statement under rule 62.9;

(b) 'complainant' meant an applicant; and

(c) 'defendant' meant the respondent.

(3) Those sections are—

(a) section 51 (issue of summons on complaint);

(b) section 54 (adjournment);

(c) section 55 (non-appearance of defendant);

(d) section 97(1) (summons to witness);

(e) section 121(1) (constitution and place of sitting of court);

(f) section 123 (defect in process).

(4) Section 127 of the 1980 Act (limitation of time) does not apply.

R-405E Court's power to vary requirements under Section 3

62.17 (1) The court may shorten or extend (even after it has expired) a time limit under rule 62.11, 62.14 or 62.15..

(2) A person who wants an extension of time must—

(a) apply when serving the statement, notice or application for which it is needed; and

(b) explain the delay.

PART 63 APPEAL TO THE CROWN COURT

R-406 When this Part applies

63.1 (1) This part applies where—

(a) a defendant wants to appeal under—

(i) section 108 of the Magistrates' Courts Act 1980,

(ii) section 45 of the Mental Health Act 1983,

(iii) paragraph 10 of schedule 3 to the Powers of Criminal Courts (Sentencing) Act 2000, or paragraphs 9(8) or 13(5) of Schedule 8 to the Criminal Justice Act 2003;

(b) the Criminal Cases Review Commission refers a defendant's case to the Crown Court under section 11 of the Criminal Appeal Act 1995;

(c) a prosecutor wants to appeal under—

(i) section 14A(5A) of the Football Spectators Act 1989, or

(ii) section 147(3) of the Customs and Excise Management Act 1979; or

(d) a person wants to appeal under—
(i) section 1 of the Magistrates' Courts (Appeals from Binding Over Orders) Act 1956,
(ii) section 12(5) of the Contempt of Court Act 1981,
(iii) regulation 3C or 3H of the Costs in Criminal Cases (General) Regulations 1986, or
(iv) section 22 of the Football Spectators Act 1989.

(2) A reference to an 'appellant' in this part is a reference to such a party or person.

Service of appeal notice R-407

63.2 (1) An appellant must serve an appeal notice on—
(a) the magistrates' court officer; and
(b) every other party.

(2) The appellant must serve the appeal notice—
(a) as soon after the decision appealed against as the appellant wants; but
(b) not more than 21 days after—
(i) sentence or the date sentence is deferred, whichever is earlier, if the appeal is against conviction or against a finding of guilt,
(ii) sentence, if the appeal is against sentence, or
(iii) the order or failure to make an order about which the appellant wants to appeal, in any other case.

(3) The appellant must—
(a) serve with the appeal notice any application for an extension of the time limit under this rule; and
(b) in that application, explain why the appeal notice is late.

Form of appeal notice R-408

63.3 The appeal notice must be in writing and must—
(a) specify—
(i) the conviction or finding of guilt,
(ii) the sentence, or
(iii) the order, or the failure to make an order
about which the appellant wants to appeal;
(b) summarise the issues;
(c) in an appeal against conviction—
(i) identify the prosecution witnesses whom the appellant will want to question if they are called to give oral evidence, and
(ii) say how long the trial lasted in the magistrates' court and how long the appeal is likely to last in the Crown Court;
(d) in an appeal against a finding that the appellant insulted someone or interrupted proceedings in the magistrates' court, attach—
(i) the magistrates' court's written findings of fact, and
(ii) the appellant's response to those findings;
(e) say whether the appellant has asked the magistrates' court to reconsider the case; and
(f) include a list of those on whom the appellant has served the appeal notice.

Duty of magistrates' court officer R-409

63.4 The magistrates' court officer must—
(a) as soon as practicable serve on the Crown Court officer—
(i) the appeal notice and any accompanying application served by the appellant,
(ii) details of the parties including their addresses,
(iii) a copy of each magistrates' court register entry relating to the decision under appeal and to any application for bail pending appeal, and
(iv) any report received for the purposes of sentencing;
(b) keep any document or object exhibited in the proceedings in the magistrates' court, or arrange for it to be kept by some other appropriate person, until—
(i) 6 weeks after the conclusion of those proceedings, or
(ii) the conclusion of any proceedings in the Crown Court that begin within that 6 weeks; and
(c) provide the Crown Court with any document, object or information for which the Crown Court officer asks, within such period as the Crown Court officer may require.

R-410 Duty of person keeping exhibit

63.5 A person who, under arrangements made by the magistrates' court officer, keeps a document or object exhibited in the proceedings in the magistrates' court must—
(a) keep that exhibit until—
(i) 6 weeks after the conclusion of those proceedings, or
(ii) the conclusion of any proceedings in the Crown Court that begin within that 6 weeks,
unless the magistrates' court or the Crown Court otherwise directs; and
(b) provide the Crown Court with any such document or object for which the Crown Court officer asks, within such period as the Crown Court officer may require.

R-411 Reference by the Criminal Cases Review Commission

63.6 (1) The Crown Court officer must, as soon as practicable, serve a reference by the Criminal Cases Review Commission on—
(a) the appellant;
(b) every other party; and
(c) the magistrates' court officer.
(2) The appellant may serve an appeal notice on—
(a) the Crown Court officer; and
(b) every other party,
not more than 21 days later.
(3) The Crown Court must treat the reference as the appeal notice if the appellant does not serve an appeal notice.

R-412 Hearings and decisions

63.7 (1) The Crown Court as a general rule must hear in public an appeal or reference to which this part applies, but—
(a) may order any hearing to be in private; and
(b) where a hearing is about a public interest ruling, must hold that hearing in private.
(2) The Crown Court officer must give as much notice as reasonably practicable of every hearing to—
(a) the parties;
(b) any party's custodian; and
(c) any other person whom the Crown Court requires to be notified.
(3) The Crown Court officer must serve every decision on—
(a) the parties;
(b) any other person whom the Crown Court requires to be served; and
(c) the magistrates' court officer and any party's custodian, where the decision determines an appeal.
(4) But where a hearing or decision is about a public interest ruling, the Crown Court officer must not—
(a) give notice of that hearing to; or
(b) serve that decision on,
anyone other than the prosecutor who applied for that ruling, unless the court otherwise directs.

R-413 Abandoning an appeal

63.8 (1) The appellant—
(a) may abandon an appeal without the Crown Court's permission, by serving a notice of abandonment on—
(i) the magistrates' court officer,
(ii) the Crown Court officer, and
(iii) every other party
before the hearing of the appeal begins; but
(b) after the hearing of the appeal begins, may only abandon the appeal with the Crown Court's permission.
(2) A notice of abandonment must be signed by or on behalf of the appellant.
(3) Where an appellant who is on bail pending appeal abandons an appeal—
(a) the appellant must surrender to custody as directed by the magistrates' court officer; and
(b) any conditions of bail apply until then.

Court's power to vary requirements under this Part R-414

63.9 The Crown Court may—
(a) shorten or extend (even after it has expired) a time limit under this Part;
(b) allow an appellant to vary an appeal notice that that appellant has served;
(c) direct that an appeal notice be served on any person;
(d) allow an appeal notice or a notice of abandonment to be in a different form to one set out in the Practice Direction, or to be presented orally.

Constitution of the Crown Court R-415

63.10 On the hearing of an appeal—
(a) the general rule is that the Crown Court must comprise—
(i) a judge of the High Court, a Circuit judge or a Recorder, and
(ii) no less than two and no more than four justices of the peace, none of whom took part in the decision under appeal; and
(b) if the appeal is from a youth court—
(i) each justice of the peace must be qualified to sit as a member of a youth court, and
(ii) the Crown Court must include a man and a woman; but
(c) the Crown Court may include only one justice of the peace and need not include both a man and a woman if—
(i) the presiding judge decides that otherwise the start of the appeal hearing will be delayed unreasonably, or
(ii) one or more of the justices of the peace who started hearing the appeal is absent.

Part 64 Appeal to the High Court by Way of Case Stated

Application to a magistrates' court to state a case R-416

64.1 (1) An application under section 111(1) of the Magistrates' Courts Act 1980 shall be made in writing and signed by or on behalf of the applicant and shall identify the question or questions of law or jurisdiction on which the opinion of the High Court is sought.
(2) Where one of the questions on which the opinion of the High Court is sought is whether there was evidence on which the magistrates' court could come to its decision, the particular finding of fact made by the magistrates' court which it is claimed cannot be supported by the evidence before the magistrates' court shall be specified in such application.
(3) Any such application shall be sent to a court officer for the magistrates' court whose decision is questioned.

Consideration of a draft case by a magistrates' court R-417

64.2 (1) Within 21 days after receipt of an application made in accordance with rule 64.1, a court officer for the magistrates' court whose decision is questioned shall, unless the justices refuse to state a case under section 111(5) of the Magistrates' Courts Act 1980, send a draft case in which are stated the matters required under rule 64.6 (content of case stated) to the applicant or his legal representative and shall send a copy thereof to the respondent or his legal representative.
(2) Within 21 days after receipt of the draft case under paragraph (1), each party may make representations thereon. Any such representations shall be in writing and signed by or on behalf of the party making them and shall be sent to the magistrates' court officer.
(3) Where the justices refuse to state a case under section 111(5) of the 1980 Act and they are required by a mandatory order of the High Court under section 111(6) to do so, this rule shall apply as if in paragraph (1)—
(a) for the words 'receipt of an application made in accordance with rule 64.1' there were substituted the words 'the date on which a mandatory order under section 111(6) of the 1980 Act is made'; and
(b) the words 'unless the justices refuse to state a case under section 111(5) of the 1980 Act' were omitted.

Preparation and submission of final case to a magistrates' court R-418

64.3 (1) Within 21 days after the latest day on which representations may be made under rule 64.2, the justices whose decision is questioned shall make such adjustments, if any, to the draft case prepared for the purposes of that rule as they think fit, after considering any such representations, and shall state and sign the case.

(2) A case may be stated on behalf of the justices whose decision is questioned by any 2 or more of them and may, if the justices so direct, be signed on their behalf by the justices' clerk.

(3) Forthwith after the case has been stated and signed a court officer for the court shall send it to the applicant or his legal representative, together with any statement required by rule 64.4.

R-419 **Extension of time limits by a magistrates' court**

64.4 (1) If a magistrates' court officer is unable to send to the applicant a draft case under rule 64.2(1) within the time required by that paragraph, he shall do so as soon as practicable thereafter and the provisions of that rule shall apply accordingly; but in that event a court officer shall attach to the draft case, and to the final case when it is sent to the applicant or his legal representative under rule 64.3(3), a statement of the delay and the reasons for it.

(2) If a magistrates' court officer receives an application in writing from or on behalf of the applicant or the respondent for an extension of the time within which representations on the draft case may be made under rule 64.2(2), together with reasons in writing for it, the justices' clerk may, by notice in writing sent to the applicant, or respondent as the case may be, by the magistrates' court officer, extend the time and the provisions of that paragraph and of rule 64.3 shall apply accordingly; but in that event the court officer shall attach to the final case, when it is sent to the applicant or his legal representative under rule 64.3(3), a statement of the extension and the reasons for it.

(3) If the justices are unable to state a case within the time required by rule 64.3(1), they shall do so as soon as practicable thereafter and the provisions of that rule shall apply accordingly; but in that event a court officer shall attach to the final case, when it is sent to the applicant or his legal representative under rule 64.3(3), a statement of the delay and the reasons for it.

R-420 **Content of case stated by a magistrates' courts**

64.5 (1) A case stated by the magistrates' court shall state the facts found by the court and the question or questions of law or jurisdiction on which the opinion of the High Court is sought.

(2) Where one of the questions on which the opinion of the High Court is sought is whether there was evidence on which the magistrates' court could come to its decision, the particular finding of fact which it is claimed cannot be supported by the evidence before the magistrates' court shall be specified in the case.

(3) Unless one of the questions on which the opinion of the High Court is sought is whether there was evidence on which the magistrates' court could come to its decision, the case shall not contain a statement of evidence.

R-421 **Application to the Crown Court to state a case**

64.6 (1) An application under section 28 of the Senior Courts Act 1981 to the Crown Court to state a case for the opinion of the High Court shall be made in writing to a court officer within 21 days after the date of the decision in respect of which the application is made.

(2) The application shall state the ground on which the decision of the Crown Court is questioned.

(3) After making the application, the applicant shall forthwith send a copy of it to the parties to the proceedings in the Crown Court.

(4) On receipt of the application, the Crown Court officer shall forthwith send it to the judge who presided at the proceedings in which the decision was made.

(5) On receipt of the application, the judge shall inform the Crown Court officer as to whether or not he has decided to state a case and that officer shall give notice in writing to the applicant of the judge's decision.

(6) If the judge considers that the application is frivolous, he may refuse to state a case and shall in that case, if the applicant so requires, cause a certificate stating the reasons for the refusal to be given to him.

(7) If the judge decides to state a case, the procedure to be followed shall, unless the judge in a particular case otherwise directs, be the procedure set out in paragraphs (8) to (12) of this rule.

(8) The applicant shall, within 21 days of receiving the notice referred to in paragraph (5), draft a case and send a copy of it to the Crown Court officer and to the parties to the proceedings in the Crown Court.

(9) Each party to the proceedings in the Crown Court shall, within 21 days of receiving a copy of the draft case under paragraph (8), either—

(a) give notice in writing to the applicant and the Crown Court officer that he does not intend to take part in the proceedings before the High Court;

(b) indicate in writing on the copy of the draft case that he agrees with it and send the copy to a court officer; or

(c) draft an alternative case and send it, together with the copy of the applicant's case, to the Crown Court officer.

(10) The judge shall consider the applicant's draft case and any alternative draft case sent to the Crown Court officer under paragraph (9)(c).

(11) If the Crown Court so orders, the applicant shall, before the case is stated and delivered to him, enter before the Crown Court officer into a recognizance, with or without sureties and in such sum as the Crown Court considers proper, having regard to the means of the applicant, conditioned to prosecute the appeal without delay.

(12) The judge shall state and sign a case within 14 days after either—

(a) the receipt of all the documents required to be sent to a court officer under paragraph (9); or

(b) the expiration of the period of 21 days referred to in that paragraph,

whichever is the sooner.

(13) A case stated by the Crown Court shall state the facts found by the Crown Court, the submissions of the parties (including any authorities relied on by the parties during the course of those submissions), the decision of the Crown Court in respect of which the application is made and the question on which the opinion of the High Court is sought.

(14) Any time limit referred to in this rule may be extended either before or after it expires by the Crown Court.

(15) If the judge decides not to state a case but the stating of a case is subsequently required by a mandatory order of the High Court, paragraphs (7) to (14) shall apply to the stating of the case save that—

(a) in paragraph (7) the words 'If the judge decides to state a case' shall be omitted; and

(b) in paragraph (8) for the words 'receiving the notice referred to in paragraph (5)' there shall be substituted the words 'the day on which the mandatory order was made'.

(16) The judge may determine an application to which this rule applies—

(a) at a hearing, in public or in private; or

(b) without a hearing.

PART 65 APPEAL TO THE COURT OF APPEAL: GENERAL RULES

When this Part applies R-422

65.1 (1) This Part applies to all applications, appeals and references to the Court of Appeal to which Parts 66, 67, 68, 69, 70 and 74 apply.

(2) In this Part and in those, unless the context makes it clear that something different is meant, 'court' means the Court of Appeal or any judge of that court.

Case management in the Court of Appeal R-423

65.2 (1) The court and the parties have the same duties and powers as under Part 3 (case management).

(2) The Registrar—

(a) must fulfil the duty of active case management under rule 3.2; and

(b) in fulfilling that duty may exercise any of the powers of case management under—

(i) rule 3.5 (the court's general powers of case management),

(ii) rule 3.9(3) (requiring a certificate of readiness), and

(iii) rule 3.10 (requiring a party to identify intentions and anticipated requirements) subject to the directions of the court.

(3) The Registrar must nominate a case progression officer under rule 3.4.

Power to vary requirements R-424

65.3 The court or the Registrar may—

(a) shorten a time limit or extend it (even after it has expired) unless that is inconsistent with other legislation;

(b) allow a party to vary any notice that that party has served;

(c) direct that a notice or application be served on any person;

(d) allow a notice or application to be in a different form, or presented orally.

Application for extension of time R-425

65.4 A person who wants an extension of time within which to serve a notice or make an application must—

(a) apply for that extension of time when serving that notice or making that application; and

(b) give the reasons for the application for an extension of time.

R-426 Renewing an application refused by a judge or the Registrar

65.5 (1) This rule applies where a party with the right to do so wants to renew—
(a) to a judge of the Court of Appeal an application refused by the Registrar; or
(b) to the Court of Appeal an application refused by a judge of that court.
(2) That party must—
(a) renew the application in the form set out in the Practice Direction, signed by or on behalf of the applicant;
(b) serve the renewed application on the Registrar not more than 14 days after—
(i) the refusal of the application that the applicant wants to renew; or
(ii) the Registrar serves that refusal on the applicant, if the applicant was not present in person or by live link when the original application was refused.

R-427 Hearings

65.6 (1) The general rule is that the Court of Appeal must hear in public—
(a) an application, including an application for permission to appeal; and
(b) an appeal or reference,
but it may order any hearing to be in private.
(2) Where a hearing is about a public interest ruling that hearing must be in private unless he court otherwise directs.
(3) Where the appellant wants to appeal against an order restricting public access to a trial, the court—
(a) may decide without a hearing—
(i) an application, including an application for permission to appeal; and
(ii) an appeal; but
(b) must announce its decision on such an appeal at a hearing in public.
(4) Where the appellant wants to appeal or to refer a case to the Supreme Court the court—
(a) may decide without a hearing an application—
(i) for permission to appeal or to refer a sentencing case, or
(ii) to refer a point of law; but
(b) must announce its decision on such an application at a hearing in public.
(5) A judge of the Court of Appeal and the Registrar may exercise any of their powers—
(a) at a hearing in public or in private; or
(b) without a hearing.

R-428 Notice of hearings and decisions

65.7 (1) The Registrar must give as much notice as reasonably practicable of every hearing to—
(a) the parties;
(b) any party's custodian;
(c) any other person whom the court requires to be notified; and
(d) the Crown Court officer, where Parts 66, 67 or 69 apply.
(2) The Registrar must serve every decision on—
(a) the parties;
(b) any other person whom the court requires to be served; and
(c) the Crown Court officer and any party's custodian, where the decision determines an appeal or application for permission to appeal.
(3) But where a hearing or decision is about a public interest ruling, the Registrar must not—
(a) give notice of that hearing to; or
(b) serve that decision on,
anyone other than the prosecutor who applied for that ruling, unless the court otherwise directs.

R-429 Duty of Crown Court officer

65.8 (1) The Crown Court officer must provide the Registrar with any document, object or information for which the Registrar asks within such period as the Registrar may require.
(2) Where someone may appeal to the Court of Appeal, the Crown Court officer must keep any document or object exhibited in the proceedings in the Crown Court, or arrange for it to be kept by some other appropriate person, until—
(a) 6 weeks after the conclusion of those proceedings; or
(b) the conclusion of any appeal proceedings that begin within that 6 weeks,
unless the court, the Registrar or the Crown Court otherwise directs.

(3) Where Part 66 applies (appeal to the Court of Appeal against ruling at preparatory hearing), the Crown Court officer must as soon as practicable serve on the appellant a transcript or note of—
(a) each order or ruling against which the appellant wants to appeal; and
(b) the decision by the Crown Court judge on any application for permission to appeal.
(4) Where Part 67 applies (appeal to the Court of Appeal against ruling adverse to prosecution), the Crown Court officer must as soon as practicable serve on the appellant a transcript or note of—
(a) each ruling against which the appellant wants to appeal;
(b) the decision by the Crown Court judge on any application for permission to appeal; and
(c) the decision by the Crown Court judge on any request to expedite the appeal.
(5) Where Part 68 applies (appeal to the Court of Appeal about conviction or sentence), the Crown Court officer must as soon as practicable serve on the Registrar—
(a) the appeal notice and any accompanying application that the appellant serves on the Crown Court officer;
(b) any Crown Court judge's certificate that the case is fit for appeal;
(c) the decision on any application at the Crown Court centre for bail pending appeal;
(d) such of the Crown Court case papers as the Registrar requires; and
(e) such transcript of the Crown Court proceedings as the Registrar requires.
(6) Where Part 69 applies (appeal to the Court of Appeal regarding reporting or public access) and an order is made restricting public access to a trial, the Crown Court officer must—
(a) immediately notify the Registrar of that order, if the appellant has given advance notice of intention to appeal; and
(b) as soon as practicable provide the applicant for that order with a transcript or note of the application.

Duty of person transcribing proceedings in the Crown Court R-430

65.9 A person who transcribes a recording of proceedings in the Crown Court under arrangements made by the Crown Court officer must provide the Registrar with any transcript for which the Registrar asks, within such period as the Registrar may require.

Duty of person keeping exhibit R-431

65.10 A person who under arrangements made by the Crown Court officer keeps a document or object exhibited in the proceedings in the Crown Court must—
(a) keep that exhibit until—
(i) 6 weeks after the conclusion of the Crown Court proceedings, or
(ii) the conclusion of any appeal proceedings that begin within that 6 weeks,
unless the court, the Registrar or the Crown Court otherwise directs; and
(b) provide the Registrar with any such document or object for which the Registrar asks within such period as the Registrar may require.

Registrar's duty to provide copy documents for appeal or reference R-432

65.11 Unless the court otherwise directs, for the purposes of an appeal or reference—
(a) the Registrar must—
(i) provide a party with a copy of any document or transcript held by the Registrar for such purposes, or
(ii) allow a party to inspect such a document or transcript,
on payment by that party of any charge fixed by the Treasury; but
(b) the Registrar must not provide a copy or allow the inspection of—
(i) a document provided only for the court and the Registrar, or
(ii) a transcript of a public interest ruling or of an application for such a ruling.

Declaration of incompatibility with a Convention right R-433

65.12 (1) This rule applies where a party—
(a) wants the court to make a declaration of incompatibility with a Convention right under section 4 of the Human Rights Act 1998; or
(b) raises an issue that the Registrar thinks may lead the court to make such a declaration.
(2) The Registrar must serve notice on—
(a) the relevant person named in the list published under section 17(1) of the Crown Proceedings Act 1947; or
(b) the Treasury Solicitor, if it is not clear who is the relevant person.

(3) That notice must include or attach details of—
(a) the legislation affected and the Convention right concerned;
(b) the parties to the appeal; and
(c) any other information or document that the Registrar thinks relevant.
(4) A person who has a right under the 1998 Act to become a party to the appeal must—
(a) serve notice on—
(i) the Registrar, and
(ii) the other parties, if that person wants to exercise that right; and
(b) in that notice—
(i) indicate the conclusion that that person invites the court to reach on the question of incompatibility, and
(ii) identify each ground for that invitation, concisely outlining the arguments in support.
(5) The court must not make a declaration of incompatibility—
(a) less than 21 days after the Registrar serves notice under paragraph (2); and
(b) without giving any person who serves a notice under paragraph (4) an opportunity to make representations at a hearing.

R-434 **Abandoning an appeal**

65.13 (1) This rule applies where an appellant wants to—
(a) abandon—
(i) an application to the court for permission to appeal, or
(ii) an appeal; or
(b) reinstate such an application or appeal after abandoning it.
(2) The appellant—
(a) may abandon such an application or appeal without the court's permission by serving a notice of abandonment on—
(i) the Registrar, and
(ii) any respondent
before any hearing of the application or appeal; but
(b) at any such hearing, may only abandon that application or appeal with the court's permission.
(3) A notice of abandonment must be in the form set out in the Practice Direction, signed by or on behalf of the appellant.
(4) On receiving a notice of abandonment the Registrar must—
(a) date it;
(b) serve a dated copy on—
(i) the appellant,
(ii) the appellant's custodian, if any,
(iii) the Crown Court officer, and
(iv) any other person on whom the appellant or the Registrar served the appeal notice; and
(c) treat the application or appeal as if it had been refused or dismissed by the Court of Appeal.
(5) An appellant who wants to reinstate an application or appeal after abandoning it must—
(a) apply in writing, with reasons; and
(b) serve the application on the Registrar.

R-435 **Abandoning a ground of appeal or opposition**

65.14 (1) This rule applies where a party wants to abandon—
(a) a ground of appeal identified in an appeal notice; or
(b) a ground of opposition identified in a respondent's notice.
(2) Such a party must give written notice to—
(a) the Registrar; and
(b) every other party,
before any hearing at which that ground will be considered by the court.

Part 66 Appeal to the Court of Appeal against Ruling at Preparatory Hearing

R-436 **When this Part applies**

66.1 (1) This Part applies where a party wants to appeal under—
(a) section 9(11) of the Criminal Justice Act 1987 or section 35(1) of the Criminal Procedure and Investigations Act 1996; or

(b) section 47(1) of the Criminal Justice Act 2003.

(2) A reference to an 'appellant' in this Part is a reference to such a party.

Service of appeal notice R-437

66.2 (1) An appellant must serve an appeal notice on—

(a) the Crown Court officer;

(b) the Registrar; and

(c) every party directly affected by the order or ruling against which the appellant wants to appeal.

(2) The appellant must serve the appeal notice not more than 5 business days after—

(a) the order or ruling against which the appellant wants to appeal; or

(b) the Crown Court judge gives or refuses permission to appeal.

Form of appeal notice R-438

66.3 (1) An appeal notice must be in the form set out in the Practice Direction.

(2) The appeal notice must—

(a) specify each order or ruling against which the appellant wants to appeal;

(b) identify each ground of appeal on which the appellant relies, numbering them consecutively (if there is more than one) and concisely outlining each argument in support;

(c) summarise the relevant facts;

(d) identify any relevant authorities;

(e) include or attach any application for the following, with reasons—

(i) permission to appeal, if the appellant needs the court's permission,

(ii) an extension of time within which to serve the appeal notice,

(iii) a direction to attend in person a hearing that the appellant could attend by live link, if the appellant is in custody;

(f) include a list of those on whom the appellant has served the appeal notice; and

(g) attach—

(i) a transcript or note of each order or ruling against which the appellant wants to appeal,

(ii) all relevant skeleton arguments considered by the Crown Court judge,

(iii) any written application for permission to appeal that the appellant made to the Crown Court judge,

(iv) a transcript or note of the decision by the Crown Court judge on any application for permission to appeal, and

(v) any other document or thing that the appellant thinks the court will need to decide the appeal.

Crown Court judge's permission to appeal R-439

66.4 (1) An appellant who wants the Crown Court judge to give permission to appeal must—

(a) apply orally, with reasons, immediately after the order or ruling against which the appellant wants to appeal; or

(b) apply in writing and serve the application on—

(i) the Crown Court officer, and

(ii) every party directly affected by the order or ruling not more than 2 business days after that order or ruling.

(2) A written application must include the same information (with the necessary adaptations) as an appeal notice.

Respondent's notice R-440

66.5 (1) A party on whom an appellant serves an appeal notice may serve a respondent's notice, and must do so if—

(a) that party wants to make representations to the court; or

(b) the court so directs.

(2) Such a party must serve the respondent's notice on—

(a) the appellant;

(b) the Crown Court officer;

(c) the Registrar; and

(d) any other party on whom the appellant served the appeal notice.

(3) Such a party must serve the respondent's notice not more than 5 business days after—

(a) the appellant serves the appeal notice; or

(b) a direction to do so.

(4) The respondent's notice must be in the form set out in the Practice Direction.
(5) The respondent's notice must—
(a) give the date on which the respondent was served with the appeal notice;
(b) identify each ground of opposition on which the respondent relies, numbering them consecutively (if there is more than one), concisely outlining each argument in support and identifying the ground of appeal to which each relates;
(c) summarise any relevant facts not already summarised in the appeal notice;
(d) identify any relevant authorities;
(e) include or attach any application for the following, with reasons—
(i) an extension of time within which to serve the respondent's notice,
(ii) a direction to attend in person any hearing that the respondent could attend by live link, if the respondent is in custody;
(f) identify any other document or thing that the respondent thinks the court will need to decide the appeal.

R-441 **Powers of Court of Appeal judge**

66.6 A judge of the Court of Appeal may give permission to appeal as well as exercising the powers given by other legislation (including these Rules).

R-442 **Renewing applications**

66.7 Rule 65.5 (renewing an application refused by a judge or the Registrar) applies with a time limit of 5 business days.

R-443 **Right to attend hearing**

66.8 (1) A party who is in custody has a right to attend a hearing in public.
(2) The court or the Registrar may direct that such a party is to attend a hearing by live link.

Part 67 Appeal to the Court of Appeal against Ruling Adverse to the Prosecution

R-444 **When this Part applies**

67.1 (1) This Part applies where a prosecutor wants to appeal under section 58(2) of the Criminal Justice Act 2003.
(2) A reference to an 'appellant' in this Part is a reference to such a prosecutor.

R-445 **Decision to appeal**

67.2 (1) An appellant must tell the Crown Court judge of any decision to appeal—
(a) immediately after the ruling against which the appellant wants to appeal; or
(b) on the expiry of the time to decide whether to appeal allowed under paragraph (2).
(2) If an appellant wants time to decide whether to appeal—
(a) the appellant must ask the Crown Court judge immediately after the ruling; and
(b) the general rule is that the judge must not require the appellant to decide there and then but instead must allow until the next business day.

R-446 **Service of appeal notice**

67.3 (1) An appellant must serve an appeal notice on—
(a) the Crown Court officer;
(b) the Registrar; and
(c) every defendant directly affected by the ruling against which the appellant wants to appeal.
(2) The appellant must serve the appeal notice not later than—
(a) the next business day after telling the Crown Court judge of the decision to appeal, if the judge expedites the appeal; or
(b) 5 business days after telling the Crown Court judge of that decision, if the judge does not expedite the appeal.

R-447 **Form of appeal notice**

67.4 (1) An appeal notice must be in the form set out in the Practice Direction.
(2) The appeal notice must—
(a) specify each ruling against which the appellant wants to appeal;

(b) identify each ground of appeal on which the appellant relies, numbering them consecutively (if there is more than one) and concisely outlining each argument in support;
(c) summarise the relevant facts;
(d) identify any relevant authorities;
(e) include or attach any application for the following, with reasons—
 (i) permission to appeal, if the appellant needs the court's permission,
 (ii) an extension of time within which to serve the appeal notice,
 (iii) expedition of the appeal, or revocation of a direction expediting the appeal;
(f) include a list of those on whom the appellant has served the appeal notice;
(g) attach—
 (i) a transcript or note of each ruling against which the appellant wants to appeal,
 (ii) all relevant skeleton arguments considered by the Crown Court judge,
 (iii) any written application for permission to appeal that the appellant made to the Crown Court judge,
 (iv) a transcript or note of the decision by the Crown Court judge on any application for permission to appeal,
 (v) a transcript or note of the decision by the Crown Court judge on any request to expedite the appeal, and
 (vi) any other document or thing that the appellant thinks the court will need to decide the appeal; and
(h) attach a form of respondent's notice for any defendant served with the appeal notice to complete if that defendant wants to do so.

Crown Court judge's permission to appeal R-448

67.5 (1) An appellant who wants the Crown Court judge to give permission to appeal must—
(a) apply orally, with reasons, immediately after the ruling against which the appellant wants to appeal; or
(b) apply in writing and serve the application on—
 (i) the Crown Court officer, and
 (ii) every defendant directly affected by the ruling

on the expiry of the time allowed under rule 67.2 to decide whether to appeal.

(2) A written application must include the same information (with the necessary adaptations) as an appeal notice.
(3) The Crown Court judge must allow every defendant directly affected by the ruling an opportunity to make representations.
(4) The general rule is that the Crown Court judge must decide whether or not to give permission to appeal on the day that the application for permission is made.

Expediting an appeal R-449

67.6 (1) An appellant who wants the Crown Court judge to expedite an appeal must ask, giving reasons, on telling the judge of the decision to appeal.
(2) The Crown Court judge must allow every defendant directly affected by the ruling an opportunity to make representations.
(3) The Crown Court judge may revoke a direction expediting the appeal unless the appellant has served the appeal notice.

Respondent's notice R-450

67.7 (1) A defendant on whom an appellant serves an appeal notice may serve a respondent's notice, and must do so if—
(a) the defendant wants to make representations to the court; or
(b) the court so directs.
(2) Such a defendant must serve the respondent's notice on—
(a) the appellant;
(b) the Crown Court officer;
(c) the Registrar; and
(d) any other defendant on whom the appellant served the appeal notice.
(3) Such a defendant must serve the respondent's notice—
(a) not later than the next business day after—
 (i) the appellant serves the appeal notice, or
 (ii) a direction to do so if the Crown Court judge expedites the appeal; or

(b) not more than 5 business days after—
(i) the appellant serves the appeal notice, or
(ii) a direction to do so if the Crown Court judge does not expedite the appeal.
(4) The respondent's notice must be in the form set out in the Practice Direction.
(5) The respondent's notice must—
(a) give the date on which the respondent was served with the appeal notice;
(b) identify each ground of opposition on which the respondent relies, numbering them consecutively (if there is more than one), concisely outlining each argument in support and identifying the ground of appeal to which each relates;
(c) summarise any relevant facts not already summarised in the appeal notice;
(d) identify any relevant authorities;
(e) include or attach any application for the following, with reasons—
(i) an extension of time within which to serve the respondent's notice,
(ii) a direction to attend in person any hearing that the respondent could attend by live link, if the respondent is in custody;
(f) identify any other document or thing that the respondent thinks the court will need to decide the appeal.

R-451 Public interest ruling

67.8 (1) This rule applies where the appellant wants to appeal against a public interest ruling.
(2) The appellant must not serve on any defendant directly affected by the ruling—
(a) any written application to the Crown Court judge for permission to appeal; or
(b) an appeal notice
if the appellant thinks that to do so in effect would reveal something that the appellant thinks ought not be disclosed.
(3) The appellant must not include in an appeal notice—
(a) the material that was the subject of the ruling; or
(b) any indication of what sort of material it is if the appellant thinks that to do so in effect would reveal something that the appellant thinks ought not be disclosed.
(4) The appellant must serve on the Registrar with the appeal notice an annex—
(a) marked to show that its contents are only for the court and the Registrar;
(b) containing whatever the appellant has omitted from the appeal notice, with reasons; and
(c) if relevant, explaining why the appellant has not served the appeal notice.
(5) Rules 67.5(3) and 67.6(2) do not apply.

R-452 Powers of Court of Appeal judge

67.9 A judge of the Court of Appeal may—
(a) give permission to appeal;
(b) revoke a Crown Court judge's direction expediting an appeal; and
(c) where an appellant abandons an appeal, order a defendant's acquittal, his release from custody and the payment of his costs,
as well as exercising the powers given by other legislation (including these Rules).

R-453 Renewing applications

67.10 Rule 65.5 (renewing an application refused by a judge or the Registrar) applies with a time limit of 5 business days.

R-454 Right to attend hearing

67.11 (1) A respondent who is in custody has a right to attend a hearing in public.
(2) The court or the Registrar may direct that such a respondent is to attend a hearing by live link.

Part 68 Appeal to the Court of Appeal about Conviction or Sentence

R-455 When this Part applies

68.1 (1) This Part applies where—
(a) a defendant wants to appeal under—
(i) Part 1 of the Criminal Appeal Act 1968,
(ii) section 274(3) of the Criminal Justice Act 2003,

(iii) paragraph 14 of Schedule 22 to the Criminal Justice Act 2003, or
(iv) section 42 of the Counter-Terrorism Act 2008;
(b) the Criminal Cases Review Commission refers a case to the Court of Appeal under section 9 of the Criminal Appeal Act 1995;
(c) a prosecutor wants to appeal to the Court of Appeal under section 14A(5A) of the Football Spectators Act 1989;
(d) a party wants to appeal under section 74(8) of the Serious Organised Crime and Police Act 2005;
(e) a person found to be in contempt of court wants to appeal under section 13 of the Administration of Justice Act 1960 and section 18A of the Criminal Appeal Act 1968; or
(f) a person wants to appeal to the Court of Appeal under—
(i) section 24 of the Serious Crime Act 2007, or
(ii) regulation 3C or 3H of the Costs in Criminal Cases (General) Regulations 1986.
(2) A reference to an 'appellant' in this Part is a reference to such a party or person.

Service of appeal notice **R-456**

68.2 (1) The general rule is that an appellant must serve an appeal notice—
(a) on the Crown Court officer at the Crown Court centre where there occurred—
(i) the conviction, verdict, or finding,
(ii) the sentence, or
(iii) the order, or the failure to make an order
about which the appellant wants to appeal; and
(b) not more than—
(i) 28 days after that occurred, or
(ii) 21 days after the order, in a case in which the appellant appeals against a wasted or third party costs order.
(2) But an appellant must serve an appeal notice—
(a) on the Registrar instead where—
(i) the appeal is against a minimum term review decision under section 274(3) of, or paragraph 14 of Schedule 22 to, the Criminal Justice Act 2003, or
(ii) the Criminal Cases Review Commission refers the case to the court; and
(b) not more than 28 days after—
(i) the minimum term review decision about which the appellant wants to appeal, or
(ii) the Registrar serves notice that the Commission has referred a conviction.

Form of appeal notice **R-457**

68.3 (1) An appeal notice must be in the form set out in the Practice Direction.
(2) The appeal notice must—
(a) specify—
(i) the conviction, verdict, or finding,
(ii) the sentence, or
(iii) the order, or the failure to make an order about which the appellant wants to appeal;
(b) identify each ground of appeal on which the appellant relies, numbering them consecutively (if there is more than one) and concisely outlining each argument in support;
(c) identify the transcript that the appellant thinks the court will need, if the appellant wants to appeal against a conviction;
(d) identify the relevant sentencing powers of the Crown Court, if sentence is in issue;
(e) where the Criminal Cases Review Commission refers a case to the court, explain how each ground of appeal relates (if it does) to the reasons for the reference;
(f) summarise the relevant facts;
(g) identify any relevant authorities;
(h) include or attach any application for the following, with reasons—
(i) permission to appeal, if the appellant needs the court's permission,
(ii) an extension of time within which to serve the appeal notice,
(iii) bail pending appeal,
(iv) a direction to attend in person a hearing that the appellant could attend by live link, if the appellant is in custody,
(v) the introduction of evidence, including hearsay evidence and evidence of bad character,

(vi) an order requiring a witness to attend court,
(vii) a direction for special measures for a witness,
(viii) a direction for special measures for the giving of evidence by the appellant;
(ix) identify any other document or thing that the appellant thinks the court will need to decide the appeal.

R-458 Crown Court judge's certificate that case is fit for appeal

68.4 (1) An appellant who wants the Crown Court judge to certify that a case is fit for appeal must—
(a) apply orally, with reasons, immediately after there occurs—
(i) the conviction, verdict, or finding,
(ii) the sentence, or
(iii) the order, or the failure to make an order about which the appellant wants to appeal; or
(b) apply in writing and serve the application on the Crown Court officer not more than 14 days after that occurred.
(2) A written application must include the same information (with the necessary adaptations) as an appeal notice.

R-459 Reference by Criminal Cases Review Commission

68.5 (1) The Registrar must serve on the appellant a reference by the Criminal Cases Review Commission.
(2) The court must treat that reference as the appeal notice if the appellant does not serve such a notice under rule 68.2.

R-460 Respondent's notice

68.6 (1) The Registrar—
(a) may serve an appeal notice on any party directly affected by the appeal; and
(b) must do so if the Criminal Cases Review Commission refers a conviction, verdict, finding or sentence to the court.
(2) Such a party may serve a respondent's notice, and must do so if—
(a) that party wants to make representations to the court; or
(b) the court or the Registrar so directs.
(3) Such a party must serve the respondent's notice on—
(a) the appellant;
(b) the Registrar; and
(c) any other party on whom the Registrar served the appeal notice.
(4) Such a party must serve the respondent's notice—
(a) not more than 14 days after the Registrar serves—
(i) the appeal notice, or
(ii) a direction to do so; or
(b) not more than 28 days after the Registrar serves notice that the Commission has referred a conviction.
(5) The respondent's notice must be in the form set out in the Practice Direction.
(6) The respondent's notice must—
(a) give the date on which the respondent was served with the appeal notice;
(b) identify each ground of opposition on which the respondent relies, numbering them consecutively (if there is more than one), concisely outlining each argument in support and identifying the ground of appeal to which each relates;
(c) identify the relevant sentencing powers of the Crown Court, if sentence is in issue;
(d) summarise any relevant facts not already summarised in the appeal notice;
(e) identify any relevant authorities;
(f) include or attach any application for the following, with reasons—
(i) an extension of time within which to serve the respondent's notice,
(ii) bail pending appeal,
(iii) a direction to attend in person a hearing that the respondent could attend by live link, if the respondent is in custody,
(iv) the introduction of evidence, including hearsay evidence and evidence of bad character,
(v) an order requiring a witness to attend court,
(vi) a direction for special measures for a witness; and
(g) identify any other document or thing that the respondent thinks the court will need to decide the appeal.

Adaptation of rules about introducing evidence R-461

68.7 (1) The following Parts apply with such adaptations as the court or the Registrar may direct—
(a) Part 29 (measures to assist a witness or defendant to give evidence);
(b) Part 34 (hearsay evidence);
(c) Part 35 (evidence of bad character); and
(d) Part 36 (evidence of a complainant's previous sexual behaviour).
(2) But the general rule is that—
(a) a respondent who opposes an appellant's application to which one of those Parts applies must do so in the respondent's notice, with reasons;
(b) an appellant who opposes a respondent's application to which one of those Parts applies must serve notice, with reasons, on—
(i) the Registrar, and
(ii) the respondent not more than 14 days after service of the respondent's notice; and
(c) the court or the Registrar may give directions with or without a hearing.

Application for bail pending appeal or retrial R-462

68.8 (1) This rule applies where a party wants to make an application to the court about bail pending appeal or retrial.
(2) That party must serve an application in the form set out in the Practice Direction on—
(a) the Registrar, unless the application is with the appeal notice; and
(b) the other party.
(3) The court must not decide such an application without giving the other party an opportunity to make representations, including representations about any condition or surety proposed by the applicant.

Conditions of bail pending appeal or retrial R-463

68.9 (1) This rule applies where the court grants a party bail pending appeal or retrial subject to any condition that must be met before that party is released.
(2) The court may direct how such a condition must be met.
(3) The Registrar must serve a certificate in the form set out in the Practice Direction recording any such condition and direction on—
(a) that party;
(b) that party's custodian; and
(c) any other person directly affected by any such direction.
(4) A person directly affected by any such direction need not comply with it until the Registrar serves that person with that certificate.
(5) Unless the court otherwise directs, if any such condition or direction requires someone to enter into a recognizance it must be—
(a) in the form set out in the Practice Direction and signed before—
(i) the Registrar,
(ii) the custodian, or
(iii) someone acting with the authority of the Registrar or custodian;
(b) copied immediately to the person who enters into it; and
(c) served immediately by the Registrar on the appellant's custodian or vice versa, as appropriate.
(6) Unless the court otherwise directs, if any such condition or direction requires someone to make a payment, surrender a document or take some other step—
(a) that payment, document or step must be made, surrendered or taken to or before—
(i) the Registrar,
(ii) the custodian, or
(iii) someone acting with the authority of the Registrar or custodian;
(b) the Registrar or the custodian, as appropriate, must serve immediately on the other a statement that the payment, document or step has been made, surrendered or taken, as appropriate.
(7) The custodian must release the appellant where it appears that any condition ordered by the court has been met.
(8) For the purposes of section 5 of the Bail Act 1976 (record of decision about bail), the Registrar must keep a copy of—
(a) any certificate served under paragraph (3);
(b) a notice of hearing given under rule 65.7(1); and
(c) a notice of the court's decision served under rule 65.7(2).

(9) Where the court grants bail pending retrial the Registrar must serve on the Crown Court officer copies of the documents kept under paragraph (8).

R-464 **Forfeiture of a recognizance given as a condition of bail**

68.10 (1) This rule applies where—

(a) the court grants a party bail pending appeal or retrial; and

(b) the bail is subject to a condition that that party provides a surety to guarantee that he will surrender to custody as required; but

(c) that party does not surrender to custody as required.

(2) The Registrar must serve notice on—

(a) the surety; and

(b) the prosecutor of the hearing at which the court may order the forfeiture of the recognizance given by that surety.

(3) The court must not forfeit a surety's recognizance—

(a) less than 7 days after the Registrar serves notice under paragraph (2); and

(b) without giving the surety an opportunity to make representations at a hearing.

R-465 **Right to attend hearing**

68.11 A party who is in custody has a right to attend a hearing in public unless—

(a) it is a hearing preliminary or incidental to an appeal, including the hearing of an application for permission to appeal; or

(b) that party is in custody in consequence of—

(i) a verdict of not guilty by reason of insanity, or

(ii) a finding of disability.

R-466 **Power to vary determination of appeal against sentence**

68.12 (1) This rule applies where the court decides an appeal affecting sentence in a party's absence.

(2) The court may vary such a decision if it did not take account of something relevant because that party was absent.

(3) A party who wants the court to vary such a decision must—

(a) apply in writing, with reasons;

(b) serve the application on the Registrar not more than 7 days after—

(i) the decision, if that party was represented at the appeal hearing, or

(ii) the Registrar serves the decision, if that party was not represented at that hearing.

R-467 **Directions about re-admission to hospital on dismissal of appeal**

68.13 (1) This rule applies where—

(a) an appellant subject to—

(i) an order under section 37(1) of the Mental Health Act 1983 (detention in hospital on conviction), or

(ii) an order under section 5(2) of the Criminal Procedure (Insanity) Act 1964 (detention in hospital on finding of insanity or disability)

has been released on bail pending appeal; and

(b) the court—

(i) refuses permission to appeal,

(ii) dismisses the appeal, or

(iii) affirms the order under appeal.

(2) The court must give appropriate directions for the appellant's—

(a) re-admission to hospital; and

(b) if necessary, temporary detention pending re-admission.

R-468 **Renewal or setting aside of order for retrial**

68.14 (1) This rule applies where—

(a) a prosecutor wants a defendant to be arraigned more than 2 months after the court ordered a retrial under section 7 of the Criminal Appeal Act 1968; or

(b) a defendant wants such an order set aside after 2 months have passed since it was made.

(2) That party must apply in writing, with reasons, and serve the application on—

(a) the Registrar;

(b) the other party.

Part 69 Appeal to the Court of Appeal Regarding Reporting or Public Access Restriction

When this Part applies R-469

69.1 (1) This Part applies where a person directly affected by an order to which section 159(1) of the Criminal Justice Act 1988 applies wants to appeal against that order.

(2) A reference to an 'appellant' in this Part is a reference to such a party.

Service of appeal notice R-470

69.2 (1) An appellant must serve an appeal notice on—

(a) the Crown Court officer;

(b) the Registrar;

(c) the parties; and

(d) any other person directly affected by the order against which the appellant wants to appeal.

(2) The appellant must serve the appeal notice not later than—

(a) the next business day after an order restricting public access to the trial;

(b) 10 business days after an order restricting reporting of the trial.

Form of appeal notice R-471

69.3 (1) An appeal notice must be in the form set out in the Practice Direction.

(2) The appeal notice must—

(a) specify the order against which the appellant wants to appeal;

(b) identify each ground of appeal on which the appellant relies, numbering them consecutively (if there is more than one) and concisely outlining each argument in support;

(c) summarise the relevant facts;

(d) identify any relevant authorities;

(e) include or attach, with reasons—

(i) an application for permission to appeal,

(ii) any application for an extension of time within which to serve the appeal notice,

(iii) any application for a direction to attend in person a hearing that the appellant could attend by live link, if the appellant is in custody,

(iv) any application for permission to introduce evidence, and

(v) a list of those on whom the appellant has served the appeal notice; and

(f) attach any document or thing that the appellant thinks the court will need to decide the appeal.

Advance notice of appeal against order restricting public access R-472

69.4 (1) This rule applies where the appellant wants to appeal against an order restricting public access to a trial.

(2) The appellant may serve advance written notice of intention to appeal against any such order that may be made.

(3) The appellant must serve any such advance notice—

(a) on—

(i) the Crown Court officer,

(ii) the Registrar,

(iii) the parties, and

(iv) any other person who will be directly affected by the order against which the appellant intends to appeal, if it is made; and

(b) not more than 5 business days after the Crown Court officer displays notice of the application for the order.

(4) The advance notice must include the same information (with the necessary adaptations) as an appeal notice.

(5) The court must treat that advance notice as the appeal notice if the order is made.

Duty of applicant for order restricting public access R-473

69.5 (1) This rule applies where the appellant wants to appeal against an order restricting public access to a trial.

(2) The party who applied for the order must serve on the Registrar—

(a) a transcript or note of the application for the order; and

(b) any other document or thing that that party thinks the court will need to decide the appeal.

(3) That party must serve that transcript or note and any such other document or thing as soon as practicable after—
 (a) the appellant serves the appeal notice; or
 (b) the order, where the appellant served advance notice of intention to appeal.

R-474 Respondent's notice on appeal against reporting restriction

69.6 (1) This rule applies where the appellant wants to appeal against an order restricting the reporting of a trial.
(2) A person on whom an appellant serves an appeal notice may serve a respondent's notice, and must do so if—
 (a) that person wants to make representations to the court; or
 (b) the court so directs.
(3) Such a person must serve the respondent's notice on—
 (a) the appellant;
 (b) the Crown Court officer;
 (c) the Registrar;
 (d) the parties; and
 (e) any other person on whom the appellant served the appeal notice.
(4) Such a person must serve the respondent's notice not more than 3 business days after—
 (a) the appellant serves the appeal notice; or
 (b) a direction to do so.
(5) The respondent's notice must be in the form set out in the Practice Direction.
(6) The respondent's notice must—
 (a) give the date on which the respondent was served with the appeal notice;
 (b) identify each ground of opposition on which the respondent relies, numbering them consecutively (if there is more than one), concisely outlining each argument in support and identifying the ground of appeal to which each relates;
 (c) summarise any relevant facts not already summarised in the appeal notice;
 (d) identify any relevant authorities;
 (e) include or attach any application for the following, with reasons—
  (i) an extension of time within which to serve the respondent's notice,
  (ii) a direction to attend in person any hearing that the respondent could attend by live link, if the respondent is in custody,
  (iii) permission to introduce evidence; and
 (f) identify any other document or thing that the respondent thinks the court will need to decide the appeal.

R-475 Renewing applications

69.7 Rule 65.5 (renewing an application refused by a judge or the Registrar) applies with a time limit of 5 business days.

R-476 Right to introduce evidence

69.8 No person may introduce evidence without the court's permission.

R-477 Right to attend hearing

69.9 (1) A party who is in custody has a right to attend a hearing in public of an appeal against an order restricting the reporting of a trial.
(2) The court or the Registrar may direct that such a party is to attend a hearing by live link.

Part 70 Reference to the Court of Appeal of Point of Law or Unduly Lenient Sentencing

R-478 When this Part applies

70.1 This Part applies where the Attorney General wants to—
 (a) refer a point of law to the Court of Appeal under section 36 of the Criminal Justice Act 1972; or
 (b) refer a sentencing case to the Court of Appeal under section 36 of the Criminal Justice Act 1988.

Service of notice of reference and application for permission R-479

70.2 (1) The Attorney General must—
(a) serve on the Registrar—
(i) any notice of reference, and
(ii) any application for permission to refer a sentencing case; and
(b) with a notice of reference of a point of law, give the Registrar details of—
(i) the defendant affected,
(ii) the date and place of the relevant Crown Court decision, and
(iii) the relevant verdict and sentencing.
(2) The Attorney General must serve an application for permission to refer a sentencing case not more than 28 days after the last of the sentences in that case.

Form of notice of reference and application for permission R-480

70.3 (1) A notice of reference and an application for permission to refer a sentencing case must be in the appropriate form set out in the Practice Direction, giving the year and number.
(2) A notice of reference of a point of law must—
(a) specify the point of law in issue and indicate the opinion that the Attorney General invites the court to give;
(b) identify each ground for that invitation, numbering them consecutively (if there is more than one) and concisely outlining each argument in support;
(c) exclude any reference to the defendant's name and any other reference that may identify the defendant;
(d) summarise the relevant facts; and
(e) identify any relevant authorities.
(3) An application for permission to refer a sentencing case must—
(a) give details of—
(i) the defendant affected,
(ii) the date and place of the relevant Crown Court decision, and
(iii) the relevant verdict and sentencing;
(b) explain why that sentencing appears to the Attorney General unduly lenient, concisely outlining each argument in support; and
(c) include the application for permission to refer the case to the court.
(4) A notice of reference of a sentencing case must—
(a) include the same details and explanation as the application for permission to refer the case;
(b) summarise the relevant facts; and
(c) identify any relevant authorities.
(5) Where the court gives the Attorney General permission to refer a sentencing case, it may treat the application for permission as the notice of reference.

Registrar's notice to defendant R-481

70.4 (1) The Registrar must serve on the defendant—
(a) a notice of reference;
(b) an application for permission to refer a sentencing case.
(2) Where the Attorney General refers a point of law, the Registrar must give the defendant notice that—
(a) the outcome of the reference will not make any difference to the outcome of the trial; and
(b) the defendant may serve a respondent's notice.
(3) Where the Attorney General applies for permission to refer a sentencing case, the Registrar must give the defendant notice that—
(a) the outcome of the reference may make a difference to that sentencing, and in particular may result in a more severe sentence; and
(b) the defendant may serve a respondent's notice.

Respondent's notice R-482

70.5 (1) A defendant on whom the Registrar serves a reference or an application for permission to refer a sentencing case may serve a respondent's notice, and must do so if—
(a) the defendant wants to make representations to the court; or
(b) the court so directs.

(2) Such a defendant must serve the respondent's notice on—
(a) the Attorney General; and
(b) the Registrar.
(3) Such a defendant must serve the respondent's notice—
(a) where the Attorney General refers a point of law, not more than 28 days after—
(i) the Registrar serves the reference, or
(ii) a direction to do so;
(b) where the Attorney General applies for permission to refer a sentencing case, not more than 14 days after—
(i) the Registrar serves the application, or
(ii) a direction to do so.
(4) Where the Attorney General refers a point of law, the respondent's notice must—
(a) identify each ground of opposition on which the respondent relies, numbering them consecutively (if there is more than one), concisely outlining each argument in support and identifying the Attorney General's ground or reason to which each relates;
(b) summarise any relevant facts not already summarised in the reference;
(c) identify any relevant authorities; and
(d) include or attach any application for the following, with reasons—
(i) an extension of time within which to serve the respondent's notice,
(ii) permission to attend a hearing that the respondent does not have a right to attend,
(iii) a direction to attend in person a hearing that the respondent could attend by live link, if the respondent is in custody.
(5) Where the Attorney General applies for permission to refer a sentencing case, the respondent's notice must—
(a) say if the respondent wants to make representations at the hearing of the application or reference; and
(b) include or attach any application for the following, with reasons—
(i) an extension of time within which to serve the respondent's notice,
(ii) permission to attend a hearing that the respondent does not have a right to attend,
(iii) a direction to attend in person a hearing that the respondent could attend by live link, if the respondent is in custody.

R-483 Variation or withdrawal of notice of reference or application for permission

70.6 (1) This rule applies where the Attorney General wants to vary or withdraw—
(a) a notice of reference; or
(b) an application for permission to refer a sentencing case.
(2) The Attorney General—
(a) may vary or withdraw the notice or application without the court's permission by serving notice on—
(i) the Registrar, and
(ii) the defendant
before any hearing of the reference or application; but
(b) at any such hearing, may only vary or withdraw that notice or application with the court's permission.

R-484 Right to attend hearing

70.7 (1) A respondent who is in custody has a right to attend a hearing in public unless it is a hearing preliminary or incidental to a reference, including the hearing of an application for permission to refer a sentencing case.
(2) The court or the Registrar may direct that such a respondent is to attend a hearing by live link.

R-485 Anonymity of defendant on reference of point of law

70.8 Where the Attorney General refers a point of law, the court must not allow anyone to identify the defendant during the proceedings unless the defendant gives permission.

Part 71 Appeal to the Court of Appeal under the Proceeds of Crime Act 2002: General Rules

Extension of time R-486

71.1 (1) An application to extend the time limit for giving notice of application for leave to appeal under Part 2 of the Proceeds of Crime Act 2002 must—
(a) be included in the notice of appeal; and
(b) state the grounds for the application.
(2) The parties may not agree to extend any date or time limit set by this Part, Part 72 or Part 73, or by the Proceeds of Crime Act 2002 (Appeals under Part 2) Order 2003.

Other applications R-487

71.2 Rules 68.3(2)(h) (form of appeal notice) shall apply in relation to an application—
(a) by a party to an appeal under Part 2 of the Proceeds of Crime Act 2002 that, under article 7 of the Proceeds of Crime Act 2002 (Appeals under Part 2) Order 2003, a witness be ordered to attend or that the evidence of a witness be received by the Court of Appeal; or
(b) by the defendant to be given leave by the court to be present at proceedings for which leave is required under article 6 of the 2003 Order,
as they apply in relation to applications under Part I of the Criminal Appeal Act 1968 and the form in which rules 68.15 and 68.26 require notice to be given may be modified as necessary.

Examination of witness by court R-488

71.3 Rule 65.7 (notice of hearings and decisions) shall apply in relation to an order of the court under article 7 of the Proceeds of Crime Act 2002 (Appeals under Part 2) Order 2003 to require a person to attend for examination as it applies in relation to such an order of the court under Part I of the Criminal Appeal Act 1968.

Supply of documentary and other exhibits R-489

71.4 Rule 65.11 (supply of documentary and other exhibits) shall apply in relation to an appellant or respondent under Part 2 of the Proceeds of Crime Act 2002 as it applies in relation to an appellant and respondent under Part I of the Criminal Appeal Act 1968.

Registrar's power to require information from court of trial R-490

71.5 The Registrar may require the Crown Court to provide the Court of Appeal with any assistance or information which they may require for the purposes of exercising their jurisdiction under Part 2 of the Proceeds of Crime Act 2002, the Proceeds of Crime Act 2002 (Appeals under Part 2) Order 2003, this Part or Parts 72 and 73.

Hearing by single judge R-491

71.6 Rule 65.6(5) (hearings) applies in relation to a judge exercising any of the powers referred to in article 8 of the Proceeds of Crime Act 2002 (Appeals under Part 2) Order 2003 or the powers in rules 72.2(3) and (4) (respondent's notice), 73.2(2) (notice of appeal) and 73.3(6) (respondent's notice), as it applies in relation to a judge exercising the powers referred to in section 31(2) of the Criminal Appeal Act 1968.

Determination by full court R-492

71.7 Rule 65.5 (renewing an application refused by a single judge or the registrar) shall apply where a single judge has refused an application by a party to exercise in his favour any of the powers listed in article 8 of the Proceeds of Crime Act 2002 (Appeals under Part 2) Order 2003 or the power in rule 72.2(3) or (4) as it applies where the judge has refused to exercise the powers referred to in section 31(2) of the Criminal Appeal Act 1968.

Notice of determination R-493

71.8 (1) This rule applies where a single judge or the Court of Appeal has determined an application or appeal under the Proceeds of Crime Act 2002 (Appeals under Part 2) Order 2003 or under Part 2 of the Proceeds of Crime Act 2002.
(2) The Registrar must, as soon as practicable, serve notice of the determination on all of the parties to the proceedings.

(3) Where a single judge or the Court of Appeal has disposed of an application for leave to appeal or an appeal under section 31 of the 2002 Act, the registrar must also, as soon as practicable, serve the order on a court officer of the court of trial and any magistrates' court responsible for enforcing any confiscation order which the Crown Court has made.

R-494 **Record of proceedings and transcripts**

71.9 Rule 65.8(2)(a) and (b) (duty of Crown Court officer—arranging recording of proceedings in Crown Court and arranging transcription) and rule 65.9 (duty of person transcribing proceedings in the Crown Court) apply in relation to proceedings in respect of which an appeal lies to the Court of Appeal under Part 2 of the Proceeds of Crime Act 2002 as they apply in relation to proceedings in respect of which an appeal lies to the Court of Appeal under Part I of the Criminal Appeal Act 1968.

R-495 **Appeal to Supreme Court**

71.10 (1) An application to the Court of Appeal for leave to appeal to the Supreme Court under Part 2 of the Proceeds of Crime Act 2002 must be made—

(a) orally after the decision of the Court of Appeal from which an appeal lies to the Supreme Court; or

(b) in the form set out in the Practice Direction, in accordance with article 12 of the Proceeds of Crime Act 2002 (Appeals under Part 2) Order 2003 and served on the Registrar.

(2) The application may be abandoned at any time before it is heard by the Court of Appeal by serving notice in writing on the Registrar.

(3) Rule 65.6(5) (hearings) applies in relation to a single judge exercising any of the powers referred to in article 15 of the 2003 Order, as it applies in relation to a single judge exercising the powers referred to in section 31(2) of the Criminal Appeal Act 1968.

(4) Rules 65.5 (renewing an application refused by a judge or the registrar) applies where a single judge has refused an application by a party to exercise in his favour any of the powers listed in article 15 of the 2003 Order as they apply where the judge has refused to exercise the powers referred to in section 31(2) of the 1968 Act.

(5) The form in which rule 65.5(2) requires an application to be made may be modified as necessary.

Part 72 Appeal to the Court of Appeal under Proceeds of Crime Act 2002: Prosecutor's Appeal Regarding Confiscation

R-496 **Notice of appeal**

72.1 (1) Where an appellant wishes to apply to the Court of Appeal for leave to appeal under section 31 of the Proceeds of Crime Act 2002, he must serve a notice of appeal in the form set out in the Practice Direction on—

(a) the Crown Court officer; and

(b) the defendant.

(2) When the notice of the appeal is served on the defendant, it must be accompanied by a respondent's notice in the form set out in the Practice Direction for the defendant to complete and a notice which—

(a) informs the defendant that the result of an appeal could be that the Court of Appeal would increase a confiscation order already imposed on him, make a confiscation order itself or direct the Crown Court to hold another confiscation hearing;

(b) informs the defendant of any right he has under article 6 of the Proceeds of Crime Act 2002 (Appeals under Part 2) Order 2003 to be present at the hearing of the appeal, although he may be in custody;

(c) invites the defendant to serve notice on the registrar if he wishes—

(i) to apply to the Court of Appeal for leave to be present at proceedings for which leave is required under article 6 of the 2003 Order, or

(ii) to present any argument to the Court of Appeal on the hearing of the application or, if leave is given, the appeal, and whether he wishes to present it in person or by means of a legal representative;

(d) draws to the defendant's attention the effect of rule 71.4 (supply of documentary and other exhibits); and

(e) advises the defendant to consult a solicitor as soon as possible.

(3) The appellant must provide a Crown Court officer with a certificate of service stating that he has served the notice of appeal on the defendant in accordance with paragraph (1) or explaining why he has been unable to effect service.

Respondent's notice R-497

72.2 (1) This rule applies where a defendant is served with a notice of appeal under rule 72.1.

(2) If the defendant wishes to oppose the application for leave to appeal, he must, not later than 14 days after the date on which he received the notice of appeal, serve on the Registrar and on the appellant a notice in the form set out in the Practice Direction—

(a) stating the date on which he received the notice of appeal;

(b) summarising his response to the arguments of the appellant; and

(c) specifying the authorities which he intends to cite.

(3) The time for giving notice under this rule may be extended by the Registrar, a single judge or by the Court of Appeal.

(4) Where the Registrar refuses an application under paragraph (3) for the extension of time, the defendant shall be entitled to have his application determined by a single judge.

(5) Where a single judge refuses an application under paragraph (3) or (4) for the extension of time, the defendant shall be entitled to have his application determined by the Court of Appeal.

Amendment and abandonment of appeal R-498

72.3 (1) The appellant may amend a notice of appeal served under rule 72.1 or abandon an appeal under section 31 of the Proceeds of Crime Act 2002—

(a) without the permission of the Court at any time before the Court of Appeal have begun hearing the appeal; and

(b) with the permission of the Court after the Court of Appeal have begun hearing the appeal, by serving notice in writing on the Registrar.

(2) Where the appellant serves a notice abandoning an appeal under paragraph (1), he must send a copy of it to—

(a) the defendant;

(b) a court officer of the court of trial; and

(c) the magistrates' court responsible for enforcing any confiscation order which the Crown Court has made.

(3) Where the appellant serves a notice amending a notice of appeal under paragraph (1), he must send a copy of it to the defendant.

(4) Where an appeal is abandoned under paragraph (1), the application for leave to appeal or appeal shall be treated, for the purposes of section 85 of the 2002 Act (conclusion of proceedings), as having been refused or dismissed by the Court of Appeal.

Part 73 Appeal to the Court of Appeal under POCA 2002: Restraint or Receivership Orders

Leave to appeal R-499

73.1 (1) Leave to appeal to the Court of Appeal under section 43 or section 65 of the Proceeds of Crime Act 2002 will only be given where—

(a) the Court of Appeal considers that the appeal would have a real prospect of success; or

(b) there is some other compelling reason why the appeal should be heard.

(2) An order giving leave may limit the issues to be heard and be made subject to conditions.

Notice of appeal R-500

73.2 (1) Where an appellant wishes to apply to the Court of Appeal for leave to appeal under section 43 or 65 of the Proceeds of Crime Act 2002 Act, he must serve a notice of appeal in the form set out in the Practice Direction on the Crown Court officer.

(2) Unless the Registrar, a single judge or the Court of Appeal directs otherwise, the appellant must serve the notice of appeal, accompanied by a respondent's notice in the form set out in the Practice Direction for the respondent to complete, on—

(a) each respondent;

(b) any person who holds realisable property to which the appeal relates; and

(c) any other person affected by the appeal, as soon as practicable and in any event not later than 7 days after the notice of appeal is served on a Crown Court officer.

(3) The appellant must serve the following documents with his notice of appeal—
(a) four additional copies of the notice of appeal for the Court of Appeal;
(b) four copies of any skeleton argument;
(c) one sealed copy and four unsealed copies of any order being appealed;
(d) four copies of any witness statement or affidavit in support of the application for leave to appeal;
(e) four copies of a suitable record of the reasons for judgment of the Crown Court; and
(f) four copies of the bundle of documents used in the Crown Court proceedings from which the appeal lies.

(4) Where it is not possible to serve all of the documents referred to in paragraph (3), the appellant must indicate which documents have not yet been served and the reasons why they are not currently available.

(5) The appellant must provide a Crown Court officer with a certificate of service stating that he has served the notice of appeal on each respondent in accordance with paragraph (2) and including full details of each respondent or explaining why he has been unable to effect service.

R-501 **Respondent's notice**

73.3 (1) This rule applies to an appeal under section 43 or 65 of the Proceeds of Crime Act 2002.
(2) A respondent may serve a respondent's notice on the Registrar.
(3) A respondent who—
(a) is seeking leave to appeal from the Court of Appeal; or
(b) wishes to ask the Court of Appeal to uphold the decision of the Crown Court for reasons different from or additional to those given by the Crown Court,

must serve a respondent's notice on the Registrar.

(4) A respondent's notice must be in the form set out in the Practice Direction and where the respondent seeks leave to appeal to the Court of Appeal it must be requested in the respondent's notice.
(5) A respondent's notice must be served on the Registrar not later than 14 days after—
(a) the date the respondent is served with notification that the Court of Appeal has given the appellant leave to appeal; or
(b) the date the respondent is served with notification that the application for leave to appeal and the appeal itself are to be heard together.

(6) Unless the Registrar, a single judge or the Court of Appeal directs other wise, the respondent serving a respondent's notice must serve the notice on the appellant and any other respondent—
(a) as soon as practicable; and
(b) in any event not later than seven days,

after it is served on the Registrar.

R-502 **Amendment and abandonment of appeal**

73.4 (1) The appellant may amend a notice of appeal served under rule 73.2 or abandon an appeal under section 43 or 65 of the Proceeds of Crime Act 2002—
(a) without the permission of the Court at any time before the Court of Appeal have begun hearing the appeal; and
(b) with the permission of the Court after the Court of Appeal have begun hearing the appeal,

by serving notice in writing on the Registrar.

(2) Where the appellant serves a notice under paragraph (1), he must send a copy of it to each respondent.

R-503 Stay

73.5 Unless the Court of Appeal or the Crown Court orders otherwise, an appeal under section 43 or 65 of the Proceeds of Crime Act 2002 shall not operate as a stay of any order or decision of the Crown Court.

R-504 **Striking out appeal notices and setting aside or imposing conditions on leave to appeal**

73.6 (1) The Court of Appeal may—
(a) strike out the whole or part of a notice of appeal served under rule 73.2; or
(b) impose or vary conditions upon which an appeal under section 43 or 65 of the Proceeds of Crime Act 2002 may be brought.

(2) The Court of Appeal will only exercise its powers under paragraph (1) where there is a compelling reason for doing so.
(3) Where a party is present at the hearing at which leave to appeal was given, he may not subsequently apply for an order that the Court of Appeal exercise its powers under paragraph (1)(b).

Hearing of appeals R-505

73.7 (1) This rule applies to appeals under section 43 or 65 of the Proceeds of Crime Act 2002.
(2) Every appeal will be limited to a review of the decision of the Crown Court unless the Court of Appeal considers that in the circumstances of an individual appeal it would be in the interests of justice to hold a re-hearing.
(3) The Court of Appeal will allow an appeal where the decision of the Crown Court was—
(a) wrong; or
(b) unjust because of a serious procedural or other irregularity in the proceedings in the Crown Court.
(4) The Court of Appeal may draw any inference of fact which it considers justified on the evidence.
(5) At the hearing of the appeal a party may not rely on a matter not contained in his notice of appeal unless the Court of Appeal gives permission.

Part 74 Appeal or Reference to the Supreme Court

When this Part applies R-506

74.1 (1) This Part applies where—
(a) a party wants to appeal to the Supreme Court after—
(i) an application to the Court of Appeal to which Part 41 applies (retrial following acquittal for serious offence), or
(ii) an appeal to the Court of Appeal to which applies Part 66 (appeal to the Court of Appeal against ruling at preparatory hearing), Part 67 (appeal to the Court of Appeal against ruling adverse to prosecution), or Part 68 (appeal to the Court of Appeal about conviction or sentence); or
(b) a party wants to refer a case to the Supreme Court after a reference to the Court of Appeal to which Part 70 applies (reference to the Court of Appeal of point of law or unduly lenient sentencing).
(2) A reference to an 'appellant' in this Part is a reference to such a party.

Application for permission or reference R-507

74.2 (1) An appellant must—
(a) apply orally to the Court of Appeal—
(i) for permission to appeal or to refer a sentencing case, or
(ii) to refer a point of law immediately after the court gives the reasons for its decision; or
(b) apply in writing and serve the application on the Registrar and every other party not more than—
(i) 14 days after the court gives the reasons for its decision if that decision was on a sentencing reference to which Part 70 applies (Attorney General's reference of sentencing case), or
(ii) 28 days after the court gives those reasons in any other case.
(2) An application for permission to appeal or to refer a sentencing case must—
(a) identify the point of law of general public importance that the appellant wants the court to certify is involved in the decision; and
(b) give reasons why—
(i) that point of law ought to be considered by the Supreme Court, and
(ii) the court ought to give permission to appeal.
(3) An application to refer a point of law must give reasons why that point ought to be considered by the Supreme Court.
(4) An application must include or attach any application for the following, with reasons—
(a) an extension of time within which to make the application for permission or for a reference,
(b) bail pending appeal,
(c) permission to attend any hearing in the Supreme Court, if the appellant is in custody.
(5) A written application must be in the form set out in the Practice Direction.

Determination of detention pending appeal, etc. R-508

74.3 On an application for permission to appeal the Court of Appeal must—
(a) decide whether to order the detention of a defendant who would have been liable to be detained but for the decision of the court; and

(b) determine any application for—
  (i) bail pending appeal,
  (ii) permission to attend any hearing in the Supreme Court, or
  (iii) a representation order.

R-509 **Bail pending appeal**

74.4 Rules 68.8 (Application for bail pending appeal or retrial), 68.9 (Conditions of bail pending appeal or re-trial) and 68.10 (Forfeiture of a recognizance given as a condition of bail) apply.

Part 75 Request to the European Court for a Preliminary Ruling

R-510 **When this Part applies**

75.1 This Part applies where the court can request the Court of Justice of the European Union ('the European Court') to give a preliminary ruling, under Article 267 of the Treaty on the Functioning of the European Union.

R-511 **Preparation of request**

75.2 (1) The court may—
  (a) make an order for the submission of a request—
    (i) on application by a party, or
    (ii) on its own initiative;
  (b) give directions for the preparation of the terms of such a request.
(2) The court must—
  (a) include in such a request—
    (i) the identity of the court making the request,
    (ii) the parties' identities,
    (iii) a statement of whether a party is in custody,
    (iv) a succinct statement of the question on which the court seeks the ruling of the European Court,
    (v) a succinct statement of any opinion on the answer that the court may have expressed in any judgment that it has delivered,
    (vi) a summary of the nature and history of the proceedings, including the salient facts and an indication of whether those facts are proved, admitted or assumed,
    (vii) the relevant rules of national law,
    (viii) a summary of the relevant contentions of the parties,
    (ix) an indication of the provisions of European Union law that the European Court is asked to interpret, and
    (x) an explanation of why a ruling of the European Court is requested;
  (b) express the request in terms that can be translated readily into other languages; and
  (c) set out the request in a schedule to the order.

R-512 **Submission of request**

75.3 (1) The court officer must serve the order for the submission of the request on the Senior Master of the Queen's Bench Division of the High Court.
(2) The Senior Master will—
  (a) submit the request to the European Court; but
  (b) unless the court otherwise directs, postpone the submission of the request until—
    (i) the time for any appeal against the order has expired, and
    (ii) any appeal against the order has been determined.

R-513 **Postponement of case pending request**

75.4 Where the court orders the submission of a request—
  (a) the general rule is that it will adjourn or postpone any further hearing; but
  (b) it may otherwise direct.

Part 76 Costs

Section 1: general

When this Part applies R-514

76.1 (1) This Part applies where the court can make an order about costs under—
(a) Part II of the Prosecution of Offences Act 1985 and Part II, IIA or IIB of The Costs in Criminal Cases (General) Regulations 1986;
(b) section 109 of the Magistrates' Courts Act 1980;
(c) section 52 of the Senior Courts Act 1981 and rule 76.6;
(d) section 8 of the Bankers Books Evidence Act 1879;
(e) section 2C(8) of the Criminal Procedure (Attendance of Witnesses) Act 1965;
(f) section 36(5) of the Criminal Justice Act 1972;
(g) section 159(5) and Schedule 3, paragraph 11, of the Criminal Justice Act 1988;
(h) section 14H(5) of the Football Spectators Act 1989;
(i) section 4(7) of the Dangerous Dogs Act 1991; or
(j) Part 3 of The Serious Crime Act 2007 (Appeals under Section 24) Order 2008.
(2) In this Part, 'costs' means—
(a) the fees payable to a legal representative;
(b) the disbursements paid by a legal representative; and
(c) any other expenses incurred in connection with the case.

Costs orders: general rules R-515

76.2 (1) The court must not make an order about costs unless each party and any other person directly affected—
(a) is present; or
(b) has had an opportunity—
(i) to attend, or
(ii) to make representations.
(2) The court may make an order about costs—
(a) at a hearing in public or in private; or
(b) without a hearing.
(3) In deciding what order, if any, to make about costs, the court must have regard to all the circumstances, including—
(a) the conduct of all the parties; and
(b) any costs order already made.
(4) If the court makes an order about costs, it must—
(a) specify who must, or must not, pay what, to whom; and
(b) identify the legislation under which the order is made, where there is a choice of powers.
(5) The court must give reasons if it—
(a) refuses an application for a costs order; or
(b) rejects representations opposing a costs order.
(6) If the court makes an order for the payment of costs—
(a) the general rule is that it will be for an amount that is sufficient reasonably to compensate the recipient for costs—
(i) actually, reasonably and properly incurred, and
(ii) reasonable in amount; but
(b) the court may order the payment of—
(i) a proportion of that amount,
(ii) a stated amount less than that amount,
(iii) costs from or until a certain date only,
(iv) costs relating only to particular steps taken, or
(v) costs relating only to a distinct part of the case.
(7) On an assessment of the amount of costs, relevant factors include—
(a) the conduct of all the parties;
(b) the particular complexity of the matter or the difficulty or novelty of the questions raised;
(c) the skill, effort, specialised knowledge and responsibility involved;

(d) the time spent on the case;
(e) the place where and the circumstances in which work or any part of it was done; and
(f) any direction or observations by the court that made the costs order.

(8) If the court orders a party to pay costs to be assessed under rule 76.11, it may order that party to pay an amount on account.

(9) An order for the payment of costs takes effect when the amount is assessed, unless the court exercises any power it has to order otherwise.

R-516 **Court's power to vary requirements under Sections 2, 3 and 4**

76.3 (1) The court may—
(a) extend a time limit for serving an application or representations under section 2, 3 or 4 of this Part, even after it has expired; and
(b) consider an application or representations—
(i) made in a different form to one set out in the Practice Direction, or
(ii) made orally instead of in writing.

(2) A person who wants an extension of time must—
(a) apply when serving the application or representations for which it is needed; and
(b) explain the delay.

Section 2: costs out of central funds

R-517 **Costs out of central funds**

76.4 (1) This rule applies where the court can order the payment of costs out of central funds.

(2) In this rule, costs—
(a) include—
(i) on an appeal, costs incurred in the court that made the decision under appeal, and
(ii) at a retrial, costs incurred at the initial trial and on any appeal; but
(b) do not include costs funded by the Legal Services Commission.

(3) The court may make an order—
(a) on application by the person who incurred the costs; or
(b) on its own initiative.

(4) Where a person wants the court to make an order that person must—
(a) apply as soon as practicable; and
(b) outline the type of costs and the amount claimed, if that person wants the court to direct an assessment; or
(c) specify the amount claimed, if that person wants the court to assess the amount itself.

(5) The general rule is that the court will make an order, but—
(a) the court may decline to make a defendant's costs order if, for example—
(i) the defendant is convicted of at least one offence, or
(ii) the defendant's conduct led the prosecutor reasonably to think the prosecution case stronger than it was; and
(b) the court may decline to make a prosecutor's costs order if, for example, the prosecution was started or continued unreasonably.

(6) If the court makes an order—
(a) it may direct an assessment under, as applicable—
(i) regulations 4 to 12 of The Costs in Criminal Cases (General) Regulations 1986, or
(ii) articles 21 to 28 of The Serious Crime Act 2007 (Appeals under Section 24) Order 2008;
(b) it may assess the amount itself, if the recipient agrees;
(c) it must assess the amount itself, in a case in which it decides not to allow an amount that is reasonably sufficient to compensate the recipient for expenses properly incurred in the proceedings.

Section 3: payment of costs by one party to another

R-518 **Costs on conviction and sentence**

76.5 (1) This rule applies where the court can order a defendant to pay the prosecutor's costs if the defendant is—
(a) convicted or found guilty;
(b) dealt with in the Crown Court after committal for sentence there; or
(c) dealt with for breach of a sentence.

(2) The court may make an order—
(a) on application by the prosecutor; or
(b) on its own initiative.
(3) Where the prosecutor wants the court to make an order—
(a) the prosecutor must—
(i) apply as soon as practicable, and
(ii) specify the amount claimed; and
(b) the general rule is that the court will make an order if it is satisfied that the defendant can pay; but
(c) the court may decline to do so.
(4) A defendant who wants to oppose an order must make representations as soon as practicable.
(5) If the court makes an order, it must assess the amount itself.

Costs on appeal R-519

76.6 (1) This rule—
(a) applies where a magistrates' court, the Crown Court or the Court of Appeal can order a party to pay another person's costs on an appeal, or an application for permission to appeal;
(b) authorises the Crown Court, in addition to its other powers, to order a party to pay another party's costs on an appeal to that court, except on an appeal under—
(i) section 108 of the Magistrates' Courts Act 1980, or
(ii) section 45 of the Mental Health Act 1983.
(2) In this rule, costs include—
(a) costs incurred in the court that made the decision under appeal; and
(b) costs funded by the Legal Services Commission.
(3) The court may make an order—
(a) on application by the person who incurred the costs; or
(b) on its own initiative.
(4) A person who wants the court to make an order must—
(a) apply as soon as practicable;
(b) notify each other party;
(c) specify—
(i) the amount claimed, and
(ii) against whom; and
(d) where an appellant abandons an appeal to the Crown Court by serving a notice of abandonment—
(i) apply in writing not more than 14 days later, and
(ii) serve the application on the appellant and on the Crown Court officer.
(5) A party who wants to oppose an order must—
(a) make representations as soon as practicable; and
(b) where the application was under paragraph (4)(d), serve written representations on the applicant, and on the Crown Court officer, not more than 7 days after it was served.
(6) Where the application was under paragraph (4)(d), the Crown Court officer may—
(a) submit it to the Crown Court; or
(b) serve it on the magistrates' court officer, for submission to the magistrates' court.
(7) If the court makes an order, it may direct an assessment under rule 76.11, or assess the amount itself where—
(a) the appellant abandons an appeal to the Crown Court;
(b) the Crown Court decides an appeal, except an appeal under—
(i) section 108 of the Magistrates' Courts Act 1980, or
(ii) section 45 of the Mental Health Act 1983; or
(c) the Court of Appeal decides an appeal to which Part 69 applies (appeal to the Court of Appeal regarding reporting or public access restriction).
(8) If the court makes an order in any other case, it must assess the amount itself.

Costs on an application R-520

76.7 (1) This rule applies where the court can order a party to pay another person's costs in a case in which—
(a) the court decides an application for the production in evidence of a copy of a bank record;

(b) a magistrates' court or the Crown Court decides an application to terminate—
(i) a football banning order, or
(ii) a disqualification for having custody of a dog; or
(c) the Crown Court allows an application to withdraw a witness summons.
(2) The court may make an order—
(a) on application by the person who incurred the costs; or
(b) on its own initiative.
(3) A person who wants the court to make an order must—
(a) apply as soon as practicable;
(b) notify each other party; and
(c) specify—
(i) the amount claimed, and
(ii) against whom.
(4) A party who wants to oppose an order must make representations as soon as practicable.
(5) If the court makes an order, it may direct an assessment under rule 76.11, or assess the amount itself.

R-521 Costs resulting from unnecessary or improper act, etc.

76.8 (1) This rule applies where the court can order a party to pay another party's costs incurred as a result of an unnecessary or improper act or omission by or on behalf of the first party.
(2) In this rule, costs include costs funded by the Legal Services Commission.
(3) The court may make an order—
(a) on application by the party who incurred such costs; or
(b) on its own initiative.
(4) A party who wants the court to make an order must—
(a) apply in writing as soon as practicable after becoming aware of the grounds for doing so;
(b) serve the application on—
(i) the court officer (or, in the Court of Appeal, the Registrar), and
(ii) each other party;
(c) in that application specify—
(i) the party by whom costs should be paid,
(ii) the relevant act or omission,
(iii) the reasons why that act or omission meets the criteria for making an order,
(iv) the amount claimed, and
(v) those on whom the application has been served.
(5) Where the court considers making an order on its own initiative, it must—
(a) identify the party against whom it proposes making the order; and
(b) specify—
(i) the relevant act or omission,
(ii) the reasons why that act or omission meets the criteria for making an order, and
(iii) with the assistance of the party who incurred the costs, the amount involved.
(6) A party who wants to oppose an order must—
(a) make representations as soon as practicable; and
(b) in reply to an application, serve written representations on the applicant and on the court officer (or Registrar) not more than 7 days after it was served.
(7) If the court makes an order, it must assess the amount itself.

Section 4: other costs orders

R-522 Costs against a legal representative

76.9 (1) This rule applies where—
(a) a party has incurred costs—
(i) as a result of an improper, unreasonable or negligent act or omission by a legal or other representative or representative's employee, or
(ii) which it has become unreasonable for that party to have to pay because of such an act or omission occurring after those costs were incurred; and
(b) the court can—
(i) order the representative responsible to pay such costs, or
(ii) prohibit the payment of costs to that representative.

Glossary

R-523

This glossary is a guide to the meaning of certain legal expressions as used in these rules.

Expression	Meaning
account monitoring order	an order requiring certain types of financial institution to provide certain information held by them relating to a customer for the purposes of an investigation
action plan order	a type of community sentence requiring a child or young person to comply with a three month plan relating to his actions and whereabouts and to comply with the directions of a responsible officer (e.g. probation officer)
admissible evidence	evidence allowed in proceedings (not all evidence introduced by the parties may be allowable in court)
adduce	to introduce (in evidence)
adjourn	to suspend or delay the hearing of a case
advance information	information about the case against an accused, to which the accused may be entitled before he or she enters a plea
affidavit	a written, sworn statement of evidence
affirmation	a non-religious alternative to the oath sworn by someone about to give evidence in court or swearing a statement
appellant	person who is appealing against a decision of the court
arraign	to put charges to the defendant in open court in the Crown Court
arraignment	the formal process of putting charges to the defendant in the Crown Court which consists of three parts: (1) calling him to the bar by name, (2) putting the charges to him by reading from the indictment and (3) asking him whether he pleads guilty or not guilty
authorities	judicial decisions or opinions of authors of repute used as grounds of statements of law
bill of indictment	a written accusation of a crime against one or more persons—a criminal trial in the Crown Court cannot start without a valid indictment
in camera (trial)	trial in private
case stated	an appeal to the High Court against the decision of a magistrates' court on the basis that the decision was wrong in law or in excess of the magistrates' jurisdiction
in chambers	non-trial hearing in private
committal	sending someone to a court (usually from a magistrates' court to the Crown Court) or to prison
committal for sentence	procedure whereby a person convicted in a magistrates' court is sent to the Crown Court for sentencing when the sentencing powers of the magistrates' court are not considered sufficient
committal proceedings	preliminary hearing in a magistrates' court before a case is sent to be tried before a jury in the Crown Court
compellable witness	a witness who can be forced to give evidence against an accused (not all witnesses are compellable)
compensation order	an order that a convicted person must pay compensation for loss or damage caused by the convicted person
complainant	a person who makes a formal complaint. In relation to an offence of rape or other sexual offences the complainant is the person against whom the offence is alleged to have been committed
complaint	document used to start certain types of proceedings in a magistrates' court, or the process of using such a document to start proceedings

Expression	Meaning
conditional discharge	an order which does not impose any immediate punishment on a person convicted of an offence, subject to the condition that he does not commit an offence in a specified period
confiscation order	an order that private property be taken into possession by the state
Convention right	a right under the European Convention on Human Rights
costs	the expenses involved in a court case, including the fees of the solicitors and barristers and of the court
counsel	a barrister
cross examination	questioning of a witness by a party other than the party who called the witness
custody time limit	the maximum period, as set down in statute, for which a person may be kept in custody before being brought to trial—these maximum periods may only be extended by an order of the judge
customer information order	an order requiring a financial institution to provide certain information held by them relating to a customer for the purposes of an investigation into the proceeds of crime
declaration of incompatibility	a declaration by a court that a piece of UK legislation is incompatible with the provisions of the European Convention on Human Rights
deferred sentence	a sentence which is determined after a delay to allow the court to assess any change in the person's conduct or circumstances after his or her conviction
deposition	written record of a witness' written evidence
distress warrant	court order giving the power to seize goods from a debtor to pay his debts
estreatment (of recognizance)	forfeiture
evidence in chief	the evidence given by a witness for the party who called him
examining justice	a magistrate carrying out his or her function of checking that a case appears on the face of the prosecution case papers to exist against an accused before the case is put forward for trial in the Crown Court—see committal and sending for trial
exhibit	a document or thing presented as evidence in court
forfeiture by peaceable re-entry	the re-possession by a landlord of premises occupied by tenants
guardianship order	an order appointing someone to take charge of a child's affairs and property
hearsay evidence	oral or written statements made by someone who is not a witness in the case but which the court is asked to accept as proving what they say—this expression is defined further by rule 34.1 for the purposes of Part 34, and by rule 57.1 for the purposes of Parts 57–61
hospital order	an order that an offender be admitted to and detained in a specified hospital
indictment	the document containing the formal charges against a defendant—a trial in the Crown Court cannot start without this
informant	someone who lays an information
information	statement by which a magistrate is informed of the offence for which a summons or warrant is required—the procedure by which this statement is brought to the magistrates' attention is known as laying an information
intermediary	a person who asks a witness (particularly a child) questions posed by the cross-examining legal representative
inter partes	a hearing where both parties attend and can make submissions
justice of the peace	a magistrate, either a lay magistrate or a District Judge (Magistrates' Courts);
justices' clerk	post in the magistrates' court of person who has various powers and duties in a magistrates' court, including giving advice to the magistrates on law and procedure

Expression	Meaning
leave of the court	permission granted by the court
leave to appeal	permission granted to appeal the decision of a court
letter of request	letter issued to a foreign court asking a judge to take the evidence of some person within that court's jurisdiction
to levy distress	to seize property from a debtor or a wrongdoer
local justice area	an area established for the purposes of the administration of magistrates' courts
mandatory order	order from the Divisional Court of the Queen's Bench Division ordering a body (such as a magistrates' court) to do something (such as rehear a case)
nominated court	a court nominated to take evidence pursuant to a request by a foreign court
notice of transfer	procedure used in cases of serious and complex fraud, and in certain cases involving child witnesses, whereby the prosecution can, without seeking judicial approval, have the case sent direct to the Crown Court without the need to have the accused committed for trial
offence triable either way	an offence which may be tried either in the magistrates' court or in the Crown Court
in open court	in a courtroom which is open to the public
order restricting discharge	an order restricting the discharge from hospital of patients who have been sent there for psychiatric treatment
parenting order	an order which can be made in certain circumstances where a child has been convicted of an offence which may require parents of the offender to comply with certain requirements including attendance of counselling or guidance sessions
party	a person or organisation directly involved in a criminal case, either as prosecutor or defendant
prefer, preferment	to bring or lay a charge or indictment
preparatory hearing	a hearing forming part of the trial sometimes used in long and complex cases to settle various issues without requiring the jury to attend
realisable property	property which can be sold for money
receiver	a person appointed with certain powers in respect of the property and affairs of a person who has obtained such property in the course of criminal conduct and who has been convicted of an offence—there are various types of receiver (management receiver, director's receiver, enforcement receiver)
receivership order	an order that a person's assets be put into the hands of an official with certain powers and duties to deal with that property
recognizance	formal undertaking to pay the Crown a specified sum if an accused fails to surrender to custody
register	the formal records kept by a magistrates' court
to remand	to send a person away when a case is adjourned until another date—the person may be remanded on bail (when he can leave, subject to conditions) or in custody
reparation order	an order made against a child or young person who has been convicted of an offence, requiring him or her to make specific reparations to the victim or to the community at large
representation order	an order authorising payment of legal aid for a defendant
requisition	a document issued under section 29 of the Criminal Justice Act 2003 requiring a person to appear before a magistrates' court to answer a written charge;
respondent	the other party (to the appellant) in a case which is the subject of an appeal
restraint order	an order prohibiting a person from dealing with any realisable property held by
seal	a formal mark which the court puts on a document to indicate that the document has been issued by the court

Expression	Meaning
security	money deposited to ensure that the defendant attends court
sending for trial	procedure whereby indictable offences are transferred to the Crown Court without the need for a committal hearing in the magistrates' court
skeleton argument	a document prepared by a party or their legal representative, setting out the basis of the party's argument, including any arguments based on law—the court may require such documents to be served on the court and on the other party prior to a trial
special measures	measures which can be put in place to provide protection and/or anonymity to a witness (e.g. a screen separating witness from the accused)
statutory declaration	a declaration made before a Commissioner for Oaths in a prescribed form
to stay	to halt proceedings, apart from taking any steps allowed by the Rules or the terms of the stay — proceedings may be continued if a stay is lifted
summons	a document signed by a magistrate after an information is laid before him which sets out the basis of the accusation against the accused and the time and place when he must appear
surety	a person who guarantees that a defendant will attend court
suspended sentence	sentence which takes effect only if the offender commits another offence punishable with imprisonment within the specified period
supervision order	an order placing a person who has been given a suspended sentence under the supervision of a local officer
tainted acquittal	an acquittal affected by interference with a witness or a juror
taxing authority	a body which assesses costs
territorial authority	the UK authority which has power to do certain things in connection with co-operation with other countries and international organisations in relation to the collection of or hearing of evidence etc
transfer direction (mental health)	a direction that a person who is serving a sentence of imprisonment who is suffering from a mental disorder be transferred to a hospital and be detained there for treatment
warrant of arrest	court order to arrest a person
warrant of commitment	court order sending someone to prison
warrant of distress	court order giving the power to seize goods from a debtor to pay his debts
warrant of detention	a court order authorising someone's detention
wasted costs order	an order that a barrister or solicitor is not to be paid fees that they would normally be paid by the Legal Services Commission
witness	a person who gives evidence, either by way of a written statement or orally in court
witness summons	a document served on a witness requiring him or her to attend court to give evidence
written charge	a document issued by a public prosecutor under section 29 of the Criminal Justice Act 2003 which institutes criminal proceedings by charging a person with an offence;
youth court	magistrates' courts exercising jurisdiction over offences committed by and other matters related to, children and young persons.

SENTENCING GUIDELINES

Sentencing Guidelines

This is an edited version of the various definitive sentencing guidelines, both those originally issued by the Sentencing Guidelines Council and those issued by the Sentencing Council for England and Wales. It contains all of the essential guideline material relevant to offences in *Blackstone's Criminal Practice*. Fuller versions are available on the Sentencing Council website via http://sentencingcouncil.judiciary.gov.uk/sentencing-guidelines.htm. By virtue of the Coroners and Justice Act 2009 (Commencement No. 4, Transitional and Saving Provisions) Order 2010 (SI 2010 No. 816), art. 7, guidelines issued by the SGC 'are to be treated as guidelines issued by the Sentencing Council'. For more on the status of guidelines and the duty of courts to follow them, see **E1.2** in the main work.

PART 1 REDUCTION IN SENTENCE FOR A GUILTY PLEA SG-1

[Introductory material and declaration that the guideline applies to all cases sentenced on or after *23 July 2007*.]

A. Statutory Provision

[Sets out the CJA 2003, ss. 144 (reduction in sentence for guilty plea: see **E1.6**) and 174(2)(d) (duty to give resons and explain effect of sentence: see **E1.16**).]

1.1 This guideline applies whether a case is dealt with in a magistrates' court or in the Crown Court and whenever practicable in the youth court (taking into account legislative restrictions such as those relevant to the length of Detention and Training orders).

1.2 The application of this guideline to sentencers when arriving at the appropriate minimum term for the offence of murder is set out in Section F.

. . .

B. Statement of Purpose SG-2

2.1 When imposing a custodial sentence, statute requires that a court must impose the shortest term that is commensurate with the seriousness of the offence(s).[1] Similarly, when imposing a community order, the restrictions on liberty must be commensurate with the seriousness of the offence(s).[2] Once that decision is made, a court is required to give consideration to the reduction for any guilty plea. As a result, the final sentence after the reduction for a guilty plea will be less than the seriousness of the offence requires.

2.2 A reduction in sentence is appropriate because a guilty plea avoids the need for a trial (thus enabling other cases to be disposed of more expeditiously), shortens the gap between charge and sentence, saves considerable cost, and, in the case of an early plea, saves victims and witnesses from the concern about having to give evidence. The reduction principle derives from the need for the effective administration of justice and not as an aspect of mitigation.

2.3 Where a sentencer is in doubt as to whether a custodial sentence is appropriate, the reduction attributable to a guilty plea will be a relevant consideration. Where this is amongst the factors leading to the imposition of a non-custodial sentence, there will be no need to apply a further reduction on account of the guilty plea. A similar approach is appropriate where the reduction for a guilty plea is amongst the factors leading to the imposition of a financial penalty or discharge instead of a community order.

2.4 When deciding the most appropriate length of sentence, the sentencer should address separately the issue of remorse, together with any other mitigating features, before calculating the reduction for the guilty plea. Similarly, assistance to the prosecuting or enforcement authorities is a separate issue which may attract a reduction in sentence under other procedures; care will need to be taken to ensure that there is no 'double counting'.

2.5 The implications of other offences that an offender has asked to be taken into consideration should be reflected in the sentence before the reduction for guilty plea has been applied.

2.6 A reduction in sentence should only be applied to the *punitive elements* of a penalty.[3] The guilty plea reduction has no impact on sentencing decisions in relation to ancillary orders, including orders of disqualification from driving.

---

[1] Criminal Justice Act 2003, s.153(2)

[2] Criminal Justice Act 2003, s.148(2)

[3] Where a court imposes an indeterminate sentence for public protection, the reduction principle applies in the normal way to the determination of the minimum term (see para. 5.1, footnote and para. 7 below) but release from custody requires the authorisation of the Parole Board once that minimum term has been served.

SG-3 C. **Application of the Reduction Principle**

3.1 Recommended Approach

The court decides sentence for the offences taking into account other offences that have been formally admitted (TICs),

↓

The court selects the amount of the reduction by reference to the sliding scale,

↓

The court applies the reduction,

↓

When pronouncing sentence the court should usually state what the sentence would have been if there had been no reduction as a result of the guilty plea.

SG-4 D. **Determining the Level of Reduction**

4.1 The level of reduction should be *a proportion of the total sentence* imposed, with the proportion calculated by reference to the circumstances in which the guilty plea was indicated, in particular the stage in the proceedings. The greatest reduction will be given where the plea was indicated at the 'first reasonable opportunity'.

4.2 Save where section 144(2) of the 2003 Act[4] applies, the level of the reduction will be gauged on a *sliding scale* ranging from a recommended *one third* (where the guilty plea was entered at the first reasonable opportunity in relation to the offence for which sentence is being imposed), reducing to a recommended *one quarter* (where a trial date has been set) and to a recommended *one tenth* (for a guilty plea entered at the 'door of the court' or after the trial has begun). See diagram below.

4.3 The level of reduction should reflect the stage at which the offender indicated a *willingness to admit guilt* to the offence for which he is eventually sentenced:

(i) the largest recommended reduction will not normally be given unless the offender indicated willingness to admit guilt at the *first reasonable opportunity*; when this occurs will vary from case to case. (*see Annex 1 for illustrative examples*);

(ii) where the admission of guilt comes later than the first reasonable opportunity, the reduction for guilty plea will be less than one third;

(iii) where the plea of guilty comes very late, it is still appropriate to give some reduction;

(iv) if after pleading guilty there is a *Newton* hearing and the offender's version of the circumstances of the offence is rejected, this should be taken into account in determining the level of reduction;

(v) if the not guilty plea was entered and maintained for tactical reasons (such as to retain privileges whilst on remand), a late guilty plea should attract very little, if any, discount.

In each category, there is a presumption that the recommended reduction will be given unless there are good reasons for a lower amount.

First reasonable opportunity	After trial date is set	Door of the court/ after trial has begun
= = = = = = = |	= = = = = = = = = = = = = |	= = = = = = = = = = = = = = = |
recommended 1/3	**recommended** 1/4	**recommended** 1/10

SG-5 E. **Withholding a Reduction**

On the basis of dangerousness

5.1 Where a sentence for a 'dangerous offender' is imposed under the provisions in the Criminal Justice Act 2003, whether the sentence requires the calculation of a minimum term or is an extended sentence, the approach will be the same as for any other determinate sentence (see also section G below).[5]

[4] See section A above.

[5] There will be some cases arising from offences committed before the commencement of the relevant provisions of the Criminal Justice Act 2003 in which a court will determine that a longer than commensurate, extended, or indeterminate sentence is required for the protection of the public. In such a case, the minimum custodial term (but not the protection of public element of the sentence) should be reduced to reflect the plea.

Where the prosecution case is overwhelming

5.2 The purpose of giving credit is to encourage those who are guilty to plead at the earliest opportunity. Any defendant is entitled to put the prosecution to proof and so every defendant who is guilty should be encouraged to indicate that guilt at the first reasonable opportunity.

5.3 Where the prosecution case is overwhelming, it may not be appropriate to give the full reduction that would otherwise be given. Whilst there is a presumption in favour of the full reduction being given where a plea has been indicated at the first reasonable opportunity, the fact that the prosecution case is overwhelming without relying on admissions from the defendant may be a reason justifying departure from the guideline.

5.4 Where a court is satisfied that a lower reduction should be given for this reason, a recommended reduction of 20% is likely to be appropriate where the guilty plea was indicated at the first reasonable opportunity.

5.5 A Court departing from a guideline must state the reasons for doing so.[6]

Where the maximum penalty for the offence is thought to be too low

5.6 The sentencer is bound to sentence for the offence with which the offender has been charged, and to which he has pleaded guilty. The sentencer cannot remedy perceived defects (for example an inadequate charge or maximum penalty) by refusal of the appropriate discount.

Where jurisdictional issues arise

(i) Where sentencing powers are limited to 6 months imprisonment despite multiple offences

5.7 When the total sentence for both or all of the offences is 6 months imprisonment, a court may determine to impose consecutive sentences which, even allowing for a reduction for a guilty plea where appropriate on each offence, would still result in the imposition of the maximum sentence available. In such circumstances, in order to achieve the purpose for which the reduction principle has been established,[7] some modest allowance should normally be given against the total sentence for the entry of a guilty plea.

(ii) Where a maximum sentence might still be imposed

5.8 Despite a guilty plea being entered which would normally attract a reduction in sentence, a magistrates' court may impose a sentence of imprisonment of 6 months for a single either-way offence where, but for the plea, that offence would have been committed to the Crown Court for sentence.

5.9 Similarly, a detention and training order of 24 months may be imposed on an offender aged under 18 if the offence is one which would but for the plea have attracted a sentence of long-term detention in excess of 24 months under the Powers of Criminal Courts (Sentencing) Act 2000, section 91.

F. Application to Sentencing for Murder **SG-6**

6.1 Murder has always been regarded as the most serious criminal offence and the sentence prescribed is different from other sentences. By law, the sentence for murder is imprisonment (detention) for life and an offender will remain subject to the sentence for the rest of his/her life.

6.2 The decision whether to release the offender from custody during this sentence will be taken by the Parole Board which will consider whether it is safe to release the offender on licence. The Court that imposes the sentence is required by law to set a minimum term that has to be served before the Parole Board may start to consider whether to authorise release on licence. If an offender is released, the licence continues for the rest of the offender's life and recall to prison is possible at any time.

6.3 Uniquely, Parliament has set starting points[8] (based on the circumstances of the killing) which a Court will apply when it fixes the minimum term. Parliament has further prescribed that, having identified the appropriate starting point, the Court must then consider whether to increase or reduce it in the light of aggravating or mitigating factors, some of which are listed in statute. Finally, Parliament specifically provides[9] that the obligation to have regard to any guilty plea applies to the fixing of the minimum term, by making the same statutory provisions that apply to other offences apply to murder without limiting the courts discretion (as it did with other sentences under the Powers of Criminal Courts (Sentencing) Act 2000).

6.4 There are important differences between the usual fixed term sentence and the minimum term set following the imposition of the mandatory life sentence for murder. The most significant of these,

[6] Criminal Justice Act 2003, s. 174(2)(a)
[7] See section B above.
[8] Criminal Justice Act 2003, schedule 21
[9] Criminal Justice Act 2003, schedule 1 para 12(c)

from the sentencer's point of view, is that a reduction for a plea of guilty in the case of murder will have double the effect on time served in custody when compared with a determinate sentence. This is because a determinate sentence will provide (in most circumstances) for the release of the offender[10] on licence half way through the total sentence whereas in the case of murder a minimum term is the period in custody before consideration is given by the Parole Board to whether release is appropriate.

6.5 Given this difference, the special characteristic of the offence of murder and the unique statutory provision of starting points, careful consideration will need to be given to the extent of any reduction and to the need to ensure that the minimum term properly reflects the seriousness of the offence. Whilst the general principles continue to apply (both that a guilty plea should be encouraged and that the extent of any reduction should reduce if the indication of plea is later than the first reasonable opportunity), the process of determining the level of reduction will be different.

6.6 *Approach*

1. Where a Court determines that there should be a *whole life* minimum term, there will be no reduction for a guilty plea.
2. In other circumstances,
    a) the Court will weigh carefully the overall length of the minimum term taking into account other reductions for which offenders may be eligible so as to avoid a combination leading to an inappropriately short sentence;
    b) where it is appropriate to reduce the minimum term having regard to a plea of guilty, the reduction will not exceed one sixth and will never exceed 5 years;
    c) the sliding scale will apply so that, where it is appropriate to reduce the minimum term on account of a guilty plea, the maximum reduction (one sixth or five years whichever is the less) is only available where there has been an indication of willingness to plead guilty at the first reasonable opportunity, with a recommended 5% for a late guilty plea.
    d) the Court should then review the sentence to ensure that the minimum term accurately reflects the seriousness of the offence taking account of the statutory starting point, all aggravating and mitigating factors and any guilty plea entered.

SG-7 **G. Application to other Indeterminate Sentences**

7.1 There are other circumstances in which an indeterminate sentence will be imposed. This may be a discretionary life sentence or imprisonment for public protection.

7.2 As with the mandatory life sentence imposed following conviction for murder, the Court will be obliged to fix a minimum term to be served before the Parole Board is able to consider whether the offender can be safely released.

7.3 However, the process by which that minimum term is fixed is different from that followed in relation to the mandatory life sentence and requires the Court first to determine what the equivalent determinate sentence would have been. Accordingly, the approach to the calculation of the reduction for any guilty plea should follow the process and scale adopted in relation to determinate sentences, as set out in section D above.

SG-8

Annex 1

First Reasonable Opportunity

1. The critical time for determining the reduction for a guilty plea is the first reasonable opportunity for the defendant to have indicated a willingness to plead guilty. This opportunity will vary with a wide range of factors and the Court will need to make a judgement on the particular facts of the case before it.
2. The key principle is that the purpose of giving a reduction is to recognise the benefits that come from a guilty plea both for those directly involved in the case in question but also in enabling Courts more quickly to deal with other outstanding cases.
3. This Annex seeks to help Courts to adopt a consistent approach by giving examples of circumstances where a determination will have to be made.
    (a) the first reasonable opportunity may be the first time that a defendant appears before the court and has the opportunity to plead guilty;
    (b) but the court may consider that it would be reasonable to have expected an indication of willingness even earlier, perhaps whilst under interview;
    Note: For a) and b) to apply, the Court will need to be satisfied that the defendant (and any legal adviser) would have had sufficient information about the allegations

[10] In accordance with the provisions of the Criminal Justice Act 2003

(c) where an offence triable either way is committed to the Crown Court for trial and the defendant pleads guilty at the first hearing in that Court, the reduction will be less than if there had been an indication of a guilty plea given to the magistrates' court (recommended reduction of one third) but more than if the plea had been entered after a trial date had been set (recommended reduction of one quarter), and is likely to be in the region of 30%;
(d) where an offence is triable only on indictment, it may well be that the first reasonable opportunity would have been during the police station stage; where that is not the case, the first reasonable opportunity is likely to be at the first hearing in the Crown Court;
(e) where a defendant is convicted after pleading guilty to an alternative (lesser) charge to that to which he/she had originally pleaded not guilty, the extent of any reduction will be determined by the stage at which the defendant first formally indicated to the court willingness to plead guilty to the lesser charge, and the reason why that lesser charge was proceeded with in preference to the original charge.

PART 2 NEW SENTENCES: CRIMINAL JUSTICE ACT 2003 SG-9

Foreword

[Introductory material which is not reproduced.]

This guideline applies only to sentences passed under the sentencing framework applicable to those aged 18 or over.

The guideline is divided into two sections:
- Sections 1 covers the practical aspects of implementing the non-custodial powers namely the new community sentence and the new form of deferred sentence;
- Section 2 deals with the new custodial sentence provisions relating to suspended sentences, prison sentences of 12 months or more, and intermittent custody.[11]

The Act also contains an extensive range of provisions to protect the public from dangerous offenders. These will be dealt with separately.

. . .

Section 1

Part 1—Community Sentences SG-10

A. Statutory Provisions

(i) The Thresholds for Community Sentences

1.1.1 Seriousness—Section 148 Criminal Justice Act 2003:
[Sets out the CJA 2003, s. 148(1) (restrictions on imposing community sentence: see **E8.2**).]
1.1.2 Persistent Offenders—Section 151 Criminal Justice Act 2003:
[Sets out the CJA 2003, s. 151(1) and (2) (community order for persistent offender previously fined – not yet in force: see **E8.2**).]

(ii) The Sentences Available

1.1.3 Meaning of Community Sentence—Section 147 Criminal Justice Act 2003
(1) In this Part 'community sentence' means a sentence which consists of or includes—
(a) a community order (as defined by section 177), or
(b) one or more youth community orders.
1.1.4 Offenders aged 16 or over—Section 177 Criminal Justice Act 2003:
[Sets out the CJA 2003, s. 177(1) to (4) (community order requirements: see **E8.5** ***et seq***).]

[11] References to the Probation Service reflect current roles and responsibilities. By the time these provisions come into force, some or all of those roles and responsibilities may be those of the National Offender Management Service (NOMS).

(iii) Determining Which Orders to make & Requirements to Include

1.1.5 Suitability—Section 148 Criminal Justice Act 2003

[Sets out the CJA 2003, s. 148(2) (restrictions on imposing community sentence: see **E8.2**).]

1.1.6 Restrictions on liberty—Section 149 Criminal Justice Act 2003

[Sets out the CJA 2003, s. 149(1) (passing of community sentence on offender remanded in custody: see **E8.2**)]

1.1.7 Compatibility—Section 177 Criminal Justice Act 2003

[Sets out the CJA 2003, s. 177(6) (community orders requirements: see **E8.5**).]

(iv) Electronic Monitoring

1.1.8 [Sets out the CJA 2003, s. 177(3) and (4) (electronic monitoring requirements: see **E8.18**)]

SG-11 **B. Imposing a Community Sentence—The Approach**

1.1.9 In the Seriousness guideline [at **SG-26**)] the two thresholds for the imposition of a community sentence are considered. Sentencers must consider all of the disposals available (within or below the threshold passed) at the time of sentence, and reject them before reaching the provisional decision to make a community sentence, so that even where the threshold for a community sentence has been passed a financial penalty or discharge may still be an appropriate penalty. Where an offender has a low risk of reoffending, particular care needs to be taken in the light of evidence that indicates that there are circumstances where inappropriate intervention can increase the risk of re-offending rather than decrease it. In addition, recent improvements in enforcement of financial penalties make them a more viable sentence in a wider range of cases.

1.1.10 Where an offender is being sentenced for a non-imprisonable offence or offences, great care will be needed in assessing whether a community sentence is appropriate since failure to comply could result in a custodial sentence.

1.1.11 Having decided (in consultation with the Probation Service where appropriate) that a community sentence is justified, the court must decide which requirements should be included in the community order. The requirements or orders imposed will have the effect of restricting the offender's liberty, whilst providing punishment in the community, rehabilitation for the offender, and/or ensuring that the offender engages in reparative activities.

The key issues arising are:

(i) which requirements to impose;

(ii) how to make allowance for time spent on remand; and

(iii) how to deal with breaches.

(i) Requirements

1.1.12 When deciding which requirements to include, the court must be satisfied on three matters—

(i) that the *restriction on liberty is commensurate with the seriousness* of the offence(s);[12]

(ii) that the *requirements are the most suitable* for the offender;[13] and

(iii) that, where there are two or more requirements included, they are *compatible with each other*.[14]

1.1.13 Sentencers should have the possibility of breach firmly in mind when passing sentence for the original offence. If a court is to reflect the seriousness of an offence, there is little value in setting requirements as part of a community sentence that are not demanding enough for an offender. On the other hand, there is equally little value in imposing requirements that would 'set an offender up to fail' and almost inevitably lead to sanctions for a breach.

In community sentences, the guiding principles are proportionality and suitability. Once a court has decided that the offence has crossed the community sentence threshold and that a community sentence is justified, the *initial* factor in defining which requirements to include in a community sentence should be the seriousness of the offence committed.

1.1.14 This means that 'seriousness' is an important factor in deciding whether the Court chooses the low, medium or high range (see below) but, having taken that decision, selection of the content of the order within the range will be determined by a much wider range of factors.

- **Sentencing ranges must remain flexible enough to take account of the suitability of the offender, his or her ability to comply with particular requirements and their availability in the local area.**

[12] Criminal Justice Act 2003 section 148(2)(b)
[13] ibid section 148(2)(a)
[14] ibid section 177(6)

- **The justification for imposing a community sentence in response to persistent petty offending is the persistence of the offending behaviour rather than the seriousness of the offences being committed. The requirements imposed should ensure that the restriction on liberty is proportionate to the seriousness of the offending, to reflect the fact that the offences, of themselves, are not sufficiently serious to merit a community sentence.**

(a) Information for Sentencers

1.1.15 In many cases, a pre-sentence report[15] will be pivotal in helping a sentencer decide whether to impose a custodial sentence or whether to impose a community sentence and, if so, whether particular requirements, or combinations of requirements, are suitable for an individual offender. The court must always ensure (especially where there are multiple requirements) that the restriction on liberty placed on the offender is proportionate to the seriousness of the offence committed.[16] The court must also consider the likely effect of one requirement on another, and that they do not place conflicting demands upon the offender.[17]

1.1.16 The Council supports the approach proposed by the Panel at paragraph 78 of its Advice that, having reached the provisional view that a community sentence is the most appropriate disposal, the sentencer should request a pre-sentence report, indicating which of the three sentencing ranges is relevant and the purpose(s) of sentencing that the package of requirements is required to fulfil. Usually the most helpful way for the court to do this would be to produce a written note for the report writer, copied on the court file. If it is known that the same tribunal and defence advocate will be present at the sentencing hearing and a probation officer is present in court when the request for a report is made, it may not be necessary to commit details of the request to writing. However, events may change during the period of an adjournment and it is good practice to ensure that there is a clear record of the request for the court. These two factors will guide the Probation Service in determining the nature and combination of requirements that may be appropriate and the onerousness and intensity of those requirements. A similar procedure should apply when ordering a pre-sentence report when a custodial sentence is being considered.

1.1.17 There will be occasions when any type of report may be unnecessary despite the intention to pass a community sentence though this is likely to be infrequent. A court could consider dispensing with the need to obtain a pre-sentence report for adult offenders—

- where the offence falls within the **LOW** range of seriousness (see [below]) and
- where the sentencer was minded to impose a single requirement, such as an exclusion requirement (where the circumstances of the case mean that this would be an appropriate disposal without electronic monitoring) *and*
- where the sentence will not require the involvement of the Probation Service, for example an electronically monitored curfew (subject to the court being satisfied that there is an appropriate address at which the curfew can operate).

(b) Ranges of Sentence Within the Community Sentence Band

1.1.18 To enable the court to benefit from the flexibility that community sentences provide and also to meet its statutory obligations, any structure governing the use of community requirements must allow the courts to choose the most appropriate sentence for each individual offender.

1.1.19 Sentencers have a statutory obligation to pass sentences that are commensurate with the seriousness of an offence. However, within the range of sentence justified by the seriousness of the offence(s), courts will quite properly consider those factors that heighten the risk of the offender committing further offences or causing further harm with a view to lessening that risk. The extent to which requirements are imposed must be capable of being varied to ensure that the restriction on liberty is commensurate with the seriousness of the offence.

1.1.20 The Council recognises that it would be helpful for sentencers to have a framework to help them decide on the most appropriate use of the new community sentence. While there is no single guiding principle, the seriousness of the offence that has been committed is an important factor. Three sentencing ranges (low, medium and high) within the community sentence band can be identified. It is not possible to position particular types of offence at firm points within the three ranges because the seriousness level of an offence is largely dependent upon the culpability of

[15] Under the Act, a pre-sentence report includes a full report following adjournment, a specific sentence report, a short format report or an oral report. The type of report supplied will depend on the level of information requested. Wherever it appears, the term 'pre-sentence report' includes all these types of report.

[16] Criminal Justice Act 2003 section 148(2)

[17] ibid section 177(6)

the offender and this is uniquely variable. The difficulty is particularly acute in relation to the medium range where it is clear that requirements will need to be tailored across a relatively wide range of offending behaviour.

1.1.21 In general terms, the lowest range of community sentence would be for those offenders whose offence was relatively minor within the community sentence band and would include persistent petty offenders whose offences only merit a community sentence by virtue of failing to respond to the previous imposition of fines. Such offenders would merit a 'light touch' approach, for example, normally a single requirement such as a short period of unpaid work, or a curfew, or a prohibited activity requirement or an exclusion requirement (where the circumstances of the case mean that this would be an appropriate disposal without electronic monitoring).

1.1.22 The top range would be for those offenders who have only just fallen short of a custodial sentence and for those who have passed the threshold but for whom a community sentence is deemed appropriate.

1.1.23 In all three ranges there must be sufficient flexibility to allow the sentence to be varied to take account of the suitability of particular requirements for the individual offender and whether a particular requirement or package of requirements might be more effective at reducing any identified risk of re-offending. It will fall to the sentencer to ensure that the sentence strikes the right balance between proportionality and suitability.

There should be three sentencing ranges (low medium and high) within the community sentence band based upon seriousness.

It is not intended that an offender necessarily progress from one range to the next on each sentencing occasion. The decision as to the appropriate range each time is based upon the seriousness of the new offence(s).

The decision on the nature and severity of the requirements to be included in a community sentence should be guided by:

(i) **the assessment of offence seriousness (LOW, MEDIUM OR HIGH);**
(ii) **the purpose(s) of sentencing the court wishes to achieve;**
(iii) **the risk of re-offending;**
(iv) **the ability of the offender to comply, and**
(v) **the availability of requirements in the local area.**

The resulting restrictions on liberty must be a proportionate response to the offence that was committed.

1.1.24 Below we set out a non-exhaustive description of examples of requirements that might be appropriate in the three sentencing ranges. These examples focus on punishment in the community, although it is recognised that not all packages will necessarily need to include a punitive requirement. There will clearly be other requirements of a rehabilitative nature, such as a treatment requirement or an accredited programme, which may be appropriate depending on the specific needs of the offender and assessment of suitability. Given the intensity of such interventions, it is expected that these would normally only be appropriate at medium and high levels of seriousness, and where assessed as having a medium or high risk of re-offending. In addition, when passing sentence in any one of the three ranges, the court should consider whether a rehabilitative intervention such as a programme requirement, or a restorative justice intervention might be suitable as an additional or alternative part of the sentence.

LOW

1.1.25 For offences only just crossing the community sentence threshold (such as persistent petty offending, some public order offences, some thefts from shops, or interference with a motor vehicle, where the seriousness of the offence or the nature of the offender's record means that a discharge or fine is inappropriate).

1.1.26 Suitable requirements might include:

- 40 to 80 hours of unpaid work or
- a curfew requirement within the lowest range (e.g. up to 12 hours per day for a few weeks) or
- an exclusion requirement (where the circumstances of the case mean that this would be an appropriate disposal without electronic monitoring) lasting a few months or
- a prohibited activity requirement or
- an attendance centre requirement (where available).

1.1.27 Since the restriction on liberty must be commensurate with the seriousness of the offence, particular care needs to be taken with this band to ensure that this obligation is complied with.

In most cases, only one requirement will be appropriate and the length may be curtailed if additional requirements are necessary.

MEDIUM

1.1.28 For offences that obviously fall within the community sentence band such as handling stolen goods worth less than £1000 acquired for resale or somewhat more valuable goods acquired for the handlers own use, some cases of burglary in commercial premises, some cases of taking a motor vehicle without consent, or some cases of obtaining property by deception.

1.1.29 Suitable requirements might include:

- a greater number (e.g. 80 to 150) of hours of unpaid work or
- an activity requirement in the middle range (20 to 30 days) or
- a curfew requirement within the middle range (e.g. up to 12 hours for 2–3 months) or
- an exclusion requirement lasting in the region of 6 months or
- a prohibited activity requirement.

1.1.30 Since the restriction on liberty must be commensurate with the seriousness of the offence, particular care needs to be taken with this band to ensure that this obligation is complied with.

HIGH

1.1.31 For offences that only just fall below the custody threshold or where the custody threshold is crossed but a community sentence is more appropriate in all the circumstances, for example some cases displaying the features of a standard domestic burglary committed by a first-time offender.

1.1.32 More intensive sentences which combine two or more requirements may be appropriate at this level. Suitable requirements might include an unpaid work order of between 150 and 300 hours; an activity requirement up to the maximum 60 days; an exclusion order lasting in the region of 12 months; a curfew requirement of up to 12 hours a day for 4–6 months.

(c) Electronic Monitoring

1.1.33 The court must also consider whether an electronic monitoring requirement[18] should be imposed which is mandatory[19] in some circumstances.

Electronic monitoring should be used with the primary purpose of promoting and monitoring compliance with other requirements, in circumstances where the punishment of the offender and/or the need to safeguard the public and prevent re-offending are the most important concerns.

(d) Recording the Sentence Imposed

1.1.34 Under the new framework there is only one (generic) community sentence provided by statute. This does not mean that offenders who have completed a community sentence and have then re-offended should be regarded as ineligible for a second community sentence on the basis that this has been tried and failed. Further community sentences, perhaps with different requirements, may well be justified.

1.1.35 Those imposing sentence will wish to be clear about the 'purposes' that the community sentence is designed to achieve when setting the requirements. Sharing those purposes with the offender and Probation Service will enable them to be clear about the goals that are to be achieved.

1.1.36 Any future sentencer must have full information about the requirements that were inserted by the court into the previous community sentence imposed on the offender (including whether it was a low/medium/high level order) and also about the offender's response. This will enable the court to consider the merits of imposing the same or different requirements as part of another community sentence. The requirements should be recorded in such a way as to ensure that they can be made available to another court if another offence is committed.

When an offender is required to serve a community sentence, the court records should be clearly annotated to show which particular requirements have been imposed.

(ii) Time Spent on Remand

1.1.37 The court will need to consider whether to give any credit for time spent in custody on remand.[20] (For further detail from the Panel's Advice, see Annex A)

The court should seek to give credit for time spent on remand (in custody or equivalent status) in all cases. It should make clear, when announcing sentence, whether or not credit for time on

[18] ibid section 177(3) and (4)
[19] unless the necessary facilities are not available or, in the particular circumstances of the case, the court considers it inappropriate.
[20] Criminal Justice Act 2003 section 149

remand has been given (bearing in mind that there will be no automatic reduction in sentence once section 67 of the Criminal Justice Act 1967 is repealed) and should explain its reasons for not giving credit when it considers either that this is not justified, would not be practical, or would not be in the best interests of the offender.

1.1.38 Where an offender has spent a period of time in custody on remand, there will be occasions where a custodial sentence is warranted but the length of the sentence justified by the seriousness of the offence would mean that the offender would be released immediately. Under the present framework, it may be more appropriate to pass a community sentence since that will ensure supervision on release.

1.1.39 However, given the changes in the content of the second part of a custodial sentence of 12 months or longer, a court in this situation where the custodial sentence would be 12 months or more should, under the new framework, pass a custodial sentence in the knowledge that licence requirements will be imposed on release from custody. This will ensure that the sentence imposed properly reflects the seriousness of the offence.

1.1.40 Recommendations made by the court at the point of sentence will be of particular importance in influencing the content of the licence. This will properly reflect the gravity of the offence(s) committed.

(iii) Breaches

1.1.41 Where an offender fails, without reasonable excuse, to comply with one or more requirements, the 'responsible officer'[21] can either give a warning or initiate breach proceedings. Where the offender fails to comply without reasonable excuse for the second time within a 12-month period, the 'responsible officer' must initiate proceedings.

1.1.42 In such proceedings the court must[22] either *increase the severity of the existing sentence* (i.e. impose more onerous conditions including requirements aimed at enforcement, such as a curfew or supervision requirement) or *revoke the existing sentence and proceed as though sentencing for the original offence*. The court is required to take account of the circumstances of the breach,[23] which will inevitably have an impact on its response.

1.1.43 In certain circumstances (where an offender has wilfully and persistently failed to comply with an order made in respect of an offence that is not itself punishable by imprisonment), the court can *impose a maximum of 51 weeks custody*.[24]

1.1.44 When increasing the onerousness of requirements, the court must consider the impact on the offender's ability to comply and the possibility of precipitating a custodial sentence for further breach. For that reason, and particularly where the breach occurs towards the end of the sentence, the court should take account of compliance to date and may consider that extending the supervision or operational periods will be more sensible; in other cases it might choose to add punitive or rehabilitative requirements instead. In making these changes the court must be mindful of the legislative restrictions on the overall length of community sentences and on the supervision and operational periods allowed for each type of requirement.

1.1.45 The court dealing with breach of a community sentence should have as its primary objective ensuring that the requirements of the sentence are finished, and this is important if the court is to have regard to the statutory purposes of sentencing. A court that imposes a custodial sentence for breach without giving adequate consideration to alternatives is in danger of imposing a sentence that is not commensurate with the seriousness of the original offence and is solely a punishment for breach. This risks undermining the purposes it has identified as being important. Nonetheless, courts will need to be vigilant to ensure that there is a realistic prospect of the purposes of the order being achieved.

Having decided that a community sentence is commensurate with the seriousness of the offence, the *primary* objective when sentencing for breach of requirements is to ensure that those requirements are completed.

1.1.46 A court sentencing for breach must take account of the extent to which the offender has complied with the requirements of the community order, the reasons for breach and the point at which the breach has occurred. Where a breach takes place towards the end of the operational period and the court is satisfied that the offender's appearance before the court is likely to be sufficient in itself to ensure future compliance, then given that it is not open to the court to make no order, an

[21] Criminal Justice Act 2003 schedule 8, paragraphs 5–6
[22] ibid paragraphs 9–10
[23] ibid paragraph 9(2)
[24] ibid paragraph 9(1)(c)

approach that the court might wish to adopt could be to re-sentence in a way that enables the original order to be completed properly—for example, a differently constructed community sentence that aims to secure compliance with the purposes of the original sentence.

1.1.47 If the court decides to increase the onerousness of an order, it must give careful consideration, with advice from the Probation Service, to the offender's ability to comply. A custodial sentence should be the last resort, where all reasonable efforts to ensure that an offender completes a community sentence have failed.

- **The Act allows for a custodial sentence to be imposed in response to breach of a community sentence. Custody should be the last resort, reserved for those cases of deliberate and repeated breach where all reasonable efforts to ensure that the offender complies have failed.**
- **Before increasing the onerousness of requirements, sentencers should take account of the offender's ability to comply and should avoid precipitating further breach by overloading the offender with too many or conflicting requirements.**
- **There may be cases where the court will need to consider re-sentencing to a differently constructed community sentence in order to secure compliance with the purposes of the original sentence, perhaps where there has already been partial compliance or where events since the sentence was imposed have shown that a different course of action is likely to be effective.**

Section I

Part 2—Deferred Sentences SG-12

A. Statutory Provisions

1.2.1 Under the existing legislation,[25] a court can defer a sentence for up to six months, provided the offender consents and the court considers that deferring the sentence is in the interests of justice.

1.2.2 The new provisions[26] continue to require the consent of the offender and that the court be satisfied that the making of such a decision is in the interests of justice. However, it is also stated that the power to defer sentence can only be exercised where:

'the offender undertakes to comply with any requirements as to his conduct during the period of the deferment that the court considers it appropriate to impose;'[27]

1.2.3 This enables the court to impose a wide variety of conditions (including a residence requirement).[28] The Act allows the court to appoint the probation service or other responsible person to oversee the offender's conduct during this period and prepare a report for the court at the point of sentence i.e. the end of the deferment period.

1.2.4 As under the existing legislation, if the offender commits another offence during the deferment period the court may have the power to sentence for both the original and the new offence at once. Sentence cannot be deferred for more than six months and, in most circumstances, no more than one period of deferment can be granted.[29]

1.2.5 A significant change is the provision enabling a court to deal with an offender before the end of the period of deferment.[30] For example if the court is satisfied that the offender has failed to comply with one or more requirements imposed in connection with the deferment, the offender can be brought back before the court and the court can proceed to sentence.

B. Use of Deferred Sentences SG-13

1.2.6 Under the new framework, there is a wider range of sentencing options open to the courts, including the increased availability of suspended sentences, and deferred sentences are likely to be used in very limited circumstances. A deferred sentence enables the court to review the conduct of the defendant before passing sentence, having first prescribed certain requirements. It also provides several opportunities for an offender to have some influence as to the sentence passed—

a) it tests the commitment of the offender not to re-offend;

[25] Powers of Criminal Courts (Sentencing) Act 2000 sections 1 and 2
[26] Criminal Justice Act 2003 schedule 23 repealing and replacing sections 1 and 2 of the 2000 Act
[27] ibid new section 1(3)(b) as inserted by schedule 23 to the Criminal Justice Act 2003
[28] ibid new section 1A(1)
[29] ibid new section 1(4)
[30] ibid new section 1B

b) it gives the offender an opportunity to do something where progress can be shown within a short period;

c) it provides the offender with an opportunity to behave or refrain from behaving in a particular way that will be relevant to sentence.

1.2.7 Given the new power to require undertakings and the ability to enforce those undertakings before the end of the period of deferral, the decision to defer sentence should be predominantly for a small group of cases at either the custody threshold or the community sentence threshold where the sentencer feels that there would be particular value in giving the offender the opportunities listed because, if the offender complies with the requirements, a different sentence will be justified at the end of the deferment period. This could be a community sentence instead of a custodial sentence or a fine or discharge instead of a community sentence. It may, rarely, enable a custodial sentence to be suspended rather than imposed immediately.

The use of deferred sentences should be predominantly for a small group of cases close to a significant threshold where, should the defendant be prepared to adapt his behaviour in a way clearly specified by the sentencer, the court may be prepared to impose a lesser sentence.

1.2.8 A court may impose any conditions during the period of deferment that it considers appropriate.[31] These could be specific requirements as set out in the provisions for community sentences,[32] or requirements that are drawn more widely. These should be specific, measurable conditions so that the offender knows exactly what is required and the court can assess compliance; the restriction on liberty should be limited to ensure that the offender has a reasonable expectation of being able to comply whilst maintaining his or her social responsibilities.

1.2.9 Given the need for clarity in the mind of the offender and the possibility of sentence by another court, the court should give a clear indication (and make a written record) of the type of sentence it would be minded to impose if it had not decided to defer and ensure that the offender understands the consequences of failure to comply with the court's wishes during the deferral period.

When deferring sentence, the sentencer must make clear the consequence of not complying with any requirements and should indicate the type of sentence it would be minded to impose. Sentencers should impose specific, measurable conditions that do not involve a serious restriction on liberty.

Section 2—Custodial Sentences

SG-14

Part 1—Custodial Sentences of 12 Months or More

A. Statutory Provisions

2.1.1 Under existing legislation:

- an adult offender receiving a custodial sentence of at least 12 months and below 4 years will automatically be released at the halfway point and will then be supervised under licence until the three-quarter point of the sentence. [For some, the actual release date may be earlier as a result of release on Home Detention Curfew (HDC).]
- an adult offender receiving a determinate sentence of 4 years or above will be eligible for release from the halfway point and, if not released before, will automatically be released at the two-thirds point. After release, the offender will be supervised under licence until the three-quarter point of the sentence.

2.1.2 Under the new framework, the impact of a custodial sentence will be more severe since the period in custody and under supervision will be for the whole of the sentence term set by the court. Additionally, separate provisions for the protection of the public will be introduced for those offenders designated as 'dangerous' under the Act which are designed to ensure that release only occurs when it is considered safe to do so.

2.1.3 Where a prison sentence of 12 months or more is imposed on an offender who is not classified as 'dangerous', that offender will be entitled to be released from custody after completing half of the sentence. The whole of the second half of the sentence will be subject to licence requirements. These requirements will be set shortly before release by the Secretary of State (with advice from the Governor responsible for authorising the prisoner's release in consultation with the Probation Service) but a court will be able to make recommendations at the sentencing stage on the content

[31] ibid new section 1 (3)(b) as inserted by schedule 23 to the Criminal Justice Act 2003

[32] Criminal Justice Act 2003 section 177

of those requirements.[33] The conditions that the Secretary of State may attach to a licence are to be prescribed by order.[34]

2.1.4 The Act requires that a custodial sentence for a fixed term should be for the shortest term that is commensurate with the seriousness of the offence.[35]

B. Imposition of Custodial Sentences of 12 Months or More **SG-15**

(i) Length of Sentence

2.1.5 The requirement that the second half of a prison sentence will be served in the community subject to conditions imposed prior to release is a major new development and will require offenders to be under supervision for the full duration of the sentence prescribed by the court. The Probation Service will be able to impose a number of complementary requirements on the offender during the second half of a custodial sentence and these are expected to be more demanding and involve a greater restriction on liberty than current licence conditions.

2.1.6 As well as restricting liberty to a greater extent, the new requirements will last until the very end of the sentence, rather than to the three-quarter point as at present, potentially making a custodial sentence significantly more demanding than under existing legislation. Breach of these requirements at any stage is likely to result in the offender being returned to custody and this risk continues, therefore, for longer under the new framework than under the existing legislation.

Transitional arrangements

2.1.7 In general, a fixed term custodial sentence of 12 months or more under the new framework will increase the sentence actually served (whether in custody or in the community) since it continues to the end of the term imposed. Existing guidelines issued since 1991 have been based on a different framework and so, in order to maintain consistency between the lengths of sentence under the current and the new framework, there will need to be some adjustment to the starting points for custodial sentences contained in those guidelines (subject to the special sentences under the 2003 Act where the offender is a 'dangerous' offender).

2.1.8 This aspect of the guideline will be temporary to overcome the short-term situation where sentencing guidelines (issued since implementation of the reforms to custodial sentences introduced by the Criminal Justice Act 1991) are based on a different framework and the new framework has made those sentences more demanding. As new guidelines are issued they will take into account the new framework in providing starting points and ranges of appropriate sentence lengths for offences and an adjustment will not be necessary.

2.1.9 Since there are so many factors that will vary, it is difficult to calculate precisely how much more demanding a sentence under the new framework will be. The Council's conclusion is that the sentencer should seek to achieve the best match between a sentence under the new framework and its equivalent under the old framework so as to maintain the same level of punishment. As a guide, the Council suggests the sentence length should be reduced by in the region of 15%.

2.1.10 The changes in the nature of a custodial sentence will require changes in the way the sentence is announced. Sentencers will need to continue[36] to spell out the practical implications of the sentence being imposed so that offenders, victims and the public alike all understand that the sentence does not end when the offender is released from custody. The fact that a breach of the requirements imposed in the second half of the sentence is likely to result in a return to custody should also be made very clear at the point of sentence.

- **When imposing a fixed term custodial sentence of 12 months or more under the new provisions, courts should consider reducing the overall length of the sentence that would have been imposed under the current provisions by in the region of 15%.**
- **When announcing sentence, sentencers should explain the way in which the sentence has been calculated, how it will be served and the implications of non-compliance with licence requirements. In particular, it needs to be stated clearly that the sentence is in two parts, one in custody and one under supervision in the community.**
- **This proposal does not apply to sentences for dangerous offenders, for which separate provision has been made in the Act.**

[33] Criminal Justice Act 2003 section 238(1)
[34] ibid section 250
[35] ibid section 153(2)
[36] having reference to the *Consolidated Criminal Practice Direction* [see **appendix 5**], Annex C, as suitably amended

(ii) Licence conditions

2.1.11 Under the Act, a court imposing a prison sentence of 12 months or more may recommend conditions that should be imposed by the Secretary of State (with advice from the Governor responsible for authorising the prisoner's release in consultation with the Probation Service) on release from custody.[37] Recommendations do not form part of the sentence and they are not binding on the Secretary of State.[38]

2.1.12 When passing such a sentence, the court will not know with any certainty to what extent the offender's behaviour may have been addressed in custody or what the offender's health and other personal circumstances might be on release and so it will be extremely difficult, especially in the case of longer custodial sentences, for sentencers to make an informed judgement about the most appropriate licence conditions to be imposed on release. However, in most cases, it would be extremely helpful for sentencers to indicate areas of an offender's behaviour about which they have the most concern and to make suggestions about the types of intervention whether this, in practice, takes place in prison or in the community.

2.1.13 The involvement of the Probation Service at the pre-sentence stage will clearly be pivotal. A recommendation on the likely post-release requirements included in a presentence report will assist the court with the decision on overall sentence length, although any recommendation would still have to be open to review when release is being considered. A curfew, exclusion requirement or prohibited activity requirement might be suitable conditions to recommend for the licence period. A court might also wish to suggest that the offender should complete a rehabilitation programme, for example for drug abuse, anger management, or improving skills such as literacy and could recommend that this should be considered as a licence requirement if the programme has not been undertaken or completed in custody.

2.1.14 The Governor responsible for authorising the prisoner's release, in consultation with the Probation Service, is best placed to make recommendations at the point of release; this is the case at present and continues to be provided for in the Act. *Specific* court recommendations will only generally be appropriate in the context of relatively short sentences, where it would not be unreasonable for the sentencer to anticipate the relevance of particular requirements at the point of release. Making recommendations in relation to longer sentences (other than suggestions about the types of intervention that might be appropriate at some point during the sentence) would be unrealistic. The Governor and Probation Service should have due regard to any recommendations made by the sentencing court and the final recommendation to the Secretary of State on licence conditions will need to build upon any interventions during the custodial period and any other changes in the offender's circumstances.

- **A court may sensibly suggest interventions that could be useful when passing sentence, but should only make *specific* recommendations about the requirements to be imposed on licence when announcing short sentences and where it is reasonable to anticipate their relevance at the point of release. The Governor and Probation Service should have due regard to any recommendations made by the sentencing court but its decision should be contingent upon any changed circumstances during the custodial period.**
- **The court should make it clear, at the point of sentence, that the requirements to be imposed on licence will ultimately be the responsibility of the Governor and Probation Service and that they are entitled to review any recommendations made by the court in the light of any changed circumstances.**

Section 2—Custodial Sentences

SG-16

Part 2—Suspended Sentences of Imprisonment

A. Statutory Provisions

2.2.1 *Section 189 Criminal Justice Act 2003*

[Sets out the CJA 2003, s. 189(1) to (7) (suspended sentences of imprisonment: see **E6.2** to **E6.4**).]

2.2.2 *Imposition of requirements*—Section 190 Criminal Justice Act 2003

[Sets out the CJA 2003, s. 190(1) to (5) (imposition of requirements by suspended sentence order: see **E6.5**).]

2.2.3 *Power to provide for review*—Section 191 Criminal Justice Act 2003

[Sets out the CJA 2003, s. 191(1) to (5) (power to provide for review of suspended sentence order: see **E6.7**).]

[37] Criminal Justice Act 2003 section 238(1)

[38] ibid section 250

2.2.4 *Periodic reviews*—Section 192 Criminal Justice Act 2003
[Sets out the CJA 2003, s. 192(1) to (8) (periodic review of suspended sentence order: see **E6.7**).]

2.2.5 *Breach, revocation or amendment of orders, and effect of further conviction—Section 193 Criminal Justice Act 2003*
Schedule 12 (which relates to the breach, revocation or amendment of the community requirements of suspended sentence orders, and to the effect of any further conviction) shall have effect.

B. Imposing a Suspended Sentence **SG-17**

2.2.6 A suspended sentence is a sentence of imprisonment. It is subject to the same criteria as a sentence of imprisonment which is to commence immediately. In particular, this requires a court to be satisfied that the custody threshold has been passed and that the length of the term is the shortest term commensurate with the seriousness of the offence.

2.2.7 A court which passes a prison sentence of less than 12 months may suspend it for between 6 months and 2 years (the operational period).[39] During that period, the court can impose one or more requirements for the offender to undertake in the community. The requirements are identical to those available for the new community sentence.

2.2.8 The period during which the offender undertakes community requirements is 'the supervision period' when the offender will be under the supervision of a 'responsible officer'; this period may be shorter than the operational period. The court may periodically review the progress of the offender in complying with the requirements and the reviews will be informed by a report from the responsible officer.

2.2.9 If the offender fails to comply with a requirement during the supervision period, or commits a further offence during the operational period, the suspended sentence can be activated in full or in part or the terms of the supervision made more onerous. There is a presumption that the suspended sentence will be activated either in full or in part.

(i) The decision to suspend

2.2.10 There are many similarities between the suspended sentence and the community sentence. In both cases, requirements can be imposed during the supervision period and the court can respond to breach by sending the offender to custody. The crucial difference is that the suspended sentence is a prison sentence and is appropriate only for an offence that passes the custody threshold and for which imprisonment is the only option. A community sentence may also be imposed for an offence that passes the custody threshold where the court considers that to be appropriate.

2.2.11 The full decision making process for imposition of custodial sentences under the new framework (including the custody threshold test) is set out in paragraphs 1.31–1.33 of the Seriousness guideline. For the purposes of suspended sentences the relevant steps are:
(a) has the custody threshold been passed?
(b) if so, is it unavoidable that a custodial sentence be imposed?
(c) if so, can that sentence be suspended? (sentencers should be clear that they would have imposed a custodial sentence if the power to suspend had not been available)
(d) if not, can the sentence be served intermittently?
(e) if not, impose a sentence which takes immediate effect for the term commensurate with the seriousness of the offence.

(ii) Length of sentence

2.2.12 Before making the decision to suspend sentence, the court must already have decided that a prison sentence is justified and should also have decided the length of sentence that would be the shortest term commensurate with the seriousness of the offence if it were to be imposed immediately. The decision to suspend the sentence should not lead to a longer term being imposed than if the sentence were to take effect immediately.
A prison sentence that is suspended should be for the same term that would have applied if the offender were being sentenced to immediate custody.

2.2.13 When assessing the length of the operational period of a suspended sentence, the court should have in mind the relatively short length of the sentence being suspended and the advantages to be gained by retaining the opportunity to extend the operational period at a later stage (see below).

[39] The power to suspend a sentence is expected to come into force earlier than the provisions implementing 'custody plus' and transitional provisions are expected to enable any sentence of imprisonment of under 12 months to be suspended. This guideline therefore is written in the language of the expected transitional provisions.

The operational period of a suspended sentence should reflect the length of the sentence being suspended. As an approximate guide, an operational period of up to 12 months might normally be appropriate for a suspended sentence of up to 6 months and an operational period of up to 18 months might normally be appropriate for a suspended sentence of up to 12 months.

(iii) Requirements

2.2.14 The court will set the requirements to be complied with during the supervision period. Whilst the offence for which a suspended sentence is imposed is generally likely to be more serious than one for which a community sentence is imposed, the imposition of the custodial sentence is a clear punishment and deterrent. In order to ensure that the overall terms of the sentence are commensurate with the seriousness of the offence, it is likely that the requirements to be undertaken during the supervision period would be less onerous than if a community sentence had been imposed. These requirements will need to ensure that they properly address those factors that are most likely to reduce the risk of re-offending.

Because of the very clear deterrent threat involved in a suspended sentence, requirements imposed as part of that sentence should generally be less onerous than those imposed as part of a community sentence. A court wishing to impose onerous or intensive requirements on an offender should reconsider its decision to suspend sentence and consider whether a community sentence might be more appropriate.

SG-18 C. Breaches

2.2.15 The essence of a suspended sentence is to make it abundantly clear to an offender that failure to comply with the requirements of the order or commission of another offence will almost certainly result in a custodial sentence. Where an offender has breached any of the requirements without reasonable excuse for the first time, the responsible officer must either give a warning or initiate breach proceedings.[40] Where there is a further breach within a twelve-month period, breach proceedings must be initiated.[41]

2.2.16 Where proceedings are brought the court has several options, including extending the operational period. However, the presumption (which also applies where breach is by virtue of the commission of a further offence) is that the suspended prison sentence will be activated (either with its original custodial term or a lesser term) unless the court takes the view that this would, in all the circumstances, be unjust. In reaching that decision, the court may take into account both the extent to which the offender has complied with the requirements and the facts of the new offence.[42]

2.2.17 Where a court considers that the sentence needs to be activated, it may activate it in full or with a reduced term. Again, the extent to which the requirements have been complied with will be very relevant to this decision.

2.2.18 If a court amends the order rather than activating the suspended prison sentence, it must either make the requirements more onerous, or extend the supervision or operational periods (provided that these remain within the limits defined by the Act).[43] In such cases, the court must state its reasons for not activating the prison sentence,[44] which could include the extent to which the offender has complied with requirements or the facts of the subsequent offence.

2.2.19 If an offender near the end of an operational period (having complied with the requirements imposed) commits another offence, it may be more appropriate to amend the order rather than activate it.

2.2.20 If a new offence committed is of a less serious nature than the offence for which the suspended sentence was passed, it may justify activating the sentence with a reduced term or amending the terms of the order.

2.2.21 It is expected that any activated suspended sentence will be consecutive to the sentence imposed for the new offence.

2.2.22 If the new offence is non-imprisonable, the sentencer should consider whether it is appropriate to activate the suspended sentence at all.

[40] Criminal Justice Act 2003 schedule 12, para 4
[41] ibid para 5
[42] ibid para 8(4)
[43] ibid section 189 (3) and (4)
[44] ibid schedule 12, para. 8(3)

Where the court decides to amend a suspended sentence order rather than activate the custodial sentence, it should give serious consideration to extending the supervision or operational periods (within statutory limits) rather than making the requirements more onerous.

Section 2 Custodial Sentences

Part 3—Intermittent Custody SG-19

[The relevant guidelines on intermittent custody are not reproduced in light of the Home Office announcement of November 2006 that the provisions are not to be implemented.]

Annex A SG-20

Time Spent on Remand—Sentencing Advisory Panel's Advice

The Act makes provision for a sentencer to give credit for time spent on remand in custody where a custodial sentence is passed.[45] It also empowers the court to have regard to time spent on remand in custody when determining the restrictions on liberty to be imposed by a community order or youth community order.[46] Where an offender has spent several weeks in custody, this may affect the nature of the sentence that is passed. For example, where the court decides that a custodial sentence is justified some sentencers may decide to pass a community sentence instead, on the basis that the offender has already completed the equivalent of a punitive element in a sentence. The Panel takes the view that, given the changes in the content of the second part of a custodial sentence, in such cases it will be more appropriate to pass a custodial sentence knowing that licence requirements will be imposed on release from custody (which may be immediate). Recommendations made by the court at the point of sentence will then be of particular importance in influencing the content of the licence. This will help to ensure that the record clearly shows the assessment of seriousness of the offending behaviour.

Whereas the Act clearly states that time spent on remand is to be regarded as part of a custodial sentence unless the Court considers it unjust,[47] it states that sentencers passing a community sentence *may* have regard to time spent on remand, but no further information is given on how this discretion should be exercised. The Panel recognises that giving credit for time spent on remand is likely to be easier to apply in relation to punitive requirements rather than the rehabilitative elements of a community sentence. For example, reducing the number of unpaid work hours could be fairly easy, whereas reducing the length of a rehabilitation programme might not be appropriate as it could undermine its effectiveness. Where an offender has been kept on remand, one could take the view that this action was justified by the bail provisions and that the sentencer should not, therefore, feel obliged to adjust the terms of the community sentence. However, in principle, the Panel recommends that the court should seek to give credit for time spent on remand in all cases and should explain its reasons for not doing so when it considers either that this is not justified, would not be practical, or would not be in the best interests of the offender.

The court should seek to give credit for time spent on remand in all cases. It should make clear, when announcing sentence, whether or not credit for time on remand has been given and should explain its reasons for not giving credit when it considers either that this is not justified, would not be practical, or would not be in the best interests of the offender.

Where, following a period of time spent in custody on remand, the court decides that a custodial sentence is justified then, given the changes in the content of the second part of a custodial sentence, the court should pass a custodial sentence in the knowledge that licence requirements will be imposed on release from custody. Recommendations made by the court at the point of sentence will be of particular importance in influencing the content of the licence.[48]

[45] Criminal Justice Act 2003 section 240
[46] ibid section 149
[47] ibid section 240 (which will, at a future date, replace Criminal Justice Act 1967, section 67, by which such period is now deducted automatically).
[48] This recommendation only applies to sentences of 12 months and above pending the implementation of 'custody plus'.

SG-21 PART 3 OVERARCHING PRINCIPLES: SERIOUSNESS

Foreword

Following the planned implementation of many of the sentencing provisions in the 2003 Act in April 2005, this guideline deals with the general concept of seriousness in the light of those provisions and considers how sentencers should determine when the respective sentencing thresholds have been crossed when applying the provisions of the Act.

This guideline applies only to sentences passed under the sentencing framework applicable to those aged 18 or over although there are some aspects that will assist courts assessing the seriousness of offences committed by those under 18.

. . .

SG-22 Seriousness

A. Statutory provisions

1.1 In every case where the offender is aged 18 or over at the time of conviction, the court must have regard to the five purposes of sentencing contained in section 142(1) Criminal Justice Act 2003:
   (a) the punishment of offenders
   (b) the reduction of crime (including its reduction by deterrence)
   (c) the reform and rehabilitation of offenders
   (d) the protection of the public
   (e) the making of reparation by offenders to persons affected by their offence

1.2 The Act does not indicate that any one purpose should be more important than any other and in practice they may all be relevant to a greater or lesser degree in any individual case—the sentencer has the task of determining the manner in which they apply.

1.3 The sentencer must start by considering the *seriousness* of the offence, the assessment of which will:
- determine which of the sentencing thresholds has been crossed;
- indicate whether a custodial, community or other sentence is the most appropriate;
- be the key factor in deciding the length of a custodial sentence, the onerousness of requirements to be incorporated in a community sentence and the amount of any fine imposed.

1.4 A court is required to pass a sentence that is commensurate with the seriousness of the offence. The *seriousness* of an offence is determined by two main parameters; the *culpability* of the offender and the *harm* caused or risked being caused by the offence.

1.5 Section 143(1) Criminal Justice Act 2003 provides:
'In considering the seriousness of any offence, the court must consider the offender's culpability in committing the offence and any harm which the offence caused, was intended to cause or might foreseeably have caused.'

SG-23 B. Culpability

1.6 Four levels of criminal culpability can be identified for sentencing purposes:

1.7 Where the offender;
   (i) has the *intention* to cause harm, with the highest culpability when an offence is planned. The worse the harm intended, the greater the seriousness.
   (ii) is *reckless* as to whether harm is caused, that is, where the offender appreciates at least some harm would be caused but proceeds giving no thought to the consequences even though the extent of the risk would be obvious to most people.
   (iii) has *knowledge* of the specific risks entailed by his actions even though he does not intend to cause the harm that results.
   (iv) is guilty of *negligence*.

Note: *There are offences where liability is strict and no culpability need be proved for the purposes of obtaining a conviction, but the degree of culpability is still important when deciding sentence. The extent to which recklessness, knowledge or negligence are involved in a particular offence will vary.*

SG-24 C. Harm

1.8 The relevant provision is widely drafted so that it encompasses those offences where harm is caused but also those where neither individuals nor the community suffer harm but a risk of harm is present.

To Individual Victims

1.9 The types of harm caused or risked by different types of criminal activity are diverse and victims may suffer physical injury, sexual violation, financial loss, damage to health or psychological distress. There are gradations of harm within all of these categories.

1.10 The nature of harm will depend on personal characteristics and circumstances of the victim and the court's assessment of harm will be an effective and important way of taking into consideration the impact of a particular crime on the victim.

1.11 In some cases no actual harm may have resulted and the court will be concerned with assessing the relative dangerousness of the offender's conduct; it will consider the likelihood of harm occurring and the gravity of the harm that could have resulted.

To the Community

1.12 Some offences cause harm to the community at large (instead of or as well as to an individual victim) and may include economic loss, harm to public health, or interference with the administration of justice.

Other Types of harm

1.13 There are other types of harm that are more difficult to define or categorise. For example, cruelty to animals certainly causes significant harm to the animal but there may also be a human victim who also suffers psychological distress and/or financial loss.

1.14 Some conduct is criminalised purely by reference to public feeling or social mores. In addition, public concern about the damage caused by some behaviour, both to individuals and to society as a whole, can influence public perception of the harm caused, for example, by the supply of prohibited drugs.

D. The Assessment of Culpability and Harm **SG-25**

1.15 Section 143(1) makes clear that the assessment of the seriousness of any individual offence must take account not only of any harm actually caused by the offence, but also of any harm that was intended to be caused or might foreseeably be caused by the offence.

1.16 Assessing seriousness is a difficult task, particularly where there is an imbalance between culpability and harm:

- sometimes the harm that actually results is greater than the harm intended by the offender;
- in other circumstances, the offender's culpability may be at a higher level than the harm resulting from the offence.

1.17 Harm must always be judged in the light of culpability. The precise level of culpability will be determined by such factors as motivation, whether the offence was planned or spontaneous or whether the offender was in a position of trust.

Culpability will be greater if:

- an offender deliberately causes more harm than is necessary for the commission of the offence, or
- where an offender targets a vulnerable victim (because of their old age or youth, disability or by virtue of the job they do).

1.18 Where unusually serious harm results and was unintended and beyond the control of the offender, culpability will be significantly influenced by the extent to which the harm could have been foreseen.

1.19 If much *more* harm, or much *less* harm has been caused by the offence than the offender intended or foresaw, the culpability of the offender, depending on the circumstances, may be regarded as carrying greater or lesser weight as appropriate.

The culpability of the offender in the particular circumstances of an individual case should be the initial factor in determining the seriousness of an offence.

(i) Aggravating Factors

1.20 Sentencing guidelines for a particular offence will normally include a list of aggravating features which, if present in an individual instance of the offence, would indicate *either* a higher than usual level of culpability on the part of the offender, *or* a greater than usual degree of harm caused by the offence (or sometimes both).

1.21 The lists below bring together the most important aggravating features with potential application to more than one offence or class of offences. They include some factors (such as the vulnerability of victims or abuse of trust) which are integral features of certain offences; in such cases, the presence of the aggravating factor is already reflected in the penalty for the offence and *cannot be used as justification for increasing the sentence further*. The lists are not intended to be comprehensive and the aggravating factors are not listed in any particular order of priority. On occasions, two or more of the factors listed will describe the same feature of the offence and care needs to be taken to avoid 'doublecounting'. Those factors starred with an asterisk are statutory aggravating factors where the statutory provisions are in force. Those marked with a hash are yet to be brought into force but as factors in an individual case are still relevant and should be taken into account.

1.22 *Factors indicating higher culpability:*

- Offence committed whilst on bail for other offences*
- Failure to respond to previous sentences
- Offence was racially or religiously aggravated*
- Offence motivated by, or demonstrating, hostility to the victim based on his or her sexual orientation (or presumed sexual orientation)
- Offence motivated by, or demonstrating, hostility based on the victims disability (or presumed disability)
- Previous conviction(s), particularly where a pattern of repeat offending is disclosed
- Planning of an offence
- An intention to commit more serious harm than actually resulted from the offence
- Offenders operating in groups or gangs
- 'Professional' offending
- Commission of the offence for financial gain (where this is not inherent in the offence itself)
- High level of profit from the offence
- An attempt to conceal or dispose of evidence
- Failure to respond to warnings or concerns expressed by others about the offender's behaviour
- Offence committed whilst on licence
- Offence motivated by hostility towards a minority group, or a member or members of it
- Deliberate targeting of vulnerable victim(s)
- Commission of an offence while under the influence of alcohol or drugs
- Use of a weapon to frighten or injure victim
- Deliberate and gratuitous violence or damage to property, over and above what is needed to carry out the offence
- Abuse of power
- Abuse of a position of trust

1.23 *Factors indicating a more than usually serious degree of harm:*

- Multiple victims
- An especially serious physical or psychological effect on the victim, even if unintended
- A sustained assault or repeated assaults on the same victim
- Victim is particularly vulnerable
- Location of the offence (for example, in an isolated place)
- Offence is committed against those working in the public sector or providing a service to the public
- Presence of others e.g. relatives, especially children or partner of the victim
- Additional degradation of the victim (e.g. taking photographs of a victim as part of a sexual offence)
- In property offences, high value (including sentimental value) of property to the victim, or substantial consequential loss (e.g. where the theft of equipment causes serious disruption to a victim's life or business)

(ii) Mitigating factors

1.24 Some factors may indicate that an offender's culpability is *unusually* low, or that the harm caused by an offence is less than usually serious.

1.25 *Factors indicating significantly lower culpability:*

- A greater degree of provocation than normally expected
- Mental illness or disability
- Youth or age, where it affects the responsibility of the individual defendant
- The fact that the offender played only a minor role in the offence

(iii) Personal mitigation

1.26 Section 166(1) Criminal Justice Act 2003 makes provision for a sentencer to take account of any matters that 'in the opinion of the court, are relevant in mitigation of sentence'.

1.27 When the court has formed an initial assessment of the seriousness of the offence, then it should consider any offender mitigation. The issue of remorse should be taken into account at this point along with other mitigating features such as admissions to the police in interview.

(iv) Reduction for a guilty plea

1.28 Sentencers will normally reduce the severity of a sentence to reflect an early guilty plea. This subject is covered by a separate guideline and provides a sliding scale reduction with a normal maximum one-third reduction being given to offenders who enter a guilty plea at the first reasonable opportunity.

1.29 Credit may also be given for ready co-operation with the authorities. This will depend on the particular circumstances of the individual case.

E. The Sentencing Thresholds **SG-26**

1.30 Assessing the seriousness of an offence is only the first step in the process of determining the appropriate sentence in an individual case. Matching the offence to a type and level of sentence is a separate and complex exercise assisted by the application of the respective threshold tests for custodial and community sentences.

The Custody Threshold

1.31 Section 152(2) Criminal Justice Act 2003 provides:
'The court must not pass a custodial sentence unless it is of the opinion that the offence, or the combination of the offence and one or more offences associated with it, was so serious that neither a fine alone nor a community sentence can be justified for the offence.'

1.32 In applying the threshold test, sentencers should note:
- the clear intention of the threshold test is to reserve prison as a punishment for the most serious offences;
- it is impossible to determine definitively which features of a particular offence make it serious enough to merit a custodial sentence;
- passing the custody threshold does *not* mean that a custodial sentence should be deemed inevitable, and custody can still be avoided in the light of personal mitigation or where there is a suitable intervention in the community which provides sufficient restriction (by way of punishment) while addressing the rehabilitation of the offender to prevent future crime. For example, a prolific offender who currently could expect a short custodial sentence (which, in advance of custody plus, would have no provision for supervision on release) might more appropriately receive a suitable community sentence.

1.33 The approach to the imposition of a custodial sentence under the new framework should be as follows:
(a) has the custody threshold been passed?
(b) if so, is it unavoidable that a custodial sentence be imposed?
(c) if so, can that sentence be suspended? (sentencers should be clear that they would have imposed a custodial sentence if the power to suspend had not been available)
(d) if not, can the sentence be served intermittently?
(e) if not, impose a sentence which takes immediate effect for the term commensurate with the seriousness of the offence.

The Threshold for Community Sentences

1.34 Section 148(1) Criminal Justice Act 2003 provides:
'A court must not pass a community sentence on an offender unless it is of the opinion that the offence, or the combination of the offence and one or more offences associated with it, was serious enough to warrant such a sentence.'

1.35 In addition, the threshold for a community sentence can be crossed even though the seriousness criterion is not met. Section 151 Criminal Justice Act 2003 provides that, in relation to an offender aged 16 or over on whom, on 3 or more previous occasions, sentences had been passed consisting only of a fine, a community sentence may be imposed (if it is in the interests of justice) despite the fact that the seriousness of the current offence (and others associated with it) might not warrant such a sentence.

1.36 Sentencers should consider all of the disposals available (within or below the threshold passed) at the time of sentence before reaching the provisional decision to make a community sentence, so that, even where the threshold for a community sentence has been passed, a financial penalty or discharge may still be an appropriate penalty.

Summary

1.37 It would not be feasible to provide a form of words or to devise any formula that would provide a general solution to the problem of where the custody threshold lies. Factors vary too widely between offences for this to be done. It is the task of *guidelines for individual offences* to provide more detailed guidance on what features within that offence point to a custodial sentence, and also to deal with issues such as sentence length, the appropriate requirements for a community sentence or the use of appropriate ancillary orders.

Having assessed the seriousness of an individual offence, sentencers must consult the sentencing guidelines for an offence of that type for guidance on the factors that are likely to indicate whether a custodial sentence or other disposal is most likely to be appropriate.

SG-27 **F. Prevalence**

1.38 The seriousness of an individual case should be judged on its own dimensions of harm and culpability rather than as part of a collective social harm. It is legitimate for the overall approach to sentencing levels for particular offences to be guided by their cumulative effect. However, it would be wrong to further penalise individual offenders by increasing sentence length for committing an individual offence of that type.

1.39 There may be exceptional local circumstances that arise which may lead a court to decide that prevalence should influence sentencing levels. The pivotal issue in such cases will be the harm being caused to the community. It is essential that sentencers both have supporting evidence from an external source (for example the local Criminal Justice Board) to justify claims that a particular crime is prevalent in their area and are satisfied that there is a compelling need to treat the offence more seriously than elsewhere.

The key factor in determining whether sentencing levels should be enhanced in response to prevalence will be the level of harm being caused in the locality. Enhanced sentences should be exceptional and in response to exceptional circumstances. Sentencers must sentence within the sentencing guidelines once the prevalence has been addressed.

SG-28 PART 4 MANSLAUGHTER BY REASON OF PROVOCATION

FOREWORD

. . . This guideline stems from a reference from the Home Secretary for consideration of the issue of sentencing where provocation is argued in cases of homicide, and, in particular, domestic violence homicides. For the purpose of describing 'domestic violence', the Home Secretary adopted the Crown Prosecution Service definition.[49] The guideline applies to sentencing of an adult offender for this offence in whatever circumstances it occurs. It identifies the widely varying features of both the provocation and the act of retaliation and sets out the approach to be adopted in deciding both the sentencing range and the starting point within that range.

This guideline is for use where the conviction for manslaughter is clearly founded on provocation alone. There will be additional, different and more complicated matters to be taken into account where the other main partial defence, diminished responsibility, is a factor.

The Council's Guideline *New Sentences: Criminal Justice Act 2003* recognised the potentially more demanding nature of custodial sentences of 12 months or longer imposed under the new framework introduced by the Criminal Justice Act 2003. Consequently the sentencing ranges and starting points in this guideline take that principle into account.

. . .

[49] 'Any criminal offence arising out of physical, sexual, psychological, emotional or financial abuse by one person against a current or former partner in a close relationship, or against a current or former family member.' A new definition of domestic violence was agreed in 2004 (and appears in the CPS Policy on Prosecuting cases of Domestic Violence, 2005) 'any incident of threatening behaviour, violence or abuse [psychological, physical, sexual, financial or emotional] between adults who are or have been intimate partners or family members, regardless of gender or sexuality'.

Manslaughter by Reason of Provocation

A. Statutory Provision SG-29

1.1 Murder and manslaughter are common law offences and there is no complete statutory definition of either. 'Provocation' is one of the partial defences by which an offence that would otherwise be murder may be reduced to manslaughter.

1.2 Before the issue of provocation can be considered, the Crown must have proved beyond reasonable doubt that all the elements of murder were present, including the necessary intent (i.e. the offender must have intended either to kill the victim or to cause grievous bodily harm). The court must then consider section 3 of the Homicide Act 1957, which provides:

Where on a charge of murder there is evidence on which the jury can find that the person charged was provoked (whether by things done or by things said or by both together) to lose his self-control, the question whether the provocation was enough to make a reasonable man do as he did shall be left to be determined by the jury; and in determining that question the jury shall take into account everything both done and said according to the effect which, in their opinion, it would have on a reasonable man.

Although both murder and manslaughter result in death, the difference in the level of culpability creates offences of a distinctively different character. Therefore the approach to sentencing in each should start from a different basis.

B. Establishing the Basis for Sentencing SG-30

2.1 The Court of Appeal in *Attorney General's Reference (Nos. 74, 95 and 118 of 2002) (Suratan and others)*,[50] set out a number of assumptions that a judge must make in favour of an offender found not guilty of murder but guilty of manslaughter by reason of provocation. The assumptions are required in order to be faithful to the verdict and should be applied equally in all cases whether conviction follows a trial or whether the Crown has accepted a plea of guilty to manslaughter by reason of provocation:

- first, that the offender had, at the time of the killing, lost self-control; mere loss of temper or jealous rage is not sufficient
- second, that the offender was caused to lose self-control by things said or done, normally by the person killed
- third, that the offender's loss of control was reasonable in all the circumstances, even bearing in mind that people are expected to exercise reasonable control over their emotions and that, as society advances, it ought to call for a higher measure of self control.
- fourth, that the circumstances were such as to make the loss of self-control sufficiently excusable to reduce the gravity of the offence from murder to manslaughter.

Bearing in mind the loss of life caused by manslaughter by reason of provocation, the starting point for sentencing should be a custodial sentence. Only in a very small number of cases involving very exceptional mitigating factors should a judge consider that a non-custodial sentence is justified.

The same general sentencing principles should apply in all cases of manslaughter by reason of provocation irrespective of whether or not the killing takes place in a domestic context.

C. Factors Influencing Sentence SG-31

3.1 A number of elements must be considered and balanced by the sentencer. Some of these are common to all types of manslaughter by reason of provocation; others have a particular relevance in cases of manslaughter in a domestic context.

3.2 ***The degree of provocation as shown by its nature and duration***—An assessment of the *degree* of the provocation as shown by its nature and duration is the critical factor in the sentencing decision.

(a) *In assessing the degree of provocation, account should be taken of the following factors:*

- if the provocation (which does not have to be a wrongful act) involves gross and extreme conduct on the part of the victim, it is a more significant mitigating factor than conduct which, although significant, is not as extreme
- the fact that the victim presented a threat not only to the offender, but also to children in his or her care
- the offender's previous experiences of abuse and/or domestic violence either by the victim or by other people

[50] [2003] 2 Cr App R (S) 42

- any mental condition which may affect the offender's perception of what amounts to provocation
- the nature of the conduct, the period of time over which it took place and its cumulative effect
- discovery or knowledge of the fact of infidelity on the part of a partner does not necessarily amount to *high* provocation. The gravity of such provocation depends entirely on all attendant circumstances.

(b) *Whether the provocation was suffered over a long or short period is important to the assessment of gravity. The following factors should be considered:*
- the impact of provocative behaviour on an offender can build up over a period of time
- consideration should not be limited to acts of provocation that occurred immediately before the victim was killed. For example, in domestic violence cases, cumulative provocation may eventually become intolerable, the latest incident seeming all the worse because of what went before.

(c) *When looking at the nature of the provocation the court should consider both the type of provocation and whether, in the particular case, the actions of the victim would have had a particularly marked effect on the offender:*
- actual (or anticipated) violence from the victim will generally be regarded as involving a higher degree of provocation than provocation arising from abuse, infidelity or offensive words unless that amounts to psychological bullying
- in cases involving actual or anticipated violence, the culpability of the offender will therefore generally be less than in cases involving verbal provocation
- where the offender's actions were motivated by fear or desperation, rather than by anger, frustration, resentment or a desire for revenge, the offender's culpability will generally be lower.

3.3 ***The extent and timing of the retaliation***—It is implicit in the verdict of manslaughter by reason of provocation that the killing was the result of a loss of self-control because of things said and/or done. The intensity, extent and nature of that loss of control must be assessed in the context of the provocation that preceded it.

3.4 The *circumstances of the killing* itself will be relevant to the offender's culpability, and hence to the appropriate sentence:
- in general, the offender's violent response to provocation is likely to be less culpable the shorter the time gap between the provocation (or the last provocation) and the killing—as evidenced, for example, by the use of a weapon that happened to be available rather than by one that was carried for that purpose or prepared for use in advance
- conversely, it is not necessarily the case that greater culpability will be found where there has been a significant lapse of time between the provocation (or the last provocation) and the killing. Where the provocation is cumulative, and particularly in those circumstances where the offender is found to have suffered domestic violence from the victim over a significant period of time, the required loss of self-control may not be sudden as some experience a 'slow-burn' reaction and appear calm
- choosing or taking advantage of favourable circumstances for carrying out the killing (so that the victim was unable to resist, such as where the victim was not on guard, or was asleep) may well be an aggravating factor—unless this is mitigated by the circumstances of the offender, resulting in the offender being the weaker or vulnerable party.

3.5 The *context of the relationship* between the offender and the victim must be borne in mind when assessing the nature and degree of the provocation offered by the victim before the crime and the length of time over which the provocation existed. In cases where the parties were still in a relationship at the time of the killing, it will be necessary to examine the balance of power between one party and the other and to consider other family members who may have been drawn into, or been victims of, the provocative behaviour.

Although there will usually be less culpability when the retaliation to provocation is sudden, it is not always the case that greater culpability will be found where there has been a significant lapse of time between the provocation and the killing.

It is for the sentencer to consider the impact on an offender of provocative behaviour that has built up over a period of time.

An offence should be regarded as aggravated where it is committed in the presence of a child or children or other vulnerable family member, whether or not the offence takes place in a domestic setting.

3.6 *Post-offence behaviour*—The behaviour of the offender after the killing can be relevant to sentence:
- immediate and genuine remorse may be demonstrated by the summoning of medical assistance, remaining at the scene, and co-operation with the authorities
- concealment or attempts to dispose of evidence or dismemberment of the body may aggravate the offence.

Post-offence behaviour is relevant to the sentence. It may be an aggravating or mitigating factor. When sentencing, the judge should consider the motivation behind the offender's actions.

3.7 *Use of a weapon*

(a) In relation to this offence, as in relation to many different types of offence, the carrying and use of a weapon is an aggravating factor. Courts must consider the type of weapon used and, importantly, whether it was to hand or carried to the scene and who introduced it to the incident.

(b) The use or not of a weapon is a factor heavily influenced by the gender of the offender. Whereas men can and do kill using physical strength alone, women often cannot and thus resort to using a weapon. The issue of key importance is whether the weapon was to hand or carried deliberately to the scene, although the circumstances in which the weapon was brought to the scene will need to be considered carefully.

Although there will usually be less culpability when the retaliation to provocation is sudden, it is not always the case that greater culpability will be found where there has been a significant lapse of time between the provocation and the killing.

It is for the sentencer to consider the impact on an offender of provocative behaviour that has built up over a period of time.

An offence should be regarded as aggravated where it is committed in the presence of a child or children or other vulnerable family member, whether or not the offence takes place in a domestic setting.

The use of a weapon should not necessarily move a case into another sentencing bracket.

In cases of manslaughter by reason of provocation, use of a weapon may reflect the imbalance in strength between the offender and the victim and how that weapon came to hand is likely to be far more important than the use of the weapon itself.

It will be an aggravating factor where the weapon is brought to the scene in contemplation of use *before* the loss of self-control (which may occur some time before the fatal incident).

D. Sentence Ranges and Starting Points SG-32

4.1 **Manslaughter is a 'serious offence' for the purposes of the provisions in the Criminal Justice Act 2003[51] for dealing with dangerous offenders. It is possible that a court will be required to use the sentences for public protection prescribed in the Act when sentencing an offender convicted of the offence of manslaughter by reason of provocation. An alternative is a discretionary life sentence. In accordance with normal practice, when setting the minimum term to be served within an indeterminate sentence under these provisions, that term will usually be half the equivalent determinate sentence.**

4.2 *Identifying sentence ranges*—The key factor that will be relevant in every case is the nature and the duration of the provocation.

(a) The process to be followed by the court will be:
identify the sentence range by reference to the degree of provocation
adjust the starting point within the range by reference to the length of time over which the provocation took place
take into consideration the circumstances of the killing (e.g. the length of time that had elapsed between the provocation and the retaliation and the circumstances in which any weapon was used)

(b) This guideline establishes that:
- there are three sentencing ranges defined by the degree of provocation—low, substantial and high
- within the three ranges, the starting point is based on provocation taking place over a short period of time
- the court will move from the starting point (based upon the degree of provocation) by considering the length of time over which the provocation has taken place, and by reference to any aggravating and mitigating factors

[51] Sections 224–230

SG-33

Manslaughter by Reason of Provocation

Factors to take into consideration

1. The sentences for public protection must be considered in all cases of manslaughter.
2. The presence of any of the general aggravating factors identified in the Council's Guideline *Overarching Principles: Seriousness* or any of the additional factors identified in this Guideline will indicate a sentence above the normal starting point.
3. This offence will not be an initial charge but will arise following a charge of murder. The Council Guideline *Reduction in Sentence for a Guilty Plea* will need to be applied with this in mind. In particular, consideration will need to be given to the time at which it was indicated that the defendant would plead guilty to manslaughter by reason of provocation.
4. An assessment of the *degree* of the provocation as shown by its nature and duration is the critical factor in the sentencing decision.
5. The intensity, extent and nature of the loss of control must be assessed in the context of the provocation that preceded it.
6. Although there will usually be less culpability when the retaliation to provocation is sudden, it is not always the case that greater culpability will be found where there has been a significant lapse of time between the provocation and the killing.
7. It is for the sentencer to consider the impact on an offender of provocative behaviour that has built up over a period of time.
8. The use of a weapon should not necessarily move a case into another sentencing bracket.
9. Use of a weapon may reflect the imbalance in strength between the offender and the victim and how that weapon came to hand is likely to be far more important than the use of the weapon itself.
10. It will be an aggravating factor where the weapon is brought to the scene in contemplation of use *before* the loss of self-control (which may occur some time before the fatal incident).
11. Post-offence behaviour is relevant to the sentence. It may be an aggravating or mitigating factor. When sentencing, the judge should consider the motivation behind the offender's actions.

This is a serious offence for the purposes of section 224 of the Criminal Justice Act 2003

Maximum penalty: Life imprisonment

Type/Nature of Activity	Sentence Ranges & Starting Points
Low degree of provocation: A low degree of provocation occurring over a short period	**Sentence Range: 10 years–life** **Starting Point—12 years custody**
Substantial degree of provocation: A substantial degree of provocation occurring over a short period	**Sentence Range: 4–9 years** **Starting Point—8 years custody**
High degree of provocation: A high degree of provocation occurring over a short period	**Sentence Range: if custody is necessary, up to 4 years** **Starting Point—3 years custody**

Additional aggravating factors	Additional mitigating factors
1. Concealment or attempts to dispose of evidence*	1. The offender was acting to protect another
2. Dismemberment or mutilation of the body*	2. Spontaneity and lack of premeditation
3. Offence committed in the presence of a child/children or other vulnerable family member	3. Previous experiences of abuse and/or domestic violence
	4. Evidence that the victim presented an ongoing danger to the offender or another
*subject to para 3.6 above.	5. Actual (or reasonably anticipated) violence from the victim

The Council Guideline New Sentences: Criminal Justice Act 2003 recognised the potentially more demanding nature of custodial sentences of 12 months or longer imposed under the new framework introduced by the Criminal Justice Act 2003. The sentencing ranges and starting points in the above guideline take account of this.

PART 5 ROBBERY SG-34

. . . This guideline applies to the sentencing of offenders convicted of robbery who are sentenced on or after 1 August 2006.

Part 1 of this guideline provides starting points and sentencing ranges that are applicable to three types of robbery; street robbery or 'mugging', robberies of small businesses and less sophisticated commercial robberies. For other types of robbery, relevant guidance from the Court of Appeal should be applied; this is summarised in Part 2 of this guideline.

The guideline makes clear that robbery will usually merit a custodial sentence but that exceptional circumstances may justify a non-custodial penalty for an adult and, more frequently, for a young offender. In this way it is not intended to make a significant change to current practice. Over the past ten years the majority of young offenders sentenced for robbery have been given a non-custodial sentence. This contrasts with adult offenders where the majority sentenced for robbery have been given a custodial sentence.[52]

The Council Guideline *New Sentences: Criminal Justice Act 2003* recognised the potentially more demanding nature of custodial sentences of 12 months or longer imposed under the new framework introduced by the Criminal Justice Act 2003. Consequently the sentencing ranges and starting points in this guideline take that principle into account . . .

A. Statutory Provision SG-35

Section 8(1) Theft Act 1968 provides:
A person is guilty of robbery if he steals, and immediately before or at the time of doing so, and in order to do so, he uses force on any person or puts or seeks to put any person in fear of being then and there subjected to force.

B. Forms of Robbery and Structure of the Guideline SG-36

For the purposes of this guideline, five categories of robbery have been identified and established from sentencing ranges and previous guidance. They are:
1. Street robbery or 'mugging'
2. Robberies of small businesses
3. Less sophisticated commercial robberies
4. Violent personal robberies in the home
5. Professionally planned commercial robberies

The guideline is divided into two parts.

Part 1—This part covers categories 1–3 above.

For each of the three categories, three levels of seriousness have been identified based on the extent of force used or threatened.

For each level of seriousness a sentencing range and a starting point within that range have been identified.

Adult and youth offenders are distinguished and the guideline provides for them as separate groups.

Part 2—No guideline is provided for categories 4 and 5. Violent personal robberies are often accompanied by other serious offences which affect sentencing decisions. For professionally planned commercial robberies, existing case authority is still valid and this is summarised in Part 2.

C. Part 1 SG-37

Street robbery or 'mugging'

Street robberies will usually involve some physical force (or threat) to steal modest sums, although in some cases there is significant intimidation or violence. The victim may or may not be physically injured.

Robberies of small businesses

This category covers robberies of businesses such as a small shop or post office, petrol station or public transport/taxi facility which may well lack the physical and electronic security devices available to banks or building societies and larger businesses.

[52] In 2004 37% of youths and 87% of adults sentenced for robbery were given custodial sentences.

Less sophisticated commercial robberies

This category covers a wide range of locations, extent of planning and degree of violence including less sophisticated bank robberies or where larger commercial establishments are the target but without detailed planning or high levels of organisation.

SG-38 **D. Assessing Seriousness**

(i) Levels of Seriousness

Three levels of seriousness are identified by reference to the features or type of activity that characterise an offence at each level and the degree of force or threat present. The levels apply to all three categories of robbery but it will be very rare for robberies of small businesses or less sophisticated commercial robberies to have the features of the lowest level of seriousness.

Level 1—Threat and/or use of minimal force

The offence includes the threat or use of force and removal of property such as snatching from a persons grasp causing bruising/pain and discomfort.

The relative seriousness of a level 1 offence depends on:
(a) the nature and duration of any force, threat or intimidation
(b) the extent of injury (if any) to the victim
(c) the value of the property taken
(d) the number and degree of aggravating factors

Level 2—Use of weapon to threaten and/or use of significant force

A weapon is produced and used to threaten, and/or force is used which results in injury to the victim.

The relative seriousness of a level 2 offence depends on:
(a) the nature and duration of the threat or intimidation
(b) the extent of injury (if any) to the victim
(c) the nature of the weapon used, whether it was real and, if it was a real firearm, whether it was loaded
(d) the value of the property taken
(e) the number and degree of aggravating factors

Level 3—Use of weapon and/or significant force and serious injury caused

The victim is caused serious physical injury, such as a broken limb, stab wound or internal injury, by the use of significant force and/or use of a weapon. Offences at this level are often accompanied by the presence of additional aggravating factors such as a degree of planning or the targeting of large sums of money or valuable goods.

The relative seriousness of a level 3 offence depends on:
(a) the extent of injury (if any) to the victim
(b) the nature of the weapon used
(c) the value of the property taken
(d) the number and degree of aggravating factors

(ii) Aggravating & Mitigating Factors

The presence of one or more aggravating features will indicate a more severe sentence within the suggested range. If the aggravating feature(s) are exceptionally serious, the case may move to the next level of seriousness.

Aggravating factors particularly relevant to robbery

(a) Degree of force or violence

- Use of a particular degree of force is more serious than the threat (which is not carried into effect) to use that same degree of force.
- Depending on the facts, however, a threat to use a high degree of force might properly be regarded as more serious than actual use of a lesser degree of force.

(b) Use of a weapon

- Possession of a weapon during the course of an offence will be an aggravating factor, even if it is not used, because it indicates planning.
- Possession of a firearm which is loaded is more serious than possession of a firearm which is unloaded.

- Whether the weapon is real or imitation is not a major factor in determining sentence because the amount of fear created in the victim is likely to be the same.
- In cases of robbery in which a firearm is carried by the offender, a separate offence of possession of a firearm may be charged. In such circumstances, sentencers should consider, where appropriate, the use of consecutive sentences which properly reflect the totality of the offending.

(c) **Vulnerability of the victim**

- Targeting the elderly, the young, those with disabilities and persons performing a service to the public, especially outside normal working hours, will aggravate an offence.

(d) **Number involved in the offence and roles of offenders**

- Group offending will aggravate an offence because the level of intimidation and fear caused to the victim is likely to be greater.
- It may also indicate planning or 'gang' activity.
- The precise role of each offender will be important. Being the ringleader in a group is an aggravating factor. However, an offender may have played a peripheral role in the offence and, rather than having planned to take part, may have become involved spontaneously through the influence of others (see Mitigating Factors below).

(e) **Value of items taken**

- Property value may be more important in planned/sophisticated robberies.
- The value of the property capable of being taken should be taken into account as well as the amount/value of the property actually taken.

(f) **Offence committed at night/in hours of darkness**

- A victim is more vulnerable while in darkness than during daylight, all other things being equal.
- The degree of fear experienced by the victim is likely to be greater if an offence is committed at night or during hours of darkness.

(g) **Wearing of a disguise**

- The wearing of a disguise in order to commit an offence of robbery usually indicates a degree of planning on the part of the offender.
- The deliberate selection of a particular type of disguise in advance of the offence, for example, a balaclava or a mask, will be more serious than the improvised use of items of clothing such as a hat or hood.

Mitigating factors particularly relevant to robbery:

(a) **Unplanned/opportunistic**

- Many street robberies are unplanned or opportunistic by their nature so the extent of the mitigation in such cases may be limited.

(b) **Peripheral Involvement**

- Where, as part of a group robbery, the offender has played a peripheral role in the offence this should be treated as a mitigating factor although it should be borne in mind that by participating as part of a group, even in a minor role, the offender is likely to have increased the degree of fear caused to the victim (see Aggravating Factors above).

(c) **Voluntary return of property taken**

- The point at which the property is returned will be important and, in general, the earlier the property is returned the greater the degree of mitigation the offender should receive.

The court will also take account of the presence or absence of other factors including:

- **Personal mitigation**
- **First offence of violence**
- **Clear evidence of remorse**
- **Ready co-operation with the police**
- **Response to previous sentences**

A list of the most important general aggravating and mitigating factors can be found in the Guideline *Overarching Principles: Seriousness.*[53] These factors are reproduced at Annex A for ease of reference.

[53] Paragraphs 1.22–1.25

Young Offenders

- Young offenders may have characteristics relevant to their offending behaviour which are different from adult offenders. Also, by statute, the youth justice system has the principal aim of preventing offending by children and young persons.[54] Because of this, there may be factors which are of greater significance in cases involving young offenders including:
- **Age of the offender**
- **Immaturity of the offender**
- **Group Pressure**

Sentencers should recognise the varying significance of these factors for different ages.

(iii) Reduction in Sentence for Guilty Plea

Having taking account of aggravating and mitigating factors the court should consider whether the sentence should be reduced to take account of a guilty plea and by how much, in accordance with the Guideline: *Reduction in Sentence for a Guilty Plea*.

SG-39 **E. Public Protection Sentences—Dangerous Offenders**

Robbery is a serious offence for the purposes of section 225 of the Criminal Justice Act 2003 and sentencers should consider whether a life sentence or sentence for public protection should be imposed.

SG-40 **F. Ancillary Orders**

In all cases, courts should consider making the following orders:

- Restitution Order[55]—requiring the return of property
- Compensation Order[56]—for injury, loss or damage suffered.

Where a non-custodial sentence is imposed, courts may also consider making:

- Anti-social behaviour order[57]—to protect the public from behaviour causing harassment, alarm or distress. This order may be particularly appropriate where the offence of robbery forms part of a pattern of behaviour but such an order may be unnecessary if it will simply prohibit what is already criminal conduct. It may be used to prevent some offenders associating with other offenders with whom offences of robbery have been committed.

SG-41 **G. Factors to take into consideration—Adult Offenders**

1. Robbery is a serious offence for the purposes of section 225 of the Criminal Justice Act 2003 and sentencers should consider whether a life sentence or sentence for public protection should be imposed. The following guidelines apply to offenders who have not been assessed as dangerous.
2. The sentencing ranges and presumptive starting points apply to all three categories of robbery detailed above:
   - **Street robbery or 'mugging'**
   - **Robberies of small businesses**
   - **Less sophisticated commercial robberies**
3. The 'starting points' are based upon a first time offender who pleaded not guilty.
4. A reduction to the appropriate sentence, taking account of seriousness and aggravating and mitigating factors, will need to be made if an offender has pleaded guilty. The effect of applying the reduction may be that the sentence imposed for an offence at one level of seriousness may fall within the range suggested for the next lowest level of seriousness.
5. The relative seriousness of each offence will be determined by the following factors:
   - **Degree of force and/or nature and duration of threats**
   - **Degree of injury to the victim**
   - **Degree of fear experienced by the victim**
   - **Value of property taken**
6. Use of a particular degree of force is more serious than the threat (which is not carried into effect) to use that same degree of force. Depending on the facts, however, a threat to use a high degree of force might properly be regarded as more serious than actual use of a lesser degree of force.
7. If a weapon is involved in the use or threat of force, the offence will be more serious. Possession of a weapon during the course of an offence will be an aggravating factor, even if it is not used, because it

[54] Crime and Disorder Act 1998, s. 37
[55] Powers of Criminal Courts (Sentencing) Act 2000, ss. 148–149
[56] ibid. s. 130
[57] Crime and Disorder Act 1998, s. 1 as amended

indicates planning. If the offence involves a real firearm it will be more serious if that firearm is loaded. Whether the weapon is real or imitation is not a major factor in determining sentence because the amount of fear created in the victim is likely to be the same.

8. The value of the property capable of being taken as well as the actual amount taken is important.
9. The presence of one or more aggravating features will indicate a more severe sentence within the suggested range and, if the aggravating feature(s) are exceptionally serious, the case will move up to the next level.
10. In all cases, courts should consider making a restitution order and/or a compensation order. Where a non-custodial sentence is imposed, the court may also consider making an anti-social behaviour order.
11. Passing the custody threshold does not mean that a custodial sentence should be deemed inevitable.[58]

Street Robbery or 'Mugging' Robberies of Small Businesses Less Sophisticated Commercial Robberies SG-42

Robbery is a serious offence for the purposes of sections 225 and 227 Criminal Justice Act 2003

Maximum Penalty: **Life imprisonment**

ADULT OFFENDERS

Type/nature of activity	Starting point	Sentencing Range
The offence includes custody the threat or use of minimal force and removal of property.	**12 months custody**	**Up to 3 years**
A weapon is produced and used to threaten, and/or force is used which results in injury to the victim.	**4 years custody**	**2–7 years custody**
The victim is caused serious physical injury by the use of significant force and/or use of a weapon.	**8 years custody**	**7–12 years custody**

Additional aggravating factors	Additional mitigating factors
1. More than one offender involved. 2. Being the ringleader of a group of offenders. 3. Restraint, detention or additional degradation, taken. 4. Offence was pre-planned. 5. Wearing a disguise. 6. Offence committed at night. 7. Vulnerable victim targeted. 8. Targeting of large sums of money or valuable goods. 9. Possession of a weapon that was not used.	1. Unplanned/opportunistic. 2. Peripheral involvement. 3. Voluntary return of property of the victim. 4. Clear evidence of remorse. 5. Ready co-operation with the police.

H. Factors to take into consideration—Young Offenders SG-43

1. A youth court cannot impose a custodial sentence on an offender aged 10 or 11. If the offender is aged 12, 13 or 14, a detention and training order can only be imposed by a youth court in the case of persistent young offenders. In the Crown Court, however, long term detention in accordance with the Powers of Criminal Courts (Sentencing) Act 2000 can be ordered on any young offender without the requirement of persistence. The Crown Court may also impose an extended sentence, detention for public protection or detention for life where the young offender meets the criteria for being a 'dangerous offender.' **The following guidelines apply to offenders who have *not* been assessed as dangerossus.**

[58] Guideline *Overarching Principles: Seriousness*, para 1.32

2. If a youth court is considering sending a case to the Crown Court, the court must be of the view that it is such a serious case that detention above two years is required, or that the appropriate sentence is a custodial sentence approaching the two year limit which is normally applicable to older offenders.[59]
3. The sentencing ranges and presumptive starting points apply to all three categories of robbery detailed above:
   - **Street robbery or 'mugging'**
   - **Robberies of small businesses**
   - **Less sophisticated commercial robberies**
4. The 'starting points' are based upon a first-time offender, aged 17 years old, who pleaded not guilty. For younger offenders sentencers should consider whether a lower starting point is justified in recognition of the offender's age or immaturity.
5. Young offenders may have characteristics relevant to their offending behaviour which are different from adult offenders. Also, by statute, the youth justice system has the principal aim of preventing offending by children and young persons.[60] Because of this, there may be factors which are of greater significance in cases involving young offenders. Sentencers should recognise the varying significance of such factors for different ages.
6. A reduction to the appropriate sentence, taking account of seriousness, and aggravating and mitigating factors, will need to be made if an offender has pleaded guilty. The effect of applying the reduction may be that the sentence imposed for an offence at one level of seriousness may fall within the range suggested for the next lowest level of seriousness.
7. The relative seriousness of each offence will be determined by the following factors:
   - **Degree of force and/or nature and duration of threats**
   - **Degree of injury to the victim**
   - **Degree of fear experienced by the victim**
   - **Value of property taken**
8. Use of a particular degree of force is more serious than the threat (which is not carried into effect) to use that same degree of force. Depending on the facts, however, a threat to use a high degree of force might properly be regarded as more serious than actual use of a lesser degree of force.
9. If a weapon is involved in the use or threat of force, the offence will be more serious. Possession of a weapon during the course of an offence will be an aggravating factor, even if it is not used, because it indicates planning. If the offence involves a real firearm it will be more serious if that firearm is loaded. Whether the weapon is real or imitation is not a major factor in determining sentence because the amount of fear created in the victim is likely to be the same.
10. The value of the property capable of being taken as well as the actual amount taken is important.
11. The presence of one or more aggravating features will indicate a more severe sentence within the suggested range and, if the aggravating feature(s) are exceptionally serious, the case will move up to the next level.
12. In all cases, courts should consider making a restitution order and/or a compensation order. Where a non-custodial sentence is imposed, the court may also consider making an anti-social behaviour order.
13. Courts are required by section 44(1) of the Children and Young Persons Act 1933 to have regard to the welfare of the child, and under section 37 of the Crime and Disorder Act 1998 to have regard to the overall aim of the youth justice system of preventing re-offending.
14. Passing the custody threshold does not mean that a custodial sentence should be deemed inevitable.[61]
15. Where there is evidence that the offence has been committed to fund a drug habit and that treatment for this could help tackle the offender's offending behaviour, sentencers should consider a drug treatment requirement as part of a supervision order or action plan order.

[59] *W v Southampton Youth Court, K v Wirral Borough Magistrates' Court* [2003] 1 Cr App R (S) 87
[60] Crime and Disorder Act 1998, s. 37
[61] Guideline *Overarching Principles: Seriousness*, para 1.32

Street Robbery or 'Mugging' Robberies of Small Businesses Less Sophisticated Commercial Robberies

Robbery is a serious offence for the purposes of sections 226 and 228 Criminal Justice Act 2003

YOUNG OFFENDERS*

Type/nature of activity	Starting point	Sentencing Range
The offence includes the threat or use of minimal force and removal of property.	**Community Order**	**Community Order—12 months detention and training order**
A weapon is produced and used to threaten, and/or force is used which results in injury to the victim.	**3 years detention**	**1–6 years detention**
The victim is caused serious physical injury by the use of significant force and/or use of a weapon.	**7 years detention**	**6–10 years detention**

* The 'starting points' are based upon a first-time offender aged 17 years old who pleaded not guilty. For younger offenders, sentencers should consider whether a lower starting point is justified in recognition of the offender's age or immaturity.

Maximum Penalty: **Life imprisonment**

Additional aggravating factors	Additional mitigating factors
1. More than one offender involved.	1. Unplanned/opportunistic.
2. Being the ringleader of a group of offenders.	2. Peripheral involvement
3. Restraint, detention or additional degradation, taken.	3. Voluntary return of property of the victim.
4. Offence was pre-planned.	4. Clear evidence of remorse.
5. Wearing a disguise.	5. Ready co-operation with the police.
6. Offence committed at night.	6. Age of the offender.
7. Vulnerable victim targeted.	7. Immaturity of the offender.
8. Targeting of large sums of money or valuable goods.	8. Peer group pressure.
9. Possession of a weapon that was not used.	

* The 'starting points' are based upon a first-time offender aged 17 years old who pleaded not guilty.
For younger offenders, sentencers should consider whether a lower starting point is justified in recognition of the offender's age or immaturity.

I. Part 2

Relevant guidance from the Court of Appeal (which is summarised below for ease of reference) should apply to cases falling within the final two categories of robbery.

Violent personal robberies in the home

The sentencing range for robbery in the home involving physical violence is 13–16 years for a first time offender pleading not guilty. In this type of case, the starting point reflects the high level of violence, although it is clear that longer terms will be appropriate where extreme violence is used.[62]

This category overlaps with some cases of aggravated burglary (an offence which also carries a maximum of life imprisonment) where comparable sentences are passed. Consideration will need to be given as to whether the offender is a 'dangerous offender' for the purposes of the Criminal Justice Act 2003.

[62] *O'Driscoll* (1986) 8 Cr App R (S) 121

Professionally planned commercial robberies

The leading Court of Appeal decision on sentencing for robbery is the 1975 case of *Turner*.[63] This focuses on serious commercial robberies at the upper end of the sentencing range but just below the top level—planned professional robberies of banks and security vehicles, involving firearms and high value theft, but without the additional elements that characterise the most serious cases. The Court of Appeal said it had 'come to the conclusion that the normal sentence for anyone taking part in a bank robbery or in the holdup of a security or a Post Office van should be 15 years if firearms were carried and no serious injury done.'

The Court also said that 18 years should be about the maximum for crimes which are not 'wholly abnormal' (such as the Great Train Robbery).[64]

In cases involving the most serious commercial robberies the Court has imposed 20–30 years (15–20 years after a plea of guilty).

Consideration will need to be given as to whether the offender is a 'dangerous offender' for the purposes of the Criminal Justice Act 2003.

SG-44

Annex A

[Annex A consists of extracts from the SGC Guideline, *Overarching Principles: Seriousness*, which is reproduced in full in **part 3**.]

SG-45

PART 6 BREACH OF A PROTECTIVE ORDER

Foreword

. . . This guideline applies to offenders convicted of breach of an order who are sentenced on or after 18 December 2006.

This guideline deals specifically with the sentencing of offenders who have breached either a restraining order imposed in order to prevent future conduct causing harassment or fear of violence, or a non-molestation order which prohibits a person from molesting another person.

It highlights the particular factors that courts should take into account when dealing with the criminal offence of breaching an order and includes starting points based on the different types of activity which can constitute a breach. It also identifies relevant aggravating and mitigating factors.

. . .

SG-46 **A. Statutory Provisions**

1.1 For the purposes of this guideline, two protective orders are considered:

(i) Restraining Order

1.2 It is an offence contrary to the Protection from Harassment Act 1997 to behave in a way which a person knows (or ought to know) causes someone else harassment (section 2) or fear of violence (section 4). When imposing sentence on an offender, a court may also impose a restraining order to prevent future conduct causing harassment or fear of violence.

1.3 An offence under these provisions may have occurred in a domestic context or may have occurred in other contexts. The Domestic Violence, Crime and Victims Act 2004 provides for such orders also to be made on conviction for any offence or following acquittal.[65]

1.4 It is an offence contrary to section 5(5) of the Act to fail to comply with the restraining order without reasonable excuse. That offence is punishable with a maximum of five years imprisonment.

(ii) Non-Molestation Order

1.5 Section 42 of the Family Law Act 1996 provides that, during family proceedings, a court may make a non-molestation order containing either or both of the following provisions:

- *(a) provision prohibiting a person ('the respondent') from molesting another person who is associated with the respondent;*
- *(b) provision prohibiting the respondent from molesting a relevant child.*

[63] (1975) 61 Cr App R 67

[64] *Wilson and others* (1964) 48 Cr App R 329

[65] When in force, s. 12 of the 2004 Act amends s. 5 of the 1997 Act and inserts a new s. 5A to that Act.

1.6 Section 1 of the Domestic Violence, Crime and Victims Act 2004[66] inserts a new section 42A into the 1996 Act. Section 42A (1) will provide that it is an offence to fail to comply with the order without reasonable excuse. That offence is punishable with a maximum of five years imprisonment.

1.7 In addition, breach of a non- molestation order may be dealt with as a contempt of court.

B. Sentencing for Breach SG-47

2.1 The facts that constitute a breach of a protective order may or may not also constitute a substantive offence. Where they do constitute a substantive offence, it is desirable that the substantive offence and the breach of the order should be charged as separate counts. Where necessary, consecutive sentences should be considered to reflect the seriousness of the counts and achieve the appropriate totality.

2.2 Sometimes, however, only the substantive offence or only the breach of the order will be charged. The basic principle is that the sentence should reflect all relevant aspects of the offence so that, provided the facts are not in issue, the result should be the same, regardless of whether one count or two has been charged. For example:

(i) **if the substantive offence only has been charged, the fact that it constitutes breach of a protective order should be treated as an aggravating factor;**

(ii) **if breach of the protective order only has been charged, the sentence should reflect the nature of the breach, namely, the conduct that amounts to the substantive offence, aggravated by the fact that it is also breach of an order.**

2.3 If breach of a protective order has been charged where no substantive offence was involved, the sentence should reflect the circumstances of the breach, including whether it was an isolated breach, or part of a course of conduct in breach of the order; whether it was planned or unpre-meditated; and any consequences of the breach, including psychiatric injury or distress to the person protected by the order.

C. Factors Influencing Sentencing SG-48

3.1 **In order to ensure that a protective order achieves the purpose it is intended for—protecting the victim from harm—it is important that the terms of the order are necessary and proportionate.**

3.2 The circumstances leading to the making of one of the protective orders will vary widely. Whilst a restraining order will be made in criminal proceedings, it will almost certainly result from offences of markedly different levels of seriousness or even acquittal. A nonmolestation order will have been made in civil proceedings and, again, may follow a wide variety of conduct by the subject of the order.

3.3 **In all cases the order will have been made to protect an individual from harm and action in response to breach should have as its primary aim the importance of ensuring that the order is complied with and that it achieves the protection that it was intended to achieve.**

3.4 **When sentencing for a breach of an order, the main aim should be to achieve future compliance with that order where that is realistic.**

The nature and context of the originating conduct or offence

3.5 The nature of the original conduct or offence is relevant in so far as it allows a judgement to be made on the level of harm caused to the victim by the breach and the extent to which that harm was intended by the offender.

3.6 If the original offence was serious, conduct which breaches the order might have a severe effect on the victim where in other contexts such conduct might appear minor. Even indirect contact, such as telephone calls, can cause significant harm or anxiety for a victim.

3.7 However, sentence following a breach is for the breach alone and must avoid punishing the offender again for the offence or conduct as a result of which the order was made.

The nature and context of the conduct that caused the breach

3.8 **The protective orders are designed to protect a victim. When dealing with a breach, a court will need to consider the extent to which the conduct amounting to breach put the victim at risk of harm.**

3.9 There may be exceptional cases where the nature of the breach is particularly serious but has not been dealt with by a separate offence being charged. In these cases, the risk posed by the offender and the nature of the breach will be particularly significant in determining the response. Where the order is breached by the use of physical violence, the starting point should normally be a custodial sentence.

[66] When in force.

3.10 Non-violent behaviour and/or indirect contact can also cause (or be intended to cause) a high degree of harm and anxiety. In such circumstances, it is likely that the custody threshold will have been crossed.

3.11 Where an order was made in civil proceedings, its purpose may have been to cause the subject of the order to modify behaviour rather than to imply that the conduct was especially serious. If so, it is likely to be disproportionate to impose a custodial sentence for a breach of the order if the breach did not involve threats or violence.

3.12 In some cases where a breach might result in a short custodial sentence but the court is satisfied that the offender genuinely intends to reform his or her behaviour and there is a real prospect of rehabilitation, the court may consider it appropriate to impose a sentence that will allow this. This may mean imposing a suspended sentence order or a community order (where appropriate with a requirement to attend an accredited domestic violence programme).

3.13 **Breach of a protective order will generally be more serious than breach of a conditional discharge.** Not only is a breach of a protective order an offence in its own right but it also undermines a specific prohibition imposed by the court. Breach of a conditional discharge amounts to an offender failing to take a chance that has been provided by the court.

SG-49 **D. Aggravating and Mitigating Factors**

4.1 Many of the aggravating factors which apply to an offence of violence in a domestic context will apply also to an offence arising from breach of a protective order.

Aggravating Factors

(i) Victim is particularly vulnerable

4.2 For cultural, religious, language, financial or any other reasons, some victims may be more vulnerable than others. This vulnerability means that the terms of a protective order are particularly important and a violation of those terms will warrant a higher penalty than usual.

4.3 Age, disability or the fact that the victim was pregnant or had recently given birth at the time of the offence may make a victim particularly vulnerable.

4.4 Any steps taken to prevent the victim reporting an incident or obtaining assistance will usually aggravate the offence.

(ii) Impact on children

4.5 If a protective order is imposed in order to protect children, either solely or in addition to another victim, then a breach of that order will generally be more serious.[67]

(iii) A proven history of violence or threats by the offender

4.6 Of necessity, a breach of a protective order will not be the first time an offender has caused fear or harassment towards a victim. However, the offence will be more serious if the breach is part of a series of prolonged violence or harassment towards the victim or the offender has a history of disobedience to court orders.

4.7 Where an offender has previously been convicted of an offence involving domestic violence, either against the same or a different person, or has been convicted for a breach of an order, this is likely to be a statutory aggravating factor.[68]

(iv) Using contact arrangements with a child to instigate an offence

4.8 An offence will be aggravated where an offender exploits contact arrangements with a child in order to commit an offence.

(v) Victim is forced to leave home

4.9 A breach will be aggravated if, as a consequence, the victim is forced to leave home.

(vi) Additional aggravating factors

4.10 In addition to the factors listed above, the following will aggravate a breach of an order:
- the offence is a further breach, following earlier breach proceedings;
- the breach was committed immediately or shortly after the order was made.

[67] The definition of 'harm' in s. 31(9) of the Children Act 1989 as amended by s. 120 of the Adoption and Children Act 2002 includes 'impairment suffered from seeing or hearing the ill-treatment of another'.
[68] Criminal Justice Act 2003, s. 143(2).

Mitigating Factors

(i) Breach was committed after a long period of compliance

4.11 If the court is satisfied that the offender has complied with a protective order for a substantial period before a breach is committed, the court should take this into account when imposing sentence for the breach. The history of the relationship and the specific nature of the contact will be relevant in determining its significance as a mitigating factor.

(ii) Victim initiated contact

4.12 If the conditions of an order are breached following contact from the victim, this should be considered as mitigation. It is important to consider the history of the relationship and the specific nature of the contact in determining its significance as a mitigating factor.

4.13 Nonetheless it is important for the court to make clear that it is the responsibility of the offender and not the victim to ensure that the order is complied with.

E. Factors to take into Consideration

Aims of sentencing SG-50

(a) When sentencing for a breach of a protective order (which would have been imposed to protect a victim from further harm), the main aim should be to achieve future compliance with that order.
(b) A court will need to assess the level of risk posed by the offender. If the offender requires treatment or assistance for mental health or other issues, willingness to undergo treatment or accept help may influence sentence.

1. Key Factors

(a) The nature of the conduct that caused the breach of the order, in particular, whether the contact was direct or indirect, although it is important to recognise that indirect contact is capable of causing significant harm or anxiety.
(b) **There may be exceptional cases where the nature of the breach is particularly serious but has not been dealt with by a separate offence being charged. In these cases the risk posed by the offender and the nature of the breach will be particularly significant in determining the response.**
(c) The nature of the original conduct or offence is relevant to sentencing for the breach in so far as it allows a judgement to be made on the level of harm caused to the victim by the breach, and the extent to which that harm was intended by the offender.
(d) The sentence following a breach is for the breach alone and must avoid punishing the offender again for the offence or conduct as a result of which the order was made.
(e) Where violence is used to breach a restraining order or a molestation order, custody is the starting point for sentence.
(f) Non-violent conduct in breach may cross the custody threshold where a high degree of harm or anxiety has been caused to the victim.
(g) Where an order was made in civil proceedings, its purpose may have been to cause the subject of the order to modify behaviour rather than to imply that the conduct was especially serious. If so, it is likely to be disproportionate to impose a custodial sentence for a breach of the order if the breach did not involve threats or violence.
(h) In some cases where a breach might result in a short custodial sentence but the court is satisfied that the offender genuinely intends to reform his or her behaviour and there is a real prospect of rehabilitation, the court may consider it appropriate to impose a sentence that will allow this. This may mean imposing a suspended sentence order or a community order (where appropriate with a requirement to attend an accredited domestic violence programme).
(i) While, in principle, consecutive sentences may be imposed for each breach of which the offender is convicted, the overall sentence should reflect the totality principle.

2. General

(a) Breach of a protective order should be considered more serious than a breach of a conditional discharge.
(b) The principle of reduction in sentence for a guilty plea should be applied as set out in the Council guideline *Reduction in Sentence for a Guilty Plea*.

3. Non-custodial sentences

(a) It is likely that all breaches of protective orders will pass the threshold for a community sentence. The reference in the starting points to medium and low range community orders refers to the Council guideline *New Sentences: Criminal Justice Act 2003* paragraphs 1.1.18–1.1.32.

(b) In accordance with general principle, the fact that the seriousness of an offence crosses a particular threshold does not preclude the court from imposing another type of sentence of a lower level where appropriate.

BREACH OF A PROTECTIVE ORDER

Breach of a Restraining Order
Section 5(5) Protection from Harassment Act 1997

Breach of a Non-Molestation Order
*Section 42A Family Law Act 1996**

Maximum Penalty: **5 years imprisonment**

Where the conduct is particularly serious, it would normally be charged as a separate offence. These starting points are based on the premise that the activity has either been prosecuted separately as an offence or is not of a character sufficient to justify prosecution of it as an offence in its own right.

Nature of activity	Starting points
	Custodial Sentence
Breach (whether one or more) involving significant physical violence and significant physical or psychological harm to the victim	**More than 12 months** The length of the custodial sentence imposed will depend on the nature and seriousness of the breach(es).
More than one breach involving some violence and/or significant physical or psychological harm To the victim	**26–39 weeks custody** [Medium/High Custody Plus order]**
Single breach involving some violence and/or significant physical or psychological harm to the victim	**13–26 weeks custody** [Low/Medium Custody Plus order]**
	Non-Custodial Sentence
More than one breach involving no/minimal contact or some direct contact	**MEDIUM range community order**
Single breach involving no/minimal direct contact	**LOW range community order**

Additional aggravating factors	Additional mitigating factors
1. Victim is particularly vulnerable. 2. Impact on children. 3. A proven history of violence or threats by the offender. 4. Using contact arrangements with a child to instigate an offence. 5. Victim is forced to leave home. 6. Offence is a further breach, following earlier breach proceedings. 7. Offender has a history of disobedience to court orders. 8. Breach was committed immediately or shortly after the order was made.	1. Breach occurred after a long period of compliance. 2. Victim initiated contact.

* When in force.
** When the relevant provisions of the Criminal Justice Act 2003 are in force.

SG-51 PART 7 OVERARCHING PRINCIPLES: DOMESTIC VIOLENCE

Foreword

. . . This guideline applies to offences sentenced on or after 18 December 2006.

This guideline stems from a reference from the Home Secretary for consideration of sentencing in cases of domestic violence. The referral suggested that 'domestic violence' should be described in terms of the Crown Prosecution Service definition (described on page 3) and this suggestion was adopted by the Council.

Consequently this guideline is for use for all cases that fall within the Crown Prosecution Service definition of domestic violence.

There is no specific offence of domestic violence. The definition covers a broad set of circumstances and allows conduct amounting to domestic violence to be covered by a wide range of offences. The guideline identifies the principles relevant to the sentencing of cases involving violence that has occurred in a domestic context and includes details of particular aggravating and mitigating factors.

This guideline makes clear that offences committed in a domestic context should be regarded as being no less serious than offences committed in a non-domestic context. Indeed, because an offence has been committed in a domestic context, there are likely to be aggravating factors present that make it more serious.

In many situations of domestic violence, the circumstances require the sentence to demonstrate clearly that the conduct is unacceptable. However, there will be some situations where all parties genuinely and realistically wish the relationship to continue as long as the violence stops. In those situations, and where the violence is towards the lower end of the scale of seriousness, it is likely to be appropriate for the court to impose a sentence that provides the support necessary.

...

A. Definition of Domestic Violence SG-52

1.1 There is no specific offence of domestic violence and conduct amounting to domestic violence is covered by a number of statutory provisions. For the purposes of this guideline, wherever such offending occurs, domestic violence is:

> 'Any incident of threatening behaviour, violence or abuse [psychological, physical, sexual, financial or emotional] between adults who are or have been intimate partners or family members, regardless of gender or sexuality.'[69]

1.2 Most incidents of domestic violence can be charged as one of a wide range of offences including physical assault (with or without a weapon), harassment, threats to cause injury or to kill, destroying or damaging property, false imprisonment (locking the victim in a room or preventing that person from leaving the house), and sexual offences.

1.3 This guideline covers issues which are relevant across the range of offences that might be committed in a domestic context. Under the above definition, the domestic context includes relationships involving intimate partners who are living together, intimate partners who do not live together and former intimate partners. It is also wide enough to include relationships between family members, for example between a father and a daughter, or a mother and a daughter, perhaps where the daughter is the mother's carer.

B. Assessing Seriousness SG-53

2.1 **As a starting point for sentence, offences committed in a domestic context should be regarded as being no less serious than offences committed in a non-domestic context.**

2.2 Thus, the starting point for sentencing should be the same irrespective of whether the offender and the victim are known to each other (whether by virtue of being current or former intimate partners, family members, friends or acquaintances) or unknown to each other.

2.3 A number of aggravating factors may commonly arise by virtue of the offence being committed in a domestic context and these will increase the seriousness of such offences. These are described in more detail in C below.

C. Aggravating and Mitigating Factors SG-54

3.1 Since domestic violence takes place within the context of a current or past relationship, the history of the relationship will often be relevant in assessing the gravity of the offence. Therefore, a court is entitled to take into account anything occurring within the relationship as a whole, which may reveal relevant aggravating or mitigating factors.

[69] This is the Government definition of domestic violence agreed in 2004. It is taken from *Policy on Prosecuting cases of Domestic Violence*, Crown Prosecution Service, 2005.

3.2 The following aggravating and mitigating factors (which are not intended to be exhaustive) are of particular relevance to offences committed in a domestic context, and should be read alongside the general factors set out in the Council guideline *Overarching Principles: Seriousness*.[70]

Aggravating Factors

(i) Abuse of trust and abuse of power

3.3 The guideline *Overarching Principles: Seriousness* identifies abuse of a position of trust and abuse of power as factors that indicate higher culpability. Within the nature of relationship required to meet the definition of domestic violence set out above, trust implies a mutual expectation of conduct that shows consideration, honesty, care and responsibility. In some such relationships, one of the parties will have the power to exert considerable control over the other.

3.4 In the context of domestic violence:

- an *abuse of trust*, whether through direct violence or emotional abuse, represents a violation of this understanding;
- an *abuse of power* in a relationship involves restricting another individual's autonomy which is sometimes a specific characteristic of domestic violence. This involves the exercise of control over an individual by means which may be psychological, physical, sexual, financial or emotional.

3.5 Where an abuse of trust or abuse of power is present, it will aggravate the seriousness of an offence. These factors are likely to exist in many offences of violence within a domestic context.

3.6 However, the breadth of the definition of domestic violence (set out in 1.1 above) encompasses offences committed by a former spouse or partner. Accordingly, there will be circumstances where the abuse of trust or abuse of power may be a very minor feature of an offence or may be deemed no longer to exist—for example, where the offender and victim have been separated for a long period of time.

(ii) Victim is particularly vulnerable

3.7 For cultural, religious, language, financial or any other reasons, some victims of domestic violence may be more vulnerable than others, not least because these issues may make it almost impossible for the victim to leave a violent relationship.

3.8 Where a perpetrator has exploited a victim's vulnerability (for instance, when the circumstances have been used by the perpetrator to prevent the victim from seeking and obtaining help), an offence will warrant a higher penalty.

3.9 Age, disability or the fact that the victim was pregnant or had recently given birth at the time of the offence may make a victim particularly vulnerable.

3.10 Any steps taken to prevent the victim reporting an incident or obtaining assistance will usually aggravate the offence.

(iii) Impact on children

3.11 Exposure of children to an offence (either directly or indirectly) is an aggravating factor.

3.12 Children are likely to be adversely affected by directly witnessing violence or other abuse and by being aware of it taking place while they are elsewhere in the home.[71]

(iv) Using contact arrangements with a child to instigate an offence

3.13 An offence will be aggravated where an offender exploits contact arrangements with a child in order to commit an offence.

(v) A proven history of violence or threats by the offender in a domestic setting

3.14 It is important that an assessment of the seriousness of an offence recognises the cumulative effect of a series of violent incidents or threats over a prolonged period, where such conduct has been proved or accepted.

3.15 Where an offender has previously been convicted of an offence involving domestic violence either against the same or a different partner, this is likely to be a statutory aggravating factor.[72]

[70] Published December 2004. The lists of aggravating factors from the guideline are reproduced at Annex A for ease of reference. See also www.sentencing-guidelines.gov.uk

[71] The definition of 'harm' in s. 31(9) of the Children Act 1989 as amended by s. 120 of the Adoption and Children Act 2002 includes 'impairment suffered from seeing or hearing the ill- treatment of another'.

[72] Criminal Justice Act 2003, s. 143(2).

(vi) A history of disobedience to court orders

3.16 A breach of an order that has been imposed for the purpose of protecting a victim can cause significant harm or anxiety. Where an offender's history of disobedience has had this effect, it will be an aggravating factor.

3.17 Commission of the offence in breach of a non-molestation order imposed in civil proceedings, in breach of a sentence (such as a conditional discharge) imposed for similar offending, or while subject to an ancillary order, such as a restraining order, will aggravate the seriousness of the offence.

3.18 The appropriate response to breach of a civil order is dealt with in a separate guideline *Breach of a Protective Order.*

(vii) Victim forced to leave home

3.19 An offence will be aggravated if, as a consequence, the victim is forced to leave home.

Mitigating Factors

(i) Positive good character

3.20 As a general principle of sentencing, a court will take account of an offender's positive good character. However, it is recognised that one of the factors that can allow domestic violence to continue unnoticed for lengthy periods is the ability of the perpetrator to have two personae. In respect of an offence of violence in a domestic context, an offender's good character in relation to conduct outside the home should generally be of no relevance where there is a proven pattern of behaviour.

3.21 Positive good character is of greater relevance in the rare case where the court is satisfied that the offence was an isolated incident.

(ii) Provocation

3.22 It may be asserted that the offence, at least in part, has been provoked by the conduct of the victim. Such assertions need to be treated with great care, both in determining whether they have a factual basis and in considering whether in the circumstances the alleged conduct amounts to provocation sufficient to mitigate the seriousness of the offence.

3.23 For provocation to be a mitigating factor, it will usually involve actual or anticipated violence including psychological bullying. Provocation is likely to have more of an effect as mitigation if it has taken place over a significant period of time.

D. Other factors influencing sentence SG-55

Wishes of the victim and effect of the sentence

4.1 As a matter of general principle, a sentence imposed for an offence of violence should be determined by the seriousness of the offence, not by the expressed wishes of the victim.

4.2 There are a number of reasons why it may be particularly important that this principle is observed in a case of domestic violence:

- it is undesirable that a victim should feel a responsibility for the sentence imposed;
- there is a risk that a plea for mercy made by a victim will be induced by threats made by, or by a fear of, the offender;
- the risk of such threats will be increased if it is generally believed that the severity of the sentence may be affected by the wishes of the victim.

4.3 Nonetheless, there may be circumstances in which the court can properly mitigate a sentence to give effect to the expressed wish of the victim that the relationship be permitted to continue. The court must, however, be confident that such a wish is genuine, and that giving effect to it will not expose the victim to a real risk of further violence. Critical conditions are likely to be the seriousness of the offence and the history of the relationship. It is vitally important that the court has up-to-date information in a pre-sentence report and victim personal statement.

4.4 Either the offender or the victim (or both) may ask the court to take into consideration the interests of any children and to impose a less severe sentence. The court will wish to have regard not only to the effect on the children if the relationship is disrupted but also to the likely effect on the children of any further incidents of domestic violence.

E. Factors to Take into Consideration SG-56

The following points of principle should be considered by a court when imposing sentence for any offence of violence committed in domestic context.

1. Offences committed in a domestic context should be regarded as being no less serious than offences committed in a non-domestic context.

2. Many offences of violence in a domestic context are dealt with in a magistrates' court as an offence of common assault or assault occasioning actual bodily harm because the injuries sustained are relatively minor. Offences involving serious violence will warrant a custodial sentence in the majority of cases.
3. Some offences will be specified offences for the purposes of the dangerous offender provisions.[73] In such circumstances, consideration will need to be given to whether there is a significant risk of serious harm to members of the public, which include, of course, family members. If so, the court will be required to impose a life sentence, imprisonment for public protection or an extended sentence.
4. Where the custody threshold is only just crossed, so that if a custodial sentence is imposed it will be a short sentence, the court will wish to consider whether the better option is a suspended sentence order or a community order, including in either case a requirement to attend an accredited domestic violence programme. Such an option will only be appropriate where the court is satisfied that the offender genuinely intends to reform his or her behaviour and that there is a real prospect of rehabilitation being successful. Such a situation is unlikely to arise where there has been a pattern of abuse.

Annex A

Extracts from Guideline *Overarching Principles: Seriousness*

[Omitted: the relevant Guideline is set out in full in **part 3**.]

SG-57

PART 8 SEXUAL OFFENCES ACT 2003

Foreword

. . . This guideline applies to the sentencing of offenders convicted of any of the sexual offences covered by this guideline who are sentenced on or after 14 May 2007.

The Sexual Offences Act 2003 contains a large number of new or amended offences for which there was no sentencing case law. Following implementation of this Act in May 2004, a number of cases have been considered by the Court of Appeal and guidance from those judgments has been incorporated into this guideline.

The guideline uses the starting point of 5 years for the rape of an adult with no aggravating or mitigating factors (derived from *Millberry and others*[74]) as the baseline from which all other sentences for offences in this guideline have been calculated. Since the judgment in *Millberry*, changes introduced by the CJA 2003 have both affected the structure of custodial sentences of 12 months and above and introduced new sentences for those convicted of many of the offences in this guideline where the court considers that the offender provides a significant risk of serious harm in the future.

The sentencing ranges and starting points in this guideline take account of both these changes. Accordingly, the transitional arrangements set out in paragraphs 2.1.7–2.1.10 of the Council guideline *New Sentences: Criminal Justice Act 2003* do not apply.

Sexual offences can be committed in a domestic context and so come within the definition of 'domestic violence' used in the Council guideline *Overarching Principles: Domestic Violence* published in December 2006. In such circumstances, reference should also be made to this guideline to identify additional principles and factors that should also be taken into account in assessing the seriousness of an offence and determining the appropriate sentence.

. . .

SG-58

Part 1: General Principles

Introduction

1.1 The Sexual Offences Act (SOA) 2003 came into force on 1 May 2004.—Part 1 creates a number of new sexual offences. It also includes a large number of pre-existing offences, some of which have been redefined and/or have revised maximum penalties.

[73] Criminal Justice Act 2003, part 12, chapter 5.
[74] [2003] 2 Cr App R (S) 31

1.2 The Criminal Justice Act (CJA) 2003 provides[75] that the seriousness of an offence should be determined by two main parameters: the *culpability* of the offender and the *harm* caused, or risked, by the offence, including the impact on the victim(s). The Sentencing Guidelines Council guideline on seriousness[76] provides that the seriousness of an offence is to be determined according to the relative impact of the culpability of the offender and the actual or foreseeable harm caused to the victim. Where there is an imbalance between culpability and harm, the culpability of the offender in the particular circumstances of an individual case should be the primary factor in determining the seriousness of the offence.

1.3 The guideline has been formulated on the basis of the sentencing framework that is currently in force. **For these types of offence more than for many others, the sentencing process must allow for flexibility and variability. The suggested starting points and sentencing ranges contained in the offence guidelines are not rigid, and movement within and between ranges will be dependent upon the circumstances of individual cases and, in particular, the aggravating and mitigating factors that are present.**

In order to assist in developing consistency of approach, a decision making process is set out below.

1.4 In the guideline published by the Council to support the new sentencing framework introduced by the CJA 2003,[77] in relation to custodial sentences of 12 months or more it is stated that, generally, a court should only make *specific* recommendations about the requirements to be included in the licence conditions when announcing shorter sentences where it is reasonable to anticipate the relevance of the requirement at the point of release. However, sentencing for a sexual offence is an example of an occasion where the court may sensibly suggest interventions that could be useful, either during the custodial period or on release. The court's recommendation will not form part of the sentence, but will be a helpful guide for the probation service.

1.5 Apart from the offence of rape which, when charged as a primary offence, is confined to male defendants, the SOA 2003 makes no distinction in terms of liability or maximum penalties for male and female offenders. The guidelines are proposed on the basis that they should apply irrespective of the gender of the victim or of the offender, except in specified circumstances where a distinction is justified by the nature of the offence.

Sentencing Guidelines

Seriousness SG-59

1.6 The guidelines for sentencing for serious sexual offences have been based on the guideline judgment on rape—*Millberry and others*[78]—in which the Court of Appeal stated that:

'. . . there are, broadly, three dimensions to consider in assessing the gravity of an individual offence of rape. The first is the degree of harm to the victim; the second is the level of culpability of the offender; and the third is the level of risk posed by the offender to society.'

1.7 In the subsequent *Attorney General's Reference (Nos. 91, 119, 120 of 2002)*,[79] the Court of Appeal held that 'similar dimensions should apply to other categories of sexual offences', and added that there would also be a need to deter others from acting in a similar fashion.

1.8 These statements established the general principles for assessing the seriousness of sexual offences that are now encapsulated in the provisions of the CJA 2003.

1.9 The maximum penalty and mode of trial prescribed by Parliament for each sexual offence give a general indication of the relative seriousness of different offences and these have also acted as a broad guide for the proposed sentencing starting points.

The harm caused by sexual offences SG-60

1.10 All sexual offences where the activity is non-consensual, coercive or exploitative result in harm. Harm is also inherent where victims ostensibly consent but where their capacity to give informed consent is affected by their youth or mental disorder.

1.11 The effects of sexual offending may be physical and/or psychological. The physical effects—injury, pregnancy or sexually transmitted infections—may be very serious. The psychological effects may be equally or even more serious, but much less obvious (even unascertainable) at the time of sentencing. They may include any or all of the following (although this list is not intended to be comprehensive and items are not listed in any form of priority):

- *Violation of the victims sexual autonomy*
- *Fear*

---

[75] s. 143(1)

[76] *Overarching Principles: Seriousness*, published 16 December 2004—www.sentencing-guidelines.gov.uk

[77] *New Sentences: Criminal Justice Act 2003*, published 16 December 2004—www.sentencing-guidelines.gov.uk

[78] [2003] 2 Cr App R (S) 31

[79] [2003] 2 Cr App R (S) 338

- *Humiliation*
- *Degradation*
- *Shame*
- *Embarrassment*
- *Inability to trust*
- *Inability to form personal or intimate relationships in adulthood*
- *Self harm or suicide*

SG-61 The offender's culpability in sexual offences

1.12 According to the Council's guideline on seriousness, culpability is determined by the extent to which the offender intends to cause harm—the worse the harm intended, the greater the offender's culpability. Sexual offences are somewhat different in that the offender's intention may be to obtain sexual gratification, financial gain or some other result, rather than to harm the victim. However, where the activity is in any way non-consensual, coercive or exploitative, the offence is inherently harmful and therefore the offender's culpability is high. Planning an offence makes the offender more highly culpable than engaging in opportunistic or impulsive offending.

1.13 In general, the difficulty of assessing seriousness where there is an imbalance between culpability and harm does not arise in relation to sexual offences. However, some offences in the SOA 2003 are defined in terms of the offender's intention to commit an offence that does not, in fact, take place, for example the 'incitement offences', the 'preparatory offences' and the new offence of 'meeting a child following sexual grooming etc'. In such cases, the level of actual harm to the victim may be lower than in cases involving the commission of a physical sexual offence. Here the level of culpability will be the primary factor in determining the seriousness of the offence, with the degree of harm that could have been caused to an individual victim, and the risk posed to others by the offender, being integral to the sentencing decision.

SG-62 The culpability of young offenders

1.14 The SOA 2003 makes special provision for young offenders found guilty of certain sexual offences—namely those in the 'ostensibly consensual' category—by providing that offenders aged under 18 will face a maximum penalty of 5 years' detention, as opposed to the maximum 14 years for offenders aged 18 or over. These are dealt with in Part 7 of the guideline.

1.15 The age of the offender will also be significant in the sentencing exercise in relation to non-consensual offences, where no special sentencing provisions have been provided for in the legislation. Its significance is particularly acute in relation to the strict liability offences such as 'rape of a child under 13', where the maximum penalty is life imprisonment, especially if an offender is very young and the disparity in age between the offender and the victim is very small.

1.16 Section 44(1) of the Children and Young Persons Act 1933 provides that every court dealing with a child or young person, as an offender or otherwise, 'shall have regard to the welfare of the child or young person'.

1.17 The youth and immaturity of an offender must always be potential mitigating factors for the courts to take into account when passing sentence. However, where the facts of a case are particularly serious, the youth of the offender will not necessarily mitigate the appropriate sentence.[80]

SG-63 The nature of the sexual activity

1.18 The nature of the sexual activity covered by some offences in the SOA 2003 (such as 'rape' and 'assault by penetration') is quite precisely defined whilst others—for example, 'sexual activity with a child', 'sexual activity with a child family member', 'abuse of a position of trust'—are drawn very widely and cover all forms of intentional activity involving sexual touching, including penetration.

- Sexual activity involves varying types and degrees of touching ranging from genital or oral penetration through to non-genital touching of the victim's clothed body.
- Penetrative acts are more serious than non-penetrative acts. The fact that the offender or victim (especially the victim) is totally or partially naked makes the activity more serious.
- The touching may be consensual, ostensibly consensual or non-consensual. Where the victim's ability to consent is impaired by, for example, youth or mental incapacity, this makes the activity, regardless of its nature, more serious.

[80] *R v Paiwant Asi-Akram* [2005] EWCA Crim 1543, *R v Patrick M* [2005] EWCA Crim 1679

Aggravating and mitigating factors SG-64

1.19 The Council guideline on seriousness sets out aggravating and mitigating factors that are applicable to a wide range of cases. Care needs to be taken to ensure that there is no double counting where an essential element of the offence charged might, in other circumstances, be an aggravating factor.

1.20 Sentencers should refer to paragraphs 1.20–1.27 of the Council guideline. For ease of reference, extracts from the guideline are provided below. The fact that a victim was vulnerable will be of particular relevance in cases involving sexual offences.

THESE FACTORS APPLY TO A WIDE RANGE OF OFFENCES AND NOT ALL WILL BE RELEVANT TO SEXUAL OFFENCES.

Factors indicating higher culpability:

- Offence committed whilst on bail for other offences
- Failure to respond to previous sentences
- Offence was racially or religiously aggravated
- Offence motivated by, or demonstrating, hostility to the victim based on his or her sexual orientation (or presumed sexual orientation)
- Offence motivated by, or demonstrating, hostility based on the victims disability (or presumed disability)
- Previous conviction(s), particularly where a pattern of repeat offending is disclosed
- Planning of an offence
- An intention to commit more serious harm than actually resulted from the offence
- Offenders operating in groups or gangs
- 'Professional' offending
- Commission of the offence for financial gain (where this is not inherent in the offence itself)
- High level of profit from the offence
- An attempt to conceal or dispose of evidence
- Failure to respond to warnings or concerns expressed by others about the offenders behaviour
- Offence committed whilst on licence
- Offence motivated by hostility towards a minority group, or a member or members of it
- Deliberate targeting of vulnerable victim(s)
- Commission of an offence while under the influence of alcohol or drugs
- Use of a weapon to frighten or injure victim
- Deliberate and gratuitous violence or damage to property, over and above what is needed to carry out the offence
- Abuse of power
- Abuse of a position of trust

Factors indicating a more than usually serious degree of harm:

- Multiple victims
- An especially serious physical or psychological effect on the victim, even if unintended
- A sustained assault or repeated assaults on the same victim
- Victim is particularly vulnerable
- Location of the offence (for example, in an isolated place)
- Offence is committed against those working in the public sector or providing a service to the public
- Presence of others e.g. relatives, especially children or partner of the victim
- Additional degradation of the victim (e.g. taking photographs of a victim as part of a sexual offence)
- In property offences, high value (including sentimental value) of property to the victim, or substantial consequential loss (e.g. where the theft of equipment causes serious disruption to a victims life or business)

Factors indicating significantly lower culpability:

- A greater degree of provocation than normally expected
- Mental illness or disability
- Youth or age, where it affects the responsibility of the individual defendant
- The fact that the offender played only a minor role in the offence

Personal mitigation

Section 166(1) Criminal Justice Act 2003 makes provision for a sentencer to take account of any matters that 'in the opinion of the court, are relevant in mitigation of sentence'. When the court has formed an initial assessment of the seriousness of the offence, then it should consider any offender mitigation. The issue of remorse should be taken into account at this point along with other mitigating features such as admissions to the police in interview.

SG-65 The risk of re-offending

1.21 One of the purposes of sentencing set out in the CJA 2003[81] is 'the protection of the public'. Part 2 of the Sexual Offences Act 2003 strengthens the current system of registration for sex offenders and also introduces a number of new orders, some of which are available on conviction and others by application in civil proceedings to a magistrates' court. There are also a number of sentencing options, custodial and non-custodial, open to sentencers where the risk of re-offending is high.

1.22 The arrangements for registration of sex offenders (see also paragraph 1.29 below) follow automatically on conviction, and are not part of the sentencing process. The duty to give reasons for, and to explain the effect of, sentencing is now set out in the CJA 2003.[82]

1.23 If a victim personal statement has not been produced, the court should enquire whether the victim has been given the opportunity to make one. In the absence of a victim personal statement, the court should not assume that the offence had no impact on the victim. A pre-sentence report should normally be prepared before sentence is passed for any sexual offence, as this may contain important information about the sexually deviant tendencies of an offender and an assessment of the likelihood of re-offending; a psychiatric report may also be appropriate. It is clearly in the interests of public protection to provide effective treatment for sex offenders at the earliest opportunity.

SG-66 Dangerous offenders

1.24 In relation to custodial sentences, the starting point will be the assessment of dangerousness as set out in section 229 of the CJA 2003; since the majority of the offences in the SOA 2003 are 'specified' offences (as defined in section 224 and listed in schedule 15, part 2). There are three sentencing options for offenders aged 18 or over: discretionary life sentences, indeterminate sentences of 'imprisonment for public protection', and the redefined extended sentences.[83]

1.25 The criterion for the assessment of dangerousness in all cases falling within the provisions for dangerous offenders is whether the court considers that there is a significant risk to members of the public of serious harm occasioned by the commission by the offender of further specified offences.[84] If the criterion is met, the options available depend on whether the offence is a 'serious' offence.

1.26 Where a specified offence carries a maximum penalty of life imprisonment or 10 years' imprisonment or more, it is a 'serious' offence for the purposes of section 225. In such cases, if the risk criterion is met in respect of an adult offender, a life sentence or imprisonment for public protection must be imposed.

1.27 In setting the minimum term to be served within an indeterminate sentence under these provisions, in accordance with normal practice that term will usually be half the equivalent determinate sentence. Such period will normally be reduced by time spent on remand in custody.

1.28 In relation to 'specified' offences that are not 'serious' offences, where the risk criterion is met in relation to an adult offender, under section 227 the court is required to extend the period for which the offender will be subject to a licence on release from custody; the custodial element in such cases must be for a minimum of 12 months. Within the statutory limits, the period of licence must be of such length as the court considers necessary for the purposes of protecting members of the public from serious harm occasioned by the commission of further specified offences.

SG-67 Other orders

1.29 There are a number of orders and requirements relevant to those convicted of sexual offences. Some follow automatically on conviction and others can be applied for:

- inclusion of an offender's name on a *Sex Offenders' Register*—used for risk management by local authorities and other statutory agencies to indicate that an individual may pose an ongoing risk to children—follows automatically on conviction or caution for a sexual offence;[85] and

[81] s. 142(1)
[82] s. 174
[83] Criminal Justice Act 2003, ss. 225–228
[84] Ibid. 225(1)
[85] Children and Young Persons Act 1933, schedule 1—currently subject to a cross-government review, in light of the alternative provisions that now exist to prohibit working with children

- *notification orders* which impose sex offender registration requirements on offenders living in the UK who have been convicted of a sexual offence overseas—available on application by complaint to a magistrates' court.[86]

1.30 A court has a duty to consider making two ancillary orders that require the intervention of the sentencer, namely sexual offences prevention orders (SOPO)[87] and orders disqualifying an offender from working with children:[88]

- *sexual offences prevention orders*—civil preventative orders that can be made either at the point of sentence in the Crown Court or a magistrates' court, or by complaint to a magistrates' court in respect of someone previously convicted of a sexual offence where that person's behaviour suggests the possibility of re-offending; and
- *disqualification orders*—an order disqualifying an offender convicted of an offence against a child from working with children, which *must* (or in defined circumstances *may*) be imposed unless the court is satisfied that the offender is unlikely to commit a further offence against a child.

When passing sentence for a sexual offence, the court must always consider whether or not it would be appropriate to make a sexual offences prevention order or an order disqualifying the offender from working with children.

Community orders SG-68

1.31 The availability of requirements able to be included within a community order, and the suitability of them for an individual offender, will be detailed in a pre-sentence report. Some options of direct relevance to sex offenders are considered below.

Sex offender treatment programmes

1.31.1 These are available both in prisons and in the community. Participation in a programme whilst in custody is voluntary, but programmes in the community can be a mandatory requirement of a community order where a PSR writer has made a recommendation and commented on the suitability of the offender for such a requirement.

- Accredited treatment programmes are targeted at males, who form the overwhelming majority of sex offenders, but individual programmes are devised for female offenders.
- Treatment programmes are usually only available to those who are given a long community order (normally 3 years), and may not always be available for those sentenced to shorter custodial sentences.

Before imposing sentence, the court should investigate the content and availability of such programmes and will wish to be satisfied that a programme will be able to commence within a realistic timeframe.

Curfews

1.31.2 A curfew requirement, usually associated with electronic monitoring, may be helpful in restricting an offender's right to be out in public at the same time as, for example, schoolchildren. A curfew requirement is most likely to be effective when used in conjunction with a residence requirement requiring an offender to live in approved accommodation where behaviour and compliance can be monitored. Such a requirement can be for between 2 and 12 hours per day and last up to 6 months.

When a court imposes a community order for a sexual offence, it should always consider imposing a requirement to attend a special treatment programme designed to help the offender recognise and control any sexually deviant tendencies.

Financial orders SG-69

1.32 In addition to the sentence imposed for the offence(s), the following supplementary penalties should be considered.

[86] Sexual Offences Act 2003, s. 97
[87] Sexual Offences Act 2003, s. 104
[88] Criminal Justice and Courts Services Act 2000, ss. 28 and 29, as amended by the Criminal Justice Act 2003, s. 299 and schedule 30

Confiscation orders

1.32.1 Depending on the date of the offence, the CJA 1988 or Proceeds of Crime Act 2002 set out the circumstances in which the courts are entitled or required to make a confiscation order to recover some of the proceeds of an offender's crime. The prosecution may suggest consideration of a confiscation order but, where appropriate, the court should consider making such an order of its own volition.

Deprivation orders

1.32.2 The courts should also consider whether, in the particular circumstances of the case, it would be appropriate to make an order depriving an offender of property used for the purposes of crime.[89] This will be a particularly relevant consideration where, for example, someone convicted of a voyeurism or child pornography offence possesses a camera or a computer used to make, store or circulate sexual material connected to the offence, or where a pimp convicted of controlling prostitution uses a car to drive prostitutes to their 'patch'. A Crown Court can also make a restraint order[90] in respect of realisable property held by an offender who is believed to have benefited from criminal conduct, prohibiting them from dealing with it.

Whenever an offender has profited in some way from the sexual exploitation of others, the court should give serious consideration to the making of a confiscation order to recover the proceeds of the crime.

The court should also, especially in relation to offences involving voyeurism, prostitution, pornography and trafficking, consider whether it would be appropriate to make an order depriving an offender of property used, or intended to be used, in connection with the offence.

Compensation orders

1.32.3 The court must consider making a compensation order, in accordance with the provisions of the Powers of Criminal Courts (Sentencing) Act 2000, in respect of any personal injury, loss or damage occasioned to a victim. Compensation should benefit, not inflict further harm on, the victim. Any financial recompense from the offender for a sexual offence may cause the victim additional humiliation, degradation and distress. The victim's views are properly obtained through sensitive discussion with the victim by the police or witness care unit, when it can be explained that the offender's ability to pay will ultimately determine whether, and how much, compensation is ordered. The views of the victim regarding compensation should be made known to the court and respected and, if appropriate, acknowledged at the time of sentencing. A victim may not want compensation from the offender, but this should not be assumed.

SG-70 **Summary of general principles**

(i) Except where otherwise indicated, the offence guidelines all relate to sentencing on conviction for a first-time offender after a plea of not guilty.

(ii) Starting points are based on a basic offence[91] of its category. Aggravating and mitigating factors that are particularly relevant to each offence are listed in the individual offence guidelines. The list of aggravating factors is not exhaustive and the factors are not ranked in any particular order. A factor that is an ingredient of an offence cannot also be an aggravating factor. Sexual offences will often involve some form of violence as an essential element of the offence and this has been included in fixing the starting points. Where harm is inflicted over and above that necessary to commit the offence, that will be an aggravating factor.

(iii) In relation to sexual offences, the presence of generic and offence-specific aggravating factors will significantly influence the type and length of sentence imposed. The generic list of aggravating and mitigating factors identified by the Sentencing Guidelines Council in its guideline on seriousness is reproduced at paragraph 1.20 above but *not* for each offence. **These factors apply to a wide range of offences and not all will be relevant to sexual offences.**

[89] Powers of Criminal Courts (Sentencing) Act 2000, s. 143
[90] Proceeds of Crime Act 2002, s. 41
[91] A 'basic offence' is one in which the ingredients of the offence as defined are present, and assuming no aggravating or mitigating factors.

(iv) Unless specifically stated, the starting points assume that the offender is an adult. Sentences will normally need to be reduced where the offender is sentenced as a youth, save in the most serious cases (see paragraph 1.17 above).

(v) Specific guidance on sentencing youths for one of the child sex offences that attracts a lower statutory maximum penalty where the offender is under 18 can be found in Part 7.

(vi) There are a large number of new or amended offences in the SOA 2003 for which there is no sentencing case law. The guidelines use the starting point of 5 years for the rape of an adult with no aggravating or mitigating factors (derived from *Millberry and others*[92]) as the baseline from which all other sentences have been calculated.

(vii) Where a community order is the recommended starting point, the requirements to be imposed are left for the court to decide according to the particular facts of the individual case. Where a community order is the proposed starting point for different levels of seriousness of the same offence or for a second or subsequent offence of the same level of seriousness, this should be reflected by the imposition of more onerous requirements.[93]

(viii) Treatment programmes are not specifically mentioned in the guidelines. A sentencer should always consider whether, in the circumstances of the individual case and the profile of the offending behaviour, it would be sensible to require the offender to take part in a programme designed to address sexually deviant behaviour.

(ix) Reference to 'non-custodial sentence' in any of the offence guidelines (save for those in Part 7) suggests that the court consider a community order or a fine. In most instances, an offence will have crossed the threshold for a community order. However, in accordance with normal sentencing practice, even in those circumstances a court is not precluded from imposing a financial penalty where that is determined to be the appropriate sentence.

(x) In all cases, the court must consider whether it would be appropriate to make any ancillary orders, such as an order banning the offender from working with children, an order requiring the offender to pay compensation to a victim, or an order confiscating an offender's assets or requiring the forfeiture of equipment used in connection with an offence.

The decision making process SG-71

The process set out below is intended to show that the sentencing approach for sexual offences is fluid and requires the structured exercise of discretion.

1. Identify dangerous offenders

Most sexual offences are specified offences for the purposes of the public protection provisions in the CJA 2003. The court must determine whether there is a significant risk of serious harm by the commission of a further specified offence. The starting points in the guidelines are a) for offenders who do not meet the dangerous offender criteria and b) as the basis for the setting of a minimum term within an indeterminate sentence for those who do meet the criteria.

2. Identify the appropriate starting point

Because many acts can be charged as more than one offence, consideration will have to be given to the appropriate guideline once findings of fact have been made. The sentence should reflect the facts found to exist and not just the title of the offence of which the offender is convicted.

3. Consider relevant aggravating factors, both general and those specific to the type of offence

This may result in a sentence level being identified that is higher than the suggested starting point, sometimes substantially so.

4. Consider mitigating factors and personal mitigation

There may be general or offence-specific mitigating factors and matters of personal mitigation which could result in a sentence that is lower than the suggested starting point (possibly substantially so), or a sentence of a different type.

5. Reduction for guilty plea

The court will then apply any reduction for a guilty plea following the approach set out in the Council's guideline *Reduction in Sentence for a Guilty Plea*.

[92] [2003] 2 Cr App R (S) 31

[93] For further information, see the Council guideline *New Sentences: Criminal Justice Act 2003*, section B: 'Imposing a Community Sentence—The Approach'.

6. Consider ancillary orders

The court should consider whether ancillary orders are appropriate or necessary. These are referred to in some of the offence guidelines.

7. The totality principle

The court should review the total sentence to ensure that it is proportionate to the offending behaviour and properly balanced.

8. Reasons

When a court moves from the suggested starting points and sentencing ranges identified in the guidelines, it should explain its reasons for doing so.

SG-72 **Sentencing ranges and starting points**

1. Typically, a guideline will apply to an offence that can be committed in a variety of circumstances with different levels of seriousness. It will apply to a first-time offender who has been convicted after a trial. Within the guidelines, a first-time offender is a person who does not have a conviction which, by virtue of section 143(2) of the CJA 2003, must be treated as an aggravating factor.
2. As an aid to consistency of approach, the guidelines describe a number of types of activity which would fall within the broad definition of the offence. These are set out in a column headed 'Type/ nature of activity'.
3. The expected approach is for a court to identify the description that most nearly matches the particular facts of the offence for which sentence is being imposed. This will identify a starting point from which the sentencer can depart to reflect aggravating or mitigating factors affecting the seriousness of the offence (beyond those contained within the column describing the type or nature of offence activity) to reach a provisional sentence.
4. The *sentencing range* is the bracket into which the provisional sentence will normally fall after having regard to factors which aggravate or mitigate the seriousness of the offence. The particular circumstances may, however, make it appropriate that the provisional sentence falls outside the range.
5. Where the offender has previous convictions which aggravate the seriousness of the current offence, that may take the provisional sentence beyond the range given, particularly where there are significant other aggravating factors present.
6. Once the provisional sentence has been identified by reference to those factors affecting the seriousness of the offence, the court will take into account any relevant factors of personal mitigation, which may take the sentence outside the range indicated in the guideline.
7. Where there has been a guilty plea, any reduction attributable to that plea will be applied to the sentence at this stage. This reduction may take the sentence below the range provided.
8. A court must give its reasons for imposing a sentence of a different kind or outside the range provided in the guidelines.[94]

SG-73

Part 2: Non-consensual Offences

2.1 The offences in this category include 'rape', 'assault by penetration', 'sexual assault' and causing a victim to take part in sexual activity without consent. Some offences are generic; others protect victims who are under 13 or who have a mental disorder impeding choice.

2.2 **The SOA 2003 creates a rule of law that there is no defence of consent where sexual activity is alleged in relation to a child under 13 years of age or a person who has a mental disorder impeding choice.**[95]

SG-74 **The harm caused by non-consensual offences**

2.3 All non-consensual offences involve the violation of the victim's sexual autonomy and will result in harm.

2.4 The seriousness of the violation may depend on a number of factors, but the nature of the sexual behaviour will be the primary indicator of the degree of harm caused in the first instance.

2.5 The principle that offences involving sexual penetration are more serious than non-penetrative sexual assault is reflected in the higher maximum penalty accorded in statute to these offences.

[94] Criminal Justice Act 2003, s. 174(2)(a)

[95] See, for example, the offences set out in the Sexual Offences Act 2003, ss. 5–8 and 30–33

The relationship between the victim and the offender

2.6 The guideline judgment in *Millberry and others*[96] established the principle that sentencers should adopt the same starting point for 'relationship rape' or 'acquaintance rape' as for 'stranger rape'. The Council has determined that the same principle should apply to all non-consensual offences. Any rape is a traumatic and humiliating experience and, although the particular circumstances in which the rape takes place may affect the sentence imposed, the starting point for sentencing should be the same.

The age of the victim

2.7 **The extreme youth or old age of a victim should be an aggravating factor.**

2.8 **In addition, in principle, the younger the child and the greater the age gap between the offender and the victim, the higher the sentence should be.**

2.9 **However, the youth and immaturity of the offender must also be taken into account in each case.**

2.10 The court in *Millberry* adopted the principle that a sexual offence against a child is more serious than the same offence perpetrated against an adult and attracts a higher starting point. No distinction was made between children aged 13 and over but under 16, and those aged under 13.

2.11 Special weight has subsequently been accorded to the protection of very young children by the introduction of a range of strict liability offences in the SOA 2003 specifically designed to protect children under 13:

- The offences of 'rape of a child under 13', 'assault by penetration of a child under 13' and 'causing a child under 13 to engage in sexual activity' where the activity included sexual penetration carry the maximum life penalty.
- The maximum penalty for the new offence of 'sexual assault of a child under 13' is 14 years, as opposed to a maximum of 10 years for the generic 'sexual assault' offence.

2.12 In keeping with the principles of protection established in the SOA 2003, the Council has determined that:

- **higher starting points in cases involving victims under 13 should normally apply, but there may be exceptions;**
- **particular care will need to be taken when applying the starting points in certain cases, such as those involving young offenders or offenders whose judgement is impaired by a mental disorder; and**
- **proximity in age between a young victim and an offender is also a relevant consideration.**

Victims with a mental disorder

2.13 The SOA 2003 introduces three groups of offences specifically designed to protect vulnerable adults who have a mental disorder. The aim is to protect all victims with a mental disorder, whether or not they have the capacity to consent to sexual activity, but the legislation has been drafted to make a distinction between:

(i) those persons who have a mental disorder 'impeding choice'—persons whose mental functioning is so impaired at the time of the sexual activity that they are 'unable to refuse';

(ii) those who have a mental disorder (but not falling within (i) above[97]) such that any ability to choose is easily overridden and agreement to sexual activity can be secured through relatively low levels of inducement, threat or deception; and

(iii) those who have a mental disorder, regardless of their ability to choose whether or not to take part in sexual activity, whose actions may be influenced by their familiarity with, or dependence upon, a care worker.

The latter two groups are considered in Part 3 of the guideline, which relates to offences involving ostensible consent.

2.14 The maximum penalty for non-consensual offences involving victims with a mental disorder is high, indicating the relative seriousness of such offending behaviour.

2.15 In line with the thinking relating to the protection of children under 13, the fact that the victim has a mental disorder impeding choice should always aggravate an offence, bearing in mind that it will have been proven that the offender knew, or could reasonably have been expected to know, that the victim had a mental disorder impeding choice.

The starting points for sentencing for offences involving victims with a mental disorder impeding choice should be higher than in comparable cases where the victim has no such disability.

[96] [2003] 2 Cr App R (S) 31

[97] That is, it is not of such a character that it 'impedes choice' within the meaning of the SOA 2003

Sentencing Guidelines

SG-75 **The offender's culpability in non-consensual offences**

2.16 All the non-consensual offences involve a high level of culpability on the part of the offender, since that person will have acted either deliberately without the victim's consent or without giving due consideration to whether the victim was able to or did, in fact, consent.

2.17 Notwithstanding paragraph 2.11 above, there will be cases involving victims under 13 years of age where there was, *in fact*, consent where, *in law*, it cannot be given. In such circumstances, presence of consent may be material in relation to sentence, particularly in relation to a young offender where there is close proximity in age between the victim and offender or where the mental capacity or maturity of the offender is impaired.

2.18 Where there was reasonable belief on the part of a young offender that the victim was 16, this can be taken into consideration as a mitigating factor.

2.19 The planning of an offence indicates a higher level of culpability than an opportunistic or impulsive offence.

2.20 In *Millberry*, the Court of Appeal established that the offender's culpability in a case of rape would be 'somewhat less' in cases where the victim had consented to sexual familiarity with the offender on the occasion in question than in cases where the offender had set out with the intention of committing rape.

2.21 Save in cases of breach of trust or grooming, an offender's culpability may be reduced if the offender and victim engaged in consensual sexual activity on the same occasion and immediately before the offence took place. Factors relevant to culpability in such circumstances include the type of consensual activity that occurred, similarity to what then occurs, and timing. However, the seriousness of the non-consensual act may overwhelm any other consideration.

2.22 The same principle should apply to the generic offences of 'assault by penetration' and 'sexual assault'. However, it should not apply to the equivalent offences relating to victims who are under 13 or who have a mental disorder impeding choice, given the presumption inherent in these offences that the victim cannot in law consent to any form of sexual activity, save where there is close proximity of age between the offender and the victim, or where the mental capacity or maturity of the offender is impaired.

SG-76

Part 2A: Rape and Assault by Penetration

2A.1 The SOA 2003 has redefined the offence of rape so that it now includes nonconsensual penile penetration of the mouth and has also introduced a new offence of 'assault by penetration'. Parliament agreed the same maximum penalty of life imprisonment for these offences.

2A.2 It is impossible to say that any one form of non-consensual penetration is inherently a more serious violation of the victim's sexual autonomy than another. The Council therefore has determined that the sentencing starting points established in *Millberry* should apply to all non-consensual offences involving penetration of the anus or vagina or penile penetration of the mouth.

- **5 years** is intended to be the starting point for a case involving an adult victim raped by a single offender in a case that involves *no aggravating factors at all*.
- **8 years** is the suggested starting point where any of the particular aggravating factors identified in the offence guidelines are involved.

2A.3 In addition:

- where identified aggravating factors exist and the victim is a child aged 13 or over but under 16, the recommended starting point is 10 years;
- for the rape of a child under 13 where there are no aggravating factors, a starting point of 10 years is recommended, rising to 13 years for cases involving any of the particular aggravating factors identified in the guideline.

2A.4 These are starting points. The existence of aggravating factors may significantly increase the sentence. The new sentences for public protection are designed to ensure that sexual offenders are not released into the community if they present a significant risk of serious harm.

SG-77 **Rape**

Factors to take into consideration:

1. The sentences for public protection *must* be considered in all cases of rape.
   a) As a result, imprisonment for life or an order of imprisonment for public protection will be imposed in some cases. Both sentences are designed to ensure that sexual offenders are not released into the community if they present a significant risk of serious harm.

b) Life imprisonment is the maximum for the offence. Such a sentence may be imposed either as a result of the offence itself where a number of aggravating factors are present, or because the offender meets the dangerousness criterion.

c) Within any indeterminate sentence, the minimum term will generally be half the appropriate determinate sentence. The starting points will be relevant, therefore, to the process of fixing any minimum term that may be necessary.

2. Rape includes penile penetration of the mouth.
3. There is no distinction in the starting points for penetration of the vagina, anus or mouth.
4. All the non-consensual offences involve a high level of culpability on the part of the offender, since that person will have acted either deliberately without the victim's consent or without giving due care to whether the victim was able to or did, in fact, consent.
5. The planning of an offence indicates a higher level of culpability than an opportunistic or impulsive offence.
6. An offender's culpability may be reduced if the offender and victim engaged in consensual sexual activity on the same occasion and immediately before the offence took place. Factors relevant to culpability in such circumstances include the type of consensual activity that occurred, similarity to what then occurs, and timing. However, the seriousness of the non-consensual act may overwhelm any other consideration.
7. The seriousness of the violation of the victim's sexual autonomy may depend on a number of factors, but the nature of the sexual behaviour will be the primary indicator of the degree of harm caused in the first instance.
8. The presence of any of the general aggravating factors identified in the Council guideline on seriousness or any of the additional factors identified in the guidelines will indicate a sentence above the normal starting point.

THESE ARE SERIOUS OFFENCES FOR THE PURPOSES OF SECTION 224 CJA 2003

1. **Rape** (section 1): Intentional non-consensual penile penetration of the vagina, anus or mouth
2. **Rape of a child under 13** (section 5): Intentional penile penetration of the vagina, anus or mouth of a person under 13

Maximum penalty for both offences: **Life imprisonment**

Type/nature of activity	Starting points	Sentencing ranges
Repeated rape of same victim over a course of time or rape involving multiple victims	**15 years custody**	**13–19 years custody**
Rape accompanied by any one of the following: abduction or detention; offender aware that he is suffering from a sexually transmitted infection; more than one offender acting together; abuse of trust; offence motivated by prejudice (race, religion, sexual orientation, physical disability); sustained attack	**13 years custody** if the victim is under 13	**11–17 years custody**
	10 years custody if the victim is a child aged 13 or over but under 16	**8–13 years custody**
	8 years custody if the victim is 16 or over	**6–11 years custody**
Single offence of rape by single offender	**10 years custody** if the victim is under 13	**8–13 years custody**
	8 years custody if the victim is 13 or over but under 16	**6–11 years custody**
	5 years custody if the victim is 16 or over	**4–8 years custody**

Sentencing Guidelines

Additional aggravating factors	Additional mitigating factors
1. Offender ejaculated or caused victim to ejaculate 2. Background of intimidation or coercion 3. Use of drugs, alcohol or other substance to facilitate the offence 4. Threats to prevent victim reporting the incident 5. Abduction or detention 6. Offender aware that he is suffering from a sexually transmitted infection 7. Pregnancy or infection results	*Where the victim is aged 16 or over* Victim engaged in consensual sexual activity with the offender on the same occasion and immediately before the offence *Where the victim is under 16* • Sexual activity between two children (one of whom is the offender) was mutually agreed and experimental • Reasonable belief (by a young offender) that the victim was aged 16 or over

An offender convicted of these offences is automatically subject to notification requirements.[98]

SG-78 **Assault by penetration**

Factors to take into consideration:

1. The sentences for public protection *must* be considered in all cases of assault by penetration. They are designed to ensure that sexual offenders are not released into the community if they present a significant risk of serious harm. Within any indeterminate sentence, the minimum term will generally be half the appropriate determinate sentence. The starting points will be relevant, therefore, to the process of fixing any minimum term that may be necessary.
2. This offence involves penetration of the vagina or anus only, with objects or body parts. It may include penile penetration where the means of penetration is only established during the trial.
3. All the non-consensual offences involve a high level of culpability on the part of the offender, since that person will have acted either deliberately without the victim's consent or without giving due care to whether the victim was able to or did, in fact, consent.
4. The planning of an offence indicates a higher level of culpability than an opportunistic or impulsive offence.
5. An offender's culpability may be reduced if the offender and victim engaged in consensual sexual activity on the same occasion and immediately before the offence took place. Factors relevant to culpability in such circumstances include the type of consensual activity that occurred, similarity to what then occurs, and timing. However, the seriousness of the non-consensual act may overwhelm any other consideration.
6. The seriousness of the violation of the victim's sexual autonomy may depend on a number of factors, but the nature of the sexual behaviour will be the primary indicator of the degree of harm caused in the first instance.
7. The presence of any of the general aggravating factors identified in the Council guideline on seriousness or any of the additional factors identified in the guidelines will indicate a sentence above the normal starting point.
8. Brief penetration with fingers, toes or tongue may result in a significantly lower sentence where no physical harm is caused to the victim.

THESE ARE SERIOUS OFFENCES FOR THE PURPOSES OF SECTION 224 CJA 2003

1. **Assault by penetration** (section 2): Non-consensual penetration of the vagina or anus with objects or body parts
2. **Assault of a child under 13 by penetration** (section 6): Intentional penetration of the vagina or anus of a person under 13 with objects or body parts

[98] In accordance with the SOA 2003, s. 80 and schedule 3

Maximum penalty for both offences: **Life imprisonment**

Type/nature of activity	Starting points	Sentencing Ranges
Penetration with an object or body part, accompanied by any one of the following: abduction or detention; more than one offender acting together; abuse of trust; offence motivated by prejudice (race, religion, sexual orientation, physical disability); sustained attack	**13 years custody** if the victim is under 13	**11–17 years custody**
	10 years custody if the victim is 13 or over but under 16	**8–13 years custody**
	8 years custody if the victim is 16 or over	**6–11 years custody**
Penetration with an object—in general, the larger or more dangerous the object, the higher the sentence should be	**7 years custody** if the victim is under 13	**5–10 years custody**
	5 years custody if the victim is 13 or over but under 16	**4–8 years custody**
	3 years custody if the victim is 16 or over	**2–5 years custody**
Penetration with a body part (fingers, toes or tongue) where no physical harm is sustained by the victim	**5 years custody** if the victim is under 13	**4–8 years custody**
	4 years custody if the victim is 13 or over but under 16	**3–7 years custody**
	2 years custody if the victim is 16 or over	**1–4 years custody**

Additional aggravating factors	Additional mitigating factors
1. Background of intimidation or coercion 2. Use of drugs, alcohol or other substance to facilitate the offence 3. Threats to prevent victim reporting the incident 4. Abduction or detention 5. Offender aware that he is suffering from a sexually transmitted infection 6. Physical harm arising from the penetration 7. Offender ejaculated or caused the victim to ejaculate	*Where the victim is aged 16 or over* Victim engaged in consensual sexual activity with the offender on the same occasion and immediately before the offence *Where the victim is under 16* • Sexual activity between two children (one of whom is the offender) was mutually agreed and experimental • Reasonable belief (by a young offender) that the victim was aged 16 or over Penetration is minimal or for a short duration

An offender convicted of these offences is automatically subject to notification requirements.[99]

PART 2B: SEXUAL ASSAULT

SG-79

2B.1 Various activities previously covered by the offence of 'indecent assault' now fall within the definitions of other offences in the SOA 2003:

- Forcible penile penetration of the mouth now comes within the definition of 'rape'.
- Penetration of the vagina or anus with a body part or other object is covered by the offence of 'assault by penetration'.
- All forms of ostensibly consensual sexual activity involving children under 16 (who cannot in law give any consent to prevent an act being an assault) now fall within a range of child sex offences.

[99] In accordance with the SOA 2003, s. 80 and schedule 3

- Vulnerable adults subjected to a sexual assault are now protected by the offences of 'sexual activity with a person with a mental disorder impeding choice' and 'causing or inciting a person with a mental disorder impeding choice to engage in sexual activity'.

2B.2 The offence of 'sexual assault' covers all forms of sexual touching and will largely be used in relation to the lesser forms of assault that would have previously fallen at the lower end of the penalty scale.

2B.3 The exact nature of the sexual activity should be the key factor in assessing the seriousness of a sexual assault and should be used as the starting point from which to begin the process of assessing the overall seriousness of the offending behaviour.

2B.4 The presence of aggravating factors can make an offence significantly more serious than the nature of the activity alone might suggest.

- **The nature of the sexual activity will be the *primary* factor in assessing the seriousness of an offence of sexual assault.**
- **In all cases, the fact that the offender has ejaculated or has caused the victim to ejaculate will increase the seriousness of the offence.**

SG-80 **Sexual assault**

Factors to take into consideration:

1. The sentences for public protection *must* be considered in all cases of sexual assault. They are designed to ensure that sexual offenders are not released into the community if they present a significant risk of serious harm.
2. The offence of 'sexual assault' covers all forms of sexual touching and therefore covers a wide range of offending behaviour. Some offences may justify a lesser sentence where the actions were more offensive than threatening and comprised a single act rather than more persistent behaviour.
3. The nature of the sexual activity will be the *primary* factor in assessing the seriousness of an offence and should be use as the starting point from which to begin the process of assessing the overall seriousness of the offending behaviour.
4. The presence of aggravating factors can make an offence significantly more serious than the nature of the activity alone might suggest.
5. For the purpose of the guideline, types of sexual touching are broadly grouped in terms of seriousness. An offence may involve activities from more than one group. In all cases, the fact that the offender has ejaculated or has caused the victim to ejaculate will increase the seriousness of the offence.
6. An offender's culpability may be reduced if the offender and victim engaged in consensual sexual activity on the same occasion and immediately before the offence took place. Factors relevant to culpability in such circumstances include the type of consensual activity that occurred, similarity to what then occurs, and timing. However, the seriousness of the non-consensual act may overwhelm any other consideration.
7. Where this offence is being dealt with in a magistrates' court, more detailed guidance is provided in the Magistrates' Court Sentencing Guidelines (MCSG) [see **SG-232**].

THESE ARE SERIOUS OFFENCES FOR THE PURPOSES OF SECTION 224 CJA 2003

1. **Sexual assault** (section 3): Non-consensual sexual touching

Maximum penalty: **10 years**

2. **Sexual assault of a child under 13** (section 7): Intentional sexual touching of a person under 13

Maximum penalty: **14 years**

Type/nature of activity	Starting points	Sentencing ranges
Contact between naked genitalia of offender and naked genitalia, face or mouth of the victim	**5 years custody** if the victim is under 13	**4–8 years custody**
	3 years custody if the victim is aged 13 or over	**2–5 years custody**
Contact between naked genitalia of offender and another part of victim's body	**2 years custody** if the victim is under 13	**1–4 years custody**
Contact with genitalia of victim by offender using part of his or her body other than the genitalia, or an object	**12 months custody** if the victim is aged 13 or over	**26 weeks–2 years custody**

Type/nature of activity	Starting points	Sentencing ranges
Contact between either the clothed genitalia of offender and naked genitalia of victim or naked genitalia of offender and clothed genitalia of victim		
Contact between part of offender's body (other than the genitalia) with part of the victim's body (other than the genitalia)	**26 weeks custody** if the victim is under 13	**4 weeks–18 months custody**
	Community order if the victim is aged 13 or over	**An appropriate non-custodial sentence**

* 'Non-custodial sentence' in this context suggests a community order or a fine. In most instances, an offence will have crossed the threshold for a community order. However, in accordance with normal sentencing practice, a court is not precluded from imposing a financial penalty where that is determined to be the appropriate sentence.

Additional aggravating factors	Additional mitigating factors
1. Offender ejaculated or caused victim to ejaculate 2. Background of intimidation or coercion 3. Use of drugs, alcohol or other substance to facilitate the offence 4. Threats to prevent victim reporting the incident 5. Abduction or detention 6. Offender aware that he or she is suffering from a sexually transmitted infection 7. Physical harm caused 8. Prolonged activity or contact	*Where the victim is aged 16 or over* Victim engaged in consensual sexual activity with the offender on the same occasion and immediately before the offence *Where the victim is under 16* • Sexual activity between two children (one of whom is the offender) was mutually agreed and experimental • Reasonable belief (by a young offender) that the victim was aged 16 or over Youth and immaturity of the offender Minimal or fleeting contact

An offender convicted of these offences is automatically subject to notification requirements.[100]

Part 2C: Causing or Inciting Sexual Activity

SG-81

2C.1 There are three offences in this category covering a wide range of sexual activity:

- Causing a person to engage in sexual activity without consent
- Causing or inciting a child under 13 to engage in sexual activity
- Causing or inciting a person with a mental disorder impeding choice to engage in sexual activity

2C.2 The maximum penalty for the second and third of these offences is the same whether the sexual activity is *caused or incited.* This recognises that, with vulnerable victims, incitement to indulge in sexual activity is, of itself, likely to result in harm.

2C.3 Deciding sentence may be complex where an incited offence did not actually take place. Whilst the effect of the incitement is of no relevance to whether or not the offence incited was *committed,* it is likely to be relevant to the sentence imposed.

[100] In accordance with the SOA 2003, s. 80 and schedule 3

2C.4 Accordingly, the starting point should be the same whether or not the sexual activity takes place. Where it does not take place, the harm (and sometimes the culpability) is likely to be less, and the sentence should be reduced appropriately to reflect this.

2C.5 If the activity does not take place because the offender desists of his or her own accord, culpability (and sometimes harm) will be reduced. This should be treated as a mitigating factor for sentencing purposes and does not affect the principle that starting points for 'causing' or 'inciting' an activity should be the same.

2C.6 If the offender is prevented from achieving his or her aim by reasons outside their control, culpability may not be reduced, but it is possible that the harm will be less than if the activity had taken place.

2C.7 Culpability must be the primary indicator for sentencing in such cases, but it would make no sense for courts to pass the same sentence for an incited offence that did not actually take place as it would for the substantive offence itself. In these circumstances, the sentence should be calculated using the starting point for the substantive offence, taking account of the nature of the harm that would have been caused had the offence taken place, and the degree to which an intended victim may have suffered as a result of knowing or believing that the incited offence would take place, but nevertheless reflecting the facts if no actual harm has been caused to a victim.

- **The starting point should be the same whether an offender causes an act to take place or incites an act which does not take place.**
- **A reduction will generally be appropriate where the incited activity does not take place.**
- **Where an offender voluntarily desists from any action taken to incite a sexual act, or personally and of their own volition intervenes to prevent a sexual act from taking place, this will be an additional mitigating factor.**
- **Whether or not the sexual activity takes place, the degree of harm done to the victim will be a material consideration when considering the sentence.**

2C.8 The offence of 'causing a person to engage in sexual activity without consent' covers situations where, for example, a victim is forced to carry out a sexual act involving his or her own person, such as self-masturbation, or to engage in sexual activity with a third party, or situations in which the victim is forced to engage in sexual activity with the offender.

2C.9 The underlying purpose is to create offences that carry the same level of penalties for what amounts to the same type of offending behaviour, regardless of the gender or sexual orientation of the offender. This is reflected in the recommended starting points for penetrative acts charged within this category.

2C.10 The two main factors determining the seriousness of an offence of causing or inciting sexual activity without consent will be the nature of the sexual activity (as an indication of the degree of harm caused, or likely to be caused, to the victim) and the level of the offender's culpability. Culpability will be higher if the victim is forced to engage in sexual activity with the offender, or with another victim, than in cases where there is no sexual contact between the victim and the offender or anyone else. In all cases, the degree of force or coercion used by the offender will be an indication of the offender's level of culpability and may also exacerbate the harm suffered by the victim.

2C.11 The same sentencing starting points for offences involving non-consensual penetration of the vagina or anus of another person will apply regardless of whether the offender is male or female. There should be no differentiation between the starting point for 'rape' and an offence where a female offender causes or incites a non-consenting male to penetrate her vagina, anus or mouth. Similarly, where a victim is caused or incited to take part in penetrative activities with a third party or where the offender causes or incites other forms of sexual activity, there is no reason to differentiate sentence for male and female offenders.

The starting points for sentencing for sexual activity that is caused or incited by the offender without the consent of the victim(s) should mirror those for similar activity perpetrated within the offences of 'rape', 'assault by penetration' and 'sexual assault'.

SG-82 **Causing sexual activity without consent**

Factors to take into consideration:

1. The sentences for public protection *must* be considered in all cases of causing sexual activity. They are designed to ensure that sexual offenders are not released into the community if they present a significant

risk of serious harm. Within any indeterminate sentence, the minimum term will generally be half the appropriate determinate sentence. The starting points will be relevant, therefore, to the process of fixing any minimum term that may be necessary.

2. The same degree of seriousness applies whether an offender causes an act to take place, incites an act that actually takes place, or incites an act that does not take place only because it is prevented by factors beyond the control of the offender.
3. The same starting points apply whether the activity was caused or incited and whether or not the incited activity took place, but some reduction will generally be appropriate when the incited activity does not, in fact, take place.
4. Where an offender voluntarily desists from any action taken to incite a sexual act or personally, and of their own volition, intervenes to prevent from taking place a sexual act that he or she has incited, this should be treated as a mitigating factor.
5. The effect of the incitement is relevant to the length of the sentence to be imposed. A court should take into account the degree to which the intended victim may have suffered as a result of knowing or believing that an offence would take place.

THESE ARE SERIOUS OFFENCES FOR THE PURPOSES OF SECTION 224 CJA 2003

1. **Causing a person to engage in sexual activity without consent** (section 4): Forcing someone else to perform a sexual act on him or herself or another person

Maximum penalty: **Life imprisonment** if the activity involves penetration; **10 years** if the activity does not involve penetration

2. **Causing or inciting a child under 13 to engage in sexual activity** (section 8): Causing or inciting a person under 13 to perform a sexual act on him or herself or another person

Maximum penalty: **Life imprisonment** if the activity involves penetration; **14 years** if the activity does not involve penetration

3. **Causing or inciting a person with a mental disorder impeding choice to engage in sexual activity** (section 31): Intentionally causing or inciting a person with a mental disorder impeding choice to engage in sexual activity.

Maximum penalty: **Life imprisonment** if the activity involves penetration; **14 years** if penetration not involved

Type/nature of activity	Starting points	Sentencing ranges
Penetration with any one of the following aggravating factors: abduction or detention; offender aware that he or she is suffering from a sexually transmitted infection; more than one offender acting together; abuse of trust; offence motivated by prejudice (race, religion, sexual orientation, physical disability); sustained attack	**13 years custody** if the victim is a child under 13 or a person with a mental disorder	**11–17 years custody**
	10 years custody if the victim is 13 or over but under 16	**8–13 years custody**
	8 years custody if the victim is 16 or over	**6–11 years custody**
Single offence of penetration of/by single offender with no aggravating or mitigating factors	**7 years custody** if the victim is a child under 13 or a person with a mental disorder	**5–10 years custody**
	5 years custody if the victim is 13 or over but under 16	**4–8 years custody**
	3 years custody if the victim is 16 or over	**2–5 years custody**
Contact between naked genitalia of offender and naked genitalia of victim, *or* causing two or more victims to engage in such activity with each other, *or* causing victim to masturbate him/herself	**5 years custody** if the victim is a child under 13 or a person with a mental disorder	**4–8 years custody**
	3 years custody	**2–5 years custody**

Sentencing Guidelines

Type/nature of activity	Starting points	Sentencing ranges
Contact between naked genitalia of offender and another part of victim's body, *or* causing two or more victims to engage in such activity with each other Contact with naked genitalia of victim by offender using part of the body other than the genitalia or an object, *or* causing two or more victims to engage in such activity with each other	**2 years custody** if the victim is a child under 13 or a person with a mental disorder	**1–4 years custody**
Contact between either the clothed genitalia of offender and naked genitalia of victim, between naked genitalia of offender and clothed genitalia of victim, *or* causing two or more victims to engage in such activity with each other	**12 months custody**	**26 weeks–2 years custody**
Contact between part of offender's body (other than the genitalia) with part of victim's body (other than the genitalia)	**26 weeks custody** if the victim is a child under 13 or a person with a mental disorder **Community order**	**4 weeks–18 months custody** **An appropriate non-custodial sentence***

* 'Non-custodial sentence' in this context suggests a community order or a fine. In most instances, an offence will have crossed the threshold for a community order. However, in accordance with normal sentencing practice, a court is not precluded from imposing a financial penalty where that is determined to be the appropriate sentence.

Additional aggravating factors	Additional mitigating factors
1. Offender ejaculated or caused victim to ejaculate 2. History of intimidation or coercion 3. Use of drugs, alcohol or other substance to facilitate the offence 4. Threats to prevent victim reporting the incident 5. Abduction or detention 6. Offender aware that he or she is suffering from a sexually transmitted infection	

An offender convicted of these offences is automatically subject to notification requirements.[101]

SG-83

Part 2D: Other Non-Consensual Offences

2D.1 Four other offences fall within the general category of non-consensual offences:
- Engaging in sexual activity in the presence of a child
- Engaging in sexual activity in the presence of a person with a mental disorder impeding choice
- Causing a child to watch a sexual act
- Causing a person with a mental disorder impeding choice to watch a sexual act

2D.2 These are offences that relate to lesser forms of offending behaviour than offences that involve physical touching of the victim, but they nevertheless attract maximum penalties of 10 years' imprisonment in recognition of the fact that the victims are particularly vulnerable.

2D.3 The guidelines are predicated on the principle that the more serious the nature of the sexual activity a victim is forced to witness, the higher the sentencing starting point should be.

2D.4 These offences can cover a very wide range of sexual activity and an equally wide range of circumstances in which a victim is subjected to witnessing it.

2D.5 However, any form of sexual activity in the presence of a child or person with a mental disorder impeding choice may well be serious enough to merit a custodial starting point. It is always within the power of the court in an individual case to consider whether there are particular factors that mitigate sentence and should move it back below the custodial threshold.

[101] In accordance with the SOA 2003, s. 80 and schedule 3

- **The same starting points for sentencing should apply in relation to the various levels of activity falling within the offences of 'engaging in sexual activity in the presence of a child' and 'engaging in sexual activity in the presence of a person with a mental disorder impeding choice'. Similarly, the same starting points should apply in relation to the offences of 'causing a child to watch a sexual act' and 'causing a person with a mental disorder impeding choice to watch a sexual act'.**
- **An offence involving an offender who intentionally commits a sexual act in the presence of a child or a person with a mental disorder impeding choice in order to obtain sexual gratification will potentially be serious enough to merit a custodial sentence. In an individual case the court will need to consider whether there are particular mitigating factors that move the sentence below the custodial threshold.**

Sexual activity in the presence of another person SG-84

Factors to take into consideration:

1. The sentences for public protection *must* be considered in all cases of engaging in sexual activity in the presence of another person. They are designed to ensure that sexual offenders are not released into the community if they present a significant risk of serious harm.
2. These offences involve intentionally, and for the purpose of obtaining sexual gratification, engaging in sexual activity in the presence of a person under 16, or a person with a mental disorder, knowing or believing that person to be aware of the activity.
3. The guidelines are predicated on the principle that the more serious the nature of the sexual activity a victim is forced to witness, the higher the sentencing starting point should be.
4. These offences will potentially be serious enough to merit a custodial sentence. In an individual case the court will need to consider whether there are particular mitigating factors that move the sentence below the custodial threshold.

THESE ARE SERIOUS OFFENCES FOR THE PURPOSES OF SECTION 224 CJA 2003

1. **Engaging in sexual activity in the presence of a child** (section 11)

Maximum penalty: **10 years (5 years** if offender is under 18)

2. **Engaging in sexual activity in the presence of a person with a mental disorder impeding choice** (section 32)

Maximum penalty: **10 years**

Type/nature of activity	Starting points	Sentencing ranges
Consensual intercourse or other forms of consensual penetration	**2 years custody**	**1–4 years custody**
Masturbation (of oneself or another person)	**18 months custody**	**12 months–2 years 6 months custody**
Consensual sexual touching involving naked genitalia	**12 months custody**	**26 weeks–18 months custody**
Consensual sexual touching of naked body parts but not involving naked genitalia	**26 weeks custody**	**4 weeks–18 months custody**

Additional aggravating factors	Additional mitigating factors
1. Background of intimidation or coercion 2. Use of drugs, alcohol or other substance to facilitate the offence 3. Threats to prevent victim reporting the incident 4. Abduction or detention	

An offender convicted of these offences is automatically subject to notification requirements.[102]

[102] In accordance with the SOA 2003, s. 80 and schedule 3

SG-85 **Causing or inciting another person to watch a sexual act**

Factors to take into consideration:

1. The sentences for public protection *must* be considered in all cases. They are designed to ensure that sexual offenders are not released into the community if they present a significant risk of serious harm.
2. These offences include intentionally causing or inciting, for the purpose of sexual gratification, a person under 16, or a person with a mental disorder, to watch sexual activity or look at a photograph or pseudo-photograph of sexual activity.
3. The guidelines are predicated on the principle that the more serious the nature of the sexual activity a victim is caused to witness, the higher the sentencing starting point should be.
4. These offences will potentially be serious enough to merit a custodial sentence. In an individual case the court will need to consider whether there are particular mitigating factors that should move the sentence below the custodial threshold.
5. The same starting points apply whether the activity was caused or incited and whether or not the incited activity took place.

THESE ARE SERIOUS OFFENCES FOR THE PURPOSES OF SECTION 224 CJA 2003

1. **Causing a child to watch a sexual act** (section 12)

Maximum penalty: **10 years (5 years** if offender is under 18)

2. **Causing a person with a mental disorder impeding choice, to watch a sexual act** (section 33)

Maximum penalty: **10 years**

Type/nature of activity	Starting points	Sentencing ranges
Live sexual activity	**18 months custody**	**12 months–2 years custody**
Moving or still images of people engaged in sexual activity involving penetration	**32 weeks custody**	**26 weeks–12 months custody**
Moving or still images of people engaged in sexual activity other than penetration	**Community order**	**Community order–26 weeks custody**

An offender convicted of these offences is automatically subject to notification requirements.[103]

Additional aggravating factors	Additional mitigating factors
1. Background of intimidation or coercion 2. Use of drugs, alcohol or other substance to facilitate the offence 3. Threats to prevent victim reporting the incident 4. Abduction or detention 5. Images of violent activity	

SG-86 ## Part 3: Offences Involving Ostensible Consent

3.1 There are several groups of offences in the SOA 2003 that involve a compliant or willing partner. Any sexual activity involving a person below the age of consent is unlawful notwithstanding any ostensible consent. In addition, there are circumstances where sexual activity takes place with the ostensible consent of both parties but where one of the parties is in such a great position of power over the other that the sexual activity is wrong.

3.2 There are two categories of offence within this broad grouping:

- Part 3A—sexual activity with children under 16—or under 18 where there is an imbalance of power (for example, within the family unit) or an abuse of trust (for example, between a teacher and a pupil); and

[103] In accordance with the SOA 2003, s. 80 and schedule 3

- Part 3B—sexual activity with adults who have the capacity to consent but who, by reason of, or for reasons related to, a mental disorder are susceptible to coercion and exploitation.

Part 3A: Offences Involving Children SG-87

3A.1 In addition to the range of non-consensual sexual offences designed to protect children under 13, there are three further groups of offences that cover all forms of ostensibly consensual sexual activity involving children under 16 and also provide additional protection for older children:

(i) 'child sex offences' (covering unlawful sexual activity with children under 16) including 'arranging or facilitating the commission of a child sex offence';

(ii) 'familial child sex offences' (relating to offences committed by members of the child's family or household and primarily intended to ensure that charges can be brought in relation to victims aged 16 or 17); and

(iii) 'abuse of a position of trust' (another offence that enables the prosecution of sexual activity involving victims aged 16 or 17, in this case where the offender has a relationship of trust with the child, such as that of a teacher or care worker).

3A.2 A 'reasonable' belief that the child was aged 16 or over is a defence to all the child sex offences, provided the child was, in fact, aged 13 or over. With the same proviso, a reasonable belief that the victim was aged 18 or over is a defence to the familial child sex offences and the abuse of trust offences.

3A.3 The maximum penalties for the offences in these groups give some indication of their relative seriousness and of the factors that increase the seriousness of an offence.

3A.4 Conversely, the lower maximum penalties for offenders aged under 18 indicate that the offence is less serious when the age gap between the victim and the offender is relatively narrow. The young age of an offender may often be seen as a mitigating factor for sentencing. This principle has already largely been catered for in the child sex offences by the provision in statute of lower maximum penalties for young offenders, which are designed to take account of their immaturity (see Part 7). However, the extreme youth of an offender and close proximity in age between the offender and the victim are both factors that will still be relevant for the court to consider when deciding sentence.

The significance of family relationships SG-88

3A.5 Family relationships, as defined in the SOA 2003 in relation to the offences of sexual activity with a child family member and inciting a child family member to engage in sexual activity, are not restricted to blood relationships and include relationships formed through adoption, fostering, marriage or partnership.

3A.6 Some relationships, such as parents and siblings, are automatically covered. Others, such as step-parents and cousins, fall within the definition of 'family member' only if they live, or have lived, in the same household as the child or if they are, or have been, regularly involved in caring for, training, supervising or being in sole charge of the child.

3A.7 More distant 'relationships', such as lodgers and au pairs, are covered only if they were living in the same household as the child at the time of the offence and were regularly involved in caring for, training, supervising or being in sole charge of the child at that time.

3A.8 These offences bring ostensibly consensual sexual activity between persons over the age of consent (which would not otherwise be unlawful) within the scope of the criminal law.

All children, even those aged 16 or 17, are potentially vulnerable to exploitation within the family unit and the offences attract the same maximum penalty regardless of the age of the victim. The Council's view is that the worst aspect of child sexual abuse within the family is that the offender is one of the very people to whom the child would normally expect to turn for support and protection.

3A.9 Victims aged 16 or 17 may have been 'groomed' by a family member from a very young age before sexual activity takes place. Evidence of grooming can be treated as an aggravating factor for sentencing purposes, as can the extreme youth of a victim. However, the closeness of the relationship in such cases increases the seriousness of the offence regardless of the age of the victim and should be reflected in the sentencing starting points.

3A.10 There is a clear difference between a young person being coerced into sexual activity by an adult who holds a position of trust in his or her life outside the family unit and being coerced into a sexual relationship by someone (adult or child) who holds a position of trust within the family unit.

3A.11 The starting points for sentencing where the child is aged 13 or over but under 16 should be higher than for the equivalent child sex offences, to reflect the inherent abuse of trust. The amount of enhancement should vary to reflect the wide range of 'familial' relationships covered by this offence—on the basis that abuse by a parent is more serious than abuse by, for example, a foster sibling or lodger.

The starting points for sentencing for the familial child sex offences should be between 25% and 50% higher than those for the generic child sex offences in all cases where the victim is aged 13 or over but under 16; the closer the familial relationship, using the statutory definitions as a guide, the higher the increase that should be applied.

3A.12 Where a victim is over the age of consent, the starting points should only be significant where the offender is a close relative and where the abuse of a familial relationship is most serious. Where the activity is commenced when the victim is already aged 16 or 17 and the sexual relationship is unlawful only because it takes place within a familial setting (e.g. the activity is between foster siblings or involves an au pair or lodger), the starting points for sentencing should be lower than those for 'sexual activity with a child' and should be matched with the starting points for the 'abuse of trust' offences.

- **Where the victim of a familial child sex offence is aged 16 or 17 when the sexual activity is commenced and the sexual relationship is unlawful only because it takes place within a familial setting, the starting points for sentencing should be in line with those for the generic abuse of trust offences.**
- **Evidence that a victim has been 'groomed' by the offender to agree to take part in sexual activity will aggravate sentence.**

SG-89 **Abuse of a position of trust**

3A.13 These offences criminalise sexual activity by adults over 18 with children under 18 in situations where the adults are looking after the children in educational establishments or in various residential settings, or where their duties involve them in the regular unsupervised contact of children in the community.

3A.14 The maximum penalty for the offences of abuse of trust (5 years) is relatively low because the offences are primarily designed to protect young people who are over the legal age of consent (i. e. aged 16 or 17) from being persuaded to engage in sexual activity that would not be criminal except for the offender's position of trust in relation to the victim.

3A.15 In view of the fact that these offences will only be charged where the victim is aged 16 or 17, the sentencing starting points in the guidelines are significantly lower than those for a child sex offence involving the same type of sexual activity. The potential harm caused to victims who have been coerced and manipulated into undesirable sexual relationships has not been underestimated, and evidence of serious coercion, threats or trauma would all be aggravating factors that would move a sentence well beyond the starting point. However, some relationships caught within the scope of these offences, although unlawful, will be wholly consensual. The length of time over which a relationship has been sustained and the proximity in age between the parties could point to a relationship born out of genuine affection. Each case must be considered carefully on its own facts.

When sentencing for an abuse of trust offence, serious coercion, threats or trauma are aggravating factors that should move a sentence well beyond the starting point.

Assessing the seriousness of sexual offences against children SG-90

3A.16 The culpability of the offender will be the primary indicator of offence seriousness, and the nature of the sexual activity will provide a guide as to the seriousness of the harm caused to the victim, for any of the offences in the three categories involving ostensibly consensual activity with children. Other factors will include:

- the age and degree of vulnerability of the victim—as a general indication, the younger the child, the more vulnerable he or she is likely to be, although older children may also suffer serious and long-term psychological damage as a result of sexual abuse;
- the age gap between the child and the offender;
- the youth and immaturity of the offender; and
- except where it is inherent in an offence, any breach of trust arising from a family relationship between the child and the offender, or from the offender's professional or other responsibility for the child's welfare, will make an offence more serious.

Sexual activity with a child SG-91

Factors to take into consideration:

1. The sentences for public protection *must* be considered in all cases. They are designed to ensure that sexual offenders are not released into the community if they present a significant risk of serious harm.
2. The culpability of the offender will be the primary indicator of offence seriousness, and the nature of the sexual activity will provide a guide as to the seriousness of the harm caused to the victim. Other factors will include:
   - the age and degree of vulnerability of the victim—as a general indication, the younger the child, the more vulnerable he or she is likely to be, although older children may also suffer serious and long-term psychological damage as a result of sexual abuse;
   - the age gap between the child and the offender;
   - the youth and immaturity of the offender; and
   - except where it is inherent in an offence, any breach of trust arising from a family relationship between the child and the offender, or from the offender's professional or other responsibility for the child's welfare, will make an offence more serious.
3. The same starting points apply whether the activity was caused or incited. Where an offence was incited but did not take place as a result of the voluntary intervention of the offender, that is likely to reduce the severity of the sentence imposed.

THESE ARE SERIOUS OFFENCES FOR THE PURPOSES OF SECTION 224 CJA 2003

1. **Sexual activity with a child** (section 9): Intentional sexual touching of a person under 16
2. **Causing or inciting a child to engage in sexual activity** (section 10): Intentionally causing or inciting a person under 16 to engage in sexual activity

Maximum penalty for both offences: **14 years** (**5 years** if offender is under 18)

Type/nature of activity	Starting points	Sentencing ranges
Penile penetration of the vagina, anus or mouth *or* penetration of the vagina or anus with another body part or an object	4 years custody	3–7 years custody
Contact between naked genitalia of offender and naked genitalia or another part of victim's body, particularly face or mouth	2 years custody	1–4 years custody
Contact between naked genitalia of offender *or* victim and clothed genitalia of victim or offender or contact with naked genitalia of victim by offender using part of his or her body other than the genitalia or an object	12 months custody	26 weeks–2 years custody
Contact between part of offender's body (other than the genitalia) with part of the victim's body (other than the genitalia)	**Community order**	**An appropriate non-custodial sentence**

* 'Non-custodial sentence' in this context suggests a community order or a fine. In most instances, an offence will have crossed the threshold for a community order. However, in accordance with normal sentencing practice, a court is not precluded from imposing a financial penalty where that is determined to be the appropriate sentence.

Additional aggravating factors	Additional mitigating factors
1. Offender ejaculated or caused victim to ejaculate 2. Threats to prevent victim reporting the incident 3. Offender aware that he or she is suffering from a sexually transmitted infection	1. Offender intervenes to prevent incited offence from taking place 2. Small disparity in age between the offender and the victim

An offender convicted of these offences is automatically subject to notification requirements.[104]

SG-92 **Familial child sex offences**

Factors to take into consideration:

1. The new sentences for public protection *must* be considered in all cases. They are designed to ensure that sexual offenders are not released into the community if they present a significant risk of serious harm.
2. The culpability of the offender will be the primary indicator of offence seriousness, and the nature of the sexual activity will provide a guide as to the seriousness of the harm caused to the victim. Other factors will include:
   - the age and degree of vulnerability of the victim—as a general indication, the younger the child, the more vulnerable he or she is likely to be, although older children may also suffer serious and long-term psychological damage as a result of sexual abuse;
   - the age gap between the child and the offender; and
   - the youth and immaturity of the offender.
3. The starting points for sentencing for the familial child sex offences should be between 25% and 50% higher than those for the generic child sex offences in all cases where the victim is aged 13 or over but under 16; the closer the familial relationship, using the statutory definitions as a guide, the higher the increase that should be applied.
4. Where a victim is over the age of consent, the starting points assume that the offender is a close relative.
5. Where the victim of a familial child sex offence is aged 16 or 17 when the sexual activity is commenced and the sexual relationship is unlawful only because it takes place within a familial setting, the starting points for sentencing should be in line with those for the generic abuse of trust offences.
6. Evidence that a victim has been 'groomed' by the offender to agree to take part in sexual activity will aggravate the seriousness of the offence.

THESE ARE SERIOUS OFFENCES FOR THE PURPOSES OF SECTION 224 CJA 2003

1. **Sexual activity with a child family member** (section 25)
2. **Inciting a child family member to engage in sexual activity** (section 26)

Maximum penalty for both offences: **14 years** (**5 years** if offender is under 18)

For use in cases where:

(a) the victim is 13 or over but under 16, regardless of the familial relationship with the offender; (b) he victim is 16 or 17 but the sexual relationship commenced when the victim was under 16; or (c) the victim is aged 16 or 17 and the offender is a blood relative.

[104] In accordance with the SOA 2003, s. 80 and schedule 3

Type/nature of activity	Starting points	Sentencing ranges
Penile penetration of the vagina, anus or mouth *or* penetration of the vagina or anus with another body part or an object	**5 years custody**	**4–8 years custody**
Contact between naked genitalia of offender and naked genitalia of victim	**4 years custody**	**3–7 years custody**
Contact between naked genitalia of offender or victim and clothed genitalia of the victim or offender	**18 months custody**	**12 months–2 years 6 months custody**
Contact between naked genitalia of victim by another part of the offender's body or an object, *or* between the naked genitalia of offender and another part of victim's body		
Contact between part of offender's body (other than the genitalia) with part of the victim's body (other than the genitalia)	**Community order**	**An appropriate non-custodial sentence***

* 'Non-custodial sentence' in this context suggests a community order or a fine. In most instances, an offence will have crossed the threshold for a community order. However, in accordance with normal sentencing practice, a court is not precluded from imposing a financial penalty where that is determined to be the appropriate sentence.

For use in cases where the victim was aged 16 or 17 when the sexual relationship commenced and the relationship is only unlawful because of the abuse of trust implicit in the offence.

Type/nature of activity	Starting points	Sentencing ranges
Penile penetration of the vagina, anus or mouth *or* penetration of the vagina or anus with another body part or an object	**2 years custody**	**1–4 years custody**
Any other form of nonpenetrative sexual activity involving the naked contact between the offender and victim	**12 months custody**	**26 weeks–2 years custody**
Contact between clothed part of offender's body (other than the genitalia) with clothed part of victim's body (other than the genitalia)	**Community order**	**An appropriate non-custodial sentence***

* 'Non-custodial sentence' in this context suggests a community order or a fine. In most instances, an offence will have crossed the threshold for a community order. However, in accordance with normal sentencing practice, a court is not precluded from imposing a financial penalty where that is determined to be the appropriate sentence.

Additional aggravating factors	Additional mitigating factors
1. Background of intimidation or coercion 2. Use of drugs, alcohol or other substance 3. Threats deterring the victim from reporting the incident 4. Offender aware that he or she is suffering from a sexually transmitted infection 5. Closeness of familial relationship	1. Small disparity in age between victim and offender

An offender convicted of these offences is automatically subject to notification requirements.[105]

Abuse of trust: sexual activity with a person under 18 SG-93

Factors to take into consideration:

1. The sentences for public protection *must* be considered in all cases. They are designed to ensure that sexual offenders are not released into the community if they present a significant risk of serious harm.
2. The culpability of the offender will be the primary indicator of offence seriousness, and the nature of the sexual activity will provide a guide as to the seriousness of the harm caused to the victim. Other factors will include:
    - the age and degree of vulnerability of the victim—as a general indication, the younger the child, the more vulnerable he or she is likely to be, although older children may also suffer serious and long-term psychological damage as a result of sexual abuse;
    - the age gap between the child and the offender; and
    - the youth and immaturity of the offender.

[105] In accordance with the SOA 2003, s. 80 and schedule 3

3. These offences will only be charged where the victim is aged 16 or 17. Therefore, the sentencing starting points in the guidelines are only intended for those cases and are significantly lower than those for a child sex offence involving the same type of sexual activity, which should be applied in all other cases.
4. When sentencing for an abuse of trust offence, evidence of serious coercion, threats or trauma are aggravating factors that should move a sentence well beyond the starting point.
5. Some relationships caught within the scope of these offences, although unlawful, will be wholly consensual. The length of time over which a relationship has been sustained and the proximity in age between the parties could point to a relationship born out of genuine affection. Each case must be considered carefully on its own facts.
6. The same starting points apply whether the activity was caused or incited. Where an offence was incited but did not take place as a result of the voluntary intervention of the offender, that is likely to reduce the severity of the sentence imposed.

THESE ARE SPECIFIED OFFENCES FOR THE PURPOSES OF SECTION 224 CJA 2003

1. **Abuse of position of trust: sexual activity with a child** (section 16): Intentional sexual touching of a child under 18 by a person aged 18 or over who is in a position of trust in relation to the child
2. **Abuse of position of trust: Causing or inciting a child to engage in sexual activity** (section 17): Intentional causing or inciting of a child under 18 to engage in sexual activity, by a person aged 18 or over who is in a position of trust in relation to the child

Maximum penalty for both offences: 5 years

The starting points shown below are intended to be used only in relation to victims aged 16 or 17. Where the victim is a child under 16, one of the child sex offences in sections 9 to 13 should normally be charged. If one of the abuse of trust offences has nevertheless been charged, the starting points should be the same as they would be for the relevant child sex offence.

Type/nature of activity	Starting points	Sentencing ranges
Penile penetration of the vagina, anus or mouth *or* penetration of the vagina or anus with another body part or an object	**18 months custody**	**12 months–2 years 6 months custody**
Other forms of non-penetrative activity	**26 weeks custody**	**4 weeks–18 months custody**
Contact between part of offender's body (other than the genitalia) with part of the victim's body (other than the genitalia)	**Community order**	**An appropriate non-custodial sentence***

* 'Non-custodial sentence' in this context suggests a community order or a fine. In most instances, an offence will have crossed the threshold for a community order. However, in accordance with normal sentencing practice, a court is not precluded from imposing a financial penalty where that is determined to be the appropriate sentence.

Additional aggravating factors	Additional mitigating factors
1. Background of intimidation or coercion 2. Offender ejaculated or caused the victim to ejaculate 3. Use of drugs, alcohol or other substance to facilitate the offence 4. Offender aware that he or she is suffering from a sexually transmitted infection	1. Small disparity in age between victim and offender 2. Relationship of genuine affection 3. No element of corruption

An offender convicted of these offences is automatically subject to notification requirements.[106]

SG-94 **Abuse of trust: sexual activity in presence of a person under 18**

Factors to take into consideration:

1. The sentences for public protection *must* be considered in all cases. They are designed to ensure that sexual offenders are not released into the community if they present a significant risk of serious harm.

[106] In accordance with the SOA 2003, s. 80 and schedule 3

2. The guidelines are predicated on the principle that the more serious the nature of the sexual activity a victim is forced to witness, the higher the sentencing starting point should be.
3. These offences will only be charged where the victim is aged 16 or 17. Therefore, the sentencing starting points in the guidelines are only intended for those cases and are significantly lower than those for a child sex offence involving the same type of sexual activity, which should be applied in all other cases.
4. These offences will potentially be serious enough to merit a custodial sentence. In an individual case, the court will need to consider whether there are particular mitigating factors that should move the sentence below the custodial threshold.

THIS IS A SPECIFIED OFFENCE FOR THE PURPOSES OF SECTION 224 CJA 2003

Abuse of trust: sexual activity in the presence of a child (section 18): Intentionally, and for the purpose of obtaining sexual gratification, engaging in sexual activity in the presence of a person under 18 (abuse of trust), knowing or believing that person to be aware of the activity

Maximum penalty: **5 years**

Type/nature of activity	Starting points	Sentencing ranges
Consensual intercourse or other forms of consensual penetration	**2 years custody**	**1–4 years custody**
Masturbation (of oneself or another person)	**18 months custody**	**12 months–2 years 6 months custody**
Consensual sexual touching involving naked genitalia	**12 months custody**	**26 weeks–2 years custody**
Consensual sexual touching of naked body parts but not involving naked genitalia	**26 weeks custody**	**4 weeks–18 months custody**

Additional aggravating factors	Additional mitigating factors
1. Background of intimidation or coercion 2. Use of drugs, alcohol or other substance to facilitate the offence 3. Threats to prevent victim reporting the incident 4. Abduction or detention	

An offender convicted of this offence is automatically subject to notification requirements.[107]

Abuse of trust: cause a person under 18 to watch a sexual act SG-95

Factors to take into consideration:

1. The sentences for public protection *must* be considered in all cases. They are designed to ensure that sexual offenders are not released into the community if they present a significant risk of serious harm.
2. The culpability of the offender will be the primary indicator of offence seriousness, and the nature of the sexual activity will provide a guide as to the seriousness of the harm caused to the victim. Other factors will include:
   - the age and degree of vulnerability of the victim—as a general indication, the younger the child, the more vulnerable he or she is likely to be, although older children may also suffer serious and long-term psychological damage as a result of sexual abuse;
   - the age gap between the child and the offender; and
   - the youth and immaturity of the offender.
3. Serious coercion, threats, corruption or trauma are aggravating factors that should move a sentence well beyond the starting point.

[107] In accordance with the SOA 2003, s. 80 and schedule 3

4. Some relationships caught within the scope of these offences, although unlawful, will be wholly consensual. The length of time over which a relationship has been sustained and the proximity in age between the parties could point to a relationship born out of genuine affection. Each case must be considered carefully on its own facts.
5. These offences will only be charged where the victim is aged 16 or 17. Therefore, the sentencing starting points in the guidelines are only intended for those cases and are significantly lower than those for a child sex offence involving the same type of sexual activity, which should be applied in all other cases.
6. The guideline is predicated on the principle that the more serious the nature of the sexual activity a victim is forced to witness, the higher the sentencing starting point should be.
7. The offence will potentially be serious enough to merit a custodial sentence. In an individual case, the court will need to consider whether there are particular mitigating factors that should move the sentence below the custodial threshold.

THIS IS A SPECIFIED OFFENCE FOR THE PURPOSES OF SECTION 224 CJA 2003

Abuse of position of trust: causing a child to watch a sexual act (section 19): Intentionally causing or inciting, for the purpose of sexual gratification, a person under 18 (abuse of trust) to watch sexual activity or look at a photograph or pseudo-photograph of sexual activity

Maximum penalty: **5 years**

Type/nature of activity	**Starting points**	**Sentencing ranges**
Live sexual activity	**18 months custody**	**12 months–2 years custody**
Moving or still images of people engaged in sexual activity involving penetration	**32 weeks custody**	**26 weeks–12 months custody**
Moving or still images of people engaging in sexual activity other than penetration	**Community order**	**Community order–26 weeks custody**

Additional aggravating factors	**Additional mitigating factors**
1. Background of intimidation or coercion 2. Use of drugs, alcohol or other substance to facilitate the offence 3. Threats to prevent victim reporting the incident 4. Abduction or detention 5. Images of violent activity	1. Small disparity in age between victim and offender

An offender convicted of this offence is automatically subject to notification requirements.[108]

SG-96 **Arranging a child sex offence**

Factors to take into consideration:

1. The sentences for public protection *must* be considered in all cases. They are designed to ensure that sexual offenders are not released into the community if they present a significant risk of serious harm.
2. Sentencers should refer to the individual guideline for the substantive offence under sections 9–13 of the SOA 2003 that was arranged or facilitated.
3. In cases where there is no commercial exploitation, the range of behaviour within, and the type of offender charged with, this offence will be wide. In some cases, a starting point below the suggested starting point for the substantive child sex offence may be appropriate.

[108] In accordance with the SOA 2003, s. 80 and schedule 3

THIS IS A SERIOUS OFFENCE FOR THE PURPOSES OF SECTION 224 CJA 2003

Arranging or facilitating commission of a child sex offence (section 14): Intentionally arranging or facilitating the commission of a child sex offence by the defendant or another person, anywhere in the world

Maximum penalty: **14 years**

Type/nature of activity	Starting points and sentencing ranges
Where the activity is arranged or facilitated as part of a commercial enterprise, even if the offender is under 18	As this offence is primarily aimed at persons organising the commission of relevant sexual offences for gain, and sometimes across international borders, this is the most likely aggravating factor. Starting points and sentencing ranges should be increased above those for the relevant substantive offence under sections 9–13.
Basic offence as defined in the SOA 2003 assuming no aggravating or mitigating factors.	The starting point and sentencing range should be commensurate with that for the relevant substantive offence under sections 9–13.

Additional aggravating factors	Additional mitigating factors
1. Background of intimidation or coercion 2. Use of drugs, alcohol or other substance to facilitate the offence 3. Threats to prevent victim reporting the incident 4. Abduction or detention 5. Number of victims involved	

Sentencing Guidelines

An offender convicted of this offence is automatically subject to notification requirements.[109]

Part 3B: Offences Against Vulnerable Adults SG-97

3B.1 The offences in the SOA 2003 that are designed to protect those who have a mental disorder impeding choice are referred to in Part 1.

3B.2 In addition, the Act includes a group of offences designed to protect adults whose mental impairment is not so severe that they are unable to make a choice, but who are nevertheless vulnerable to relatively low levels of inducement, threats or deception.

3B.3 The structure of these offences broadly parallels that of the offences against children, but the maximum penalties for the offences are higher and mirror those for the offences relating to persons with a mental disorder impeding choice. Charges brought under these offences relate to ostensibly consensual activity, but cases will be brought in circumstances where there is clear evidence to suggest that agreement has been secured unlawfully.

3B.4 Although the level of mental impairment of the victim is different between the offences in Part 1 and those in this part, the prosecution is required in all cases to prove that the offender knew of the victim's mental disorder. Thus the victim's capacity to consent will be irrelevant to a finding of guilt, and the level of offender culpability is high.

3B.5 Where a victim is unable to refuse, the sexual activity may, or may not, have been forced upon the victim. Where a victim has the capacity to consent but is vulnerable to coercion, the activity will be ostensibly consensual, but the level of trauma and harm caused, or risked, to the victim may be very high.

3B.6 The level of protection accorded to the victim should be the same, and sentencing starting points for the two groups of offences should also be comparable.

The starting points for sentencing for a sexual offence should be the same whether the victim has a mental disorder impeding choice, or has a mental disorder and the activity has been procured by inducement, threat or deception.

[109] In accordance with the SOA 2003, s. 80 and schedule 3

3B.7 There is a further group of offences designed to protect those with a mental disorder, which consists of four offences relating to sexual activity by care workers. As with the abuse of trust offences protecting children, these offences primarily relate to ostensibly consensual sexual activity with persons over 16 that is only criminal because of the care worker relationship.

3B.8 These offences are primarily designed to be charged where victims have the capacity to choose and where there is no clear evidence of inducement, threat or deception. The maximum penalties, therefore, are lower than those arising from the other two groups of 'mental disorder' offences and it follows that starting points for sentencing should be proportionately lower. The maximum penalties, however, are more significant than those for the range of abuse of trust offences, in recognition of the fact that these offences are designed to protect a particularly vulnerable group of victims, and this has been taken into account in the guideline.

3B.9 The nature of the sexual activity and the degree of vulnerability of the victim will be the main determinants of the seriousness of an offence in these categories. The aggravating factors identified in the Council guideline on seriousness and in Part 1 are relevant to these offences.

3B.10 The period of time during which sexual activity has taken place will be relevant in determining the seriousness of an offender's behaviour but could, depending on the particular circumstances, be considered as either an aggravating or a mitigating factor. The fact that an offender has repeatedly involved a victim in exploitative behaviour over a period of time will normally be an aggravating feature for sentencing purposes. However, in cases involving ostensibly consensual sexual activity with a person over the age of consent who has a low-level mental disorder that does not impair his or her ability to choose, evidence of a long-term relationship between the parties may indicate the existence of genuine feelings of love and affection that deserve to be treated as a mitigating factor for sentencing. As with the abuse of trust offences, each case must be carefully considered on its facts.

SG-98 **Sexual activity with a person who has a mental disorder**

Factors to take into consideration:

1. The sentences for public protection *must* be considered in all cases. They are designed to ensure that sexual offenders are not released into the community if they present a significant risk of serious harm. Within any indeterminate sentence, the minimum term will generally be half the appropriate determinate sentence. The starting points will be relevant, therefore, to the process of fixing any minimum term that may be necessary.
2. The starting points for sentencing for a sexual offence should be the same whether the victim has a mental disorder impeding choice, or has a mental disorder that makes him or her vulnerable to inducement, threat or deception.
3. The same starting points apply whether the activity was caused or incited. Where an offence was incited but did not take place as a result of the voluntary intervention of the offender, that is likely to reduce the severity of the sentence imposed.

THESE ARE SERIOUS OFFENCES FOR THE PURPOSES OF SECTION 224 CJA 2003

1. **Sexual activity with a person with a mental disorder impeding choice** (section 30): Intentional sexual touching of a person with a mental disorder
2. **Inducement, threat or deception to procure sexual activity with a person with a mental disorder** (section 34): Intentional sexual touching of someone with a mental disorder whose agreement has been obtained by the giving or offering of an inducement, the making of a threat or the practice of a deception
3. **Causing a person with a mental disorder to engage in, or agree to engage in, sexual activity by inducement, threat or deception** (section 35): Using inducement, threat or deception to secure the agreement of a person with a mental disorder impeding choice to perform a sexual act on him or herself or another person.

Maximum penalty: **Life** if activity involves penetration; **14 years** if no penetration

Type/nature of activity	Starting points	Sentencing ranges
Penetration with any of the aggravating factors: abduction or detention; offender aware that he or she is suffering from a sexually transmitted infection; more than one offender acting together; offence motivated by prejudice (race, religion, sexual orientation, physical disability); sustained or repeated activity	**13 years custody**	**11–17 years custody**
Single offence of penetration of/by single offender with no aggravating or mitigating factors	**10 years custody**	**8–13 years custody**
Contact between naked genitalia of offender and naked genitalia of victim	**5 years custody**	**4–8 years custody**
Contact between naked genitalia of offender and another part of victim's body *or* naked genitalia of victim by offender using part of his or her body other than the genitalia Contact between clothed genitalia of offender and naked genitalia of victim *or* naked genitalia of offender and clothed genitalia of victim	**15 months custody**	**36 weeks–3 years custody**
Contact between part of offender's body (other than the genitalia) with parts of victim's body (other than the genitalia)	**26 weeks custody**	**4 weeks–18 months custody**

Additional aggravating factors	Additional mitigating factors
1. Background of intimidation or coercion 2. Offender ejaculated or caused the victim to ejaculate 3. Use of drugs, alcohol or other substance to facilitate the offence 4. Threats to prevent the victim reporting the incident 5. Abduction or detention 6. Offender is aware that he or she is suffering from a sexually transmitted infection	1. Relationship of genuine affection 2. Offender had a mental disorder at the time of the offence that significantly affected his or her culpability

An offender convicted of these offences is automatically subject to notification requirements.[110]

Care workers: sexual activity with a person who has a mental disorder SG-99

Factors to take into consideration:

1. The sentences for public protection *must* be considered in all cases. They are designed to ensure that sexual offenders are not released into the community if they present a significant risk of serious harm.
2. The starting points for sentencing are predicated on the fact that these offences are designed to be charged where victims have the capacity to choose and where there is no clear evidence of inducement, threat or deception.

THESE ARE SERIOUS OFFENCES FOR THE PURPOSES OF SECTION 224 CJA 2003

1. **Care workers: sexual activity with a person with a mental disorder** (section 38): Intentional sexual touching of a person with a mental disorder by someone involved in his or her care
2. **Care workers: causing or inciting sexual activity** (section 39): Someone involved in the care of a person with a mental disorder intentionally causing or inciting that person to engage in sexual activity

[110] In accordance with the SOA 2003, s. 80 and schedule 3

Maximum penalty: **14 years** if activity involves penetration; **10 years** if activity does not involve penetration

Type/nature of activity	Starting points	Sentencing ranges
Basic offence of sexual activity involving penetration, assuming no aggravating or mitigating factors	**3 years custody**	**2–5 years custody**
Other forms of nonpenetrative activity	**12 months custody**	**26 weeks–2 years custody**
Naked contact between part of the offender's body with part of the victim's body	**Community order**	**An appropriate non-custodial sentence**

* 'Non-custodial sentence' in this context suggests a community order or a fine. In most instances, an offence will have crossed the threshold for a community order. However, in accordance with normal sentencing practice, a court is not precluded from imposing a financial penalty where that is determined to be the appropriate sentence.

Additional aggravating factors	Additional mitigating factors
1. History of intimidation 2. Use of drugs, alcohol or other substance to facilitate the offence 3. Threats to prevent victim reporting the incident 4. Abduction or detention 5. Offender aware that he or she is suffering from a sexually transmitted infection	1. Relationship of genuine affection

An offender convicted of these offences is automatically subject to notification requirements.[111]

SG-100 **Sexual activity in the presence of a person with a mental disorder**

Factors to take into consideration:

1. The sentences for public protection *must* be considered in all cases. They are designed to ensure that sexual offenders are not released into the community if they present a significant risk of serious harm.
2. The starting points for sentencing for a sexual offence should be the same whether the victim has a mental disorder impeding choice, or has a mental disorder that makes him or her vulnerable to inducement, threat or deception.
3. The guidelines are predicated on the principle that the more serious the nature of the sexual activity a victim is forced to witness, the higher the sentencing starting point should be.
4. These offences will potentially be serious enough to merit a custodial sentence. In an individual case, the court will need to consider whether there are particular mitigating factors that should move the sentence below the custodial threshold.

OFFENCES UNDER SECTION 36 ARE SERIOUS OFFENCES FOR THE PURPOSES OF SECTION 224 CJA 2003

OFFENCES UNDER SECTION 40 ARE SPECIFIED OFFENCES FOR THE PURPOSES OF SECTION 224 CJA 2003

1. **Engaging in sexual activity in the presence, secured by inducement, threat or deception, of a person with a mental disorder** (section 36): Intentionally, and for the purpose of obtaining sexual gratification, engaging in sexual activity in the presence of a person with a mental disorder, knowing or believing that person to be aware of the activity

Maximum penalty: **10 years**

2. **Care workers: sexual activity in the presence of a person with a mental disorder** (section 40): Care worker intentionally, and for the purpose of obtaining sexual gratification, engaging in sexual activity in the presence of a person with a mental disorder, knowing or believing that person to be aware of the activity

[111] In accordance with the SOA 2003, s. 80 and schedule 3

Maximum penalty: **7 years**

Type/nature of activity	Starting points	Sentencing ranges
Consensual intercourse or other forms of consensual penetration	2 years custody	1–4 years custody
Masturbation (of oneself or another person)	18 months custody	12 months–2 years 6 months custody
Consensual sexual touching involving naked genitalia	12 months custody	26 weeks–2 years custody
Consensual sexual touching of naked body parts but not involving naked genitalia	26 weeks custody	4 weeks–18 months custody

Additional aggravating factors	Additional mitigating factors
1. Background of intimidation or coercion 2. Use of drugs, alcohol or other substance to facilitate the offence 3. Threats to prevent victim reporting the incident 4. Abduction or detention	

An offender convicted of these offences is automatically subject to notification requirements.[112]

Causing or inciting a person with a mental disorder to watch a sexual act SG-101

Factors to take into consideration:

1. The sentences for public protection *must* be considered in all cases. They are designed to ensure that sexual offenders are not released into the community if they present a significant risk of serious harm.
2. The starting points for sentencing for a sexual offence should be the same whether the victim has a mental disorder impeding choice, or has a mental disorder that makes him or her vulnerable to inducement, threat or deception.
3. The guidelines are predicated on the principle that the more serious the nature of the sexual activity a victim is forced to witness, the higher the sentencing starting point should be.
4. These offences will potentially be serious enough to merit a custodial sentence. In an individual case, the court will need to consider whether there are particular mitigating factors that move the sentence below the custodial threshold.
5. The same starting points apply whether the activity was caused or incited. Where an offence was incited but did not take place as a result of the voluntary intervention of the offender, that is likely to reduce the severity of the sentence imposed.

OFFENCES UNDER SECTION 37 ARE SERIOUS OFFENCES FOR THE PURPOSES OF SECTION 224 CJA 2003

OFFENCES UNDER SECTION 41 ARE SPECIFIED OFFENCES FOR THE PURPOSES OF SECTION 224 CJA 2003

1. **Causing a person with a mental disorder to watch a sexual act by inducement, threat or deception** (section 37): Intentionally causing by inducement, threat or deception, for the purpose of sexual gratification, a person with a mental disorder to watch sexual activity or look at a photograph or pseudo-photograph of sexual activity

Maximum penalty: **10 years**

2. **Care workers: causing a person with a mental disorder to watch a sexual act** (section 41): Intentionally causing, for the purpose of sexual gratification, a person with a mental disorder to watch sexual activity or look at a photograph or pseudo-photograph of sexual activity

[112] In accordance with the SOA 2003, s. 80 and schedule 3

Maximum penalty: 7 years

Type/nature of activity	Starting points	Sentencing ranges
Live sexual activity	**18 months custody**	**12 months–2 years custody**
Moving or still images of people engaged in sexual activity involving penetration	**32 weeks custody**	**26 weeks–12 months custody**
Moving or still images of people engaging in sexual activity other than penetration	**Community order**	**Community order–26 weeks**

Additional aggravating factors	Additional mitigating factors
1. Background of intimidation or coercion 2. Use of drugs, alcohol or other substance to facilitate the offence 3. Threats to prevent victim reporting the incident 4. Abduction or detention 5. Images of violent activity	

An offender convicted of this offence is automatically subject to notification requirements.[113]

SG-102

Part 4: Preparatory Offences

4.1 The characteristic feature of this group of offences is that the offender intended to commit a sexual offence that was not, in fact, carried out, either because the act was interrupted or because of a change of mind.

4.2 In some circumstances, an offender may be charged with both the preparatory and the substantive offence.

4.3 The new offence of 'meeting a child following sexual grooming etc' has been included within this category.

The following offences are covered in this section:

- Sexual grooming
- Committing another offence with intent
- Trespass with intent
- Administering a substance with intent

SG-103 **Sexual grooming**

Factors to take into consideration:

1. The sentences for public protection *must* be considered in all cases. They are designed to ensure that sexual offenders are not released into the community if they present a significant risk of serious harm.
2. In a case where no substantive sexual offence has in fact been committed, the main dimension of seriousness will be the offender's *intention*—the more serious the offence intended, the higher the offender's culpability.
3. The *harm* to the victim in such cases will invariably be less than that resulting from a completed offence, although the *risk* to which the victim has been put is always a relevant factor.
4. In some cases, where the offender has come quite close to fulfilling his or her intention, the victim may have been put in considerable fear, and physical injury to the victim is a possible feature.
5. In addition to the generic aggravating factors identified in the Council guideline on seriousness, the main factors determining the seriousness of a preparatory offence are:
   - the seriousness of the intended offence (which will affect both the offender's culpability and the degree of risk to which the victim has been exposed);
   - the degree to which the offence was planned;
   - the sophistication of the grooming;
   - the determination of the offender;
   - how close the offender came to success;
   - the reason why the offender did not succeed, i. e. whether it was a change of mind or whether someone or something prevented the offender from continuing; and
   - any physical or psychological injury suffered by the victim.

[113] In accordance with the SOA 2003, s. 80 and schedule 3

6. The starting point should be commensurate with that for the preparatory offence actually committed, with an enhancement to reflect the nature and severity of the intended sexual offence.

THIS IS A SERIOUS OFFENCE FOR THE PURPOSES OF SECTION 224 CJA 2003

Meeting a child following sexual grooming etc (section 15): An offender aged 18 or over meeting, or travelling to meet, a child under 16 (having met or communicated with the child on at least two previous occasions) with the intention of committing a sexual offence against the child

Maximum penalty: **10 years**

Type/nature of activity	Starting points	Sentencing ranges
Where the intent is to commit an assault by penetration or rape	**4 years custody** if the victim is under 13 **2 years custody** if the victim is 13 or over but under 16	**3–7 years custody** **1–4 years custody**
Where the intent is to coerce the child into sexual activity	**2 years custody** if the victim is under 13 **18 months custody** if the victim is 13 or over but under 16	**1–4 years custody** **12 months–2 years** **6 months custody**

An offender convicted of this offence is automatically subject to notification requirements.[114]

Additional aggravating factors	Additional mitigating factors
1. Background of intimidation or coercion 2. Use of drugs, alcohol or other substance to facilitate the offence 3. Offender aware that he or she is suffering from a sexually transmitted infection 4. Abduction or detention	

Committing another offence with intent **SG-104**

Factors to take into consideration:

This guideline assumes that the intended sexual offence was not committed.

1. The sentences for public protection *must* be considered in all cases. They are designed to ensure that sexual offenders are not released into the community if they present a significant risk of serious harm. Within any indeterminate sentence, the minimum term will generally be half the appropriate determinate sentence. The starting points will be relevant, therefore, to the process of fixing any minimum term that may be necessary.
2. In a case where no substantive sexual offence has in fact been committed, the main dimension of seriousness will be the offender's *intention*—the more serious the offence intended, the higher the offender's culpability.
3. The *harm* to the victim in such cases will invariably be less than that resulting from a completed offence, although the *risk* to which the victim has been put is always a relevant factor.
4. In some cases, where the offender has come quite close to fulfilling his or her intention, the victim may have been put in considerable fear, and physical injury to the victim is a possible feature.
5. In addition to the generic aggravating factors identified in the Council guideline on seriousness, the main factors determining the seriousness of a preparatory offence are:
   - the seriousness of the intended offence (which will affect both the offender's culpability and the degree of risk to which the victim has been exposed);
   - the degree to which the offence was planned;
   - the determination of the offender;
   - how close the offender came to success;
   - the reason why the offender did not succeed, i. e. whether it was a change of mind or whether someone or something prevented the offender from continuing; and
   - any physical or psychological injury suffered by the victim.
6. The starting point should be commensurate with that for the preparatory offence actually committed, with an enhancement to reflect the nature and severity of the intended sexual offence.

[114] In accordance with the SOA 2003, s. 80 and schedule 3

THIS IS A SERIOUS OFFENCE FOR THE PURPOSES OF SECTION 224 CJA 2003

Committing an offence with intent to commit a sexual offence (section 62)

Maximum penalty: **Life imprisonment** if offence is kidnapping or false imprisonment; **10 years** for any other criminal offence

Type/nature of activity	Starting points and sentencing ranges
Any offence committed with intent to commit a sexual offence, e.g. assault (see item 4 of 'Factors to take into consideration' above)	The starting point and sentencing range should be commensurate with that for the preliminary offence actually committed, but with an enhancement to reflect the intention to commit a sexual offence. The enhancement will need to be varied depending on the nature and seriousness of the intended sexual offence, but **2 years** is suggested as a suitable enhancement where the intent was to commit rape or an assault by penetration.

Additional aggravating factors	Additional mitigating factors
1. Use of drugs, alcohol or other substance to facilitate the offence 2. Offender aware that he or she is suffering from a sexually transmitted infection (where the intended offence would have involved penile penetration)	1. Offender decides, of his or her own volition, not to proceed with the intended sexual offence 2. Incident of brief duration

An offender convicted of this offence is automatically subject to notification requirements.[115]

SG-105 **Trespass with intent**

Factors to take into consideration:

1. The sentences for public protection *must* be considered in all cases. They are designed to ensure that sexual offenders are not released into the community if they present a significant risk of serious harm.
2. In a case where no substantive sexual offence has in fact been committed, the main dimension of seriousness will be the offender's *intention*—the more serious the offence intended, the higher the offender's culpability.
3. The *harm* to the victim in such cases will invariably be less than that resulting from a completed offence, although the *risk* to which the victim has been put is always a relevant factor.
4. In some cases, where the offender has come quite close to fulfilling his or her intention, the victim may have been put in considerable fear, and physical injury to the victim is a possible feature.
5. In addition to the generic aggravating factors identified in the Council guideline on seriousness, the main factors determining the seriousness of a preparatory offence are:
    - the seriousness of the intended offence (which will affect both the offender's culpability and the degree of risk to which the victim has been exposed);
    - the degree to which the offence was planned;
    - the determination of the offender;
    - how close the offender came to success;
    - the reason why the offender did not succeed, i. e. whether it was a change of mind or whether someone or something prevented the offender from continuing; and
    - any physical or psychological injury suffered by the victim.
6. The starting point should be commensurate with that for the preparatory offence actually committed, with an enhancement to reflect the nature and severity of the intended sexual offence.

[115] In accordance with the SOA 2003, s. 80 and schedule 3

THIS IS A SERIOUS OFFENCE FOR THE PURPOSES OF SECTION 224 CJA 2003

Trespass with intent to commit a sexual offence (section 63): Knowingly or recklessly trespassing on any premises with intent to commit a sexual offence on those premises

Maximum penalty: **10 years**

Type/nature of activity	Starting points	Sentencing ranges
The intention is to commit rape or an assault by penetration	4 years custody	3–7 years custody
The intended sexual offence is other than rape or assault by penetration	2 years custody	1–4 years custody

Additional aggravating factors	Additional mitigating factors
1. Offender aware that he or she is suffering from a sexually transmitted infection (where intended offence would have involved penile penetration) 2. Targeting of a vulnerable victim 3. Significant impact on persons present in the premises	1. Offender decides, of his or her own volition, not to commit the intended sexual offence

An offender convicted of this offence is automatically subject to notification requirements.[116]

Administering a substance with intent SG-106

Factors to take into consideration:

1. The sentences for public protection *must* be considered in all cases. They are designed to ensure that sexual offenders are not released into the community if they present a significant risk of serious harm.
2. In a case where no substantive sexual offence has in fact been committed, the main dimension of seriousness will be the offender's *intention*—the more serious the offence intended, the higher the offender's culpability. This is equally so where the offence is committed by an offender for the benefit of another.
3. The *harm* to the victim in such cases will invariably be less than that resulting from a completed offence, although the *risk* to which the victim has been put is always a relevant factor.
4. In some cases, where the offender has come quite close to fulfilling his or her intention, the victim may have been put in considerable fear, and physical injury to the victim is a possible feature, in particular for this offence.
5. In addition to the generic aggravating factors identified in the Council guideline on seriousness, the main factors determining the seriousness of a preparatory offence are:
   - the seriousness of the intended offence (which will affect both the offender's culpability and the degree of risk to which the victim has been exposed);
   - the degree to which the offence was planned;
   - the determination of the offender;
   - how close the offender came to success;
   - the reason why the offender did not succeed, i. e. whether it was a change of mind or whether someone or something prevented the offender from continuing; and
   - any physical or psychological injury suffered by the victim.
6. The starting point should be commensurate with that for the preparatory offence actually committed, with an enhancement to reflect the nature and severity of the intended sexual offence.

THIS IS A SERIOUS OFFENCE FOR THE PURPOSES OF SECTION 224 CJA 2003

Administering a substance with intent (section 61): Administering a substance, without the consent of the victim, with the intention of overpowering or stupefying the victim in order to enable any person to engage in sexual activity involving the victim

[116] In accordance with the SOA 2003, s. 80 and schedule 3

Maximum penalty: **10 years**

Type/nature of activity	Starting points	Sentencing ranges
If intended offence is rape or assault by penetration	**8 years custody** if the victim is under 13	**6–9 years custody**
	6 years custody otherwise	**4–9 years custody**
If intended offence is any sexual offence other than rape or assault by penetration **6 years custody** if the victim is under 13	**6 years custody** if the victim is under 13	**4–9 years custody**
	4 years custody otherwise	**3–7 years custody**

Additional aggravating factors	Additional mitigating factors
1. Threats to prevent the victim reporting an offence 2. Abduction or detention 3. Offender aware that he or she, or the person planning to commit the sexual offence, is suffering from a sexually transmitted infection 4. Targeting of the victim	1. Offender intervenes to prevent the intended sexual offence from taking place

An offender convicted of this offence is automatically subject to notification requirements.[117]

SG-107

PART 5: OTHER OFFENCES

5.1 This category covers a small number of relatively minor offences, none of which involves direct sexual contact with a person who was not consenting:
- Prohibited adult sexual relationships: sex with an adult relative
- Sexual activity in a public lavatory
- Exposure
- Voyeurism
- Intercourse with an animal
- Sexual penetration of a corpse

SG-108 **Prohibited adult sexual relationships: sex with an adult relative**

Factors to take into consideration:

1. The sentences for public protection *must* be considered in all cases. They are designed to ensure that sexual offenders are not released into the community if they present a significant risk of serious harm.
2. The two offences within this category are triable either way and carry a maximum penalty of 2 years' imprisonment on conviction on indictment. The relatively low maximum penalty for these offences reflects the fact that they involve sexual relationships between consenting adults.
3. For these offences, unlike those against child family members, the relationship between offender and victim is narrowly defined in terms of close blood relationships only: 'a parent, grandparent, child, grandchild, brother, sister, half-brother, half-sister, uncle, aunt, nephew or niece'.
4. It is a defence to both offences that the offender was unaware of the blood relationship, unless it is proved that he or she could reasonably have been expected to be aware of it.
5. These offences could be charged in a wide range of circumstances and the most important issue for the sentencer to consider is the particular circumstances in which an offence has taken place and the harm that has been caused or risked:
   - Where an offence involves no harm to a victim (other than the offensiveness of the conduct to society at large), the starting point for sentencing should normally be a community order.
   - Where there is evidence of the exploitation of a victim or significant aggravation, the normal starting point should be a custodial sentence.
   - The presence of certain aggravating factors should merit a higher custodial starting point.
6. Examples of aggravating factors especially relevant to these offences include:
   - high level of coercion or humiliation of the victim;
   - imbalance of power;

[117] In accordance with the SOA 2003, s. 80 and schedule 3

- evidence of grooming;
- age gap between the parties;
- history of sexual offending;
- sexual intercourse with the express intention of conceiving a child or resulting in the conception of a child; and
- no attempt taken to prevent the transmission of a sexual infection.

THESE ARE SPECIFIED OFFENCES FOR THE PURPOSES OF SECTION 224 CJA 2003

1. **Sex with an adult relative: penetration** (section 64): Intentional penetration of the vagina or anus of an adult blood relative with a body part or object; or penetration of the vagina, anus or mouth with the penis
2. **Sex with an adult relative: consenting to penetration** (section 65): Consenting to intentional penetration of the vagina or anus by an adult blood relative with a body part or object; or penetration of the vagina, anus or mouth with the penis

Type/nature of activity	Starting points	Sentencing ranges
Where there is evidence of long-term grooming that took place at a time when the person being groomed was under 18	**12 months custody** if offender is 18 or over	**26 weeks–2 years custody**
Where there is evidence of grooming of one party by the other at a time when both parties were over the age of 18	**Community order**	**An appropriate non-custodial sentence**
Sexual penetration with no aggravating factors	**Community order**	**An appropriate non-custodial sentence***

* 'Non-custodial sentence' in this context suggests a community order or a fine. In most instances, an offence will have crossed the threshold for a community order. However, in accordance with normal sentencing practice, a court is not precluded from imposing a financial penalty where that is determined to be the appropriate sentence.

Additional aggravating factors	Additional mitigating factors
1. Background of intimidation or coercion 2. Use of drugs, alcohol or other substance to facilitate the offence 3. Threats to prevent the victim reporting an offence 4. Evidence of long-term grooming 5. Offender aware that he or she is suffering from a sexually transmitted infection 6. Where there is evidence that no effort was made to avoid pregnancy or the sexual transmission of infection	1. Small disparity in age between victim and offender 2. Relationship of genuine affection

Maximum penalty for both offences: **2 years**

An offender convicted of these offences is automatically subject to notification requirements.[118]

Sexual activity in a public lavatory SG-109

Factors to take into consideration:

1. This offence has been introduced to give adults and children the freedom to use public lavatories for the purpose for which they are designed, without the fear of being an unwilling witness to overtly sexual behaviour of a kind that most people would not expect to be conducted in public.
2. This offence, being a public order offence rather than a sexual offence, carries the lowest maximum penalty in the SOA 2003–6 months' imprisonment—and the starting point for sentencing reflects this.
3. More detailed guidance is provided in the Magistrates' Court Sentencing Guidelines (MCSG) [see **SG-231**].

Sexual activity in a public lavatory (section 71): Intentionally engaging in sexual activity in a public lavatory

[118] In accordance with the SOA 2003, s. 80 and schedule 3

Maximum penalty: **6 months**

Type/nature of activity	Starting points	Sentencing ranges
Repeat offending and/or aggravating factors	**Community order**	**An appropriate non-custodial sentence**
Basic offence as defined in the SOA 2003, assuming no aggravating or mitigating factors	**Fine**	**An appropriate non-custodial sentence**

* 'Non-custodial sentence' in this context suggests a community order or a fine. In most instances, an offence will have crossed the threshold for a community order. However, in accordance with normal sentencing practice, a court is not precluded from imposing a financial penalty where that is determined to be the appropriate sentence.

Additional aggravating factors	Additional mitigating factors
1. Intimidating behaviour/threats of violence to member(s) of the public	

SG-110 **Exposure**

Factors to take into consideration:

1. The sentences for public protection *must* be considered in all cases. They are designed to ensure that sexual offenders are not released into the community if they present a significant risk of serious harm.
2. The offence replaces section 4 of the Vagrancy Act 1824 and section 28 of the Town Police Clauses Act 1847. It is gender neutral (covering exposure of male or female genitalia to a male or female witness) and carries a maximum penalty of 2 years' imprisonment.
3. These offences are sometimes more serious than they may, at first, appear. Although there is no physical contact with the victim, the offence may cause serious alarm or distress, especially when the offender behaves aggressively or uses obscenities.
4. A pre-sentence report,[119] which can identify sexually deviant tendencies, will be extremely helpful in determining the most appropriate disposal. It will also help determine whether an offender would benefit from participation in a programme designed to help them address those tendencies.
5. A person convicted of this offence is subject to notification requirements.[120]
6. Where this offence is being dealt with in a magistrates' court, more detailed guidance is provided in the Magistrates' Court Sentencing Guidelines (MCSG) [see **SG-202**].

THIS IS A SPECIFIED OFFENCE FOR THE PURPOSES OF SECTION 224 CJA 2003

Exposure (section 66): Intentional exposure of the offender's genitals, intending that someone will see them and be caused alarm or distress

Maximum penalty: **2 years**

Type/nature of activity	Starting points	Sentencing ranges
Repeat offender	**12 weeks custody**	**4 weeks– 26 weeks custody**
Basic offence as defined in the SOA 2003, assuming no aggravating or mitigating factors, or some offences with aggravating factors	**Community order**	**An appropriate non-custodial sentence***

* 'Non-custodial sentence' in this context suggests a community order or a fine. In most instances, an offence will have crossed the threshold for a community order. However, in accordance with normal sentencing practice, a court is not precluded from imposing a financial penalty where that is determined to be the appropriate sentence.

[119] As defined in the Criminal Justice Act 2003, s. 158

[120] In accordance with the Sexual Offences Act 2003, s. 80 and schedule 3

Additional aggravating factors	Additional mitigating factors
1. Threats to prevent the victim reporting an offence 2. Intimidating behaviour/threats of violence 3. Victim is a child	

An offender convicted of this offence is automatically subject to notification requirements.[121]

Voyeurism **SG-111**

Factors to take into consideration:

1. The sentences for public protection *must* be considered in all cases. They are designed to ensure that sexual offenders are not released into the community if they present a significant risk of serious harm.
2. The offence of voyeurism covers cases where someone who has a reasonable expectation of privacy is secretly observed. The offence may be committed in a number of ways:
   - by direct observation on the part of the offender;
   - by operating equipment with the intention of enabling someone else to observe the victim;
   - by recording someone doing a private act, with the intention that the recorded image will be viewed by the offender or another person; or
   - by installing equipment or constructing or adapting a structure with the intention of enabling the offender or another person to observe a private act.
3. In all cases the observation, or intended observation, must be for the purpose of obtaining sexual gratification and must take place, or be intended to take place, without the consent of the person observed.
4. The SOA 2003 defines a 'private act', in the context of this offence, as an act carried out in a place which, in the circumstances, would reasonably be expected to provide privacy, and where the victim's genitals, buttocks or breasts are exposed or covered only in underwear; *or* the victim is using a lavatory; *or* the person is 'doing a sexual act that is not of a kind ordinarily done in public'.
5. The harm inherent in this offence is intrusion of the victim's privacy. Whilst less serious than nonconsensual touching, it may nevertheless cause severe distress, embarrassment or humiliation to the victim, especially in cases where a private act is not simply observed by one person, but where an image of it is disseminated for wider viewing. A higher sentencing starting point is recommended for cases where the offender records and shares images with others.
6. For offences involving the lowest level of offending behaviour, i. e. spying on someone for private pleasure, a non-custodial sentence is recommended as the starting point.
7. A pre-sentence report,[122] which can identify sexually deviant tendencies, will be extremely helpful in determining the most appropriate disposal. It will also help determine whether an offender would benefit from participation in a programme designed to help them address those tendencies.
8. Where this offence is being dealt with in a magistrates' court, more detailed guidance is provided in the Magistrates' Court Sentencing Guidelines (MCSG) [see **SG-251**].

THIS IS A SPECIFIED OFFENCE FOR THE PURPOSES OF SECTION 224 CJA 2003

Voyeurism (section 67): For the purpose of obtaining sexual gratification, and knowing that the other person does not consent to being observed, observing another person engaged in a private act

Maximum penalty: **2 years**

[121] In accordance with the Sexual Offences Act 2003, s. 80 and schedule 3
[122] As defined in the Criminal Justice Act 2003, s. 158

Type/nature of activity	Starting points	Sentencing ranges
Offence with serious aggravating factors such as recording sexual activity and placing it on a website or circulating it for commercial gain	**12 months custody**	**26 weeks–2 years custody**
Offence with aggravating factors such as recording sexual activity and showing it to others	**26 weeks custody**	**4 weeks–18 months custody**
Basic offence as defined in the SOA 2003, assuming no aggravating or mitigating factors, e.g. the offender spies through a hole he or she has made in a changing room wall	**Community order**	**An appropriate non-custodial sentence***

* 'Non-custodial sentence' in this context suggests a community order or a fine. In most instances, an offence will have crossed the threshold for a community order. However, in accordance with normal sentencing practice, a court is not precluded from imposing a financial penalty where that is determined to be the appropriate sentence.

Additional aggravating factors	Additional mitigating factors
1. Threats to prevent the victim reporting an offence 2. Recording activity and circulating pictures/videos 3. Circulating pictures or videos for commercial gain—particularly if victim is vulnerable, e.g. a child or person with a mental or physical disorder 4. Distress to victim, e.g. where the pictures/videos are circulated to people known to the victim	

An offender convicted of this offence is automatically subject to notification requirements.[123]

SG-112 **Intercourse with an animal**

Factors to take into consideration:

1. The sentences for public protection *must* be considered in all cases. They are designed to ensure that sexual offenders are not released into the community if they present a significant risk of serious harm.
2. This replaces the previous offence of 'buggery' with an animal, for which the maximum penalty was life imprisonment. The maximum penalty of 2 years' imprisonment attached to this offence is sufficient to recognise an offender's predisposition towards unnatural sexual activity.
3. A custodial sentence for an adult for this offence will result in an obligation to comply with notification requirements and this seems to be the most appropriate course of action for a repeat offender. The offence can be charged in addition to existing offences relating to cruelty to animals.
4. A pre-sentence report,[124] which can identify sexually deviant tendencies, will be extremely helpful in determining the most appropriate disposal. It will also help determine whether an offender would benefit from participation in a programme designed to help them address those tendencies.

THIS IS A SPECIFIED OFFENCE FOR THE PURPOSES OF SECTION 224 CJA 2003

Intercourse with an animal (section 69): Intentionally penetrating a live animal's anus or vagina with the offender's penis; or intentionally causing or allowing a person's anus or vagina to be penetrated by the penis of a live animal

Maximum penalty: 2 years

Type/nature of activity	Starting points	Sentencing ranges
Basic offence as defined in the SOA 2003, assuming no aggravating or mitigating factors	**Community order**	**An appropriate non-custodial sentence**

* 'Non-custodial sentence' in this context suggests a community order or a fine. In most instances, an offence will have crossed the threshold for a community order. However, in accordance with normal sentencing practice, a court is not precluded from imposing a financial penalty where that is determined to be the appropriate sentence.

[123] In accordance with the Sexual Offences Act 2003, s. 80 and schedule 3
[124] As defined in the Criminal Justice Act 2003, s. 158

Additional aggravating factors	Additional mitigating factors
1. Recording activity and/or circulating pictures or videos	1. Symptom of isolation rather than depravity

An offender convicted of this offence is automatically subject to notification requirements.[125]

Sexual penetration of a corpse SG-113

Factors to take into consideration:

1. The sentences for public protection *must* be considered in all cases. They are designed to ensure that sexual offenders are not released into the community if they present a significant risk of serious harm.
2. Necrophilia is associated with 'other very deviant behaviour', and killers who use the bodies of their victims for sexual gratification cannot, under the existing law, be formally recognised as, or treated as, sexual offenders.
3. A pre-sentence report[126] (and in some cases a psychiatric report), which can identify sexually deviant tendencies, will be extremely helpful in determining the most appropriate disposal. It will also help determine whether an offender would benefit from participation in a programme designed to help them address those tendencies.

THIS IS A SPECIFIED OFFENCE FOR THE PURPOSES OF SECTION 224 CJA 2003

Sexual penetration of a corpse (section 70): Intentional sexual penetration of part of the body of a dead person with a part of the offender's body or an object

Maximum penalty: **2 years**

Type/nature of activity	Starting points	Sentencing ranges
Repeat offending and/or aggravating factors	**26 weeks custody**	**4 weeks–18 months custody**
Basic offence as defined in the SOA 2003, assuming no aggravating or mitigating factors	**Community order**	**An appropriate non-custodial sentence***

* 'Non-custodial sentence' in this context suggests a community order or a fine. In most instances, an offence will have crossed the threshold for a community order. However, in accordance with normal sentencing practice, a court is not precluded from imposing a financial penalty where that is determined to be the appropriate sentence.

Additional aggravating factors	Additional mitigating factors
1. Distress caused to relatives or friends of the deceased 2. Physical damage caused to body of the deceased 3. The corpse was that of a child 4. The offence was committed in a funeral home or mortuary	

An offender convicted of this offence is automatically subject to notification requirements.[127]

Part 6: Exploitation Offences SG-114

6.1 Whilst all sexual offences involve, to a greater or lesser degree, the exploitation or abuse of a victim or victims, the specific sexual exploitation offences involve a high degree of offender culpability, with offenders intentionally exploiting vulnerable individuals. In some cases, for example the prostitution offences, the sexual acts themselves may not be unlawful, but the purpose of the legislation is to address the behaviour of those who are prepared to exploit others by causing, inciting or controlling their sexual activities, whether or not for gain.

The harm caused by the offences SG-115

6.2 Section 54 of the SOA 2003 defines 'gain' as:

(a) *any financial advantage, including the discharge of an obligation to pay or the provision of goods or services (including sexual services) gratuitously or at a discount; or*

[125] In accordance with the SOA 2003, s. 80 and schedule 3
[126] As defined in the Criminal Justice Act 2003, s. 158
[127] In accordance with the SOA 2003, s. 80 and schedule 3

(b) *the goodwill of any person which is, or appears likely, in time, to bring financial advantage.*

6.3 The sexual exploitation offences cover a range of offending behaviour that is broken down into four groups in the SOA 2003:
(i) indecent photographs of children;
(ii) abuse of children through prostitution and pornography;
(iii) exploitation of prostitution; and
(iv) trafficking.

6.4 Groups (i) and (ii) specifically relate to the exploitation and abuse of children; for the purposes of these offences, 'child' means anyone under the age of 18.

6.5 The 'exploitation of prostitution' offences relate to adult victims. The offences in group (iii) include the specific element that the activity was carried out 'for gain'. However, whether or not it is implicit in the offence that the prosecution is seeking to prove, in most cases someone will secure an advantage from the exploitation.

6.6 The 'trafficking' offences are designed to protect victims of all ages.

6.7 The term 'prostitution', which is used in most of the offences in these groups, is defined as 'providing sexual services for payment or promise of payment' and 'payment' is defined as being 'any financial advantage'.

6.8 The offences that do not require the prosecution to prove that the offender acted 'for gain' have the effect that offenders cannot avoid prosecution by claiming that they did not stand to benefit by their involvement. For these offences, the starting points for sentencing are based solely on the criminality of taking part in sexual exploitation without taking into account any benefits, financial or otherwise, that the defendant may receive.

Where a sexual exploitation offence does not require the prosecution to prove that the offender acted for gain, the degree of personal involvement of the offender and the levels of personal or financial gain should be treated as aggravating factors for sentencing.

6.9 Confiscation and compensation orders have particular relevance in the context of exploitation offences, where it is extremely likely both that there will be property that can be seized from the offender and also that exploited victims will have been caused a degree of harm that might merit compensation.

6.10 The 'for gain' element is inherent in the 'exploitation of prostitution' offences; therefore, it cannot be treated as an aggravating factor and is reflected in the starting points for sentencing. This group of offences relates to offenders who control the activities of those over the age of consent, and the maximum penalties are lower than for offences where the prosecution is not required to prove that the defendant acted 'for gain'. However, the commercial sexual exploitation of another person's vulnerability is serious and socially unacceptable offending behaviour, and the starting point for these offences should still be significant.

Where a sexual exploitation offence requires the prosecution to prove that the offender acted for personal gain and this is already reflected in the starting point for sentencing, evidence of substantial financial or other advantage to a value in the region of £5000 and upwards (in line with the provisions of section 75(4) of the Proceeds of Crime Act 2002) should be treated as an aggravating factor.

6.11 Although the courts must bear in mind the actual 'recoverable amount'[128] when making a confiscation order, they can legitimately take into account, as an aggravating factor for sentencing purposes, not only the benefits secured by the offender in fact, but also the benefits that he or she would have accrued from the offence had the activity not been intercepted or disrupted. Courts should also take into account non-monetary profits such as payment in kind, gifts or favours, which will need to be carefully assessed in each individual case.[129]

[128] Proceeds of Crime Act 2002, s. 9
[129] ibid. ss. 79–81

The offender's culpability SG-116

6.12 In the Council's guideline on seriousness, it is stated that, in broad terms, an intention to cause harm is at the highest level of criminal culpability—the worse the harm intended, the higher the offender's culpability—and planning an offence makes the offender more highly culpable than impulsive offending.

6.13 The common thread of the exploitation offences is the planned abuse of vulnerable victims, with the main purpose of the offender being to secure some form of personal advantage, whether this is financial gain or reward, sexual services or personal sexual gratification (as in the offence of 'paying for sexual services of a child').

6.14 As the combination of culpability with harm determines the seriousness of an offence, it follows that the offences covered in this section are at the higher end of the scale of seriousness, and robust sentencing provisions are needed.

Evidence of an offender's involvement in, or management of, a well-planned or large-scale commercial operation resulting in sexual exploitation should be treated as an aggravating factor for sentencing: the greater the offender's degree of involvement, the more serious the offence.

The age of the victim SG-117

- **In general the younger the age of the child the higher the sentence should be for an offence involving the sexual exploitation of a child.**
- **In particular the starting points for sentencing should be higher where the victim is under 13. The starting points for offences involving victims aged 16 or 17 should be lower than those for victims aged 13 or over but under 16 to recognise that they are over the legal age of consent but any evidence of grooming coercion threats or intimidation should increase a sentence in line with that which would apply if the victim were aged 13 or over but under 16.**

The risk of re-offending SG-118

6.15 The sexual exploitation offences are of a level of seriousness that suggests a custodial sentence will normally be appropriate, but the way in which the risk of re-offending should be addressed will depend on the nature of, and the motivation for, the offences committed.

6.16 A person found guilty of, for example, 'paying for sexual services of a child' or, in some cases, 'causing or inciting child prostitution or pornography' may very well benefit from taking part in a sex offender treatment programme, which will help the offender to recognise and control sexually deviant tendencies. There is a need to ensure that offenders are assessed for their suitability to take part in such programmes and that periods spent on licence in the community are of a sufficient length to enable such programmes to take place.

6.17 However, different issues arise where the courts are sentencing someone whose behaviour has nothing to do with personal sexual deviance but instead involves the exploitation of the sexual appetites or deviancies of others, whether or not for gain. In such cases, sex offender treatment programmes are unlikely to be appropriate. The use of fines or community orders containing requirements such as a curfew, residence, unpaid work and prohibited activity may be effective in discouraging future offending.

Part 6A: Indecent Photographs of Children SG-119

6A.1 The SOA 2003 makes amendments to the Protection of Children Act 1978 and the Criminal Justice Act 1988. It is now a crime to take, make, permit to take, distribute, show, possess, possess with intent to distribute, or to advertise indecent photographs or pseudo-photographs of any person below the age of 18.

6A.2 The levels for sentencing of offences involving pornographic images were established in the case of *R v Oliver, Hartrey and Baldwin*.[130] These levels have been reviewed in terms of the nature of the images falling into each level:

- Images depicting non-penetrative activity are less serious than images depicting penetrative activity.

[130] [2003] 2 Cr App R(S) 15

- Images of non-penetrative activity between children are generally less serious than images depicting non-penetrative activity between adults and children.
- All acts falling within the definitions of rape and assault by penetration, which carry the maximum life penalty, should be classified as level 4.

The levels of seriousness (in ascending order) for sentencing for offences involving pornographic images are:

Level 1 Images depicting erotic posing with no sexual activity
Level 2 Non-penetrative sexual activity between children, or solo masturbation by a child
Level 3 Non-penetrative sexual activity between adults and children
Level 4 Penetrative sexual activity involving a child or children, or both children and adults
Level 5 Sadism or penetration of, or by, an animal

Offences involving any form of sexual penetration of the vagina or anus, or penile penetration of the mouth (except where they involve sadism or intercourse with an animal, which fall within level 5), should be classified as activity at level 4.

6A.3 Pseudo-photographs should generally be treated as less serious than real images. However, they can be just as serious as photographs of a real child, for example where the imagery is particularly grotesque and beyond the scope of normal photography.

6A.4 The aggravating and mitigating factors set out in the case of *Oliver* remain relevant and are included in the guideline for this offence.

6A.5 An adult (aged 18 or over) who is given any sentence (including a conditional discharge) in relation to offences involving a victim or victims aged under 16 will be subject to registration requirements.[131] Where the offences involved a victim or victims aged 16 or 17, the requirement to register is triggered by a sentence other than an absolute or conditional discharge. Where the imposition of a conditional discharge would not result in registration, it should not be imposed purely to avoid the requirement for registration.

6A.6 Courts have the discretion to make an order disqualifying an offender (adult or juvenile) from working with children regardless of the sentence imposed.[132]

SG-120 **Possession of indecent photographs where the child depicted is aged 16 or 17**

6A.7 The starting points for sentencing should reflect the fundamental facts of a case, including that the victim is over the legal age of consent.

Sentences should be lower than those involving photographs of children under 16 where:

- **an offender possesses only a few indecent photographs, none of which includes sadism or penetration of, or by, an animal; and**
- **the images are of children aged 16 or 17; and**
- **the photographs are retained solely for the use of the offender.**

6A.8 The presence of any aggravating factors will substantially increase a sentence, and the principle of lower sentences should not be applied where an offender possesses images at level 5 as these will involve either non-consensual or unlawful activity.

6A.9 Where it cannot be established that a victim was under 13, penalties will need to be based on the sentencing starting points for children aged 13 or over but under 16. In many cases, however, the extreme youth of the child in a photograph or pseudo-photograph will either be a matter of proven fact or will be a question that is beyond reasonable doubt. Where the nature of the image indicates that the victim is likely to have suffered particularly serious harm, this should always aggravate the sentence.

Starting points for sentencing for possession of indecent photographs should be higher where the victim is a child under 13.

[131] Sexual Offences Act 2003, s. 134
[132] Criminal Justice and Court Services Act 2000, s. 29A as inserted by the Criminal Justice Act 2003, schedule 30

6A.10 The court cannot make inferences about the status of unknown material, because of the fundamental principle that a person may only be convicted and sentenced according to the facts that have been proved. However, if an offender has used devices to destroy or hide material then it falls within the general aggravating factor 'An attempt to conceal or dispose of evidence'.

Showing or distributing and the element of financial gain SG-121

6A.11 The starting points in the guideline reflect the differences in terms of relative seriousness and maximum penalty available for possessing indecent photographs or pseudo-photographs (5 years) and taking or making, distributing or showing, etc such photographs (10 years).

6A.12 Showing or distributing indecent photographs or pseudo-photographs, even on a very small scale, is regarded as serious offending behaviour. Wide-scale distribution is in the most serious category of offending behaviour.

6A.13 Where the material is shown or distributed without the victims consent, the fact that the victim is over the age of consent should not have any bearing on sentencing levels, even if the material was originally taken and possessed with his or her consent.

6A.14 Where the offence involves a victim aged 16 or 17, the starting points for sentencing should reflect the fact that the victim is above the age of consent. The fact that the victim was not coerced or forced into the activity must be relevant for sentencing purposes, and starting points should be lower to encourage consistency. Any evidence of threats or intimidation to induce consent should have the effect of increasing sentence in an individual case.

6A.15 Any profit for the victim, financial or otherwise, actual or anticipated, should be neutral for sentencing purposes.

The showing or distribution of pornographic images of children under 16, or of children aged 16 or 17 without their consent is an aggravating factor for sentencing purposes.

Indecent photographs of children SG-122

Factors to take into consideration:

1. The levels of seriousness (in ascending order) for sentencing for offences involving pornographic images are:
   Level 1 Images depicting erotic posing with no sexual activity
   Level 2 Non-penetrative sexual activity between children, or solo masturbation by a child
   Level 3 Non-penetrative sexual activity between adults and children
   Level 4 Penetrative sexual activity involving a child or children, or both children and adults
   Level 5 Sadism or penetration of, or by, an animal
2. Offences involving any form of sexual penetration of the vagina or anus, or penile penetration of the mouth (except where they involve sadism or intercourse with an animal, which fall within level 5), should be classified as activity at level 4.
3. Pseudo-photographs generally should be treated less seriously than real photographs.
4. Sentences should be lower than those involving photographs of children under 16 where:
   - an offender possesses only a few indecent photographs, none of which includes sadism or penetration of, or by, an animal; and
   - the images are of children aged 16 or 17; and
   - the photographs are retained solely for the use of the offender.
5. The fact that the subject of the indecent photograph(s) is aged 16 or 17 has *no* impact on sentencing starting points where the activity depicted is at level 5.
6. Starting points for sentencing for possession of indecent photographs should be higher where the subject of the indecent photograph(s) is a child under 13.
7. Registration requirements attach to a conviction for this offence dependent upon the age of the subject portrayed in the indecent photograph(s) and the sentence imposed.
8. Courts should consider making an order disqualifying an offender (adult or juvenile) from working with children regardless of the sentence imposed.
9. Courts should consider making an order for the forfeiture of any possessions (for example, computers or cameras) used in connection with the commission of the offence.

THESE OFFENCES ARE SERIOUS OFFENCES FOR THE PURPOSES OF SECTION 224 CJA 2003, EXCEPT WHERE THEY INVOLVE ONLY POSSESSION, WHEN THEY ARE SPECIFIED OFFENCES FOR THE PURPOSES OF SECTION 227

Indecent photographs of children (section 1 of the Protection of Children Act 1978 and section 160 of the Criminal Justice Act 1988, as amended by section 45 of the SOA 2003): Taking, making, permitting to take, possessing, possessing with intent to distribute, distributing or advertising indecent photographs or pseudo-photographs of children under 18.

Maximum penalty: **5 years** for possession; otherwise **10 years**

Type/nature of activity	Starting points	Sentencing ranges
Offender commissioned or encouraged the production of level 4 or 5 images Offender involved in the production of level 4 or 5 images	6 years custody	4–9 years custody
Level 4 or 5 images shown or distributed	3 years custody	2–5 years custody
Offender involved in the production of, or has traded in, material at levels 1–3	2 years custody	1–4 years custody
Possession of a large quantity of level 4 or 5 material for personal use only Large number of level 3 images shown or distributed	12 months custody	26 weeks–2 years custody
Possession of a large quantity of level 3 material for personal use Possession of a small number of images at level 4 or 5 Large number of level 2 images shown or distributed Small number of level 3 images shown or distributed	26 weeks custody	4 weeks–18 months custody
Offender in possession of a large amount of material at level 2 or a small amount at level 3 Offender has shown or distributed material at level1 or 2 on a limited scale Offender has exchanged images at level 1 or 2 with other collectors, but with no element of financial gain	12 weeks custody	4 weeks–26 weeks custody
Possession of a large amount of level 1 material and/or no more than a small amount of level 2, and the material is for personal use and has not been distributed or shown to others	Community order	An appropriate non-custodial sentence*

* 'Non-custodial sentence' in this context suggests a community order or a fine. In most instances, an offence will have crossed the threshold for a community order. However, in accordance with normal sentencing practice, a court is not precluded from imposing a financial penalty where that is determined to be the appropriate sentence.

Additional aggravating factors	Additional mitigating factors
1. Images shown or distributed to others, especially children 2. Collection is systematically stored or organised, indicating a sophisticated approach to trading or a high level of personal interest 3. Images stored, made available or distributed in such a way that they can be inadvertently accessed by others 4. Use of drugs, alcohol or other substance to facilitate the offence of making or taking 5. Background of intimidation or coercion 6. Threats to prevent victim reporting the activity 7. Threats to disclose victim's activity to friends or relatives 8. Financial or other gain	1. A few images held solely for personal use 2. Images viewed but not stored 3. A few images held solely for personal use and it is established both that the subject is aged 16 or 17 and that he or she was consenting

An offender convicted of this offence is automatically subject to notification requirements.[133]

PART 6B: ABUSE OF CHILDREN THROUGH PROSTITUTION AND PORNOGRAPHY SG-123

6B.1 The four offences in this category are:

- Paying for sexual services of a child
- Causing or inciting child prostitution or pornography
- Controlling a child prostitute or a child involved in pornography
- Arranging or facilitating child prostitution or pornography

Paying for sexual services of a child **SG-124**

Factors to take into consideration:

1. The sentences for public protection *must* be considered in all cases. They are designed to ensure that sexual offenders are not released into the community if they present a significant risk of serious harm. Within any indeterminate sentence, the minimum term will generally be half the appropriate determinate sentence. The starting points will be relevant, therefore, to the process of fixing any minimum term that may be necessary.
2. The offence of 'paying for sexual services of a child' is the only offence in this group that involves actual physical sexual activity between an offender and a victim.
3. It carries staged maximum penalties according to the age of the victim (in this case under 16, or over 16 but under 18) and also, specifically in relation to victims under 13, whether the sexual services provided or offered involved penetrative activity.
4. The starting points for sentencing for the offence of 'paying for sexual services of a child', where the victim is aged 13 or over but under 16, are higher than those for the offence of 'sexual activity with a child', to reflect the fact that the victim has been commercially exploited.
5. Starting points for victims aged 16 or 17 are lower than the equivalent starting points for victims aged 13 to 15, in line with the difference in the maximum penalty, to reflect the fact that the victim is above the legal age of consent.
6. The starting points where the victim is aged 13 or over but under 16 are higher than those for the offence of 'sexual activity with a child', to reflect the fact that the victim has been commercially exploited.
7. The starting points for sentencing for the offence of 'paying for sexual services of a child' where the victim is under 13 are higher than those for the specific 'under 13' offences covering the same type of sexual activity, to reflect the fact that the victim has been commercially exploited.
8. The offence of 'paying for sexual services of a child' includes higher maximum penalties to cater for those (albeit rare) cases where the age of the victim is only established during the course of a trial. The same principle has been applied to the starting points for sentencing.

THIS IS A SERIOUS OFFENCE FOR THE PURPOSES OF SECTION 224 CJA 2003

Paying for sexual services of a child (section 47): Intentionally obtaining the sexual services of a child having made or promised payment or knowing that another person has made or promised payment

Maximum penalty: **Life imprisonment** for offences involving penetration where the child is under 13, otherwise **14 years; 14 years** where the child is aged 13 or over but under 16; **7 years** where the child is aged 16 or 17

Type/nature of activity	Starting points	Sentencing ranges
History of paying for penetrative sex with children under 18	If the victim is under 13, the offence of 'rape of a child under 13' or 'assault of a child under 13 by penetration' would normally be charged. Any commercial element to the offence and any history of repeat offending would be aggravating factors. However, if this offence is charged—**15 years custody**	**13–19 years custody**
	7 years custody if the victim is 13 or over but under 16	**5–10 years custody**
	3 years custody if the victim is aged 16 or 17	**2–5 years custody**

[133] In accordance with the SOA 2003, s. 80 and schedule 3

Type/nature of activity	Starting points	Sentencing ranges
Penile penetration of the vagina, anus or mouth *or* penetration of the vagina or anus with another body part or an object	If the victim is under 13, the offence of 'rape of a child under 13' or 'assault of a child under 13 by penetration' would normally be charged. Any commercial element to the offence would be an aggravating factor. However, if this offence is charged—**12 years custody**	**10–16 years custody**
	5 years custody if the victim is 13 or over but under 16	**4–8 years custody**
	2 years custody if the victim is aged 16 or 17	**1–4 years custody**
Sexual touching falling short of penetration	If the victim is under 13, the offence of 'sexual assault of a child under 13' would normally be charged. Any commercial element to the offence would be an aggravating factor. However, if this offence is charged—**5 years custody**	**4–8 years custody**
	4 years custody if the victim is 13 or over but under 16	**3–7 years custody**
	12 months custody if the victim is aged 16 or 17	**26 weeks–2 years custody**

Additional aggravating factors	Additional mitigating factors
1. Use of drugs, alcohol or other substance to secure the victim's compliance 2. Abduction or detention 3. Threats to prevent victim reporting the activity 4. Threats to disclose victim's activity to friends or relatives 5. Offender aware that he or she is suffering from a sexually transmitted infection	

An offender convicted of this offence is automatically subject to notification requirements.[134]

SG-125 Child prostitution or pornography

Factors to take into consideration:

1. The sentences for public protection *must* be considered in all cases. They are designed to ensure that sexual offenders are not released into the community if they present a significant risk of serious harm.
2. Three offences fall within this group:
   - Causing or inciting child prostitution or child pornography
   - Controlling a child prostitute or a child involved in pornography
   - Arranging or facilitating child prostitution or pornography
3. The level of involvement of the offender is a fundamental element of the 'abuse of children through prostitution and pornography' offences.
4. Financial reward may not always be a factor in someone's involvement in these offences. Thus the offences cover anyone who takes part in any way, for whatever reason, in a child's involvement in prostitution or pornography. However, most offenders will stand to gain in some way from their involvement, and sentencing starting points need to be relatively high, in line with established principles about the serious nature of commercial exploitation.
5. The courts should consider making an order confiscating any profits stemming from the offender's criminal lifestyle or forfeiting any possessions (for example cameras, computers, property) used in connection with the commission of the offence.
6. Evidence of an offender's involvement in, or management of, a well-planned or large-scale commercial operation resulting in sexual exploitation should be treated as an aggravating factor for sentencing: the greater the offender's degree of involvement, the more serious the offence.
7. The starting point for the child prostitution and pornography offences will always be a custodial sentence.
8. The same starting points apply whether the activity was caused or incited. Where an offence was incited but did not take place as a result of the voluntary intervention of the offender, that is likely to reduce the severity of the sentence imposed.

[134] In accordance with the SOA 2003, s. 80 and schedule 3

9. The presence of any of the general aggravating factors identified in the Council guideline on seriousness or any of the additional factors identified in the guidelines will indicate a sentence above the normal starting point.
10. In cases where a number of children are involved, consecutive sentences may be appropriate, leading to cumulative sentences significantly higher than the suggested starting points for individual offences.
11. In cases where the offender is, to a degree, another victim, a court may wish to take a more lenient stance. A court might consider whether the circumstances of the offender should mitigate sentence. This will depend on the merits of each case.

THESE ARE SERIOUS OFFENCES FOR THE PURPOSES OF SECTION 224 CJA 2003

1. **Causing or inciting child prostitution or pornography** (section 48): Intentionally causing or inciting a child to become a prostitute, or to be involved in pornography, anywhere in the world
2. **Controlling a child prostitute or a child involved in pornography** (section 49): Intentionally controlling any of the activities of a child under 18 where those activities relate to child's prostitution, or involvement in pornography, anywhere in the world
3. **Arranging or facilitating child prostitution or pornography** (section 50): Intentionally arranging or facilitating the prostitution of a child, or the child's involvement in pornography, anywhere in the world

Maximum penalty for all offences: **14 years**

Type/nature of activity: Penetrative activity	**Starting points**	**Sentencing ranges**
Organised commercial exploitation	If the victim is under 13, the offence of 'causing or inciting a child under 13 to engage in sexual activity' would normally be charged. The commercial element of the offence would be an aggravating factor. However, if this offence is charged—**10 years custody**	**8–13 years custody**
	8 years custody if the victim is 13 or over but under 16	**6–11 years custody**
	4 years custody if the victim is aged 16 or 17	**3–7 years custody**
Offender's involvement is minimal and not perpetrated for gain	If the victim is under 13, the offence of 'causing or inciting a child under 13 to engage in sexual activity' would normally be charged. The commercial element of the offence would be an aggravating factor. However, if this offence is charged—**8 years custody**	**6–11 years custody**
	5 years custody if the victim is 13 or over but under 16	**4–8 years custody**
	2 years custody if the victim is aged 16 or 17	**1–4 years custody**
Organised commercial exploitation	If the victim is under 13, the offence of 'causing or inciting a child under 13 to engage in sexual activity' would normally be charged. The commercial element of the offence would be an aggravating factor. However, if this offence is charged—**8 years custody**	**6–11 years custody**
	6 years custody if the victim is 13 or over but under 16	**4–9 years custody**
	3 years custody if the victim is aged 16 or 17	**2–5 years custody**
Offender's involvement is minimal and not perpetrated for gain	If the victim is under 13, the offence of 'causing or inciting a child under 13 to engage in sexual activity' would normally be charged. The commercial element of the offence would be an aggravating factor. However, if this offence is charged—**6 years custody**	**4–9 years custody**
	3 years custody if the victim is aged 13 or over but under 16	**2–5 years custody**
	12 months custody if the victim is aged 16 or 17	**26 weeks–2 years custody**

Additional aggravating factors	Additional mitigating factors
1. Background of threats or intimidation 2. Large-scale commercial operation 3. Use of drugs, alcohol or other substance to secure the victim's compliance 4. Induced dependency on drugs 5. Forcing a victim to violate another person 6. Victim has been manipulated into physical and emotional dependence on the offender 7. Abduction or detention 8. Threats to prevent victim reporting the activity 9. Threats to disclose victim's activity to friends or relatives 10. Storing, making available or distributing images in such a way that they can be inadvertently accessed by others 11. Images distributed to other children or persons known to the victim 12. Financial or other gain	1. Offender also being controlled in prostitution or pornography and subject to threats or intimidation

An offender convicted of this offence is automatically subject to notification requirements.[135]

SG-126

Part 6C: Exploitation of Prostitution

6C.1 The offences in this section relate to the exploitation of adults who work as prostitutes, replacing gender-specific offences in the Sexual Offences Act 1956. Offenders who cause, incite or control the activities of a prostitute for their own gain, or for the gain of a third person, can be prosecuted under two new offences.

6C.2 The offences 'causing or inciting prostitution for gain' and 'controlling prostitution for gain' cover two levels of criminal activity:

(i) the coercion of another person into prostitution; and
(ii) controlling his or her activities for gain.

SG-127

Exploitation of prostitution

Factors to take into consideration:

1. The sentences for public protection *must* be considered in all cases. They are designed to ensure that sexual offenders are not released into the community if they present a significant risk of serious harm.
2. The degree of coercion, both in terms of recruitment and subsequent control of a prostitute's activities, is highly relevant to sentencing.
3. The degree to which a victim is exploited or controlled, the harm suffered as a result, the level of involvement of the offender, the scale of the operation and the timescale over which it has been run will all be relevant in terms of assessing the seriousness of the offence.
4. Where an offender has profited from his or her involvement in the prostitution of others, the courts should always consider making a confiscation order approximately equivalent to the profits enjoyed.
5. The presence of any of the general aggravating factors identified in the Council guideline on seriousness or any of the additional factors identified in the guidelines will indicate a sentence above the normal starting point.
6. Where there is evidence that an offender convicted of an exploitation of prostitution offence is not actively involved in the coercion or control of the victim(s), that he or she acted through fear or intimidation and that he or she is trying to exit prostitution, the courts may wish to consider whether, in the particular circumstances of the case, this should mitigate sentence.
7. The starting points are the same whether prostitution was caused or incited and whether or not the incited activity took place. Where the offence was incited, the sentencer should begin from the starting point that the offence was incited, taking account of the nature of the harm that would have been caused had the offence taken place and calculating the final sentence to reflect that no actual harm was occasioned to the victim, but being mindful that the intended victim may have suffered as a result of knowing or believing the offence would take place.

[135] In accordance with the SOA 2003, s. 80 and schedule 3

8. The starting point for the exploitation of prostitution offences where an offender's involvement was minimal, and he or she has not actively engaged in the coercion or control of those engaged in prostitution, is a non-custodial sentence.
9. A fine may be more appropriate for very minimal involvement.
10. Where an offender has profited from his or her involvement in the prostitution of others, the court should consider making a confiscation order[136] approximately equivalent to the profits enjoyed.
11. Where this offence is being dealt with in a magistrates' court, more detailed guidance is provided in the Magistrates' Court Sentencing Guidelines (MCSG) [see **SG-202**].

THESE ARE SPECIFIED OFFENCES FOR THE PURPOSES OF SECTION 227 CJA 2003

1. **Causing or inciting prostitution for gain** (section 52): Intentionally causing or inciting another person to become a prostitute anywhere in the world
2. **Controlling prostitution for gain** (section 53): Intentionally controlling any of the activities of another person relating to that person's prostitution in any part of the world

Maximum penalty for both offences: 7 **years**

Type/nature of activity	Starting points	Sentencing ranges
Offender is the keeper of a brothel and has made substantial profits in the region of £5000 and upwards	**2 years custody**	**1–4 years custody**
Offender is the keeper of the brothel and is personally involved in its management	**12 months custody**	**26 weeks–2 years custody**
Involvement of the offender was minimal	**Community order**	**An appropriate non-custodial sentence***

* 'Non-custodial sentence' in this context suggests a community order or a fine. In most instances, an offence will have crossed the threshold for a community order. However, in accordance with normal sentencing practice, a court is not precluded from imposing a financial penalty where that is determined to be the appropriate sentence.

Additional aggravating factors	Additional mitigating factors
1. Background of threats, intimidation or coercion 2. Large-scale commercial operation 3. Substantial gain (in the region of £5000 and upwards) 4. Use of drugs, alcohol or other substance to secure the victim's compliance 5. Induced dependency on drugs 6. Abduction or detention 7. Threats to prevent victim reporting the activity 8. Threats to disclose victim's activity to friends or relatives	1. Offender also being controlled in prostitution and subject to threats or intimidation

Keeping a brothel used for prostitution **SG-128**

Factors to take into consideration:

1. The sentences for public protection *must* be considered in all cases. They are designed to ensure that sexual offenders are not released into the community if they present a significant risk of serious harm.
2. The offence covers anyone who keeps, manages or acts or assists in the management of a brothel. The degree of coercion, both in terms of recruitment and subsequent control of a prostitute's activities, is highly relevant to sentencing.
3. The degree to which a victim is exploited or controlled, the harm suffered as a result, the level of involvement of the offender, the scale of the operation and the timescale over which it has been run will all be relevant in terms of assessing the seriousness of the offence.
4. The presence of any of the general aggravating factors identified in the Council guideline on seriousness or any of the additional factors identified in the guidelines will indicate a sentence above the normal starting point.

[136] Criminal Justice Act 1988 as amended by the Proceeds of Crime Act 2002

5. Where there is evidence that an offender convicted of an exploitation of prostitution offence is not actively involved in the coercion or control of the victim(s), that he or she acted through fear or intimidation and that he or she is trying to exit prostitution, the courts may wish to consider whether, in the particular circumstances of the case, this should mitigate sentence.
6. The starting points are the same whether prostitution was caused or incited and whether or not the incited activity took place. Where the offence was incited, the sentencer should begin from the starting point that the offence was incited, taking account of the nature of the harm that would have been caused had the offence taken place and calculating the final sentence to reflect that no actual harm was occasioned to the victim, but being mindful that the intended victim may have suffered as a result of knowing or believing the offence would take place.
7. A non-custodial sentence may be appropriate for very minimal involvement.
8. Where an offender has profited from his or her involvement in the prostitution of others, the courts should always consider making a confiscation order approximately equivalent to the profits enjoyed.
9. Where this offence is being dealt with in a magistrates' court, more detailed guidance is provided in the Magistrates' Court Sentencing Guidelines (MCSG) [see **SG-218**].

Keeping a brothel used for prostitution (section 33A of the Sexual Offences Act 1956 as inserted by section 55 of the SOA 2003): Keeping, managing, or acting or assisting in the management of a brothel

Maximum penalty: 7 years

Type/nature of activity	Starting points	Sentencing ranges
Evidence of physical and/or mental coercion	**3 years custody**	**2–5 years custody**
No coercion or corruption, but the offender is closely involved in the victim's prostitution	**12 months custody**	**26 weeks–2 years custody**
No evidence that the victim was physically coerced or corrupted, and the involvement of the offender was minimal	**Community order**	**An appropriate non-custodial sentence***

* 'Non-custodial sentence' in this context suggests a community order or a fine. In most instances, an offence will have crossed the threshold for a community order. However, in accordance with normal sentencing practice, a court is not precluded from imposing a financial penalty where that is determined to be the appropriate sentence.

Additional aggravating factors	Additional mitigating factors
1. Background of threats, intimidation or coercion 2. Large-scale commercial operation 3. Personal involvement in the prostitution of others 4. Abduction or detention 5. Financial or other gain	1. Using employment as a route out of prostitution and not actively involved in exploitation 2. Coercion by third party

SENTENCERS ARE REMINDED THAT A NUMBER OF FINANCIAL ORDERS CAN BE MADE IN ADDITION TO THE SENTENCE IMPOSED FOR THIS OFFENCE (SEE PART 1, PARAGRAPH 1.32 ABOVE).

SG-129

Part 6D: Trafficking

Factors to take into consideration:

1. The sentences for public protection *must* be considered in all cases. They are designed to ensure that sexual offenders are not released into the community if they present a significant risk of serious harm.
2. The type of activity covered by the various trafficking offences in the SOA 2003 is broadly the same, the only difference being the geographical area within which the trafficked persons are moved. The harm being addressed is sexual exploitation, but here either children or adults may be involved as victims.
3. The offences are designed to cover anyone involved in any stage of the trafficking operation, whether or not there is evidence of gain. This is serious offending behaviour, which society as a whole finds repugnant, and a financial or community penalty would rarely be an appropriate disposal.

4. The degree of coercion used and the level of control over the trafficked person's liberty will be relevant to assessing the seriousness of the offender's behaviour. The nature of the sexual exploitation to which the victim is exposed will also be relevant, as will the victim's age and vulnerability.
5. In general terms the greater the level of involvement, the more serious the crime. Those at the top of an organised trafficking chain may have very little personal involvement with day-to-day operations and may have no knowledge at all of individual victims. However, being in control of a money-making operation that is based on the degradation, exploitation and abuse of vulnerable people may be equally, if not more, serious than the actions of an individual who is personally involved at an operational level.
6. The presence of any of the general aggravating factors identified in the Council guideline on seriousness or any of the additional factors identified in the guidelines will indicate a sentence above the normal starting point.
7. Circumstances such as the fact that the offender is also a victim of trafficking and that their actions were governed by fear could be a mitigating factor if not accepted as a defence.
8. The starting point for sentencing for offences of trafficking for sexual exploitation should be a custodial sentence. Aggravating factors such as participation in a large-scale commercial enterprise involving a high degree of planning, organisation or sophistication, financial or other gain, and the coercion and vulnerability of victims should move sentences towards the maximum 14 years.
9. In cases where a number of children are involved, consecutive sentences may be appropriate, leading to cumulative sentences significantly higher than the suggested starting points for individual offences.
10. Where an offender has profited from his or her involvement in the prostitution of others, the court should consider making a confiscation order[137] approximately equivalent to the profits enjoyed.
11. The court may order the forfeiture of a vehicle used, or intended to be used, in connection with the offence.[138]

THESE ARE SERIOUS OFFENCES FOR THE PURPOSES OF SECTION 224 CJA 2003

Trafficking into/within/out of the UK for sexual exploitation (sections 57, 58 and 59): Intentionally arranging or facilitating a person's arrival/travel within/departure from the UK, intending or believing that a sexual offence will be committed

Maximum penalty for all offences: **14 years**

Type/nature of activity	Starting points	Sentencing ranges
Involvement at any level in any stage of the trafficking operation where the victim was coerced	6 years custody	4–9 years custody
Involvement at any level in any stage of the trafficking operation where there was no coercion of the victim	2 years custody	1–4 years custody

Note: if the victim is under 13, one of the specific under-13 offences would normally be charged. Any commercial exploitation element would be an aggravating factor.

Additional aggravating factors	Additional mitigating factors
1. Large-scale commercial operation 2. High degree of planning or sophistication 3. Large number of people trafficked 4. Substantial financial (in the region of £5000 and upwards) or other gain 5. Fraud 6. Financial extortion of the victim 7. Deception 8. Use of force, threats of force or other forms of coercion 9. Threats against victim or members of victim's family 10. Abduction or detention 11. Restriction of victim's liberty 12. Inhumane treatment 13. Confiscation of victim's passport	1. Coercion of the offender by a third party 2. No evidence of personal gain 3. Limited involvement

[137] Proceeds of Crime Act 2002, part 2
[138] Sexual Offences Act 2003, s. 60A as inserted by the Violent Crime Reduction Act 2006, s. 54 and schedule 4

Sentencing Guidelines

SG-130

Part 7: Sentencing Young Offenders—Offences with a Lower Statutory Maximum

7.1 The SOA 2003 makes special provision in respect of the maximum sentence that can be imposed for certain offences where committed by a person under the age of 18 (a young offender). The sentencing framework that applies to the sentencing of young offenders is also different.

7.2 This section deals with those offences within the context of the framework that currently applies. Many cases will be sentenced in the youth court, but a significant proportion may also be dealt with in the Crown Court. The essential elements of each offence, relevant charging standards and any other general issues pertaining to the offence are set out in the offence guidelines at pages 135–139.

7.3 The offences with which Part 7 is concerned are:
(i) Sexual activity with a child
(ii) Causing or inciting a child to engage in sexual activity
(iii) Engaging in sexual activity in the presence of a child
(iv) Causing a child to watch a sexual act
(v) Sexual activity with a child family member
(vi) Inciting a child family member to engage in sexual activity

7.4 In relation to each offence, the maximum sentence for an offence committed by a young offender is 5 years' custody compared with a maximum of 14 years or 10 years for an offender aged 18 or over. Offences under (i), (ii), (v) and (vi) above can be committed to the Crown Court where it is considered that sentencing powers greater than those available in a magistrates' court may be needed.[139]

7.5 The provisions relating to the sentencing of dangerous offenders apply to young offenders with some variation and, where appropriate, cases should be sent for trial or committed for sentence in the Crown Court. The offences in this section are 'serious' offences for the purposes of the provisions. Where the significant harm criterion is met, the court is required[140] to impose one of the sentences for public protection, which in the case of those under 18 are discretionary detention for life, indeterminate detention for public protection or an extended sentence.

7.6 The following guidelines are for those offences where the court considers that the facts found by the court justify the involvement of the criminal law—these findings may be different from those on which the decision to prosecute was made.

7.7 The sentencing framework that applies to young offenders is different from that for adult offenders. The significant factors are set out below.

7.8 For each offence, the circumstances that would suggest that a custodial sentence should be passed where it is available to the court and those that would suggest that a case should be dealt with in the Crown Court (as 'grave crimes') are set out. As for adult offenders, these guidelines relate to sentencing on conviction for a first-time offender after a plea of not guilty.

7.9 The principal aim for all involved in the youth justice system is to prevent offending by children and young persons.[141]

7.10 A court imposing sentence on a youth must have regard to the welfare,[142] maturity, sexual development and intelligence of the youth. These are always important factors.

7.11 Where a young offender pleads guilty to one of these offences and it is the first offence of which they are convicted, a youth court may impose an absolute discharge, a mental health disposal, a custodial sentence, or make a referral order.

7.12 Except where the dangerous offender provisions apply:
(i) Where the young offender is aged 12, 13 or 14, a custodial sentence may only be imposed if the youth is a 'persistent offender' or has committed a 'grave crime' warranting detention for a period in excess of 2 years.[143]
(ii) Where a young offender is aged 10 or 11, no custodial sentence is available in the youth court.
(iii) Where a custodial sentence is imposed in the youth court, it must be a Detention and Training Order (DTO), which can only be for 4/6/8/10/12/18 or 24 months.
(iv) Where a custodial sentence is imposed in the Crown Court, it may be a DTO or it may be detention for a period up to the maximum for the offence.

---

[139] Powers of Criminal Courts (Sentencing) Act 2000, s. 91
[140] Criminal Justice Act 2003, ss. 226 and 228
[141] Crime and Disorder Act 1998, s. 37
[142] Children and Young Persons Act 1933, s. 44
[143] Powers of Criminal Courts (Sentencing) Act 2000, s. 100

Sexual activity with a child SG-131
(when committed by a person under the age of 18)

THIS IS A SPECIFIED OFFENCE FOR THE PURPOSES OF SECTION 224 CJA 2003

Intentional sexual touching of a person under 16 (sections 9 and 13)

Maximum penalty: **5 years** (**14 years** if offender is 18 or over)

The starting points below are based upon a first-time offender aged 17 years old who pleaded not guilty. For younger offenders, sentencers should consider whether a lower starting point is justified in recognition of the offender's age or immaturity.

Type/nature of activity	Starting points	Sentencing ranges
Offence involving penetration where one or more aggravating factors exist or where there is a substantial age gap between the parties	**Detention and Training Order 12 months**	**Detention and Training Order 6–24 months**
CUSTODY THRESHOLD		
Any form of sexual activity (non-penetrative or penetrative) not involving any aggravating factors	**Community order**	**An appropriate noncustodial sentence***

* 'Non-custodial sentence' in this context suggests a youth community order (as defined in the Criminal Justice Act 2003, section 147(2)) or a fine. In most instances, an offence will have crossed the threshold for a community order. However, in accordance with normal sentencing practice, a court is not precluded from imposing a financial penalty where that is determined to be the appropriate sentence.

Aggravating factors	Mitigating factors
1. Background of intimidation or coercion 2. Use of drugs, alcohol or other substance to facilitate the offence 3. Threats to prevent victim reporting the incident 4. Abduction or detention 5. Offender aware that he or she is suffering from a sexually transmitted infection	1. Relationship of genuine affection 2. Youth and immaturity of offender

An offender convicted of this offence is automatically subject to notification requirements when sentenced to imprisonment for a term of at least 12 months.[144]

Causing or inciting a child to engage in sexual activity SG-132
(when committed by a person under the age of 18)

THIS IS A SPECIFIED OFFENCE FOR THE PURPOSES OF SECTION 224 CJA 2003

Intentional causing/inciting of person under 16 to engage in sexual activity (sections 10 and 13)

Maximum penalty: **5 years** (**14 years** if offender is 18 or over)

The same starting points apply whether the activity was caused or incited and whether or not the incited activity took place.

The starting points below are based upon a first-time offender aged 17 years old who pleaded not guilty. For younger offenders, sentencers should consider whether a lower starting point is justified in recognition of the offender's age or immaturity

[144] In accordance with the SOA 2003, s. 80 and schedule 3

Type/nature of activity	Starting points	Sentencing ranges
Sexual activity involving penetration where one or more aggravating factors exist	**Detention and Training Order 12 months**	**Detention and Training Order 6–24 months**
CUSTODY THRESHOLD		
Any form of sexual activity (non-penetrative or penetrative) not involving any aggravating factors	**Community order**	**An appropriate non-custodial sentence***

* 'Non-custodial sentence' in this context suggests a youth community order (as defined in the Criminal Justice Act 2003, section 147(2)) or a fine. In most instances, an offence will have crossed the threshold for a community order. However, in accordance with normal sentencing practice, a court is not precluded from imposing a financial penalty where that is determined to be the appropriate sentence.

Aggravating factors	Mitigating factors
1. Background of intimidation or coercion 2. Use of drugs, alcohol or other substance to facilitate the offence 3. Threats to prevent victim reporting the incident 4. Abduction or detention 5. Offender aware that he or she is suffering from a sexually transmitted infection	1. Relationship of genuine affection 2. Offender intervenes to prevent incited offence from taking place 3. Youth and immaturity of offender

An offender convicted of this offence is automatically subject to notification requirements when sentenced to imprisonment for a term of at least 12 months.[145]

SG-133 **Engaging in sexual activity in the presence of a child**
(when committed by a person under the age of 18)

THIS IS A SPECIFIED OFFENCE FOR THE PURPOSES OF SECTION 224 CJA 2003

Intentionally and for the purpose of obtaining sexual gratification, engaging in sexual activity in the presence of a person under 16, knowing or believing that the child is aware of the activity (sections 11 and 13)

Maximum penalty: **5 years** (**10 years** if offender is 18 or over)

The starting points below are based upon a first-time offender aged 17 years old who pleaded not guilty. For younger offenders, sentencers should consider whether a lower starting point is justified in recognition of the offender's age or immaturity.

Type/nature of activity	Starting points	Sentencing ranges
Sexual activity involving penetration where one or more aggravating factors exist	**Detention and Training Order 12 months**	**Detention and Training Order 6–24 months**
CUSTODY THRESHOLD		
Any form of sexual activity (non-penetrative or penetrative) not involving any aggravating factors	**Community order**	**An appropriate non-custodial sentence***

* 'Non-custodial sentence' in this context suggests a youth community order (as defined in the Criminal Justice Act 2003, section 147(2)) or a fine. In most instances, an offence will have crossed the threshold for a community order. However, in accordance with normal sentencing practice, a court is not precluded from imposing a financial penalty where that is determined to be the appropriate sentence.

Aggravating factors	Mitigating factors
1. Background of intimidation or coercion 2. Use of drugs, alcohol or other substance to facilitate the offence 3. Threats to prevent victim reporting the incident 4. Abduction or detention	1. Youth and immaturity of offender

[145] In accordance with the SOA 2003, s. 80 and schedule 3

An offender convicted of this offence is automatically subject to notification requirements when sentenced to imprisonment for a term of at least 12 months.[146]

Causing a child to watch a sexual act SG-134
(when committed by a person under the age of 18)

THIS IS A SPECIFIED OFFENCE FOR THE PURPOSES OF SECTION 224 CJA 2003

Intentionally causing a person under 16 to watch sexual activity or look at a photograph or pseudo-photograph of sexual activity for the purpose of obtaining sexual gratification (sections 12 and 13)

Maximum penalty: **5 years** (**10 years** if offender is 18 or over)

The starting points below are based upon a first-time offender aged 17 years old who pleaded not guilty. For younger offenders, sentencers should consider whether a lower starting point is justified in recognition of the offender's age or immaturity.

Type/nature of activity	Starting points	Sentencing ranges
Live sexual activity	**Detention and Training Order 8 months**	**Detention and Training Order 6–12 months**
CUSTODY THRESHOLD		
Moving or still images of people engaged in sexual acts involving penetration	**Community order**	**An appropriate non-custodial sentence***
Moving or still images of people engaged in sexual acts other than penetration	**Community order**	**An appropriate non-custodial sentence***

* 'Non-custodial sentence' in this context suggests a youth community order (as defined in the Criminal Justice Act 2003, section 147(2)) or a fine. In most instances, an offence will have crossed the threshold for a community order. However, in accordance with normal sentencing practice, a court is not precluded from imposing a financial penalty where that is determined to be the appropriate sentence.

Aggravating factors	Mitigating factors
1. Background of intimidation or coercion 2. Use of drugs, alcohol or other substance to facilitate the offence 3. Threats to prevent victim reporting the incident 4. Abduction or detention 5. Images of violent activity	1. Youth and immaturity of offender

An offender convicted of this offence is automatically subject to notification requirements when sentenced to imprisonment for a term of at least 12 months.[147]

Sexual activity with a child family member and Inciting a child family member to engage in sexual activity SG-135
(when committed by a person under the age of 18)

THIS IS A SERIOUS OFFENCE FOR THE PURPOSES OF SECTION 224 CJA 2003

Intentional sexual touching with a child family member (section 25)

Intentionally inciting sexual touching by a child family member (section 26)

Maximum penalty for both offences: **5 years** (**14 years** if offender is 18 or over)

The starting points below are based upon a first-time offender aged 17 years old who pleaded not guilty. For younger offenders, sentencers should consider whether a lower starting point is justified in recognition of the offender's age or immaturity.

[146] In accordance with the SOA 2003, s. 80 and schedule 3
[147] In accordance with the SOA 2003, s. 80 and schedule 3

Type/nature of activity	Starting points	Sentencing ranges
Offence involving penetration where one or more aggravating factors exist or where there is a substantial age gap between the parties	**Detention and Training Order 18 months**	**Detention and Training Order 6–24 months**
CUSTODY THRESHOLD		
Any form of sexual activity that does not involve any aggravating factors	**Community order**	**An appropriate non-custodial sentence***

* 'Non-custodial sentence' in this context suggests a youth community order (as defined in the Criminal Justice Act 2003, section 147(2)) or a fine. In most instances, an offence will have crossed the threshold for a community order. However, in accordance with normal sentencing practice, a court is not precluded from imposing a financial penalty where that is determined to be the appropriate sentence.

Aggravating factors	Mitigating factors
1. Background of intimidation or coercion 2. Use of drugs, alcohol or other substance 3. Threats deterring the victim from reporting the incident 4. Offender aware that he or she is suffering from a sexually transmitted infection	1. Small disparity in age between victim and offender 2. Relationship of genuine affection 3. Youth and immaturity of offender

An offender convicted of this offence is automatically subject to notification requirements when sentenced to imprisonment for a term of at least 12 months.[148]

SG-136

PART 9 FAIL TO SURRENDER TO BAIL

Foreword

This guideline applies to the sentencing of offenders convicted of failing to surrender to bail who are sentenced on or after **10 December 2007**. Bail Act offences are committed in significant numbers each year and are a major cause of disruption, delay and unnecessary cost for the criminal justice system. A prime objective of courts is to bring criminal proceedings to a conclusion as soon as practicable, and a rigorous and consistent response when offenders fail to answer bail is needed to help achieve this. This, in turn, may help to discourage future offending. Where it is not possible to dispose of the original offence, sentencing for a Bail Act offence should normally be undertaken separately and carried out as soon as appropriate in light of the circumstances of an individual case.

When a Bail Act offence has been committed, the sentence must be commensurate with the seriousness of the offence and must take into account both the reason why the offender failed to surrender and the degree of harm intended or caused. For these purposes, 'harm' is not only that caused to individual victims and witnesses but includes the consequential effect on police and court resources and the wider negative impact on public confidence in the criminal justice system.

As the considerations for offences committed by youths will differ markedly from those relevant for adult offenders, this guideline relates to the sentencing of adult offenders only.

SG-137

Fail to Surrender to Bail

A. Statutory provision

1. [Sets out the Bail Act 1976, s. 6 (see **D7.96**.)]
2. An offence under subsection (1) or (2) is punishable either on summary conviction or, in the Crown Court, as if it were a criminal contempt of court. The maximum sentence in a magistrates' court is 3 months imprisonment.[149] If the matter is committed to the Crown Court for sentence, or dealt with

[148] In accordance with the SOA 2003, s. 80 and schedule 3

[149] Police and Justice Act 2006, s.34 amends various sections of the Criminal Justice Act 2003 so that this maximum sentence is not affected by the general provisions relating to custodial sentences of less than 12 months when in force

there, the maximum sentence is 12 months custody and the sentence is subject to the usual appellate procedures.[150]

B. Assessing Seriousness **SG-138**

3. When assessing the seriousness of an offence, the court must consider the offender's culpability and any harm which the offence caused, was intended to cause or might foreseeably have caused.[151]
4. In assessing **culpability**, a court will need to consider whether the failure to surrender was intended to cause harm and, if so, what level of harm. In assessing **harm**, a court will need to consider to what extent the failure to surrender impeded the course of justice. When applied to Bail Act offences, 'harm' includes not only the harm caused to individual victims and witnesses but the consequential drain on police and court resources and the wider negative impact on public confidence in the criminal justice system.
5. The same *approach* to sentencing should be adopted whether the offence is committed contrary to section 6(1) or to section 6(2). However, the offence contrary to section 6(2) requires that there had been a reasonable excuse not to attend on the original date and so the degree of harm arising from the failure to attend as soon as reasonably practicable after that date is likely to be less. Accordingly, the seriousness of the offence is likely to be less also.

(i) Culpability

6. The obligation on a person who is granted bail is to surrender to custody at the court or the police station as required. The assessment of culpability requires consideration of the immediate reason why the defendant failed to appear. This can range from forgetfulness (comparable to the category of culpability described as 'negligence' in the Council guideline on seriousness[152]) or fear of the outcome of the hearing through to a deliberate act. Where the failure to surrender was deliberate, it will be relevant whether it was designed to disrupt the system to the defendant's advantage or whether the defendant simply gave no thought at all to the consequences.

(ii) Harm

7. Some degree of harm, even if only a minor delay or inconvenience to the authorities, will always be caused when a defendant fails to surrender. The degree of harm *actually* caused will vary considerably depending on the particular circumstances of the offence. The harm that the offence might foreseeably have caused[153] must also be taken into account.
8. **Failure to surrender to a court** for any reason (whether bail is granted by the police or by a court) inevitably delays justice. Potentially, it will result in additional distress to victims and witnesses. It will almost always waste public money in the form of court time and the resources of the prosecution, the police and the defence.
   (a) Where a defendant fails to appear for a first court hearing but attends shortly afterwards, the only harm caused is likely to be the financial cost to the system. Procedural delays may also be caused by the prosecution, the defence or the Courts Service at various stages of the process and, where a case could not have proceeded even if the defendant had surrendered to bail, this should be taken into account when assessing the harm actually caused.
   (b) Where a defendant appears for trial on the wrong day but enters a late guilty plea enabling the case to be disposed of to some degree at least (albeit with some delay and disruption), the harm caused by the delay may be offset by the benefits stemming from the change of plea.
   (c) The most serious harm is likely to result when a defendant fails to appear for trial, especially if this results in witnesses being sent away. A lengthy aborted trial in the Crown Court will be more harmful than a short hearing in a magistrates' court though each situation has the potential to affect public confidence in the system.
   (d) Where a court decides not to proceed to trial in the absence of the defendant (see paragraphs 34–39), interference with the course of justice may be particularly acute. Memories may become less certain with the passage of time. Victims and witnesses, many of whom find the prospect of preparing for and attending court daunting, are likely to be caused distress and/or inconvenience. They may find it more difficult to attend court on the second or subsequent occasion, to the extent that they may not even appear at all. In such circumstances the harm is very high

Sentencing Guidelines

[150] Administration of Justice Act 1960, s.13
[151] Criminal Justice Act 2003, s.143(1)
[152] *Overarching Principles: Seriousness*, page 4, www.sentencing-guidelines.gov.uk
[153] Criminal Justice Act, s.143(1)

because justice will be prevented. Victims of violent or sexual offences are particularly likely to be distressed to learn that the accused is 'at large' in defiance of the court.

(e) The level of harm is likely to be assessed as high where an offender fails to appear for sentence and is also seen to be flouting the authority of the court, such as where the avoidance of sentence results in the consequential avoidance of ancillary orders such as disqualification from driving or from working with children or vulnerable adults, the payment of compensation or registration as a sex offender. This may increase the level of harm whenever the offender continues to present a risk to public safety.

9. In general terms, the same approach to sentencing should be adopted whether the offence involves a failure to surrender to a court or to a police station since the legal obligation is the same. However, the harm that results from failure to surrender to a court will usually be greater than that resulting from failure to surrender to a police station and this will affect the assessment of the seriousness of an individual offence.

10. **Failure to surrender to a police station** results in police time being wasted and the course of justice being impeded; potentially, it can also result in victims and witnesses being distressed and concerned about their safety and the ability of the system to protect the public and deliver justice. However, the circumstances in which such bail is granted are less formal than the grant of court bail and the history of the individual case should be examined. There may be less culpability where bail has been enlarged on a number of occasions and less harm if *court* proceedings are not significantly delayed.

(iii) Nature and seriousness of original offence

11. Failure to surrender to custody is an offence in its own right and the sentence imposed should be proportionate to the seriousness of the offending behaviour itself. Where the Bail Act offence is sentenced in advance of the offence in relation to which bail was granted the assessment of seriousness will take place without reference to the seriousness of, or likely sentence for, the original offence.

12. However, the specific nature of the original offence may significantly affect the harm or likelihood of harm caused by the failure to surrender. Particular types of offence (such as violent or sexual offences) may have implications for public protection and safety and the offender's failure to surrender might cause fear and distress to witnesses.

13. Seriousness is not reduced automatically by subsequent acquittal of the original offence. Whilst it may seem harsh that a defendant before the court for an offence of which he is not guilty should be punished for the ancillary offence of failure to surrender during the course of the prosecution of that offence, both the culpability and the likely harm – delay, distress and inconvenience to witnesses, and additional costs—are the same. Moreover, one of the most serious effects of a Bail Act offence can be that a trial cannot take place because of the failure to surrender and it will often be invidious to expect a court to identify genuinely innocent defendants.

(iv) Aggravating and mitigating factors

14. Since 'recent and relevant' previous convictions aggravate the seriousness of an offence,[154] defendants who repeatedly fail to attend court are likely to receive more severe sentences.

15. The period of time for which a defendant absconds is also likely to influence the court when considering sentence. Whilst being absent for a long period of time will aggravate an offence, the fact that a defendant arrives at court only a few days, or even only a few hours, late, is not a factor that will necessarily mitigate sentence; in many cases, the harm will already have been done (for example, the trial may have been put back, witnesses may have been inconvenienced and there may be an increased likelihood that witnesses will fail to attend at a future hearing).

16. Leaving the jurisdiction is an aggravating factor as are other actions designed to avoid the jurisdiction of the court such as changing identity and appearance.

17. **The following aggravating factors are particularly relevant to an offence of failing to surrender to bail:**
    - Repeat offending
    - Offender's absence causes a lengthy delay to the administration of justice
    - Determined attempt to avoid the jurisdiction of the court

18. Prompt voluntary surrender might mitigate sentence where it saves police time in tracing and arresting an offender. It may also be an indication of remorse. This must be weighed against the degree of harm caused by the offence, which may still be significant. Surrender initiated by the offender merits consideration as a mitigating factor. Surrender in response to follow up action has no significance.

[154] ibid. s.143(2)

19. The fact that an offender has a disorganised or chaotic lifestyle, which may be due to a dependency on drugs or alcohol, does not of itself reduce the seriousness of the offence. Depending on the particular facts, it may be regarded as personal mitigation.
20. A misunderstanding (which does not amount to a defence) may be a mitigating factor but must be differentiated from a mistake on the part of the defendant, where the error must be regarded as his or her own responsibility.[155]
21. Where an offender has literacy or language difficulties, steps should normally be taken by the police or the court to address this when bail is granted. Such difficulties may be mitigation (where they do not amount to a defence but contribute to the offender failing to surrender to bail) where potential problems were not identified and/or appropriate steps were not taken to mitigate the risk in the circumstances as known at the time that bail is granted.
22. An offender's position as the sole or primary carer of dependant relatives may be personal mitigation when it is the reason why the offender has failed to surrender to custody.
23. **The following mitigating factors are particularly relevant to an offence of failing to surrender:**
    - prompt voluntary surrender;

    and, where they are not sufficient to amount to a defence:
    - misunderstanding;
    - a failure to comprehend the requirements or significance of bail;
    - caring responsibilities.

C. Procedural issues SG-139

(i) When to sentence

24. The key principle is that a court should *deal* with a defendant who fails to surrender *as soon as is practicable* even if the trial or other hearing for the offence that led to the grant of bail is adjourned.[156] The following factors are relevant to the decision as to what is practicable:
    - when the proceedings in respect of which bail was granted are expected to conclude;
    - the seriousness of the offence for which the defendant is already being prosecuted;
    - the type of penalty that might be imposed for the breach of bail and for the original offence;
    - any other relevant circumstances.
25. Whether or not the defendant is guilty of a Bail Act offence should be determined as soon as possible. It will be central to the issue of whether bail should now be granted or refused. Even where the offence is denied, a trial is normally short; it should be held on the first appearance after arrest or surrender, unless an adjournment is necessary (for example, for the defence to obtain medical evidence).
26. When there is a plea or finding of guilt, sentence should be imposed *as soon as practicable*. The point at which it becomes possible to sentence an offence and the point at which it is practicable to do so will vary widely from case to case; a decision about timing is best made according to individual circumstances.
27. A key relevant circumstance is whether the substantive offence is to be adjourned, either for a pre-sentence report or for trial, and whether the remand is to be on bail or in custody.
28. Where the defendant is remanded in custody, the sentencing options for the Bail Act offence are limited.
29. Where the defendant is to regain his or her liberty, there is the possibility of a noncustodial sentence. A community order, including an electronically monitored curfew requirement and, perhaps, a supervision requirement or an activity requirement may be helpful in ensuring attendance at future court hearings.
30. In more serious cases in which the custody threshold has been passed, a suspended sentence order could serve the same purpose.
31. These factors support sentencing without delay or with a short delay for a presentence report. On the other hand, there will be occasions when it is more appropriate that all outstanding matters should be dealt with on one sentencing occasion. This may be where the totality of offending may affect sentence type (for example where two or more offences together pass the custody threshold, but individually do not) or where the harm caused by the failure to surrender cannot be assessed at an early stage (for example, where witnesses may no longer be available).
32. A magistrates' court will be constrained by the maximum sentence available. In certain circumstances, Bail Act offences that would normally be dealt with in a magistrates' court may be committed to the Crown Court to be dealt with.[157]

[155] See, for example, *Laidlaw v Atkinson* Queen's Bench Division CO/275/86
[156] See Consolidated Criminal Practice Direction last revised April 2007— www.hmcourtsservice.gov.uk/cms/pds.htm
[157] Bail Act 1976, s.6(6)

(ii) Consecutive and concurrent custodial sentences

33. Where a custodial sentence is imposed for the original offence and a custodial sentence is also deemed appropriate for a Bail Act offence, a court should normally impose a consecutive sentence. However, a concurrent sentence will be appropriate where otherwise the overall sentence would be disproportionate to the combined seriousness of the offences.

(iii) Conducting trials in the absence of the defendant

34. A defendant has a duty to surrender to bail and a right to be present at his or her trial. However, where a defendant is absent voluntarily, having breached the duty to surrender, a court may proceed to hear a case in the defendant's absence. In a magistrates' court this is a statutory power.[158] While some sentences may be imposed in a defendant's absence, it is not possible to impose a custodial sentence or a community order, and it is undesirable to impose a disqualification from driving.
35. The Consolidated Criminal Practice Direction[159] reinforces the encouragement to courts to proceed in absence and identifies factors to be taken into account before so doing which include:
    - the conduct of the defendant;
    - the disadvantage to the defendant;
    - the public interest;
    - the effect of any delay; and
    - whether the attendance of the defendant could be secured at a later hearing.
36. Additional factors for a magistrates' court to consider include:
    - there is less risk of either a magistrate or a district judge drawing an impermissible inference from a defendant's absence than would be the case with a jury; and
    - in a magistrates' court the finder of fact may ask questions and test the evidence of prosecution witnesses.
37. The overriding concern of the court is to ensure that a trial conducted in the absence of the defendant is as fair as circumstances permit and, in particular, that the defendant's rights under Article 6 of the European Convention on Human Rights (ECHR)[160] are not infringed.
38. Proceeding to trial in the absence of the defendant may reduce the harm arising from a Bail Act offence. When considering the degree to which this should influence sentence, it must be borne in mind that the position in a magistrates' court is different from that in the Crown Court. An appeal against conviction from a magistrates' court can result in a re-hearing, whereas that is not the case after a jury trial. There is also the discretionary power under section 142 of the Magistrates' Courts Act 1980 to set aside a conviction and order a re-hearing in a magistrates' court. If an application to set aside a conviction is successful, witnesses will be required to give evidence again at a later date. It will be relevant to an assessment of harm whether either of those provisions has been used.
39. Where it has proved possible to proceed to trial or conclude proceedings in the absence of the defendant, this should have no bearing on *culpability* for a Bail Act offence as the intention of the defendant remains unchanged. It may, however, be relevant to the assessment of *harm* as this may have been reduced or avoided because of the decision to proceed in absence.

SG-140 **D. Sentencing ranges and starting points**

(i) This guideline applies to a first time offender who has been convicted after a trial. A first time offender is a person who does not have a conviction which, by virtue of section 143(2) of the Criminal Justice Act 2003, must be treated as an aggravating factor.

(ii) The guideline establishes levels of seriousness based upon both offender culpability and the resulting consequences. These are set out in the column headed 'nature of failure and harm'.

(iii) A court will identify the description that most nearly matches the particular facts of the offence and this will identify a starting point from which the sentencer can depart to reflect any aggravating or mitigating factors affecting the *seriousness of the offence* to reach a provisional sentence.

(iv) The sentencing range is the bracket into which the provisional sentence will normally fall. The particular circumstances may, however, make it appropriate that the provisional sentence falls outside the range.

(v) Where the offender has previous convictions which aggravate the seriousness of the current offence, that may take the provisional sentence beyond the range given particularly where there are significant other aggravating factors present.

---

[158] Magistrates' Courts Act 1980, s.11

[159] Last revised April 2007—www.hmcourts-service.gov.uk/cms/pds.htm

[160] Right to a fair trial

(vi) Once the provisional sentence has been identified by reference to those factors affecting the seriousness of the offence, the court will take into account any relevant factors of personal mitigation, which may take the sentence beyond the range given.
(vii) Where there has been a guilty plea, any reduction attributable to that plea will be applied to the sentence at this stage. Again, this reduction may take the sentence below the range provided.
(viii) A court must give its reasons for imposing a sentence of a different kind or outside the range provided in the guidelines.[161]

The Decision Making Process

[Sets out the standard sequential decision making process: identify starting point, consider aggravating factors, consider mitigating factors, apply reduction for guilty plea, review in light of the totality principle and give reasons.]

E. Factors to take into consideration **SG-141**

1. Whilst the approach to sentencing should generally be the same whether the defendant failed to surrender to a court or to a police station and whether the offence is contrary to section 6(1) or 6(2), the court must examine all the relevant circumstances.
2. Whilst the seriousness of the original offence does not of itself aggravate or mitigate the seriousness of the offence of failing to surrender, the circumstances surrounding the original offence may be relevant in assessing the harm arising from this offence.
3. Where it has proved possible to conclude proceedings in the absence of the defendant, this may be relevant to the assessment of harm caused.
4. Where the failure to surrender to custody was 'deliberate';
    - at or near the bottom of the range will be cases where the defendant gave no thought at all to the consequences, or other mitigating factors are present, and the degree of delay or interference with the progress of the case was not significant in all the circumstances;
    - at or near the top of the range will be cases where any of aggravating factors 1–3 are present if there is also a significant delay and/or interference with the progress of the case.
5. Only the most common aggravating and mitigating factors specifically relevant to Bail Act offences are included in the guideline. When assessing the seriousness of an offence, the courts must always have regard to the full list of aggravating and mitigating factors in the Council guideline on Seriousness.[162]
6. A previous conviction that is likely to be 'relevant' for the purposes of this offence is one which demonstrates failure to comply with an order of a court.
7. Acquittal of the original offence does not automatically mitigate this offence.
8. The fact that an offender has a disorganised or chaotic lifestyle should not normally be treated as mitigation of the offence, but may be regarded as personal mitigation depending on the particular facts of a case.
9. Once the provisional sentence has been identified by reference to factors affecting the seriousness of the offence, the court will take into account any relevant factors of personal mitigation, and any reduction where a guilty plea was entered.[163]
10. The sentence for this offence should normally be in addition to any sentence for the original offence. Where custodial sentences are being imposed for a Bail Act offence and the original offence at the same time, the normal approach should be for the sentences to be consecutive. The length of any custodial sentence imposed must be commensurate with the seriousness of the offence(s).[164]
11. If an offence is serious enough to justify imposition of a community order, a curfew requirement with an electronic monitoring requirement may be a particularly appropriate part of such an order in any of the three sentencing ranges.
12. Power exists for magistrates' courts to impose one day's detention in appropriate cases.[165]

BAIL ACT 1976, ss. 6(1) & 6(2) **SG-142**

Maximum penalty: 12 months imprisonment in the Crown Court
3 months imprisonment in a magistrates' court

[161] Criminal Justice Act 2003, s.174(2)(a)
[162] *Overarching Principles: Seriousness*, pages 6–7, published 16 December 2004, www.sentencing-guidelines.gov.uk
[163] Reduction in sentence for a guilty plea (revised), published July 2007, www.sentencing-guidelines.gov.uk
[164] Criminal Justice Act 2003, s.152(2)
[165] Magistrates' Courts Act 1980, s.135

The following starting points and sentencing ranges are for a first time offender aged 18 or over who pleaded not guilty. They should be applied as set out . . . above.

Nature of failure & harm	Starting point	Sentencing range
Deliberate failure to attend causing delay and/or interference with the administration of justice. *The type and degree of harm actually caused will affect where in the range the case falls. See guidance. . .*	**14 days custody**	*Crown Court* **Community order (medium)— 40 weeks custody** *Magistrates' court* **Community order (low)— 10 weeks custody**
Negligent or non-deliberate failure to attend causing delay and/or interference with the administration of justice	**Fine**	**Fine—Community order (medium)**
Surrenders late on day but case proceeds as planned	**Fine**	**Fine**

Additional aggravating factors	Additional mitigating factors
1. Lengthy absence 2. Serious attempts to evade justice 3. Determined attempt seriously to undermine the course of justice 4. Previous relevant convictions and/or repeated breach of court orders or police bail	1. Prompt voluntary surrender *When not amounting to a defence:* 2. Misunderstanding 3. A failure to comprehend bail significance or requirements 4. Caring responsibilities [see para. 22 for further detail.]

SG-143 PART 10 ASSAULT DEFINITIVE GUIDELINE (CROWN COURT)

[Note: This definitive guideline was the first to be issued by the Sentencing Council: see **E1.2**.]

SG-144 Applicability of Guideline

In accordance with section 120 of the Coroners and Justice Act 2009, the Sentencing Council issues this definitive guideline. It applies to all offenders aged 18 and older, who are sentenced on or after 13 June 2011, regardless of the date of the offence.

Section 125(1) of the Coroners and Justice Act 2009 provides that when sentencing offences committed after 6 April 2010:

'Every court—

(a) must, in sentencing an offender, follow any sentencing guideline which is relevant to the offender's case, and

(b) must, in exercising any other function relating to the sentencing of offenders, follow any sentencing guidelines which are relevant to the exercise of the function,

unless the court is satisfied that it would be contrary to the interests of justice to do so.'

This guideline applies only to offenders aged 18 and older. General principles to be considered in the sentencing of youths are in the Sentencing Guidelines Council's definitive guideline, *Overarching Principles—Sentencing Youths* [see **SG-406**].

SG-145 Structure, ranges and starting points

For the purposes of section 125(3)–(4) of the Coroners and Justice Act 2009, the guideline specifies *offence ranges*—the range of sentences appropriate for each type of offence. Within each offence, the Council has specified three *categories* which reflect varying degrees of seriousness. The offence range is split into *category ranges*—sentences appropriate for each level of seriousness. The Council has also identified a starting point within each category.

Starting points define the position within a category range from which to start calculating the provisional sentence. **Starting points apply to all offences within the corresponding category and are applicable to all offenders in all cases irrespective of plea or previous convictions.** Once the starting point is established the court should consider further aggravating and mitigating factors and previous convictions so as to adjust the sentence within the range. Credit for a guilty plea is taken into consideration only at step 4 in the process, after the appropriate sentence has been identified.

Information on community orders and fine bands is [available at **SG-282**].

Causing Grievous Bodily Harm with Intent to do Grievous Bodily Harm/ Wounding with Intent to do Grievous Bodily Harm **SG-146**

Offences against the Person Act 1861 (section 18)

This is a serious specified offence for the purposes of section 224 of the Criminal Justice Act 2003

Triable only on indictment
Maximum: Life imprisonment

Offence range: 3–16 years' custody

STEP ONE Determining the offence category

The court should determine the offence category using the table below.

Category 1	Greater harm (serious injury must normally be present) **and** higher culpability
Category 2	Greater harm (serious injury must normally be present) **and** lower culpability; **or** lesser harm **and** higher culpability
Category 3	Lesser harm **and** lower culpability

The court should determine the offender's culpability and the harm caused, or intended, by reference only to the factors below (as demonstrated by the presence of one or more). These factors comprise the principal factual elements of the offence and should determine the category.

Factors indicating greater harm Injury (which includes disease transmission and/or psychological harm) which is serious in the context of the offence (must normally be present) Victim is particularly vulnerable because of personal circumstances Sustained or repeated assault on the same victim **Factors indicating lesser harm** Injury which is less serious in the context of the offence	**Factors indicating higher culpability** *Statutory aggravating factors:* Offence racially or religiously aggravated Offence motivated by, or demonstrating, hostility to the victim based on his or her sexual orientation (or presumed sexual orientation) Offence motivated by, or demonstrating, hostility to the victim based on the victim's disability (or presumed disability) *Other aggravating factors:* A significant degree of premeditation Use of weapon or weapon equivalent (for example, shod foot, headbutting, use of acid, use of animal) Intention to commit more serious harm than actually resulted from the offence Deliberately causes more harm than is necessary for commission of offence Deliberate targeting of vulnerable victim Leading role in group or gang Offence motivated by, or demonstrating, hostility based on the victim's age, sex, gender identity (or presumed gender identity) **Factors indicating lower culpability** Subordinate role in group or gang A greater degree of provocation than normally expected Lack of premeditation Mental disorder or learning disability, where linked to commission of the offence Excessive self defence

STEP TWO Starting point and category range

Having determined the category, the court should use the corresponding starting points to reach a sentence within the category range below. The starting point applies to all offenders irrespective of plea or previous convictions. A case of particular gravity, reflected by multiple features of culpability in step one, could merit upward adjustment from the starting point before further adjustment for aggravating or mitigating features, set out below.

Offence category	Starting Point (*Applicable to all Offenders*)	Category Range (*Applicable to all Offenders*)
Category 1	12 years' custody	9–16 years' custody
Category 2	6 years' custody	5–9 years' custody
Category 3	4 years' custody	3–5 years' custody

The table below contains a non-exhaustive list of additional factual elements providing the context of the offence and factors relating to the offender. Identify whether any combination of these, or other relevant factors, should result in an upward or downward adjustment from the starting point. In some cases, having considered these factors, it may be appropriate to move outside the identified category range.

Factors increasing seriousness *Statutory aggravating factors:* Previous convictions, having regard to a) the nature of the offence to which the conviction relates and its relevance to the current offence; and b) the time that has elapsed since the conviction Offence committed whilst on bail *Other aggravating factors include:* Location of the offence Timing of the offence Ongoing effect upon the victim Offence committed against those working in the public sector or providing a service to the public Presence of others including relatives, especially children or partner of the victim Gratuitous degradation of victim In domestic violence cases, victim forced to leave their home Failure to comply with current court orders Offence committed whilst on licence An attempt to conceal or dispose of evidence Failure to respond to warnings or concerns expressed by others about the offender's behaviour Commission of offence whilst under the influence of alcohol or drugs Abuse of power and/or position of trust	Exploiting contact arrangements with a child to commit an offence Previous violence or threats to the same victim Established evidence of community impact Any steps taken to prevent the victim reporting an incident, or obtaining assistance and/or from assisting or supporting the prosecution Offences taken into consideration (TICs) **Factors reducing seriousness or reflecting personal mitigation** No previous convictions **or** no relevant/recent convictions Single blow Remorse Good character and/or exemplary conduct Determination, and/or demonstration of steps taken to address addiction or offending behaviour Serious medical conditions requiring urgent, intensive or long-term treatment Isolated incident Age and/or lack of maturity where it affects the responsibility of the offender Lapse of time since the offence where this is not the fault of the offender Mental disorder or learning disability, where **not** linked to the commission of the offence Sole or primary carer for dependent relatives

STEP THREE **Consider any other factors which indicate a reduction, such as assistance to the prosecution**

The court should take into account sections 73 and 74 of the Serious Organised Crime and Police Act 2005 (assistance by defendants: reduction or review of sentence) and any other rule of law by virtue of which an offender may receive a discounted sentence in consequence of assistance given (or offered) to the prosecutor or investigator.

STEP FOUR **Reduction for Guilty Pleas**

The court should take account of any potential reduction for a guilty plea in accordance with section 144 of the Criminal Justice Act 2003 and the *Guilty Plea* guideline.

STEP FIVE **Dangerousness**

Causing grievous bodily harm with intent to do grievous bodily harm/wounding with intent to do grievous bodily harm is a serious offence within the meaning of Chapter 5 of the Criminal Justice Act 2003 and at this stage the court should consider whether having regard to the criteria contained in that Chapter it would be appropriate to award a life sentence, imprisonment for public protection or an extended sentence. Where offenders meet the dangerousness criteria, the notional determinate sentence should be used as the basis for the setting of a minimum term.

STEP SIX **Totality Principle**

If sentencing an offender for more than one offence, or where the offender is already serving a sentence, consider whether the total sentence is just and proportionate to the offending behaviour.

STEP SEVEN **Compensation and ancillary orders**

In all cases, the court should consider whether to make compensation and/or other ancillary orders.

STEP EIGHT Reasons

Section 174 of the Criminal Justice Act 2003 imposes a duty to give reasons for, and explain the effect of, the sentence.

STEP NINE Consideration for remand time

Sentencers should take into consideration any remand time served in relation to the final sentence. The court should consider whether to give credit for time spent on remand in custody or on bail in accordance with sections 240 and 240A of the Criminal Justice Act 2003.

Inflicting Grievous Bodily Harm/Unlawful Wounding SG-147

Offences against the Person Act 1861 (section 20)

Racially/Religiously Aggravated GBH/Unlawful Wounding

Crime and Disorder Act 1998 (section 29)

These are specified offences for the purposes of section 224 of the Criminal Justice Act 2003

Triable either way
Maximum (section 20): 5 years
Maximum (section 29): 7 years

Offence range: Community order—4 years' custody

STEP ONE Determining the offence category

Category 1	Greater harm (serious injury must normally be present) **and** higher culpability
Category 2	Greater harm (serious injury must normally be present) **and** lower culpability; **or** lesser harm **and** higher culpability
Category 3	Lesser harm **and** lower culpability

The court should determine the offender's culpability and the harm caused, or intended, by reference only to the factors below (as demonstrated by the presence of one or more). These factors comprise the principal factual elements of the offence and should determine the category.

Factors indicating greater harm Injury (which includes disease transmission and/or psychological harm) which is serious in the context of the offence (must normally be present) Victim is particularly vulnerable because of personal circumstances Sustained or repeated assault on the same victim	**Factors indicating lesser harm** Injury which is less serious in the context of the offence
Factors indicating higher culpability *Statutory aggravating factors:* Offence motivated by, or demonstrating, hostility to the victim based on his or her sexual orientation (or presumed sexual orientation) Offence motivated by, or demonstrating, hostility to the victim based on the victim's disability (or presumed disability) *Other aggravating factors:* A significant degree of premeditation Use of weapon or weapon equivalent (for example, shod foot, headbutting, use of acid, use of animal) Intention to commit more serious harm than actually resulted from the offence Deliberately causes more harm than is necessary for commission of offence Deliberate targeting of vulnerable victim Leading role in group or gang Offence motivated by, or demonstrating, hostility based on the victim's age, sex, gender identity (or presumed gender identity)	**Factors indicating lower culpability** Subordinate role in a group or gang A greater degree of provocation than normally expected Lack of premeditation Mental disorder or learning disability, where linked to commission of the offence Excessive self defence

STEP TWO Starting Point and Category Range

Having determined the category, the court should use the corresponding starting points to reach a sentence within the category range below. The starting point applies to all offenders irrespective of plea or previous convictions. A case of particular gravity, reflected by multiple features of culpability in step one, could merit upward adjustment from the starting point before further adjustment for aggravating or mitigating features, set out below.

Offence Category	Starting Point (*Applicable to all offenders*)	Category Range (*Applicable to all offenders*)
Category 1	3 years' custody	2 years 6 months'—4 years' custody
Category 2	1 year 6 months' custody	1–3 years' custody
Category 3	High level community order	Low level community order—51 weeks' custody

The table below contains a **non-exhaustive** list of additional factual elements providing the context of the offence and factors relating to the offender. Identify whether any combination of these, or other relevant factors, should result in an upward or downward adjustment from the starting point. In some cases, having considered these factors, it may be appropriate to move outside the identified category range.

When sentencing **category 3 offences**, the court should also consider the custody threshold as follows:

- has the custody threshold been passed?
- if so, is it unavoidable that a custodial sentence be imposed?
- if so, can that sentence be suspended?

Factors increasing seriousness	Factors reducing seriousness or reflecting personal mitigation
Statutory aggravating factors: Previous convictions, having regard to a) the nature of the offence to which the conviction relates and its relevance to the current offence; and b) the time that has elapsed since the conviction Offence committed whilst on bail *Other aggravating factors include:* Location of the offence Timing of the offence Ongoing effect upon the victim Offence committed against those working in the public sector or providing a service to the public Presence of others including relatives, especially children or partner of the victim Gratuitous degradation of victim In domestic violence cases, victim forced to leave their home Failure to comply with current court orders Offence committed whilst on licence An attempt to conceal or dispose of evidence Failure to respond to warnings or concerns expressed by others about the offender's behaviour Commission of offence whilst under the influence of alcohol or drugs Abuse of power and/or position of trust Exploiting contact arrangements with a child to commit an offence Established evidence of community impact Any steps taken to prevent the victim reporting an incident, obtaining assistance and/or from assisting or supporting the prosecution Offences taken into consideration (TICs)	No previous convictions **or** no relevant/recent convictions Single blow Remorse Good character and/or exemplary conduct Determination and/or demonstration of steps taken to address addiction or offending behaviour Serious medical conditions requiring urgent, intensive or long-term treatment Isolated incident Age and/or lack of maturity where it affects the responsibility of the offender Lapse of time since the offence where this is not the fault of the offender Mental disorder or learning disability, where **not** linked to the commission of the offence Sole or primary carer for dependent relatives

Section 29 offences only: The court should determine the appropriate sentence for the offence without taking account of the element of aggravation and then make an addition to the sentence, considering the level of aggravation involved. It may be appropriate to move outside the identified category range, taking into account the increased statutory maximum.

STEP THREE Consider any other factors which indicate a reduction, such as assistance to the prosecution

The court should take into account sections 73 and 74 of the Serious Organised Crime and Police Act 2005 (assistance by defendants: reduction or review of sentence) and any other rule of law by virtue of which an offender may receive a discounted sentence in consequence of assistance given (or offered) to the prosecutor or investigator.

STEP FOUR Reduction for guilty pleas

The court should take account of any potential reduction for a guilty plea in accordance with section 144 of the Criminal Justice Act 2003 and the *Guilty Plea* guideline.

STEP FIVE Dangerousness

Inflicting grievous bodily harm/Unlawful wounding and racially/religiously aggravated GBH/Unlawful wounding are specified offences within the meaning of Chapter 5 of the Criminal Justice Act 2003 and at this stage the court should consider whether having regard to the criteria contained in that Chapter it would be appropriate to award an extended sentence.

[Steps Six to Nine are almost identical to those which apply for causing grievous bodily harm with intent: see **SG-146**.]

Assault Occasioning Actual Bodily Harm **SG-148**

Offences against the Person Act 1861 (section 47)

Racially/Religiously Aggravated ABH

Crime and Disorder Act 1998 (section 29)

These are specified offences for the purposes of section 224 of the Criminal Justice Act 2003

Triable either way
Maximum (section 47): 5 years' custody
Maximum (section 29): 7 years' custody

Offence range: Fine—3 years' custody

STEP ONE Determining the offence category

The court should determine the offence category using the table below.

Category 1	Greater harm (serious injury must normally be present) **and** higher culpability
Category 2	Greater harm (serious injury must normally be present) **and** lower culpability; **or** lesser harm **and** higher culpability
Category 3	Lesser harm **and** lower culpability

The court should determine the offender's culpability and the harm caused, or intended, by reference only to the factors identified in the table below (as demonstrated by the presence of one or more). These factors comprise the principal factual elements of the offence and should determine the category.

Factors indicating greater harm	Factors indicating lesser harm
Injury (which includes disease transmission and/or psychological harm) which is serious in the context of the offence (must normally be present) Victim is particularly vulnerable because of personal circumstances Sustained or repeated assault on the same victim	Injury which is less serious in the context of the offence
Factors indicating higher culpability *Statutory aggravating factors:* Offence motivated by, or demonstrating, hostility to the victim based on his or her sexual orientation (or presumed sexual orientation) Offence motivated by, or demonstrating, hostility to the victim based on the victim's disability (or presumed disability) *Other aggravating factors:* A significant degree of premeditation Use of weapon or weapon equivalent (for example, shod foot, headbutting, use of acid, use of animal) Intention to commit more serious harm than actually resulted from the offence Deliberately causes more harm than is necessary for commission of offence Deliberate targeting of vulnerable victim Leading role in group or gang Offence motivated by, or demonstrating, hostility based on the victim's age, sex, gender identity (or presumed gender identity)	**Factors indicating lower culpability** Subordinate role in group or gang A greater degree of provocation than normally expected Lack of premeditation Mental disorder or learning disability, where linked to commission of the offence Excessive self defence

STEP TWO Starting Point and Category Range

Having determined the category, the court should use the corresponding starting points to reach a sentence within the category range below. The starting point applies to all offenders irrespective of plea or previous convictions. A case of particular gravity, reflected by multiple features of culpability in step one, could merit upward adjustment from the starting point before further adjustment for aggravating or mitigating features, set out below.

Offence category	Starting Point (*Applicable to all offenders*)	Category Range (*Applicable to all offenders*)
Category 1	1 year 6 months' custody	1–3 years' custody
Category 2	26 weeks' custody	Low level community order—51 weeks' custody
Category3	Medium level community order	Band A fine—High level community order

The table below contains a **non-exhaustive** list of additional factual elements providing the context of the offence and factors relating to the offender. Identify whether any combination of these, or other relevant factors, should result in an upward or downward adjustment from the starting point. In some cases, having considered these factors, it may be appropriate to move outside the identified category range.

When sentencing **category 2** offences, the court should also consider the custody threshold as follows:

- as the custody threshold been passed?
- if so, is it unavoidable that a custodial sentence be imposed?
- if so, can that sentence be suspended?

When sentencing **category 3** offences, the court should also consider the community order threshold as follows:

- has the community order threshold been passed?

Factors increasing seriousness	Factors reducing seriousness or reflecting personal mitigation
Statutory aggravating factors: Previous convictions, having regard to a) the nature of the offence to which the conviction relates and its relevance to the current offence; and b) the time that has elapsed since the conviction Offence committed whilst on bail *Other aggravating factors include:* Location of the offence Timing of the offence Ongoing effect upon the victim Offence committed against those working in the public sector or providing a service to the public Presence of others including relatives, especially children or partner of the victim Gratuitous degradation of victim In domestic violence cases, victim forced to leave their home Failure to comply with current court orders Offence committed whilst on licence An attempt to conceal or dispose of evidence Failure to respond to warnings or concerns expressed by others about the offender's behaviour Commission of offence whilst under the influence of alcohol or drugs Abuse of power and/or position of trust Exploiting contact arrangements with a child to commit an offence Established evidence of community impact Any steps taken to prevent the victim reporting an incident, obtaining assistance and/or from assisting or supporting the prosecution Offences taken into consideration (TICs)	No previous convictions **or** no relevant/recent convictions Single blow Remorse Good character and/or exemplary conduct Determination and/or demonstration of steps taken to address addiction or offending behaviour Serious medical conditions requiring urgent, intensive or long-term treatment Isolated incident Age and/or lack of maturity where it affects the responsibility of the offender Lapse of time since the offence where this is not the fault of the offender Mental disorder or learning disability, where **not** linked to the commission of the offence Sole or primary carer for dependent relatives

Section 29 offences only: The court should determine the appropriate sentence for the offence without taking account of the element of aggravation and then make an addition to the sentence, considering the level of aggravation involved. It may be appropriate to move outside the identified category range, taking into account the increased statutory maximum.

[Steps Three to Nine are almost identical to those for inflicting grievous bodily harm: see **SG-146**.]

Assault with Intent to Resist Arrest **SG-149**

Offences against the Person Act 1861 (section 38)

This is a specified offence for the purposes of section 224 of the Criminal Justice Act 2003

Triable either way
Maximum 2 years' custody

Offence range: Fine—51 weeks' custody

STEP ONE Determining the offence category

The court should determine the offence category using the table below.

Category 1	Greater harm **and** higher culpability
Category 2	Greater harm **and** lower culpability; **or** lesser harm **and** higher culpability
Category 3	Lesser harm **and** lower culpability

The court should determine the offender's culpability and the harm caused, or intended, by reference **only** to the factors identified in the table below (as demonstrated by the presence of one or more). These factors comprise the principal factual elements of the offence and should determine the category.

Factors indicating greater harm Sustained or repeated assault on the same victim **Factors indicating higher culpability** *Statutory aggravating factors:* Offence racially or religiously aggravated Offence motivated by, or demonstrating, hostility to the victim based on his or her sexual orientation (or presumed sexual orientation) Offence motivated by, or demonstrating, hostility to the victim based on the victim's disability (or presumed disability) *Other aggravating factors:* A significant degree of premeditation Use of weapon or weapon equivalent (for example, shod foot, headbutting, use of acid, use of animal) Intention to commit more serious harm than actually resulted from the offence Deliberately causes more harm than is necessary for commission of offence Leading role in group or gang Offence motivated by, or demonstrating, hostility based on the victim's age, sex, gender identity (or presumed gender identity)	**Factors indicating lesser harm** Injury which is less serious in the context of the offence **Factors indicating lower culpability** Subordinate role in group or gang Lack of premeditation Mental disorder or learning disability, where linked to commission of the offence

STEP TWO Starting Point and Category Range

Having determined the category, the court should use the corresponding starting points to reach a sentence within the category range below. The starting point applies to all offenders irrespective of plea or previous convictions. A case of particular gravity, reflected by multiple features of culpability in step one, could merit upward adjustment from the starting point before further adjustment for aggravating or mitigating features, set out below.

Offence Category	**Starting Point** (*Applicable to all offenders*)	**Category Range** (*Applicable to all offenders*)
Category 1	26 weeks' custody	12 weeks'—51 weeks' custody
Category 2	Medium level community order	Low level community order—High level community order
Category 3	Band B fine	Band A fine—Band C fine

The table below contains a **non-exhaustive** list of additional factual elements providing the context of the offence and factors relating to the offender. Identify whether any combination of these, or other relevant factors, should result in an upward or downward adjustment from the starting point. In some cases, having considered these factors, it may be appropriate to move outside the identified category range.

When sentencing **category 1** offences, the court should consider whether the sentence can be suspended.

Factors increasing seriousness	Factors reducing seriousness or reflecting personal mitigation
Statutory aggravating factors: Previous convictions, having regard to a) the nature of the offence to which the conviction relates and its relevance to the current offence; and b) the time that has elapsed since the conviction Offence committed whilst on bail *Other aggravating factors include:* Location of the offence Timing of the offence Ongoing effect upon the victim Gratuitous degradation of victim Failure to comply with current court orders Offence committed whilst on licence An attempt to conceal or dispose of evidence Failure to respond to warnings or concerns expressed by others about the offender's behaviour Commission of offence whilst under the influence of alcohol or drugs Established evidence of community impact Any steps taken to prevent the victim reporting an incident, obtaining assistance and/or from assisting or supporting the prosecution Offences taken into consideration (TICs)	No previous convictions **or** no relevant/recent convictions Single blow Remorse Good character and/or exemplary conduct Determination and/or demonstration of steps taken to address addiction or offending behaviour Serious medical conditions requiring urgent, intensive or long-term treatment Isolated incident Age and/or lack of maturity where it affects the responsibility of the defendant Mental disorder or learning disability, where **not** linked to the commission of the offence Sole or primary carer for dependent relatives

[Steps Three to Nine are almost identical to those for inflicting grievous bodily harm: see **SG-146**.]

Assault on a Police Constable in Execution of his Duty **SG-150**

Police Act 1996 (section 89)

Triable only summarily
Maximum: 26 weeks' custody

Offence range: Fine—26 weeks' custody

STEP ONE Determining the offence category

The court should determine the offence category using the table below.

Category 1	Greater harm **and** higher culpability
Category 2	Greater harm **and** lower culpability; **or** lesser harm **and** higher culpability
Category 3	Lesser harm **and** lower culpability

The court should determine the offender's culpability and the harm caused, or intended, by reference only to the factors below (as demonstrated by the presence of one or more). These factors comprise the principal factual elements of the offence and should determine the category.

Factors indicating greater harm	Factors indicating lesser harm
Sustained or repeated assault on the same victim	Injury which is less serious in the context of the offence
Factors indicating higher culpability *Statutory aggravating factors:* Offence racially or religiously aggravated Offence motivated by, or demonstrating, hostility to the victim based on his or her sexual orientation (or presumed sexual orientation) Offence motivated by, or demonstrating, hostility to the victim based on the victim's disability(or presumed disability) *Other aggravating factors:* A significant degree of premeditation Use of weapon or weapon equivalent (for example, shod foot, headbutting, use of acid, use of animal) Intention to commit more serious harm than actually resulted from the offence Deliberately causes more harm than is necessary for commission of offence Leading role in group or gang Offence motivated by, or demonstrating, hostility based on the victim's age, sex, gender identity (or presumed gender identity)	**Factors indicating lower culpability** Subordinate role in group or gang Lack of premeditation Mental disorder of learning disability where linked to commission of the offence

STEP TWO Starting point and category range

Having determined the category, the court should use the corresponding starting points to reach a sentence within the category range below. The starting point applies to all offenders irrespective of plea or previous convictions. A case of particular gravity, reflected by multiple features of culpability in step one, could merit upward adjustment from the starting point before further adjustment for aggravating or mitigating features, set out below.

Offence Category	Starting Point (*Applicable to all offenders*)	Category Range (*Applicable to all offenders*)
Category 1	12 weeks' custody	Low level community order—26 weeks' custody
Category 2	Medium level community order	Low level community order—High level community order
Category 3	Band B fine	Band A fine—Band C fine

The table below contains a **non-exhaustive** list of additional factual elements providing the context of the offence and factors relating to the offender. Identify whether any combination of these, or other relevant factors, should result in an upward or downward adjustment from the starting point. In some cases, having considered these factors, it may be appropriate to move outside the identified category range.

When sentencing **category 1** offences, the court should also consider the custody threshold as follows:

- has the custody threshold been passed?
- if so, is it unavoidable that a custodial sentence be imposed?
- if so, can that sentence be suspended?

Factors increasing seriousness	Factors reducing seriousness or reflecting personal mitigation
Statutory aggravating factors: Previous convictions, having regard to a) the nature of the offence to which the conviction relates and its relevance to the current offence; and b) the time that has elapsed since the conviction Offence committed whilst on bail *Other aggravating factors include:* Location of the offence Timing of the offence Ongoing effect upon the victim Gratuitous degradation of victim Failure to comply with current court orders Offence committed whilst on licence An attempt to conceal or dispose of evidence Failure to respond to warnings or concerns expressed by others about the offender's behaviour Commission of offence whilst under the influence of alcohol or drugs Any evidence of community impact Any steps taken to prevent the victim reporting an incident, obtaining assistance and/or from assisting or supporting the prosecution Offences taken into consideration (TICs)	No previous convictions **or** no relevant/recent convictions Single blow Remorse Good character and/or exemplary conduct Determination and/or demonstration of steps taken to address addiction or offending behaviour Serious medical conditions requiring urgent, intensive or long-term treatment Isolated incident Age and/or lack of maturity where it affects the responsibility of the offender Lapse of time since the offence where this is not the fault of the offender Mental disorder or learning disability, where **not** linked to the commission of the offence Sole or primary carer for dependent relatives

[Steps Three to Eight are almost identical to those for inflicting grievous bodily harm (see **SG-146**) but with the omission of Step Five (Dangerousness).]

Common Assault **SG-151**

Criminal Justice Act 1988 (section 39)

Racially/Religiously Aggravated Common Assault

Crime and Disorder Act 1998 (section 29)

Racially/religiously aggravated assault is a specified offence for the purposes of section 224 of the Criminal Justice Act 2003

Triable only summarily
Maximum (section 39): 26 weeks' custody

Triable either way
Maximum (section 29): 2 years' custody

Offence range: Discharge—26 weeks' custody

STEP ONE Determining the Offence Category

The court should determine the offence category using the table below.

Category 1	Greater harm (injury or fear of injury must normally be present) **and** higher culpability
Category 2	Greater harm (injury or fear of injury must normally be present) **and** lower culpability; **or** lesser harm and higher culpability
Category 3	Lesser harm **and** lower culpability

The court should determine the offender's culpability and the harm caused, or intended, by reference only to the factors below (as demonstrated by the presence of one or more). These factors comprise the principal factual elements of the offence and should determine the category.

Factors indicating greater harm Injury or fear of injury which is s erious in the context of the offence (must normally be present) Victim is particularly vulnerable because of personal circumstances Sustained or repeated assault on the same victim	**Factors indicating lesser harm** Injury which is less serious in the context of the offence
Factors indicating higher culpability *Statutory aggravating factors:* Offence motivated by, or demonstrating, hostility to the victim based on his or her sexual orientation (or presumed sexual orientation) Offence motivated by, or demonstrating, hostility to the victim based on the victim's disability (or presumed disability) *Other aggravating factors:* A significant degree of premeditation Threatened or actual use of weapon or weapon equivalent (for example, shod foot, headbutting, use of acid, use of animal) Intention to commit more serious harm than actually resulted from the offence Deliberately causes more harm than is necessary for commission of offence Deliberate targeting of vulnerable victim Leading role in group or gang Offence motivated by, or demonstrating, hostility based on the victim's age, sex, gender identity (or presumed gender identity)	**Factors indicating lower culpability** Subordinate role in group or gang A greater degree of provocation than normally expected Lack of premeditation Mental disorder or learning disability, where linked to commission of the offence Excessive self defence

STEP TWO **Starting point and category range**

Having determined the category, the court should use the corresponding starting points to reach a sentence within the category range below. The starting point applies to all offenders irrespective of plea or previous convictions. A case of particular gravity, reflected by multiple features of culpability in step one, could merit upward adjustment from the starting point before further adjustment for aggravating or mitigating features, set out below.

Offence Category	**Starting Point** (*Applicable to all offenders*)	**Category Range** (*Applicable to all offenders*)
Category 1	High level community order	Low level community order—26 weeks' custody
Category 2	Medium level community order	Band A fine—High level community order
Category 3	Band A fine	Discharge—Band C fine

The table below contains a **non-exhaustive** list of additional factual elements providing the context of the offence and factors relating to the offender. Identify whether any combination of these, or other relevant factors, should result in an upward or downward adjustment from the starting point. In some cases, having considered these factors, it may be appropriate to move outside the identified category range.

When sentencing **category** 1 offences, the court should also consider the custody threshold as follows:

- has the custody threshold been passed?
- if so, is it unavoidable that a custodial sentence be imposed?
- if so, can that sentence be suspended?

When sentencing **category 2** offences, the court should also consider the community order threshold as follows:

- has the community order threshold been passed?

Factors increasing seriousness	Factors reducing seriousness or reflecting personal mitigation
Statutory aggravating factors: Previous convictions, having regard to a) the nature of the offence to which the conviction relates and its relevance to the current offence; and b) the time that has elapsed since the conviction Offence committed whilst on bail *Other aggravating factors include:* Location of the offence Timing of the offence Ongoing effect upon the victim Offence committed against those working in the public sector or providing a service to the public Presence of others including relatives, especially children or partner of the victim Gratuitous degradation of victim In domestic violence cases, victim forced to leave their home Failure to comply with current court orders Offence committed whilst on licence An attempt to conceal or dispose of evidence Failure to respond to warnings or concerns expressed by others about the offender's behaviour Commission of offence whilst under the influence of alcohol or drugs Abuse of power and/or position of trust Exploiting contact arrangements with a child to commit an offence Established evidence of community impact Any steps taken to prevent the victim reporting an incident, obtaining assistance and/or from assisting or supporting the prosecution Offences taken into consideration (TICs)	No previous convictions **or** no relevant/recent convictions Single blow Remorse Good character and/or exemplary conduct Determination and/or demonstration of steps taken to address addiction or offending behaviour Serious medical conditions requiring urgent, intensive or long-term treatment Isolated incident Age and/or lack of maturity where it affects the responsibility of the offender Lapse of time since the offence where this is not the fault of the offender Mental disorder or learning disability, where **not** linked to the commission of the offence Sole or primary carer for dependent relatives

Section 29 offences only: The court should determine the appropriate sentence for the offence without taking account of the element of aggravation and then make an addition to the sentence, considering the level of aggravation involved. It may be appropriate to move outside the identified category range, taking into account the increased statutory maximum.

[Steps Three to Nine are almost identical to those for inflicting grievous bodily harm: see **SG-146**.]

ANNEX **SG-152**

[*Fine bands - Not reproduced: see* **SG-282.**]

Community Orders

In this guideline, community sentences are expressed as one of three levels (low, medium and high).

A non-exhaustive description of examples of requirements that might be appropriate for each level is provided below. Where two or more requirements are ordered, they must be compatible with each other.

LOW	MEDIUM	HIGH
In general, only one requirement will be appropriate and the length may be curtailed if additional requirements are necessary		More intensive sentences which combine two or more requirements may be appropriate
Suitable requirements might include: • 40–80 hours unpaid work • Curfew requirement within the lowest range (e.g. up to 12 hours per day for a few weeks) • Exclusion requirement, without electronic monitoring, for a few months • Prohibited activity requirement • Attendance centre requirement (where available)	Suitable requirements might include: • Greater number of hours of unpaid work (e.g. 80–150 hours) • An activity requirement in the middle range (20 to 30 days) • Curfew requirement within the middle range (e.g. up to 12 hours for 2–3 months) • Exclusion requirement, lasting in the region of 6 months • Prohibited activity requirement	Suitable requirements might include: • 150–300 hours unpaid work • Activity requirement up to the maximum of 60 days • Curfew requirement up to 12 hours per day for 4–6 months • Exclusion order lasting in the region of 12 months

The tables above are also set out in the *Magistrates' Court Sentencing Guidelines* which includes further guidance on fines and community orders.

SG-153

PART 11 OVERARCHING PRINCIPLES: ASSAULTS ON CHILDREN AND CRUELTY TO A CHILD

Foreword

. . . This guideline applies to the sentencing of offenders on or after 3 March 2008.

In a separate guideline the Council has set out the principles and guidance relevant to the sentencing of assault offences ranging from common assault at the lowest end of the seriousness scale, up to wounding or causing grievous bodily harm with intent.

This guideline details additional relevant principles for sentencing where the assault was on a child.

In addition, this guideline defines sentencing principles, starting points and ranges for the offence of cruelty to a child which may involve a variety of types of conduct and stem from a pattern of offending behaviour against a child rather than an isolated assault. . ..

SG-154 **Introduction and structure of the guideline**[166]

1. The Council has produced a separate guideline covering offences of assault which do not result in the death of the victim, ranging in seriousness from common assault to wounding or causing grievous bodily harm with intent. Those offences involve the infliction of permanent or temporary harm on a victim by direct action, or an intention to cause harm to a victim even if harm does not in fact result.
2. That guideline applies only to the sentencing of offenders aged 18 and older convicted of assault, primarily where the victim of the assault is aged 16 or over. It covers:
    - assessing the culpability of the offender and the harm caused;
    - relevant aggravating and mitigating factors;
    - use of a weapon and particular parts of the body;
    - aggravated assaults;
    - provocation as mitigation;
    - compensating victims, and
    - ancillary orders.
3. In **Part 1** of this guideline additional principles are set out which should be considered when the victim of an assault is a child (aged 15 years and under).
4. **Part 2** provides guidance in relation to the offence of cruelty to a child[167] which has a wide-ranging definition that can include assault but also other forms of conduct likely to cause a child under 16 years of age unnecessary suffering or injury to health.

[166] Assault and other offences against the person; www.sentencing-guidelines.gov.uk
[167] Children and Young Persons Act 1933, s.1(1)

Part 1: Assaults on children: General principles

A. Assessing seriousness SG-155

5. The primary factor in considering sentence is the seriousness of the offence committed; that is determined by assessing the culpability of the offender and the harm caused, intended or reasonably foreseeable.[168] A community sentence can be imposed only if the court considers that the offence is serious enough to justify it[169] and a custodial sentence can be imposed only if the court considers that a community sentence or a fine alone cannot be justified in view of the seriousness of the offence.[170] The Council has published a definitive guideline that guides sentencers determining whether the respective thresholds have been crossed.[171]
6. In considering the seriousness of an offence committed by an offender who has one or more previous convictions, the court must consider whether it should treat any of them as an aggravating factor having regard to the nature of the offence to which each conviction relates and its relevance to the current offence, and the time that has elapsed since the conviction.[172]
7. When dealing with cases involving assaults committed by adults against children, many of which involved some of the aggravating factors described below, the Court of Appeal has given a consistent message that an assault against a child will normally merit a custodial sentence. The Council's view is that such a presumption will not always be appropriate, but in all cases, the fact that the victim is a child is likely to aggravate the seriousness of the offence where the offender is an adult.

(i) Aggravation

8. The fact that the victim of an assault is a child will often mean that the offence involves a particularly vulnerable victim.
9. For all offences of assault, where the offence has been committed by an adult offender and the victim is a child under 16 years, the most relevant aggravating factors, as listed in the Council guideline *Overarching Principles: Seriousness*, are likely to be those set out below. Many of those are most likely to be present where the defendant has caring responsibilities for the child:
   - victim is particularly vulnerable;
   - abuse of power;
   - abuse of position of trust;
   - an especially serious physical or psychological effect on the victim, even if unintended;
   - presence of others e.g. relatives, especially other children;
   - additional degradation of the victim.

   Additional aggravating factors are:
   - sadistic behaviour;
   - threats to prevent the victim reporting the offence;
   - deliberate concealment of the victim from the authorities; and
   - failure to seek medical help.
10. Many offences committed by adults against children will involve an abuse of power and many also will include an abuse of a position of trust. The Education Act 1996 abolished the right of teachers and other school staff to administer corporal punishment.[173]
11. The location of the offence, for example the fact that an offence takes place in the child's home, and the particular circumstances, such as the fact that the victim is isolated—common aggravating factors in cases of child cruelty—may also be present in relation to individual offences of assault against children.

(ii) Mitigation

12. An offender might seek to argue that any harm caused to the child amounted to lawful chastisement and a court might form the view that the offender held a genuine belief that his or her actions amounted to no more than a legitimate form of physical punishment. The defence of lawful chastisement is available only in relation to a charge of common assault. Where that defence is not available, or, in relation to a charge of common assault, such a defence has failed, sentence for the offence would normally be approached in the same way as any other assault.

[168] Criminal Justice Act 2003, s.152(2)
[169] ibid, s.148(1)
[170] ibid, s.152(2)
[171] *Overarching Principles: Seriousness* published on 16 December 2004; www.sentencing-guidelines.gov.uk
[172] Criminal Justice Act 2003, s.143(2)
[173] s. 548

13. There will be circumstances where the defendant has been charged with an assault occasioning actual bodily harm and the court finds as fact that the defendant only intended to administer lawful chastisement to the child, and the injury that was inflicted was neither intended nor foreseen by the defendant.
14. Although the defendant would have intended nothing more than lawful chastisement (as currently allowed by the law), he or she would have no defence to such a charge because an assault occasioning actual bodily harm does not require the offender to intend or even foresee that his act will result in any physical harm; it is sufficient that it did. Such a finding of fact should result in a substantial reduction in sentence and should not normally result in a custodial sentence. Where not only was the injury neither intended nor foreseen, but was not even reasonably foreseeable, then a discharge might be appropriate.

SG-156 **B. Other factors relevant to sentencing**

(i) The adverse effect of the sentence on the victim

15. In many circumstances, an offence of assault on a child will cause the court to conclude that only a custodial sentence can be justified. Imposition of such a sentence will often protect a victim from further harm and anguish; some children will be less traumatised once they are no longer living with an abusive carer.
16. However, where imprisonment of the offender deprives a child victim of his or her sole or main carer (and may result in the child being taken into care), it may punish and re-victimise the child.
17. In view of the seriousness of the offence committed and the risk of further harm to the victim or other children, even though a child may be distressed by separation from a parent or carer, imposing a custodial sentence on the offender may be the only option. However, where sentencing options remain more open, the court should take into account the impact that a custodial sentence for the offender might have on the victim.
18. There will be cases where the child victim is the subject of concurrent care proceedings and, indeed, the child's future care arrangements may well have been determined by the time the offender is sentenced. Both the sentencing court and the Family Court need to be aware of the progress of any concurrent proceedings.
19. **In considering whether a custodial sentence is the most appropriate disposal for an offence of assault on a child the court should take into account any available information concerning the future care of the child.**

(ii) Offenders who have primary care responsibilities

20. The gender of an offender is irrelevant for sentencing purposes. The important factor for consideration is the offender's role as sole or primary carer of the victim or other children or dependants.
21. In cases where an immediate custodial sentence of less than 12 months is justified, it is possible that a suspended sentence order (where available) might be the most appropriate sentence. This could enable the offender, subject to the necessary risk assessment being made, to resume care for, or at least have regular contact with, the child and could also open up opportunities for imposing requirements to rehabilitate and support an offender in need. In practice, this principle is likely to benefit more women than men, firstly because women commit the larger proportion of offences and secondly because men are less likely to be the sole or primary carers of children but the principle is established on the grounds of carer status and not gender.
22. **Where the offender is the sole or primary carer of the victim or other dependants, this potentially should be taken into account for sentencing purposes, regardless of whether the offender is male or female. In such cases, an immediate custodial sentence may not be appropriate and, subject to a risk assessment, the offender may be able to resume care for or have contact with the victim.**

Part 2: Cruelty to a child

SG-157 **A. Statutory provision**

23. [Sets out the CYPA 1933, s. 1(1) (see **B2.114**).][174]

[174] In addition to the Children and Young Persons Act 1933 the UN Convention on the Rights of the Child may be particularly relevant when dealing with this offence. Article 19 obliges States Parties to take all appropriate legislative, administrative, social and educational measures to protect the child from all forms of physical or mental violence, injury or abuse, neglect or negligent treatment, maltreatment or exploitation, including sexual abuse, while in the care of parent(s), legal guardian(s) or any other person who has the care of the child.

B. Forms of cruelty to a child SG-158

24. As is clear from the definition, the offence covers a variety of types of conduct that can compendiously or separately amount to child cruelty. The four generally accepted categories are:
    (i) assault and ill-treatment;
    (ii) failure to protect;
    (iii) neglect; and
    (iv) abandonment.
25. With regard to assaults, the CPS Charging Standard[175] suggests that an assault charged as child cruelty will differ in nature from that which is generally charged as an offence against the person and notes that 'the offence is particularly relevant in cases of cruelty over a period of time.' As such, it is more likely to apply to offences where there is evidence that a child was assaulted by someone with caring responsibility during a certain period but where there is no clear evidence of any particular incidents, the extent of those incidents or the specific time of the incidents.
26. Where a serious assault has been committed, the CPS Charging Standard advises that a charge of child cruelty will not be appropriate and that the most appropriate offence against the person should be charged in such circumstances.[176]
27. For the purposes of the offence, 'neglect' can mean physical and/or emotional neglect.

C. Assessing seriousness SG-159

28. It is not appropriate to identify one category of child cruelty as being automatically more serious than another; there will be a multitude of scenarios, some of which will involve more than one type of cruelty, in which the seriousness of the types of cruelty judged one against another will vary markedly. A long period of neglect, for example, could, in some circumstances, be more harmful to a child than a short period of violence.
29. In order to assess properly the seriousness of an offence, the precise nature of the offence must be established before consideration is given to a range of contingent factors, including the defendants intent, the length of time over which the cruelty took place, and the degree of physical and psychological harm suffered by the victim.

(i) Culpability

30. Although the nature and degree of harm that was caused, was intended or was reasonably foreseeable will impact on the seriousness of an offence of child cruelty, the Council guideline[177] clearly establishes that culpability should be the initial factor in determining the seriousness of an offence. In child cruelty offences, where there is such a wide variation in the nature and degree of harm that can be caused to a victim, there will similarly be a considerable variation in levels of culpability.
31. Child cruelty may be the consequence of a wide range of factors including:
    - sadism
    - violence resulting from any number of causes
    - a reduced ability to protect a child in the face of aggression from an overbearing partner
    - indifference or apathy resulting from low intelligence or induced by alcohol or drug dependence
    - immaturity or social deprivation resulting in an inability to cope with the pressures of caring for children
    - psychiatric illness
32. In the short term, an offence might arise as the result of a momentary lack of control by an otherwise responsible and loving carer. The extent to which any of these factors might have contributed to the commission of an offence will be important in determining the culpability of the offender.
33. A court must strike a balance between the need to reflect the serious view which society takes of the ill-treatment of very young children and the need to protect those children, and also the pressures upon immature and inadequate parents attempting to cope with the problems of infancy.
34. The extent to which remorse should influence sentence will always have to be judged in the light of all the circumstances surrounding the case.
35. In view of the seriousness with which society as a whole regards child cruelty, the normal sentencing starting point for an offence of child cruelty should be a custodial sentence. The length of that sentence will be influenced, however, by the circumstances in which the offence took place.

[175] The Charging Standard on Offences Against the Person; www.cps.gov.uk
[176] *Child Cruelty: Charging Practice*; www.cps.gov.uk/legal/section7
[177] *Overarching Principles: Seriousness*, page 5, published on 16 December 2004; www.sentencing-guidelines.gov.uk

(ii) Harm

36. In order to assist a court in assessing the exact nature and seriousness of an offence of child cruelty, the CPS Charging Standard[178] advises that 'it may be preferable to have two or more alternative allegations in order that conduct complained of is appropriately described' and this certainly seems to be of benefit to sentencers. Where an offender has been convicted of an offence of child cruelty and the indictment clearly states the nature of the offender's conduct—neglect for example—the sentencer can be clear about the nature of the conduct for which the offender is to be sentenced.
37. However, even if the nature of the offending behaviour can be identified, statute is silent as to the relative seriousness of the different types of child cruelty identified above, creating obvious difficulties for the sentencing court.
38. There is a significant distinction between cases of wilful ill-treatment which usually involve positive acts of abuse and physical violence, and cases of neglect which are typified by the absence of actions.
39. In some cases there will be physical injury, whether resulting directly from an assault or ill-treatment or resulting from a period of abandonment or neglect. In other cases the harm occasioned may be lack of proper care, attention or supervision or exposure to the risk of harm.
40. As to whether one form of cruelty is worse than another will depend not only on the degree to which the victim suffers as a result but also on the motivation and culpability of the offender, which can range from inadequate parenting skills and an inability to cope, or constantly prioritising the needs of the offender or the offender's partner over those of the child, through to purposeful, sadistic and systematic abuse.

(iii) Aggravating and mitigating factors

41. The *Seriousness* guideline[179] sets out aggravating and mitigating factors that are applicable to a wide range of cases. Not all will be relevant to the offence of cruelty to a child. Care needs to be taken to ensure that there is no double counting where an essential element of the offence charged might, in other circumstances, be an aggravating factor. The sentencing starting points for the offence of child cruelty have been calculated to reflect the inherent abuse of trust or power and these cannot be treated as aggravating factors.
42. The following additional factors will aggravate offences of child cruelty:
    - targeting one particular child from the family
    - sadistic behaviour
    - threats to prevent the victim from reporting the offence
    - deliberate concealment of the victim from the authorities
    - failure to seek medical help
43. The following additional factor will mitigate offences of child cruelty:
    - seeking medical help or bringing the situation to the notice of the authorities

SG-160 **D. Other factors relevant to sentencing**

(i) Long-term psychological harm

44. There is no immediately predictable link between a type of offending behaviour and the impact it may have on the victim, either in the immediate or long term. The innate resilience of children and the presence of protection from another adult or the wider environment are also important factors that will influence the impact of the offence upon the child.
45. However, victims of child cruelty will frequently suffer psychological as well as physical harm. The evidence of emotional and behavioural consequences of child abuse is frequently presented by the following characteristics:[180]
    - impaired capacity to enjoy life—abused children often appear sad, preoccupied and listless;
    - psychiatric or psychosomatic stress symptoms, for example, bed-wetting, tantrums, bizarre behaviour, eating problems etc;
    - low self-esteem—children who have been abused often think they must be worthless to deserve such treatment;
    - school learning problems, such as lack of concentration;
    - withdrawal—many abused children withdraw from relationships with other children and become isolated and depressed;

[178] The Charging Standard on Offences Against the Person; www.cps.gov.uk

[179] *Overarching Principles: Seriousness*, paragraphs 1.20–1.27, published on 16 December 2004; www.sentencing-guidelines.gov.uk

[180] 'The Effects of Physical Abuse and Neglect' in Wendy Stanton Rogers et al ed, *Child Abuse and Neglect*, The Open University 1992 page 206, citing a study by Martin, H.P. and Beezley P., 'Behavioural observations of abused children', *Developmental Medicine and Child Neurology*, Vol 19 (1977), pages 373–87

- opposition/defiance—a generally negative, uncooperative attitude;
- hyper-vigilance—typified in the 'frozen watchfulness' expression;
- compulsivity—abused children sometimes compulsively carry out certain activities or rituals;
- pseudo-mature behaviour—a false appearance of independence or being excessively 'good' all the time or offering indiscriminate affection to any adult who takes an interest.

46. Abuse can also be evidenced by 'learned behaviour aggression' and a tendency for a victim of child cruelty to inflict violence on others. Victims may also mature into adults with poor parenting skills who perpetrate similar acts of cruelty on their own children.

47. There is an established general principle that the sentence imposed for an offence can be based both on what is known about the harm caused to an individual victim and, in some cases, what is known about the harm caused to society as a whole.

48. Whilst objective evidence about the degree of physical harm should be available at the point of sentence, psychological harm, especially that which may or may not manifest itself in the future, will be extremely difficult, and often impossible, to assess at the point of sentence. Where there is objective expert evidence about the particularly severe psychological trauma suffered by an individual victim, which indicates a more than usually serious degree of harm, this would be captured by the generic aggravating factor in the Council guideline—*An especially serious physical or psychological effect on the victim, even if unintended*.[181]

49. **The sentencing starting points for the offence of child cruelty have been calculated to reflect the likelihood of psychological harm and this cannot be treated as aggravating factors. Where there is an especially serious physical or psychological effect on the victim, even if unintended, this should increase sentence.**

(ii) The adverse effect of the sentence on the victim

50. Imposing a custodial sentence for an offence of child cruelty is the most appropriate outcome in most cases in that it properly reflects society's view of the seriousness of this type of offending behaviour and protects victims from further harm and anguish. In addition, it is not unreasonable to suppose that some children will be less traumatised once they are no longer living with an abusive carer.

51. However, there is a counter argument that, as the imprisonment of the offender may deprive a child victim of his or her sole or main carer and may result in the child being taken into care, a custodial sentence effectively punishes and re-victimises the child and, it is argued, should only be considered in the most serious of cases.

52. In some cases, even though a child may be distressed by separation from a parent or carer, imposing a custodial sentence on the offender may be the only option in view of the seriousness of the offence committed and the risk of further harm to the victim or other children. However, where sentencing options remain open, the court should take into account the impact that a custodial sentence for the offender might have on the victim.

53. In many cases the child victim will be the subject of concurrent care proceedings and, indeed, the child's future care arrangements may well have been determined by the time the offender is sentenced. Both the sentencing court and the Family Court need to be aware of the progress of any concurrent proceedings.

54. **In considering whether a custodial sentence is the most appropriate disposal for an offence of child cruelty, the court should take into account any available information concerning the future care of the child.**

(iii) Offenders who have primary care responsibilities

55. The gender of an offender is irrelevant for sentencing purposes. The important factor for consideration is the offender's role as sole or primary carer of the victim or other children or dependants.

56. In cases where an immediate custodial sentence of less than 12 months is justified, it is possible that a suspended sentence order might be the most appropriate sentence. This could enable the offender, subject to the necessary risk assessment being made, to resume care for, or at least have regular contact with, the child and could also open up opportunities for imposing requirements to rehabilitate and support an offender in need. In practice, this principle is likely to benefit more women than men, firstly because women commit the larger proportion of offences and secondly because men are less likely to be the sole or primary carers of children but the principle is established on the grounds of carer status and not gender.

57. **Where the offender is the sole or primary carer of the victim or other dependants, this potentially should be taken into account for sentencing purposes, regardless of whether the offender is male or**

[181] *Overarching Principles: Seriousness*, page 7, published on 16 December 2004; www.sentencing-guidelines.gov.uk

female. In such cases, an immediate custodial sentence may not be appropriate and, subject to a risk assessment, the offender may be able to resume care for or have contact with the victim.

(iv) Personal mitigation

58. There may be other factors that impact on an offender's behaviour towards children in his or her care and should legitimately influence the nature and length of the sentence passed in child cruelty cases.
59. In relation to the offence of cruelty to a child, the most relevant areas of personal mitigation are likely to be:
    - Mental illness/depression
    - Inability to cope with the pressures of parenthood
    - Lack of support
    - Sleep deprivation
    - Offender dominated by an abusive or stronger partner
    - Extreme behavioural difficulties in the child, often coupled with a lack of support
    - Inability to secure assistance or support services in spite of every effort having been made by the offender
60. It must be noted, however, that some of the factors identified above, in particular sleep deprivation, lack of support and an inability to cope could be regarded as an inherent part of caring for children, especially when a child is very young. Thus, such factors could be put forward in mitigation by most carers charged with an offence of child cruelty. It follows that, before being accepted in mitigation, there must be evidence that these factors were present to a high degree and had an identifiable and significant impact on the offender's behaviour.

SG-161 **E. Starting points and sentencing ranges**

1. Typically, a guideline will apply to an offence that can be committed in a variety of circumstances with different levels of seriousness. It will apply to a first-time offender who has been convicted after a trial. Within the guidelines, a first-time offender is a person who does not have a conviction which, by virtue of section 143(2) of the CJA 2003, must be treated as an aggravating factor.
2. As an aid to consistency of approach, the guidelines describe a number of types of activity which would fall within the broad definition of the offence. These are set out in a column headed 'Type/nature of activity'.
3. The expected approach is for a court to identify the description that most nearly matches the particular facts of the offence for which sentence is being imposed. This will identify a starting point from which the sentencer can depart to reflect aggravating or mitigating factors affecting the seriousness of the offence (beyond those contained within the column describing the type or nature of offence activity) to reach a provisional sentence.
4. The *sentencing range* is the bracket into which the provisional sentence will normally fall after having regard to factors which aggravate or mitigate the seriousness of the offence. The particular circumstances may, however, make it appropriate that the provisional sentence falls outside the range.
5. Where the offender has previous convictions which aggravate the seriousness of the current offence, that may take the provisional sentence beyond the range given, particularly where there are significant other aggravating factors present.
6. Once the provisional sentence has been identified by reference to those factors affecting the seriousness of the offence, the court will take into account any relevant factors of personal mitigation, which may take the sentence outside the range indicated in the guideline.
7. Where there has been a guilty plea, any reduction attributable to that plea will be applied to the sentence at this stage. This reduction may take the sentence below the range provided.
8. A court must give its reasons for imposing a sentence of a different kind or outside the range provided in the guidelines.[182]

SG-162 **The Decision Making Process**

The process . . . is intended to show that the sentencing approach for the offence of cruelty to a child is fluid and requires the structured exercise of discretion.

[Sets out the standard sequential decision making process: identify dangerous offenders, identify starting point, consider aggravating factors, consider mitigating factors, apply reduction for guilty plea, consider ancillary orders, review in light of the totality principle and give reasons.]

[182] Criminal Justice Act 2003, s. 174(2)(a)

F. Factors to take into consideration SG-163

1. Cruelty to a child is a specified offence for the purposes of section 224 of the Criminal Justice Act 2003 and sentencers should consider whether a sentence for public protection should be imposed. **The following guideline applies to offenders who have *not* been assessed as dangerous.**
2. The suggested starting points and sentencing ranges in the guideline are based upon a first-time adult offender convicted after a trial (see . . . above).
3. The same starting point and sentencing range is proposed for offences which might fall into the four categories (assault; ill-treatment or neglect; and abandonment). These are designed to take into account the fact that the victim is particularly vulnerable, assuming an abuse of trust or power and the likelihood of psychological harm, and designed to reflect the seriousness with which society as a whole regards these offences, is proposed for an offence in each.
4. Only additional aggravating and mitigating factors specifically relevant to this offence are included in the guideline. When assessing the seriousness of any offence, the courts must always refer to the full list of aggravating and mitigating factors in the Council guideline on Seriousness.[183]
5. Where there is an especially serious physical or psychological effect on the victim, even if unintended, this should increase sentence.
6. In considering whether a custodial sentence is the most appropriate disposal for an offence of child cruelty, the court should take into account any available information concerning the future care of the child.
7. Where the offender is the sole or primary carer of the victim or other dependants, this potentially should be taken into account for sentencing purposes, regardless of whether the offender is male or female. In such cases, an immediate custodial sentence may not be appropriate.
8. Sentencers should take into account relevant matters of personal mitigation such as those suggested at paragraph 59 above.

Cruelty to a child SG-164

Children and Young Persons Act 1933 (section 1(1))

THIS IS A SERIOUS OFFENCE FOR THE PURPOSES OF SECTION 224 CRIMINAL JUSTICE ACT 2003.

Maximum penalty: 10 years imprisonment

Nature of failure & harm	Starting point	Sentencing range
(i) Serious cruelty over a period of time. (ii) Serious long-term neglect. (iii) Failure to protect a child from either of the above.	**6 years custody**	**5–9 years custody**
(i) Series of assaults (the more serious the individual assaults and the longer the period over which they are perpetrated, the more serious the offence). (ii) Protracted neglect or ill-treatment (the longer the period of ill-treatment or neglect and the longer the period over which it takes place, the more serious the offence). (iii) Failure to protect a child from either of the above.	**3 years custody**	**2–5 years custody**
(i) Assault(s) resulting in injuries consistent with ABH. (ii) More than one incident of neglect or ill-treatment (but not amounting to long-term behaviour). (iii) Single incident of long-term abandonment OR regular incidents of short-term abandonment (the longer the period of long-term abandonment or the greater the number of incidents of short-term abandonment) the more serious the offence). (iv) Failure to protect a child from any of the above.	**36 weeks custody**	**26 weeks–2 years custody**
(i) Short-term neglect or ill-treatment. (ii) Single incident of short-term abandonment. (iii) Failure to protect a child from any of the above.	**12 weeks custody**	**Community Order (LOW)—26 weeks custody**

[183] *Overarching Principles: Seriousness*, published on 16 December 2004; www.sentencing-guidelines.gov.uk

Additional aggravating factors	Additional mitigating factors
1. Targeting one particular child from the family. 2. Sadistic behaviour. 3. Threats to prevent the victim from reporting the offence. 4. Deliberate concealment of the victim from the authorities. 5. Failure to seek medical help.	1. Seeking medical help or bringing the situation to the notice of the authorities.

SG-165 PART 12 MAGISTRATES' COURT SENTENCING GUIDELINES

...

These guidelines cover offences for which sentence is frequently imposed in a magistrates' court when dealing with adult offenders. They apply to allocation (mode of trial) decisions and to sentences imposed on or after 4 August 2008 and replace the guidelines effective from 1 January 2004.

When dealing with an either way offence for which there is no plea or an indication of a not guilty plea, these guidelines will be relevant to the mode of trial decision and should be consulted at this stage. This is important because, in some cases, the ability to commit an offender to the Crown Court for sentence after trial may be limited. Where an offence is included in these guidelines, the guideline supersedes the equivalent part of the Mode of Trial guidelines in Part V.51 of the Consolidated Criminal Practice Direction.

These guidelines apply to sentencing in a magistrates' court whatever the composition of the court. They apply also to the Crown Court when dealing with appeals against sentences imposed in a magistrates' court and when sentencing for summary only offences. In all other cases, the Crown Court must have regard to any other definitive Council guidelines which are relevant to the offender's case.

[Extract from the CJA 2003, s. 172(1), which is now repealed.]

The guidelines provide greater guidance on both starting points and sentence ranges than the previous edition. They have been expanded to cover additional offences, the explanatory material has been revised and, in respect of offence guidelines, a new format has been adopted to reflect better the sentencing framework established by the Criminal Justice Act 2003. Where appropriate, guidelines issued by the Council or Court of Appeal are incorporated. What is included is necessarily a summary; *the original guideline or Court of Appeal judgment should be consulted for comprehensive guidance*. . ..

SG-166 User Guide

1. Assess offence seriousness (culpability and harm)

Offence seriousness is the starting point for sentencing under the Criminal Justice Act 2003. The court's assessment of offence seriousness will:

- determine which of the sentencing thresholds has been crossed;
- indicate whether a custodial, community or other sentence is the most appropriate;
- be the key factor in deciding the length of a custodial sentence, the onerousness of requirements to be incorporated in a community sentence and the amount of any fine

When considering the seriousness of any offence, the court must consider the offender's *culpability* in committing the offence and any *harm* which the offence caused, was intended to cause, or might forseeably have caused.[184] In using these guidelines, this assessment should be approached in two stages:

SG-167 **1. Offence seriousness (culpability and harm)**

A. Identify the appropriate starting point

The guidelines set out *examples* of the nature of activity which may constitute the offence, progressing from less to more serious conduct, and provide a *starting point* based on a *first time offender pleading not guilty*. The guidelines also specify a sentencing *range for* each example of activity. Refer [below] for further guidance on the meaning of the terms 'starting point', 'range' and 'first time offender'.

[184] Criminal Justice Act 2003, s.143(1)

Sentencers should begin by considering which of the examples of offence activity corresponds most closely to the circumstances of the particular case in order to identify the appropriate *starting point:*

- where the starting point is a fine, this is indicated as band A, B or C. The approach to assessing fines is set out [below];
- where the community sentence threshold is passed, the guideline sets out whether the starting point should be a low, medium or high level community order. Refer [below] for further guidance;
- where the starting point is a custodial sentence, refer [below] for further guidance.

The Council's definitive guideline *Overarching Principles: Seriousness*, published 16 December 2004 [see **SG-21**], identifies four levels of culpability for sentencing purposes (intention, recklessness, knowledge and negligence). The starting points in the individual offence guidelines assume that culpability is at the highest level applicable to the offence (often, but not always, intention). *Where a lower level of culpability is present, this should be taken into account.*

1. **Offence seriousness (culpability and harm)** **SG-168**

B. Consider the effect of aggravating and mitigating factors

Once the starting point has been identified, the court can add to or reduce this to reflect any aggravating or mitigating factors that impact on the *culpability* of the offender and/or *harm* caused by the offence to reach a provisional sentence. Any factors contained in the description of the activity used to reach the starting point must not be counted again.

The *range* is the bracket into which the provisional sentence will normally fall after having regard to factors which aggravate or mitigate the seriousness of the offence.

However:

- the court is not precluded from going outside the range where the facts justify it;
- previous convictions which aggravate the seriousness of the current offence may take the provisional sentence beyond the range, especially where there are significant other aggravating factors present.

In addition, where an offender is being sentenced for multiple offences, the courts assessment of the totality of the offending may result in a sentence above the range indicated for the individual offences, including a sentence of a different type. Refer [below] for further guidance.

The guidelines identify aggravating and mitigating factors which may be particularly relevant to each individual offence. These include some factors drawn from the general list of aggravating and mitigating factors in the Council's definitive guideline *Overarching Principles: Seriousness*. . .. In each case, sentencers should have regard to the full list, which includes the factors that, by statute, make an offence more serious:

- offence committed while on bail for other offences;
- offence was racially or religiously aggravated;
- offence was motivated by, or demonstrates, hostility based on the victim's sexual orientation (or presumed sexual orientation);
- offence was motivated by, or demonstrates, hostility based on the victim's disability (or presumed disability);
- offender has previous convictions that the court considers can reasonably be treated as aggravating factors having regard to their relevance to the current offence and the time that has elapsed since conviction.

While the lists . . . aim to identify the most common aggravating and mitigating factors, *they are not intended to be exhaustive.* Sentencers should always consider whether there are any other factors that make the offence more or less serious.

2. Form a preliminary view of the appropriate sentence, then consider offender mitigation **SG-169**

When the court has reached a provisional sentence based on its assessment of offence seriousness, it should take into account matters of offender mitigation. The Council guideline *Overarching Principles: Seriousness* states that the issue of remorse should be taken into account at this point along with other mitigating features such as admissions to the police in interview.

3. Consider a reduction for a guilty plea **SG-170**

The Council guideline *Reduction in Sentence for a Guilty Plea* [set out in full in **part 1**] states that the *punitive* elements of the sentence should be reduced to recognise an offender's guilty plea. The reduction has no impact on sentencing decisions in relation to ancillary orders, including disqualification.

The level of the reduction should reflect the stage at which the offender indicated a willingness to admit guilt and will be gauged on a sliding scale, ranging from a *recommended* one third (where the guilty plea was entered at the first reasonable opportunity), reducing to a *recommended* one quarter (where a trial date has been set) and to a *recommended* one tenth (for a guilty plea entered at the 'door of the court' or after the trial has begun). There is a presumption that the recommended reduction will be given unless there are good reasons for a lower amount.

The application of the reduction may affect the type, as well as the severity, of the sentence. It may also take the sentence below the *range* in some cases.

The court must state that it has reduced a sentence to reflect a guilty plea.[185] It should usually indicate what the sentence would have been if there had been no reduction as a result of the plea.

SG-171 **4. Consider ancillary orders, including compensation**

Ancillary orders of particular relevance to individual offences are identified in the relevant guidelines . . .

The court must *always* consider making a compensation order where the offending has resulted in personal injury, loss or damage.[186] The court is required to give reasons if it decides not to make such an order.[187]

SG-172 **5. Decide sentence: Give reasons**

Sentencers must state reasons for the sentence passed in every case, including for any ancillary orders imposed.[188] It is particularly important to identify any aggravating or mitigating factors, or matters of offender mitigation, that have resulted in a sentence more or less severe than the suggested starting point.

If a court imposes a sentence of a different kind or outside the *range* indicated in the guidelines, *it must state its reasons for doing so.*[189]

The court should also give its reasons for not making an order that has been canvassed before it or that it might have been expected to make.

Offences

Alcohol Sale Offences

SG-173 *Licensing Act 2003, s. 141 (sale of alcohol to drunk person); s. 146 (sale of alcohol to children); s. 147 (allowing sale of alcohol to children)*

Triable only summarily:
Maximum: Level 3 fine (s.141); Level 5 fine (ss.146 and 147)

Offence seriousness (culpability and harm)

A. Identify the appropriate starting point
Starting points based on first time offender pleading not guilty

Examples of nature of activity	Starting point	Range
Sale to a child (i.e. person under 18)/to a drunk person	**Band B fine**	**Band A fine to band C fine**

Note: refer to [below] for approach to fines for offences committed for commercial purposes

B. Consider the effect of aggravating and mitigating factors (other than those within examples above)

Common aggravating and mitigating factors are identified [elsewhere]—the following may be particularly relevant but these lists are not exhaustive

Factors indicating higher culpability	Factors indicating greater degree of harm
1. No attempt made to establish age 2. Spirits/high alcohol level of drink 3. Drunk person highly intoxicated 4. Large quantity of alcohol supplied 5. Sale intended for consumption by group of children/drunk people 6. Offender in senior or management position	1. Younger child/children 2. Drunk person causing distress to others 3. Drunk person aggressive

[185] Criminal Justice Act 2003, s.174(2)(d)
[186] Powers of Criminal Courts (Sentencing) Act 2000, s.130(1)
[187] ibid., s.130(3)
[188] Criminal Justice Act 2003, s.174(1)
[189] ibid., s.174(2)(a)

[Sets out the standard sequential sentencing procedure but specifies the need to consider the forfeiture or suspension of a personal liquor licence.]

Note: Section 23 of the Violent Crime Reduction Act 2006 created a new offence of persistently selling alcohol to children, which came into force on 6 April 2007. This is committed if, on three or more different occasions within a period of three consecutive months, alcohol is unlawfully sold on the same premises to a person under 18. The offence is summary only and the maximum penalty is a £10,000 fine. *Consult your legal adviser for guidance on the approach to sentencing and the court's powers in relation to liquor licences.*

ALCOHOL/TOBACCO, FRAUDULENTLY EVADE DUTY SG-174

Customs and Excise Management Act 1979, s. 170

Triable either way:
Maximum when tried summarily: Level 5 fine or three times the value of the goods (whichever is greater) and/or 6 months
Maximum when tried on indictment: 7 years

Refer to guideline *Fraud—banking and insurance fraud and obtaining credit through fraud, benefit fraud and revenue fraud* [see **SG-206** ***et seq.***].

ANIMAL CRUELTY SG-175

Animal Welfare Act 2006, s. 4 (unnecessary suffering); s. 8 (fighting etc.); s. 9 (breach of duty of person responsible for animal to ensure welfare)

Triable only summarily:
Maximum: £20,000 fine and/or 6 months (ss. 4 and 8) Level 5 fine and/or 6 months (s. 9)

Offence seriousness (culpability and harm)

A. Identify the appropriate starting point

Starting points based on first time offender pleading not guilty

Examples of nature of activity	Starting point	Range
One impulsive act causing little or no injury; short term neglect	**Band C fine**	**Band B fine to medium level community order**
Several incidents of deliberate ill-treatment/ frightening animal(s); medium term neglect	**High level community order**	**Medium level community order to 12 weeks custody**
Attempt to kill/torture; animal baiting/ conducting or permitting cock-fighting etc.; prolonged neglect	**18 weeks custody**	**12 to 26 weeks custody**

Offence seriousness (culpability and harm)

B. Consider the effect of aggravating and mitigating factors (other than those within examples above)

Common aggravating and mitigating factors are identified [elsewhere] – the following may be particularly relevant but these lists are not exhaustive

Factors indicating higher culpability	Factors indicating greater degree of harm
1. Offender in position of special responsibility 2. Adult involves children in offending 3. Animal(s) kept for livelihood 4. Use of weapon 5. Offender ignored advice/warnings 6. Offence committed for commercial gain	1. Serious injury or death 2. Several animals affected **Factors indicating lower culpability** 1. Offender induced by others 2. Ignorance of appropriate care 3. Offender with limited capacity

[Sets out the standard sequential sentencing procedure but also mentions the need to consider disqualification from ownership of animal.]

SG-176

Anti-social Behaviour Order, Breach Of

Factors to take into consideration

This guideline and accompanying notes are taken from the Sentencing Guidelines Council's definitive guideline *Breach of an Anti-Social Behaviour Order*, published 9 December 2008 [see **SG-379**].

Key factors

(a) An ASBO may be breached in a very wide range of circumstances and may involve one or more terms not being complied with. The examples given below are intended to illustrate how the scale of the conduct that led to the breach, taken as a whole, might come within the three levels of seriousness:

- No harm caused or intended—in the absence of intimidation or the causing of fear of violence, breaches involving being drunk or begging may be at this level, as may prohibited use of public transport or entry into a prohibited area, where there is no evidence that harassment, alarm or distress was caused or intended.
- Lesser degree of harm intended or likely—examples may include lesser degrees of threats or intimidation, the use of seriously abusive language, or causing more than minor damage to property.
- Serious harm caused or intended—breach at this level of seriousness will involve the use of violence, significant threats or intimidation or the targeting of individuals or groups of people in a manner that leads to a fear of violence.

(b) The suggested starting points are based on the assumption that the offender had the highest level of culpability.

(c) In the most serious cases, involving repeat offending and a breach causing serious harassment together with the presence of several aggravating factors, such as the use of violence, a sentence beyond the highest range will be justified.

(d) When imposing a community order, the court must ensure that the requirements imposed are proportionate to the seriousness of the breach, compatible with each other, and also with the prohibitions of the ASBO if the latter is to remain in force. Even where the threshold for a custodial sentence is crossed, a custodial sentence is not inevitable.

(e) An offender may be sentenced for more than one offence of breach, which occurred on different days. While consecutive sentences may be imposed in such cases, the overall sentence should reflect the totality principle.

Guidelines

Crime and Disorder Act 1988, s.1(10)

Triable either way:
Maximum when tried summarily: Level 5 fine and/or 6 months
Maximum when tried on indictment: 5 years

Note: A conditional discharge is not available as a sentence for this offence

Offence seriousness (culpability and harm)

A. Identify the appropriate starting point

Starting points based on first time offender* pleading not guilty

Examples of nature of activity	Starting point	Range
Breach where no harassment, alarm or distress was caused or intended	**Low level community order**	**Band B fine to medium level community order**
Breach involving a lesser degree of actual or intended harassment, alarm or distress than in the box below, or where such harm would have been likely had the offender not been apprehended	**6 weeks custody**	**Medium level community order to 26 weeks custody**
Breach involving serious actual or intended harassment, alarm or distress	**26 weeks custody**	**Custody threshold to Crown Court**

Offence seriousness (culpability and harm)

B. Consider the effect of aggravating and mitigating factors (other than those within examples above)

Common aggravating and mitigating factors are identified [elsewhere]—the following may be particularly relevant but these lists are not exhaustive

Factors indicating higher culpability	Factors indicating lower culpability
1. Offender has a history of disobedience to court orders 2. Breach was committed immediately or shortly after the order was made 3. Breach was committed subsequent to earlier breach proceedings arising from the same order 4. Targeting of a person the order was made to protect or a witness in the original proceedings	1. Breach occurred after a long period of compliance 2. The prohibition(s) breached was not fully understood, especially where an interim order was made without notice

[Sets out the standard sequential sentencing procedure.]

**For the purposes of this guideline a "first time offender" is one who does not have a previous conviction for breach of an ASBO*

Arson (Criminal Damage by Fire) SG-177

Criminal Damage Act 1971, s. 1

Triable either way:
Maximum when tried summarily: Level 5 fine and/or 6 months
Maximum when tried on indictment: Life

Where offence committed in domestic context, refer [below] for guidance.

Identify dangerous offenders

This is a serious offence for the purposes of the public protection provisions in the Criminal Justice Act 2003 . . .

Offence seriousness (culpability and harm)

A. Identify the appropriate starting point

Starting points based on first time offender pleading not guilty

Examples of nature of activity	Starting point	Range
Minor damage by fire	**High level community order**	**Medium level community order to 12 weeks custody**
Moderate damage by fire	**12 weeks custody**	**6 to 26 weeks custody**
Significant damage by fire	**Crown Court**	**Crown Court**

Offence seriousness (culpability and harm)

B. Consider the effect of aggravating and mitigating factors (other than those within examples above)

Common aggravating and mitigating factors are identified [elsewhere]—the following may be particularly relevant but these lists are not exhaustive

Factors indicating higher culpability	Factor indicating lower culpability
1. Revenge attack **Factors indicating greater degree of harm** 1. Damage to emergency equipment 2. Damage to public amenity 3. Significant public or private fear caused e.g. in domestic context	1. Damage caused recklessly

[Sets out the standard sequential sentencing procedure.]

Sentencing Guidelines

SG-178 Assault Occasioning Actual Bodily Harm

Offences against the Person Act 1861 (section 47)

Racially/Religiously Aggravated ABH

Crime and Disorder Act 1998 (section 29)

[This guideline was published by the Sentencing Council and has effect in respect of all sentences passed after 13 June 2011 on offenders aged 18 or older. It replaces the guideline which previously applied and which continued to have effect until that date.]

These are specified offences for the purposes of section 224 of the Criminal Justice Act 2003

Triable either way

Section 47
Maximum when tried summarily: Level 5 fine and/or 26 weeks' custody
Maximum when tried on indictment: 5 years' custody

Section 29
Maximum when tried summarily: Level 5 fine and/or 26 weeks' custody
Maximum when tried on indictment: 7 years' custody

Offence range: Fine – 3 years' custody

This guideline applies to all offenders aged 18 and older, who are sentenced on or after 13 June 2011. The definitions [at **SG-273**] of 'starting point' and 'first time offender' do not apply for this guideline. Starting point and category ranges apply to all offenders in all cases, irrespective of plea or previous convictions.

STEP ONE Determining the offence category

The court should determine the offence category using the table below.

Category 1	Greater harm (serious injury must normally be present) **and** higher culpability
Category 2	Greater harm (serious injury must normally be present) **and** lower culpability; **or** lesser harm and higher culpability
Category 3	Lesser harm and lower culpability

The court should determine the offender's culpability and the harm caused, or intended, by reference only to the factors identified in the table below (as demonstrated by the presence of one or more). These factors comprise the principal factual elements of the offence and should determine the category.

Factors indicating greater harm Injury (which includes disease transmission and/or psychological harm) which is serious in the context of the offence (must normally be present) Victim is particularly vulnerable because of personal circumstances Sustained or repeated assault on the same victim	**Factors indicating lesser harm** Injury which is less serious in the context of the offence
Factors indicating higher culpability *Statutory aggravating factors:* Offence motivated by, or demonstrating, hostility to the victim based on his or her sexual orientation (or presumed sexual orientation) Offence motivated by, or demonstrating, hostility to the victim based on the victim's disability (or presumed disability) *Other aggravating factors:* A significant degree of premeditation Use of weapon or weapon equivalent (for example, shod foot, headbutting, use of acid, use of animal) Intention to commit more serious harm than actually resulted from the offence Deliberately causes more harm than is necessary for commission of offence Deliberate targeting of vulnerable victim Leading role in group or gang Offence motivated by, or demonstrating, hostility based on the victim's age, sex, gender identity (or presumed gender identity)	**Factors indicating lower culpability** Subordinate role in group or gang A greater degree of provocation than normally expected Lack of premeditation Mental disorder or learning disability, where linked to commission of the offence Excessive self defence

STEP TWO Starting point and category range

Having determined the category, the court should use the corresponding starting points to reach a sentence within the category range below. The starting point applies to all offenders irrespective of plea or previous convictions. A case of particular gravity, reflected by multiple features of culpability in step one, could merit upward adjustment from the starting point before further adjustment for aggravating or mitigating features, set out below.

Offence Category	Starting Point (*Applicable to all offenders*)	Category Range (*Applicable to all offenders*)
Category 1	Crown Court	Crown Court
Category 2	26 weeks' custody	Low level community order – Crown Court (51 weeks' custody)
Category 3	Medium level community order	Band A fine—High level community order

The table below contains a **non-exhaustive** list of additional factual elements providing the context of the offence and factors relating to the offender. Identify whether any combination of these, or other relevant factors, should result in an upward or downward adjustment from the starting point. In some cases, having considered these factors, it may be appropriate to move outside the identified category range.

When sentencing **category 2** offences, the court should also consider the custody threshold as follows:

- has the custody threshold been passed?
- if so, is it unavoidable that a custodial sentence be imposed?
- if so, can that sentence be suspended?

When sentencing **category 3** offences, the court should also consider the community order threshold as follows:

- has the community order threshold been passed?

Factors increasing seriousness	**Factors reducing seriousness or reflecting personal mitigation**
Statutory aggravating factors: Previous convictions, having regard to a) the nature of the offence to which the conviction relates and its relevance to the current offence; and b) the time that has elapsed since the conviction Offence committed whilst on bail *Other aggravating factors include:* Location of the offence Timing of the offence Ongoing effect upon the victim Offence committed against those working in the public sector or providing a service to the public Presence of others including relatives, especially children or partner of the victim Gratuitous degradation of victim In domestic violence cases, victim forced to leave their home Failure to comply with current court orders Offence committed whilst on licence An attempt to conceal or dispose of evidence Failure to respond to warnings or concerns expressed by others about the offender's behaviour Commission of offence whilst under the influence of alcohol or drugs Abuse of power and/or position of trust Exploiting contact arrangements with a child to commit an offence Established evidence of community impact Any steps taken to prevent the victim reporting an incident, obtaining assistance and/or from assisting or supporting the prosecution Offences taken into consideration (TICs)	No previous convictions **or** no relevant/recent convictions Single blow Remorse Good character and/or exemplary conduct Determination and/or demonstration of steps taken to address addiction or offending behaviour Serious medical conditions requiring urgent, intensive or long-term treatment Isolated incident Age and/or lack of maturity where it affects the responsibility of the offender Lapse of time since the offence where this is not the fault of the offender Mental disorder or learning disability, where **not** linked to the commission of the offence Sole or primary carer for dependent relatives

Section 29 offences only: The court should determine the appropriate sentence for the offence without taking account of the element of aggravation and then make an addition to the sentence, considering the level of aggravation involved. It may be appropriate to move outside the identified category range, taking into account the increased statutory maximum.

STEP THREE Consider any other factors which indicate a reduction, such as assistance to the prosecution

The court should take into account any rule of law by virtue of which an offender may receive a discounted sentence in consequence of assistance given (or offered) to the prosecutor or investigator.

STEP FOUR Reduction for guilty pleas

The court should take account of any potential reduction for a guilty plea in accordance with section 144 of the Criminal Justice Act 2003 and the Guilty Plea guideline.

STEP FIVE Dangerousness

Inflicting grievous bodily harm/Unlawful wounding and racially/religiously aggravated GBH/Unlawful wounding are specified offences within the meaning of Chapter 5 of the Criminal Justice Act 2003 and at this stage the court should consider whether having regard to the criteria contained in that Chapter it would be appropriate to award an extended sentence.

STEP SIX Totality principle

If sentencing an offender for more than one offence, or where the offender is already serving a sentence, consider whether the total sentence is just and proportionate to the offending behaviour.

STEP SEVEN Compensation and ancillary orders

In all cases, the court should consider whether to make compensation and/or other ancillary orders.

STEP EIGHT Reasons

Section 174 of the Criminal Justice Act 2003 imposes a duty to give reasons for, and explain the effect of, the sentence.

STEP NINE Consideration for remand time

Sentencers should take into consideration any remand time served in relation to the final sentence. The court should consider whether to give credit for time spent on remand in custody or on bail in accordance with sections 240 and 240A of the Criminal Justice Act 2003.

SG-179

Assault with Intent to Resist Arrest

Offences against the Person Act 1861 (section 38)

[This guideline was published by the Sentencing Council and has effect in respect of all sentences passed after 13 June 2011 on offenders aged 18 or older. It replaces the guideline which previously applied and which continued to have effect until that date.]

This is a specified offence for the purposes of section 224 of the Criminal Justice Act 2003

Triable either way
Maximum when tried summarily: Level 5 fine and/or 26 weeks' custody
Maximum when tried on indictment: 2 years' custody

Offence range: Fine—51 weeks' custody

This guideline applies to all offenders aged 18 and older, who are sentenced on or after 13 June 2011. The definitions [at **SG-273**] of 'starting point' and 'first time offender' do not apply for this guideline. Starting point and category ranges apply to all offenders in all cases, irrespective of plea or previous convictions.

STEP ONE Determining the offence category

The court should determine the offence category using the table below.

Category 1	Greater harm **and** higher culpability
Category 2	Greater harm **and** lower culpability; **or** lesser harm **and** higher culpability
Category 3	Lesser harm **and** lower culpability

The court should determine the offender's culpability and the harm caused, or intended, by reference only to the factors identified in the table below (as demonstrated by the presence of one or more). These factors comprise the principal factual elements of the offence and should determine the category.

Factors indicating greater harm Sustained or repeated assault on the same victim	**Factors indicating lesser harm** Injury which is less serious in the context of the offence
Factors indicating higher culpability *Statutory aggravating factors:* Offence racially or religiously aggravated Offence motivated by, or demonstrating, hostility to the victim based on his or her sexual orientation(or presumed sexual orientation) Offence motivated by, or demonstrating, hostility to the victim based on the victim's disability (or presumed disability) *Other aggravating factors:* A significant degree of premeditation Use of weapon or weapon equivalent (for example, shod foot, headbutting, use of acid, use of animal) Intention to commit more serious harm than actually resulted from the offence Deliberately causes more harm than is necessary for commission of offence Leading role in group or gang Offence motivated by, or demonstrating, hostility based on the victim's age, sex, gender identity (or presumed gender identity)	**Factors indicating lower culpability** Subordinate role in group or gang Lack of premeditation Mental disorder or learning disability, where linked to commission of the offence

STEP TWO Starting point and category range

Having determined the category, the court should use the corresponding starting points to reach a sentence within the category range below. The starting point applies to all offenders irrespective of plea or previous convictions. A case of particular gravity, reflected by multiple features of culpability in step one, could merit upward adjustment from the starting point before further adjustment for aggravating or mitigating features, set out below.

Offence Category	Starting Point (*Applicable to all offenders*)	Category Range (*Applicable to all offenders*)
Category 1	26 weeks' custody	12 weeks' custody—Crown Court (51 weeks' custody)
Category 2	Medium level community order	Low level community order—High level community order
Category 3	Band B fine	Band A fine—Band C fine

The table below contains a **non-exhaustive** list of additional factual elements providing the context of the offence and factors relating to the offender. Identify whether any combination of these, or other relevant factors, should result in an upward or downward adjustment from the starting point. In some cases, having considered these factors, it may be appropriate to move outside the identified category range.

When sentencing **category 1** offences, the court should consider whether the sentence can be suspended.

Factors increasing seriousness	**Factors reducing seriousness or reflecting personal mitigation**
Statutory aggravating factors: Previous convictions, having regard to a) the nature of the offence to which the conviction relates and its relevance to the current offence; and b) the time that has elapsed since the conviction Offence committed whilst on bail *Other aggravating factors include:* Location of the offence Timing of the offence Ongoing effect upon the victim Gratuitous degradation of victim Failure to comply with current court orders Offence committed whilst on licence An attempt to conceal or dispose of evidence Failure to respond to warnings or concerns expressed by others about the offender's behaviour Commission of offence whilst under the influence of alcohol or drugs Established evidence of community impact Any steps taken to prevent the victim reporting an incident, obtaining assistance and/or from assisting or supporting the prosecution Offences taken into consideration (TICs)	No previous convictions **or** no relevant/recent convictions Single blow Remorse Good character and/or exemplary conduct Determination and/or demonstration of steps taken to address addiction or offending behaviour Serious medical conditions requiring urgent, intensive or long-term treatment Isolated incident Age and/or lack of maturity where it affects the responsibility of the defendant Mental disorder or learning disability, where **not** linked to the commission of the offence Sole or primary carer for dependent relatives

[Steps Three to Nine are almost identical to those which apply to assault occasioning actual bodily harm: see **SG-178**.]

SG-180 Assault on a Police Constable in Execution of his Duty

Police Act 1996 (section 89)

[This guideline was published by the Sentencing Council and has effect in respect of all sentences passed after 13 June 2011 on offenders aged 18 or older. It replaces the guideline which previously applied and which continued to have effect until that date.]

Triable only summarily
Maximum: Level 5 fine and/or 26 weeks' custody

Offence range: Fine—26 weeks' custody

This guideline applies to all offenders aged 18 and older, who are sentenced on or after 13 June 2011. The definitions [at **SG-273**] of 'starting point' and 'first time offender' do not apply for this guideline. Starting point and category ranges apply to all offenders in all cases, irrespective of plea or previous convictions.

STEP ONE Determining the offence category

The court should determine the offence category using the table below.

Category 1	Greater harm **and** higher culpability
Category 2	Greater harm **and** lower culpability; or lesser harm **and** higher culpability
Category 3	Lesser harm **and** lower culpability

The court should determine the offender's culpability and the harm caused, or intended, by reference only to the factors below (as demonstrated by the presence of one or more). These factors comprise the principal factual elements of the offence and should determine the category.

Factors indicating greater harm Sustained or repeated assault on the same victim	**Factors indicating lesser harm** Injury which is less serious in the context of the offence
Factors indicating higher culpability *Statutory aggravating factors:* Offence racially or religiously aggravated Offence motivated by, or demonstrating, hostility to the victim based on his or her sexual orientation (or presumed sexual orientation) Offence motivated by, or demonstrating, hostility to the victim based on the victim's disability (or presumed disability) *Other aggravating factors:* A significant degree of premeditation Use of weapon or weapon equivalent (for example, shod foot, headbutting, use of acid, use of animal) Intention to commit more serious harm than actually resulted from the offence Deliberately causes more harm than is necessary for commission of offence Leading role in group or gang Offence motivated by, or demonstrating, hostility based on the victim's age, sex, gender identity (or presumed gender identity)	**Factors indicating lower culpability** Subordinate role in group or gang Lack of premeditation Mental disorder or learning disability, where linked to commission of the offence

STEP TWO Starting point and category range

Having determined the category, the court should use the corresponding starting points to reach a sentence within the category range below. The starting point applies to all offenders irrespective of plea or previous convictions. A case of particular gravity, reflected by multiple features of culpability in step one, could merit upward adjustment from the starting point before further adjustment for aggravating or mitigating features, set out below.

Offence Category	Starting Point (*Applicable to all offenders*)	Category Range (*Applicable to all offenders*)
Category 1	12 weeks' custody	Low level community order—26 weeks' custody
Category 2	Medium level community order	Low level community order—High level community order
Category 3	Band B fine	Band A fine—Band C fine

The table below contains a **non-exhaustive** list of additional factual elements providing the context of the offence and factors relating to the offender. Identify whether any combination of these, or other relevant factors, should result in an upward or downward adjustment from the starting point. In some cases, having considered these factors, it may be appropriate to move outside the identified category range.

When sentencing **category 1** offences, the court should also consider the custody threshold as follows:

- has the custody threshold been passed?
- if so, is it unavoidable that a custodial sentence be imposed?
- if so, can that sentence be suspended?

Factors increasing seriousness	**Factors reducing seriousness or reflecting personal mitigation**
Statutory aggravating factors: Previous convictions, having regard to a) the nature of the offence to which the conviction relates and its relevance to the current offence; and b) the time that has elapsed since the conviction Offence committed whilst on bail *Other aggravating factors include:* Location of the offence Timing of the offence Ongoing effect upon the victim Gratuitous degradation of victim Failure to comply with current court orders Offence committed whilst on licence An attempt to conceal or dispose of evidence Failure to respond to warnings or concerns expressed by others about the offender's behaviour Commission of offence whilst under the influence of alcohol or drugs Established evidence of community impact Any steps taken to prevent the victim reporting an incident, obtaining assistance and/or from assisting or supporting the prosecution Offences taken into consideration (TICs)	No previous convictions **or** no relevant/recent convictions Single blow Remorse Good character and/or exemplary conduct Determination and/or demonstration of steps taken to address addiction or offending behaviour Serious medical conditions requiring urgent, intensive or long-term treatment Isolated incident Age and/or lack of maturity where it affects the responsibility of the offender Lapse of time since the offence where this is not the fault of the offender Mental disorder or learning disability, where **not** linked to the commission of the offence Sole or primary carer for dependent relatives

[Steps Three to Eight are almost identical to Steps Three to Nine which apply to assault occasioning actual bodily harm (see **SG-178**) but Step Five (Dangerousness) is omitted.]

SG-181

Bail, Failure to Surrender

Factors to take into consideration
This guideline and accompanying notes are taken from the Sentencing Guidelines Council's definitive guideline *Fail to Surrender to Bail*, published 29 November 2007 [see **SG-136**]

Key factors

(a) Whilst the approach to sentencing should generally be the same whether the offender failed to surrender to a court or to a police station *and* whether the offence is contrary to ss. 6(1) or 6(2), the court must examine all the relevant circumstances.

(b) The following factors may be relevant when assessing the harm caused by the offence:
- Where an offender fails to appear for a first court hearing but attends shortly afterwards, the only harm caused is likely to be the financial cost to the system. Where a case could not have proceeded even if the offender had surrendered to bail, this should be taken into account.
- Where an offender appears for trial on the wrong day but enters a late guilty plea enabling the case to be disposed of to some degree at least, the harm caused by the delay may be offset by the benefits stemming from the change of plea.
- The most serious harm is likely to result when an offender fails to appear for trial, especially if this results in witnesses being sent away. Where it has been possible to conclude proceedings in the absence of the offender, this may be relevant to the assessment of harm caused.
- The level of harm is likely to be assessed as high where an offender fails to appear for sentence and is also seen to be flouting the authority of the court, such as where the avoidance of sentence results in the consequential avoidance of ancillary orders such as disqualification from driving, the payment of compensation or registration as a sex offender. This may increase the level of harm whenever the offender continues to present a risk to public safety.
- Whilst the seriousness of the original offence does not of itself aggravate or mitigate the seriousness of the offence of failing to surrender, the circumstances surrounding the original offence may be relevant in assessing the harm arising from the Bail Act offence.

- The circumstances in which bail to return to a police station is granted are less formal than the grant of court bail and the history of the individual case should be examined. There may be less culpability where bail has been enlarged on a number of occasions and less harm if court proceedings are not significantly delayed.

(c) Where the failure to surrender to custody was 'deliberate':
- at or near the bottom of the sentencing range will be cases where the offender gave no thought at all to the consequences, or other mitigating factors are present, and the degree of delay or interference with the progress of the case was not significant in all the circumstances;
- at or near the top of the range will be cases where aggravating factors 1, 2 or 4 opposite are present if there is also a significant delay and/or interference with the progress of the case.

(d) A previous conviction that is likely to be 'relevant' for the purposes of this offence is one which demonstrates failure to comply with an order of a court.
(e) Acquittal of the original offence does not automatically mitigate the Bail Act offence.
(f) The fact that an offender has a disorganised or chaotic lifestyle should not normally be treated as offence mitigation, but may be regarded as offender mitigation depending on the particular facts.
(g) A misunderstanding which does not amount to a defence may be a mitigating factor whereas a mistake on the part of the offender is his or her own responsibility.
(h) Where an offender has literacy or language difficulties, these may be mitigation (where they do not amount to a defence) where potential problems were not identified and/or appropriate steps were not taken to mitigate the risk in the circumstances as known at the time that bail was granted.
(i) An offenders position as the sole or primary carer of dependent relatives may be offender mitigation when it is the reason why the offender failed to surrender to custody.
(j) The sentence for this offence should usually be in addition to any sentence for the original offence. Where custodial sentences are being imposed for a Bail Act offence and the original offence at the same time, the normal approach should be for the sentences to be consecutive. The length of any custodial sentence imposed must be commensurate with the seriousness of the offence(s).
(k) If an offence is serious enough to justify the imposition of a community order, a curfew requirement with an electronic monitoring requirement may be particularly appropriate—see [below].

Guidelines

Bail Act 1976, ss. 6(1) and 6(2)

Triable either way:
Maximum when tried summarily: Level 5 fine and/or 3 months
Maximum when tried on indictment: 12 months

In certain circumstances, a magistrates' court may commit to the Crown Court for sentence. *Consult your legal adviser for guidance.*

Offence seriousness (culpability and harm)

A. Identify the appropriate starting point

Starting points based on first time offender pleading not guilty

Examples of nature of activity	Starting point	Range
Surrenders late on day but case proceeds as planned	**Band A fine**	**Band A fine to Band B fine**
Negligent or non-deliberate failure to attend causing delay and/or interference with the administration of justice	**Band C fine**	**Band B fine to medium level community order**
Deliberate failure to attend causing delay and/or interference with the administration of justice *The type and degree of harm actually caused will affect where in the range the case falls—see note (c) opposite*	**14 days custody**	**Low level community order to 10 weeks custody**

B. Consider the effect of aggravating and mitigating factors (other than those within examples above)

Common aggravating and mitigating factors are identified [elsewhere]—the following may be particularly relevant but these lists are not exhaustive

Factors indicating higher culpability	Factors indicating lower culpability
1. Serious attempts to evade justice 2. Determined attempt seriously to undermine the course of justice 3. Previous relevant convictions and/or breach of court orders or police bail	Where not amounting to a defence: 1. Misunderstanding 2. Failure to comprehend bail significance or requirements 3. Caring responsibilities—see note (i) opposite
Factor indicating greater degree of harm	**Factor indicating lesser degree of harm**
4. Lengthy absence	4. Prompt voluntary surrender

[Sets out the standard sequential sentencing procedure.]

In appropriate cases, a magistrates' court may impose one day's detention: Magistrates' Courts Act 1980, s. 135

SG-182 Bladed Article/Offensive Weapon, Possession Of

Factors to take into consideration

These guidelines and accompanying notes are drawn from the Court of Appeal's decision in *R v Celaire and Poulton* [2003] 1 Cr App R (S) 116. [But see the note issued as to the effect of *Povey* [2009] 1 Cr App R (S) 228, discussed at B12.120.]

Key factors

(a) Concurrent sentences may be appropriate if the weapons offence is ancillary to a more serious offence; consecutive sentences may be appropriate if the offences are distinct and independent. . ..
(b) When assessing offence seriousness, consider the offender's intention, the circumstances of the offence and the nature of the weapon involved.
(c) Some weapons are inherently more dangerous than others but the nature of the weapon is not the primary determinant of offence seriousness. A relatively less dangerous weapon, such as a billiard cue or knuckle-duster, may be used to create fear and such an offence may be at least as serious as one in which a more obviously dangerous weapon, such as a knife or an acid spray, is being carried for self-defence or no actual attempt has been made by the offender to use it.
(d) Nevertheless, the fact that the offender was carrying a weapon which is offensive per se may shed light on his or her intentions.

Guidelines

Triable either way:
Maximum when tried summarily: Level 5 fine and/or 6 months
Maximum when tried on indictment: 4 years

Offence seriousness (culpability and harm)

A. Identify the appropriate starting point

Starting points based on first time offender pleading not guilty

Examples of nature of activity	Starting point	Range
Weapon not used to threaten or cause fear	**High level community order**	**Band C fine to 12 weeks custody**
Weapon not used to threaten or cause fear but offence committed in dangerous circumstances	**6 weeks custody**	**High level community order to Crown Court**
Weapon used to threaten or cause fear and offence committed in dangerous circumstances	**Crown Court**	**Crown Court**

B. Consider the effect of aggravating and mitigating factors (other than those within examples above)

Common aggravating and mitigating factors are identified [elsewhere]—the following may be particularly relevant but these lists are not exhaustive

Factors indicating higher culpability	Factors indicating greater degree of harm
1. Particularly dangerous weapon 2. Specifically planned use of weapon to commit violence, threaten violence or intimidate 3. Offence motivated by hostility towards minority individual or group 4. Offender under influence of drink or drugs 5. Offender operating in group or gang	1. Offence committed at school, hospital or other place where vulnerable persons may be present 2. Offence committed on premises where people carrying out public services 3. Offence committed on or outside licensed premises 4. Offence committed on public transport 5. Offence committed at large public gathering, especially where there may be risk of disorder **Factors indicating lower culpability** 1. Weapon carried only on temporary basis 2. Original possession legitimate e.g. in course of trade or business

[Sets out the standard sequential sentencing procedure and mentions need to consider deprivation of property (including weapon).]

BURGLARY IN A DWELLING **SG-183**

[The Guidelines are subject to a note issued following the judgment in *Saw* [2009] EWCA Crim 1 (see **SG-184**). The note is set out in italics below. It is expressed to be additional to, rather a replacement for, the original Guidelines although aspects of the two conflict.]

Factors to take into consideration

These guidelines and accompanying notes are drawn from the Court of Appeal's decision in *R v McInerney and Keating* [2002] EWCA Crim 3003

Key factors

(a) Even where the custody threshold is passed, consider whether a community order is appropriate (*McInerney and Keating* and refer also [below]).
(b) Cases in the Crown Court category may be suitable for a community order (see note (a) above), but should nevertheless be committed to the Crown Court for trial/sentence so that any breach of the order can be sentenced within the powers of that Court.
(c) For attempted burglary or burglary under s. 9(1)(a) of the Theft Act 1968, it is the offender's intention that will determine which of the three categories opposite the offence falls into, not the fact that nothing was stolen.
(d) Relevant convictions that will aggravate offence seriousness in accordance with s. 143(2) of the Criminal Justice Act 2003 may include convictions for both property and violent offences.

Guidelines

Theft Act 1968, s. 9

Triable either way:
Maximum when tried summarily: Level 5 fine and/or 6 months
Maximum when tried on indictment: 14 years

Allocation
Consult legal adviser for guidance

Offence is indictable only and must be sent to the Crown Court if:
(1) The offender has been convicted of two other domestic burglaries committed on separate occasions after 30 November 1999 and one was committed after conviction for the other: Powers of Criminal Courts (Sentencing) Act 2000, s. 111;
(2) Any person was subjected to violence or the threat of violence: Magistrates' Courts Act 1980, sch. 1

Offence seriousness (culpability and harm)

A. Identify the appropriate starting point

Starting points based on first time offender pleading not guilty

Examples of nature of activity	Starting point	Range
Unforced entry and low value theft with no aggravating features	**Medium level community order**	**Low level community order to 12 weeks custody**
Forced entry, goods stolen not high value, no aggravating features	**12 weeks custody**	**High level community order to Crown Court**
Goods stolen high value or any aggravating feature present	**Crown Court**	**Crown Court**

B. Consider the effect of aggravating and mitigating factors (other than those within examples above)

Common aggravating and mitigating factors are identified [elsewhere]—the following may be particularly relevant but these lists are not exhaustive

Factors indicating higher culpability	Factors indicating lower culpability
1. Ransacking property 2. Professionalism 3. Victim deliberately targeted e.g. out of spite 4. Housebreaking implements or weapons carried **Factors indicating greater degree of harm** 1. Occupier at home or returns home while offender present 2. Goods stolen of sentimental value	1. Offender played only a minor role in the burglary 2. Offence committed on impulse **Factor indicating lesser degree of harm** 1. No damage or disturbance to property

[Sets out the standard sequential sentencing procedure and mentions need to consider deprivation of property.]

SG-184 *Burglary in a dwelling*

[The above] provides a summary of the effect of the Court of Appeal guideline judgment in McInerney and Keating as it applies both to mode of trial (allocation) and to sentencing decisions in a magistrates' court. In the light of experience and pending any fuller consideration by the Sentencing Guidelines Council, that judgment has been reviewed and clarified by the Court of Appeal in R v Saw and others [2009] EWCA Crim 1.

The purpose of this note is to clarify the effect of the decision on the application of this part of the Magistrates' Court Sentencing Guidelines.

Approach to sentencing—Key points

1. The aim of the judgment is to achieve consistency of approach, clearly recognising the seriousness of this offence—not only is it an offence against property but it is also an offence against the person. Particular focus is required on the impact of the offence on those living in the burgled house; sentences should reflect the level of harmful consequences even when not intended by the offender.

2. The sentence must reflect the criminality of the offender. Previous convictions and the record of an offender are of more significance than in the case of some other crimes. Burglary of a dwelling should be treated as more serious when committed by an offender with previous convictions for relevant dishonesty than an identical offence committed by a first offender.

3. The judgment states that it does not add anything to the Magistrates' Court Sentencing Guidelines, emphasising the importance of addressing the aggravating and mitigating factors referred to in the judgment. The Magistrates' Court Sentencing Guidelines currently provide for committal to the Crown Court where an aggravating feature is present and sentence within the powers of the Crown Court is included within the range in some other circumstances.

4. A non-exhaustive list of aggravating and mitigating features commonly encountered in burglary is provided in the judgment; this is more extensive than the list in the Magistrates' Court Sentencing Guidelines derived from McInerney and Keating. They are summarised at the end of this note. The importance of the aggravating features derives from the increase in the impact of the offence that results from them, or from the increase in the culpability of the offender that they demonstrate, or from a combination of the two.

The guideline—categories of seriousness
The Magistrates' Court Sentencing Guidelines set out three categories of offence seriousness:

Category 1—Offences likely to be able to be sentenced within the jurisdiction of a magistrates' court (when committed by a first time offender) are those where the entry to the premises was unforced, the property stolen of low value and there were no aggravating features; the starting point is a community sentence. In determining whether an aggravating feature was present, the court should refer to the list set out in Saw and others.

Category 2—Where the entry was forced the goods were not of high value, and there were no aggravating features, the sentencing range commences within the jurisdiction of a magistrates' court but ends within the jurisdiction of the Crown Court; the starting point is 12 weeks custody. In determining whether an aggravating feature was present, the court should refer to the list set out in Saw and others.

Although Saw and others requires particular focus on the impact of the offence on the victim, it confirms that a low level burglary with minimal loss and minimal damage and without raised culpability or raised impact, committed by a first time offender, may be dealt with by way of a community order rather than an immediate custodial penalty.

Category 3—An offence would be expected to be committed to the Crown Court where the goods stolen were of high value or any aggravating feature was present.

Saw and others provides that the court must address the overall criminality of the offender (in the light of previous convictions) and the impact of the offence on the victim(s):

- *where there is limited raised culpability and/or impact, it is likely that the sentence will be within a general range of 9 to18 months custody; a shorter sentence (including the making of a community order) may be appropriate where it is established that the offender played a subsidiary role or was exploited by other offenders;*
- *where there is seriously raised culpability and/or serious impact, the starting point should be a custodial sentence in excess of 18 months; a community order should be considered only in the most extreme and exceptional circumstances.*

As noted [above], where a case otherwise appropriate for sentence in the Crown Court is, on its own particular facts likely to attract a community order, it should nonetheless be sentenced in the Crown Court so that any sanction for non-compliance can be imposed with the powers of that court rather than within the more limited powers of a magistrates' court.

Aggravating and Mitigating Features (not exhaustive)
Aggravating features:

- *the use or threat of force on or against the victim (NB: this would make the offence triable on indictment only),*
- *trauma to the victim beyond that normally associated with this type of offence,*
- *pre-meditation and professional planning or organisation, such as by offenders working in groups or when housebreaking implements are carried*
- *vandalism of the premises burgled,*
- *deliberate targeting of any vulnerable victim,*
- *deliberate targeting of any victim,*
- *the presence of the occupier whether at night or during the day,*
- *high economic or sentimental value of the property stolen or damaged,*
- *offence committed on bail or shortly after imposition of a non-custodial sentence,*
- *two or more burglaries of homes rather than a single offence,*
- *the offender's previous convictions.*

Mitigating features:

- *nothing, or only property of very low value is taken,*
- *offender played a minor part in the burglary, and treated by others in group as if he were on the fringes*
- *exploited by others*
- *offence committed on impulse*

- *age and state of health (mental and physical)*
- *good character*
- *evidence of genuine regret and remorse*
- *ready co-operation with the police*
- *positive response to previous sentences*

CONSULT YOUR LEGAL ADVISER FOR GUIDANCE

SG-185

Burglary in a Building other than a Dwelling

Factors to take into consideration

This guideline and accompanying notes are taken from the Sentencing Guidelines Council's definitive guideline Theft and Burglary in a building other than a dwelling, published 9 December 2008 [see **SG-368**]

Key factors

(a) This guideline is concerned solely with burglary committed in a building other than a dwelling where an offender enters as a trespasser with intent to steal or, having entered as a trespasser, actually goes on to steal.

(b) The starting points and sentencing ranges in this guideline are based on the assumption that the offender was motivated by greed or a desire to live beyond his or her means. To avoid double counting, such a motivation should not be treated as a factor that increases culpability.

(c) The starting point is based on the loss suffered by the victim. Whilst, in general, the greater the loss, the more serious the offence, the monetary value of the loss may not reflect the full extent of the harm caused by the offence. The court should also take into account the impact of the offence on the victim (which may be significantly greater than the monetary value of the loss; this may be particularly important where the value of the loss is high in proportion to the victims financial circumstances even though relatively low in absolute terms), any harm to persons other than the direct victim, and any harm in the form of public concern or erosion of public confidence.

(d) Offences of this type will be aggravated where the offender targets premises because high value, often easily disposable, property is likely to be found there as this indicates professionalism and organisation in the offending, as well as an intention to derive a high level of gain. Targeting of vulnerable community premises may result in a higher than usual degree of harm due to the inconvenience, distress and expense caused to the victim. Where premises which have been burgled on a prior occasion are targeted, this indicates planning, organisation and professionalism and, therefore, should be regarded as increasing the offenders culpability. Repeat victimisation may also increase the harm caused by the offence in terms of distress, inconvenience and expense to the victim.

(e) The Council has identified the following matters of offender mitigation which may be relevant to this offence:

(i) *Return of stolen property*
Whether and the degree to which the return of stolen property constitutes a matter of personal mitigation will depend on an assessment of the circumstances and, in particular, the voluntariness and timeliness of the return.

(ii) *Impact on sentence of offender's dependency*
Where an offence is motivated by an addiction (often to drugs, alcohol or gambling) this does not mitigate the seriousness of the offence, but a dependency may properly influence the type of sentence imposed. In particular, it may sometimes be appropriate to impose a drug rehabilitation requirement, an alcohol treatment requirement (for dependent drinkers) or an activity or supervision requirement including alcohol specific information, advice and support (for harmful and hazardous drinkers) as part of a community order or a suspended sentence order in an attempt to break the cycle of addiction and offending, even if an immediate custodial sentence would otherwise be warranted.

(iii) *Offender motivated by desperation or need*
The fact that an offence has been committed in desperation or need arising from particular hardship may count as personal mitigation in exceptional circumstances.

Guidelines

Theft Act 1968, s. 9

Triable either way:
Maximum when tried summarily: Level 5 fine and/or 6 months
Maximum when tried on indictment: 10 years

Offence seriousness (culpability and harm)

A. Identify the appropriate starting point

Starting points based on first time offender pleading not guilty

Examples of nature of activity	Starting point	Range
Burglary involving goods valued at less than £2,000	**Medium level community order**	**Band B fine to 26 weeks custody**
Burglary involving goods valued at £2,000 or more but less than £20,000	**18 weeks custody**	**High level community order to Crown Court**
Burglary involving goods valued at £20,000 or more	**Crown Court**	**Crown Court**

B. Consider the effect of aggravating and mitigating factors (other than those within examples above)

Common aggravating and mitigating factors are identified [elsewhere]—the following may be particularly relevant but these lists are not exhaustive

Factors indicating higher culpability
1. Targeting premises containing property of high value
2. Targeting vulnerable community premises
3. Targeting premises which have been burgled on prior occasion(s)
4. Possession of a weapon (where this is not charged separately)

[Sets out the standard sequential sentencing procedure.]

Child Prostitution and Pornography **SG-186**

Factors to take into consideration

This guideline is taken from the Sentencing Guidelines Council's definitive guideline Sexual Offences Act 2003, published 30 April 2007 [see **SG-125**]

Key factors

(a) Few cases will be suitable to be dealt with in a magistrates' court for the following reasons:
- The courts should consider making an order confiscating any profits stemming from the offender's criminal life-style or forfeiting any possessions (e.g. cameras, computers, property) used in connection with the commission of the offence. Only the Crown Court can make a confiscation order.
- The starting point for the child prostitution and pornography offences will always be a custodial sentence.
- In cases where a number of children are involved, consecutive sentences may be appropriate, leading to cumulative sentences significantly higher than the starting points for individual offences.

(b) In accordance with s. 80 [of] and sch. 3 [to] the Sexual Offences Act 2003, automatic notification requirements apply upon conviction to an offender aged 18 or over.

Guidelines

Sexual Offences Act 2003, s. 48 (causing or inciting child prostitution or pornography);
s. 49 (controlling a child prostitute or a child involved in pornography);
s. 50 (arranging or facilitating child prostitution or pornography)

Triable either way:
Maximum when tried summarily: Level 5 fine and/or 6 months
Maximum when tried on indictment: 14 years

Identify dangerous offenders

These are serious offences for the purposes of the public protection provisions in the Criminal Justice Act 2003 . . .

Offence seriousness (culpability and harm)

A. Identify the appropriate starting point

Starting points based on first time offender pleading not guilty

These offences should normally be dealt with in the Crown Court. However, there may be rare cases of non-penetrative activity involving a victim aged 16 or 17 where the offender's involvement is minimal and not perpetrated for gain in which a custodial sentence within the jurisdiction of a magistrates' court may be appropriate. *Consult your legal adviser for further guidance.*

B. Consider the effect of aggravating and mitigating factors (other than those within examples above)

Common aggravating and mitigating factors are identified [elsewhere]—the following may be particularly relevant but these lists are not exhaustive

Factors indicating higher culpability 1. Background of threats or intimidation 2. Large-scale commercial operation 3. Use of drugs, alcohol or other substance to secure the victim's compliance 4. Forcing a victim to violate another person 5. Abduction or detention 6. Threats to prevent the victim reporting the activity 7. Threats to disclose victim's activity to friends/relatives 8. Images distributed to other children or persons known to the victim 9. Financial or other gain **Factors indicating greater degree of harm** 1. Induced dependency on drugs 2. Victim has been manipulated into physical and emotional dependence on the offender 3. Storing, making available or distributing images in such a way that they can be inadvertently accessed by others	**Factor indicating lower culpability** 1. Offender also being controlled in prostitution or pornography and subject to threats or intimidation

[Sets out the standard sequential sentencing procedure.]

SG-187

Common Assault

Criminal Justice Act 1988 (section 39)

Racially/Religiously Aggravated Common Assault

Crime and Disorder Act 1998 (section 29)

[This guideline was published by the Sentencing Council and has effect in respect of all sentences passed after 13 June 2011 on offenders aged 18 or older. It replaces the guideline which previously applied and which continued to have effect until that date.]

Racially/religiously aggravated assault is a specified offence for the purposes of section 224 of the Criminal Justice Act 2003

Section 39
Triable only summarily
Maximum when tried summarily: Level 5 fine and/or 26 weeks' custody

Section 29
Triable either way
Maximum when tried summarily: Level 5 fine and/or 26 weeks' custody
Maximum when tried on indictment: 2 years' custody

Offence range: Discharge—26 weeks' custody

This guideline applies to all offenders aged 18 and older, who are sentenced on or after 13 June 2011. The definitions [at **SG-273**] of 'starting point' and 'first time offender' do not apply for this guideline. Starting point and category ranges apply to all offenders in all cases, irrespective of plea or previous convictions.

STEP ONE Determining the offence category

The court should determine the offence category using the table below.

Category 1	Greater harm (injury or fear of injury must normally be present) **and** higher culpability
Category 2	Greater harm (injury or fear of injury must normally be present) **and** lower culpability; **or** lesser harm and higher culpability
Category 3	Lesser harm **and** lower culpability

The court should determine the offender's culpability and the harm caused, or intended, by reference only to the factors below (as demonstrated by the presence of one or more). These factors comprise the principal factual elements of the offence and should determine the category.

Factors indicating greater harm Injury or fear of injury which is serious in the context of the offence (must normally be present) Victim is particularly vulnerable because of personal circumstances Sustained or repeated assault on the same victim	**Factors indicating lesser harm** Injury which is less serious in the context of the offence
Factors indicating higher culpability *Statutory aggravating factors:* Offence motivated by, or demonstrating, hostility to the victim based on his or her sexual orientation (or presumed sexual orientation) Offence motivated by, or demonstrating, hostility to the victim based on the victim's disability (or presumed disability) *Other aggravating factors:* A significant degree of premeditation Threatened or actual use of weapon or weapon equivalent (for example, shod foot, headbutting, use of acid, use of animal) Intention to commit more serious harm than actually resulted from the offence Deliberately causes more harm than is necessary for commission of offence Deliberate targeting of vulnerable victim Leading role in group or gang Offence motivated by, or demonstrating, hostility based on the victim's age, sex, gender identity (or presumed gender identity)	**Factors indicating lower culpability** Subordinate role in group or gang A greater degree of provocation than normally expected Lack of premeditation Mental disorder or learning disability, where linked to commission of the offence Excessive self defence

STEP TWO Starting point and category range

Having determined the category, the court should use the corresponding starting points to reach a sentence within the category range below. The starting point applies to all offenders irrespective of plea or previous convictions. A case of particular gravity, reflected by multiple features of culpability in step one, could merit upward adjustment from the starting point before further adjustment for aggravating or mitigating features, set out below.

Offence Category	**Starting Point** (*Applicable to all offenders*)	**Category Range** (*Applicable to all offenders*)
Category 1	High level community order	Low level community order—26 weeks' custody
Category 2	Medium level community order	Band A fine—High level community order
Category 3	Band A fine	Discharge—Band C fine

Sentencing Guidelines

The table below contains a **non-exhaustive** list of additional factual elements providing the context of the offence and factors relating to the offender. Identify whether any combination of these, or other relevant factors, should result in an upward or downward adjustment from the starting point. In some cases, having considered these factors, it may be appropriate to move outside the identified category range.

When sentencing **category 1** offences, the court should also consider the custody threshold as follows:

- has the custody threshold been passed?
- if so, is it unavoidable that a custodial sentence be imposed?
- if so, can that sentence be suspended?

When sentencing **category 2** offences, the court should also consider the community order threshold as follows:

- has the community order threshold been passed?

Factors increasing seriousness	Factors reducing seriousness or reflecting personal mitigation
Statutory aggravating factors: Previous convictions, having regard to a) the nature of the offence to which the conviction relates and its relevance to the current offence; and b) the time that has elapsed since the conviction Offence committed whilst on bail *Other aggravating factors include:* Location of the offence Timing of the offence Ongoing effect upon the victim Offence committed against those working in the public sector or providing a service to the public Presence of others including relatives, especially children or partner of the victim Gratuitous degradation of victim In domestic violence cases, victim forced to leave their home Failure to comply with current court orders Offence committed whilst on licence An attempt to conceal or dispose of evidence Failure to respond to warnings or concerns expressed by others about the offender's behaviour Commission of offence whilst under the influence of alcohol or drugs Abuse of power and/or position of trust Exploiting contact arrangements with a child to commit an offence Established evidence of community impact Any steps taken to prevent the victim reporting an incident, obtaining assistance and/or from assisting or supporting the prosecution Offences taken into consideration (TICs)	No previous convictions or no relevant/recent convictions Single blow Remorse Good character and/or exemplary conduct Determination and/or demonstration of steps taken to address addiction or offending behaviour Serious medical conditions requiring urgent, intensive or long-term treatment Isolated incident Age and/or lack of maturity where it affects the responsibility of the offender Lapse of time since the offence where this is not the fault of the offender Mental disorder or learning disability, where not linked to the commission of the offence Sole or primary carer for dependent relatives

Section 29 offences only: The court should determine the appropriate sentence for the offence without taking account of the element of aggravation and then make an addition to the sentence, considering the level of aggravation involved. It may be appropriate to move outside the identified category range, taking into account the increased statutory maximum.

[Steps Three to Nine are almost identical to those which apply to assault occasioning actual bodily harm: see **SG-178**.]

Communication Network Offences

SG-188

Communications Act 2003, ss. 127(1) and 127(2)

Triable only summarily:
Maximum: Level 5 fine and/or 6 months

Offence seriousness (culpability and harm)

A. Identify the appropriate starting point

Starting points based on first time offender pleading not guilty

Sending grossly offensive, indecent, obscene or menacing messages (s.127(1))		
Examples of nature of activity	**Starting point**	**Range**
Single offensive, indecent, obscene or menacing call of short duration, having no significant impact on receiver	**Band B fine**	**Band A fine to band C fine**
Single call where extreme language used, having only moderate impact on receiver	**Medium level community order**	**Low level community order to high level community order**
Single call where extreme language used and substantial distress or fear caused to receiver; OR One of a series of similar calls as described in box above	**6 weeks custody**	**High level community order to 12 weeks custody**

Sending false message/persistent use of communications network for purpose of causing annoyance, inconvenience or needless anxiety (s.127(2))		
Examples of nature of activity	**Starting point**	**Range**
Persistent silent calls over short period to private individual, causing inconvenience or annoyance	**Band B fine**	**Band A fine to band C fine**
Single hoax call to public or private organisation resulting in moderate disruption or anxiety	**Medium level community order**	**Low level community order to high level community order**
Single hoax call resulting in major disruption or substantial public fear or distress; OR One of a series of similar calls as described in box above	**12 weeks custody**	**High level community order to 18 weeks custody**

B. Consider the effect of aggravating and mitigating factors (other than those within examples above)

Common aggravating and mitigating factors are identified [elsewhere]

[Sets out the standard sequential sentencing procedure.]

Community Order, Breach Of

SG-189

Criminal Justice Act 2003, sch. 8

These notes are taken from the Sentencing Guidelines Council's definitive guideline *New Sentences: Criminal Justice Act 2003*, published 16 December 2004[190] [see **SG-11**]

Options in breach proceedings:
When dealing with breaches of community orders for offences committed after 4 April 2005, the court must either:

- amend the terms of the original order so as to impose more onerous requirements. The court may extend the duration of particular requirements within the order, but it cannot extend the overall length of the original order; or
- revoke the original order and proceed to sentence for the original offence. Where an offender has wilfully and persistently failed to comply with an order made in respect of an offence that is not punishable by imprisonment, the court can impose up to six months' custody.

[190] Criminal Justice Act 2003, sch.8, para. 9(1)(c)

Approach:

- having decided that a community order is commensurate with the seriousness of the offence, the primary objective when sentencing for breach of requirements is to ensure that those requirements are completed;
- a court sentencing for breach must take account of the extent to which the offender has complied with the requirements of the original order, the reasons for the breach, and the point at which the breach has occurred;
- if increasing the onerousness of requirements, sentencers should take account of the offender's ability to comply and should avoid precipitating further breach by overloading the offender with too many or conflicting requirements;
- there may be cases where the court will need to consider re-sentencing to a differently constructed community order in order to secure compliance with the purposes of the original sentence, perhaps where there has already been partial compliance or where events since the sentence was imposed have shown that a different course of action is likely to be effective;
- where available, custody should be the last resort, reserved for those cases of deliberate and repeated breach where all reasonable efforts to ensure that the offender complies have failed.

Where the original order was made by the Crown Court, breach proceedings must be commenced in that court unless the order provided that any failure to comply with its requirements may be dealt with in a magistrates' court. . . .

SG-190

Criminal Damage (other than by Fire)

Racially Or Religiously Aggravated Criminal Damage

Criminal Damage Act 1971, s. 1(1)

Crime and Disorder Act 1998, s. 30

Criminal damage: triable only summarily if value involved does not exceed £5,000:
Maximum: Level 4 fine and/or 3 months
Triable either way if value involved exceeds £5,000:
Maximum when tried summarily: Level 5 fine and/or 6 months
Maximum when tried on indictment: 10 years

Racially or religiously aggravated criminal damage: triable either way
Maximum when tried summarily: Level 5 fine and/or 6 months
Maximum when tried on indictment: 14 years

Where offence committed in domestic context, refer [below] for guidance

Offence seriousness (culpability and harm)

A. Identify the appropriate starting point

Starting points based on first time offender pleading not guilty

Examples of nature of activity	Starting point	Range
Minor damage e.g. breaking small window; small amount of graffiti	**Band B fine**	**Conditional discharge to band C fine**
Moderate damage e.g. breaking large plate-glass or shop window; widespread graffiti	**Low level community order**	**Band C fine to medium level community order**
Significant damage up to £5,000 e.g. damage caused as part of a spree	**High level community order**	**Medium level community order to 12 weeks custody**
Damage between £5,000 and £10,000	**12 weeks custody**	**6 to 26 weeks custody**
Damage over £10,000	**Crown Court**	**Crown Court**

B. Consider the effect of aggravating and mitigating factors (other than those within examples above)

Common aggravating and mitigating factors are identified [elsewhere]—the following may be particularly relevant but these lists are not exhaustive

Factors indicating higher culpability	Factors indicating lower culpability
1. Revenge attack 2. Targeting vulnerable victim **Factors indicating greater degree of harm** 1. Damage to emergency equipment 2. Damage to public amenity 3. Significant public or private fear caused e.g. in domestic context	1. Damage caused recklessly 2. Provocation

[Sets out the standard sequential sentencing procedure. Notes that 'If offender charged and convicted of the racially or religiously aggravated offence, increase the sentence to reflect this element']

Cruelty to a Child

SG-191

Factors to take into consideration

This guideline and accompanying notes are taken from the Sentencing Guidelines Council's definitive guidelines *Overarching Principles: Assaults on children and Cruelty to a child*, published 20 February 2008 [see **SG-153**]

Key factors

(a) The same starting point and sentencing range is proposed for offences which might fall into the four categories (assault; ill-treatment or neglect; abandonment; and failure to protect). These are designed to take into account the fact that the victim is particularly vulnerable, assuming an abuse of trust or power and the likelihood of psychological harm, and designed to reflect the seriousness with which society as a whole regards these offences.

(b) As noted above, the starting points have been calculated to reflect the likelihood of psychological harm and this cannot be treated as an aggravating factor. Where there is an especially serious physical or psychological effect on the victim, even if unintended, this should increase sentence.

(c) The normal sentencing starting point for an offence of child cruelty should be a custodial sentence. The length of that sentence will be influenced by the circumstances in which the offence took place.

(d) However, in considering whether a custodial sentence is the most appropriate disposal, the court should take into account any available information concerning the future care of the child.

(e) Where the offender is the sole or primary carer of the victim or other dependants, this potentially should be taken into account for sentencing purposes, regardless of whether the offender is male or female. In such cases, an immediate custodial sentence may not be appropriate.

(f) The most relevant areas of personal mitigation are likely to be:
- Mental illness/depression
- Inability to cope with the pressures of parenthood
- Lack of support
- Sleep deprivation
- Offender dominated by an abusive or stronger partner
- Extreme behavioural difficulties in the child, often coupled with a lack of support
- Inability to secure assistance or support services in spite of every effort having been made by the offender.

Some of the factors identified above, in particular sleep deprivation, lack of support and an inability to cope, could be regarded as an inherent part of caring for children, especially when a child is very young and could be put forward as mitigation by most carers charged with an offence of child cruelty. It follows that, before being accepted as mitigation, there must be evidence that these factors were present to a high degree and had an identifiable and significant impact on the offender's behaviour.

Guidelines

Children and Young Persons Act 1933, s.1(1)

Triable either way:
Maximum when tried summarily: Level 5 fine and/or 6 months
Maximum when tried on indictment: 10 years

Identify dangerous offenders

This is a serious offence for the purposes of the public protection provisions in the Criminal Justice Act 2003 . . .

Offence seriousness (culpability and harm)

A. Identify the appropriate starting point

Starting points based on first time offender pleading not guilty

Examples of nature of activity	Starting point	Range
(i) Short term neglect or ill-treatment (ii) Single incident of short-term abandonment (iii) Failure to protect a child from any of the above	**12 weeks custody**	**Low level community order to 26 weeks custody**
(i) Assault(s) resulting in injuries consistent with ABH (ii) More than one incident of neglect or ill-treatment (but not amounting to long-term behaviour) (iii) Single incident of long-term abandonment OR regular incidents of short-term abandonment (the longer the period of long-term abandonment or the greater the number of incidents of short-term abandonment, the more serious the offence) (iv) Failure to protect a child from any of the above	**Crown Court**	**26 weeks custody to Crown Court**
(i) Series of assaults (ii) Protracted neglect or ill-treatment (iii) Serious cruelty over a period of time (iv) Failure to protect a child from any of the above	**Crown Court**	**Crown Court**

B. Consider the effect of aggravating and mitigating factors (other than those within examples above)

Common aggravating and mitigating factors are identified [elsewhere]—the following may be particularly relevant but these lists are not exhaustive

1. Targeting one particular child from the family 2. Sadistic behaviour 3. Threats to prevent the victim from reporting the offence 4. Deliberate concealment of the victim from the authorities 5. Failure to seek medical help	1. Seeking medical help or bringing the situation to the notice of the authorities

[Sets out the standard sequential sentencing procedure.]

SG-192

Drugs—Class A—Fail to Attend/Remain for Initial Assessment

Drugs Act 2005, s. 12

Triable only summarily:
Maximum: Level 4 fine and/or 3 months
Offence seriousness (culpability and harm)

A. Identify the appropriate starting point

Starting points based on first time offender pleading not guilty

Examples of nature of activity	Starting point	Range
Failure to attend at the appointed place and time	**Medium level community order**	**Band C fine to high level community order**

B. Consider the effect of aggravating and mitigating factors (other than those within examples above)

Common aggravating and mitigating factors are identified [elsewhere]—the following may be particularly relevant but these lists are not exhaustive

Factors indicating greater degree of harm	Factors indicating lower culpability
1. Threats or abuse to assessor or other staff	1. Offender turns up but at wrong place or time or fails to remain for duration of appointment 2. Subsequent voluntary contact to rearrange appointment

[Sets out the standard sequential sentencing procedure.]

DRUGS—CLASS A—FAIL/REFUSE TO PROVIDE A SAMPLE SG-193

Police and Criminal Evidence Act 1984, s. 63B

Triable only summarily:
Maximum: Level 4 fine and/or 3 months

Offence seriousness (culpability and harm)

A. Identify the appropriate starting point

Starting points based on first time offender pleading not guilty

Examples of nature of activity	Starting point	Range
Refusal to provide sample without good cause when required by police officer	**Medium level community order**	**Band C fine to high level community order**

B. Consider the effect of aggravating and mitigating factors (other than those within examples above)

Common aggravating and mitigating factors are identified [elsewhere]—the following may be particularly relevant but these lists are not exhaustive

Factor indicating greater degree of harm	Factors indicating lower culpability
1. Threats or abuse to staff	1. Subsequent voluntary contact with drug workers 2. Subsequent compliance with testing on arrest/charge

[Sets out the standard sequential sentencing procedure.]

DRUGS—CLASS A—POSSESSION SG-194

Misuse of Drugs Act 1971, s. 5(2)

Triable either way:
Maximum when tried summarily: Level 5 fine and/or 6 months
Maximum when tried on indictment: 7 years

Offence seriousness (culpability and harm)

A. Identify the appropriate starting point

Starting points based on first time offender pleading not guilty

Examples of nature of activity	Starting point	Range
Possession of a very small quantity of the drug e.g. one small wrap or tablet	**Band C fine**	**Band B fine to medium level community order**
More than a very small quantity of the drug e.g. up to six wraps or tablets	**Medium level community order**	**Low level community order to high level community order**
Larger amounts	**High level community order**	**Medium level community order to Crown Court**
Possession of drug in prison—whether by prisoner or another	**Crown Court**	**Crown Court**

B. Consider the effect of aggravating and mitigating factors (other than those within examples above)

Common aggravating and mitigating factors are identified [elsewhere]—the following may be particularly relevant but these lists are not exhaustive

Factor indicating higher culpability 1. Offender exercising or acting in position of special responsibility **Factor indicating greater degree of harm** 1. Possession of drug in a public place or school	

[Sets out the standard sequential sentencing procedure, but also indicates need to consider forfeiture and destruction of drug.]

SG-195 Drugs—Class A—Produce, Supply, Possess with Intent to Supply

Misuse of Drugs Act 1971, ss. 4(2), 4(3), 5(3)

Triable either way:
Maximum when tried summarily: Level 5 fine and/or 6 months
Maximum when tried on indictment: Life

Offence seriousness (culpability and harm)

A. Identify the appropriate starting point

Starting points based on first time offender pleading not guilty

These offences should normally be dealt with in the Crown Court. However, there may be very rare cases involving non-commercial supply (e.g. between equals) of a very small amount (e.g. one small wrap or tablet) in which a custodial sentence within the jurisdiction of a magistrates' court may be appropriate.

SG-196 Drugs—Class B and C—Possession

Misuse of Drugs Act 1971, s. 5(2)

Triable either way:
Maximum when tried summarily: Level 4 fine and/or 3 months (class B); level 3 fine and/or 3 months (class C)
Maximum when tried on indictment: 5 years (class B); 2 years (class C)

Offence seriousness (culpability and harm)

A. Identify the appropriate starting point

Starting points based on first time offender pleading not guilty

Examples of nature of activity	Starting point	Range
Possession of a small amount of class B drug for personal use	**Band B fine**	**Band A fine to low level community order**
Possession of large amount of class B drug for personal use	**Band C fine**	**Band B fine to 12 weeks custody**

B. Consider the effect of aggravating and mitigating factors (other than those within examples above)

Common aggravating and mitigating factors are identified [elsewhere]—the following may be particularly relevant but these lists are not exhaustive

Factor indicating higher culpability 1. Offender exercising or acting in position of special responsibility **Factor indicating greater degree of harm** 1. Possession of drugs in a public place or school	Factors indicating lower culpability 1. Possession of Class C rather than Class B drug 2. Evidence that use was to help cope with a medical condition

[Sets out the standard sequential sentencing procedure, but also indicates need to consider forfeiture and destruction of drug.]

Drugs—Class B and C—Supply, Possess with Intent to Supply SG-197

Misuse of Drugs Act 1971, ss. 4(3) and 5(3)

Triable either way:
Maximum when tried summarily: Level 5 fine and/or 6 months (class B); level 4 fine and/or 3 months (class C)

Maximum when tried on indictment: 14 years (class B and class C)

Offence seriousness (culpability and harm)

A. Identify the appropriate starting point

Starting points based on first time offender pleading not guilty

Examples of nature of activity	Starting point	Range
Sharing minimal quantity between equals on a non-commercial basis e.g. a reefer	**Band C fine**	**Band B fine to low level community order**
Small scale retail supply to consumer	**High level community order (class C) 6 weeks custody (class B)**	**Low level community order to 6 weeks custody (class C) Medium level community order to 26 weeks custody (class B)**
Any other supply, including small scale supply in prison—whether by prisoner or another	**Crown Court**	**Crown Court**

B. Consider the effect of aggravating and mitigating factors (other than those within examples above)

Common aggravating and mitigating factors are identified [elsewhere]—the following may be particularly relevant but these lists are not exhaustive

Factors indicating higher culpability 1. Offender exercising or acting in position of special responsibility **Factors indicating greater degree of harm** 1. Supply to vulnerable persons including children 2. Offence committed on/in vicinity of school premises (Note: supply on or in the vicinity of school premises is a statutory aggravating factor: Misuse of Drugs Act 1971, s.4A. Consult your legal adviser for guidance.)	

[Sets out the standard sequential sentencing procedure, but also indicates need to consider forfeiture and destruction of drug and forfeiture or suspension of personal liquor licence.]

Drugs—Cultivation of Cannabis SG-198

Misuse of Drugs Act 1971, s. 6(2)

Triable either way:
Maximum when tried summarily: Level 5 fine and/or 6 months
Maximum when tried on indictment: 14 years
Offence seriousness (culpability and harm)

A. Identify the appropriate starting point

Starting points based on first time offender pleading not guilty

Examples of nature of activity	Starting point	Range
Very small scale cultivation for personal use only i.e. one or two plants	**Band C fine**	**Band B fine to low level community order**
Small scale cultivation for personal use and noncommercial supply to small circle of friends	**High level community order**	**Medium level community order to 12 weeks custody**
Commercial cultivation	**Crown Court**	**Crown Court**

B. Consider the effect of aggravating and mitigating factors (other than those within examples above)

Common aggravating and mitigating factors are identified [elsewhere]—the following may be particularly relevant but these lists are not exhaustive

Factors indicating higher culpability	Factors indicating lower culpability
1. Use of sophisticated growing system 2. Use of sophisticated system of concealment 3. Persistent use/cultivation of cannabis **Factor indicating greater degree of harm** 1. Involvement of vulnerable/young persons	1. Evidence drug used to help with a medical condition 2. Original planting carried out by others

[Sets out the standard sequential sentencing procedure, but also indicates need to consider forfeiture and destruction of drug.]

SG-199

Drunk and Disorderly in a Public Place

Criminal Justice Act 1967, s. 91

Triable only summarily:
Maximum: Level 3 fine

Offence seriousness (culpability and harm)

A. Identify the appropriate starting point

Starting points based on first time offender pleading not guilty

Examples of nature of activity	Starting point	Range
Shouting, causing disturbance for some minutes	**Band A fine**	**Conditional discharge to band B fine**
Substantial disturbance caused	**Band B fine**	**Band A fine to band C fine**

B. Consider the effect of aggravating and mitigating factors (other than those within examples above)

Common aggravating and mitigating factors are identified [elsewhere]—the following may be particularly relevant but these lists are not exhaustive

Factors indicating higher culpability	Factors indicating lower culpability
1. Offensive words or behaviour involved 2. Lengthy incident 3. Group action **Factors indicating greater degree of harm** 1. Offence committed at school, hospital or other place where vulnerable persons may be present 2. Offence committed on public transport 3. Victim providing public service	1. Minor and non-threatening 2. Stopped as soon as police arrived

[Sets out the standard sequential sentencing procedure and includes mention of need to consider football banning order.]

SG-200

Electricity, Abstract/Use without Authority

Factors to take into consideration

Key factors

(a) The starting points and sentencing ranges in this guideline are based on the assumption that the offender was motivated by greed or a desire to live beyond his or her means. To avoid double counting, such a motivation should not be treated as a factor that increases culpability.

(b) When assessing the harm caused by this offence, the starting point should be the loss suffered by the victim. In general, the greater the loss, the more serious the offence. However, the monetary value of the loss may not reflect the full extent of the harm caused by the offence. The court should also take into account the impact of the offence on the victim, any harm to persons other than the direct victim, and any harm in the form of public alarm or erosion of public confidence.

(c) The following matters of offender mitigation may be relevant to this offence:

(i) *Offender motivated by desperation or need*
The fact that an offence has been committed in desperation or need arising from particular hardship may count as offender mitigation in exceptional circumstances.

(ii) *Voluntary restitution*
Whether and the degree to which payment for stolen electricity constitutes a matter of offender mitigation will depend on an assessment of the circumstances and, in particular, the voluntariness and timeliness of the payment.

(iii) *Impact on sentence of offender's dependency*
Many offenders convicted of acquisitive crimes are motivated by an addiction, often to drugs, alcohol or gambling. This does not mitigate the seriousness of the offence, but an offender's dependency may properly influence the type of sentence imposed. In particular, it may sometimes be appropriate to impose a drug rehabilitation requirement or an alcohol treatment requirement as part of a community order or a suspended sentence order in an attempt to break the cycle of addiction and offending, even if an immediate custodial sentence would otherwise be warranted.[191]

Guidelines

Theft Act 1968, s. 13

Triable either way:
Maximum when tried summarily: Level 5 fine and/or 6 months
Maximum when tried on indictment: 5 years

Offence seriousness (culpability and harm)

A. Identify the appropriate starting point

Starting points based on first time offender pleading not guilty

Examples of nature of activity	Starting point	Range
Where the offence results in substantial commercial gain, a custodial sentence may be appropriate		
Offence involving evidence of planning and indication that the offending was intended to be continuing, such as using a device to interfere with the electricity meter or re-wiring to by-pass the meter	**Medium level community order**	**Band A fine to high level community order**

B. Consider the effect of aggravating and mitigating factors (other than those within examples above)

Common aggravating and mitigating factors are identified [elsewhere]—the following may be particularly relevant but these lists are not exhaustive

Factor indicating greater degree of harm	
1. Risk of danger caused to property and/or life	

[Sets out the standard sequential sentencing procedure.]

[191] See para.2 on p.163. The Court of Appeal gave guidance on the approach to making drug treatment and testing orders, which also applies to imposing a drug rehabilitation requirement in *Attorney General's Reference No. 64 of 2003 (Boujettif and Harrison)* [2003] EWCA Crim 3514 and *Woods and Collins* [2005] EWCA Crim 2065 summarised in the Sentencing Guidelines Council *Guideline Judgments Case Compendium* (section (A) Generic Sentencing Principles) available at: www.sentencing-guidelines.gov.uk

SG-201

Exploitation of Prostitution

Sexual Offences Act 2003, s. 52 (causing or inciting prostitution for gain); s. 53 (controlling prostitution for gain)

Triable either way:
Maximum when tried summarily: Level 5 fine or 6 months
Maximum when tried on indictment: 7 years

This guideline is taken from the Sentencing Guidelines Council's definitive guideline *Sexual Offences Act 2003*, published 30 April 2007 [see **SG-126**]

Identify dangerous offenders

These are specified offences for the purposes of the public protection provisions in the Criminal Justice Act 2003 . . .

Offence seriousness (culpability and harm)

A. Identify the appropriate starting point

Starting points based on first time offender pleading not guilty

Examples of nature of activity	Starting point	Range
No evidence victim was physically coerced or corrupted, and the involvement of the offender was minimal	**Medium level community order**	**Band C fine to high level community order**
No coercion or corruption but the offender is closely involved in the victim's prostitution	**Crown Court**	**26 weeks custody to Crown Court**
Evidence of physical and/or mental coercion	**Crown Court**	**Crown Court**

B. Consider the effect of aggravating and mitigating factors (other than those within examples above)

Common aggravating and mitigating factors are identified [elsewhere]—the following may be particularly relevant but these lists are not exhaustive

Factors indicating higher culpability	Factor indicating greater degree of harm
1. Background of threats, intimidation or coercion 2. Large-scale commercial operation 3. Substantial gain (in the region of £5,000 and up) 4. Use of drugs, alcohol or other substance to secure the victim's compliance 5. Abduction or detention 6. Threats to prevent the victim reporting the activity 7. Threats to disclose victim's activity to friends/relatives	1. Induced dependency on drugs **Factor indicating lower culpability** 1. Offender also being controlled in prostitution and subject to threats or intimidation

[Sets out the standard sequential sentencing procedure.]

Note: Where an offender has profited from his or her involvement in the prostitution of others, the court should consider making a confiscation order approximately equivalent to the profits enjoyed. Such an order may be made only in the Crown Court.

SG-202

Exposure

Sexual Offences Act 2003, s. 66

Triable either way:
Maximum when tried summarily: Level 5 fine or 6 months
Maximum when tried on indictment: 2 years

This guideline is taken from the Sentencing Guidelines Council's definitive guideline *Sexual Offences Act 2003*, published 30 April 2007 [see **SG-110**]

Key factors

(a) This offence is committed where an offender intentionally exposes his or her genitals and intends that someone will see them and be caused alarm or distress. It is gender neutral, covering exposure of male or female genitalia to a male or female witness.

(b) The Sentencing Guidelines Council guideline provides that, when dealing with a repeat offender, the starting point should be 12 weeks custody with a range of 4 to 26 weeks custody. The presence of aggravating factors may suggest that a sentence above the range is appropriate and that the case should be committed to the Crown Court.
(c) In accordance with s.80 and sch.3 of the Sexual Offences Act 2003, automatic notification requirements apply upon conviction to an offender aged 18 or over where:
   (1) the victim was under 18; or
   (2) a term of imprisonment or a community sentence of at least 12 months is imposed.
(d) This guideline may be relevant by way of analogy to conduct charged as the common law offence of outraging public decency; the offence is triable either way and has a maximum penalty of a level 5 fine and/or 6 months imprisonment when tried summarily.

Identify dangerous offenders

This is a specified offence for the purposes of the public protection provisions in the Criminal Justice Act 2003 . . .

Offence seriousness (culpability and harm)

A. Identify the appropriate starting point

Starting points based on first time offender pleading not guilty

Examples of nature of activity	Starting point	Range
Basic offence as defined in the Act, assuming no aggravating or mitigating factors	**Low level community order**	**Band B fine to medium level community order**
Offence with an aggravating factor	**Medium level community order**	**Low level community order to high level community order**
Two or more aggravating factors	**12 weeks custody**	**6 weeks custody to Crown Court**

B. Consider the effect of aggravating and mitigating factors (other than those within examples above)

Common aggravating and mitigating factors are identified [elsewhere]—the following may be particularly relevant but these lists are not exhaustive

Factors indicating higher culpability	Factor indicating greater degree of harm
1. Threats to prevent the victim reporting an offence 2. Intimidating behaviour/threats of violence	1. Victim is a child

[Sets out the standard sequential sentencing procedure.]

False Accounting **SG-203**

Theft Act 1968, s. 17

Triable either way:
Maximum when tried summarily: Level 5 fine and/or 6 months
Maximum when tried on indictment: 7 years

Refer to guideline *Fraud— banking and insurance fraud and obtaining credit through fraud, benefit fraud and revenue fraud* [see **SG-206** ***et seq.***].

Firearm, Carrying in Public Place **SG-204**

Firearms Act 1968, s. 19

Triable either way (but triable only summarily if the firearm is an air weapon):
Maximum when tried summarily: Level 5 fine and/or 6 months
Maximum when tried on indictment: 7 years (12 months for imitation firearms)

Offence seriousness (culpability and harm)

A. Identify the appropriate starting point

Starting points based on first time offender pleading not guilty

Examples of nature of activity	Starting point	Range
Carrying an unloaded air weapon	**Low level community order**	**Band B fine to medium level community order**
Carrying loaded air weapon/imitation firearm/unloaded shot gun without ammunition	**High level community order**	**Medium level community order to 26 weeks custody (air weapon) Medium level community order to Crown Court (imitation firearm, unloaded shot gun)**
Carrying loaded shot gun/carrying shot gun or any other firearm together with ammunition for it	**Crown Court**	**Crown Court**

B. Consider the effect of aggravating and mitigating factors (other than those within examples above)

Common aggravating and mitigating factors are identified [elsewhere]—the following may be particularly relevant but these lists are not exhaustive

Factors indicating higher culpability	Factors indicating lower culpability
1. Brandishing the firearm 2. Carrying firearm in a busy place 3. Planned illegal use **Factors indicating greater degree of harm** 1. Person or people put in fear 2. Offender participating in violent incident	1. Firearm not in sight 2. No intention to use firearm 3. Firearm to be used for lawful purpose (not amounting to a defence)

[Sets out the standard sequential sentencing procedure, ancillary orders to be considered include compensation, forfeiture or suspension of personal liquor licence and football banning order (where appropriate).]

Football Related Offences

SG-205 *Sporting Events (Control of Alcohol etc.) Act 1985: s. 2(1) (possession of alcohol whilst entering or trying to enter ground); s.2(2) (being drunk in, or whilst trying to enter, ground) Football Offences Act 1991: s. 2 (throwing missile); s. 3 (indecent or racist chanting); s. 4 (going onto prohibited areas)*

Criminal Justice and Public Order Act 1994: s. 166 (unauthorised sale or attempted sale of tickets)

Triable only summarily:
Maximum: Level 2 fine (being drunk in ground) Level 3 fine (throwing missile; indecent or racist chanting; going onto prohibited areas) Level 5 fine (unauthorised sale of tickets) Level 3 fine and/or 3 months (possession of alcohol)

Offence seriousness (culpability and harm)

A. Identify the appropriate starting point

Starting points based on first time offender pleading not guilty

Examples of nature of activity	Starting point	Range
Being drunk in, or whilst trying to enter, ground	**Band A fine**	**Conditional discharge to band B fine**
Going onto playing or other prohibited area; Unauthorised sale or attempted sale of tickets	**Band B fine**	**Band A fine to band C fine**
Throwing missile; Indecent or racist chanting	**Band C fine**	**Band C fine**
Possession of alcohol whilst entering or trying to enter ground	**Band C fine**	**Band B fine to high level community order**

B. Consider the effect of aggravating and mitigating factors (other than those within examples above)

Common aggravating and mitigating factors are identified [elsewhere]—the following may be particularly relevant but these lists are not exhaustive

Factors indicating higher culpability 1. Commercial ticket operation; potential high cash value; counterfeit tickets 2. Inciting others to misbehave 3. Possession of large quantity of alcohol 4. Offensive language or behaviour (where not an element of the offence) **Factors indicating greater degree of harm** 1. Missile likely to cause serious injury e.g. coin, glass, bottle, stone	

[Sets out the standard sequential sentencing procedure and mentions need to consider a football banning order.]

Fraud—Banking and Insurance Fraud, and Obtaining Credit through Fraud, Benefit Fraud, and Revenue Fraud **SG-206**

Factors to take into consideration

This guideline and accompanying notes are taken from the Sentencing Guidelines Council's definitive guideline *Sentencing for Fraud— Statutory offences*, published 26 October 2009 [see **SG-393**]. The starting points and ranges for fraud against HM Revenue and Customs, for benefit fraud and for banking and insurance and obtaining credit through fraud are the same since the seriousness of all offences of organisational fraud derives from the extent of the fraudulent activity (culpability) and the financial loss caused or likely to be caused (harm).

Key factors common to these types of fraud

(a) As the determinants of seriousness include the 'value of property or consequential loss involved', the table provides both a fixed amount (on which the starting point is based) and a band (on which the sentencing range is based). Where the value is larger or smaller than the amount on which the starting point is based, this should lead to upward or downward movement from the starting point as appropriate. Where the amount the offender intended to obtain cannot be established, the appropriate measure will be the amount that was likely to be achieved in all the circumstances. Where the offender was entitled to part or all of the amount obtained, the starting point should be based on the amount to which they were not entitled.

(b) A further determinant of seriousness is whether the fraud was a single fraudulent transaction or a multiple fraud. Where one false declaration or a failure to disclose a change in circumstances results in multiple payments, this should be regarded as multiple fraud.

(c) In general terms, the greater the loss, the more serious will be the offence. However, the financial value of the loss may not reflect the full extent of the harm caused. The court should also take into account; the impact of the offence on the victim (particularly where the loss may be significantly greater than the monetary value); harm to persons other than the direct victim (including the aggravation and stress of unscrambling the consequences of an offence); erosion of public confidence; and the difference between the loss intended and that which results (which may involve adjusting the assessment of seriousness to reflect the degree of loss caused).

(d) When the offending involves a number of people acting co-operatively, this will aggravate an offence as it indicates planning or professional activity, and may also increase the degree of loss caused or intended. The role of each offender is important in determining the appropriate level of seriousness and movement above or below the starting point within the applicable level.

(e) Use of another person's identity is an aggravating factor; the extent to which it aggravates an offence will be based on the degree of planning and the impact that the offence has had on the living victim or relatives of the deceased – whether the identity belongs to a living or deceased person is neutral for this purpose.

(f) Matters of offender mitigation which may be particularly relevant to these types of fraud include:

- *Voluntary cessation of offending* — a claim, supported by objective evidence, that an offender stopped offending before being apprehended should be treated as mitigation, particularly where accompanied by a genuine expression of remorse. The lapse of time since commission of the last offence is relevant to whether the claim is genuine, and reasons for the cessation will assist the court in determining whether it amounts to mitigation and if so, to what degree.
- *Complete and unprompted disclosure of the extent of the fraud* — an admission that a greater sum has been obtained than that known to the authorities ensures that an offender is sentenced for

the complete extent of the fraud. This is ready co-operation with the authorities and should be treated as mitigation. Provision of information about others involved in the fraud should also be treated as mitigation. Generally, the earlier the disclosure is given and the higher the degree of assistance, the greater the allowance for mitigation.

- *Voluntary restitution* — the timing of the voluntary restitution will indicate the degree to which it reflects genuine remorse. Generally, the earlier the property or money is returned the greater the degree of mitigation the offender should receive. If circumstances beyond the control of the offender prevent return of defrauded items, the degree of mitigation will depend on the point in time at which, and the determination with which the offender tried to return the items.
- *Financial pressure* — financial pressure neither increases nor diminishes an offender's culpability. However, where such pressure is **exceptional** and not of the offenders own making, it may in very rare circumstances constitute mitigation.

(g) A court should be aware that a confiscation order is an important sanction. Such an order may only be made in the Crown Court. The court must commit the offender to the Crown Court where this is requested by the prosecution with a view to an order being considered.

(h) Ancillary orders should be considered in all cases, principally compensation, deprivation and disqualification from driving, as well as other powers particular to the type of offending behaviour.

Additional notes:

Banking and insurance fraud and obtaining credit through fraud:

(i) A payment card or bank account fraud is unlikely to be committed in circumstances where the offender's intention was not fraudulent from the outset.

(ii) Use of another person's identity is a feature of nearly all payment card and bank account frauds since in most cases the offender claims to be the account holder or a person authorised to deal with the account. Courts should therefore increase the starting point to reflect the presence of this aggravating factor.

Benefit fraud:

(i) This guideline is based on an understanding that the prosecutor will generally seek summary trial for appropriate benefit fraud cases involving sums up to £35,000.

(ii) The fact that defrauded sums may have been recovered is not relevant to the choice of the type of sentence to be imposed.

(iii) The court should have regard to personal and family circumstances of offenders which will vary greatly and may be particularly significant to sentencing this type of fraud.

Revenue fraud:

(i) The proposals for the sentencing of revenue fraud take as a starting point an offender who acts intentionally. Where the offender has acted recklessly (relevant only to offences under the Value Added Tax Act 1994), courts should adjust the assessment of seriousness to take account of this lower level of culpability.

(ii) Payments to HMRC may be evaded in order to increase the profitability of a legitimate business or the level of an individual's legitimate remuneration; payments may be fraudulently obtained from HMRC without any underlying legitimate activity at all as in a Carousel Fraud. Although the type of harm is the same since both result in a loss to HMRC, where payment is sought from HMRC in such circumstances, culpability is likely to be higher. Accordingly, such offences are likely to be regarded as more serious.

Guidelines

Fraud Act 2006, s.1

Theft Act 1968, s.17

Social Security Administration Act 1992, ss.111A(1), 111A(1A), 111A(1B), 111A(1D) and 111(1E)

Tax Credits Act 2002, s.35

Value Added Tax Act 1994, ss.72(1), (3) and (8)

Finance Act 2000, s.144

Customs and Excise Management Act 1979, ss.170(1)(a)(i) and (ii), 170(1)(b), 170(2)(a), 170B, 50(1)(a) and 50(2)

All offences: Triable either way
Maximum when tried summarily: Level 5 fine and/or 6 months
Maximum when tried on indictment: Fraud, 10 years; other offences, 7 years

Offences under s.112, Social Security Administration Act 1992 are not covered by this guideline.

This guideline does not apply to offences under s.50 or s.170, Customs and Excise Management Act 1979 which involve prohibited weapons and have a maximum penalty of 10 years.

Offence seriousness (culpability and harm)

A. Identify the appropriate starting point

Starting points based on first time offender pleading not guilty

Examples of nature of activity	Starting point	Range
Single fraudulent transaction, not fraudulent from the outset	Value £2,500 – **Band B fine** Value £12,500 – **Medium level community order** Value £60,000 – **12 weeks custody**	Value less than £5,000 – **Band A fine to low level community order** Value £5,000 to less than £20,000 – **Band B fine to 6 weeks custody** Value £20,000 to less than £100,000 – **Medium level community order to Crown Court**
Single fraudulent transaction, fraudulent from the outset	Value £2,500 – **Low level community order** Value £12,500 – **High level community order** Value £60,000 – **26 weeks custody**	Value less than £5,000 – **Band A fine to medium level community order** Value £5,000 to less than £20,000 – **Band C fine to 18 weeks custody** Value £20,000 to less than £100,000 – **6 weeks custody to Crown Court**
Not fraudulent from the outset, **and either** • fraud carried out over a significant period of time **or** • multiple frauds **Where value exceeds £100,000**	Value £2,500 – **Medium level community order** Value £12,500 – **6 weeks custody** Value £60,000 – **Crown Court** **Crown Court**	Value less than £5,000 – **Band B fine to high level community order** Value £5,000 to less than £20,000 – **Medium level community order to 26 weeks custody** Value £20,000 to less than £100,000 – **12 weeks custody to Crown Court** **Crown Court**
Fraudulent from the outset, **and either** • fraud carried out over a significant period of time **or** • multiple frauds **Where value £100,000 or more or fraud was professionally planned**	Value £2,500 – **High level community order** Value £12,500 – **12 weeks custody** Value £60,000 – **Crown Court** **Crown Court**	Value less than £5,000 – **Low level community order to 6 weeks custody** Value £5,000 to less than £20,000 – **High level community order to Crown Court** Value £20,000 to less than £100,000 – **18 weeks custody to Crown Court** **Crown Court**

*Where the actual amount is greater or smaller than the value on which the starting point is based, that is likely to be one of the factors that will move the sentence within the range (see (a) [under Key Factors above])

B. Consider the effect of aggravating and mitigating factors
(other than those within examples above)

Common aggravating and mitigating factors are identified [elsewhere] - the following may be particularly relevant but **these lists are not exhaustive**

Factors indicating higher culpability	Factors indicating lower culpability
1. Number involved in the offence and role of the offender 2. Making repeated importations, particularly in the face of warnings from the authorities 3. Dealing in goods with an additional health risk **Factors indicating greater degree of harm** 1. Use of another person's identity 2. Disposing of goods to under-aged purchasers	1. Peripheral involvement 2. Misleading or incomplete advice

[Sets out the standard sequential sentencing procedure.]

SG-207

Fraud – Confidence

Factors to take into consideration

This guideline and accompanying notes are taken from the Sentencing Guidelines Council's definitive guideline *Sentencing for Fraud – Statutory offences*, published 26 October 2009 [see **SG-393**].

Key factors

(a) This type of offending involves a victim transferring money and/or property as a result of being deceived or misled by the offender. An example of a simple confidence fraud is a person claiming to be collecting money for charity when, in fact, he or she intends to keep the money. Other examples of common confidence frauds are *Advance fee frauds* (such as lottery/prize draw scams and foreign money-making frauds) and *Fraudulent sales of goods and services* (where goods or services are never received/performed or are worth less than represented.

(b) As the determinants of seriousness include the 'value of property or consequential loss involved', the table provides both a fixed amount (on which the starting point is based) and a band (on which the sentencing range is based). Where the value is larger or smaller than the amount on which the starting point is based, this should lead to upward or downward movement as appropriate. Where the amount the offender intended to obtain cannot be established, the appropriate measure will be the amount that was likely to be achieved in all the circumstances.

(c) A further determinant of seriousness is whether the fraud was a single fraudulent transaction or a multiple fraud. Most confidence frauds will by their nature involve many actual or potential victims and multiple transactions and should be regarded as multiple fraud.

(d) Targeting a vulnerable victim is also a determinant of seriousness. A victim might be vulnerable as a result of old age, youth or disability. In addition, some victims of advance fee frauds may have personalities which make them 'vulnerable in a way and to a degree not typical of the general population' because they fall for scams many times and may be targeted using 'sucker lists' of people who have previously fallen victim to scams. Care should be taken to ensure that where targeting a vulnerable victim is used to determine the appropriate level of seriousness and starting point, that it is not used again as an aggravating factor to move within the sentencing range.

(e) In general terms, the greater the loss, the more serious will be the offence. However, the financial value of the loss may not reflect the full extent of the harm caused. The court should also take into account; the impact of the offence on the victim (particularly where the loss may be significantly greater than the monetary value); harm to persons other than the direct victim (including the aggravation and stress of unscrambling the consequences of an offence); erosion of public confidence; and the difference between the loss intended and that which results (which may involve adjusting the assessment of seriousness to reflect the degree of loss caused).

(f) When the offending involves a number of people acting co-operatively, this will aggravate an offence as it indicates planning or professional activity, and may also increase the degree of loss caused or intended. The role of each offender is important in determining the appropriate level of seriousness and movement above or below the starting point within the applicable level.

(g) Use of another persons identity is an aggravating factor; the extent to which it aggravates an offence will be based on the degree of planning and the impact that the offence has had on the living victim or relatives of the deceased – whether the identity belongs to a living or deceased person is neutral for this purpose.

(h) Matters of offender mitigation which may be particularly relevant to this type of fraud include:

- *Voluntary cessation of offending* — a claim, supported by objective evidence, that an offender stopped offending before being apprehended should be treated as mitigation, particularly where accompanied by a genuine expression of remorse. The lapse of time since commission of the last offence is relevant to whether the claim is genuine, and reasons for the cessation will assist the court in determining whether it amounts to mitigation and if so, to what degree.
- *Complete and unprompted disclosure of the extent of the fraud* — an admission that a greater sum has been obtained than that known to the authorities ensures that an offender is sentenced for the complete extent of the fraud. This amounts to ready co-operation with the authorities and should be treated as mitigation. Provision of information about others involved in the fraud should also be treated as mitigation. Generally, the earlier the disclosure is given and the higher the degree of assistance, the greater the allowance for mitigation.
- *Voluntary restitution* — the timing of the voluntary restitution will indicate the degree to which it reflects genuine remorse. Generally, the earlier the property or money is returned the greater

the degree of mitigation the offender should receive. If circumstances beyond the control of the offender prevent return of defrauded items, the degree of mitigation will depend on the point in time at which, and the determination with which the offender tried to return the items.

- *Financial pressure* — financial pressure neither increases nor diminishes an offender's culpability. However, where such pressure is **exceptional** and not of the offender's own making, it may in very rare circumstances constitute mitigation.

(i) A court should be aware that a confiscation order is an important sanction. Such an order may only be made in the Crown Court. The court must commit the offender to the Crown Court where this is requested by the prosecution with a view to an order being considered.

(j) Ancillary orders should be considered in all cases, principally compensation and deprivation.

Guidelines

Fraud Act 2006, s. 1

Theft Act 1968, s. 17

All offences: Triable either way
Maximum when tried summarily: Level 5 fine and/or 6 months
Maximum when tried on indictment: Fraud, 10 years; other offences, 7 years

Offence seriousness (culpability and harm)

A. Identify the appropriate starting point

Starting points based on first time offender pleading not guilty

Examples of nature of activity	Starting point	Range
Single fraudulent transaction confidence fraud not targeting a vulnerable victim, and involving no or limited planning	Value £10,000 – **Medium level community order** Value £60,000 – **12 weeks custody**	Value less than £20,000 – **Band B fine to 6 weeks custody** Value £20,000 to less than £100,000 – **Medium level community order to Crown Court**
Single fraudulent transaction confidence fraud involving targeting of a vulnerable victim	Value £10,000 – **6 weeks custody** Value £60,000 – **26 weeks custody**	Value less than £20,000 – **Medium level community order to 26 weeks custody** Value £20,000 to less than £100,000 – **High level community order to Crown Court**
Lower scale advance fee fraud **or** other confidence fraud characterised by a degree of planning and/or multiple transactions	Value £10,000 – **Crown Court** Value £60,000 – **Crown Court**	Value less than £20,000 – **26 weeks custody to Crown Court** Value £20,000 to less than £100,000 – **Crown Court**
Large scale advance fee fraud **or** other confidence fraud involving the deliberate targeting of a large number of vulnerable victims	Value £10,000 – **Crown Court** Value £60,000 – **Crown Court**	Value less than £20,000 – **Crown Court** Value £20,000 to less than £100,000 – **Crown Court**

*Where the actual amount is greater or smaller than the value on which the starting point is based, that is likely to be one of the factors that will move the sentence within the range (see (b) [under Key Factors above])

B. Consider the effect of aggravating and mitigating factors
(other than those within examples above)

Common aggravating and mitigating factors are identified [elsewhere] — the following may be particularly relevant but **these lists are not exhaustive**

Factors indicating higher culpability	Factors indicating lower culpability
1. Number involved in the offence and role of the offender 2. Offending carried out over a significant period of time **Factors indicating greater degree of harm** 1.Use of another person's identity 2. Offence has lasting effect on the victim	1. Peripheral involvement 2. Behaviour not fraudulent from the outset 3. Misleading or inaccurate advice

[Sets out the standard sequential sentencing procedure.]

SG-208 FRAUD — POSSESSING, MAKING OR SUPPLYING ARTICLES FOR USE IN FRAUD

Factors to take into consideration

This guideline and accompanying notes are taken from the Sentencing Guidelines Council's definitive guideline *Sentencing for Fraud — Statutory offences*, published 26 October 2009 [see **SG-393**].

Key factors

(a) There are many ways in which offenders may commit this group of offences. 'Articles' will include any electronic programs or data stored electronically false fronts for cash machines, computer programs for generating credit card numbers, lists of credit card or bank account details, 'sucker lists' and draft letters or emails for use in advance fee frauds.

(b) Offenders who possess, make or supply articles for use in fraud intend their actions to lead to a fraud, and therefore have the highest level of culpability. The three offences in this group all involve an element of planning (whether by the offender or by another person) which indicates a higher level of culpability; this has been incorporated into the proposed starting points.

(c) In relation to harm, the value of the fraud (either that intended by the offender where that can be ascertained, or that which was likely to be achieved) is not a determinant of seriousness for these offences but is a factor that should be taken into account in determining the appropriate sentence within the sentencing range.

(d) Whilst in many cases no financial harm will have been caused, in some cases, particularly where the 'article' is a list of credit card or bank account details, the victim(s) may have been inconvenienced despite not suffering any financial loss. In all cases, the harm must be judged in light of the offender's culpability.

(e) When the offending involves a number of people acting co-operatively, this will aggravate an offence as it indicates planning or professional activity, and may also increase the degree of loss caused or intended. The role of each offender is important in determining the appropriate level of seriousness and movement above or below the starting point within the applicable level.

(f) Matters of offender mitigation which may be particularly relevant to this type of fraud include:

- *Voluntary cessation of offending* — a claim, supported by objective evidence, that an offender stopped offending before being apprehended should be treated as mitigation, particularly where accompanied by a genuine expression of remorse. The lapse of time since commission of the last offence is relevant to whether the claim is genuine, and reasons for the cessation will assist the court in determining whether it amounts to mitigation and if so, to what degree.
- *Complete and unprompted disclosure of the extent of the fraud* — an admission that a greater sum has been obtained than that known to the authorities ensures that an offender is sentenced for the complete extent of the fraud. This amounts to ready co-operation with the authorities and should be treated as mitigation. Provision of information about others involved in the fraud should also be treated as mitigation. Generally, the earlier the disclosure is given and the higher the degree of assistance, the greater the allowance for mitigation.
- *Voluntary restitution* — the timing of the voluntary restitution will indicate the degree to which it reflects genuine remorse. Generally, the earlier the property or money is returned the greater the degree of mitigation the offender should receive. If circumstances beyond the control of the offender prevent return of defrauded items, the degree of mitigation will depend on the point in time at which, and the determination with which the offender tried to return the items.
- *Financial pressure* — financial pressure neither increases nor diminishes an offender's culpability. However, where such pressure is **exceptional** and not of the offender's own making, it may in very rare circumstances constitute mitigation.

(g) A court should be aware that a confiscation order is an important sanction. Such an order may only be made in the Crown Court. The court must commit the offender to the Crown Court where this is requested by the prosecution with a view to an order being considered.

(h) Ancillary orders should be considered in all cases, principally compensation and deprivation.

Guidelines

Fraud Act 2006, s.6

Fraud Act 2006, s.7

Fraud Act 2006, s.1

Possession of articles: Triable either way
Maximum when tried summarily: Level 5 fine and/or 6 months
Maximum when tried on indictment: 5 years

Making or supplying articles, and Fraud (s.1): Triable either way
Maximum when tried summarily: Level 5 fine and/or 6 months
Maximum when tried on indictment: 10 years

Offence seriousness (culpability and harm)

A. Identify the appropriate starting point

Starting points based on first time offender pleading not guilty

Examples of nature of activity	Starting point	Range
Possessing articles intended for use in a less extensive and less skilfully planned fraud	**Medium level community order**	**Low level community order to 26 weeks custody**
Possessing articles for use in an extensive and skilfully planned fraud	**Crown Court**	**6 weeks custody to Crown Court**
Making or adapting, supplying or offering to supply articles intended for use in a less extensive and less skilfully planned fraud	**26 weeks custody**	**High level community order to Crown Court**
Making or adapting, supplying or offering to supply articles for use in an extensive and skilfully planned fraud	**Crown Court**	**Crown Court**

B. Consider the effect of aggravating and mitigating factors (other than those within examples above)

Common aggravating and mitigating factors are identified [elsewhere] — the following may be particularly relevant but **these lists are not exhaustive**

Factors indicating higher culpability	Factor indicating lower culpability
1. Number involved in the offence and role of the offender 2. Offending carried out over a significant period of time **Factors indicating greater degree of harm** 1. Use of another person's identity 2. Offence has lasting effect on the victim	1. Peripheral involvement

[Sets out the standard sequential sentencing procedure.]

GOING EQUIPPED, FOR THEFT SG-209

Theft Act 1968, s. 25

Triable either way:
Maximum when tried summarily: Level 5 fine and/or 6 months
Maximum when tried on indictment: 3 years

May disqualify if offence committed with reference to theft or taking of motor vehicles (no points available)

Offence seriousness (culpability and harm)

A. Identify the appropriate starting point

Starting points based on first time offender pleading not guilty

Examples of nature of activity	Starting point	Range
Possession of items for theft from shop or of vehicle	**Medium level community order**	**Band C fine to high level community order**
Possession of items for burglary, robbery	**High level community order**	**Medium level community order to Crown Court**

B. Consider the effect of aggravating and mitigating factors (other than those within examples above)

Common aggravating and mitigating factors are identified [elsewhere]—the following may be particularly relevant but these lists are not exhaustive

Factors indicating higher culpability 1. Circumstances suggest offender equipped for particularly serious offence 2. Items to conceal identity	

[Sets out the standard sequential sentencing procedure and notes need to consider disqualification from driving and deprivation of property.]

SG-210 Grievous Bodily Harm/Unlawful Wounding & Racially or Religiously Aggravated Grievous Bodily Harm/Unlawful Wounding

[See now 'Inflicting Grievous Bodily Harm/Unlawful Wounding' at **SG-217**, the new Guideline from the Sentencing Council which has effect from 13 June 2011.]

SG-211 Handling Stolen Goods

Theft Act 1968, s. 22

Triable either way:
Maximum when tried summarily: Level 5 fine and/or 6 months
Maximum when tried on indictment: 14 years

These guidelines are drawn from the Court of Appeal's decision in *R v Webbe and others* [2001] EWCA Crim 1217

Offence seriousness (culpability and harm)

A. Identify the appropriate starting point

Starting points based on first time offender pleading not guilty

Examples of nature of activity	Starting point	Range
Property worth £1,000 or less acquired for offender's own use	**Band B fine**	**Band B fine to low level community order**
Property worth £1,000 or less acquired for re-sale; or Property worth more than £1,000 acquired for offender's own use; or Presence of at least one aggravating factor listed below—regardless of value	**Medium level community order**	**Low level community order to 12 weeks custody** **Note:** the custody threshold is likely to be passed if the offender has a record of dishonesty offences
Sophisticated offending; or Presence of at least two aggravating factors listed below	**12 weeks custody**	**6 weeks custody to Crown Court**
Offence committed in context of a business; or Offender acts as organiser/distributor of proceeds of crime; or Offender makes self available to other criminals as willing to handle the proceeds of thefts or burglaries; or Offending highly organised, professional; or Particularly serious original offence, such as armed robbery	**Crown Court**	**Crown Court**

B. Consider the effect of aggravating and mitigating factors
(other than those within examples above)

Common aggravating and mitigating factors are identified [elsewhere]—the following may be particularly relevant but these lists are not exhaustive

Factors indicating higher culpability	Factors indicating lower culpability
1. Closeness of offender to primary offence. Closeness may be geographical, arising from presence at or near the primary offence when it was committed, or temporal, where the handler instigated or encouraged the primary offence beforehand, or, soon after, provided a safe haven or route for disposal 2. High level of profit made or expected by offender **Factors indicating greater degree of harm** 1. Seriousness of the primary offence, including domestic burglary 2. High value of goods to victim, including sentimental value 3. Threats of violence or abuse of power by offender over others, such as an adult commissioning criminal activity by children, or a drug dealer pressurising addicts to steal in order to pay for their habit	1. Little or no benefit to offender 2. Voluntary restitution to victim **Factor indicating lower degree of harm** 1. Low value of goods

[Sets out the standard sequential sentencing procedure and mentions need to consider deprivation of property]

Harassment—Putting People in Fear of Violence Racially or Religiously Aggravated Harassment—Putting People in Fear of Violence SG-212

Protection from Harassment Act 1997, s. 4

Crime and Disorder Act 1998, s. 32

Harassment: triable either way
Maximum when tried summarily: Level 5 fine and/or 6 months
Maximum when tried on indictment: 5 years

Racially or religiously aggravated harassment: triable either way
Maximum when tried summarily: Level 5 fine and/or 6 months
Maximum when tried on indictment: 7 years

Where offence committed in domestic context, refer [below] for guidance

Identify dangerous offenders

This is a specified offence for the purposes of the public protection provisions in the Criminal Justice Act 2003. . .

Offence seriousness (culpability and harm)

A. Identify the appropriate starting point

Starting points based on first time offender pleading not guilty

Examples of nature of activity	Starting point	Range
A pattern of two or more incidents of unwanted contact	**6 weeks custody**	**High level community order to 18 weeks custody**
Deliberate threats, persistent action over a longer period; or Intention to cause fear of violence	**18 weeks custody**	**12 weeks custody to Crown Court**
Sexual threats, vulnerable person targeted	**Crown Court**	**Crown Court**

B. Consider the effect of aggravating and mitigating factors (other than those within examples above)

Common aggravating and mitigating factors are identified [elsewhere]—the following may be particularly relevant but these lists are not exhaustive

Factors indicating higher culpability	Factors indicating lower culpability
1. Planning 2. Offender ignores obvious distress 3. Visits in person to victims home or workplace 4. Offender involves others 5. Using contact arrangements with a child to instigate offence **Factors indicating greater degree of harm** 1. Victim needs medical help/counselling 2. Physical violence used 3. Victim aware that offender has history of using violence 4. Grossly violent or offensive material sent 5. Children frightened 6. Evidence that victim changed lifestyle to avoid contact	1. Limited understanding of effect on victim 2. Initial provocation

[Sets out the standard sequential sentencing procedure. Notes that 'If offender charged and convicted of the racially or religiously aggravated offence, increase the sentence to reflect this element'.]

SG-213

Harassment (Without Violence)
Racially or Religiously Aggravated Harassment (Non Violent)

Protection from Harassment Act 1997, s.2
Crime and Disorder Act 1998, s.32

Harassment: triable only summarily
Maximum: Level 5 fine and/or 6 months

Racially or religiously aggravated harassment: triable either way
Maximum when tried summarily: Level 5 fine and/or 6 months
Maximum when tried on indictment: 2 years

Where offence committed in domestic context, refer [below] for guidance

Offence seriousness (culpability and harm)

A. Identify the appropriate starting point

Starting points based on first time offender pleading not guilty

Examples of nature of activity	Starting point	Range
Small number of incidents	**Medium level community order**	**Band C fine to high level community order**
Constant contact at night, trying to come into workplace or home, involving others	**6 weeks custody**	**Medium level community order to 12 weeks custody**
Threatening violence, taking personal photographs, sending offensive material	**18 weeks custody**	**12 to 26 weeks custody**

B. Consider the effect of aggravating and mitigating factors (other than those within examples above)

Common aggravating and mitigating factors are identified [elsewhere]—the following may be particularly relevant but these lists are not exhaustive

Factors indicating higher culpability	Factors indicating lower culpability
1. Planning 2. Offender ignores obvious distress 3. Offender involves others 4. Using contact arrangements with a child to instigate offence **Factors indicating greater degree of harm** 1. Victim needs medical help/counselling 2. Action over long period 3. Children frightened 4. Use or distribution of photographs	1. Limited understanding of effect on victim 2. Initial provocation

[Sets out the standard sequential sentencing procedure. Notes that 'If offender charged and convicted of the racially or religiously aggravated offence, increase the sentence to reflect this element'.]

Identity Documents—Possess False/Another's/Improperly Obtained SG-214

Identity Cards Act 2006, s. 25(5)
(possession of a false identity document (as defined in s. 26—includes a passport))

Triable either way:
Maximum when tried summarily: Level 5 fine and/or 6 months
Maximum when tried on indictment: 2 years (s.25(5))

Note: possession of a false identity document with the intention of using it is an indictable-only offence (Identity Cards Act 2006, s. 25(1)). The maximum penalty is 10 years imprisonment.

Offence seriousness (culpability and harm)

A. Identify the appropriate starting point

Starting points based on first time offender pleading not guilty

Examples of nature of activity	Starting point	Range
Single document possessed	**Medium level community order**	**Band C fine to high level community order**
Small number of documents, no evidence of dealing	**12 weeks custody**	**6 weeks custody to Crown Court**
Considerable number of documents possessed, evidence of involvement in larger operation	**Crown Court**	**Crown Court**

B. Consider the effect of aggravating and mitigating factors (other than those within examples above)

Common aggravating and mitigating factors are identified [elsewhere]—the following may be particularly relevant but these lists are not exhaustive

Factors indicating higher culpability	Factor indicating lower culpability
1. Clear knowledge that documents false 2. Number of documents possessed (where not in offence descriptions above) **Factors indicating greater degree of harm** 1. Group activity 2. Potential impact of use (where not in offence descriptions above)	1. Genuine mistake or ignorance

[Sets out the standard sequential sentencing procedure.]

Income Tax Evasion SG-215

Finance Act 2000, s. 144

Triable either way:
Maximum when tried summarily: Level 5 fine and/or 6 months
Maximum when tried on indictment: 7 years

Refer to guideline *Fraud — banking and insurance fraud and obtaining credit through fraud, benefit fraud and revenue fraud* [see **SG-206 *et seq.***].

Indecent Photographs of Children SG-216

Protection of Children Act 1978, s. 1
Criminal Justice Act 1988, s. 160

Triable either way:
Maximum when tried summarily: Level 5 fine or 6 months
Maximum when tried on indictment: 5 years for possession; otherwise 10 years

This guideline is taken from the Sentencing Guidelines Council's definitive guideline *Sexual Offences Act 2003*, published 30 April 2007 [see **SG-119**]

Key factors

(a) The levels of seriousness (in ascending order) for sentencing for offences involving pornographic images are:
Level 1 Images depicting erotic posing with no sexual activity
Level 2 Non-penetrative sexual activity between children, or solo masturbation by a child
Level 3 Non-penetrative sexual activity between adults and children
Level 4 Penetrative sexual activity involving a child or children, or both children and adults
Level 5 Sadism or penetration of, or by, an animal.

(b) Pseudo-photographs generally should be treated less seriously than real photographs.

(c) Starting points should be higher where the subject of the indecent photograph(s) is a child under 13.

(d) In accordance with section 80 [of] and schedule 3 [to] the Sexual Offences Act 2003, automatic notification requirements apply upon conviction to an offender aged 18 or over where the offence involved photographs of children aged under 16.

Offence seriousness (culpability and harm)

A. Identify the appropriate starting point

Starting points based on first time offender pleading not guilty

Examples of nature of activity	Starting point	Range
Possession of a large amount of level 1 material and/or no more than a small amount of level 2, and the material is for personal use and has not been distributed or shown to others	**Medium level community order**	**Band C fine to high level community order**
Offender in possession of a large amount of material at level 2 or a small amount at level 3 Offender has shown or distributed material at level 1 on a limited scale Offender has exchanged images at level 1 or 2 with other collectors, but with no element of financial gain	**12 weeks custody**	**4 to 26 weeks custody**
Possession of a large quantity of level 3 material for personal use Possession of a small number of images at level 4 or 5 Large number of level 2 images shown or distributed Small number of level 3 images shown or distributed	**26 weeks custody**	**4 weeks custody to Crown Court**
Large number of level 3 images shown or distributed	**Crown Court**	**26 weeks custody to Crown Court**
Offender traded material at levels 1–3 Level 4 or 5 images shown or distributed Offender involved in the production of material of any level	**Crown Court**	**Crown Court**

B. Consider the effect of aggravating and mitigating factors (other than those within examples above)

Common aggravating and mitigating factors are identified [elsewhere]—the following may be particularly relevant but these lists are not exhaustive

Factors indicating higher culpability	Factors indicating lower culpability
1. Collection is systematically stored or organised, indicating a sophisticated approach to trading or a high level of personal interest 2. Use of drugs, alcohol or other substance to facilitate the offence of making or taking 3. Background of intimidation or coercion 4. Threats to prevent victim reporting the activity 5. Threats to disclose victim's activity to friends/relatives 6. Financial or other gain **Factors indicating greater degree of harm** 1. Images shown or distributed to others, especially children 2. Images stored, made available or distributed in such a way that they can be inadvertently accessed by others	1. A few images held solely for personal use 2. Images viewed but not stored 3. A few images held solely for personal use and it is established that the subject is aged 16 or 17 and that he or she was consenting

[Sets out the standard sequential sentencing procedure and mentions need to consider deprivation of property used to commit offence.]

Inflicting Grievous Bodily Harm/Unlawful Wounding SG-217

Offences against the Person Act 1861 (section 20)

Racially/Religiously Aggravated GBH/Unlawful Wounding

Crime and Disorder Act 1998 (section 29)

[This guideline was published by the Sentencing Council and has effect in respect of all sentences passed after 13 June 2011 on offenders aged 18 or older. It replaces the guideline which previously applied and which continued to have effect until that date.]

These are specified offences for the purposes of section 224 of the Criminal Justice Act 2003

Triable either way

Section 20
Maximum when tried summarily: Level 5 fine and/or 26 weeks' custody
Maximum when tried on indictment: 5 years' custody

Section 29
Maximum when tried summarily: Level 5 fine and/or 26 weeks' custody
Maximum when tried on indictment: 7 years' custody

Offence range: Community order—4 years' custody

This guideline applies to all offenders aged 18 and older, who are sentenced on or after 13 June 2011. The definitions at [**SG-273**] of 'starting point' and 'first time offender' do not apply for this guideline. Starting point and category ranges apply to all offenders in all cas-es, irrespective of plea or previous convictions.

STEP ONE Determining the offence category

The court should determine the offence category using the table below:

Category 1	Greater harm (serious injury must normally be present) **and** higher culpability
Category 2	Greater harm (serious injury must normally be present) **and** lower culpability; **or** lesser harm and higher culpability
Category 3	Lesser harm and lower culpability

The court should determine the offender's culpability and the harm caused, or intended, by reference only to the factors below (as demonstrated by the presence of one or more). These factors comprise the principal factual elements of the offence and should determine the category.

Factors indicating greater harm Injury (which includes disease transmission and/or psychological harm) which is serious in the context of the offence (must normally be present) Victim is particularly vulnerable because of personal circumstances Sustained or repeated assault on the same victim **Factors indicating higher culpability** *Statutory aggravating factors:* Offence motivated by, or demonstrating, hostility to the victim based on his or her sexual orientation (or presumed sexual orientation) Offence motivated by, or demonstrating, hostility to the victim based on the victim's disability (or presumed disability)	**Factors indicating lesser harm** Injury which is less serious in the context of the offence **Factors indicating lower culpability** Subordinate role in a group or gang A greater degree of provocation than normally expected Lack of premeditation Mental disorder or learning disability, where linked to commission of the offence Excessive self defence

Other aggravating factors: A significant degree of premeditation Use of weapon or weapon equivalent (for example, shod foot, headbutting, use of acid, use of animal) Intention to commit more serious harm than actually resulted from the offence Deliberately causes more harm than is necessary for commission of offence Deliberate targeting of vulnerable victim Leading role in group or gang Offence motivated by, or demonstrating, hostility based on the victim's age, sex, gender identity (or presumed gender identity)	

STEP TWO Starting point and category range

Having determined the category, the court should use the corresponding starting points to reach a sentence within the category range below. The starting point applies to all offenders irrespective of plea or previous convictions.

A case of particular gravity, reflected by multiple features of culpability in step one, could merit upward adjustment from the starting point before further adjustment for aggravating or mitigating features, set out below.

Offence Category	Starting Point (*Applicable to all offenders*)	Category Range (*Applicable to all offenders*)
Category 1	Crown Court	Crown Court
Category 2	Crown Court	Crown Court
Category 3	High level community order	Low level community order—Crown Court (51 weeks' custody)

The table below contains a **non-exhaustive** list of additional factual elements providing the context of the offence and factors relating to the offender. Identify whether any combination of these, or other relevant factors, should result in an upward or downward adjustment from the starting point. In some cases, having considered these factors, it may be appropriate to move outside the identified category range.

When sentencing **category 3** offences, the court should also consider the custody threshold as follows:

- has the custody threshold been passed?
- if so, is it unavoidable that a custodial sentence be imposed?
- if so, can that sentence be suspended?

Factors increasing seriousness	Factors reducing seriousness or reflecting personal mitigation
Statutory aggravating factors: Previous convictions, having regard to a) the nature of the offence to which the conviction relates and its relevance to the current offence; and b) the time that has elapsed since the conviction Offence committed whilst on bail	No previous convictions or no relevant/recent convictions Single blow Remorse Good character and/or exemplary conduct

Other aggravating factors include: Location of the offence Timing of the offence Ongoing effect upon the victim Offence committed against those working in the public sector or providing a service to the public Presence of others including relatives, especially children or partner of the victim Gratuitous degradation of victim In domestic violence cases, victim forced to leave their home Failure to comply with current court orders Offence committed whilst on licence An attempt to conceal or dispose of evidence Failure to respond to warnings or concerns expressed by others about the offender's behaviour Commission of offence whilst under the influence of alcohol or drugs Abuse of power and/or position of trust Exploiting contact arrangements with a child to commit an offence Established evidence of community impact Any steps taken to prevent the victim reporting an incident, obtaining assistance and/or from assisting or supporting the prosecution Offences taken into consideration (TICs)	Determination and/or demonstration of steps taken to address addiction or offending behaviour Serious medical conditions requiring urgent, intensive or long-term treatment Isolated incident Age and/or lack of maturity where it affects the responsibility of the offender Lapse of time since the offence where this is not the fault of the offender Mental disorder or learning disability, where not linked to the commission of the offence Sole or primary carer for dependent relatives

Section 29 offences only: The court should determine the appropriate sentence for the offence without taking account of the element of aggravation and then make an addition to the sentence, considering the level of aggravation involved. It may be appropriate to move outside the identified category range, taking into account the increased statutory maximum.

[Steps Three to Nine are almost identical to those which apply to assault occasioning actual bodily harm: see **SG-178**.]

Keeping a Brothel used for Prostitution **SG-218**

Sexual Offences Act 2003, s. 55

Triable either way:
Maximum when tried summarily: Level 5 fine and/or 6 months
Maximum when tried on indictment: 7 years

This guideline is taken from the Sentencing Guidelines Council's definitive guideline *Sexual Offences Act 2003*, published 30 April 2007 [see **part 8**]

Offence seriousness (culpability and harm)

A. Identify the appropriate starting point

Starting points based on first time offender pleading not guilty

Examples of nature of activity	Starting point	Range
Involvement of the offender was minimal	**Medium level community order**	**Band C fine to high level community order**
Offender is the keeper of the brothel and is personally involved in its management	Crown Court	**26 weeks to Crown Court**
Offender is the keeper of a brothel and has made substantial profits in the region of £5,000 and upwards	Crown Court	Crown Court

B. Consider the effect of aggravating and mitigating factors (other than those within examples above)

Common aggravating and mitigating factors are identified [elsewhere]—the following may be particularly relevant but these lists are not exhaustive

Factors indicating higher culpability	Factors indicating lower culpability
1. Background of threats, intimidation or coercion 2. Large-scale commercial operation 3. Personal involvement in the prostitution of others 4. Abduction or detention 5. Financial or other gain	1. Using employment as a route out of prostitution and not actively involved in exploitation 2. Coercion by third party

[Sets out the standard sequential sentencing procedure.]

Note: Where an offender has profited from his or her involvement in the prostitution of others, the courts should always consider making a confiscation order approximately equivalent to the profits enjoyed. Such an order may be made only in the Crown Court.

SG-219

Making off Without Payment

Factors to take into consideration

Key factors

(a) The starting points and sentencing ranges in this guideline are based on the assumption that the offender was motivated by greed or a desire to live beyond his or her means. To avoid double counting, such a motivation should not be treated as a factor that increases culpability.

(b) When assessing the harm caused by this offence, the starting point should be the loss suffered by the victim. In general, the greater the loss, the more serious the offence. However, the monetary value of the loss may not reflect the full extent of the harm caused by the offence. The court should also take into account the impact of the offence on the victim, any harm to persons other than the direct victim, and any harm in the form of public alarm or erosion of public confidence.

(c) The following matters of offender mitigation may be relevant to this offence:

(i) Offender motivated by desperation or need
The fact that an offence has been committed in desperation or need arising from particular hardship may count as offender mitigation in exceptional circumstances.

(ii) Voluntary return of stolen property
Whether and the degree to which the return of stolen property constitutes a matter of offender mitigation will depend on an assessment of the circumstances and, in particular, the voluntariness and timeliness of the return.

(iii) Impact on sentence of offender's dependency
Many offenders convicted of acquisitive crimes are motivated by an addiction, often to drugs, alcohol or gambling. This does not mitigate the seriousness of the offence, but an offender's dependency may properly influence the type of sentence imposed. In particular, it may sometimes be appropriate to impose a drug rehabilitation requirement or an alcohol treatment requirement as part of a community order or a suspended sentence order in an attempt to break the cycle of addiction and offending, even if an immediate custodial sentence would otherwise be warranted.[192]

[192] See para.2 on p.163. The Court of Appeal gave guidance on the approach to making drug treatment and testing orders, which also applies to imposing a drug rehabilitation requirement in *Attorney General's Reference No. 64 of 2003 (Boujettif and Harrison)* [2003] EWCA Crim 2514 and *Woods and Collins* [2005] EWCA Crim 2065 summarised in the Sentencing Guidelines Council *Guideline Judgments Case Compendium* (section (A) Generic Sentencing Principles) available at: www.sentencing-guidelines.gov.uk

Guidelines

Theft Act 1978, s. 3

Triable either way:
Maximum when tried summarily: Level 5 fine and/or 6 months
Maximum when tried on indictment: 2 years

Offence seriousness (culpability and harm)

A. Identify the appropriate starting point

Starting points based on first time offender pleading not guilty

Examples of nature of activity	Starting point	Range
Single offence committed by an offender acting alone with evidence of little or no planning, goods or services worth less than £200	**Band C fine**	**Band A fine to high level community order**
Offence displaying one or more of the following: – offender acting in unison with others – evidence of planning – offence part of a 'spree' – intimidation of victim – goods or services worth £200 or more	**Medium level community order**	**Low level community order to 12 weeks custody**

B. Consider the effect of aggravating and mitigating factors (other than those within examples above)

Common aggravating and mitigating factors are identified [elsewhere]—the following may be particularly relevant but these lists are not exhaustive
[Sets out the standard sequential sentencing procedure.]

Obstruct/Resist a Police Constable in Execution of Duty SG-220

Police Act 1996, s. 89(2)

Triable only summarily:
Maximum: Level 3 fine and/or one month

Offence seriousness (culpability and harm)

A. Identify the appropriate starting point

Starting points based on first time offender pleading not guilty

Examples of nature of activity	Starting point	Range
Failure to move when required to do so	**Band A fine**	**Conditional discharge to band B fine**
Attempt to prevent arrest or other lawful police action; or giving false details	**Band B fine**	**Band A fine to band C fine**
Several people attempting to prevent arrest or other lawful police action	**Low level community order**	**Band C fine to medium level community order**

B. Consider the effect of aggravating and mitigating factors (other than those within examples above)

Common aggravating and mitigating factors are identified [elsewhere]—the following may be particularly relevant but these lists are not exhaustive

Factors indicating higher culpability	Factors indicating lower culpability
1. Premeditated action 2. Aggressive words/threats 3. Aggressive group action	1. Genuine mistake or misjudgement 2. Brief incident

[Sets out the standard sequential sentencing procedure.]

SG-221

Obtaining Services Dishonestly

Fraud Act 2006, s. 11

Triable either way:
Maximum when tried summarily: Level 5 fine and/or 6 months
Maximum when tried on indictment: 5 years

The offence of obtaining services dishonestly may be committed in circumstances that otherwise could be charged as an offence contrary to section 1 of the Fraud Act 2006 or may be more akin to making off without payment, contrary to section 3 of the Theft Act 1978. For this reason, it has not been included specifically within any of the guidelines for fraud, and one of the following approaches should be used:

- where it involves conduct which can be characterised as a fraud offence (such as obtaining credit through fraud or payment card fraud), the court should apply the guideline for the relevant type of fraud (see [above]); or
- where the conduct could be characterised as making off without payment (that is, where an offender, knowing that payment on the spot for any goods supplied or service done is required or expected, dishonestly makes off without having paid and with intent to avoid payment), the guideline for that offence should be used (see [above]).

SG-222

Protective Order, Breach Of

Factors to take into consideration

This guideline and accompanying notes are taken from the Sentencing Guidelines Council's definitive guideline *Breach of a Protective Order*, published 7 December 2006 [see **SG-45**]

Aims of sentencing

(a) The main aim of sentencing for breach of a protective order (which would have been imposed to protect a victim from future harm) should be to achieve future compliance with that order.
(b) The court will need to assess the level of risk posed by the offender. Willingness to undergo treatment or accept help may influence sentence.

Key factors

(i) The nature of the conduct that caused the breach of the order. In particular, whether the contact was direct or indirect, although it is important to recognise that indirect contact is capable of causing significant harm or anxiety.
(ii) There may be exceptional cases where the nature of the breach is particularly serious but has not been dealt with by a separate offence being charged. In these cases the risk posed by the offender and the nature of the breach will be particularly significant in determining the response.
(iii) The nature of the original conduct or offence is relevant in so far as it allows a judgement to be made on the level of harm caused to the victim by the breach, and the extent to which that harm was intended.
(iv) The sentence following a breach is for the breach alone and must avoid punishing the offender again for the offence or conduct as a result of which the order was made.
(v) It is likely that all breaches of protective orders will pass the threshold for a community sentence. Custody is the starting point where violence is used. Non-violent conduct may also cross the custody threshold where a high degree of harm or anxiety has been caused.
(vi) Where an order was made in civil proceedings, its purpose may have been to cause the subject of the order to modify behaviour rather than to imply that the conduct was especially serious. If so, it is likely to be disproportionate to impose a custodial sentence if the breach of the order did not involve threats or violence.
(vii) In some cases where a breach might result in a short custodial sentence but the court is satisfied that the offender genuinely intends to reform his or her behaviour and there is a real prospect of rehabilitation, the court may consider it appropriate to impose a sentence that will allow this. This may mean imposing a suspended sentence order or a community order (where appropriate with a requirement to attend an accredited domestic violence programme).

Guidelines

Protection from Harassment Act 1997, s. 5(5) (breach of restraining order)

Family Law Act 1996, s. 42A (breach of non-molestation order)

Triable either way:
Maximum when tried summarily: Level 5 fine and/or 6 months
Maximum when tried on indictment: 5 years

Where the conduct is particularly serious, it would normally be charged as a separate offence. These starting points are based on the premise that the activity has either been prosecuted separately as an offence or is not of a character sufficient to justify prosecution of it as an offence in its own right.

Where offence committed in domestic context, refer [below] for guidance

Offence seriousness (culpability and harm)

A. Identify the appropriate starting point

Starting points based on first time offender pleading not guilty

Examples of nature of activity	Starting point	Range
Single breach involving no/minimal direct contact	**Low level community order**	**Band C fine to medium level community order**
More than one breach involving no/minimal contact or some direct contact	**Medium level community order**	**Low level community order to high level community order**
Single breach involving some violence and/or significant physical or psychological harm to the victim	**18 weeks custody**	**13 to 26 weeks custody**
More than one breach involving some violence and/or significant physical or psychological harm to the victim	**Crown Court**	**26 weeks custody to Crown Court**
Breach (whether one or more) involving significant physical violence and significant physical or psychological harm to the victim	**Crown Court**	**Crown Court**

B. Consider the effect of aggravating and mitigating factors (other than those within examples above)

Common aggravating and mitigating factors are identified [elsewhere]—the following may be particularly relevant but these lists are not exhaustive

Factors indicating higher culpability	Factors indicating greater degree of harm
1. Proven history of violence or threats by the offender 2. Using contact arrangements with a child to instigate offence 3. Offence is a further breach, following earlier breach proceedings 4. Offender has history of disobedience to court orders 5. Breach committed immediately or shortly after order made	1. Victim is particularly vulnerable 2. Impact on children 3. Victim is forced to leave home **Factors indicating lower culpability** 1. Breach occurred after long period of compliance 2. Victim initiated contact

[Sets out the standard sequential sentencing procedure.]

Public Order Act, s. 2—Violent Disorder SG-223

Public Order Act 1986, s. 2

Triable either way:
Maximum when tried summarily: Level 5 fine and/or 6 months
Maximum when tried on indictment: 5 years

Identify dangerous offenders

This is a specified offence for the purposes of the public protection provisions in the Criminal Justice Act 2003. . .

Offence seriousness (culpability and harm)

A. Identify the appropriate starting point

Starting points based on first time offender pleading not guilty

These offences should normally be dealt with in the Crown Court. However, there may be rare cases involving minor violence or threats of violence leading to no or minor injury, with few people involved and no weapon or missiles, in which a custodial sentence within the jurisdiction of a magistrates' court may be appropriate.

SG-224 PUBLIC ORDER ACT, S. 3—AFFRAY

Public Order Act 1986, s. 3

Triable either way:
Maximum when tried summarily: Level 5 fine and/or 6 months
Maximum when tried on indictment: 3 years

Identify dangerous offenders

This is a specified offence for the purposes of the public protection provisions in the Criminal Justice Act 2003. . .

Offence seriousness (culpability and harm)

A. Identify the appropriate starting point

Starting points based on first time offender pleading not guilty

Examples of nature of activity	Starting point	Range
Brief offence involving low-level violence, no substantial fear created	**Low level community order**	**Band C fine to medium level community order**
Degree of fighting or violence that causes substantial fear	**High level community order**	**Medium level community order to 12 weeks custody**
Fight involving a weapon/throwing objects, or conduct causing risk of serious injury	**18 weeks custody**	**12 weeks custody to Crown Court**

B. Consider the effect of aggravating and mitigating factors (other than those within examples above)

Common aggravating and mitigating factors are identified [elsewhere]—the following may be particularly relevant but these lists are not exhaustive

Factors indicating higher culpability	Factors indicating lower culpability
1. Group action 2. Threats 3. Lengthy incident **Factors indicating greater degree of harm** 1. Vulnerable person(s) present 2. Injuries caused 3. Damage to property	1. Did not start the trouble 2. Provocation 3. Stopped as soon as police arrived

Sets out the standard sequential sentencing procedure and mentions the need to consider a football banning order.]

SG-225 PUBLIC ORDER ACT, S. 4—THREATENING BEHAVIOUR—FEAR OR PROVOCATION OF VIOLENCE RACIALLY OR RELIGIOUSLY AGGRAVATED THREATENING BEHAVIOUR

Public Order Act 1986, s. 4

Crime and Disorder Act 1998, s. 31

Threatening behaviour: triable only summarily
Maximum: Level 5 fine and/or 6 months

Racially or religiously aggravated threatening behaviour: triable either way
Maximum when tried summarily: Level 5 fine and/or 6 months
Maximum when tried on indictment: 2 years

Where offence committed in domestic context, refer [below] for guidance

Offence seriousness (culpability and harm)

A. Identify the appropriate starting point

Starting points based on first time offender pleading not guilty

Examples of nature of activity	Starting point	Range
Fear or threat of low level immediate unlawful violence such as push, shove or spit	**Low level community order**	**Band B fine to medium level community order**
Fear or threat of medium level immediate unlawful violence such as punch	**High level community order**	**Low level community order to 12 weeks custody**
Fear or threat of high level immediate unlawful violence such as use of weapon; missile thrown; gang involvement	**12 weeks custody**	**6 to 26 weeks custody**

B. Consider the effect of aggravating and mitigating factors (other than those within examples above)

Common aggravating and mitigating factors are identified [elsewhere]—the following may be particularly relevant but these lists are not exhaustive

Factors indicating higher culpability	Factors indicating lower culpability
1. Planning 2. Offender deliberately isolates victim 3. Group action 4. Threat directed at victim because of job 5. History of antagonism towards victim **Factors indicating greater degree of harm** 1. Offence committed at school, hospital or other place where vulnerable persons may be present 2. Offence committed on enclosed premises such as public transport 3. Vulnerable victim(s) 4. Victim needs medical help/counseling	1. Impulsive action 2. Short duration 3. Provocation

[Sets out the standard sequential sentencing procedure and mentions the need to consider a football banning order. Notes that 'If offender charged and convicted of the racially or religiously aggravated offence, increase the sentence to reflect this element'.]

Public Order Act, s. 4A—Disorderly Behaviour with Intent to Cause Harassment, Alarm or Distress **SG-226**

Racially Or Religiously Aggravated Disorderly Behaviour With Intent To Cause Harassment, Alarm Or Distress

Public Order Act 1986, s. 4A

Crime and Disorder Act 1998, s. 31

Disorderly behaviour with intent to cause harassment, alarm or distress: triable only summarily
Maximum: Level 5 fine and/or 6 months

Racially or religiously aggravated disorderly behaviour with intent to cause harassment etc.: triable either way

Maximum when tried summarily: Level 5 fine and/or 6 months
Maximum when tried on indictment: 2 years

Offence seriousness (culpability and harm)

A. Identify the appropriate starting point

Starting points based on first time offender pleading not guilty

Examples of nature of activity	Starting point	Range
Threats, abuse or insults made more than once but on same occasion against the same person e.g. while following down the street	**Band C fine**	**Band B fine to low level community order**
Group action or deliberately planned action against targeted victim	**Medium level community order**	**Low level community order to 12 weeks custody**
Weapon brandished or used or threats against vulnerable victim—course of conduct over longer period	**12 weeks custody**	**High level community order to 26 weeks custody**

B. Consider the effect of aggravating and mitigating factors (other than those within examples above)

Common aggravating and mitigating factors are identified [elsewhere]—the following may be particularly relevant but these lists are not exhaustive

Factors indicating higher culpability	Factors indicating lower culpability
1. High degree of planning 2. Offender deliberately isolates victim **Factors indicating greater degree of harm** 1. Offence committed in vicinity of victims home 2. Large number of people in vicinity 3. Actual or potential escalation into violence 4. Particularly serious impact on victim	1. Very short period 2. Provocation

[Sets out the standard sequential sentencing procedure and mentions the need to consider a football banning order. Notes that 'If offender charged and convicted of the racially or religiously aggravated offence, increase the sentence to reflect this element'.]

SG-227 Public Order Act, s.5—Disorderly Behaviour (Harassment, Alarm or Distress) Racially or religiously Aggravated Disorderly Behaviour

Public Order Act 1986, s. 5

Crime and Disorder Act 1998, s. 31

Disorderly behaviour: triable only summarily
Maximum: Level 3 fine

Racially or religiously aggravated disorderly behaviour: triable only summarily
Maximum: Level 4 fine

Offence seriousness (culpability and harm)

A. Identify the appropriate starting point

Starting points based on first time offender pleading not guilty

Examples of nature of activity	Starting point	Range
Shouting, causing disturbance for some minutes	**Band A fine**	**Conditional discharge to band B fine**
Substantial disturbance caused	**Band B fine**	**Band A fine to band C fine**

B. Consider the effect of aggravating and mitigating factors (other than those within examples above)

Common aggravating and mitigating factors are identified [elsewhere]—the following may be particularly relevant but these lists are not exhaustive

Factors indicating higher culpability	Factors indicating lower culpability
1. Group action 2. Lengthy incident **Factors indicating greater degree of harm** 1. Vulnerable person(s) present 2. Offence committed at school, hospital or other place where vulnerable persons may be present 3. Victim providing public service	1. Stopped as soon as police arrived 2. Brief/minor incident 3. Provocation

[Sets out the standard sequential sentencing procedure and mentions the need to consider a football banning order. Notes that 'If offender charged and convicted of the racially or religiously aggravated offence, increase the sentence to reflect this element'.]

Railway Fare Evasion SG-228

Regulation of Railways Act 1889, s. 5(3) (travelling on railway without paying fare, with intent to avoid payment); s. 5(1) (failing to produce ticket)

Triable only summarily:
Maximum: Level 3 fine or 3 months (s. 5(3)); level 2 fine (s. 5(1))

Offence seriousness (culpability and harm)

A. Identify the appropriate starting point

Starting points based on first time offender pleading not guilty

Examples of nature of activity	Starting point	Range
Failing to produce ticket or pay fare on request	**Band A fine**	**Conditional discharge to band B fine**
Travelling on railway without having paid the fare or knowingly and wilfully travelling beyond the distance paid for, with intent to avoid payment	**Band B fine**	**Band A fine to band C fine**

B. Consider the effect of aggravating and mitigating factors (other than those within examples above)

Common aggravating and mitigating factors are identified [elsewhere]—the following may be particularly relevant but these lists are not exhaustive

Factor indicating higher culpability	Factor indicating greater degree of harm
1. Offensive or intimidating language or behaviour towards railway staff	1. High level of loss caused or intended to be caused

[Sets out the standard sequential sentencing procedure.]

School Non-attendance SG-229

Education Act 1996, s. 444(1) (parent fails to secure regular attendance at school of registered pupil); s. 444(1A) (parent knowingly fails to secure regular attendance at school of registered pupil)

Triable only summarily
Maximum: Level 3 fine (s. 444(1)); level 4 fine and/or 3 months (s. 444(1A))

Offence seriousness (culpability and harm)

A. Identify the appropriate starting point

Starting points based on first time offender pleading not guilty

Examples of nature of activity	Starting point	Range
Short period following previous good attendance (s.444(1))	**Band A fine**	**Conditional discharge to band A fine**
Erratic attendance for long period (s. 444(1))	**Band B fine**	**Band B fine to Band C fine**
Colluding in and condoning non-attendance or deliberately instigating non-attendance (s. 444(1A))	**Medium level community order**	**Low level community order to high level community order**

B. Consider the effect of aggravating and mitigating factors (other than those within examples above)

Common aggravating and mitigating factors are identified [elsewhere]—the following may be particularly relevant but these lists are not exhaustive

Sentencing Guidelines

Factors indicating higher culpability	Factors indicating lower culpability
1. Parental collusion (s.444(1) only) 2. Lack of parental effort to ensure attendance (s.444(1) only) 3. Threats to teachers and/or officials 4. Refusal to co-operate with school and/or officials **Factors indicating greater degree of harm** 1. More than one child 2. Harmful effect on other children in family	1. Parent unaware of child's whereabouts 2. Parent tried to ensure attendance 3. Parent concerned by child's allegations of bullying/unable to get school to address bullying

[Sets out the standard sequential sentencing procedure and mentions need to consider a parenting order.]

SG-230 Sex Offenders Register—Fail to Comply with Notification Requirements

Sexual Offences Act 2003, s. 91(1)(a) (fail to comply with notification requirements); s. 91(1)(b) (supply false information)

Triable either way:
Maximum when tried summarily: Level 5 fine and/or 6 months
Maximum when tried on indictment: 5 years

Offence seriousness (culpability and harm)

A. Identify the appropriate starting point

Starting points based on first time offender pleading not guilty

Examples of nature of activity	Starting point	Range
Negligent or inadvertent failure to comply with requirements	**Medium level community order**	**Band C fine to high level community order**
Deliberate failure to comply with requirements OR Supply of information known to be false	**6 weeks custody**	**High level community order to 26 weeks custody**
Conduct as described in box above AND Long period of non-compliance OR Attempts to avoid detection	**18 weeks custody**	**6 weeks custody to Crown Court**

B. Consider the effect of aggravating and mitigating factors (other than those within examples above)

Common aggravating and mitigating factors are identified [elsewhere]—the following may be particularly relevant but these lists are not exhaustive

Factor indicating higher culpability	Factor indicating lower culpability
1. Long period of non-compliance (where not in the examples above) **Factor indicating greater degree of harm** 1. Alarm or distress caused to victim 2. Particularly serious original offence	1. Genuine misunderstanding

[Sets out the standard sequential sentencing procedure.]

Note
An offender convicted of this offence will always have at least one relevant previous conviction for the offence that resulted in the notification requirements being imposed. The starting points and ranges take this into account; any other previous convictions should be considered in the usual way...

SG-231 Sexual Activity in a Public Lavatory

Sexual Offences Act 2003, s. 71

Triable only summarily
Maximum: Level 5 fine and/or 6 months

This guideline and accompanying notes are taken from the Sentencing Guidelines Council's definitive guideline *Sexual Offences Act 2003*, published 30 April 2007 [see **SG-109**]

Key factors

(a) This offence is committed where an offender intentionally engages in sexual activity in a public lavatory. It was introduced to give adults and children the freedom to use public lavatories for the purpose for which they are designed, without the fear of being an unwilling witness to overtly sexual behaviour of a kind that most people would not expect to be conducted in public. It is primarily a public order offence rather than a sexual offence.
(b) When dealing with a repeat offender, the starting point should be a low level community order with a range of Band C fine to medium level community order. The presence of aggravating factors may suggest that a sentence above the range is appropriate.
(c) This guideline may be relevant by way of analogy to conduct charged as the common law offence of outraging public decency; the offence is triable either way and has a maximum penalty of a level 5 fine and/or 6 months imprisonment when tried summarily.

Offence seriousness (culpability and harm)

A. Identify the appropriate starting point

Starting points based on first time offender pleading not guilty

Examples of nature of activity	Starting point	Range
Basic offence as defined in the Act, assuming no aggravating or mitigating factors	**Band C fine**	**Band C fine**
Offence with aggravating factors	**Low level community order**	**Band C fine to medium level community order**

B. Consider the effect of aggravating and mitigating factors (other than those within examples above)

Common aggravating and mitigating factors are identified [elsewhere]—the following may be particularly relevant but these lists are not exhaustive

Factors indicating higher culpability 1. Intimidating behaviour/threats of violence to member(s) of the public 2. Blatant behaviour	

[Sets out the standard sequential sentencing procedure.]

Sexual Assault **SG-232**

Sexual Offences Act 2003, ss. 3 and 7 (sexual assault of child under 13)

Triable either way:
Maximum when tried summarily: Level 5 fine and/or 6 months
Maximum when tried on indictment: 10 years (s.3), 14 years (s.7)

This guideline is taken from the Sentencing Guidelines Council's definitive guideline *Sexual Offences Act 2003*, published 30 April 2007 [see **SG-79**]

Identify dangerous offenders

These are serious offences for the purposes of the public protection provisions in the Criminal Justice Act 2003. . .

Offence seriousness (culpability and harm)

A. Identify the appropriate starting point

Starting points based on first time offender pleading not guilty

Examples of nature of activity	Starting point	Range
Contact between part of offenders body (other than the genitalia) with part of the victims body (other than the genitalia)	**26 weeks custody** if the victim is under 13 **Medium level community order** if the victim is aged 13 or over	**4 weeks custody to Crown Court** **Band C fine to 6 weeks custody**
Contact between naked genitalia of offender and another part of victim's body Contact with naked genitalia of victim by offender using part of his or her body other than the genitalia, or an object Contact between either the clothed genitalia of offender and naked genitalia of victim or naked genitalia of offender and clothed genitalia of victim	**Crown Court** if the victim is under 13 **Crown Court** if the victim is aged 13 or over	**Crown Court** **26 weeks custody to Crown Court**
Contact between naked genitalia of offender and naked genitalia, face or mouth of the victim	**Crown Court**	**Crown Court**

B. Consider the effect of aggravating and mitigating factors (other than those within examples above)

Common aggravating and mitigating factors are identified [elsewhere]—the following may be particularly relevant but these lists are not exhaustive

Factors indicating higher culpability	Factors indicating lower culpability
1. Background of intimidation or coercion 2. Use of drugs, alcohol or other substance to facilitate the offence 3. Threats to prevent the victim reporting the incident 4. Abduction or detention 5. Offender aware that he or she is suffering from a sexually transmitted infection 6. Prolonged activity or contact **Factors indicating greater degree of harm** 1. Offender ejaculated or caused victim to ejaculate 2. Physical harm caused	1. Youth and immaturity of the offender 2. Minimal or fleeting contact *Where the victim is aged 16 or over* 3. Victim engaged in consensual activity with the offender on the same occasion and immediately before the offence *Where the victim is under 16* 4. Sexual activity between two children (one of whom is the offender) was mutually agreed and experimental

[Sets out the standard sequential sentencing procedure.]

Note:

(a) In accordance with section 80 [of] and schedule 3 [to] the Sexual Offences Act 2003, automatic notification requirements apply upon conviction to an offender aged 18 or over where:
    (1) the victim was under 18; or
    (2) a term of imprisonment or a community sentence of at least 12 months is imposed.

SG-233 Social Security Benefit, False Statement/Representation to Obtain

Social Security Administration Act 1992, s. 112
(makes statement/representation known to be false)

Triable only summarily
Maximum: Level 5 fine and/or 3 months

For offences under s. 111A, refer to guideline *Fraud — banking and insurance fraud and obtaining credit through fraud, benefit fraud and revenue fraud* [see **SG-206** ***et seq.***].

Offence seriousness (culpability and harm)

A. Identify the appropriate starting point

Starting points based on first time offender pleading not guilty

Examples of nature of activity	Starting point	Range
Claim fraudulent from the start, up to £5,000 obtained	**Medium level community order**	**Band B fine to high level community order**

B. Consider the effect of aggravating and mitigating factors (other than those within examples above)

Common aggravating and mitigating factors are identified [elsewhere]—the following may be particularly relevant but these lists are not exhaustive

Factors indicating higher culpability	Factors indicating lower culpability
1. Offending carried out over a long period 2. Offender acting in unison with one or more others 3. Planning 4. Offender motivated by greed or desire to live beyond his/her means 5. False identities or other personal details used 6. False or forged documents used 7. Official documents altered or falsified	1. Pressurised by others 2. Claim initially legitimate **Factor indicating lesser degree of harm** 1. Voluntary repayment of amounts overpaid

[Sets out the standard sequential sentencing procedure.]

Note: A maximum of £5,000 compensation may be imposed for each offence of which the offender has been convicted. The above guidelines have been drafted on the assumption that, in most cases, the Department for Work and Pensions will take separate steps to recover the overpayment.

Tax Credit Fraud SG-234

Tax Credits Act 2002, s. 35

Triable either way:
Maximum when tried summarily: Level 5 fine and/or 6 months
Maximum when tried on indictment: 7 years

Refer to guideline *Fraud — banking and insurance fraud and obtaining credit through fraud, benefit fraud and revenue fraud* [see **SG-206 *et seq.***].

Taxi Touting/Soliciting for Hire SG-235

Criminal Justice and Public Order Act 1994, s. 167

Triable only summarily:

Maximum: Level 4 fine

Offence seriousness (culpability and harm)

A. Identify the appropriate starting point

Starting points based on first time offender pleading not guilty

Examples of nature of activity	Starting point	Range
Licensed taxi-driver touting for trade (i.e. making approach rather than waiting for a person to initiate hiring)	**Band A fine**	**Conditional discharge to band A fine and consider disqualification 1–3 months**
PHV licence held but touting for trade rather than being booked through an operator; an accomplice to touting	**Band B fine**	**Band A fine to band C fine and consider disqualification 3–6 months**
No PHV licence held	**Band C fine**	**Band B fine to Band C fine and disqualification 6–12 months**

Note: refer [below] for approach to fines for offences committed for commercial purposes

B. Consider the effect of aggravating and mitigating factors (other than those within examples above)

Common aggravating and mitigating factors are identified [elsewhere]—the following may be particularly relevant but these lists are not exhaustive

Factors indicating higher culpability	Factor indicating lower culpability
1. Commercial business/large scale operation 2. No insurance/invalid insurance 3. No driving licence and/or no MOT 4. Vehicle not roadworthy **Factors indicating greater degree of harm** 1. Deliberately diverting trade from taxi rank 2. PHV licence had been refused/offender ineligible for licence	1. Providing a service when no licensed taxi available

[Sets out the standard sequential sentencing procedure and mentions need to consider disqualification from driving and deprivation of property]

SG-236

Theft—General Principles

1. The guideline *Theft and Burglary in a building other than a dwelling*, published by the Sentencing Guidelines Council 9 December 2008 [see **SG-368**] covers four forms of theft. However, the principles relating to the assessment of seriousness in the guideline are of general application and are likely to be of assistance where a court is sentencing for a form of theft not covered by a specific guideline. These are summarised below for ease of reference.

Assessing seriousness

(i) Culpability and harm

2. As it is an essential element of the offence of theft that the offender acted dishonestly, an offender convicted of theft will have a high level of culpability. Even so, the precise level of culpability will vary according to factors such as the offender's motivation, whether the offence was planned or spontaneous and whether the offender was in a position of trust. An offence will be aggravated where there is evidence of planning.
3. When assessing the harm caused by a theft offence, the starting point is normally based on the loss suffered by the victim. Whilst, in general, the greater the loss, the more serious the offence, the monetary value of the loss may not reflect the full extent of the harm caused by the offence. The court should also take into account the impact of the offence on the victim (which may be significantly greater than the monetary value of the loss; this may be particularly important where the value of the loss is high in proportion to the victim's financial circumstances even though relatively low in absolute terms), any harm to persons other than the direct victim, and any harm in the form of public concern or erosion of public confidence.

(ii) Aggravating and mitigating factors

4. The most common factors that are likely to aggravate an offence of theft are:
   factors indicating higher culpability: planning of an offence, offenders operating in groups or gangs, and deliberate targeting of vulnerable victims.
   factors indicating a more than usually serious degree of harm: victim is particularly vulnerable, high level of gain from the offence, and high value (including sentimental value) of property to the victim or substantial consequential loss.

(iii) Offender mitigation

5. The Council has identified the following matters of offender mitigation that might apply to offences of theft:
   (a) *Return of stolen property*—depending on the circumstances and in particular, the voluntariness and timeliness of the return.
   (b) *Impact on sentence of offender's dependency*—where an offence is motivated by an addiction (often to drugs, alcohol or gambling) this does not mitigate the seriousness of the offence, but a dependency may properly influence the type of sentence imposed. In particular, it may sometimes be appropriate to impose a drug rehabilitation requirement, an alcohol treatment requirement (for dependent drinkers) or an activity or supervision requirement including alcohol specific information, advice and support (for harmful and hazardous drinkers) as part of a community order or a suspended sentence order in an attempt to break the cycle of addiction and offending, even if an immediate custodial sentence would otherwise be warranted.
   (c) *Offender motivated by desperation or need*—the fact that an offence has been committed in desperation or need arising from particular hardship may count as offender mitigation in **exceptional circumstances**.

THEFT—BREACH OF TRUST—FACTORS TO TAKE INTO CONSIDERATION SG-237

This guideline and accompanying notes are taken from the Sentencing Guidelines Council's definitive guideline *Theft and Burglary in a building other than a dwelling*, published 9 December 2008 [see SG-371]

Key factors

(a) When assessing the harm caused by this offence, the starting point should be the loss suffered by the victim. In general, the greater the loss, the more serious the offence. However, the monetary value of the loss may not reflect the full extent of the harm caused by the offence. The court should also take into account the impact of the offence on the victim (which may be significant and disproportionate to the value of the loss having regard to their financial circumstances), any harm to persons other than the direct victim, and any harm in the form of public concern or erosion of public confidence.

(b) In general terms, the seriousness of the offence will increase in line with the level of trust breached. The extent to which the nature and degree of trust placed in an offender should be regarded as increasing seriousness will depend on a careful assessment of the circumstances of each individual case, including the type and terms of the relationship between the offender and victim.

(c) The concept of breach of trust for the purposes of the offence of theft includes employer/employee relationships and those between a professional adviser and client. It also extends to relationships in which a person is in a position of authority in relation to the victim or would be expected to have a duty to protect the interests of the victim, such as medical, social or care workers. The targeting of a vulnerable victim by an offender through a relationship or position of trust will indicate a higher level of culpability.

(d) The Council has identified the following matters of offender mitigation which may be relevant to this offence:

(i) *Return of stolen property*
Whether and the degree to which the return of stolen property constitutes a matter of offender mitigation will depend on an assessment of the circumstances and, in particular, the voluntariness and timeliness of the return.

(ii) *Impact on sentence of offender's dependency*
Where an offence is motivated by an addiction (often to drugs, alcohol or gambling) this does not mitigate the seriousness of the offence, but a dependency may properly influence the type of sentence imposed. In particular, it may sometimes be appropriate to impose a drug rehabilitation requirement, an alcohol treatment requirement (for dependent drinkers) or an activity or supervision requirement including alcohol specific information, advice and support (for harmful and hazardous drinkers) as part of a community order or a suspended sentence order in an attempt to break the cycle of addiction and offending, even if an immediate custodial sentence would otherwise be warranted.

(iii) *Offender motivated by desperation or need*
The fact that an offence has been committed in desperation or need arising from particular hardship may count as offender mitigation in exceptional circumstances.

(iv) *Inappropriate degree of trust or responsibility*
The fact that an offender succumbed to temptation having been placed in a position of trust or given responsibility to an inappropriate degree may be regarded as offender mitigation.

(v) *Voluntary cessation of offending*
The fact that an offender voluntarily ceased offending before being discovered does not reduce the seriousness of the offence. However, if the claim to have stopped offending is genuine, it may constitute offender mitigation, particularly if it is evidence of remorse.

(vi) *Reporting an undiscovered offence*
Where an offender brings the offending to the attention of his or her employer or the authorities, this may be treated as offender mitigation.

(f) In many cases of theft in breach of trust, termination of an offender's employment will be a natural consequence of committing the offence. Other than in the most exceptional of circumstances, loss of employment and any consequential hardship should not constitute offender mitigation.

(g) Where a court is satisfied that a custodial sentence is appropriate for an offence of theft in breach of trust, consideration should be given to whether that sentence can be suspended in accordance with the criteria in the Council guideline *New Sentences: Criminal Justice Act 2003*. A suspended sentence may be particularly appropriate where this would allow for reparation to be made either to the victim or to the community at large.

SG-238 THEFT—BREACH OF TRUST

Theft Act 1968, s. 1

Triable either way:
Maximum when tried summarily: Level 5 fine and/or 6 months
Maximum when tried on indictment: 7 years
Offence seriousness (culpability and harm)

A. Identify the appropriate starting point

Starting points based on first time offender pleading not guilty

Examples of nature of activity	**Starting point**	**Range**
Theft of less than £2,000	**Medium level community order**	**Band B fine to 26 weeks custody**
Theft of £2,000 or more but less than £20,000 OR Theft of less than £2,000 in breach of a high degree of trust	**18 weeks custody**	**High level community order to Crown Court**
Theft of £20,000 or more OR Theft of £2,000 or more in breach of a high degree of trust	**Crown Court**	**Crown Court**

B. Consider the effect of aggravating and mitigating factors (other than those within examples above)

Common aggravating and mitigating factors are identified [elsewhere]—the following may be particularly relevant but these lists are not exhaustive

Factors indicating higher culpability 1. Long course of offending 2. Suspicion deliberately thrown on others 3. Offender motivated by intention to cause harm or out of revenge	

SG-239 THEFT—DWELLING

Factors to take into consideration

This guideline and accompanying notes are taken from the Sentencing Guidelines Council's definitive guideline *Theft and Burglary in a building other than a dwelling*, published 9 December 2008 [see **SG-375**]

Key factors

(a) The category of theft in a dwelling covers the situation where a theft is committed by an offender who is present in a dwelling with the authority of the owner or occupier. Examples include thefts by lodgers or visitors to the victim's residence, such as friends, relatives or salespeople. Such offences involve a violation of the privacy of the victim's home and constitute an abuse of the victim's trust. Where an offender enters a dwelling as a trespasser in order to commit theft, his or her conduct will generally constitute the more serious offence of burglary; this guideline does not apply where the offender has been convicted of burglary—see [above] for guidance.

(b) The starting points and sentencing ranges in this guideline are based on the assumption that the offender was motivated by greed or a desire to live beyond his or her means. To avoid double counting, such a motivation should not be treated as a factor that increases culpability.

(c) For the purpose of this guideline, a 'vulnerable victim' is a person targeted by the offender because it is anticipated that he or she is unlikely or unable to resist the theft. The exploitation of a vulnerable victim indicates a high level of culpability and will influence the category of seriousness into which the offence falls.

(d) The guideline is based on the assumption that most thefts in a dwelling do not involve property of high monetary value or of high value to the victim. Where the property stolen is of high monetary value or of high value (including sentimental value) to the victim, the appropriate sentence may be beyond the range into which the offence otherwise would fall. For the purpose of this form of theft, property worth more than £2,000 should generally be regarded as being of 'high monetary value', although this will depend on an assessment of all the circumstances of the particular case.

(e) A sentence beyond the range into which the offence otherwise would fall may also be appropriate where the effect on the victim is particularly severe or where substantial consequential loss results (such as where the theft of equipment causes serious disruption to the victim's life or business).

(f) The Council has identified the following matters of offender mitigation which may be relevant to this offence:
   (i) *Return of stolen property*
   Whether and the degree to which the return of stolen property constitutes a matter of offender mitigation will depend on an assessment of the circumstances and, in particular, the voluntariness and timeliness of the return.
   (ii) *Impact on sentence of offender's dependency*
   Where an offence is motivated by an addiction (often to drugs, alcohol or gambling) this does not mitigate the seriousness of the offence, but a dependency may properly influence the type of sentence imposed. In particular, it may sometimes be appropriate to impose a drug rehabilitation requirement, an alcohol treatment requirement (for dependent drinkers) or an activity or supervision requirement including alcohol specific information, advice and support (for harmful and hazardous drinkers) as part of a community order or a suspended sentence order in an attempt to break the cycle of addiction and offending, even if an immediate custodial sentence would otherwise be warranted.
   (iii) *Offender motivated by desperation or need*
   The fact that an offence has been committed in desperation or need arising from particular hardship may count as offender mitigation in exceptional circumstances.

Guidelines

Theft Act 1968, s. 1

Triable either way:
Maximum when tried summarily: Level 5 fine and/or 6 months
Maximum when tried on indictment: 7 years

Offence seriousness (culpability and harm)

A. Identify the appropriate starting point

Starting points based on first time offender pleading not guilty

Examples of nature of activity	Starting point	Range
Where the effect on the victim is particularly severe, the stolen property is of high value (as defined in note (d) opposite), or substantial consequential loss results, a sentence higher than the range into which the offence otherwise would fall may be appropriate		
Theft in a dwelling not involving vulnerable victim	**Medium level community order**	**Band B fine to 18 weeks custody**
Theft from a vulnerable victim (as defined in note (c) [above])	**18 weeks custody**	**High level community order to Crown Court**
Theft from a vulnerable victim (as defined in note (c) [above]) involving intimidation or the use or threat of force (falling short of robbery) or the use of deception	**Crown Court**	**Crown Court**

B. Consider the effect of aggravating and mitigating factors (other than those within examples above)

Common aggravating and mitigating factors are identified [elsewhere]—the following may be particularly relevant but these lists are not exhaustive

Factors indicating higher culpability 1. Offender motivated by intention to cause harm or out of revenge **Factors indicating greater degree of harm** 1. Intimidation or face-to-face confrontation with victim [except where this raises the offence into a higher sentencing range] 2. Use of force, or threat of force, against victim (not amounting to robbery) [except where this raises the offence into a higher sentencing range] 3. Use of deception [except where this raises the offence into a higher sentencing range] 4. Offender takes steps to prevent the victim from reporting the crime or seeking help	

[Sets out the standard sequential sentencing procedure.]

SG-240

Theft—Person

Factors to take into consideration

This guideline and accompanying notes are taken from the Sentencing Guidelines Council's definitive guideline *Theft and Burglary in a building other than a dwelling*, published 9 December 2008 [see **SG-373**]

Key factors

(a) Theft from the person may encompass conduct such as 'pick-pocketing', where the victim is unaware that the property is being stolen, as well as the snatching of handbags, wallets, jewellery and mobile telephones from the victim's possession or from the vicinity of the victim. The offence constitutes an invasion of the victim's privacy and may cause the victim to experience distress, fear and inconvenience either during or after the event. While in some cases the conduct may be similar, this guideline does not apply where the offender has been convicted of robbery; sentencers should instead refer to the Council guideline on robbery.

(b) The starting points and sentencing ranges in this guideline are based on the assumption that the offender was motivated by greed or a desire to live beyond his or her means. To avoid double counting, such a motivation should not be treated as a factor that increases culpability.

(c) For the purpose of this guideline, a 'vulnerable victim' is a person targeted by the offender because it is anticipated that he or she is unlikely or unable to resist the theft. Young or elderly persons, or those with disabilities may fall into this category. The exploitation of a vulnerable victim indicates a high level of culpability and will influence the category of seriousness into which the offence falls.

(d) Offences of this type will be aggravated where there is evidence of planning, such as where tourists are targeted because of their unfamiliarity with an area and a perception that they will not be available to give evidence.

(e) The guideline is based on the assumption that most thefts from the person do not involve property of high monetary value or of high value to the victim. Where the stolen property is of high monetary value or of high value (including sentimental value) to the victim, the appropriate sentence may be beyond the range into which the offence otherwise would fall. For the purposes of this form of theft, 'high monetary value' is defined as more than £2,000.

(f) A sentence beyond the range into which the offence otherwise would fall may also be appropriate where the effect on the victim is particularly severe or where substantial consequential loss results (such as where the theft of equipment causes serious disruption to the victim's life or business).

(g) The Council has identified the following matters of offender mitigation which may be relevant to this offence:

(i) *Return of stolen property*
Whether and the degree to which the return of stolen property constitutes a matter of offender mitigation will depend on an assessment of the circumstances and, in particular, the voluntariness and timeliness of the return.

(ii) *Impact on sentence of offender's dependency*
Where an offence is motivated by an addiction (often to drugs, alcohol or gambling) this does not mitigate the seriousness of the offence, but a dependency may properly influence the type of sentence imposed. In particular, it may sometimes be appropriate to impose a drug rehabilitation requirement, an alcohol treatment requirement (for dependent drinkers) or an activity or supervision requirement including alcohol specific information, advice and support (for harmful and hazardous drinkers) as part of a community order or a suspended sentence order in an attempt to break the cycle of addiction and offending, even if an immediate custodial sentence would otherwise be warranted.

(iii) *Offender motivated by desperation or need*
The fact that an offence has been committed in desperation or need arising from particular hardship may count as offender mitigation in exceptional circumstances.

Guidelines

Theft Act 1968, s. 1

Triable either way:
Maximum when tried summarily: Level 5 fine and/or 6 months
Maximum when tried on indictment: 7 years

Offence seriousness (culpability and harm)

A. Identify the appropriate starting point

Starting points based on first time offender pleading not guilty

Examples of nature of activity	Starting point	Range
Where the effect on the victim is particularly severe, the stolen property is of high value (as defined in note (f) opposite), or substantial consequential loss results, a sentence higher than the range into which the offence otherwise would fall may be appropriate		
Theft from the person not involving vulnerable victim	**Medium level community order**	**Band B fine to 18 weeks custody**
Theft from a vulnerable victim (as defined in note (c) [above])	**18 weeks custody**	**High level community order to Crown Court**
Theft involving the use or threat of force (falling short of robbery) against a vulnerable victim (as defined in note (c) [above])	**Crown Court**	**Crown Court**

B. Consider the effect of aggravating and mitigating factors (other than those within examples above)

Common aggravating and mitigating factors are identified [elsewhere]—the following may be particularly relevant but these lists are not exhaustive

Factors indicating higher culpability 1. Offender motivated by intention to cause harm or out of revenge **Factors indicating greater degree of harm** 1. Intimidation or face-to-face confrontation with victim [except where this raises the offence into a higher sentencing range] 2. Use of force, or threat of force, against victim (not amounting to robbery) [except where this raises the offence into a higher sentencing range] 3. High level of inconvenience caused to victim, e.g. replacing house keys, credit cards etc	

[Sets out the standard sequential sentencing procedure.]

Theft—Shop SG-241

Factors to take into consideration

This guideline and accompanying notes are taken from the Sentencing Guidelines Council's definitive guideline *Theft and Burglary in a building other than a dwelling*, published 9 December 2008 [see **SG-377**]

Key factors

(a) The circumstances of this offence can vary significantly. At the least serious end of the scale are thefts involving low value goods, no (or little) planning and no violence or damage; a non-custodial sentence will usually be appropriate for a first time offender. At the higher end of the spectrum are thefts involving organised gangs o groups or the threat or use of force and a custodial starting point will usually be appropriate.

(b) The starting points and sentencing ranges in this guideline are based on the assumption that the offender was motivated by greed or a desire to live beyond his or her means. To avoid double counting, such a motivation should not be treated as a factor that increases culpability.

(c) When assessing the level of harm, the circumstances of the retailer are a proper consideration; a greater level of harm may be caused where the theft is against a small retailer.

(d) Retailers may suffer additional loss as a result of this type of offending such as the cost of preventative security measures, higher insurance premiums and time spent by staff dealing with the prosecution of offenders. However, the seriousness of an individual case must be judged on its own dimension of harm and culpability and the sentence on an individual offender should not be increased to reflect the harm caused to retailers in general by the totality of this type of offending.

(e) Any recent previous convictions for theft and dishonesty offences will need to be taken into account in sentencing. Where an offender demonstrates a level of 'persistent' or 'seriously persistent' offending, the community and custody thresholds may be crossed even though the other characteristics of the offence would otherwise warrant a lesser sentence.

(f) The list of aggravating and mitigating factors on the pullout card identifies high value as an aggravating factor in property offences. In cases of theft from a shop, theft of high value goods may be associated with other aggravating factors such as the degree of planning, professionalism and/or operating in a group, and care will need to be taken to avoid double counting. Deliberately targeting high value goods will always make an offence more serious.

(g) The Council has identified the following matters of offender mitigation which may be relevant to this offence:
  (i) *Return of stolen property*
  Whether and the degree to which the return of stolen property constitutes a matter of offender mitigation will depend on an assessment of the circumstances and, in particular, the voluntariness and timeliness of the return.
  (ii) *Impact on sentence of offender's dependency*
  Where an offence is motivated by an addiction (often to drugs, alcohol or gambling) this does not mitigate the seriousness of the offence, but a dependency may properly influence the type of sentence imposed. In particular, it may sometimes be appropriate to impose a drug rehabilitation requirement, an alcohol treatment requirement (for dependent drinkers) or an activity or supervision requirement including alcohol specific information, advice and support (for harmful and hazardous drinkers) as part of a community order or a suspended sentence order in an attempt to break the cycle of addiction and offending, even if an immediate custodial sentence would otherwise be warranted.
  (iii) *Offender motivated by desperation or need*
  The fact that an offence has been committed in desperation or need arising from particular hardship may count as offender mitigation in exceptional circumstances.

Guidelines

Theft Act 1968, s. 1

Triable either way:
Maximum when tried summarily: Level 5 fine and/or 6 months
Maximum when tried on indictment: 7 years

Offence seriousness (culpability and harm)

A. Identify the appropriate starting point

Starting points based on first time offender pleading not guilty

Examples of nature of activity	**Starting point**	**Range**
Little or no planning or sophistication and Goods stolen of low value	**Band B fine**	**Conditional discharge to low level community order**
Low level intimidation or threats or Some planning e.g. a session of stealing on the same day or going equipped or Some related damage	**Low level community order**	**Band B fine to medium level community order**
Significant intimidation or threats or Use of force resulting in slight injury or Very high level of planning or Significant related damage	**6 weeks custody**	**High level community order to Crown Court**
Organised gang/group and Intimidation or the use or threat of force (short of robbery)	**Crown Court**	**Crown Court**

B. Consider the effect of aggravating and mitigating factors (other than those within examples above)

Common aggravating and mitigating factors are identified [elsewhere]—the following may be particularly relevant but these lists are not exhaustive

Factors indicating higher culpability 1. Child accompanying offender is involved or aware of theft 2. Offender is subject to a banning order that includes the store targeted 3. Offender motivated by intention to cause harm or out of revenge 4. Professional offending **Factors indicating greater degree of harm** 1. Victim particularly vulnerable (e.g. small independent shop) 2. Offender targeted high value goods	

[Sets out the standard sequential sentencing procedure.]

Threats to Kill SG-242

Offences Against the Person Act 1861, s. 16

Triable either way:
Maximum when tried summarily: Level 5 fine and/or 6 months
Maximum when tried on indictment: 10 years

Where offence committed in domestic context, refer [below] for guidance

Identify dangerous offenders

This is a serious offence for the purposes of the public protection provisions in the Criminal Justice Act 2003. . .

Offence seriousness (culpability and harm)

A. Identify the appropriate starting point

Starting points based on first time offender pleading not guilty

Examples of nature of activity	Starting point	Range
One threat uttered in the heat of the moment, no more than fleeting impact on victim	**Medium level community order**	**Low level community order to high level community order**
Single calculated threat or victim fears that threat will be carried out	**12 weeks custody**	**6 to 26 weeks custody**
Repeated threats or visible weapon	**Crown Court**	**Crown Court**

B. Consider the effect of aggravating and mitigating factors (other than those within examples above)

Common aggravating and mitigating factors are identified [elsewhere]—the following may be particularly relevant but these lists are not exhaustive

Factors indicating higher culpability	Factor indicating lower culpability
1. Planning 2. Offender deliberately isolates victim 3. Group action 4. Threat directed at victim because of job 5. History of antagonism towards victim **Factors indicating greater degree of harm** 1. Vulnerable victim 2. Victim needs medical help/counseling	1. Provocation

[Sets out the standard sequential sentencing procedure and mentions need to consider football banning order.]

Trade Mark, Unauthorised use of etc. SG-243

Trade Marks Act 1994, s. 92

Triable either way:
Maximum when tried summarily: Level 5 fine and/or 6 months
Maximum when tried on indictment: 10 years

Offence seriousness (culpability and harm)

A. Identify the appropriate starting point

Starting points based on first time offender pleading not guilty

Examples of nature of activity	Starting point	Range
Small number of counterfeit items	**Band C fine**	**Band B fine to low level community order**
Larger number of counterfeit items but no involvement in wider operation	**Medium level community order, plus fine***	**Low level community order to 12 weeks custody, plus fine***
High number of counterfeit items or involvement in wider operation e.g. manufacture or distribution	**12 weeks custody**	**6 weeks custody to Crown Court**
Central role in large-scale operation	**Crown Court**	**Crown Court**

* This may be an offence for which it is appropriate to combine a fine with a community order. Consult your legal adviser for further guidance.

B. Consider the effect of aggravating and mitigating factors (other than those within examples above)

Common aggravating and mitigating factors are identified [elsewhere]—the following may be particularly relevant but these lists are not exhaustive

Factors indicating higher culpability	Factor indicating lower culpability
1. High degree of professionalism 2. High level of profit **Factor indicating greater degree of harm** 1. Purchasers at risk of harm e.g. from counterfeit drugs	1. Mistake or ignorance about provenance of goods

[Sets out the standard sequential sentencing procedure and mentions need to consider ordering forfeiture and destruction of the goods.]

SG-244

TV Licence Payment Evasion

Communications Act 2003, s. 363

Triable only summarily:
Maximum: Level 3 fine

Offence seriousness (culpability and harm)

A. Identify the appropriate starting point

Starting points based on first time offender pleading not guilty

Examples of nature of activity	Starting point	Range
Up to 6 months unlicensed use	**Band A fine**	**Band A fine**
Over 6 months unlicensed use	**Band B Fine**	**Band A fine to band B fine**

B. Consider the effect of aggravating and mitigating factors (other than those within examples above)

Common aggravating and mitigating factors are identified [elsewhere]—the following may be particularly relevant but these lists are not exhaustive

	Factors indicating lower culpability
	1. Accidental oversight or belief licence held 2. Confusion of responsibility 3. Licence immediately obtained

[Sets out the standard sequential sentencing procedure.]

SG-245

VAT Evasion

Value Added Tax Act 1994, s. 72

Triable either way:
Maximum when tried summarily: Level 5 fine and/or 6 months
Maximum when tried on indictment: 7 years

Refer to guideline *Fraud — banking and insurance fraud and obtaining credit through fraud, benefit fraud and revenue fraud* [see **SG-206 *et seq.***].

Vehicle Interference

SG-246

Criminal Attempts Act 1981, s. 9

Triable only summarily:
Maximum: Level 4 fine and/or 3 months

Offence seriousness (culpability and harm)

A. Identify the appropriate starting point

Starting points based on first time offender pleading not guilty

Examples of nature of activity	Starting point	Range
Trying door handles; no entry gained to vehicle; no damage caused	**Band C fine**	**Band A fine to low level community order**
Entering vehicle, little or no damage caused	**Medium level community order**	**Band C fine to high level community order**
Entering vehicle, with damage caused	**High level community order**	**Medium level community order to 12 weeks custody**

B. Consider the effect of aggravating and mitigating factors (other than those within examples above)

Common aggravating and mitigating factors are identified [elsewhere]—the following may be particularly relevant but these lists are not exhaustive

Factor indicating higher culpability 1. Targeting vehicle in dark/isolated location **Factors indicating greater degree of harm** 1. Emergency services vehicle 2. Disabled driver's vehicle 3. Part of series	

[Sets out the standard sequential sentencing procedure.]

Vehicle Licence/Registration Fraud

SG-247

Vehicle Excise and Registration Act 1994, s.44

Triable either way:
Maximum when tried summarily: Level 5 fine
Maximum when tried on indictment: 2 years

Offence seriousness (culpability and harm)

A. Identify the appropriate starting point

Starting points based on first time offender pleading not guilty

Examples of nature of activity	Starting point	Range
Use of unaltered licence from another vehicle	**Band B fine**	**Band B fine**
Forged licence bought for own use, or forged/altered for own use	**Band C fine**	**Band C fine**
Use of number plates from another vehicle; or Licence/number plates forged or altered for sale to another	**High level community order (in Crown Court)**	**Medium level community order to Crown Court (Note:** community order and custody available only in Crown Court)

B. Consider the effect of aggravating and mitigating factors (other than those within examples above)

Common aggravating and mitigating factors are identified [elsewhere]—the following may be particularly relevant but these lists are not exhaustive

Factors indicating higher culpability	Factors indicating lower culpability
1. LGV, PSV, taxi etc. 2. Long-term fraudulent use **Factors indicating greater degree of harm** 1. High financial gain 2. Innocent victim deceived 3. Legitimate owner inconvenienced	1. Licence/registration mark from another vehicle owned by defendant 2. Short-term use

[Sets out the standard sequential sentencing procedure and mentions the need to consider disqualification from driving and deprivation of property (including vehicle).]

SG-248

Vehicle Taking, without Consent

Theft Act 1968, s. 12

Triable only summarily:
Maximum: Level 5 fine and/or 6 months
May disqualify (no points available)

Offence seriousness (culpability and harm)

A. Identify the appropriate starting point

Starting points based on first time offender pleading not guilty

Examples of nature of activity	Starting point	Range
Exceeding authorised use of e.g. employer's or relative's vehicle; retention of hire car beyond return date	**Low level community order**	**Band B fine to medium level community order**
As above with damage caused to lock/ignition; OR Stranger's vehicle involved but no damage caused	**Medium level community order**	**Low level community order to high level community order**
Taking vehicle from private premises; OR Causing damage to e.g. lock/ignition of stranger's vehicle	**High level community order**	**Medium level community order to 26 weeks custody**

B. Consider the effect of aggravating and mitigating factors
(other than those within examples above)

Common aggravating and mitigating factors are identified [elsewhere]—the following may be particularly relevant but these lists are not exhaustive

Factors indicating greater degree of harm	Factor indicating lower culpability
1. Vehicle later burnt 2. Vehicle belonging to elderly/disabled person 3. Emergency services vehicle 4. Medium to large goods vehicle 5. Passengers carried	1. Misunderstanding with owner **Factor indicating lesser degree of harm** 1. Offender voluntarily returned vehicle to owner

[Sets out the standard sequential sentencing procedure and mentions need to consider disqualification from driving.]

SG-249

Vehicle Taking (Aggravated)

Damage caused to Property other than the Vehicle in Accident or damage Caused to the Vehicle

Theft Act 1968, ss. 12A(2)(c) and (d)

Triable either way (triable only summarily if damage under £5,000):
Maximum when tried summarily: Level 5 fine and/or 6 months
Maximum when tried on indictment: 2 years

- Must endorse and disqualify for at least 12 months
- Must disqualify for *at least* 2 years if offender has had two or more disqualifications for periods of 56 days or more in preceding 3 years. . .

If there is a delay in sentencing after conviction, consider interim disqualification

Offence seriousness (culpability and harm)

A. Identify the appropriate starting point

Starting points based on first time offender pleading not guilty

Examples of nature of activity	Starting point	Range
Exceeding authorised use of e.g. employer's or relative's vehicle; retention of hire car beyond return date; minor damage to taken vehicle	**Medium level community order**	**Low level community order to high level community order**
Greater damage to taken vehicle and/or moderate damage to another vehicle and/or property	**High level community order**	**Medium level community order to 12 weeks custody**
Vehicle taken as part of burglary or from private premises; severe damage	**18 weeks custody**	**12 to 26 weeks custody (Crown Court if damage over £5,000)**

B. Consider the effect of aggravating and mitigating factors (other than those within examples above)

Common aggravating and mitigating factors are identified [elsewhere]—the following may be particularly relevant but these lists are not exhaustive

Factors indicating higher culpability	Factors indicating lower culpability
1. Vehicle deliberately damaged/destroyed 2. Offender under influence of alcohol/drugs **Factors indicating greater degree of harm** 1. Passenger(s) carried 2. Vehicle belonging to elderly or disabled person 3. Emergency services vehicle 4. Medium to large goods vehicle 5. Damage caused in moving traffic accident	1. Misunderstanding with owner 2. Damage resulting from actions of another (where this does not provide a defence)

[Sets out the standard sequential sentencing procedure.]

Vehicle Taking (Aggravated) Dangerous Driving or Accident Causing Injury SG-250

Theft Act 1968, ss. 12A(2)(a) and (b)

Triable either way:
Maximum when tried summarily: Level 5 fine and/or 6 months
Maximum when tried on indictment: 2 years; 14 years if accident caused death

- Must endorse and disqualify for at least 12 months
- Must disqualify for *at least* 2 years if offender has had two or more disqualifications for periods of 56 days or more in preceding 3 years. . .

If there is a delay in sentencing after conviction, consider interim disqualification

Offence seriousness (culpability and harm)

A. Identify the appropriate starting point

Starting points based on first time offender pleading not guilty

Examples of nature of activity	Starting point	Range
Taken vehicle involved in single incident of bad driving where little or no damage or risk of personal injury	**High level community order**	**Medium level community order to 12 weeks custody**
Taken vehicle involved in incident(s) involving excessive speed or showing off, especially on busy roads or in built-up area	**18 weeks custody**	**12 to 26 weeks custody**
Taken vehicle involved in prolonged bad driving involving deliberate disregard for safety of others	**Crown Court**	**Crown Court**

B. Consider the effect of aggravating and mitigating factors (other than those within examples above)

Common aggravating and mitigating factors are identified [elsewhere]—the following may be particularly relevant but these lists are not exhaustive

Factors indicating higher culpability	Factors indicating greater degree of harm
1. Disregarding warnings of others 2. Evidence of alcohol or drugs 3. Carrying out other tasks while driving 4. Carrying passengers or heavy load 5. Tiredness 6. Trying to avoid arrest 7. Aggressive driving, such as driving much too close to vehicle in front, inappropriate attempts to overtake, or cutting in after overtaking	1. Injury to others 2. Damage to other vehicles or property

[Sets out the standard sequential sentencing procedure and mentions the need to consider ordering disqualification until appropriate driving test passed.]

SG-251

Voyeurism

Factors to take into consideration

This guideline is taken from the Sentencing Guidelines Council's definitive guideline *Sexual Offences Act 2003*, published 30 April 2007 [see **SG-111**]

Key factors

(a) This offence is committed where, for the purpose of obtaining sexual gratification, an offender observes a person doing a private act and knows that the other person does not consent to being observed. It may be committed in a number of ways such as by direct observation on the part of the offender, by recording someone doing a private act with the intention that the recorded image will be viewed by the offender or another person, or by installing equipment or constructing or adapting a structure with the intention of enabling the offender or another person to observe a private act. For the purposes of this offence, 'private act' means an act carried out in a place which, in the circumstances, would reasonably be expected to provide privacy and: the persons genitals, buttocks or breasts are exposed or covered only in underwear; or the person is using a lavatory; or the person is doing a sexual act that is not of a kind ordinarily done in public.

(b) In accordance with section 80 [of] and schedule 3 [to] the Sexual Offences Act 2003, automatic notification requirements apply upon conviction to an offender aged 18 or over where:
  (1) the victim was under 18; or
  (2) a term of imprisonment or a community sentence of at least 12 months is imposed.

Guidelines

Sexual Offences Act 2003, s. 67

Triable either way:
Maximum when tried summarily: Level 5 fine and/or 6 months
Maximum when tried on indictment: 2 years

Identify dangerous offenders

This is a specified offence for the purposes of the public protection provisions in the Criminal Justice Act 2003...

Offence seriousness (culpability and harm)

A. Identify the appropriate starting point

Starting points based on first time offender pleading not guilty

Examples of nature of activity	Starting point	Range
Basic offence as defined in the Act, assuming no aggravating or mitigating factors, e.g. the offender spies through a hole he or she has made in a changing room wall	**Low level community order**	**Band B fine to high level community order**
Offence with aggravating factors such as recording sexual activity and showing it to others	**26 weeks custody**	**4 weeks custody to Crown Court**
Offence with serious aggravating factors such as recording sexual activity and placing it on a website or circulating it for commercial gain	**Crown Court**	**26 weeks to Crown Court**

B. Consider the effect of aggravating and mitigating factors (other than those within examples above)

Common aggravating and mitigating factors are identified [elsewhere]—the following may be particularly relevant but these lists are not exhaustive

Factors indicating higher culpability	Factor indicating greater degree of harm
1. Threats to prevent the victim reporting an offence 2. Recording activity and circulating pictures/videos 3. Circulating pictures or videos for commercial gain—particularly if victim is vulnerable e.g. a child or a person with a mental or physical disorder	1. Distress to victim e.g. where the pictures/videos are circulated to people known to the victim

[Sets out the standard sequential sentencing procedure.]

Witness Intimidation SG-252

Criminal Justice and Public Order Act 1994, s. 51

Triable either way:
Maximum when tried summarily: 6 months or level 5 fine
Maximum when tried on indictment: 5 years

Where offence committed in domestic context, refer [below] for guidance

Offence seriousness (culpability and harm)

A. Identify the appropriate starting point

Starting points based on first time offender pleading not guilty

Examples of nature of activity	Starting point	Range
Sudden outburst in chance encounter	**6 weeks custody**	**Medium level community order to 18 weeks custody**
Conduct amounting to a threat; staring at, approaching or following witnesses; talking about the case; trying to alter or stop evidence	**18 weeks custody**	**12 weeks custody to Crown Court**
Threats of violence to witnesses and/or their families; deliberately seeking out witnesses	**Crown Court**	**Crown Court**

B. Consider the effect of aggravating and mitigating factors (other than those within examples above)

Common aggravating and mitigating factors are identified [elsewhere]—the following may be particularly relevant but these lists are not exhaustive

Factors indicating higher culpability 1. Breach of bail conditions 2. Offender involves others **Factors indicating greater degree of harm** 1. Detrimental impact on administration of justice 2. Contact made at or in vicinity of victim's home	

[Sets out the standard sequential sentencing procedure.]

Motoring Offences

SG-253 ## Careless Driving (Drive Without Due Care and Attention)

Road Traffic Act 1988, s. 3

Triable only summarily: Maximum: Level 5 fine
Must endorse and may disqualify. If no disqualification, impose 3–9 points

Offence seriousness (culpability and harm)

A. Identify the appropriate starting point

Starting points based on first time offender pleading not guilty

Examples of nature of activity	Starting point	Range
Momentary lapse of concentration or misjudgement at low speed	**Band A fine**	**Band A fine** **3–4 points**
Loss of control due to speed, mishandling or insufficient attention to road conditions, or carelessly turning right across on-coming traffic	**Band B fine**	**Band B fine** **5–6 points**
Overtaking manoeuvre at speed resulting in collision of vehicles, or driving bordering on the dangerous	**Band C fine**	**Band C fine** **Consider disqualification OR 7–9 points**

B. Consider the effect of aggravating and mitigating factors
(other than those within examples above)

Common aggravating and mitigating factors are identified [elsewhere]—the following may be particularly relevant but these lists are not exhaustive

Factors indicating higher culpability	Factors indicating lower culpability
1. Excessive speed 2. Carrying out other tasks while driving 3. Carrying passengers or heavy load 4. Tiredness **Factors indicating greater degree of harm** 1. Injury to others 2. Damage to other vehicles or property 3. High level of traffic or pedestrians in vicinity 4. Location e.g. near school when children are likely to be present	1. Minor risk 2. Inexperience of driver 3. Sudden change in road or weather conditions

[Sets out the standard sequential sentencing procedure and mentions need to consider ordering disqualification until appropriate driving test passed.] . . .

SG-254 ## Causing Death by Careless or Inconsiderate Driving

Factors to take into consideration

This guideline and accompanying notes are taken from the Sentencing Guidelines Council's definitive guideline *Causing Death by Driving*, published 15 July 2008 [see **SG-365**].

Key factors

(a) It is unavoidable that some cases will be on the borderline between *dangerous* and *careless* driving, or may involve a number of factors that significantly increase the seriousness of an offence. As a result, the guideline for this offence identifies three levels of seriousness, the range for the highest of which overlaps with ranges for the lower levels of seriousness for *causing death by dangerous driving*.

(b) The three levels of seriousness are defined by the degree of carelessness involved in the standard of driving:
 - the most serious level for this offence is where the offender's driving fell *not that far short of dangerous*;
 - the least serious group of offences relates to those cases where the level of culpability is low—for example in a case involving an offender who misjudges the speed of another vehicle, or turns without seeing an oncoming vehicle because of restricted visibility;
 - other cases will fall into the intermediate level.

(c) Where the level of carelessness is low and there are no aggravating factors, even the fact that death was caused is not sufficient to justify a prison sentence.

(d) A fine is unlikely to be an appropriate sentence for this offence; where a non-custodial sentence is considered appropriate, this should be a community order. The nature of the requirements will be determined by the purpose identified by the court as of primary importance. Requirements most likely to be relevant include unpaid work requirement, activity requirement, programme requirement and curfew requirement.

(e) Offender mitigation particularly relevant to this offence includes conduct after the offence such as where the offender gave direct, positive, assistance at the scene of a collision to victim(s). It may also include remorse—whilst it can be expected that anyone who has caused a death by driving would be remorseful, this cannot undermine its importance for sentencing purposes. It is for the court to determine whether an expression of remorse is genuine.

(f) Where an offender has a good driving record, this is not a factor that automatically should be treated as mitigation, especially now that the presence of previous convictions is a statutory aggravating factor. However, any evidence to show that an offender has previously been an exemplary driver, for example having driven an ambulance, police vehicle, bus, taxi or similar vehicle conscientiously and without incident for many years, is a fact that the courts may well wish to take into account by way of offender mitigation. This is likely to have even greater effect where the driver is driving on public duty (for example, on ambulance, fire services or police duties) and was responding to an emergency.

(g) Disqualification of the offender from driving and endorsement of the offender's driving licence are mandatory, and the offence carries between 3 and 11 penalty points when the court finds special reasons for not imposing disqualification. There is a discretionary power to order an extended driving test/re-test where a person is convicted of this offence.

Guidelines

Road Traffic Act 1988, s. 2B

Triable either way:
Maximum when tried summarily: Level 5 fine and/or 6 months
Maximum when tried on indictment: 5 years

Offence seriousness (culpability and harm)

A. Identify the appropriate starting point

Starting points based on first time offender pleading not guilty

Examples of nature of activity	**Starting point**	**Range**
Careless or inconsiderate driving arising from momentary inattention with no aggravating factors	**Medium level community order**	**Low level community order to high level community order**
Other cases of careless or inconsiderate driving	**Crown Court**	**High level community order to Crown Court**
Careless or inconsiderate driving falling not far short of dangerous driving	**Crown Court**	**Crown Court**

B. Consider the effect of aggravating and mitigating factors (other than those within examples above)

Common aggravating and mitigating factors are identified [elsewhere]—the following may be particularly relevant but these lists are not exhaustive

Factors indicating higher culpability	Factors indicating lower culpability
1. Other offences committed at the same time, such as driving other than in accordance with the terms of a valid licence; driving while disqualified; driving without insurance; taking a vehicle without consent; driving a stolen vehicle 2. Previous convictions for motoring offences, particularly offences that involve bad driving 3. Irresponsible behaviour, such as failing to stop or falsely claiming that one of the victims was responsible for the collision **Factors indicating greater degree of harm** 1. More than one person was killed as a result of the offence 2. Serious injury to one or more persons in addition to the death(s)	1. Offender seriously injured in the collision 2. The victim was a close friend or relative 3. The actions of the victim or a third party contributed to the commission of the offence 4. The offender's lack of driving experience contributed significantly to the likelihood of a collision occurring and/or death resulting 5. The driving was in response to a proven and genuine emergency falling short of a defence

[Sets out the standard sequential sentencing procedure and mentions need to consider ordering disqualification and deprivation of property]

SG-255 Causing Death by Driving: Unlicensed, Disqualified or Uninsured Drivers

Factors to take into consideration

Key factors

(a) Culpability arises from the offender driving a vehicle on a road or other public place when, by law, not allowed to do so; the offence does not involve any fault in the standard of driving.

(b) Since driving whilst disqualified is more culpable than driving whilst unlicensed or uninsured, a higher starting point is proposed when the offender was disqualified from driving at the time of the offence.

(c) Being uninsured, unlicensed or disqualified are the only determinants of seriousness for this offence, as there are no factors relating to the standard of driving. The list of aggravating factors identified is slightly different as the emphasis is on the decision to drive by an offender who is not permitted by law to do so.

(d) A fine is unlikely to be an appropriate sentence for this offence; where a non-custodial sentence is considered appropriate, this should be a community order.

(e) Where the *decision to drive was brought about by a genuine and proven emergency*, that may mitigate offence seriousness and so it is included as an additional mitigating factor.

(f) An additional mitigating factor covers those situations where an offender genuinely believed that there was valid insurance or a valid licence.

(g) Offender mitigation particularly relevant to this offence includes conduct after the offence such as where the offender gave direct, positive, assistance at the scene of a collision to victim(s). It may also include remorse—whilst it can be expected that anyone who has caused a death by driving would be remorseful, this cannot undermine its importance for sentencing purposes. It is for the court to determine whether an expression of remorse is genuine.

(h) Where an offender has a good driving record, this is not a factor that automatically should be treated as mitigation, especially now that the presence of previous convictions is a statutory aggravating factor. However, any evidence to show that an offender has previously been an exemplary driver, for example having driven an ambulance, police vehicle, bus, taxi or similar vehicle conscientiously and without incident for many years, is a fact that the courts may well wish to take into account by way of offender mitigation. This is likely to have even greater effect where the driver is driving on public duty (for example, on ambulance, fire services or police duties) and was responding to an emergency.

(i) Disqualification of the offender from driving and endorsement of the offender's driving licence are mandatory, and the offence carries between 3 and 11 penalty points when the court finds special reasons for not imposing disqualification. There is a discretionary power[193] to order an extended driving test/re-test where a person is convicted of this offence.

Guidelines

[193] Road Traffic Offenders Act 1988, s.36(4)

Road Traffic Act 1988, s. 3ZB

Triable either way:
Maximum when tried summarily: Level 5 fine and/or 6 months
Maximum when tried on indictment: 2 years

Offence seriousness (culpability and harm)

A. Identify the appropriate starting point

Starting points based on first time offender pleading not guilty

Examples of nature of activity	Starting point	Range
The offender was unlicensed or uninsured—no aggravating factors	**Medium level community order**	**Low level community order to high level community order**
The offender was unlicensed or uninsured plus at least 1 aggravating factor from the list below	**26 weeks custody**	**High level community order to Crown Court**
The offender was disqualified from driving **OR** The offender was unlicensed or uninsured plus 2 or more aggravating factors from the list below	**Crown Court**	**Crown Court**

B. Consider the effect of aggravating and mitigating factors (other than those within examples above)

Common aggravating and mitigating factors are identified [elsewhere]—the following may be particularly relevant but these lists are not exhaustive

Factors indicating higher culpability	Factors indicating lower culpability
1. Previous convictions for motoring offences, whether involving bad driving or involving an offence of the same kind that forms part of the present conviction (i.e. unlicensed, disqualified or uninsured driving) 2. Irresponsible behaviour such as failing to stop or falsely claiming that someone else was driving **Factors indicating greater degree of harm** 1. More than one person was killed as a result of the offence 2. Serious injury to one or more persons in addition to the death(s)	1. The decision to drive was brought about by a proven and genuine emergency falling short of a defence 2. The offender genuinely believed that he or she was insured or licensed to drive 3. The offender was seriously injured as a result of the collision 4. The victim was a close friend or relative

[Sets out the standard sequential sentencing procedure and mentions need to consider ordering disqualification and deprivation of property]

Dangerous Driving SG-256

Road Traffic Act 1988, s. 2

Triable either way:
Maximum when tried summarily: Level 5 fine and/or 6 months
Maximum when tried on indictment: 2 years

- Must endorse and disqualify for *at least* 12 months. Must order extended re-test
- Must disqualify for *at least* 2 years if offender has had two or more disqualifications for periods of 56 days or more in preceding 3 years If there is a delay in sentencing after conviction, consider interim disqualification

Offence seriousness (culpability and harm)

A. Identify the appropriate starting point

Starting points based on first time offender pleading not guilty

Examples of nature of activity	Starting point	Range
Single incident where little or no damage or risk of personal injury	**Medium level community order**	**Low level community order to high level community order** **Disqualify 12–15 months**
Incident(s) involving excessive speed or showing off, especially on busy roads or in built-up area; OR Single incident where little or no damage or risk of personal injury but offender was disqualified driver	**12 weeks custody**	**High level community order to 26 weeks custody** **Disqualify 15–24 months**
Prolonged bad driving involving deliberate disregard for safety of others; OR Incident(s) involving excessive speed or showing off, especially on busy roads or in built-up area, by disqualified driver; OR Driving as described in box above while being pursued by police	**Crown Court**	**Crown Court**

B. Consider the effect of aggravating and mitigating factors (other than those within examples above)

Common aggravating and mitigating factors are identified [elsewhere]—the following may be particularly relevant but these lists are not exhaustive

Factors indicating higher culpability	Factors indicating lower culpability
1. Disregarding warnings of others 2. Evidence of alcohol or drugs 3. Carrying out other tasks while driving 4. Carrying passengers or heavy load 5. Tiredness 6. Aggressive driving, such as driving much too close to vehicle in front, racing, inappropriate attempts to overtake, or cutting in after overtaking 7. Driving when knowingly suffering from a medical condition which significantly impairs the offender's driving skills 8. Driving a poorly maintained or dangerously loaded vehicle, especially where motivated by commercial concerns **Factors indicating greater degree of harm** 1. Injury to others 2. Damage to other vehicles or property	1. Genuine emergency 2. Speed not excessive 3. Offence due to inexperience rather than irresponsibility of driver

[Sets out the standard sequential sentencing procedure and mentions need to consider order for deprivation of property.]

SG-257

Drive Whilst Disqualified

Road Traffic Act 1988, s. 103

Triable only summarily: Maximum: Level 5 fine and/or 6 months
Must endorse and may disqualify. If no disqualification, impose 6 points

Offence seriousness (culpability and harm)

A. Identify the appropriate starting point

Starting points based on first time offender pleading not guilty

Examples of nature of activity	Starting point	Range
Full period expired but retest not taken	**Low level community order**	**Band C fine to medium level community order 6 points or disqualify for 3–6 months**
Lengthy period of ban already served	**High level community order**	**Medium level community order to 12 weeks custody** **Lengthen disqualification for 6–12 months beyond expiry of current ban**
Recently imposed ban	**12 weeks custody**	**High level community order to 26 weeks custody** **Lengthen disqualification for 12–18 months beyond expiry of current ban**

B. Consider the effect of aggravating and mitigating factors
(other than those within examples above)

Common aggravating and mitigating factors are identified [elsewhere]—the following may be particularly relevant but these lists are not exhaustive

Factors indicating higher culpability	Factors indicating lower culpability
1. Never passed test 2. Planned long-term evasion 3. Vehicle obtained during ban 4. Driving for remuneration **Factors indicating greater degree of harm** 1. Distance driven 2. Evidence of associated bad driving 3. Offender caused accident	1. Defendant not present when disqualification imposed and genuine reason why unaware of ban 2. Genuine emergency established

[Sets out the standard sequential sentencing procedure and mentions need to consider order for deprivation of property.]

Note: An offender convicted of this offence will always have at least one relevant previous conviction for the offence that resulted in disqualification. The starting points and ranges take this into account; any other previous convictions should be considered in the usual way. . .

Excess Alcohol (Drive/Attempt to Drive) SG-258

Road Traffic Act 1988, s. 5(1)(a)

Triable only summarily: Maximum: Level 5 fine and/or 6 months

- Must endorse and disqualify for at least 12 months
- Must disqualify for *at least* 2 years if offender has had two or more disqualifications for periods of 56 days or more in preceding 3 years—refer [below]. . .
- Must disqualify for *at least* 3 years if offender has been convicted of a relevant offence in preceding 10 years—refer [below]. . .

If there is a delay in sentencing after conviction, consider interim disqualification

Note: the final column below provides guidance regarding the length of disqualification that may be appropriate in cases to which the 3 year minimum applies. The period to be imposed in any individual case will depend on an assessment of all the relevant circumstances, including the length of time since the earlier ban was imposed and the gravity of the current offence.

Offence seriousness (culpability and harm)

A. Identify the appropriate starting point

Starting points based on first time offender pleading not guilty

Level of alcohol			Starting point	Range	Disqualification	Disqual. 2nd offence in 10 years—see note above
Breath (mg)	Blood (ml)	Urine (ml)				
36–59	81–137	108–183	Band C fine	Band C fine	12–16 months	36–40 months
60–89	138–206	184–274	Band C fine	Band C fine	17–22 months	36–46 months
90–119	207–275	275–366	Medium level community order	Low level community order to high level community order	23–28 months	36–52 months
120–150 and above	276–345 and above	367–459 and above	12 weeks custody	High level community order to 26 weeks custody	29–36 months	36–60 months

B. Consider the effect of aggravating and mitigating factors
(other than those within examples above)

Common aggravating and mitigating factors are identified [elsewhere]—the following may be particularly relevant but these lists are not exhaustive

Factors indicating higher culpability	Factors indicating lower culpability
1. LGV, HGV, PSV etc. 2. Poor road or weather conditions 3. Carrying passengers 4. Driving for hire or reward 5. Evidence of unacceptable standard of driving **Factors indicating greater degree of harm** 1.Involved in accident 2. Location e.g. near school 3. High level of traffic or pedestrians in the vicinity	1. Genuine emergency established* 2. Spiked drinks* 3. Very short distance driven* *even where not amounting to special reasons

[Sets out the standard sequential sentencing procedure and mentions need to consider offering drink/drive rehabilitation course and forfeiture or suspension of personal liquor licence].

SG-259

Excess Alcohol (In Charge)

Road Traffic Act 1988, s. 5(1)(b)

Triable only summarily: Maximum: Level 4 fine and/or 3 months
Must endorse and may disqualify. If no disqualification, impose 10 points

Offence seriousness (culpability and harm)

A. Identify the appropriate starting point

Starting points based on first time offender pleading not guilty

Level of alcohol			Starting point	Range
Breath (mg)	**Blood (ml)**	**Urine (ml)**		
36–59	81–137	108–183	**Band B fine**	**Band B fine** **10 points**
60–89	138–206	184–274	**Band B fine**	**Band B fine** **10 points OR consider disqualification**
90–119	207–275	275–366	**Band C fine**	**Band C fine to medium level community order Consider disqualification up to 6 months OR 10 points**
120–150 and above	276–345 and above	367–459 and above	**Medium level community order**	**Low level community order to 6 weeks custody Disqualify 6–12 months**

B. Consider the effect of aggravating and mitigating factors
(other than those within examples above)

Common aggravating and mitigating factors are identified [elsewhere] – the following may be particularly relevant but these lists are not exhaustive

Factors indicating higher culpability	Factor indicating lower culpability
1. LGV, HGV, PSV etc. 2. Ability to drive seriously impaired 3. High likelihood of driving 4. Driving for hire or reward	1. Low likelihood of driving

[Sets out the standard sequential sentencing procedure and mentions need to consider forfeiture or suspension of personal liquor licence.]

Sentencing Guidelines

Fail to Stop/Report Road Accident SG-260

Road Traffic Act 1988, s. 170(4)

Triable only summarily: Maximum: Level 5 fine and/or 6 months
Must endorse and may disqualify. If no disqualification, impose 5–10 points

Offence seriousness (culpability and harm)

A. Identify the appropriate starting point

Starting points based on first time offender pleading not guilty

Examples of nature of activity	Starting point	Range
Minor damage/injury or stopped at scene but failed to exchange particulars or report	**Band B fine**	**Band B fine** **5–6 points**
Moderate damage/injury or failed to stop and failed to report	**Band C fine**	**Band C fine** **7–8 points** **Consider disqualification**
Serious damage/injury and/or evidence of bad driving	**High level community order**	**Band C fine to 26 weeks custody** **Disqualify 6–12 months OR 9–10 points**

B. Consider the effect of aggravating and mitigating factors
(other than those within examples above)

Common aggravating and mitigating factors are identified [elsewhere]—the following may be particularly relevant but these lists are not exhaustive

Factors indicating higher culpability	Factors indicating lower culpability
1. Evidence of drink or drugs/evasion of test 2. Knowledge/suspicion that personal injury caused (where not an element of the offence) 3. Leaving injured party at scene 4. Giving false details	1. Believed identity known 2. Genuine fear of retribution 3. Subsequently reported

[Sets out the standard sequential sentencing procedure.] . . .

Fail to Provide Specimen for Analysis (Drive/Attempt to Drive) SG-261

Road Traffic Act 1988, s. 7(6)

Triable only summarily: Maximum: Level 5 fine and/or 6 months

- Must endorse and disqualify for at least 12 months
- Must disqualify for *at least* 2 years if offender has had two or more disqualifications for periods of 56 days or more in preceding 3 years—refer [below] . . .
- Must disqualify for *at least* 3 years if offender has been convicted of a relevant offence in preceding 10 years—refer [below] . . .

If there is a delay in sentencing after conviction, consider interim disqualification

Note: the final column below provides guidance regarding the length of disqualification that may be appropriate in cases to which the 3 year minimum applies. The period to be imposed in any individual case will depend on an assessment of all the relevant circumstances, including the length of time since the earlier ban was imposed and the gravity of the current offence.

Offence seriousness (culpability and harm)

A. Identify the appropriate starting point

Starting points based on first time offender pleading not guilty

Examples of nature of activity	Starting point	Range	Disqualification	Disqual. 2nd offence in 10 years
Defendant refused test when had honestly held but unreasonable excuse	**Band C fine**	**Band C fine**	**12–16 months**	**36–40 months**
Deliberate refusal or deliberate failure	**Low level community order**	**Band C fine to high level community order**	**17–28 months**	**36–52 months**
Deliberate refusal or deliberate failure where evidence of serious impairment	**12 weeks custody**	**High level community order to 26 weeks custody**	**29–36 months**	**36–60 months**

B. Consider the effect of aggravating and mitigating factors (other than those within examples above)

Common aggravating and mitigating factors are identified [elsewhere]—the following may be particularly relevant but these lists are not exhaustive

Factors indicating higher culpability	Factor indicating lower culpability
1. Evidence of unacceptable standard of driving 2. LGV, HGV, PSV etc. 3. Obvious state of intoxication 4. Driving for hire or reward **Factor indicating greater degree of harm** 1. Involved in accident	1. Genuine but unsuccessful attempt to provide specimen

[Sets out the standard sequential sentencing procedure and mentions need to consider offering drink/drive rehabilitation course.

SG-262

Fail to Provide Specimen for Analysis (In Charge)

Road Traffic Act 1988, s. 7(6)

Triable only summarily: Maximum: Level 4 fine and/or 3 months
Must endorse and may disqualify. If no disqualification, impose 10 points

Offence seriousness (culpability and harm)

A. Identify the appropriate starting point

Starting points based on first time offender pleading not guilty

Examples of nature of activity	Starting point	Range
Defendant refused test when had honestly held but unreasonable excuse	**Band B fine**	**Band B fine** **10 points**
Deliberate refusal or deliberate failure	**Band C fine**	**Band C fine to medium level community order** **Consider disqualification OR 10 points**
Deliberate refusal or deliberate failure where evidence of serious impairment	**Medium level community order**	**Low level community order to 6 weeks custody** **Disqualify 6–12 months**

B. Consider the effect of aggravating and mitigating factors (other than those within examples above)

Common aggravating and mitigating factors are identified [elsewhere]—the following may be particularly relevant but these lists are not exhaustive

Factors indicating higher culpability	Factors indicating lower culpability
1. Obvious state of intoxication 2. LGV, HGV, PSV etc. 3. High likelihood of driving 4. Driving for hire or reward	1. Genuine but unsuccessful attempt to provide specimen 2. Low likelihood of driving

[Sets out the standard sequential sentencing procedure.] . . .

No Insurance SG-263

Road Traffic Act 1988, s. 143

Triable only summarily: Maximum: Level 5 fine
Must endorse and may disqualify. If no disqualification, impose 6–8 points—see notes below

Offence seriousness (culpability and harm)

A. Identify the appropriate starting point

Starting points based on first time offender pleading not guilty

Examples of nature of activity	Starting point	Range
Using a motor vehicle on a road or other public place without insurance	**Band C fine**	**Band C fine 6 points—12 months disqualification—see notes below**

B. Consider the effect of aggravating and mitigating factors (other than those within examples above)

Common aggravating and mitigating factors are identified [elsewhere]—the following may be particularly relevant but these lists are not exhaustive

Factors indicating higher culpability	Factors indicating lower culpability
1. Never passed test 2. Gave false details 3. Driving LGV, HGV, PSV etc. 4. Driving for hire or reward 5. Evidence of sustained uninsured use **Factor indicating greater degree of harm** 1. Involved in accident 2. Accident resulting in injury	1. Responsibility for providing insurance rests with another 2. Genuine misunderstanding 3. Recent failure to renew or failure to transfer vehicle details where insurance was in existence 4. Vehicle not being driven

[Sets out the standard sequential sentencing procedure.] . . .

Notes Consider range from 7 points–2 months disqualification where vehicle was being driven and no evidence that the offender has held insurance. Consider disqualification of 6–12 months if evidence of sustained uninsured use and/or involvement in accident.

Speeding SG-264

Road Traffic Regulation Act 1984, s. 89(10)

Triable only summarily: Maximum: Level 3 fine (level 4 if motorway)
Must endorse and may disqualify. If no disqualification, impose 3–6 points

Offence seriousness (culpability and harm)

A. Identify the appropriate starting point

Starting points based on first time offender pleading not guilty

Speed limit (mph)	Recorded speed (mph)		
20	21–30	31–40	41–50
30	31–40	41–50	51–60
40	41–55	56–65	66–75
50	51–65	66–75	76–85
60	61–80	81–90	91–100
70	71–90	91–100	101–110
Starting point	**Band A fine**	**Band B fine**	**Band B fine**
Range	**Band A fine**	**Band B fine**	**Band B fine**
Points/disqualification	**3 points**	**4–6 points OR Disqualify 7–28 days**	**Disqualify 7–56 days OR 6 points**

B. Consider the effect of aggravating and mitigating factors
(other than those within examples above)

Common aggravating and mitigating factors are identified [elsewhere]—the following may be particularly relevant but these lists are not exhaustive

Factors indicating higher culpability	Factor indicating lower culpability
1. Poor road or weather conditions 2. LGV, HGV, PSV etc. 3. Towing caravan/trailer 4. Carrying passengers or heavy load 5. Driving for hire or reward 6. Evidence of unacceptable standard of driving over and above speed **Factors indicating greater degree of harm** 1. Location e.g. near school 2. High level of traffic or pedestrians in the vicinity	1. Genuine emergency established

[Sets out the standard sequential sentencing procedure.] . . .

SG-265 Unfit Through Drink or Drugs (Drive/Attempt to Drive)

Road Traffic Act 1988, s. 4(1)

Triable only summarily: Maximum: Level 5 fine and/or 6 months

- Must endorse and disqualify for at least 12 months
- Must disqualify for *at least* 2 years if offender has had two or more disqualifications for periods of 56 days or more in preceding 3 years—refer [below] . . .
- Must disqualify for *at least* 3 years if offender has been convicted of a relevant offence in preceding 10 years—refer [below] . . .

If there is a delay in sentencing after conviction, consider interim disqualification

Note: the final column below provides guidance regarding the length of disqualification that may be appropriate in cases to which the 3 year minimum applies. The period to be imposed in any individual case will depend on an assessment of all the relevant circumstances, including the length of time since the earlier ban was imposed and the gravity of the current offence.

Offence seriousness (culpability and harm)

A. Identify the appropriate starting point

Starting points based on first time offender pleading not guilty

Examples of nature of activity	Starting point	Range	Disqualification	Disqual. 2nd offence in 10 years
Evidence of moderate level of impairment and no aggravating factors	**Band C fine**	**Band C fine**	**12–16 months**	**36–40 months**
Evidence of moderate level of impairment and presence of one or more aggravating factors listed below	**Band C fine**	**Band C fine**	**17–22 months**	**36–46 months**
Evidence of high level of impairment and no aggravating factors	**Medium level community order**	**Low level community order to high level community order**	**23–28 months**	**36–52months**
Evidence of high level of impairment and presence of one or more aggravating factors listed below	**12 weeks custody**	**High level community order to 26 weeks custody**	**29–36 months**	**36–60 months**

B. Consider the effect of aggravating and mitigating factors
(other than those within examples above)

Common aggravating and mitigating factors are identified [elsewhere]—the following may be particularly relevant but these lists are not exhaustive

Factors indicating higher culpability	Factors indicating lower culpability
1. LGV, HGV, PSV etc. 2. Poor road or weather conditions 3. Carrying passengers 4. Driving for hire or reward 5. Evidence of unacceptable standard of driving **Factors indicating greater degree of harm** 1. Involved in accident 2. Location e.g. near school 3. High level of traffic or pedestrians in the vicinity	1. Genuine emergency established* 2. Spiked drinks* 3. Very short distance driven* *even where not amounting to special reasons

[Sets out the standard sequential sentencing procedure and mentions need to consider offering a drink/drive rehabilitation course.

Sentencing Guidelines

Unfit Through Drink or Drugs (In Charge) SG-266

Road Traffic Act 1988, s. 4(2)

Triable only summarily: Maximum: Level 4 fine and/or 3 months

Must endorse and may disqualify. If no disqualification, impose 10 points

Offence seriousness (culpability and harm)

A. Identify the appropriate starting point

Starting points based on first time offender pleading not guilty

Examples of nature of activity	Starting point	Range
Evidence of moderate level of impairment and no aggravating factors	**Band B fine**	**Band B fine** **10 points**
Evidence of moderate level of impairment and presence of one or more aggravating factors listed below	**Band B fine**	**Band B fine** **10 points or consider disqualification**
Evidence of high level of impairment and no aggravating factors	**Band C fine**	**Band C fine to medium level community order 10 points or consider disqualification**
Evidence of high level of impairment and presence of one or more aggravating factors listed below	**High level community order**	**Medium level community order to 12 weeks custody** **Consider disqualification OR 10 points**

B. Consider the effect of aggravating and mitigating factors (other than those within examples above)

Common aggravating and mitigating factors are identified [elsewhere]—the following may be particularly relevant but these lists are not exhaustive

Factors indicating higher culpability	Factor indicating lower culpability
1. LGV, HGV, PSV etc. 2. High likelihood of driving 3. Driving for hire or reward	1. Low likelihood of driving

[Sets out the standard sequential sentencing procedure and mentions need to consider offering a drink/drive rehabilitation course.]

SG-267 OFFENCES APPROPRIATE FOR IMPOSITION OF FINE OR DISCHARGE

SG-268 **Part 1: Offences concerning the driver**

Offence	Maximum	Points	Starting point	Special considerations
Fail to co-operate with preliminary (roadside) breath test	L3	4	B	
Fail to give information of driver's identity as required	L3	6	C	For limited companies, endorsement is not available; a fine is the only available penalty
Fail to produce insurance certificate	L4	–	A	Fine per offence, not per document
Fail to produce test certificate	L3	–	A	
Drive otherwise than in accordance with licence (where could be covered)	L3	–	A	
Drive otherwise than in accordance with licence	L3	3–6	A	Aggravating factor if no licence ever held

Part 2: Offences concerning the vehicle SG-269

*The guidelines for some of the offences below differentiate between three types of offender when the offence is committed in the course of business: driver, owner-driver and owner-company. *For owner-driver, the starting point is the same as for driver; however, the court should consider an uplift of at least 25%.*

Offence	Maximum	Points	Starting point	Special considerations
No excise licence	**L3 or 5 times annual duty, whichever is greater**	–	**A (1–3 months unpaid) B (4–6 months unpaid) C (7–12 months unpaid)**	Add duty lost
Fail to notify change of ownership to DVLA	L3	–	A	If offence committed in course of business: A (driver) A* (owner-driver) B (owner-company)
No test certificate	L3	–	A	If offence committed in course of business: A (driver) A* (owner-driver) B (owner-company)
Brakes defective	L4	3	B	If offence committed in course of business: B (driver) B* (owner-driver) C (owner-company) L5 if goods vehicle—see Part 5 below
Steering defective	L4	3	B	If offence committed in course of business: B (driver) B* (owner-driver) C (owner-company) L5 if goods vehicle—see Part 5 below
Tyres defective	L4	3	B	If offence committed in course of business: B (driver) B* (owner-driver) C (owner-company) L5 if goods vehicle—see Part 5 below Penalty per tyre
Condition of vehicle/accessories/ Equipment involving danger of injury (Road Traffic Act 1988, s.40A)	L4	3	B	Must disqualify for at least 6 months if offender has one or more previous convictions for same offence within three years If offence committed in course of business: B (driver) B* (owner-driver) C (owner-company) L5 if goods vehicle—see Part 5 below
Exhaust defective	L3	–	A	If offence committed in course of business: A (driver) A* (owner-driver) B (owner-company)
Lights defective	L3	–	A	If offence committed in course of business: A (driver) A* (owner-driver) B (owner-company)

Part 3: Offences concerning use of vehicle SG-270

*The guidelines for some of the offences below differentiate between three types of offender when the offence is committed in the course of business: driver, owner-driver and owner-company. **For owner-driver, the starting point is the same as for driver; however, the court should consider an uplift of at least 25%.**

Offence	Maximum	Points	Starting point	Special considerations
Weight, position or distribution of load or manner in which load secured involving danger of injury (Road Traffic Act 1988, s.40A)	L4	3	B	Must disqualify for at least 6 months if offender has one or more previous convictions for same offence within three years If offence committed in course of business: A (driver) A* (owner-driver) B (owner-company) L5 if goods vehicle—see Part 5 below
Number of passengers or way carried involving danger of injury (Road Traffic Act 1988, s.40A)	L4	3	B	If offence committed in course of business: A (driver) A* (owner-driver) B (owner-company) L5 if goods vehicle—see Part 5 below
Position or manner in which load secured (not involving danger) (Road Traffic Act 1988, s.42)	L3	–	A	L4 if goods vehicle—see Part 5 below
Overloading/exceeding axle weight	L5	–	A	Starting point caters for cases where the overload is up to and including 10%. Thereafter, 10% should be added to the penalty for each additional 1% of overload Penalty per axle If offence committed in course of business: A (driver) A* (owner-driver) B (owner-company) If goods vehicle—see Part 5 below
Dangerous parking	L3	3	A	
Pelican/zebra crossing contravention	L3	3	A	
Fail to comply with traffic sign (e.g. red traffic light, stop sign, double white lines, no entry sign)	L3	3	A	
Fail to comply with traffic sign (e.g. give way sign, keep left sign, temporary signs)	L3	–	A	
Fail to comply with police constable directing traffic	L3	3	A	
Fail to stop when required by police constable	**L5 (mechanically propelled vehicle) L3 (cycle)**	–	B	
Use of mobile telephone	L3	3	A	
Seat belt offences	**L2 (adult or child in front) L2 (child in rear)**	–	A	
Fail to use appropriate child car seat	L2	–	A	

Part 4: Motorway offences SG-271

Offence	Maximum	Points	Starting point	Special considerations
Drive in reverse or wrong way on slip road	L4	3	B	
Drive in reverse or wrong way on motorway	L4	3	C	
Drive off carriageway (central reservation or hard shoulder)	L4	3	B	
Make U turn	L4	3	C	
Learner driver or excluded vehicle	L4	3	B	
Stop on hard shoulder	L4	–	A	
Vehicle in prohibited lane	L4	3	A	
Walk on motorway, slip road or hard shoulder	L4	–	A	

Part 5: Offences re buses/goods vehicles over 3.5 tonnes (GVW) SG-272

* The guidelines for these offences differentiate between three types of offender: driver; owner-driver; and owner-company. **For owner-driver, the starting point is the same as for driver; however, the court should consider an uplift of at least 25%.**

** In all cases, take safety, damage to roads and commercial gain into account. Refer [below] for approach to fines for 'commercially motivated' offences.

Offence	Maximum	Points	Starting point	Special considerations
No goods vehicle plating certificate	L3	–	A (driver) A* (owner-driver) B (owner-company)	
No goods vehicle test certificate	L4	–	B (driver) B* (owner-driver) C (owner-company)	
Brakes defective	L5	3	B (driver) B* (owner-driver) C (owner-company)	
Steering defective	L5	3	B (driver) B* (owner-driver) C (owner-company)	
Tyres defective	L5	3	B (driver) B* (owner-driver) C (owner-company)	Penalty per tyre
Exhaust emission	L4	–	B (driver) B* (owner-driver) C (owner-company)	
Condition of vehicle/ accessories/equipment involving danger of injury (Road Traffic Act 1988, s.40A)	L5	3	B (driver) B* (owner-driver) C (owner-company)	Must disqualify for at least 6 months if offender has one or more previous convictions for same offence within three years
Number of passengers or way carried involving danger of injury (Road Traffic Act 1988, s.40A)	L5	3	B (driver) B* (owner-driver) C (owner-company)	Must disqualify for at least 6 months if offender has one or more previous convictions for same offence within three years

Offence	Maximum	Points	Starting point	Special considerations
Weight, position or distribution of load or manner in which load secured involving danger of injury (Road Traffic Act 1988, s.40A)	L5	3	B (driver) B* (owner-driver) C (owner- company)	Must disqualify for at least 6 months if offender has one or more previous convictions for same offence within three years
Position or manner in which load secured (not involving danger) (Road Traffic Act 1988, s.42)	L4	–	B (driver) B* (owner-driver) C (owner company)	
Overloading/exceeding axle weight	L5	–	B (driver) B* (owner-driver) C (owner company)	Starting points cater for cases where the overload is up to and including 10%. Thereafter, 10% should be added to the penalty for each additional 1% of overload Penalty per axle
No operators licence	L4	–	B (driver) B* (owner-driver) C (owner company)	
Speed limiter not used or incorrectly calibrated	L4	–	B (driver) B* (owner-driver) C (owner company)	
Tachograph not used/not working	L5	–	B (driver) B* (owner-driver) C (owner company)	
Exceed permitted driving time/periods of duty	L4	–	B (driver) B* (owner-driver) C (owner company)	
Fail to keep/return written record sheets	L4	–	B (driver) B* (owner-driver) C (owner company)	
Falsify or alter records with intent to deceive	L5/2 years	–	B (driver) B* (owner-driver) C (owner company)	Either way offence

Explanatory Material

SG-273 **Meaning of 'range', 'starting point' and 'first time offender'**

. . ., these guidelines are for *a first time offender* convicted after a trial. They provide a *starting point* based on an assessment of the seriousness of the offence and a *range* within which the sentence will normally fall in most cases.
A clear, consistent understanding of each of these terms is essential and the Council and the Sentencing Advisory Panel have agreed the meanings set out in paragraphs 1(a)–(d) below.

They are explained in a format that follows the structured approach to the sentencing decision which identifies first those aspects that affect the assessment of the seriousness of the offence, then those aspects that form part of personal mitigation and, finally, any reduction for a guilty plea.

In practice, the boundaries between these stages will not always be as clear cut but the underlying principles will remain the same.

In accordance with section 174 of the Criminal Justice Act 2003, a court is obliged to '*state in open court, in ordinary language and in general terms, its reasons for deciding on the sentence passed*'. In particular, '*where guidelines indicate that a sentence of a particular kind, or within a particular range, would normally be appropriate and the sentence is of a different kind, or is outside that range*' the court must give its reasons for imposing a sentence of a different kind or outside the range.

Assessing the seriousness of the offence SG-274

1. a) These guidelines apply to an offence that can be committed in a variety of circumstances with different levels of seriousness. They apply to a *first time offender* who has been convicted after a trial.[194] Within the guidelines, a *first time offender* is a person who does not have a conviction which, by virtue of section 143(2) of the Criminal Justice Act 2003, must be treated as an aggravating factor.
   b) As an aid to consistency of approach, a guideline will describe a number of types of activity falling within the broad definition of the offence. These are set out in a column headed 'examples of nature of activity'.
   c) The expected approach is for a court to identify the description that most nearly matches the particular facts of the offence for which sentence is being imposed. This will identify a *starting point* from which the sentencer can depart to reflect aggravating or mitigating factors affecting the seriousness of the *offence* (beyond those contained in the description itself) to reach a *provisional sentence.*
   d) The range is the bracket into which the *provisional sentence* will normally fall after having regard to factors which aggravate or mitigate the seriousness of the offence. The particular circumstances may, however, make it appropriate that the *provisional sentence* falls outside the *range.*
2. Where the offender has previous convictions which aggravate the seriousness of the current offence, that may take the *provisional sentence* beyond the *range* given particularly where there are significant other aggravating factors present.

Offender Mitigation SG-275

3. Once the *provisional sentence* has been identified (by reference to the factors affecting the seriousness of the *offence*), the court will take into account any relevant factors of *offender* mitigation. Again, this may take the provisional sentence outside the range.

Reduction for guilty plea SG-276

4. Where there has been a guilty plea, any reduction attributable to that plea will be applied to the sentence at this stage. This reduction may take the sentence below the *range* provided.

Fine band starting points and ranges SG-277

In these guidelines, where the starting point or range for an offence is or includes a fine, it is expressed as one of three fine bands (A, B or C). As detailed . . . below, each fine band has both a starting point and a range.

On some offence guidelines, both the starting point and the range are expressed as a single fine band; see for example careless driving . . . where the starting point and range for the first level of offence activity are 'band A fine'. This means that the starting point will be the starting point for fine band A (50% of the offender's relevant weekly income) and the range will be the range for fine band A (25–75% of relevant weekly income). On other guidelines, the range encompasses more than one fine band; see for example drunk and disorderly in a public place . . . where the starting point for the second level of offence activity is 'band B fine' and the range is 'band A fine to band C fine'. This means that the starting point will be the starting point for fine band B (100% of relevant weekly income) and the range will be the lowest point of the range for fine band A to the highest point of the range for fine band C (25%–175% of relevant weekly income).

Sentencing for multiple offences SG-278

The starting points and ranges indicated in the individual offence guidelines assume that the offender is being sentenced for a single offence. Where an offender is being sentenced for multiple offences, the overall sentence must be just and appropriate having regard to the totality of the offending; the court should not simply aggregate the sentences considered suitable for the individual offences. The court's assessment of the totality of the offending may result in an overall sentence above the range indicated for the individual offences, including a sentence of a different type.[195] While concurrent sentences are generally to be preferred where the offences arose out of a single incident, consecutive sentences may be desirable in some circumstances. . . .

[194] This means any case in which there is no guilty plea including, e.g., where an offender is convicted in absence after evidence has been heard

[195] When considering whether the threshold for a community or custodial sentence is passed, ss.148(1) and 152(2) of the Criminal Justice Act 2003 confirm that the court may have regard to the combination of the offence and one or more offences associated with it.

SG-279 **Offences not included in the guidelines**

A number of offences are currently under consideration by the Council and will be included in the MCSG by way of an update when agreed. In the interim, the relevant guideline from the previous version of the MCSG has been included for ease of reference—*these do not constitute formal guidelines issued by the Council.* Where there is no guideline for an offence, it may assist in determining sentence to consider the starting points and ranges indicated for offences that are of a similar level of seriousness. When sentencing for the breach of any order for which there is not a specific guideline, the primary objective will be to ensure compliance. Reference to existing guidelines in respect of breaches of orders may provide a helpful point of comparison (see in particular . . . (breach of community order) and . . . (breach of protective order)). . ..

SG-280 APPROACH TO THE ASSESSMENT OF FINES

SG-281 **Introduction**

1. The amount of a fine must reflect the *seriousness* of the offence.[196]
2. The court must also take into account the *financial circumstances* of the offender; this applies whether it has the effect of increasing or reducing the fine.[197] Normally a fine should be of an amount that is capable of being paid within 12 months.
3. The aim is for the fine to have an equal impact on offenders with different financial circumstances; it should be a hardship but should not force the offender below a reasonable 'subsistence' level.
4. The guidance below aims to establish a clear, consistent and principled approach to the assessment of fines that will apply fairly in the majority of cases. However, it is impossible to anticipate every situation that may be encountered and in each case the court will need to exercise its judgement to ensure that the fine properly reflects the *seriousness of the offence* and takes into account the *financial circumstances* of the offender.

SG-282 **Fine bands**

5. For the purpose of the offence guidelines, a fine is based on one of three bands (A, B or C).[198] The selection of the relevant fine band, and the position of the individual offence within that band, is determined by the seriousness of the offence.

	Starting point	**Range**
Fine Band A	**50% of relevant weekly income**	**25–75% of relevant weekly income**
Fine Band B	**100% of relevant weekly income**	**75–125% of relevant weekly income**
Fine Band C	**150% of relevant weekly income**	**125–175% of relevant weekly income**

6. For an explanation of the meaning of starting point and range, both generally and in relation to fines, see [above].

SG-283 **Definition of relevant weekly income**

7. The *seriousness* of an offence determines the choice of fine band and the position of the offence within the range for that band. The offender's *financial circumstances* are taken into account by expressing that position as a proportion of the offender's *relevant weekly income.*
8. Where an offender is in receipt of income from employment or is self-employed *and* that income is more than £100 per week after deduction of tax and national insurance (or equivalent where the offender is self-employed), the actual income is the *relevant weekly income.*
9. Where an offender's only source of income is state benefit (including where there is relatively low additional income as permitted by the benefit regulations) or the offender is in receipt of income from employment or is self-employed but the amount of income after deduction of tax and national insurance is £100 or less, the *relevant weekly income is deemed to be £100.* Additional information about the basis for this approach is set out [below].
10. In calculating relevant weekly income, no account should be taken of tax credits, housing benefit, child benefit or similar.

[196] Criminal Justice Act 2003, s.164(2)
[197] ibid., ss.164(1) and 164(4)
[198] As detailed in paras. 36–38 below, two further bands are provided which apply where the offence has passed the threshold for a community order (Band D) or a custodial sentence (Band E) but the court decides that it need not impose such a sentence and that a financial penalty is appropriate

No reliable information SG-284

11. Where an offender has failed to provide information, or the court is not satisfied that it has been given sufficient reliable information, it is entitled to make such determination as it thinks fit regarding the financial circumstances of the offender.[199] Any determination should be clearly stated on the court records for use in any subsequent variation or enforcement proceedings. In such cases, a record should also be made of the applicable fine band and the court's assessment of the position of the offence within that band based on the seriousness of the offence.
12. Where there is no information on which a determination can be made, the court should proceed on the basis of an *assumed relevant weekly income of £350*. This is derived from national median pre-tax earnings; a gross figure is used as, in the absence of financial information from the offender, it is not possible to calculate appropriate deductions.[200]
13. Where there is some information that tends to suggest a significantly lower or higher income than the recommended £350 default sum, the court should make a determination based on that information.
14. A court is empowered to remit a fine in whole or part if the offender subsequently provides information as to means.[201] The assessment of offence seriousness and, therefore, the appropriate fine band and the position of the offence within that band is not affected by the provision of this information.

Assessment of financial circumstances SG-285

15. While the initial consideration for the assessment of a fine is the offender's relevant weekly income, the court is required to take account of the offender's *financial circumstances* more broadly. Guidance on important parts of this assessment is set out below.
16. An offender's financial circumstances may have the effect of increasing or reducing the amount of the fine; however, they are **not** relevant to the assessment of offence seriousness. They should be considered separately from the selection of the appropriate fine band and the court's assessment of the position of the offence within the range for that band.

Out of the ordinary expenses SG-286

17. In deciding the proportions of relevant weekly income that are the starting points and ranges for each fine band, account has been taken of reasonable living expenses. Accordingly, no further allowance should normally be made for these. In addition, no allowance should normally be made where the offender has dependants.
18. Outgoings will be relevant to the amount of the fine only where the expenditure is *out of the ordinary* and *substantially* reduces the ability to pay a financial penalty so that the requirement to pay a fine based on the standard approach would lead to *undue* hardship.

Unusually low outgoings SG-287

19. Where the offender's living expenses are substantially **lower** than would normally be expected, it may be appropriate to adjust the amount of the fine to reflect this. This may apply, for example, where an offender does not make any financial contribution towards his or her living costs.

Savings SG-288

20. Where an offender has savings these will not normally be relevant to the assessment of the amount of a fine although they may influence the decision on time to pay.
21. However, where an offender has little or no income but has substantial savings, the court may consider it appropriate to adjust the amount of the fine to reflect this.

Household has more than one source of income SG-289

22. Where the household of which the offender is a part has more than one source of income, the fine should normally be based on the income of the offender alone.

[199] Criminal Justice Act 2003, s.164(5)
[200] For 2004–05, the median pre-tax income of all tax payers was £315 per week: HMRC Survey of Personal Incomes. This figure has been increased to take account of inflation
[201] Criminal Justice Act 2003, s.165(2)

23. However, where the offender's part of the income is very small (or the offender is wholly dependent on the income of another), the court may have regard to the extent of the household's income and assets which will be available to meet any fine imposed on the offender.[202]

SG-290 **Potential earning capacity**

24. Where there is reason to believe that an offender's potential earning capacity is greater than his or her current income, the court may wish to adjust the amount of the fine to reflect this.[203] This may apply, for example, where an unemployed offender states an expectation to gain paid employment within a short time. The basis for the calculation of fine should be recorded in order to ensure that there is a clear record for use in variation or enforcement proceedings.

SG-291 **High income offenders**

25. Where the offender is in receipt of very high income, a fine based on a proportion of relevant weekly income may be disproportionately high when compared with the seriousness of the offence. In such cases, the court should adjust the fine to an appropriate level; as a general indication, in most cases the fine for a first time offender pleading not guilty should not exceed 75% of the maximum fine.

SG-292 **Offence committed for 'commercial' purposes**

26. Some offences are committed with the intention of gaining a significant commercial benefit. These often occur where, in order to carry out an activity lawfully, a person has to comply with certain processes which may be expensive. They include, for example, 'taxi-touting' (where unauthorised persons seek to operate as taxi drivers) and 'fly-tipping' (where the cost of lawful disposal is considerable).
27. In some of these cases, a fine based on the standard approach set out above may not reflect the level of financial gain achieved or sought through the offending. Accordingly:
    a. where the offender has generated income or avoided expenditure to a level that can be calculated or estimated, the court may wish to consider that amount when determining the financial penalty;
    b. where it is not possible to calculate or estimate that amount, the court may wish to draw on information from the enforcing authorities about the general costs of operating within the law.

SG-293 **Reduction for a guilty plea**

28. Where a guilty plea has been entered, the amount of the fine should be reduced by the appropriate proportion. See . . . the user guide for guidance.

SG-294 **Other considerations**

Maximum fines

29. A fine must not exceed the statutory limit. Where this is expressed in terms of a 'level', the maxima are:

Level 1	£200
Level 2	£500
Level 3	£1,000
Level 4	£2,500
Level 5	£5,000

Victims surcharge

30. Whenever a court imposes a fine in respect of an offence committed after 1 April 2007, it *must* order the offender to pay a surcharge of £15.[204]
31. Where the offender is of adequate means, the court must not reduce the fine to allow for imposition of the surcharge. Where the offender does not have sufficient means to pay the total financial penalty considered appropriate by the court, the order of priority is compensation, surcharge, fine, costs.
32. Further guidance is set out in *Guidance on Victims Surcharge* issued by the Justices' Clerks' Society and Magistrates' Association (30 March 2007).

[202] *R v Engen* [2004] EWCA Crim 1536 (CA)
[203] *R v Little* (unreported) 14 April 1976 (CA)
[204] Criminal Justice Act 2003, ss.161A and 161B

Costs

33. See [below] for guidance on the approach to costs. Where the offender does not have sufficient means to pay the total financial penalty considered appropriate by the court, the order of priority is compensation, surcharge, fine, costs.

Multiple offences

34. Where an offender is to be fined for two or more offences that arose out of the same incident, it will often be appropriate to impose on the most serious offence a fine which reflects the totality of the offending where this can be achieved within the maximum penalty for that offence. 'No separate penalty' should be imposed for the other offences.
35. Where compensation is being ordered, that will need to be attributed to the relevant offence as will any necessary ancillary orders.

Fine Bands D and E

36. Two further fine bands are provided to assist a court in calculating a fine where the offence and general circumstances would otherwise warrant a community order (band D) or a custodial sentence (band E) but the court has decided that it need not impose such a sentence and that a financial penalty is appropriate. See pages 160 and 163 for further guidance.
37. The following starting points and ranges apply:

	Starting point	Range
Fine Band D	**250% of relevant weekly income**	**200–300% of relevant weekly income**
Fine Band E	**400% of relevant weekly income**	**300–500% of relevant weekly income**

38. In cases where these fine bands apply, it may be appropriate for the fine to be of an amount that is larger than can be repaid within 12 months. See paragraph 43 below.

Imposition of fines with custodial sentences

39. A fine and a custodial sentence may be imposed for the same offence although there will be few circumstances in which this is appropriate, particularly where the custodial sentence is to be served immediately. One example might be where an offender has profited financially from an offence but there is no obvious victim to whom compensation can be awarded. Combining these sentences is most likely to be appropriate only where the custodial sentence is short and/or the offender clearly has, or will have, the means to pay.
40. Care must be taken to ensure that the overall sentence is proportionate to the seriousness of the offence and that better off offenders are not able to 'buy themselves out of custody'.

Consult your legal adviser in any case in which you are considering combining a fine with a custodial sentence.

Payment

41. A fine is payable in full on the day on which it is imposed. The offender should always be asked for immediate payment when present in court and some payment on the day should be required wherever possible.
42. Where that is not possible, the court may, in certain circumstances, require the offender to be detained. More commonly, a court will allow payments to be made over a period set by the court:
    a. if periodic payments are allowed, the fine should normally be payable within a maximum of 12 months. However, it may be unrealistic to expect those on very low incomes to maintain payments for as long as a year;
    b. compensation should normally be payable within 12 months. However, in exceptional circumstances it may be appropriate to allow it to be paid over a period of up to 3 years.
43. Where fine bands D and E apply (see paragraphs 36–38 above), it may be appropriate for the fine to be of an amount that is larger than can be repaid within 12 months. In such cases, the fine should normally be payable within a maximum of 18 months (band D) or 2 years (band E).
44. It is generally recognised that the maximum weekly payment by a person in receipt of state benefit should rarely exceed £5.
45. When allowing payment by instalments by an offender in receipt of earned income, the following approach may be useful. If the offender has dependants or larger than usual commitments, the weekly payment is likely to be decreased.

Net weekly income	Starting point for weekly payment
£60	£5
£120	£10
£200	£25
£250	£30
£300	£50
£400	£80

46. The payment terms must be included in any collection order made in respect of the amount imposed; see [below].

SG-295 *Assessment of fines: sentencing structure*

1. Decide that a fine is appropriate

2. Offence seriousness
A. Identify the appropriate fine band

- In the offence guidelines, the starting point for a fine is identified as fine band A, B or C
- Each fine band provides a **starting point** and a **range** related to the **seriousness** of the offence expressed as a proportion of the offender's **relevant weekly income**. . .

2. Offence seriousness
B. Consider the effect of aggravating and mitigating factors

- **Move up or down from the starting point** to reflect aggravating or mitigating factors that affect the **seriousness** of the offence—this will usually be within the indicated **range** for the fine band but the court is not precluded from going outside the range where the facts justify it. . .

3. Consider offender mitigation

- The court may consider it appropriate to make a further adjustment to the starting point in light of any matters of offender mitigation. . .

4. **Form a view of the position of the offence within the range for the fine band then take into account the offenders financial circumstances**

- Require the offender to provide a statement of **financial circumstances**. Obtain further information through questioning if necessary. Failure to provide the information when required is an offence
- The provision of financial information does not affect the seriousness of the offence or, therefore, the position of the offence within the range for the applicable fine band
- The initial consideration for the assessment of the fine is the offender's **relevant weekly income**. . .
- However, the court must take account of the offender's financial circumstances more broadly. These may have the effect of **increasing or reducing** the amount of the fine. . .
- Where the court has **insufficient information** to make a proper determination of the offender's financial circumstances, it may make such determination as it thinks fit. . .

5. Consider a reduction for a guilty plea

- Reduce the fine by the appropriate proportion. . .

6. Consider ancillary orders, including compensation

- Consider compensation in every case where the offending has resulted in personal injury, loss or damage—give reasons if order not made. . .. Compensation takes priority over a fine where there are insufficient resources to pay both. . .

7. Decide sentence Give reasons

- The resulting fine must reflect the seriousness of the offence and must take into account the offender's financial circumstances
- Consider the proposed total financial penalty, including compensation, victims surcharge and costs. Where there are insufficient resources to pay the total amount, the order of priority is compensation, surcharge, fine, costs
- Give reasons for the sentence passed, including any ancillary orders
- State if the sentence has been reduced to reflect a guilty plea; indicate what the sentence would otherwise have been
- Explain if the sentence is of a different kind or outside the range indicated in the guidelines
- Expect immediate payment. If payment by instalments allowed, the court must make a collection order unless this would be impracticable or inappropriate. . .

Additional information: approach to offenders on low income SG-296

1. An offender whose primary source of income is state benefit will generally receive a base level of benefit (e.g. job seekers' allowance, a relevant disability benefit or income support) and may also be eligible for supplementary benefits depending on his or her individual circumstances (such as child tax credits, housing benefit, council tax benefit and similar).
2. If relevant weekly income were defined as the amount of benefit received, this would usually result in higher fines being imposed on offenders with a higher level of need; in most circumstances that would not properly balance the seriousness of the offence with the financial circumstances of the offender. While it might be possible to exclude from the calculation any allowance above the basic entitlement of a single person, that could be complicated and time consuming.
3. Similar issues can arise where an offender is in receipt of a low earned income since this may trigger eligibility for means related benefits such as working tax credits and housing benefit depending on the particular circumstances. It will not always be possible to determine with any confidence whether such a person's financial circumstances are significantly different from those of a person whose primary source of income is state benefit.
4. For these reasons, a simpler and fairer approach to cases involving offenders in receipt of low income (whether primarily earned or as a result of benefit) is to identify an amount that is deemed to represent the offender's relevant weekly income.
5. While a precise calculation is neither possible nor desirable, it is considered that an amount that is approximately half-way between the base rate for job seekers' allowance and the net weekly income of an adult earning the minimum wage for 30 hours per week represents a starting point that is both realistic and appropriate; *this is currently £100.*[205] The calculation is based on a 30 hour working week in recognition of the fact that many of those on minimum wage do not work a full 37 hour week and that lower minimum wage rates apply to younger people.
6. It is expected that this figure will remain in use until 31 March 2011. Future revisions of the guideline will update the amount in accordance with current benefit and minimum wage levels.

Enforcement of Fines SG-297

1. The Courts Act 2003 created a new fines collection scheme which provides for greater administrative enforcement of fines. The main features are set out below. . ..

Attachment of earnings orders/applications for benefit deductions SG-298

2. Unless it would be impracticable or inappropriate to do so, the court must make an attachment of earnings order (AEO) or application for benefit deductions (ABD) whenever:
   - compensation is imposed;[206] or
   - the court concludes that the offender is an existing defaulter and that the existing default cannot be disregarded.[207]
3. In other cases, the court may make an AEO or ABD with the offender's consent.[208]

[205] With effect from 1 October 2007, the minimum wage is £5.52 per hour for an adult aged 22 or over. Based on a 30 hour week, this equates to approximately £149.14 after deductions for tax and national insurance. To ensure equivalence of approach, the level of job seekers' allowance for a single person aged 22 has been used for the purpose of calculating the mid point; this is currently £46.85
[206] Courts Act 2003, sch.5, para.7A
[207] ibid., para.8
[208] ibid., para.9

SG-299 **Collection orders**

4. The court must make a collection order in every case in which a fine or compensation order is imposed unless this would be impracticable or inappropriate.[209] The collection order must state:
   - the amount of the sum due, including the amount of any fine, compensation order or other sum;
   - whether the court considers the offender to be an existing defaulter;
   - whether an AEO or ABD has been made and information about the effect of the order;
   - if the court has not made an AEO or ABD, the payment terms;
   - if an AEO or ABD has been made, the reserve terms (i.e. the payment terms that will apply if the AEO or ABD fails). It will often be appropriate to set a reserve term of payment in full within 14 days.
5. If an offender defaults on a collection order and is not already subject to an AEO or ABD, a fines officer must make an AEO or ABD.[210] Where this would be impracticable or inappropriate, or where the offender is already subject to an AEO or ABD, a fines officer must either:[211]
   - issue a 'further steps' notice advising that the officer intends to take any of the enforcement action listed below; or
   - refer the case to a magistrates' court.
6. The following enforcement action is available to a fines officer:[212]
   - making an AEO or ABD;
   - issuing a distress warrant;
   - registering the sum in the register of judgments and orders;
   - making a clamping order. A magistrates' court may order the sale of the vehicle if the sum remains unpaid one month after the vehicle was clamped;[213]
   - taking enforcement proceedings in the High Court or county court.
7. Where a fines officer refers the case to a magistrates' court, the court may:[214]
   - vary the payment terms or reserve terms;
   - take any of the enforcement steps available to fines officers listed above;
   - where the court is satisfied that the default is due to wilful refusal or culpable neglect, increase the fine by up to 50 per cent;[215]
   - discharge the collection order and exercise any of the court's standard fine enforcement powers.
8. The case may also be referred to a magistrates' court if an offender appeals against a 'further steps' notice issued by a fines officer.[216]

SG-300 **Standard fine enforcement powers**

9. These powers are normally available if:
   - a collection order is not made; or
   - a case is referred to a magistrates' court by a fines officer; or
   - an offender appeals against a 'further steps' notice issued by a fines officer.

SG-301 **Remission of fine**

10. The court can remit a fine 'if it thinks it just to do so having regard to a change of circumstances since the date of conviction'.[217] This requirement may be satisfied where:
    - the defaulter's means have changed since the fine was imposed;
    - arrears have accumulated by the imposition of additional fines to a level which makes repayment of the total amount within a reasonable time unlikely;
    - the defaulter is serving a term of imprisonment; remission may be more practical than lodging concurrent warrants of imprisonment.
11. There is no power to remit excise penalties (which include fines and back duty for using an untaxed vehicle).[218]

---

[209] ibid., para.12
[210] ibid., para.26
[211] ibid., para.37
[212] ibid., para.38
[213] Courts Act 2003, sch.5, para.41
[214] ibid., para.39
[215] ibid., para.42A
[216] ibid., para.37
[217] Magistrates' Courts Act 1980, s.85
[218] Criminal Justice Act 2003, s.165

12. Compensation and costs cannot be remitted but, where payment is unlikely or impractical due to the defaulter's means or circumstances, the sum may be discharged or reduced. Victims and claimants should be consulted and given an opportunity to attend the hearing.
13. The court is also empowered to remit a fine that was imposed in the absence of information about the offender's means.

Imprisonment in default of payment SG-302

14. A court may issue a warrant of commitment if the defaulter is already serving a custodial sentence.[219]
15. If a means inquiry establishes that the defaulter has the ability to pay immediately, and the offence was punishable by imprisonment, the court can commit him or her to prison.[220]
16. Otherwise, the court may issue a warrant of commitment only if there has been a means inquiry and the court:[221]
    - is satisfied that the default is due to wilful refusal or culpable neglect; and
    - has considered or tried all other methods of enforcing payment and concluded that they are inappropriate or unsuccessful.
17. The other methods that the court is required to have considered or tried are:
    - money payment supervision order;[222]
    - application for deductions from benefit;
    - attachment of earnings order;
    - distress warrant;
    - taking enforcement proceedings in the High Court or county court
    - if the offender is aged under 25, an attendance centre order (where available).[223]
18. The period of commitment should be the shortest which is likely to succeed in obtaining payment; the periods prescribed in schedule 4 of the Magistrates' Courts Act 1980 . . . should be regarded as maxima rather than the norm. The period of imprisonment may be suspended on condition that regular payments are made. Where such payments are not made, the defaulter should be brought back before the court for consideration of whether the period of imprisonment should be implemented.

Maximum periods of imprisonment in default of payment	
Amount not exceeding £200	7 days
Amount exceeding £200 but not exceeding £500	14 days
Amount exceeding £500 but not exceeding £1,000	28 days
Amount exceeding £1,000 but not exceeding £2,500	45 days
Amount exceeding £2,500 but not exceeding £5,000	3 months
Amount exceeding £5,000 but not exceeding £10,000	6 months
Amount exceeding £10,000	12 months

Detention in the precincts of the court or at a police station SG-303

19. The court may order that an offender be detained for a specified period ending no later than 8pm on the day on which the order is made:[224] this is available both as a sentence in its own right and as an order in respect of unpaid fines where it can be used as an alternative to remission. No means inquiry is required.

Warrant for detention in police station overnight SG-304

20. The court may issue a warrant for the overnight detention of a defaulter in a police station.[225] The defaulter must be released at 8am the following day, or the same day if arrested after midnight.

[219] Magistrates' Courts Act 1980, s.82(3)
[220] Magistrates' Courts Act 1980, s.82(4)(a)
[221] ibid., s.82(4)(b)
[222] ibid., s.88
[223] Powers of Criminal Courts (Sentencing) Act 2000, s.60
[224] Magistrates' Courts Act 1980, s.135
[225] ibid., s.136

SG-305 **Discharge of fines by unpaid work (being piloted in specified areas until 31 March 2009)**

21. Schedule 6 [to] the Courts Act 2003 empowers the court to order that an offender discharge a fine by performing work for a specified number of hours. This is not a community order; it is an enforcement provision that may be invoked following a court's decision on the information before it that a fine was an appropriate sentence for the offence.
22. The order can be made only where other means of enforcing the sum are likely to be impracticable or inappropriate. The offender must be suitable for unpaid work and consent to the order. The number of hours is determined by dividing the sum due by the 'prescribed hourly sum' (currently £6 per hour).

SG-306

Community Orders

1. Community orders have the effect of restricting the offender's liberty while providing punishment in the community, rehabilitation for the offender, and/or ensuring that the offender engages in reparative activities. They are available in respect of all offences, including those for which the maximum penalty is a fine.
2. A community order must not be imposed unless the offence is 'serious enough to warrant such a sentence'.[226] For detailed guidance regarding this threshold and the approach to community orders, sentencers should refer to the Sentencing Guidelines Council's definitive guideline *New Sentences: Criminal Justice Act 2003*, published 16 December 2004 [see **SG-9**], and the National Standards for the Probation Service. The Council guideline emphasises that:
   - sentencers must consider all available disposals at the time of sentence; even where the threshold for a community sentence has been passed, a fine or discharge may be an appropriate penalty;
   - where an offender is being sentenced for a non-imprisonable offence, great care is needed in assessing whether a community sentence is appropriate since failure to comply could result in a custodial sentence (see page 43).[227]
3. Community orders consist of one or more of the following requirements:
   - unpaid work requirement;
   - activity requirement;
   - programme requirement;
   - prohibited activity requirement;
   - curfew requirement;
   - exclusion requirement;
   - residence requirement;
   - mental health treatment requirement;
   - drug rehabilitation requirement;
   - alcohol treatment requirement;
   - supervision requirement;
   - in a case where the offender is aged under 25, attendance centre requirement (where available).
4. The court must ensure that the restriction on the offender's liberty is commensurate with the seriousness of the offence and that the requirements are the most suitable for the offender.[228] Where two or more requirements are included, they must be compatible with each other.[229]
5. The Council guideline provides that the seriousness of the offence should be the ***initial*** factor in determining which requirements to include in a community order. It establishes three sentencing ranges within the community order band based on offence seriousness (low, medium and high), and identifies non-exhaustive examples of requirements that might be appropriate in each. These are set out below. The examples focus on punishment in the community; other requirements of a rehabilitative nature may be more appropriate in some cases.

[226] Criminal Justice Act 2003, s.148
[227] The power to make a community order for a non-imprisonable offence will be removed by provisions in the Criminal Justice and Immigration Act 2008 when in force
[228] Criminal Justice Act 2003, ss.148(2)(a) and 148(2)(b)
[229] ibid., s.177(6)

Low	Medium	High
Offences only just cross community order threshold, where the seriousness of the offence or the nature of the offender's record means that a discharge or fine is inappropriate	Offences that obviously fall within the community order band	Offences only just fall below the custody threshold or the custody threshold is crossed but a community order is more appropriate in the circumstances
In general, only one requirement will be appropriate and the length may be curtailed if additional requirements are necessary		More intensive sentences which combine two or more requirements may be appropriate
Suitable requirements might include: • 40–80 hours unpaid work • Curfew requirement within the lowest range (e.g. up to 12 hours per day for a few weeks) • Exclusion requirement, without electronic monitoring, for a few months • Prohibited activity requirement • Attendance centre requirement (where available)	• Suitable requirements might include: • Greater number of hours of unpaid work (e.g. 80–150 hours) • Curfew requirement within the middle range (e.g. up to 12 hours for 2–3 months) • Exclusion requirement lasting in the region of 6 months • Prohibited activity requirement	Suitable requirements might include: • 150–300 hours unpaid work • Activity requirement up to the maximum of 60 days • Curfew requirement up to 12 hours per day for 4–6 months • Exclusion order lasting in the region of 12 months

6. The particular requirements imposed within the range must be suitable for the individual offender and will be influenced by a wide range of factors including the stated purpose(s) of the sentence, the risk of re-offending, the ability of the offender to comply, and the availability of the requirements in the local area. Sentencers must ensure that the sentence strikes the right balance between proportionality and suitability. The resulting restriction on liberty must be a proportionate response to the offence that was committed.
7. In many cases, a pre-sentence report will be pivotal in helping the court decide whether to impose a community order and, if so, whether particular requirements or combinations of requirements are suitable for an individual offender. Whenever the court reaches the provisional view that a community order may be appropriate, it should usually request a pre-sentence report. It will be helpful to indicate the court's preliminary opinion as to which of the three sentencing ranges is relevant and the purpose(s) of sentencing that the package of requirements is expected to fulfil. Ideally this should be provided to the Probation Service in written form, with a copy retained on the court file for the benefit of the sentencing bench.

Electronic monitoring **SG-307**

8. Subject to limited exceptions, the court must impose an electronic monitoring requirement where it makes a community order with a curfew or exclusion requirement, and may do so in all other cases.[230] Electronic monitoring should be used with the primary purpose of promoting and monitoring compliance with other requirements, in circumstances where the punishment of the offender and/or the need to safeguard the public and prevent re-offending are the most important concerns.

Breach of Community Order **SG-308**

9. Refer to [the specific guideline above] for guidance on the approach to sentencing for breaches of community orders.

[230] Criminal Justice Act 2003, ss.177(3) and 177(4)

SG-309

Custodial Sentences

1. A custodial sentence must not be imposed unless the offence 'was so serious that neither a fine alone nor a community sentence can be justified for the offence'.[231] Guidance regarding this threshold and the approach to the imposition of custodial sentences is set out in the Sentencing Guidelines Council's definitive guideline *Overarching Principles*: Seriousness, published 16 December 2004 [see **SG-21**].
2. The guideline emphasises that:
   - the clear intention of the threshold test is to reserve prison as a punishment for the most serious offences;
   - passing the custody threshold does not mean that a custodial sentence should be deemed inevitable; custody can still be avoided in light of offender mitigation or where there is a suitable intervention in the community which provides sufficient restriction (by way of punishment) while addressing the rehabilitation of the offender to prevent future crime. However, where the offence would otherwise appear to warrant a term of imprisonment within the Crown Court's jurisdiction, it is for the Crown Court to make that judgement;
   - the approach to the imposition of a custodial sentence should be as follows:
     (a) Has the custody threshold been passed?
     (b) If so, is it unavoidable that a custodial sentence be imposed?
     (c) If so, can that sentence be suspended? (Sentencers should be clear that they would have imposed a custodial sentence if the power to suspend had not been available.)
     (d) If not, impose a sentence which takes immediate effect for the shortest term commensurate with the seriousness of the offence.[232]

Suspended sentences

3. If the court imposes a term of imprisonment between 14 days and six months,[233] it may suspend the sentence for between 6 months and 2 years (the 'operational period').[234] Where the court imposes two or more sentences to be served consecutively, the power to suspend the sentence is not available in relation to any of them unless the aggregate of the terms does not exceed six months.[235]
4. When the court suspends a sentence, it must impose one or more requirements for the offender to undertake in the community. The requirements are identical to those available for community orders.
5. If the offender fails to comply with a community requirement or commits a further offence, the court must <u>either</u> activate the suspended sentence in full or in part <u>or</u> amend the order so as to:[236]
   a) extend the period during which the offender is subject to community requirements;
   b) make the community requirements more onerous; or
   c) extend the operational period.
6. There are many similarities between suspended sentences and community orders: requirements can be imposed on the offender and the court can respond to breach by sending him or her to custody. The crucial difference is that a suspended sentence is a prison sentence; it may be imposed only where the court is satisfied both that the custodial threshold has been passed and that it is not appropriate to impose a community order, fine or other non-custodial sentence.
7. A further difference is the approach to any breach; when sentencing for breach of a community order, the primary objective is to ensure that the requirements of the order are complied with. When responding to breach of a suspended sentence, the statutory presumption is that the custodial sentence will be activated.[237]
8. Detailed guidance regarding suspended sentences and the appropriate response to breaches is set out in the Sentencing Guidelines Council's definitive guideline *New Sentences: Criminal Justice Act 2003*, published 16 December 2004 [see **SG-9**]. The guideline emphasises that:
   - a custodial sentence that is suspended should be for the same term that would have applied if the sentence was to be served immediately;

[231] Criminal Justice Act 2003, s.152(2)
[232] ibid., s.153(2)
[233] When implemented, provisions in the Criminal Justice and Immigration Act 2008 will restrict the use of this power in magistrates' courts
[234] Criminal Justice Act 2003, s.189(1)
[235] ibid., s.189(2) as amended by art.2(2)(b) of the Criminal Justice Act 2003 (Sentencing) (Transitory Provisions) Order 2005
[236] ibid., sch.12, para.8
[237] Criminal Justice Act 2003, sch.12, para.8(3)

- the time for which a sentence is suspended should reflect the length of the sentence; up to 12 months might normally be appropriate for a suspended sentence of up to 6 months;
- the imposition of a custodial sentence is both punishment and a deterrent; to ensure that the overall terms of the sentence are commensurate with offence seriousness, requirements imposed as part of the sentence should generally be less onerous than if a community order had been imposed;
- a court wishing to impose onerous or intensive requirements should reconsider whether a community sentence might be more appropriate (refer to pages 160–162);
- where an offender has breached a suspended sentence, there is a presumption that the suspended prison term will be activated in full or in part. Relevant considerations will include the extent to which (if any) the offender complied with the requirements, and the circumstances of the breach.

9. When the court imposes a suspended sentence, it may also order that the sentence be reviewed periodically at a review hearing.[238]

COMPENSATION

SG-310

1. The court *must* consider making a compensation order in any case where personal injury, loss or damage has resulted from the offence.[239] It can either be a sentence in its own right or an ancillary order. The court must give reasons if it decides not to order compensation.
2. Up to £5,000 compensation may be imposed in respect of each offence of which the offender has been convicted.[240] Compensation may also be ordered in respect of offences taken into consideration. The total amount of compensation must not exceed the maximum available for the offence(s) of which the offender has been convicted so that, e.g., where an offender has been convicted of two offences, the maximum amount of compensation able to be awarded is £10,000 regardless of the number of offences taken into consideration.
3. Where the personal injury, loss or damage arises from a road accident, a compensation order may be made only if there is a conviction for an offence under the Theft Act 1968, or the offender is uninsured and the Motor Insurers' Bureau will not cover the loss.[241] Compensation paid by the Motor Insurers' Bureau is subject to an excess of £300.
4. Subject to consideration of the victim's views (see paragraph 6 below), the court must order compensation wherever possible and should not have regard to the availability of other sources such as civil litigation or the Criminal Injuries Compensation Scheme. Any amount paid by an offender under a compensation order will generally be deducted from a subsequent civil award or payment under the Scheme to avoid double compensation.[242]
5. Compensation may be ordered for such amount as the court considers appropriate having regard to any evidence and any representations made by the offender or prosecutor.[243] The court must also take into account the offender's means (see also paragraphs 11–13 below).[244]
6. Compensation should benefit, not inflict further harm on, the victim. Any financial recompense from the offender may cause distress. A victim may or may not want compensation from the offender and assumptions should not be made either way. The victim's views are properly obtained through sensitive discussion by the police or witness care unit, when it can be explained that the offender's ability to pay will ultimately determine whether, and how much, compensation is ordered and whether the compensation will be paid in one lump sum or by instalments. If the victim does not want compensation, this should be made known to the court and respected.
7. In cases where it is difficult to ascertain the full amount of the loss suffered by the victim, consideration should be given to making a compensation order for an amount representing the agreed or likely loss. Where relevant information is not immediately available, it may be appropriate to grant an adjournment for it to be obtained.
8. The court should consider two types of loss:
   - financial loss sustained as a result of the offence such as the cost of repairing damage or, in case of injury, any loss of earnings or medical expenses;

[238] ibid., s.191
[239] Powers of Criminal Courts (Sentencing) Act 2000, s.130
[240] ibid., s.131(1)
[241] ibid., s.130(6)
[242] The minimum amount payable under the Criminal Injuries Compensation Scheme is £1,000
[243] Powers of Criminal Courts (Sentencing) Act 2000, s.130(4)
[244] ibid., s.130(11)

- pain and suffering caused by the injury (including terror, shock or distress) and any loss of facility. This should be assessed in light of all factors that appear to the court to be relevant, including any medical evidence, the victim's age and personal circumstances.

9. The tables below suggest starting points for compensating physical and mental injuries commonly encountered in a magistrates' court. They have been developed to be consistent with the approach in the Criminal Injuries Compensation Authority tariff (revised 2001), available at: www.cica.gov.uk.

SG-311 **Physical injury**

Type of injury	Description	Starting point
Graze	Depending on size	Up to £75
Bruise	Depending on size	Up to £100
Cut: no permanent scar	Depending on size and whether stitched	£100 – 500
Black eye		£125
Eye	Blurred or double vision lasting up to 6 weeks Blurred or double vision lasting for 6 to 13 weeks Blurred or double vision lasting for more than 13 weeks (recovery expected)	Up to £1,000 £1,000 £1,750
Brain	Concussion lasting one week	£1,500
Nose	Undisplaced fracture of nasal bone Displaced fracture requiring manipulation Deviated nasal septum requiring septoplasty	£1,000 £2,000 £2,000
Loss of non-front tooth Loss of front tooth	Depending on cosmetic effect	£1,250 £1,750
Facial scar	Minor disfigurement (permanent)	£1,500
Arm	Fractured humerus, radius, ulna (substantial recovery)	£3,300
Shoulder	Dislocated (substantial recovery)	£1,750
Wrist	Dislocated/fractured—including scaphoid fracture (substantial recovery) Fractured—colles type (substantial recovery)	£3,300 £4,400
Sprained wrist, ankle	Disabling for up to 6 weeks Disabling for 6 to 13 weeks Disabling for more than 13 weeks	Up to £1,000 £1,000 £2,500
Finger	Fractured finger other than index finger (substantial recovery) Fractured index finger (substantial recovery) Fractured thumb (substantial recovery)	£1,000 £1,750 £2,000
Leg	Fractured fibula (substantial recovery) Fractured femur, tibia (substantial recovery)	£2,500 £3,800
Abdomen	Injury requiring laparotomy	£3,800

SG-312 **Mental injury**

Description	Starting point
Temporary mental anxiety (including terror, shock, distress), not medically verified	Up to £1,000
Disabling mental anxiety, lasting more than 6 weeks, medically verified	£1,000
Disability mental illness, lasting up to 28 weeks, confirmed by psychiatric diagnosis	£2,500

*In this context, 'disabling' means a person's functioning is significantly impaired in some important aspect of his or her life, such as impaired work or school performance or significant adverse effects on social relationships.

10. The following table, which is also based on the Criminal Injuries Compensation Authority tariff, sets out suggested starting points for compensating physical and sexual abuse. It will be rare for cases involving this type of harm to be dealt with in a magistrates' court and it will be important to consult your legal adviser for guidance in these situations.

Physical and sexual abuse SG-313

Type of abuse	Description	Starting point
Physical abuse of adult	Intermittent physical assaults resulting in accumulation of healed wounds, burns or scalds, but with no appreciable disfigurement	£2,000
Physical abuse of child	Isolated or intermittent assault(s) resulting in weals, hair pulled from scalp etc.	£1,000
	Intermittent physical assaults resulting in accumulation of healed wounds, burns or scalds, but with no appreciable disfigurement	£2,000
Sexual abuse of adult	Non-penetrative indecent physical acts over clothing	£1,000
	Non-penetrative indecent act(s) under clothing	£2,000
Sexual abuse of child (under 18)	Non-penetrative indecent physical act(s) over clothing	£1,000
	Non-penetrative frequent assaults over clothing or non-penetrative indecent act under clothing	£2,000
	Repetitive indecent acts under clothing	£3,300

11. Once the court has formed a preliminary view of the appropriate level of compensation, it must have regard to the means of the offender so far as they are known. Where the offender has little money, the order may have to be scaled down or additional time allowed to pay; the court may allow compensation to be paid over a period of up to three years in appropriate cases.
12. The fact that a custodial sentence is imposed does not, in itself, make it inappropriate to order compensation; however, it may be relevant to whether the offender has the means to satisfy the order.
13. Where the court considers that it would be appropriate to impose a fine and a compensation order but the offender has insufficient means to pay both, priority should be given to compensation. Compensation also takes priority over the victim surcharge where the offender's means are an issue.

Ancillary Orders SG-314

1. There are several ancillary orders available in a magistrates' court which should be considered in appropriate cases. Annex A lists the offences in respect of which certain orders are available [not reproduced]. The individual offence guidelines above also identify ancillary orders particularly likely to be relevant to the offence. In all cases, consult your legal adviser regarding available orders and their specific requirements and effects.
2. Ancillary orders should be taken into account when assessing whether the overall penalty is commensurate with offence seriousness.

Anti-social behaviour orders SG-315

- The court may make an anti-social behaviour order (ASBO) in respect of any person convicted of an offence.[245]
- Before making an order, the court must find that the offender acted in an anti-social manner, i.e. in a manner likely to cause harassment, alarm or distress.
- The court must also consider that the order is necessary to protect the public from further anti-social acts by the offender.
- The order must have effect for at least two years. If the offender is sentenced to custody, the provisions of the order may be suspended until release.
- An ASBO may include only prohibitions; there is no power to impose positive obligations.
- The following is a summary of principles and other considerations relevant to the making of an ASBO in relation to adults and youths taken from the Sentencing Guidelines Council's definitive guideline *Breach of an Anti-Social Behaviour Order* [see **SG-379**]:
  (1) Proceedings for the imposition of an ASBO are civil in nature, so that hearsay evidence is admissible, but a court must be satisfied to a criminal standard that the individual has acted in the anti-social manner alleged.
  (2) The test of 'necessity' requires the exercise of judgement or evaluation; it does not require proof beyond reasonable doubt that the order is "necessary".

[245] Crime and Disorder Act 1998, s.1C

(3) It is particularly important that the findings of fact giving rise to the making of the order are recorded by the court.

(4) As the ASBO is a preventative order it is unlawful to use it as a punishment; so, when sentencing an offender, a court must not allow itself to be diverted into making an ASBO as an alternative or additional sanction.

(5) The police have powers to arrest an individual for any criminal offence, and the court should not impose an order which prohibits the subject from committing an offence if it will not add significantly to the existing powers of the police to protect others from anti-social behaviour by the subject. An order must not prohibit a criminal offence merely to increase the sentence range available for that offence.

(6) The terms of the order made must be precise and capable of being understood by the subject. Where the subject is aged under 18, it is important for both the subject and the parent or guardian to confirm their understanding of the order and its terms. The prohibitions must be enforceable in the sense that they should allow a breach to be readily identified and capable of being proved.

(7) An order should not impose a 'standard list' of prohibitions, but should identify and prohibit the particular type of anti-social behaviour that gives rise to the necessity of an ASBO. Each separate prohibition must be necessary to protect persons from anti-social behaviour by the subject, and each order must be specifically fashioned to deal with the individual concerned.

(8) The order must be proportionate to the legitimate aim pursued and commensurate with the risk guarded against. The court should avoid making compliance very difficult through the imposition of numerous prohibitions, and those that will cause great disruption to the subject should be considered with particular care. It is advisable to make an order for a specific period; when considering the duration of an order imposed on a youth, the potential for the subject to mature may be a relevant factor.

(9) Not all prohibitions set out in an ASBO have to run for the full term of the ASBO itself. The test must always be what is necessary to deal with the particular anti-social behaviour of the offender and what is proportionate in the circumstances. At least one of the prohibitions must last for the duration of the order but not all are required to last for the 2 years that is the minimum length of an order. The court can vary the terms of an order at any time upon application by the subject (or the applicant in the case of an order made upon application).

(10) When making an order upon conviction, the court has the power to suspend its terms until the offender has been released from a custodial sentence. However, where a custodial sentence of 12 months or more is imposed and the offender is liable to be released on licence and thus subject to recall, an order will not generally be necessary. There might be cases where geographical restraints could supplement licence conditions.

(11) Other considerations:

   (i) Where an ASBO is imposed on a subject aged 10–17, the court must consider whether a Parenting order would be desirable in the interests of preventing repetition of the antisocial behaviour.[246] Such an order *must* be made where the offender is aged under 16 and the condition is met, but is discretionary where the offender is aged 16 or 17.

   (ii) Where a magistrates' court imposes a stand-alone ASBO, it must also consider whether an Individual support order (ISO) would be desirable to tackle the underlying causes of the behaviour.[247]

   (iii) In the case of an adult, the court may make an Intervention order if the underlying causes of the anti-social behaviour are drug-related and appropriate treatment is available.[248]

(12) Interim orders:

Where a decision to impose an order (either upon application or conviction) is pending, the court may make an interim order if it considers it just to do so.[249] The court must balance the seriousness of the behaviour and the urgency with which it is necessary to take steps to control it, with the likely impact of an interim order upon the potential subject.[250]

---

[246] Crime and Disorder Act 1998, s.8. The Anti-social Behaviour Act 2003 now provides for a court to impose stand-alone Parenting Orders, if it is satisfied that the child has engaged in criminal or anti-social behaviour. The ASBA also provides for certain agencies to enter into Parenting Contracts which, as an alternative to legal action, have much in common with the nonstatutory Acceptable Behaviour Contracts

[247] ibid., s.1AA

[248] ibid., s.1G

[249] ibid., s.1D

[250] *Leeds Magistrates Court, ex parte Kenny; Secretary of State for Constitutional Affairs and another, ex parte M* [2004] EWCA Civ 312

- Further guidance is set out in A Guide for the Judiciary (third edition) January 2007 (supplement January 2008) published by the Judicial Studies Board.[251] Refer also to Anti-Social Behaviour Orders—A Guide to Law and Procedure in the Magistrates' Court published by the Justices' Clerks' Society.[252]

Binding over orders **SG-316**

- The court has the power to bind an individual over to keep the peace.[253]
- The order is designed to prevent future misconduct and requires the individual to promise to pay a specified sum if the terms of the order are breached. Exercise of the power does not depend upon conviction.
- Guidance on the making of binding over orders is set out in part III.31 of the Consolidated Criminal Practice Direction, as amended in March 2007. Key principles include:
  (1) before imposing the order, the court must be satisfied beyond reasonable doubt that a breach of the peace involving violence or an imminent threat of violence has occurred, or that there is a real risk of violence in the future. The court should hear evidence and the parties before making any order;
  (2) the court should state its reasons for making the order;
  (3) the order should identify the specific conduct or activity from which the individual must refrain, the length of the order and the amount of the recognisance;
  (4) the length of the order should be proportionate to the harm sought to be avoided and should not generally exceed 12 months;
  (5) when fixing the amount of the recognisance, the court should have regard to the individual's financial resources.

Confiscation orders **SG-317**

- Confiscation orders under the Proceeds of Crime Act 2002 may only be made by the Crown Court.
- An offender convicted of an offence in a magistrates' court must be committed to the Crown Court where this is requested by the prosecution with a view to a confiscation order being considered.[254]
- If the committal is made in respect of an either way offence, the court must state whether it would have committed the offender to the Crown Court for sentencing had the issue of a confiscation order not arisen.

Deprivation orders **SG-318**

- The court has the power to deprive an offender of property used for the purpose of committing or facilitating the commission of an offence, whether or not it deals with the offender in any other way.[255]
- Before making the order, the court must have regard to the value of the property and the likely financial and other effects on the offender.
- Without limiting the circumstances in which the court may exercise the power, a vehicle is deemed to have been used for the purpose of committing the offence where the offence is punishable by imprisonment and consists of:
  (1) driving, attempting to drive, or being in charge of a motor vehicle;
  (2) failing to provide a specimen; or
  (3) failing to stop and/or report an accident.[256]

Deprivation of ownership of animal **SG-319**

- Where an offender is convicted of one of the following offences under the Animal Welfare Act 2006, the court may make an order depriving him or her of ownership of the animal and for its disposal:[257]
  (1) causing unnecessary suffering (s. 4);
  (2) mutilation (s. 5);
  (3) docking of dogs' tails (ss. 6(1) and 6(2));
  (4) fighting etc. (s. 8);
  (5) breach of duty to ensure welfare (s. 9);
  (6) breach of disqualification order (s. 36(9)).

[251] www.jsboard.co.uk
[252] www.jc-society.com/File/ASBO_updated_GPG_May_2006.pdf
[253] Justices of the Peace Act 1361, Magistrates Court Act 1980, s.115
[254] Proceeds of Crime Act 2002, s.70
[255] Powers of Criminal Courts (Sentencing) Act 2000, s.143
[256] ibid., ss.143(6) and 143(7)
[257] Animal Welfare Act 2006, s.33

- The court is required to give reasons if it decides not to make such an order.
- Deprivation of ownership may be ordered instead of or in addition to dealing with the offender in any other way.

SG-320 **Disqualification from ownership of animals**

- Where an offender is convicted of one of the following offences under the Animal Welfare Act 2006, the court may disqualify him or her from owning or keeping animals, dealing in animals, and/or transporting animals:[258]
  (1) causing unnecessary suffering (s. 4);
  (2) mutilation (s. 5);
  (3) docking of dogs' tails (ss. 6(1) and 6(2));
  (4) administration of poisons etc. (s. 7);
  (5) fighting etc. (s. 8);
  (6) breach of duty to ensure welfare (s. 9);
  (7) breach of licensing or registration requirements (s. 13(6));
  (8) breach of disqualification order (s. 36(9)).
- The court is required to give reasons if it decides not to make such an order.
- The court may specify a period during which an offender may not apply for termination of the order under section 43 of the Animal Welfare Act 2006; if no period is specified, an offender may not apply for termination of the order until one year after the order was made.
- Disqualification may be imposed instead of or in addition to dealing with the offender in any other way.

SG-321 **Disqualification orders**

- The court may disqualify any person convicted of an offence from driving for such period as it thinks fit.[259] This may be instead of or in addition to dealing with the offender in any other way.
- The section does not require the offence to be connected to the use of a vehicle. The Court of Appeal has held that the power is available as part of the overall punitive element of a sentence, and the only restrictions on the exercise of the power are those in the statutory provision.[260]

SG-322 **Disqualification of company directors**

- The Company Directors Disqualification Act 1986 empowers the court to disqualify an offender from being a director or taking part in the promotion, formation or management of a company for up to five years.
- An order may be made in two situations:
  (1) where an offender has been convicted of an indictable offence in connection with the promotion, formation, management, liquidation or striking off of a company;[261] or
  (2) where an offender has been convicted of an offence involving a failure to file documents with, or give notice to, the registrar of companies. If the offence is triable only summarily, disqualification can be ordered only where the offender has been the subject of three default orders or convictions in the preceding five years.[262]

SG-323 **Drinking banning orders (when in force)**

- Where an offender is convicted of an offence which was committed while under the influence of alcohol, the court must consider whether a drinking banning order is necessary for the purpose of protecting others from further criminal or disorderly conduct by the offender while he or she is under the influence of alcohol.[263] If the court decides not to make such an order, it must state its reasons.
- A drinking banning order may impose any prohibition on the offender which is necessary for the purpose identified above, and must include such prohibition as the court considers necessary on the offender's entering licensed premises.[264]
- The court must specify the duration of the order, which must be between two months and two years.[265]

[258] ibid., s.34
[259] Powers of Criminal Courts (Sentencing) Act 2000., s.146
[260] *R v Sofekun* [2008] EWCA Crim 2035
[261] Company Directors Disqualification Act 1988, s.2
[262] ibid., s.5
[263] Violent Crime Reduction Act 2006, s.6
[264] ibid., s.1
[265] ibid., s.2

- The court may direct that the order will cease to have effect before the end of the specified period if the offender completes an approved course;[266] consult your legal adviser for guidance on this provision. The court is required to give reasons if it does not include such a direction in the order.

Exclusion orders SG-324

- The court may make an exclusion order where an offender has been convicted of an offence committed on licensed premises involving the use or threat of violence.
- The order prohibits the offender from entering specified licensed premises without the consent of the licensee.[267]
- The term of the order must be between three months and two years.
- Note that the provisions regarding exclusion orders will be repealed when the power to impose drinking banning orders is brought into force.

Football banning orders SG-325

- The court must make a football banning order where an offender has been convicted of a relevant offence and it is satisfied that there are reasonable grounds to believe that making a banning order would help to prevent violence or disorder.[268] If the court is not so satisfied, it must state that fact and give its reasons.
- Relevant offences are those set out in schedule 1 [to] the Football Spectators Act 1989. . .
- The order requires the offender to report to a police station within five days, may require the offender to surrender his or her passport, and may impose requirements on the offender in relation to any regulated football matches.
- Where the order is imposed in addition to a sentence of immediate imprisonment, the term of the order must be between six and ten years. In other cases, the term of the order must be between three and five years.

Forfeiture and destruction of drugs SG-326

- Where an offender is convicted of an offence under the Misuse of Drugs Act 1971, the court may order forfeiture and destruction of anything shown to the satisfaction of the court to relate to the offence.[269]

Forfeiture and destruction of goods bearing unauthorised trade mark SG-327

- Where the court is satisfied that an offence under section 92 of the Trade Marks Act 1994 has been committed, it must (on the application of a person who has come into possession of the goods in connection with the investigation or prosecution of the offence) order forfeiture of the goods.[270]
- If it considers it appropriate, instead of ordering destruction of the goods, the court may direct that they be released to a specified person on condition that the offending sign is erased, removed or obliterated.

Forfeiture or suspension of liquor licence SG-328

- Where an offender who holds a personal licence to supply alcohol is charged with a 'relevant offence', he or she is required to produce the licence to the court, or inform the court of its existence, no later than his or her first appearance.
- 'Relevant offences' are listed in schedule 4 of the Licensing Act 2003. . .
- Where the offender is convicted, the court may order forfeiture of the licence or suspend it for up to six months.[271] When deciding whether to order forfeiture or suspension, the court may take account of the offender's previous convictions for 'relevant offences'.[272]
- Whether or not forfeiture or suspension is ordered, the court is required to notify the licensing authority of the offender's conviction and the sentence imposed.

Parenting orders SG-329

- The court may make a parenting order where an offender has been convicted of an offence under section 444 of the Education Act 1996 (failing to secure regular attendance at school) and the court

[266] ibid., ss.2(3)–(8)
[267] Licensed Premises (Exclusion of Certain Persons) Act 1980, s.1
[268] Football Spectators Act 1989, s.14A
[269] Misuse of Drugs Act 1971, s.27(1)
[270] Trade Marks Act 1994, s.97
[271] Licensing Act 2003, s.129(2)
[272] ibid., s.129(3)

is satisfied that the order would be desirable in the interests of preventing the commission of any further offence under that section.[273]

- The order may impose such requirements that the court considers desirable in the interests of preventing the commission of a further offence under section 444.
- A requirement to attend a counselling or guidance programme may be included only if the offender has been the subject of a parenting order on a previous occasion.
- The term of the order must not exceed 12 months.

SG-330 **Restitution orders**

- Where goods have been stolen and an offender is convicted of any offence with reference to theft of those goods, the court may make a restitution order.[274]
- The court may:
  (1) order anyone in possession or control of the stolen goods to restore them to the victim;
  (2) on the application of the victim, order that goods directly or indirectly representing the stolen goods (as being the proceeds of any disposal or realisation of the stolen goods) be transferred to the victim; or
  (3) order that a sum not exceeding the value of the stolen goods be paid to the victim out of any money taken out of the offender's possession on his or her apprehension.

SG-331 **Restraining orders**

- Where an offender is convicted of harassment or conduct causing fear of violence, the court may make a restraining order.[275]
- The order may prohibit the offender from doing anything for the purpose of protecting the victim of the offence, or any other person mentioned in the order, from further conduct which amounts to harassment or will cause a fear of violence.[276]
- The order may have effect for a specified period or until further order.[277]
- When in force, section 5A of the Protection from Harassment Act 1997 will enable the court to make a restraining order in respect of an offender who has been acquitted of an offence if the court considers that it is necessary to protect a person from harassment. Consult your legal adviser for guidance.

SG-332 **Sexual offences prevention orders**

- The court may make a sexual offences prevention order where it deals with an offender in respect of an offence listed in schedules 3 or 5 [to] the Sexual Offences Act 2003. . .
- The court must be satisfied that the order is necessary to protect others from 'serious sexual harm' from the offender; the prohibitions in the order must also be necessary for this purpose.
- 'Serious sexual harm' means serious physical or psychological harm caused by the offender committing an offence listed in schedule 3 [to] the Sexual Offences Act 2003.
- The order may include only negative prohibitions; there is no power to impose positive obligations.
- The order must have effect for at least five years.

SG-333

Costs

1. Where an offender is convicted of an offence, the court has discretion to make such order as to costs as it considers just and reasonable.[278]
2. The Court of Appeal has given the following guidance:[279]
   - an order for costs should never exceed the sum which, having regard to the offender's means and any other financial order imposed, he or she is able to pay and which it is reasonable to order him or her to pay;
   - an order for costs should never exceed the sum which the prosecutor actually and reasonably incurred;
   - the purpose of the order is to compensate the prosecutor. Where the conduct of the defence has put the prosecutor to avoidable expense, the offender may be ordered to pay some or all of that sum to the prosecutor but the offender must not be punished for exercising the right to defend himself or herself;

[273] Crime and Disorder Act 1998, s.8
[274] Powers of Criminal Courts (Sentencing) Act 2000, s.148
[275] Protection from Harassment Act 1997, s.5
[276] ibid., s.5(2)
[277] ibid., s.5(3)
[278] Prosecution of Offences Act 1985, s.18
[279] *R v Northallerton Magistrates' Court, ex parte Dove* [2000] 1 Cr App R (S) 136 (CA)

- the costs ordered to be paid should not be grossly disproportionate to any fine imposed for the offence. This principle was affirmed in *BPS Advertising Limited v London Borough of Barnet*[280] in which the Court held that, while there is no question of an arithmetical relationship, the question of costs should be viewed in the context of the maximum penalty considered by Parliament to be appropriate for the seriousness of the offence;
- if the combined total of the proposed fine and the costs sought by the prosecutor exceeds the sum which the offender could reasonably be ordered to pay, the costs order should be reduced rather than the fine;
- it is for the offender to provide details of his or her financial position so as to enable the court to assess what he or she can reasonably afford to pay. If the offender fails to do so, the court is entitled to draw reasonable inferences as to means from all the circumstances of the case;
- if the court proposes to make any financial order against the offender, it must give him or her fair opportunity to adduce any relevant financial information and to make appropriate submissions.

3. A costs award may cover the costs of investigation as well as prosecution. However, where the investigation was carried out as part of a council officer's routine duties, for which he or she would have been paid in the normal way, this is a relevant factor to be taken into account when deciding the appropriate amount of any costs order.[281]
4. Where the court wishes to impose costs in addition to a fine, compensation and/or the victim surcharge but the offender has insufficient resources to pay the total amount, the order of priority is:
   i) compensation;
   ii) victim surcharge;
   iii) fine;
   iv) costs.

Sentencing Guidelines

Deferred Sentences SG-334

1. The court is empowered to defer passing sentence for up to six months.[282] The court may impose any conditions during the period of deferment that it considers appropriate. These could be specific requirements as set out in the provisions for community sentences, or requirements that are drawn more widely. The purpose of deferment is to enable the court to have regard to the offender's conduct after conviction or any change in his or her circumstances, including the extent to which the offender has complied with any requirements imposed by the court.
2. Three conditions must be satisfied before sentence can be deferred:
   - the offender must consent;
   - the offender must undertake to comply with requirements imposed by the court; and
   - the court must be satisfied that deferment is in the interests of justice.
3. Guidance regarding deferred sentences is set out in the Sentencing Guidelines Council's definitive guideline *New Sentences: Criminal Justice Act 2003*, published 16 December 2004 [see **part 2**]. The guideline emphasises that:
   - deferred sentences will be appropriate in very limited circumstances;
   - deferred sentences are likely to be relevant predominantly in a small group of cases close to either the community or custodial sentence threshold where, should the offender be prepared to adapt his behaviour in a way clearly specified by the sentencer, the court may be prepared to impose a lesser sentence;
   - sentencers should impose specific and measurable conditions that do not involve a serious restriction on liberty;
   - the court should give a clear indication of the type of sentence it would have imposed if it had decided not to defer;
   - the court should also ensure that the offender understands the consequences of failure to comply with the court's wishes during the deferment period.
4. If the offender fails to comply with any requirement imposed in connection with the deferment, or commits another offence, he or she can be brought back to court before the end of the deferment period and the court can proceed to sentence.

[280] [2006] EWCA 3335 (Admin) QBD
[281] ibid.
[282] Powers of Criminal Courts (Sentencing) Act 2000, s.1 as amended by Criminal Justice Act 2003, s.278 and sch.23, para.1

SG-335 Offences Committed in a Domestic Context

1. When sentencing an offence committed in a domestic context, refer to the Sentencing Guidelines Council's definitive guideline *Overarching Principles: Domestic Violence*, published 7 December 2006. [See **SG-51**.]

SG-336 Aggravation Related to Race, Religion, Disability or Sexual Orientation

SG-337 Racial or religious aggravation—statutory provisions

1. Sections 29 to 32 of the Crime and Disorder Act 1998 create specific racially or religiously aggravated offences, which have higher maximum penalties than the non-aggravated versions of those offences. The individual offence guidelines indicate whether there is a specifically aggravated form of the offence.
2. An offence is racially or religiously aggravated for the purposes of sections 29–32 of the Act if the offender demonstrates hostility towards the victim based on his or her membership (or presumed membership) of a racial or religious group, or if the offence is racially or religiously motivated.[283]
3. For all other offences, section 145 of the Criminal Justice Act 2003 provides that the court must regard racial or religious aggravation as an aggravating factor.
4. The court should not treat an offence as racially or religiously aggravated for the purposes of section 145 where a racially or religiously aggravated form of the offence was charged but resulted in an acquittal.[284] The court should not normally treat an offence as racially or religiously aggravated if a racially or religiously aggravated form of the offence was available but was not charged.[285] Consult your legal adviser for further guidance in these situations.

SG-338 Aggravation related to disability or sexual orientation—statutory provisions

5. Under section 146 of the Criminal Justice Act 2003, the court must treat as an aggravating factor the fact that:
   - an offender demonstrated hostility towards the victim based on his or her sexual orientation or disability (or presumed sexual orientation or disability); or
   - the offence was motivated by hostility towards persons who are of a particular sexual orientation or who have a particular disability.

SG-339 Approach to sentencing

6. A court should not conclude that offending involved aggravation related to race, religion, disability or sexual orientation without first putting the offender on notice and allowing him or her to challenge the allegation.
7. When sentencing any offence where such aggravation is found to be present, the following approach should be followed. This applies both to the specific racially or religiously aggravated offences under the Crime and Disorder Act 1998 and to offences which are regarded as aggravated under section 145 or 146 of the Criminal Justice Act 2003:[286]
   - sentencers should first determine the appropriate sentence, leaving aside the element of aggravation related to race, religion, disability or sexual orientation but taking into account all other aggravating or mitigating factors;
   - the sentence should then be increased to take account of the aggravation related to race, religion, disability or sexual orientation;
   - the increase may mean that a more onerous penalty of the same type is appropriate, or that the threshold for a more severe type of sentence is passed;
   - the sentencer must state in open court that the offence was aggravated by reason of race, religion, disability or sexual orientation;
   - the sentencer should state what the sentence would have been without that element of aggravation.
8. The extent to which the sentence is increased will depend on the seriousness of the aggravation. The following factors could be taken as indicating a high level of aggravation:

SG-340 Offender's intention

- The element of aggravation based on race, religion, disability or sexual orientation was planned

---

[283] Crime and Disorder Act 1988, s.28

[284] Refer to *R v McGillivray* [2005] EWCA Crim 604 (CA)

[285] Refer to *R v O'Callaghan* [2005] EWCA Crim 317 (CA)

[286] Refer to *R v Kelly and Donnelly* [2001] EWCA Crim 170 in which the Court considered the approach to sentencing in cases involving racial or religious aggravation

- The offence was part of a pattern of offending by the offender
- The offender was a member of, or was associated with, a group promoting hostility based on race, religion, disability or sexual orientation
- The incident was deliberately set up to be offensive or humiliating to the victim or to the group of which the victim is a member

Impact on the victim or others SG-341

- The offence was committed in the victim's home
- The victim was providing a service to the public
- The timing or location of the offence was calculated to maximise the harm or distress it caused
- The expressions of hostility were repeated or prolonged
- The offence caused fear and distress throughout a local community or more widely
- The offence caused particular distress to the victim and/or the victim's family.

9. At the lower end of the scale, the aggravation may be regarded as less serious if:
   - It was limited in scope or duration
   - The offence was not motivated by hostility on the basis of race, religion, disability or sexual orientation, and the element of hostility or abuse was minor or incidental
10. In these guidelines, the specific racially or religiously aggravated offences under the Crime and Disorder Act 1998 are addressed on the same page as the 'basic offence'; the starting points and ranges indicated on the guideline relate to the 'basic' (i.e. non-aggravated) offence. The increase for the element of racial or religious aggravation may result in a sentence above the range; this will not constitute a departure from the guideline for which reasons must be given.

Environmental/Health and Safety Offences SG-342

[Omitted.]

Road Traffic Offences SG-343

Disqualification SG-344

Obligatory disqualification

1. Some offences carry obligatory disqualification for a minimum of 12 months.[287] The minimum period is automatically increased where there have been certain previous convictions and disqualifications.
2. An offender must be disqualified for *at least two years* if he or she has been disqualified two or more times for a period of at least 56 days in the three years preceding the commission of the offence.[288] The following disqualifications are to be disregarded for the purposes of this provision:
   - interim disqualification;
   - disqualification where vehicle used for the purpose of crime;
   - disqualification for stealing or taking a vehicle or going equipped to steal or take a vehicle.
3. An offender must be disqualified for *at least three years* if he or she is convicted of one of the following offences *and* has within the ten years preceding the commission of the offence been convicted of any of these offences:[289]
   - causing death by careless driving when under the influence of drink or drugs;
   - driving or attempting to drive while unfit;
   - driving or attempting to drive with excess alcohol;
   - failing to provide a specimen (drive/attempting to drive).
4. The individual offence guidelines above indicate whether disqualification is mandatory for the offence and the applicable minimum period. Consult your legal adviser for further guidance.

[287] Road Traffic Offenders Act 1988, s.34
[288] ibid., s.34(4)
[289] ibid., s.34(3)

5. The period of disqualification may be reduced or avoided if there are special reasons.[290] These must relate to the offence; circumstances peculiar to the offender cannot constitute special reasons.[291] The Court of Appeal has established that, to constitute a special reason, a matter must:[292]
    - be a mitigating or extenuating circumstance;
    - not amount in law to a defence to the charge;
    - be directly connected with the commission of the offence;
    - be one which the court ought properly to take into consideration when imposing sentence.
6. Consult your legal adviser for further guidance on special reasons applications.

'Totting up' disqualification

7. Disqualification for a *minimum* of six months must be ordered if an offender incurs 12 penalty points or more within a three-year period.[293] The minimum period may be automatically increased if the offender has been disqualified within the preceding three years. Totting up disqualifications, unlike other disqualifications, erase all penalty points.
8. The period of a totting up disqualification can be reduced or avoided for exceptional hardship or other mitigating circumstances. No account is to be taken of hardship that is not exceptional hardship or circumstances alleged to make the offence not serious. Any circumstances taken into account in the preceding three years to reduce or avoid a totting disqualification must be disregarded.[294]
9. Consult your legal adviser for further guidance on exceptional hardship applications.

Discretionary disqualification

10. Whenever an offender is convicted of an endorsable offence or of taking a vehicle without consent, the court has a discretionary power to disqualify instead of imposing penalty points. The individual offence guidelines above indicate whether the offence is endorsable and the number or range of penalty points it carries.
11. The number of variable points or the period of disqualification should reflect the seriousness of the offence. Some of the individual offence guidelines above include penalty points and/or periods of disqualification in the sentence starting points and ranges; however, the court is not precluded from sentencing outside the range where the facts justify it. Where a disqualification is for less than 56 days, there are some differences in effect compared with disqualification for a longer period; in particular, the licence will automatically come back into effect at the end of the disqualification period (instead of requiring application by the driver) and the disqualification is not taken into account for the purpose of increasing subsequent obligatory periods of disqualification.[295]
12. In some cases in which the court is considering discretionary disqualification, the offender may already have sufficient penalty points on his or her licence that he or she would be liable to a 'totting up' disqualification if further points were imposed. In these circumstances, the court should impose penalty points rather than discretionary disqualification so that the minimum totting up disqualification period applies (see paragraph 7 above).

Disqualification until a test is passed

13. Where an offender is convicted of dangerous driving, the court must order disqualification until an extended driving test is passed.
14. The court has discretion to disqualify until a test is passed where an offender is convicted of any endorsable offence.[296] Where disqualification is obligatory, the extended test applies. In other cases, it will be the ordinary test.
15. An offender disqualified as a 'totter' under the penalty points provisions may also be ordered to re-take a driving test; in this case, the extended test applies.
16. The discretion to order a re-test is likely to be exercised where there is evidence of inexperience, incompetence or infirmity, or the disqualification period is lengthy (that is, the offender is going to be 'off the road' for a considerable time).

---

[290] ibid., s.34(1)
[291] *Whittal v Kirby* [1946] 2 All ER 552 (CA)
[292] *R v Wickens* (1958) 42 Cr App R 436 (CA)
[293] Road Traffic Offenders Act 1988, s.35
[294] ibid.
[295] ibid., ss.34(4), 35(2), 37(1A)
[296] ibid., s.36(4)

Reduced period of disqualification for completion of rehabilitation course

17. Where an offender is disqualified for 12 months or more in respect of an alcohol-related driving offence, the court may order that the period of disqualification will be reduced if the offender satisfactorily completes an approved rehabilitation course.[297]
18. Before offering an offender the opportunity to attend a course, the court must be satisfied that an approved course is available and must inform the offender of the effect of the order, the fees that the offender is required to pay, and when he or she must pay them.
19. The court should also explain that the offender may be required to satisfy the Secretary of State that he or she does not have a drink problem and is fit to drive before the offender's licence will be returned at the end of the disqualification period.[298]
20. In general, a court should consider offering the opportunity to attend a course to all offenders convicted of a relevant offence for the first time. The court should be willing to consider offering an offender the opportunity to attend a second course where it considers there are good reasons. It will not usually be appropriate to give an offender the opportunity to attend a third course.
21. The reduction must be at least three months but cannot be more than one quarter of the total period of disqualification:
    - a period of 12 months disqualification must be reduced to nine months;
    - in other cases, a reduction of one week should be made for every month of the disqualification so that, for example, a disqualification of 24 months will be reduced by 24 weeks.
22. When it makes the order, the court must specify a date for completion of the course which is at least two months before the end of the reduced period of disqualification.

Disqualification in the offender's absence

23. A court is able to disqualify an offender in absence provided that he or she has been given adequate notice of the hearing and that disqualification is to be considered.[299] It is recommended, however, that the court should avoid exercising this power wherever possible unless it is sure that the offender is aware of the hearing and the likely imposition of disqualification. This is because an offender who is disqualified in absence commits an offence by driving from the time the order is made, even if he or she has not yet received notification of it, and, as a result of the disqualification, is likely to be uninsured in relation to any injury or damage caused.

New drivers SG-345

24. Drivers who incur six points or more during the two-year probationary period after passing the driving test will have their licence revoked automatically by the Secretary of State; they will be able to drive only after application for a provisional licence pending the passing of a further test.[300]
25. An offender liable for an endorsement which will cause the licence to be revoked under the new drivers' provisions may ask the court to disqualify rather than impose points. This will avoid the requirement to take a further test. Generally, this would be inappropriate since it would circumvent the clear intention of Parliament.

Dangerous Offenders SG-346

1. The Criminal Justice Act 2003 established a new regime for dealing with dangerous offenders. The provisions apply where an offender is convicted of a specified violent or sexual offence. They have been substantially amended by the Criminal Justice and Immigration Act 2008.
2. Specified offences are listed in schedule 15 to the Act and include affray, assault occasioning actual bodily harm, putting people in fear of violence, sexual assault and violent disorder. The individual offence guidelines above indicate whether the offence is specified under the Act. A specified offence which (in the case of a person aged 18 years or over) is punishable with a maximum of life imprisonment or imprisonment for 10 years or more is defined as a 'serious offence'.
3. Where an offender is convicted of a specified offence that is not a 'serious offence', the court may impose an extended sentence of imprisonment.
4. Where an offender is convicted of a specified offence that is a 'serious offence', the court may impose a life sentence (where that is the maximum sentence for the offence), imprisonment for public protection or an extended sentence of imprisonment.

[297] Road Traffic Offenders Act 1988, s.34A
[298] Road Traffic Act 1988, s.94 and Motor Vehicles (Driving Licences) Regulations 1999, reg.74
[299] Magistrates' Courts Act 1980, s.11(4)
[300] Road Traffic (New Drivers) Act 1995

5. All these sentences may be imposed only in the Crown Court and only if the court is satisfied that there is a significant risk of serious harm from the offender committing a further specified offence. Even in such circumstances, a court has a discretion whether or not to impose a sentence under the dangerous offender provisions.
6. A significant change has been the requirement that (except where the offender has a previous conviction for one of the offences listed in schedule 15A to the 2003 Act)[301] a sentence under these provisions may be imposed only if the equivalent determinate sentence would have been at least 4 years.
7. Accordingly, it is very unlikely that a magistrates' court will need to consider these provisions specifically since an offence likely to result in a sentence of 4 years or more will be committed for trial or sentence under other provisions.
8. Consult your legal adviser for further guidance.

SG-347

Informal Warnings, Cannabis Warnings and Simple Cautions

1. There are several alternatives to formal charges available to police, including informal warnings, cannabis warnings and simple cautions.
2. A cannabis warning may be given where the offender is found in possession of a small amount of cannabis consistent with personal use and the offender admits the elements of the offence.
3. A simple caution may be issued where there is evidence that the offender has committed an offence, the offender admits to the offence, and the offender agrees to being given the caution.
4. When sentencing an offender who has received a warning or simple caution on a previous occasion:
   - the warning or simple caution is not a previous conviction and, therefore, is not a statutory aggravating factor;
   - the earlier warning or simple caution does not increase the seriousness of the current offence.

SG-348

Conditional Cautions

1. The Criminal Justice Act 2003 empowers the Crown Prosecution Service to issue a conditional caution, which requires an offender to comply with rehabilitative and/or reparative conditions, as an alternative to prosecution. Before the caution can be given, the offender must admit the offence and consent to the conditions.

Approach to sentencing for offence for which offender was cautioned but failed to comply with conditions

2. If the offender fails, without reasonable cause, to comply with the conditional caution, he or she may be prosecuted for the original offence. When sentencing in such a case:
   - the offender's non-compliance with the conditional caution does not increase the seriousness of the original offence and must not be regarded as an aggravating factor;
   - the offender's non-compliance may be relevant to selection of the type of sentence. For example, it may indicate that it is inappropriate to include certain requirements as part of a community order. The circumstances of the offender's failure to satisfy the conditions, and any partial compliance, will be relevant to this assessment.

Approach to sentencing for later offence where offender has had a previous conditional caution

3. When sentencing an offender who has received a conditional caution in respect of an earlier offence:
   - a conditional caution is not a previous conviction and, therefore, is not a statutory aggravating factor;
   - the earlier conditional caution does not increase the level of seriousness of the current offence;
   - nevertheless, the offender's response to the caution may properly influence the court's assessment of the offender's suitability for a particular sentence, so long as it remains within the limits established by the seriousness of the current offence.

SG-349

Penalty Notices—Fixed Penalty Notices and Penalty Notices for Disorder

1. Penalty notices may be issued as an alternative to prosecution in respect of a range of offences. Unlike conditional cautions, an admission of guilt is not a prerequisite to issuing a penalty notice.

[301] as inserted by Schedule 5 to the Criminal Justice and Immigration Act 2008

2. An offender who is issued with a penalty notice may nevertheless be prosecuted for the offence if he or she:
   - asks to be tried for the offence;
   - fails to pay the penalty within the period stipulated in the notice and the prosecutor decides to proceed with charges.[302]

Approach to sentencing for offence for which penalty notice was available

3. When sentencing in cases in which a penalty notice was available:
   - the fact that the offender did not take advantage of the penalty (whether that was by requesting a hearing or failing to pay within the specified timeframe) does not increase the seriousness of the offence and must not be regarded as an aggravating factor. The appropriate sentence must be determined in accordance with the sentencing principles set out above (including the amount of any fine, which must take an offender's financial circumstances into account), disregarding the availability of the penalty;
   - where a penalty notice was not offered or taken up for reasons unconnected with the offence itself, such as administrative difficulties, the starting point should be a fine equivalent to the amount of the penalty and no order of costs should be imposed. The offender should not be disadvantaged by the unavailability of the penalty notice in these circumstances. A list of offences for which penalty notices are available, and the amount of the penalty, is set out in Annex B.

Approach to sentencing for later offence where offender has had previous penalty notices

4. The fact that an offender has previously been issued with a penalty notice does not increase the seriousness of the current offence and must not be regarded as an aggravating factor. It may, however, properly influence the court's assessment of the offender's suitability for a particular sentence, so long as it remains within the limits established by the seriousness of the current offence.

Pre-sentence Reports SG-350

1. The purpose of a pre-sentence report ('PSR') is to provide information to help the court decide on the most suitable sentence. In relation to an offender aged 18 or over, unless the court considers a report to be unnecessary, it is required to request a report before deciding:
   - that the community or custody threshold is passed;
   - what is the shortest term of a custodial sentence that is commensurate with the seriousness of the offence;
   - whether the restrictions on liberty within a community order are commensurate with the seriousness of the offence; and
   - whether the requirements are suitable for the offender.[303]
2. A report should not normally be requested where the court considers that it is appropriate to impose a fine.
3. A report may be oral or written.
4. Written reports may be either:

Fast delivery reports ('FDR') SG-351

- Completed without a full OASys assessment.
- Where community orders are being considered, generally appropriate for low or medium seriousness cases and may be appropriate in some high seriousness cases.
- Should normally be available within 24 hours.

Standard delivery reports ('SDR') SG-352

- Based on a full OASys assessment.
- Generally appropriate where a custodial sentence is being considered, although in some straightforward cases a fast delivery PSR may be sufficient.
- Where community orders are being considered, generally appropriate for high seriousness cases.
- Should normally be available within 15 working days; 10 working days if the offender is in custody.

[302] In some cases of non-payment, the penalty is automatically registered and enforceable as a fine without need for recourse to the courts. This procedure applies to penalty notices for disorder and fixed penalty notices issued in respect of certain road traffic offences but not to fixed penalty notices issued for most other criminal offences

[303] Criminal Justice Act 2003, ss.156(3) and 156(4)

Probation staff are able to determine the most appropriate type of report based on the circumstances of the case and the requirements of the court.

5. Every report should contain:[304]
   - basic facts about the offender and the sources used to prepare the report;
   - an offence analysis;
   - an assessment of the offender;
   - an assessment of the risk of harm to the public and the likelihood of re-offending;
   - a sentencing proposal.

SG-353

Victim Personal Statements

1. Victim personal statements give victims a formal opportunity to say how a crime has affected them. Where the victim has chosen to make such a statement, a court should consider and take it into account prior to passing sentence.
2. The Consolidated Criminal Practice Direction (as amended March 2007) emphasises that:
   - evidence of the effects of an offence on the victim must be in the form of a witness statement under section 9 of the Criminal Justice Act 1967 or an expert's report;
   - the statement must be served on the defence prior to sentence;
   - except where inferences can properly be drawn from the nature of or circumstances surrounding the offence, the court must not make assumptions unsupported by evidence about the effects of an offence on the victim;
   - the court must pass what it judges to be the appropriate sentence having regard to the circumstances of the offence and the offender, taking into account, so far as the court considers it appropriate, the consequences to the victim;
   - the opinions of the victim or the victim's close relatives as to what the sentence should be are not relevant.
3. For cases involving sexual offences, see also page 165 regarding the relevance of the victim's views to any compensation order that may be imposed.

SG-354

Annex A: Availability of Ancillary Orders

[Annex A consists of a list of offences covered in the MCSG for which particular ancillary orders are available and is omitted. For guidance on the various available ancillary orders, see the relevant material in the main work.]

SG-355

Annex B: Offences for which Penalty Notices are Available

The tables below list the offences covered in the MCSG for which penalty notices are available and the amount of the penalty. Consult your legal adviser for further guidance.

SG-356 **Penalty notices for disorder**

Offence	Legislation	Amount
Criminal damage (where damage under £500 in value, and not normally where damage over £300)	Criminal Damage Act 1971, s.1	£80
Disorderly behaviour	Public Order Act 1986, s.5	£80
Drunk and disorderly	Criminal Justice Act 1967, s.91	£80
Sale of alcohol to drunk person on relevant premises (not including off-licenses)	Licensing Act 2003, s.141	£80
Sale of alcohol to person under 18 (staff only; licensees should be subject of a summons)	Licensing Act 2003, s.146	£80
Theft from a shop (where goods under £200 in value, and not normally where goods over £100)	Theft Act 1968, s.1	£80

[304] Probation Bench Handbook (2005)

Fixed penalty notices SG-357

Offence	Legislation	Amount	Penalty points
Brakes, steering or tyres defective	Road Traffic Act 1988, s.41A	£60	3
Breach of other construction and use requirements	Road Traffic Act 1988, s.42	£60	3
Driving other than in accordance with licence	Road Traffic Act 1988, s.87(1)	£60	3
Failing to comply with police officer signal	Road Traffic Act 1988, s.35	£30	3
Failing to comply with traffic sign	Road Traffic Act 1988, s.36	£60	3
Failing to supply details of driver's identity	Road Traffic Act 1988, s.172	£120	6
No insurance	Road Traffic Act 1988, s.143	£200	6
No test certificate	Road Traffic Act 1988, s.47	£30	–
Overloading/exceeding axle weight	Road Traffic Act 1988, s.41B	£30	–
Pelican/zebra crossing contravention	Road Traffic Regulation Act 1984, s.25(5)	£60	3
Railway fare evasion (where penalty notice scheme in operation by train operator)	Railways (Penalty Fares) Regulations 1994	£20 or twice the full single fare to next stop, whichever is greater	–
Seat belt offences	Road Traffic Act 1988, s.14	£30	–
School non-attendance	Education Act 1996, s.444(1)	£50 if paid within 28 days; £100 if paid within 42 days	–
Speeding	Road Traffic Regulation Act 1984, s.89(1)	£60	3
Using hand-held mobile phone while driving	Road Traffic Act 1988, s.41D	£60	3
Using vehicle in dangerous condition	Road Traffic Act 1988, s.40A	£60	3

PART 13 CAUSING DEATH BY DRIVING SG-358

Foreword

. . . This guideline applies to the sentencing of offenders convicted of any of the offences dealt with herein who are sentenced on or after **4 August 2008**.

This guideline applies only to the sentencing of offenders aged 18 and older. The legislative provisions relating to the sentencing of youths are different; the younger the age, the greater the difference. A separate guideline setting out general principles relating to the sentencing of youths is planned.

. . .

Introduction SG-359

1. This guideline applies to the four offences of *causing death by dangerous driving, causing death by driving under the influence of alcohol or drugs, causing death by careless driving and causing death by driving: unlicensed, disqualified or uninsured drivers.*
2. The Crown Prosecution Service's *Policy for Prosecuting Cases of Bad Driving* sets out the approach for prosecutors when considering the appropriate charge based on an assessment of the standard of the offender's driving. This has been taken into account when formulating this guideline. Annex A sets out the statutory definitions for dangerous, careless and inconsiderate driving together with examples of the types of driving behaviour likely to result in the charge of one offence rather than another.

3. Because the principal harm done by these offences (the death of a person) is an element of the offence, the factor that primarily determines the starting point for sentence is the culpability of the offender. Accordingly, for all offences other than *causing death by driving: unlicensed, disqualified or uninsured drivers*, the central feature should be an evaluation of the quality of the driving involved and the degree of danger that it foreseeably created. These guidelines draw a distinction between those factors of an offence that are intrinsic to the quality of driving (referred to as 'determinants of seriousness') and those which, while they aggravate the offence, are not.
4. The levels of seriousness in the guidelines for those offences based on dangerous or careless driving alone have been determined by reference *only* to determinants of seriousness. Aggravating factors will have the effect of either increasing the starting point within the sentencing range provided or, in certain circumstances, of moving the offence up to the next sentencing range. The outcome will depend on both the number of aggravating factors present and the potency of those factors. Thus, the same outcome could follow from the presence of one particularly bad aggravating factor or two or more less serious factors.
5. The determinants of seriousness likely to be relevant in relation to *causing death by careless driving under the influence* are both the degree of carelessness and the level of intoxication. The guideline sets out an approach to assessing both those aspects but giving greater weight to the degree of intoxication since Parliament has provided for a maximum of 14 years imprisonment rather than the maximum of 5 years where the death is caused by careless driving only.
6. Since there will be no allegation of bad driving, the guideline for *causing death by driving; unlicensed, disqualified or uninsured drivers* links the assessment of offender culpability to the nature of the prohibition on the offender's driving and includes a list of factors that may aggravate an offence.
7. The degree to which an aggravating factor is present (and its interaction with any other aggravating and mitigating factors) will be immensely variable and the court is best placed to judge the appropriate impact on sentence. Clear identification of those factors relating to the standard of driving as the initial determinants of offence seriousness is intended to assist the adoption of a common approach.

SG-360 **A. Assessing seriousness**

(i) Determinants of seriousness

8. There are five factors that may be regarded as determinants of offence seriousness, each of which can be demonstrated in a number of ways. Common examples of each of the determinants are set out below and key issues are discussed in the text that follows . . .

   Examples of the determinants are:

   - *Awareness of risk*
     (a) a prolonged, persistent and deliberate course of very bad driving
   - *Effect of alcohol or drugs*
     (b) consumption of alcohol above the legal limit
     (c) consumption of alcohol at or below the legal limit where this impaired the offender's ability to drive
     (d) failure to supply a specimen for analysis
     (e) consumption of illegal drugs, where this impaired the offender's ability to drive
     (f) consumption of legal drugs or medication where this impaired the offender's ability to drive (including legal medication known to cause drowsiness) where the driver knew, or should have known, about the likelihood of impairment
   - *Inappropriate speed of vehicle*
     (g) greatly excessive speed; racing; competitive driving against another vehicle
     (h) driving above the speed limit
     (i) driving at a speed that is inappropriate for the prevailing road or weather conditions
     (j) driving a PSV, HGV or other goods vehicle at a speed that is inappropriate either because of the nature of the vehicle or its load, especially when carrying passengers
   - *Seriously culpable behaviour of offender*
     (k) aggressive driving (such as driving much too close to the vehicle in front, persistent inappropriate attempts to overtake, or cutting in after overtaking)
     (l) driving while using a hand-held mobile phone
     (m) driving whilst the driver's attention is avoidably distracted, for example by reading or adjusting the controls of electronic equipment such as a radio, hands-free mobile phone or satellite navigation equipment
     (n) driving when knowingly suffering from a medical or physical condition that significantly impairs the offender's driving skills, including failure to take prescribed medication

(o) driving when knowingly deprived of adequate sleep or rest, especially where commercial concerns had a bearing on the commission of the offence
(p) driving a poorly maintained or dangerously loaded vehicle, especially where commercial concerns had a bearing on the commission of the offence

- *Victim*
  (q) failing to have proper regard to vulnerable road users

9. Issues relating to the determinants of seriousness are considered below.

(a) Alcohol/drugs

10. For those offences where the presence of alcohol or drugs is not an element of the offence, where there is sufficient evidence of driving impairment attributable to alcohol or drugs, the consumption of alcohol or drugs prior to driving will make an offence more serious. Where the drugs were legally purchased or prescribed, the offence will only be regarded as more serious if the offender knew or should have known that the drugs were likely to impair driving ability.
11. Unless inherent in the offence or charged separately, failure to provide a specimen for analysis (or to allow a blood specimen taken without consent to be analysed) should be regarded as a determinant of offence seriousness.
12. Where it is established to the satisfaction of the court that an offender had consumed alcohol or drugs unwittingly before driving, that may be regarded as a mitigating factor. However, consideration should be given to the circumstances in which the offender decided to drive or continue to drive when driving ability was impaired.

(b) Avoidable distractions

13. A distinction has been drawn between **ordinary** avoidable distractions and those that are more significant because they divert the attention of the driver for longer periods or to a greater extent; in this guideline these are referred to as a **gross** avoidable distraction. The guideline for causing *death by dangerous driving* provides for a gross avoidable distraction to place the offence in a higher level of seriousness.
14. Any avoidable distraction will make an offence more serious but the degree to which an offender's driving will be impaired will vary. Where the reaction to the distraction is significant, it may be the factor that determines whether the offence is based on *dangerous* driving or on *careless* driving; in those circumstances, care must be taken to avoid 'double counting'.
15. Using a hand-held mobile phone when driving is, in itself, an unlawful act; the fact that an offender was avoidably distracted by using a hand-held mobile phone when a causing death by driving offence was committed will always make an offence more serious. Reading or composing text messages *over a period of time will be a gross* avoidable distraction and is likely to result in an offence of causing death by dangerous driving being in a higher level of seriousness.
16. Where it is proved that an offender was briefly distracted by reading a text message or adjusting a hands-free set or its controls at the time of the collision, this would be on a par with consulting a map or adjusting a radio or satellite navigation equipment, activities that would be considered an avoidable distraction.

(c) Vulnerable road users

17. Cyclists, motorbike riders, horse riders, pedestrians and those working in the road are vulnerable road users and a driver is expected to take extra care when driving near them. Driving too close to a bike or horse; allowing a vehicle to mount the pavement; driving into a cycle lane; and driving without the care needed in the vicinity of a pedestrian crossing, hospital, school or residential home, are all examples of factors that should be taken into account when determining the seriousness of an offence. See paragraph 24 below for the approach where the actions of another person contributed to the collision.
18. The fact that the victim of a causing death by driving offence was a particularly vulnerable road user is a factor that should be taken into account when determining the seriousness of an offence.

(ii) Aggravating and mitigating factors

(a) More than one person killed

19. The seriousness of any offence included in these guidelines will generally be greater where more than one person is killed since it is inevitable that the degree of harm will be greater. In relation to the assessment of culpability, whilst there will be circumstances in which a driver could reasonably anticipate the possible death of more than one person (for example, the driver of a vehicle with passengers (whether that is a bus, taxi or private car) or a person driving badly in an area where there are many

people), there will be many circumstances where the driver could not anticipate the number of people who would be killed.

20. The greater obligation on those responsible for driving other people is not an element essential to the quality of the driving and so has not been included amongst the determinants of seriousness that affect the choice of sentencing range. In practical terms, separate charges are likely to be brought in relation to each death caused. Although concurrent sentences are likely to be imposed (in recognition of the fact that the charges relate to one episode of offending behaviour), each individual sentence is likely to be higher because the offence is aggravated by the fact that more than one death has been caused.
21. Where more than one person is killed, that will aggravate the seriousness of the offence because of the increase in harm. Where the number of people killed is high *and* that was reasonably foreseeable, the number of deaths is likely to provide sufficient justification for moving an offence into the next highest sentencing band.

(b) Effect on offender

22. Injury to the offender may be a mitigating factor when the offender has suffered very serious injuries. In most circumstances, the weighting it is given will be dictated by the circumstances of the offence and the effect should bear a direct relationship to the extent to which the offender's driving was at fault—the greater the fault, the less the effect on mitigation; this distinction will be of particular relevance where an offence did not involve any fault in the offender's standard of driving.
23. Where one or more of the victims was in a close personal or family relationship with the offender, this may be a mitigating factor. In line with the approach where the offender is very seriously injured, the degree to which the relationship influences the sentence should be linked to offender culpability in relation to the commission of the offence; mitigation for this reason is likely to have less effect where the culpability of the driver is particularly high.

(c) Actions of others

24. Where the actions of the victim or a third party contributed to the commission of an offence, this should be acknowledged and taken into account as a mitigating factor.

(d) Offender's age/lack of driving experience

25. The Council guideline *Overarching Principles: Seriousness* [see **SG-21**] includes a generic mitigating factor '*youth or age, where it affects the responsibility of the individual defendant*'. There is a great deal of difference between recklessness or irresponsibility—which may be due to youth—and inexperience in dealing with prevailing conditions or an unexpected or unusual situation that presents itself—which may be present regardless of the age of the offender. The fact that an offender's lack of driving experience contributed to the commission of an offence should be treated as a mitigating factor; in this regard, the age of the offender is not relevant.

(iii) Personal mitigation

(a) Good driving record

26. This is not a factor that automatically should be treated as a mitigating factor, especially now that the presence of previous convictions is a statutory aggravating factor. However, any evidence to show that an offender has previously been an exemplary driver, for example having driven an ambulance, police vehicle, bus, taxi or similar vehicle conscientiously and without incident for many years, is a fact that the courts may well wish to take into account by way of personal mitigation. This is likely to have even greater effect where the driver is driving on public duty (for example, on ambulance, fire services or police duties) and was responding to an emergency.

(b) Conduct after the offence

—Giving assistance at the scene

27. There may be many reasons why an offender does not offer help to the victims at the scene—the offender may be injured, traumatised by shock, afraid of causing further injury or simply have no idea what action to take—and it would be inappropriate to assess the offence as more serious on this ground (and so increase the level of sentence). However, where an offender gave direct, positive, assistance to victim(s) at the scene of a collision, this should be regarded as personal mitigation.

—Remorse

28. Whilst it can be expected that anyone who has caused death by driving would be expected to feel remorseful, this cannot undermine its importance for sentencing purposes. Remorse is identified as

personal mitigation in [*Overarching Principles: Seriousness*: see **SG-21**] and the Council can see no reason for it to be treated differently for this group of offences. It is for the court to determine whether an expression of remorse is genuine; where it is, this should be taken into account as personal mitigation.

(c) Summary

29. Evidence that an offender is normally a careful and conscientious driver, giving direct, positive assistance to a victim and genuine remorse may be taken into account as personal mitigation and may justify a reduction in sentence.

B. Ancillary orders **SG-361**

(i) Disqualification for driving

30. For each offence, disqualification is a mandatory part of the sentence (subject to the usual (very limited) exceptions), and therefore an important element of the overall punishment for the offence. In addition, an order that the disqualification continues until the offender passes an extended driving test order is compulsory[305] for those convicted of causing death by dangerous driving or by careless driving when under the influence, and discretionary[306] in relation to the two other offences.
31. Any disqualification is effective from the date on which it is imposed. When ordering disqualification from driving, the duration of the order should allow for the length of any custodial period in order to ensure that the disqualification has the desired impact. In principle, the minimum period of disqualification should either equate to the length of the custodial sentence imposed (in the knowledge that the offender is likely to be released having served half of that term), or the relevant statutory minimum disqualification period, whichever results in the longer period of disqualification.

(ii) Deprivation order

32. A general sentencing power exists which enables courts to deprive an offender of property used for the purposes of committing an offence.[307] A vehicle used to commit an offence included in this guideline can be regarded as being used for the purposes of committing the offence.

C. Sentencing ranges and starting points **SG-362**

1. Typically, a guideline will apply to an offence that can be committed in a variety of circumstances with different levels of seriousness. It will apply to a first-time offender who has been convicted after a trial. Within the guidelines, a first-time offender is a person who does not have a conviction which, by virtue of section 143(2) of the CJA 2003, must be treated as an aggravating factor.
2. As an aid to consistency of approach, the guidelines describe a number of types of activity which would fall within the broad definition of the offence. These are set out in a column headed 'Type/nature of activity'.
3. The expected approach is for a court to identify the description that most nearly matches the particular facts of the offence for which sentence is being imposed. This will identify a starting point from which the sentencer can depart to reflect aggravating or mitigating factors affecting the seriousness of the offence (beyond those contained within the column describing the type or nature of offence activity) to reach a provisional sentence.
4. The *sentencing range* is the bracket into which the provisional sentence will normally fall after having regard to factors which aggravate or mitigate the seriousness of the offence. The particular circumstances may, however, make it appropriate that the provisional sentence falls outside the range.
5. Where the offender has previous convictions which aggravate the seriousness of the current offence, that may take the provisional sentence beyond the range given, particularly where there are significant other aggravating factors present.
6. Once the provisional sentence has been identified by reference to those factors affecting the seriousness of the offence, the court will take into account any relevant factors of personal mitigation, which may take the sentence outside the range indicated in the guideline.
7. Where there has been a guilty plea, any reduction attributable to that plea will be applied to the sentence at this stage. This reduction may take the sentence below the range provided.
8. A court must give its reasons for imposing a sentence of a different kind or outside the range provided in the guidelines.[308]

[305] Road Traffic Offenders Act 1988, s. 36(1)
[306] ibid., s. 36(4)
[307] Powers of Criminal Courts (Sentencing) Act 2000, s. 143
[308] Criminal Justice Act 2003, s. 174(2)(a)

The decision making process

The process set out below is intended to show that the sentencing approach for offences of causing death by driving is fluid and requires the structured exercise of discretion.

[Sets out the standard decision making process: identify dangerous offenders, identify starting point, consider aggravating factors, consider mitigating factors, apply reduction for guilty plea, consider ancillary orders, review in light of totality principle and give reasons.]

SG-363 **D. Offence guidelines**

Causing death by dangerous driving
Factors to take into consideration

1. The following guideline applies to a 'first-time offender' aged 18 or over convicted after trial (see . . . above), who has not been assessed as a dangerous offender requiring a sentence under ss. 224–228 Criminal Justice Act 2003 (as amended).
2. When assessing the seriousness of any offence, the court must always refer to the full list of aggravating and mitigating factors in the Council guideline on Seriousness[309] as well as those set out in the adjacent table as being particularly relevant to this type of offending behaviour.

3. Levels of seriousness

The 3 levels are distinguished by factors related predominantly to the standard of driving; the general description of the degree of risk is complemented by examples of the type of bad driving arising. The presence of aggravating factors or combinations of a small number of determinants of seriousness will increase the starting point within the range. Where there is a larger group of determinants of seriousness and/or aggravating factors, this may justify moving the starting point to the next level.

Level 1—The most serious offences encompassing driving that involved a deliberate decision to ignore (or a flagrant disregard for) the rules of the road and an apparent disregard for the great danger being caused to others. Such offences are likely to be characterised by:

- *A prolonged, persistent and deliberate course of very bad driving* ***AND/OR***
- *Consumption of substantial amounts of alcohol or drugs leading to gross impairment* ***AND/OR***
- *A group of determinants of seriousness which in isolation or smaller number would place the offence in level 2*

Level 1 is that for which the increase in maximum penalty was aimed primarily. Where an offence involves both of the determinants of seriousness identified, particularly if accompanied by aggravating factors such as multiple deaths or injuries, or a very bad driving record, this may move an offence towards the top of the sentencing range.

Level 2—This is driving that created a substantial risk of danger and is likely to be characterised by:

- *Greatly excessive speed, racing or competitive driving against another driver* ***OR***
- *Gross avoidable distraction such as reading or composing text messages over a period of time* ***OR***
- *Driving whilst ability to drive is impaired as a result of consumption of alcohol or drugs, failing to take prescribed medication or as a result of a known medical condition* ***OR***
- *A group of determinants of seriousness which in isolation or smaller number would place the offence in level 3*

Level 3 – This is driving that created a significant risk of danger and is likely to be characterised by:

- *Driving above the speed limit/at a speed that is inappropriate for the prevailing conditions* ***OR***
- *Driving when knowingly deprived of adequate sleep or rest or knowing that the vehicle has a dangerous defect or is poorly maintained or is dangerously loaded* ***OR***
- *A brief but obvious danger arising from a seriously dangerous manoeuvre* ***OR***
- *Driving whilst avoidably distracted* ***OR***
- *Failing to have proper regard to vulnerable road users*

The starting point and range overlap with Level 2 is to allow the breadth of discretion necessary to accommodate circumstances where there are significant aggravating factors.

4. Sentencers should take into account relevant matters of personal mitigation; see in particular guidance on **good driving record, giving assistance at the scene** and **remorse** . . . above.

[309] *Overarching Principles: Seriousness*, published 16 December 2004, www.sentencing-guidelines.gov.uk

Causing Death by Dangerous Driving

Road Traffic Act 1988 (section 1)

This is a serious offence for the purposes of section 224 Criminal Justice Act 2003

Maximum penalty: 14 years imprisonment minimum disqualification of 2 years with compulsory extended re-test

Nature of offence	Starting point	Sentencing range
Level 1 The most serious offences encompassing driving that involved a deliberate decision to ignore (or a flagrant disregard for) the rules of the road and an apparent disregard for the great danger being caused to others	8 years custody	7–14 years custody
Level 2 Driving that created a *substantial* risk of danger	5 years custody	4–7 years custody
Level 3 Driving that created a *significant* risk of danger *[Where the driving is markedly less culpable than for this level, reference should be made to the starting point and range for the most serious level of causing death by careless driving]*	3 years custody	2–5 years custody

Additional aggravating factors	Additional mitigating factors
1. Previous convictions for motoring offences, particularly offences that involve bad driving or the consumption of excessive alcohol or drugs before driving 2. More than one person killed as a result of the offence 3. Serious injury to one or more victims, in addition to the death(s) 4. Disregard of warnings 5. Other offences committed at the same time, such as driving other than in accordance with the terms of a valid licence; driving while disqualified; driving without insurance; taking a vehicle without consent; driving a stolen vehicle 6. The offender's irresponsible behaviour such as failing to stop, falsely claiming that one of the victims was responsible for the collision, or trying to throw the victim off the car by swerving in order to escape 7. Driving off in an attempt to avoid detection or apprehension	1. Alcohol or drugs consumed unwittingly 2. Offender was seriously injured in the collision 3. The victim was a close friend or relative 4. Actions of the victim or a third party contributed significantly to the likelihood of a collision occurring and/or death resulting 5. The offender's lack of driving experience contributed to the commission of the offence 6. The driving was in response to a proven and genuine emergency falling short of a defence

Causing death by careless driving when under the influence of drink or drugs or having failed without reasonable excuse either to provide a specimen for analysis or to permit the analysis of a blood sample SG-364

Factors to take into consideration

1. The following guideline applies to a 'first-time offender' aged 18 or over convicted after trial (see . . . above), who has not been assessed as a dangerous offender requiring a sentence under ss. 224–228 Criminal Justice Act 2003 (as amended).
2. When assessing the seriousness of any offence, the court must always refer to the full list of aggravating and mitigating factors in the Council guideline on Seriousness[310] as well as those set out in the adjacent table as being particularly relevant to this type of offending behaviour.
3. This offence can be committed through:
   (i) being unfit to drive through drink or drugs;
   (ii) having consumed so much alcohol as to be over the prescribed limit;
   (iii) failing without reasonable excuse to provide a specimen for analysis within the timescale allowed; or

[310] *Overarching Principles: Seriousness*, published 16 December 2004, www.sentencing-guidelines.gov.uk

(iv) failing without reasonable excuse to permit the analysis of a blood sample taken when incapable of giving consent.

4. In comparison with *causing death by dangerous driving*, the level of culpability in the actual manner of driving is lower but that culpability is increased in all cases by the fact that the offender has driven after consuming drugs or an excessive amount of alcohol. Accordingly, there is considerable parity in the levels of seriousness with the deliberate decision to drive after consuming alcohol or drugs aggravating the *careless* standard of driving onto a par with *dangerous* driving.
5. The fact that the offender was under the influence of drink or drugs is an inherent element of this offence. For discussion on the significance of driving after having consumed drink or drugs, see . . . above.
6. The guideline is based both on the level of alcohol or drug consumption and on the degree of carelessness.
7. The increase in sentence is more marked where there is an increase in the level of intoxication than where there is an increase in the degree of carelessness reflecting the 14 year imprisonment maximum for this offence compared with a 5 year maximum for causing death by careless or inconsiderate driving alone.
8. A refusal to supply a specimen for analysis may be a calculated step by an offender to avoid prosecution for driving when having consumed in excess of the prescribed amount of alcohol, with a view to seeking to persuade the court that the amount consumed was relatively small. A court is entitled to draw adverse inferences from a refusal to supply a specimen without reasonable excuse and should treat with caution any attempt to persuade the court that only a limited amount of alcohol had been consumed.[311] The three levels of seriousness where the offence has been committed in this way derive from the classification in the Magistrates' Court Sentencing Guidelines.
9. Sentencers should take into account relevant matters of personal mitigation; see in particular guidance on **good driving record, giving assistance at the scene** and **remorse** . . . above.

Causing Death by Careless Driving when Under the Influence of Drink or Drugs or having Failed either to Provide a Specimen for Analysis or to Permit Analysis of a Blood Sample

Road Traffic Act 1988 (section 3A)

This is a serious offence for the purposes of section 224 Criminal Justice Act 2003

Maximum penalty: 14 years imprisonment;
minimum disqualification of 2 years with compulsory extended re-test

The legal limit of alcohol is 35 µg breath (80 mg in blood and 107 mg in urine)	**Careless/inconsiderate driving arising from momentary inattention with no aggravating factors**	**Other cases of careless/inconsiderate driving**	**Careless/inconsiderate driving falling not far short of dangerousness**
71 µ or above of alcohol/high quantity of drugs OR deliberate non-provision of specimen where evidence of serious impairment	**Starting point:** 6 years custody **Sentencing range:** 5–10 years custody	**Starting point:** 7 years custody **Sentencing range:** 6–12 years custody	**Starting point:** 8 years custody **Sentencing range:** 7–14 years custody
51–70 µg of alcohol/moderate quantity of drugs OR deliberate non-provision of specimen	**Starting point:** 4 years custody **Sentencing range:** 3–7 years custody	**Starting point:** 5 years custody **Sentencing range:** 4–8 years custody	**Starting point:** 6 years custody **Sentencing range:** 5–9 years custody
35–50 µg of alcohol/minimum quantity of drugs OR test refused because of honestly held but unreasonable belief	**Starting point:** 18 months custody **Sentencing range:** 26 weeks–4 years custody	**Starting point:** 3 years custody **Sentencing range:** 2–5 years custody	**Starting point:** 4 years custody **Sentencing range:** 3–6 years custody

[311] *Attorney-General's Reference No. 21 of 2000* [2001] 1 Cr App R (S) 173

Additional aggravating factors	Additional mitigating factors
1. Other offences committed at the same time, such as driving other than in accordance with the terms of a valid licence; driving while disqualified; driving without insurance; taking a vehicle without consent; driving a stolen vehicle 2. Previous convictions for motoring offences, particularly offences that involve bad driving or the consumption of excessive alcohol before driving 3. More than one person was killed as a result of the offence 4. Serious injury to one or more persons in addition to the death(s) 5. Irresponsible behaviour such as failing to stop or falsely claiming that one of the victims was responsible for the collision	1. Alcohol or drugs consumed unwittingly 2. Offender was seriously injured in the collision 3. The victim was a close friend or relative 4. The actions of the victim or a third party contributed significantly to the likelihood of a collision occurring and/or death resulting 5. The driving was in response to a proven and genuine emergency falling short of a defence

Causing death by careless or inconsiderate driving SG-365

Factors to take into consideration

1. The following guideline applies to a 'first-time offender' aged 18 or over convicted after trial (see . . . above), who has not been assessed as a dangerous offender requiring a sentence under ss. 224–228 Criminal Justice Act 2003 (as amended).
2. When assessing the seriousness of any offence, the court must always refer to the full list of aggravating and mitigating factors in the Council guideline on Seriousness[312] as well as those set out in the adjacent table as being particularly relevant to this type of offending behaviour.
3. The maximum penalty on indictment is 5 years imprisonment. The offence is triable either way and, in a magistrates' court, statute provides that the maximum sentence is 12 months imprisonment; this will be revised to 6 months imprisonment until such time as the statutory provisions increasing the sentencing powers of a magistrates' court are implemented.[313]
4. Disqualification of the offender from driving and endorsement of the offender's driving licence are mandatory, and the offence carries between 3 and 11 penalty points when the court finds special reasons for not imposing disqualification. There is a discretionary power[314] to order an extended driving test where a person is convicted of this offence.
5. Since the maximum sentence has been set at 5 years imprisonment, the sentence ranges are generally lower for this offence than for the offences of *causing death by dangerous driving* or *causing death by careless driving under the influence*, for which the maximum sentence is 14 years imprisonment. However, it is unavoidable that some cases will be on the borderline between *dangerous* and *careless* driving, or may involve a number of factors that significantly increase the seriousness of an offence. As a result, the guideline for this offence identifies three levels of seriousness, the range for the highest of which overlaps with ranges for the lowest level of seriousness for *causing death by dangerous driving*.
6. The three levels of seriousness are defined by the degree of carelessness involved in the standard of driving. The most serious level for this offence is where the offender's driving fell *not that far short of dangerous*. The least serious group of offences relates to those cases where the level of culpability is low—for example in a case involving an offender who misjudges the speed of another vehicle, or turns without seeing an oncoming vehicle because of restricted visibility. Other cases will fall into the intermediate level.
7. The starting point for the most serious offence of *causing death by careless driving* is lower than that for the least serious offence of *causing death by dangerous driving* in recognition of the different standards of driving behaviour. However, the range still leaves scope, within the 5 year maximum, to impose longer sentences where the case is particularly serious.
8. Where the level of carelessness is low and there are no aggravating factors, even the fact that death was caused is not sufficient to justify a prison sentence.
9. A fine is unlikely to be an appropriate sentence for this offence; where a non-custodial sentence is considered appropriate, this should be a community order. The nature of the requirements will be determined by the purpose[315] identified by the court as of primary importance. Requirements most

[312] *Overarching Principles: Seriousness*, published 16 December 2004, www.sentencing-guidelines.gov.uk
[313] Criminal Justice Act 2003, ss. 154(1) and 282; Road Safety Act 2006, s. 61(5)
[314] Road Traffic Offenders Act 1988, s. 36(4)
[315] Criminal Justice Act 2003, s. 142(1)

likely to be relevant include unpaid work requirement, activity requirement, programme requirement and curfew requirement.

10. Sentencers should take into account relevant matters of personal mitigation; see in particular guidance on **good driving record, giving assistance at the scene** and **remorse** . . . above.

Causing Death by Careless or Inconsiderate Driving

Road Traffic Act 1988 (section 2B)

Maximum penalty: 5 years imprisonment minimum disqualification of 12 months, discretionary re-test

Nature of offence	Starting point	Sentencing range
Careless or inconsiderate driving falling not far short of dangerous driving	**15 months custody**	**36 weeks–3 years custody**
Other cases of careless or inconsiderate driving	**36 weeks custody**	**Community order (HIGH)—2 years custody**
Careless or inconsiderate driving arising from momentary inattention with no aggravating factors	**Community order (MEDIUM)**	**Community order (LOW)—Community order (HIGH)**

Additional aggravating factors	Additional mitigating factors
1. Other offences committed at the same time, such as driving other than in accordance with the terms of a valid licence; driving while disqualified; driving without insurance; taking a vehicle without consent; driving a stolen vehicle 2. Previous convictions for motoring offences, particularly offences that involve bad driving 3. More than one person was killed as a result of the offence 4. Serious injury to one or more persons in addition to the death(s) 5. Irresponsible behaviour, such as failing to stop or falsely claiming that one of the victims was responsible for the collision	1. Offender was seriously injured in the collision 2. The victim was a close friend or relative 3. The actions of the victim or a third party contributed to the commission of the offence 4. The offender's lack of driving experience contributed significantly to the likelihood of a collision occurring and/or death resulting 5. The driving was in response to a proven and genuine emergency falling short of a defence

SG-366 **Causing death by driving: unlicensed, disqualified or uninsured drivers**

Factors to take into consideration

1. The following guideline applies to a 'first-time offender' aged 18 or over convicted after trial (see . . . above), who has not been assessed as a dangerous offender requiring a sentence under ss. 224–228 Criminal Justice Act 2003 (as amended).
2. When assessing the seriousness of any offence, the court must always refer to the full list of aggravating and mitigating factors in the Council guideline on Seriousness[316] as well as those set out in the adjacent table as being particularly relevant to this type of offending behaviour.
3. This offence has a maximum penalty of 2 years imprisonment and is triable either way. In a magistrates' court, statute provides that the maximum sentence is 12 months imprisonment; this will be revised to 6 months imprisonment until such time as the statutory provisions increasing the sentencing powers of a magistrates' court are implemented.[317]
4. Disqualification of the offender from driving and endorsement of the offender's driving licence are mandatory, and the offence carries between 3 and 11 penalty points when the court finds special reasons for not imposing disqualification. There is a discretionary power[318] to order an extended driving test where a person is convicted of this offence.
5. Culpability arises from the offender driving a vehicle on a road or other public place when, by law, not allowed to do so; the offence does not require proof of any fault in the standard of driving.

[316] *Overarching Principles: Seriousness*, published 16 December 2004, www.sentencing-guidelines.gov.uk

[317] Criminal Justice Act 2003, ss. 154(1) and 282; Road Safety Act 2006, s. 61(5)

[318] Road Traffic Offenders Act 1988, s. 36(4)

6. Because of the significantly lower maximum penalty, the sentencing ranges are considerably lower than for the other three offences covered in this guideline; many cases may be sentenced in a magistrates' court, particularly where there is an early guilty plea.
7. A fine is unlikely to be an appropriate sentence for this offence; where a noncustodial sentence is considered appropriate, this should be a community order.
8. Since driving whilst disqualified is more culpable than driving whilst unlicensed or uninsured, a higher starting point is proposed when the offender was disqualified from driving at the time of the offence.
9. Being uninsured, unlicensed or disqualified are the only determinants of seriousness for this offence, as there are no factors relating to the standard of driving. The list of aggravating factors identified is slightly different as the emphasis is on the decision to drive by an offender who is not permitted by law to do so.
10. In some cases, the extreme circumstances that led an offender to drive whilst unlicensed, disqualified or uninsured may result in a successful defence of 'duress of circumstances'.[319] In less extreme circumstances, where the *decision to drive was brought about by a genuine and proven emergency*, that may mitigate offence seriousness and so it is included as an additional mitigating factor.
11. A driver may hold a reasonable belief in relation to the validity of insurance (for example having just missed a renewal date or relied on a third party to make an application) and also the validity of a licence (for example incorrectly believing that a licence covered a particular category of vehicle). In light of this, an additional mitigating factor covers those situations where an offender genuinely believed that there was valid insurance or a valid licence.
12. Sentencers should take into account relevant matters of personal mitigation; see in particular guidance on **good driving record, giving assistance at the scene** and **remorse** . . . above.

Causing Death by Driving: Unlicensed, Disqualified or Uninsured Drivers

Road Traffic Act 1988 (section 3ZB)

Maximum penalty: 2 years imprisonment minimum disqualification of 12 months, discretionary re-test

Nature of offence	Starting point	Sentencing range
The offender was disqualified from driving **OR** The offender was unlicensed or uninsured plus 2 or more aggravating factors from the list below	**12 months custody**	**36 weeks–2 years custody**
The offender was unlicensed or uninsured plus at least 1 aggravating factor from the list below	**26 weeks custody**	**Community order (HIGH)—36 weeks custody**
The offender was unlicensed or uninsured—no aggravating factors	**Community order (MEDIUM)**	**Community order (LOW)—Community order (HIGH)**

Additional aggravating factors	Additional mitigating factors
1. Previous convictions for motoring offences, whether involving bad driving or involving an offence of the same kind that forms part of the present conviction (i.e. unlicensed, disqualified or uninsured driving) 2. More than one person was killed as a result of the offence 3. Serious injury to one or more persons in addition to the death(s) 4. Irresponsible behaviour such as failing to stop or falsely claiming that someone else was driving	1. The decision to drive was brought about by a proven and genuine emergency falling short of a defence 2. The offender genuinely believed that he or she was insured or licensed to drive 3. The offender was seriously injured as a result of the collision 4. The victim was a close friend or relative

Annex A: Dangerous and Careless Driving

SG-367

Statutory definitions and examples

[Omitted—see the relevant material in **part C**]

[319] In *DPP v Mullally* [2006] EWHC 3448 the Divisional Court held that the defence of necessity must be strictly controlled and that it must be proved that the actions of the defendant were reasonable in the given circumstances. See also *Hasan* [2005] UKHL 22

SG-368

PART 14 THEFT AND BURGLARY IN A BUILDING OTHER THAN A DWELLING

. . . This guideline applies to the sentencing of offenders convicted of theft or burglary in a building other than a dwelling who are sentenced on or after 5 January 2009.

. . .

This guideline applies only to the sentencing of offenders aged 18 and over. . . .

SG-369

A. Statutory provisions

1. The forms of theft and burglary covered by this guideline are:
   - theft in breach of trust;
   - theft in a dwelling;
   - theft from the person;
   - theft from a shop;
   - burglary in a building other than a dwelling.
2. [Sets out the Theft Act 1968, s. 1.]
   Although this guideline covers four particular forms of theft, the principles covered in paragraphs 5 to 30 are of general application and are likely to be of assistance where a court is sentencing for a form of theft not covered by a specific guideline.
3. [Sets out the Theft Act 1968, s. 9.]
   The guideline for burglary relates solely to the situation in which an offender enters a building other than a dwelling as a trespasser with intent to steal or, having entered a building as a trespasser, actually goes on to steal.
4. Offences under sections 1 and 9 of the Theft Act are punishable either on summary conviction or on indictment. The maximum sentence in a magistrates' court is 6 months imprisonment. In the Crown Court, the maximum sentence is 7 years custody for theft and 10 years for burglary in a building other than a dwelling.

SG-370

B. Assessing seriousness

5. The primary factor in considering sentence is the seriousness of the offence; that is determined by assessing the culpability of the offender and any harm which the offence caused, was intended to cause or might foreseeably have caused.[320] A community sentence can be imposed only if a court considers that the offence is serious enough to justify it,[321] and a custodial sentence can be imposed only if a court considers that a community order or a fine alone cannot be justified in view of the seriousness of the offence.[322] The Council has published a definitive guideline on seriousness that guides sentencers through the process of determining whether the respective sentencing thresholds have been crossed.[323]

(i) Culpability and harm

6. The culpability of the offender is the initial factor in determining offence seriousness. It is an essential element of the offences addressed in this guideline that the offender acted dishonestly. This requires that:[324]
   - the conduct was dishonest according to ordinary standards of reasonable and honest people and
   - the offender knew that the conduct was by those standards dishonest.

   Accordingly, an offender convicted of these offences will have demonstrated a high level of culpability.
7. Even so, the precise level of culpability will vary according to factors such as the offender's motivation, whether the offence was planned or spontaneous and whether the offender was in a position of trust.[325] An offence will be aggravated where there is evidence of planning.
8. The starting points and sentencing ranges in this guideline are based on the assumption that the offender was motivated by greed or a desire to live beyond his or her means. To avoid double counting, such a motivation should not be treated as a factor that increases culpability. Where an offence of theft is motivated by an intention to cause harm, or out of revenge, this will aggravate the offence.

---

320 Criminal Justice Act 2003, s.143(1)
321 ibid., s.148(1)
322 ibid., s.152(2)
323 *Overarching Principles: Seriousness*, published 16 December 2004, www.sentencing-guidelines.gov.uk
324 *R v Ghosh* [1982] QB 1053
325 *Overarching Principles: Seriousness*, published 16 December 2004, www.sentencing-guidelines.gov.uk

9. When assessing the harm caused by theft and burglary in a building other than a dwelling offences, the starting point should be the loss suffered by the victim. In general, the greater the loss, the more serious the offence. However, the monetary value of the loss may not reflect the full extent of the harm caused by the offence. The court should also take into account the impact of the offence on the victim (which may be significantly greater than the monetary value of the loss; this may be particularly important where the value of the loss is high in proportion to the victim's financial circumstances even though relatively low in absolute terms), any harm to persons other than the direct victim, and any harm in the form of public concern or erosion of public confidence.
10. In some theft and burglary in a building other than a dwelling cases, the harm that results from an offence may be greater than the harm intended by the offender. In others, the offender may have intended more harm than actually results.[326]

(ii) Aggravating and mitigating factors

11. The Council guideline *Overarching Principles: Seriousness* identifies a number of factors that might increase or mitigate the seriousness of an offence. For ease of reference, the factors are set out in Annex A.
12. The most common factors that are likely to aggravate an offence of theft or burglary in a building other than a dwelling are:

Factors indicating higher culpability

- planning of an offence;
- offenders operating in groups or gangs; and
- deliberate targeting of vulnerable victims.

Factors indicating a more than usually serious degree of harm

- victim is particularly vulnerable;
- high level of gain from the offence; and
- high value (including sentimental value) of property to the victim or substantial consequential loss.

13. In the offence guidelines that follow, the Council has identified aggravating factors in addition to those from the general list that may be of particular relevance to the individual offences. The Council has not identified any additional offence mitigating factors pertinent to the offences in this guideline.

(iii) Personal mitigation

14. The Council has identified the following matters of personal mitigation that might apply to the offences contained in this guideline.

(a) Return of stolen property

15. Whether and the degree to which the return of stolen property constitutes a matter of personal mitigation will depend on an assessment of the circumstances and, in particular, the voluntariness and timeliness of the return.

(b) Impact on sentence of offender's dependency

16. Many offenders convicted of acquisitive crimes are motivated by an addiction, often to drugs, alcohol or gambling. This does not mitigate the seriousness of the offence, but an offender's dependency may properly influence the type of sentence imposed. In particular, it may sometimes be appropriate to impose:
    - a drug rehabilitation requirement (which can be part of a community order within all the community sentencing bands from low to high seriousness), or
    - an alcohol treatment requirement (for dependent drinkers), or
    - an activity or supervision requirement including alcohol specific information, advice and support (for harmful and hazardous drinkers)

    as part of a community order or a suspended sentence order in an attempt to break the cycle of addiction and offending, even if an immediate custodial sentence would otherwise be warranted.[327]

[326] see *Overarching Principles: Seriousness*, para.1.17, published 16 December 2004, www.sentencing-guidelines.gov.uk
[327] *New Sentences: Criminal Justice Act 2003*, published 16 December 2004, www.sentencing-guidelines.gov.uk. The Court of Appeal gave guidance on the approach to making drug treatment and testing orders, which also applies to imposing a drug rehabilitation requirement, *in Attorney General's Reference No. 64 of 2003 (Boujettif and Harrison)* [2003] EWCA Crim 3514 and *Woods and Collins* [2005] EWCA Crim 2065 summarised in the Sentencing Guidelines Council *Guideline Judgments Case Compendium* (section (A) Generic Sentencing Principles) available at www.sentencing-guidelines.gov.uk

(c) Offender motivated by desperation or need

17. The fact that an offence has been committed in desperation or need arising from particular hardship may count as personal mitigation in **exceptional circumstances.**

SG-371 C. **Ancillary and other orders**

(i) **Restitution order**

18. Under section 148 of the Powers of Criminal Courts (Sentencing) Act 2000, a court may order that stolen goods be restored to the victim or that a sum not exceeding the value of the goods be paid to the victim from money taken out of the offender's possession at the time of apprehension. Further, on the application of the victim, the court may order that other goods representing the proceeds of disposal or realisation of the stolen goods be transferred to the victim. Where the stolen property cannot be traced or the offender is not in possession of sufficient money at the time of apprehension, a restitution order will not be available and a compensation order should be considered instead.
19. A restitution order should not normally impact on or influence the choice of sentence as the offender has no control over the making of the order.

(ii) **Compensation order**

20. Under section 130 of the Powers of Criminal Courts (Sentencing) Act 2000, the court must consider making a compensation order in any case where an offence has resulted in personal injury, loss or damage. Compensation can either be a sentence in its own right or an ancillary order.
21. Compensation should benefit, not inflict further harm on, the victim. A victim may or may not want compensation from the offender and assumptions should not be made either way. The victim's views are properly obtained through sensitive discussion with the police when it can be explained that the offender's ability to pay will ultimately determine whether, and how much, compensation is ordered and whether the compensation will be paid in one lump sum or by instalments. If the victim does not want compensation, this should be made known to the court and respected.
22. In cases where it is difficult to ascertain the full amount of the loss suffered by the victim, consideration should be given to making a compensation order for an amount representing the agreed or likely loss. Where relevant information is not immediately available, it may be appropriate to grant an adjournment for it to be obtained.
23. When imposed as an ancillary order, a compensation order normally should not impact on or influence the choice of sentence. However, in cases where the court considers that it is appropriate to impose both a fine and compensation order and the offender has insufficient means to pay both, priority must be given to the compensation order.[328]
24. Where an offender has acted (as opposed to offered) to free assets in order to pay compensation, this is akin to making voluntary restitution and may be regarded as personal mitigation.

(iii) **Confiscation order**

25. Where there is evidence in a case before the Crown Court that the offender has benefited financially from his or her offending, the court must, in accordance with the Proceeds of Crime Act 2002, consider whether to make a confiscation order. A magistrates' court may commit the offender to the Crown Court for sentence with a view to such an order being made.
26. If the court makes a confiscation order, it must take account of the order before it imposes a fine or a deprivation order.[329]
27. Except as provided in paragraph 26 above, the court must not take account of the confiscation order in deciding the appropriate sentence.[330]
28. Where a court makes both a compensation order and a confiscation order and it believes that the offender does not have sufficient means to satisfy both orders, it must direct that the compensation is paid from the confiscated assets.[331]

(iv) **Deprivation order**

29. Under section 143 of the Powers of Criminal Courts (Sentencing) Act 2000, a court may deprive an offender of property used or intended to be used to commit or facilitate the commission of an offence.

[328] Powers of Criminal Courts (Sentencing) Act 2000, s.130(12). The court must also impose a surcharge of £15 in any case in which a fine is imposed. Where there are insufficient means, compensation will take priority over the surcharge but the surcharge will take priority over a fine.
[329] Proceeds of Crime Act 2002, ss.13(2) and (3)
[330] ibid., s.13(4)
[331] ibid., ss.13(5) and (6)

30. Where the property has an 'innocent use' but can also be used to commit or facilitate the commission of an offence, a deprivation order must be taken into account when considering whether the overall penalty is commensurate with the seriousness of the offence.[332] However, where the property can be used only for the purpose of crime, a deprivation order should not be taken into account when determining the appropriate sentence.

D. Sentencing ranges and starting points SG-372

1. Typically, a guideline will apply to an offence that can be committed in a variety of circumstances with different levels of seriousness. It will apply to a first time offender who has been **convicted after a trial**. Within the guidelines, a "first time offender" is a person who does not have a conviction which, by virtue of section 143(2) of the Criminal Justice Act 2003, must be treated as an aggravating factor.
2. As an aid to consistency of approach, the guidelines describe a number of types of activity which would fall within the broad definition of the offence. These are set out in a column headed 'type/nature of activity'.
3. The expected approach is for a court to identify the description that most nearly matches the particular facts of the offence for which sentence is being imposed. This will identify a **starting point** from which the sentencer can depart to reflect aggravating or mitigating factors affecting the seriousness of the offence (beyond those contained within the column describing the type or nature of offence activity) to reach a **provisional sentence**.
4. The **sentencing range** is the bracket into which the provisional sentence will normally fall after having regard to factors which aggravate or mitigate the seriousness of the offence. The particular circumstances may, however, make it appropriate that the provisional sentence falls outside the range.
5. Where the offender has previous convictions which aggravate the seriousness of the current offence, that may take the provisional sentence beyond the range given particularly where there are significant other aggravating factors present.
6. Once the provisional sentence has been identified by reference to those factors affecting the seriousness of the offence, the court will take into account any relevant factors of personal mitigation, which may take the sentence beyond the range given.
7. Where there has been a guilty plea, any reduction attributable to that plea will be applied to the sentence at this stage. Again, this reduction may take the sentence below the range provided.
8. A court must give its reasons for imposing a sentence of a different kind or outside the range provided in the guidelines.[333]

The decision making process

[Sets out the standard sequential decision making process: identify starting point, consider aggravating factors, consider mitigating factors, apply reduction for guilty plea, consider ancillary orders, review in light of the totality principle and give reasons.]

E. Offence guidelines SG-373

Theft in breach of trust SG-374

Factors to take into consideration

1. The following starting points and sentencing ranges are for a first time offender aged 18 or over who pleaded not guilty. They should be applied as set out . . . above.
2. In relation to harm, in general, the greater the loss, the more serious the offence. However, this is subject to the considerations set out in the rest of this paragraph. The guideline is based on the monetary value of the amount involved but, the monetary value may not reflect the full extent of the harm caused by the offence. The court should also take into account the impact of the offence on the victim (which may be significantly greater than the monetary value of the loss; this may be particularly important where the value of the loss is high in proportion to the victim's financial circumstances even though relatively low in absolute terms), any harm to persons other than the direct victim, and any harm in the form of public concern or erosion of public confidence.
3. In general terms, the seriousness of the offence will increase in line with the level of trust breached. The extent to which the nature and degree of trust placed in an offender should be regarded as increasing seriousness will depend on a careful assessment of the circumstances of each individual case, including the type and terms of the relationship between the offender and victim.

[332] *R v Buddo* (1982) 4 Cr App R (S) 268, *R v Joyce* and others (1989) 11 Cr App R (S) 253, *R v Priestley* [1996] 2 Cr App R (S) 144

[333] Criminal Justice Act 2003, s.174(2)(a)

4. The concept of breach of trust for the purposes of the offence of theft is wide. It includes not only employer/employee relationships and those between a professional adviser and client, but also extends more generally to relationships in which the offender was in a position of authority in relation to the victim, or one whereby they would be expected to have a duty to protect the interests of the victim, such as medical, social or care workers.
5. Thefts by offenders in whom a high degree of trust has been placed should generally attract higher sentences than thefts of similar amounts by offenders in whom a lower degree of trust is vested. The targeting of a vulnerable victim by an offender through a relationship or position of trust will indicate a higher level of culpability.
6. When assessing the seriousness of an offence, a court must always have regard to the full list of aggravating and mitigating factors in the Council guideline *Overarching Principles: Seriousness* (reproduced in Annex A [but not set out below]). Identified below are additional aggravating factors likely to be particularly relevant to this type of theft:

   (i) Long course of offending

   Offending carried out over a period of months or years represents a sustained and deliberate course of conduct and should be regarded as increasing an offender's culpability. Offending over an extended period may also result in greater harm to the victim in terms of financial loss and/or distress.

   (ii) Suspicion deliberately thrown on others

   Where an offender has taken positive steps to incriminate another, either at the time of committing the offence or subsequently, this should be regarded as an aggravating factor.

7. The Council has identified the following matters of personal mitigation which may be relevant in addition to those set out [in part B] above:

   (i) Inappropriate degree of trust or responsibility

   The fact that an offender succumbed to temptation having been placed in a position of trust or given responsibility to an inappropriate degree may be regarded as personal mitigation.

   (ii) Cessation of offending

   The fact that an offender voluntarily ceased offending before being discovered does not reduce the seriousness of the offence. However, if the claim to have stopped offending is genuine, it may constitute personal mitigation, particularly if it is evidence of remorse.[334]

   (iii) Reporting an undiscovered offence

   Where an offender brings the offending to the attention of his or her employer or the authorities, this may be treated as personal mitigation.[335]

8. In many cases of theft in breach of trust, termination of an offenders employment will be a natural consequence of committing the offence. Other than in the most exceptional of circumstances, loss of employment and any consequential hardship should not constitute personal mitigation.
9. Where a court is satisfied that a custodial sentence of 12 months or less is appropriate for an offence of theft in breach of trust, consideration should be given to whether that sentence can be suspended in accordance with the criteria in the Council guideline *New Sentences: Criminal Justice Act 2003*.[336] A suspended sentence order may be particularly appropriate where this would allow for reparation to be made either to the victim or to the community at large.

Theft in Breach of Trust

Theft Act 1968 (section 1)
Maximum penalty: 7 years imprisonment

; *Principles: Seriousness*, published 16 December 2004, www.sentencing-guidelines.gov.uk
ı.29
:0–25

Type/nature of activity	Starting point	Sentencing range
Theft of £125,000 or more **or** Theft of £20,000 or more in breach of a high degree of trust	**3 years custody**	**2–6 years custody**
Theft of £20,000 or more but less than £125,000 **or** Theft of £2,000 or more but less than £20,000 in breach of a high degree of trust	**2 years custody**	**12 months–3 years custody**
Theft of £2,000 or more but less than £20,000 **or** Theft of less than £2,000 in breach of a high degree of trust	**18 weeks custody**	**Community order (HIGH)—12 months custody**
Theft of less than £2,000	**Community order (MEDIUM)**	**Fine—26 weeks custody**

Additional aggravating factors:
1. Long course of offending 2. Suspicion deliberately thrown on others 3. Offender motivated by intention to cause harm or out of revenge

Theft in a dwelling **SG-375**

Factors to take into consideration

1. The following starting points and sentencing ranges are for a first time offender aged 18 or over who pleaded not guilty. They should be applied as set out . . . above.
2. The category of theft in a dwelling covers the situation where a theft is committed by an offender who is present in a dwelling with the authority of the owner or occupier. Examples include thefts by lodgers or visitors to the victim's residence, such as friends, relatives or salespeople. Such offences involve a violation of the privacy of the victim's home and constitute an abuse of the victim's trust. Where an offender enters a dwelling as a trespasser in order to commit theft, his or her conduct will generally constitute the more serious offence of burglary; **this guideline does not apply where the offender has been convicted of burglary.**[337]
3. For the purpose of this guideline, a 'vulnerable victim' is a person targeted by the offender because it is anticipated that he or she is unlikely or unable to resist the theft. The exploitation of a vulnerable victim indicates a high level of culpability and will influence the category of seriousness into which the offence falls.
4. The guideline is based on the assumption that most thefts in a dwelling do not involve property of high monetary value or of high value to the victim. Where the property stolen is of high monetary value or of high value (including sentimental value) to the victim, the appropriate sentence may be beyond the range into which the offence otherwise would fall. For the purpose of this form of theft, property worth more than £2,000 should generally be regarded as being of 'high monetary value', although this will depend on an assessment of all the circumstances of the particular case.
5. A sentence beyond the range into which the offence otherwise would fall may also be appropriate where the effect on the victim is particularly severe or where substantial consequential loss results (such as where the theft of equipment causes serious disruption to the victim's life or business).
6. When assessing the seriousness of an offence, a court must always have regard to the full list of aggravating and mitigating factors in the Council guideline Overarching Principles: Seriousness (reproduced in Annex A [not set out below]). Identified below are additional aggravating factors likely to be particularly relevant to this type of theft:

   (i) Confrontation with the victim

   Where there is intimidation and/or a face-to-face confrontation between the offender and victim, this should be regarded as an aggravating factor. Where the victim is a 'vulnerable victim' (as defined in para. 3 above), the use of intimidation will influence the category of seriousness into which the offence falls.

[337] The Court of Appeal issued guidance for sentencing burglary in a dwelling in *R v McInerney and Keating* [2002] EWCA Crim 3003 summarised in the Sentencing Guidelines Council *Guideline Judgments Case Compendium* (section (H) Theft Act offences/Fraud) available at www.sentencing-guidelines.gov.uk

(ii) Use of force, or threat of force

Generally, where theft in a dwelling is accompanied by force or the threat of force, it will constitute the more serious offence of robbery. However, there may be some cases involving force which are charged as theft in a dwelling, perhaps where the force was used after the theft had taken place. In such cases, an offender can be sentenced only for the offence of which he or she is convicted and the court is bound by the maximum penalty for that offence. At the same time, the court must have regard to all the circumstances of the case when determining the appropriate sentence. Where the victim is a 'vulnerable victim' (as defined in para. 3 [above]), the use or threat of force will influence the category of seriousness into which the offence falls. In other cases, it may be an aggravating factor.

(iii) Use of deception

Where an offender has deceived or tricked the victim in order to gain entry, for example by falsely claiming to be a meter reader, this should be regarded as an aggravating factor. Where the victim is a 'vulnerable victim' (as defined in para. 3 [above]), the use of deception will influence the category of seriousness into which the offence falls.

(iv) Taking steps to prevent the victim reporting the crime or seeking help

Where an offender takes steps to prevent the victim from reporting the offence or seeking help, such as by damaging a telephone, this should be regarded as increasing offence seriousness.

Theft in a Dwelling

Theft Act 1968 (section 1)

Maximum penalty: 7 years imprisonment

Type/nature of activity	Starting point	Range
Where the effect on the victim is particularly severe, the stolen property is of high value (as defined in para. 4 opposite), or substantial consequential loss results, a sentence higher than the range into which the offence otherwise would fall may be appropriate		
Theft from a vulnerable victim (as defined in para. 3 [above]) involving intimidation or the use or threat of force (falling short of robbery) or the use of deception	**18 months custody**	**12 months–3 years custody**
Theft from a vulnerable victim (as defined in para. 3 [above])	**18 weeks custody**	**Community order (HIGH)—12 months custody**
Theft in a dwelling not involving vulnerable victim	**Community order (MEDIUM)**	**Fine—18 weeks custody**

Additional aggravating factors:
1. Offender motivated by intention to cause harm or out of revenge 2. Intimidation or face-to-face confrontation with victim [except where this raises the offence into a higher sentencing range] 3. Use of force, or threat of force, against victim (not amounting to robbery) [except where this raises the offence into a higher sentencing range] 4. Use of deception [except where this raises the offence into a higher sentencing range] 5. Offender takes steps to prevent the victim from reporting the crime or seeking help

SG-376 **Theft from the person**

Factors to take into consideration

1. The following starting points and sentencing ranges are for a first time offender aged 18 or over who pleaded not guilty. They should be applied as set out . . . above. While in some cases the conduct may be similar, **this guideline does not apply where the offender has been convicted of robbery; sentencers should instead refer to the Council guideline on robbery (see also para 6(ii) below).**
2. Theft from the person may encompass conduct such as 'pick-pocketing', where the victim is unaware that the property is being stolen, as well as the snatching of handbags, wallets, jewellery and mobile

telephones from the victim's possession or from the vicinity of the victim. Where there is evidence of planning, that will be an aggravating factor. This may, for example, be demonstrated where tourists are targeted because of their unfamiliarity with an area or because of a perception that they will not be available to give evidence if a case proceeds to trial. The offence constitutes an invasion of the victim's privacy and may cause the victim to experience distress, fear and inconvenience either during or after the event.

3. For the purpose of this guideline, a 'vulnerable victim' is a person targeted by the offender because it is anticipated that he or she is unlikely or unable to resist the theft. Young or elderly persons or those with disabilities may fall into this category. The exploitation of a vulnerable victim indicates a high level of culpability and will influence the category of seriousness into which the offence falls.
4. The guideline is based on the assumption that most thefts from the person do not involve property of high monetary value or of high value to the victim. Where the property stolen is of high monetary value or of high value (including sentimental value) to the victim, the appropriate sentence may be beyond the range into which the offence otherwise would fall. For the purpose of this form of theft, 'high monetary value' is defined as more than £2,000.
5. A sentence beyond the range into which the offence otherwise would fall may also be appropriate where the effect on the victim is particularly severe or where substantial consequential loss results (such as where the theft of equipment causes serious disruption to the victim's life or business).
6. When assessing the seriousness of an offence, a court must always have regard to the full list of aggravating and mitigating factors in the Council guideline *Overarching Principles: Seriousness* (reproduced in Annex A [not set out below]). Identified below are additional aggravating factors likely to be particularly relevant to this type of theft:

   (i) Confrontation with the victim

   Where there is intimidation and/or a face-to-face confrontation between the offender and victim, this should be regarded as an aggravating factor. Where the victim is a 'vulnerable victim' (as defined in para. 3 above), the use of intimidation will influence the category of seriousness into which the offence falls.

   (ii) Use of force, or threat of force

   Where the offender uses or threatens to use force to commit the theft, the conduct may constitute the more serious offence of robbery.[338] However, there may be some cases involving force which are charged as theft from the person. In such cases, an offender can be sentenced only for the offence of which he or she is convicted and the court is bound by the maximum penalty for that offence. At the same time, the court must have regard to all the circumstances of the case when determining the appropriate sentence. Where the victim is a 'vulnerable victim' (as defined in para. 3 opposite), the use or threat of force will influence the category of seriousness into which the offence falls. In other cases, it may be an aggravating factor.

   (iii) High level of inconvenience caused to victim

   The theft of some items, such as house keys and credit cards, may cause a particularly high level of distress and inconvenience to victims and this should be regarded as an aggravating factor. Tourists are vulnerable as a target for thefts from the person (not least because it may be perceived that they will not be available to give evidence) and may experience greater distress and inconvenience than others in arranging the replacement of documents, cash and cards. Such factors should be taken into account as increasing the seriousness of the offence.

7. Previous authorities have expressed concern about the prevalence of theft against the person and the associated need for deterrence, particularly in relation to pick-pocketing.20 The Council guideline *Overarching Principles: Seriousness* sets out the approach which should be adopted when considering issues of local prevalence. Further, national prevalence should not be used by sentencers to justify including a deterrent element in sentences as this is already taken into account in Council guidelines.

THEFT FROM THE PERSON

Theft Act 1968 (section 1)

Maximum penalty: 7 years imprisonment

[338] Theft Act 1968, s.8(1)

Type/nature of activity	Starting point	Sentencing range
Where the effect on the victim is particularly severe, the stolen property is of high value (as defined in para. 4 opposite), or substantial consequential loss results, a sentence higher than the range into which the offence otherwise would fall may be appropriate.		
Theft from a vulnerable victim (as defined in para. 3 opposite) involving intimidation or the use or threat of force (falling short of robbery)	**18 months custody**	**12 months–3 years custody**
Theft from a vulnerable victim (as defined in para. 3 [above])	**18 weeks custody**	**Community order (HIGH)—12 months custody**
Theft from the person not involving vulnerable victim	**Community order (MEDIUM)**	**Fine—18 weeks custody**

Additional aggravating factors:
1. Offender motivated by intention to cause harm or out of revenge 2. Intimidation or face-to-face confrontation with victim [except where this raises the offence into a higher sentencing range] 3. Use of force, or threat of force, against victim (not amounting to robbery) [except where this raises the offence into a higher sentencing range] 4. High level of inconvenience caused to victim, e.g. replacing house keys, credit cards etc.

SG-377 **Theft from a shop**

Factors to take into consideration

1. The following starting points and sentencing ranges are for a first time offender aged 18 or over who pleaded not guilty. They should be applied as set out . . . above.
2. The circumstances of this offence can vary significantly. At the least serious end of the scale are thefts involving low value goods, no (or little) planning and no violence or damage; a non-custodial sentence will usually be appropriate for a first time offender. At the higher end of the spectrum are thefts involving organised gangs or groups or the threat or use of force and a custodial starting point will usually be appropriate.
3. When assessing the level of harm, the circumstances of the retailer are a proper consideration; a greater level of harm may be caused where the theft is against a small retailer.
4. Retailers may suffer additional loss as a result of this type of offending such as the cost of preventative security measures, higher insurance premiums and time spent by staff dealing with the prosecution of offenders. However, the seriousness of an individual case must be judged on its own dimension of harm and culpability and the sentence on an individual offender should not be increased to reflect the harm caused to retailers in general by the totality of this type of offending.
5. In accordance with section 143(2) of the Criminal Justice Act 2003, any recent previous convictions for theft and dishonesty offences will need to be taken into account in sentencing. Where an offender demonstrates a level of 'persistent' or 'seriously persistent' offending, the community and custody thresholds may be crossed even though the other characteristics of the offence would otherwise warrant a lesser sentence.
6. When assessing the seriousness of an offence, a court must always have regard to the full list of aggravating and mitigating factors in the Council guideline *Overarching Principles: Seriousness* (reproduced in Annex A [not set out below]).
7. The Council guideline on Seriousness identifies high value as an aggravating factor in property offences. In cases of theft from a shop, theft of high value goods may be associated with other aggravating factors such as the degree of planning, professionalism and/or operating in a group, and care will need to be taken to avoid double counting. Deliberately targeting high value goods will always make an offence more serious.
8. Additional aggravating factors particularly relevant to this type of theft include:

   (i) Involving a child

   Where a child accompanies an offender during the offence, it will be an aggravating factor if the child is involved in, or is likely to be aware of, the theft or could be influenced or distressed by it. However, the mere presence of a child does not make the offence more serious.

(ii) Offender subject to a banning order

The fact that an offender is subject to a banning order that includes the store in which the offence is committed is an aggravating factor. Breach of any type of order (for example a civil banning order or a shop imposed ban) will aggravate to the same degree. However, where an offender is being sentenced also for breach, care must be taken to ensure that there is no double counting.

(iii) Intimidation, threat or use of force and additional damage to property

Generally, where theft from a shop is accompanied by force or the threat of force, it will be appropriate to charge the offender with the more serious offence of robbery. However, there may be some cases involving force which are charged as theft from a shop. In such cases, an offender can be sentenced only for the offence of which he or she is convicted and the court is bound by the maximum penalty for that offence. At the same time, the court must have regard to all the circumstances of the case when determining the appropriate sentence. This may result in sentencers concluding that the offending was aggravated by the use or threat of force and that a more severe sentence is warranted. Any additional damage to property (for example caused when an offender is tackled or detained) also aggravates the seriousness of the offence.

Theft from a Shop

Theft Act 1968 (section 1)

Maximum penalty: 7 years imprisonment

Type/nature of activity	Starting point	Sentencing range
Organised gang/group **and** Intimidation or the use or threat of force (short of robbery)	**12 months custody**	**36 weeks–4 years custody**
Significant intimidation or threats **or** Use of force resulting in slight injury **or** Very high level of planning **or** Significant related damage	**6 weeks custody**	**Community order (HIGH)—36 weeks custody**
Low level intimidation or threats **or** Some planning e.g. a session of stealing on the same day or going equipped **or** Some related damage	**Community order (LOW)**	**Fine-Community order (MEDIUM)**
Little or no planning or sophistication and Goods stolen of low value	**Fine**	**Conditional discharge—Community order (LOW)**

Additional aggravating factors:
1. Child accompanying offender is involved in or aware of theft 2. Offender is subject to a banning order that includes the store targeted 3. Offender motivated by intention to cause harm or out of revenge 4. Professional offending 5. Victim particularly vulnerable (e.g. small independent shop) 6. Offender targeted high value goods

Burglary in a building other than a dwelling **SG-378**

Factors to take into consideration

1. The following starting points and sentencing ranges are for a first time offender aged 18 or over who pleaded not guilty. They should be applied as set out . . . above.
2. Section 9 of the Theft Act 1968 provides that the offence of burglary can be committed in a number of ways. This guideline is concerned solely with burglary committed in a building other than a dwelling and is limited to situations in which an offender enters a building as a trespasser with intent to steal or, having entered a building as a trespasser, actually goes on to steal.
3. The seriousness of individual instances of this offence can vary significantly. At the lower end are cases of opportunistic offending by a single offender where there was no forced entry, no damage caused and nothing stolen. Towards the other end of the spectrum are cases involving significant planning and professionalism, multiple offenders going equipped with implements to facilitate the commission

of the offence, targeting of particular premises and the theft of property or cash or damage and consequential losses of a significant value. The guideline indicates that, in these circumstances, a sentence in excess of 7 years imprisonment may be appropriate.

4. In relation to harm, the greater the loss, the more serious the offence. However, the monetary value of the loss may not reflect the full extent of the harm caused by the offence. The court should also take into account the impact of the offence on the victim (which may be significantly greater than the monetary value of the loss; this may be particularly important where the value of the loss is high in proportion to the victim's financial circumstances even though relatively low in absolute terms), any harm to persons other than the direct victim, and any harm in the form of public concern or erosion of public confidence.
5. When assessing the seriousness of an offence, the courts must always have regard to the full list of aggravating and mitigating factors in the Council guideline *Overarching Principles: Seriousness* (reproduced in Annex A [not set out below]). The following factors from the general list may be particularly relevant, alongside those set out . . . above:
   - deliberate and gratuitous violence or damage to property, over and above what is needed to carry out the offence;
   - abuse of a position of trust.
6. Identified below are additional aggravating factors which may be relevant to this offence:

   (i) Targeting premises

   Some offenders deliberately target premises because high value, often easily disposable, property is likely to be found there. This is an aggravating factor as it indicates a degree of professionalism and organisation in the offending, as well as an intention to derive a high level of gain.

   Community premises, including schools, clubrooms, places of worship and doctors' surgeries, may be particular targets. Burglaries of such premises may result in a higher than usual degree of harm in terms of, for example, the inconvenience caused by the theft of the property and this should be regarded as an aggravating factor. Premises which have been burgled on a prior occasion are also sometimes targeted, often on the assumption that security is weak or that goods stolen in the earlier burglary will have been replaced. This indicates planning, organisation and professionalism and, therefore, should be regarded as increasing the offender's culpability. Repeat victimisation may also increase the harm caused by the offence in terms of distress, inconvenience and expense to the victim.

   (ii) Possession of a weapon

   In cases where it is not clear whether the offender was in possession of a weapon at the time of entry into the building (which may fulfil the requirements for a more serious charge of aggravated burglary), an additional charge of possession of an offensive weapon may be before the court. If however, an offender found with a weapon is charged solely with burglary, possession of that weapon may be regarded as an aggravating factor, subject to the overriding principle that an offender can be sentenced only for the offence of which he or she has been convicted.

Burglary in a Building other than a Dwelling

Theft Act 1968 (section 9)

Maximum penalty: 10 years imprisonment

Type/nature of activity	Starting point	Range
Where the effect on the victim is particularly severe, the goods are of particularly high value, the cost of damage or consequential losses is significant, or there is evidence of a professional burglary and/or significant planning, a sentence of more than 7 years custody may be appropriate		
Burglary involving goods valued at £20,000 or more	**2 years custody**	**12 months–7 years custody**
Burglary involving goods valued at £2,000 or more but less than £20,000	**18 weeks custody**	**Community order (HIGH)—12 months custody**
Burglary involving goods valued at less than £2,000	**Community order (MEDIUM)**	**Fine—26 weeks custody**

Additional aggravating factors:
1. Targeting premises containing property of high value 2. Targeting vulnerable community premises 3. Targeting premises which have been burgled on prior occasion(s) 4. Possession of a weapon (where this is not charged separately)

ANNEX A: AGGRAVATING AND MITIGATING FACTORS IDENTIFIED IN THE COUNCIL GUIDELINE *OVERARCHING PRINCIPLES: SERIOUSNESS*

[Not reproduced – see **SG-21**.]

PART 15 BREACH OF AN ANTI-SOCIAL BEHAVIOUR ORDER SG-379

. . . This guideline applies to the sentencing of offenders convicted of breaching an anti-social behaviour order (ASBO) who are sentenced on or after 5 January 2009.

The Council has previously set out the approach to dealing with breaches of orders in its guidelines on New Sentences: Criminal Justice Act 20031 and Breach of Protective Orders.2 The main aim of sentencing for breach of a court order is to achieve the purpose of the order; in the case of an ASBO that is to protect the public from behaviour that is likely to cause harassment, alarm or distress.

Any perception that the courts do not treat seriously a failure to comply with a court order can undermine public confidence and is therefore an important additional consideration.

Since the ability of a court to deal appropriately with an order that has been breached depends on how it was made, Annex A to the guideline summarises the key principles and considerations applicable to the making of an ASBO.

This guideline applies to the sentencing of adult and young offenders. It is recognised that a large proportion of orders are imposed on persons under 18 years of age. Although the sentencing framework for youths is very different from that for adults, and a guideline for sentencing young offenders will follow in due course, the Council considered that sentencers would find it helpful to have guiding principles for sentencing young offenders for breach of an ASBO. . .

A. Statutory provision SG-380

1. [Sets out the CDA 1998, s. 1(10).]
2. Where a person is convicted of an offence of breach of an anti-social behaviour order (ASBO), it is not open to the court to make an order discharging the offender conditionally.[339]

B. Introduction SG-381

3. An ASBO is a preventative order that can be made in either civil or criminal proceedings; its aim is to protect the public from behaviour that causes, or is likely to cause, harassment, alarm or distress. An order may be made on application to a magistrates' court, on conviction, or in conjunction with other proceedings in the County Court.
4. Since the ability of a court to deal appropriately with an order that has been breached depends on how it was made, Annex A summarises the key principles and considerations applicable to the making of an ASBO.
5. This guideline relates to the sentencing of both adult and young offenders. As the sentencing framework that applies to offenders aged under 18 is significantly different from that for older offenders, the guidance for young offenders is in the form of principles particularly regarding the circumstances in which a custodial sentence might be justified. The maximum penalty in the case of a young offender is detention for 24 months.
6. Breach of this type of order is different from breach of a community order or failure to surrender to custody because it has the potential to affect a community or the public at large in a way that causes direct harm.

The main aim of sentencing for breach of a court order is to achieve the purpose of the order. Therefore, the sentence for breach of an ASBO should primarily reflect the harassment, alarm or distress involved; the fact that it constituted breach of a court order is a secondary consideration.

[339] Crime and Disorder Act 1998, s.1(11)

SG-382 C. **Assessing seriousness**

7. The sentence for breach of an ASBO must be commensurate with the seriousness of the offence; that is determined by assessing the culpability of the offender and any harm which the offence caused, was intended to cause or might foreseeably have caused.[340]
8. A community sentence can be imposed only if a court considers that the offence is serious enough to justify it,[341] and a custodial sentence can be imposed only if a court considers that a community sentence or a fine alone cannot be justified in view of the seriousness of the offence.[342] The Council has published a definitive guideline on seriousness that guides sentencers through the process of determining whether the respective sentencing thresholds have been crossed.[343]
9. A wide range of prohibitions can be attached to an order; consequently the degree of harm resulting from a breach will vary greatly and may be experienced by the wider community as well as by individuals.
10. In order properly to assess the seriousness of a breach of an ASBO, a court needs to be aware of the purpose of the order and the context in which it was made. A breach may be of one or more prohibitions in an order; the approach to sentencing is based on an assessment of the seriousness of the harm arising from the breach (or intended by the offender) rather than the number of prohibitions not complied with.

(i) **Culpability and harm**

11. When a court is considering the seriousness of breach of an order such as an ASBO, it will need to consider two aspects of culpability:

    (a) **The degree to which the offender intended to breach the order.**

    Culpability is variable and an offender may have:

    - intended the breach
    - been reckless as to whether the order was breached
    - been aware of the risk of breach; or
    - been unaware of this risk due to an incomplete understanding of the terms of the order.

    (b) **The degree to which the offender intended to cause the harm that resulted (or could have resulted).**

    Culpability will be higher where the offender foresaw the harm likely to be caused by the breach and will be at its highest where such harm was intended.

12. There are also two dimensions to the harm involved in breach of an ASBO:
    (a) the breach may itself cause harassment, alarm or distress, which can reduce the quality of life in a community.
    (b) breach of an ASBO contravenes an order of the court, and this can undermine public confidence in the effective administration of justice.
13. The assessment of the seriousness of an individual offence must take into account not only the harm actually caused by an offence but also any harm that was intended or might foreseeably have been caused.[344]
14. The test of foreseeability is objective[345] but as the prohibitions imposed must have been considered by a court to be necessary to prevent anti-social behaviour, some degree of harm must always be foreseeable whenever an order is breached. Where a breach causes harm that was not readily foreseeable, the level of culpability should carry more weight than harm when assessing offence seriousness.[346]

(ii) **Relevance of the originating conduct**

15. The **original conduct** that led to the making of an order is a relevant consideration in so far as it indicates the level of harm caused and whether this was intended.[347]
16. High culpability and/or harm may be indicated if the breach continues a pattern of behaviour against an identifiable victim. Conversely, where there is little connection between the breach and the behaviour that the order was aimed at, this may indicate a less serious offence.

---

[340] Criminal Justice Act 2003, s.143(1)
[341] Criminal Justice Act 2003, s.148(1)
[342] ibid., s.152(2)
[343] *Overarching Principles: Seriousness*, published 16 December 2004, www.sentencing-guidelines.gov.uk
[344] Criminal Justice Act 2003, s.143(1)
[345] Harm must have been foreseeable by 'a reasonable person'
[346] *Overarching Principles: Seriousness*, published 16 December 2004, www.sentencing-guidelines.gov.uk
[347] *Breach of a Protective Order*, published 7 December 2006, www.sentencing-guidelines.gov.uk

17. The court should examine the prohibitions of the order itself (particularly those in older orders which may have been made without the benefit of the guidance summarised in Annex A), their necessity and reasonableness in all the circumstances.[348]

(iii) Breach of an interim order

18. Breach of an interim order or a final order is equally serious and the same approach to sentencing should be taken.
19. Sentence for a breach of an interim order should be imposed as soon as possible. If the hearing regarding the final order can be brought forward, this should be done so that the two issues can be considered together. However, sentencing for the breach of the interim order should not be delayed for this purpose.
20. Where an interim order is breached the court should consider the extent to which an urgent need for specific interim prohibitions was demonstrated, or if the interim order was sought principally to obtain additional time to prepare a case for the full hearing.[349]
21. Where an interim order has been made without notice to the subject, the order does not take effect until it has been served. If doubts arise about the extent to which the subject has understood the prohibitions but the defence of reasonable excuse is not made out, a lack of understanding of the terms of the order may still mitigate the seriousness of the offence through reducing culpability.

(iv) A breach that also constitutes another criminal offence

22. Whether one offence or two has been charged, the sentence should reflect all relevant aspects of the offence so that, provided the facts are not in issue, the result should be the same.[350]
    (a) if the substantive offence only has been charged, the fact that it constitutes breach of an ASBO should be treated as an aggravating factor;
    (b) if breach of the order only has been charged, the sentence should reflect the full circumstances of the breach, which will include the conduct that could have been charged as a substantive offence.
23. Where breach of an ASBO also constitutes another offence with a lower maximum penalty than that for breach of the order, this penalty is an element to be considered in the interests of proportionality, although the court is not limited by it when sentencing an adult or youth for breach.

(v) Aggravating and mitigating factors

24. The Council guideline *Overarching Principles: Seriousness* identifies a number of factors that might increase or mitigate the seriousness of an offence. For ease of reference, the factors are set out in Annex B.

(vi) Personal mitigation

25. Offender mitigation is particularly relevant to breach of an ASBO as compliance with the order depends on the ability to understand its terms and make rational decisions in relation to these. Sentence may be mitigated where:
    - the offender has a lower level of understanding due to mental health issues or learning difficulties
    - the offender was acting under the influence of an older or more experienced offender; or
    - there has been compliance with an Individual Support Order or Intervention Order imposed when the ASBO was made.

D. Sentencing guideline—Adult offenders **SG-383**

Sentencing ranges and starting points

1. This guideline applies to a *"first time offender"* who has been **convicted after a trial**. In common with other proceedings based on breach of a court order,[351] it is likely that an offender in breach of an ASBO will have previous convictions. That has been taken into account in determining the starting points and ranges. Therefore, within this guideline, a "first time offender" is a person who does not

[348] Where appropriate, an application may be made separately for the order to be varied: Crime and Disorder Act 1998, ss.1(8) or 1CA. See also the Magistrates' Courts (Anti-Social Behaviour Orders) Rules 2002. Where the subject/offender is aged under 18, Practice Direction (Magistrates' Courts: Anti-Social Behaviour Orders: Composition of Benches) [2006] 1 AER 886 provides for the constitution of the court

[349] A report commissioned by the YJB concluded that there may be grounds for interim ASBOs only where there is an urgent need for specific prohibitions: Aikta-Reena Solanki, Tim Bateman, Gwyneth Boswell and Emily Hill, Anti-social Behaviour Orders, YJB (2006)

[350] *Breach of a Protective Order*, published 7 December 2006, www.sentencing-guidelines.gov.uk

[351] for example, failing to surrender to bail

have a conviction for breach of an ASBO rather than the usual approach which is based on the existence of any conviction which, by virtue of section 143(2) of the Criminal Justice Act 2003, must be treated as an aggravating factor.

2. As an aid to consistency of approach, the guideline describes a number of types of activity which would fall within the broad definition of the offence. These are set out in a column headed 'Nature of failure & harm'.
3. The expected approach is for a court to identify the description that most nearly matches the particular facts of the offence for which sentence is being imposed. This will identify a **starting point** from which the sentencer can depart to reflect aggravating or mitigating factors affecting the seriousness of the offence (beyond those contained within the column describing the nature of the failure or of the harm) to reach a **provisional sentence**.
4. The **sentencing range** is the bracket into which the provisional sentence will normally fall after having regard to factors which aggravate or mitigate the seriousness of the offence. The particular circumstances may, however, make it appropriate that the provisional sentence falls outside the range.
5. Where the offender has previous convictions which aggravate the seriousness of the current offence, that may take the provisional sentence beyond the range given particularly where there are significant other aggravating factors present.
6. Once the provisional sentence has been identified by reference to those factors affecting the seriousness of the offence, the court will take into account any relevant factors of personal mitigation, which may take the sentence beyond the range given.
7. Where there has been a guilty plea, any reduction attributable to that plea will be applied to the sentence at this stage. Again, this reduction may take the sentence below the range provided.
8. A court must give its reasons for imposing a sentence of a different kind or outside the range provided in the guidelines.[352]

The decision making process

[Sets out the standard sequential decision making process: identify starting point, consider aggravating factors, consider mitigating factors, apply reduction for guilty plea, consider ancillary orders, review in light of the totality principle and give reasons.]

Factors to take into consideration

1. The starting points and sentencing ranges are for a *"first time offender"* who pleaded not guilty. In this guideline, a *"first time offender"* is one who does not have a previous conviction for breach of an ASBO.
2. Where a court determines that there are other convictions which it is reasonable to treat as a factor aggravating the seriousness of the breach,[353] that factor will be taken into account at stage 2 of the sentencing process set out on page 7.
3. An ASBO may be breached in a wide range of circumstances and may involve one or more prohibitions not being complied with. The examples given below are intended to illustrate how the scale of the conduct that led to the breach, taken as a whole, might come within the three levels of seriousness:
    - Serious harm caused or intended—breach at this level of seriousness will involve the use of violence, significant threats or intimidation or the targeting of individuals or groups of people in a manner that leads to a fear of violence.
    - Lesser degree of harm intended or likely—examples may include lesser degrees of threats or intimidation, the use of seriously abusive language, or causing more than minor damage to property.
    - No harm caused or intended—in the absence of intimidation or the causing of fear of violence, breaches involving being drunk or begging may be at this level, as may prohibited use of public transport or entry into a prohibited area, where there is no evidence that harassment, alarm or distress was caused or intended.
4. The suggested starting points are based on the assumption that the offender had the highest level of culpability.
5. Aggravating and mitigating factors specifically relevant to sentencing for breach of an ASBO are included in the guideline. Care needs to be taken to ensure that there is no double counting where an element of the breach determines the level of seriousness where it might in other circumstances be an

[352] Criminal Justice Act 2003, s.174(2)(a)
[353] in accordance with Criminal Justice Act 2003, s.143(2)

aggravating factor. When assessing the seriousness of an offence, the court must always refer to the full list of aggravating and mitigating factors in the Council guideline on Seriousness (see Annex B).[354]

6. In the most serious cases, involving repeat offending and a breach causing serious harassment together with the presence of several aggravating factors, such as the use of violence, a sentence beyond the highest range will be justified.
7. Once the provisional sentence has been identified by reference to factors affecting the seriousness of the offence, the court will take into account any relevant factors of personal mitigation (see paragraph 25 above), and, in accordance with the Council guideline[355] consider reducing the sentence where a guilty plea was entered.
8. When imposing a community order, the court must ensure that the requirements imposed are proportionate to the seriousness of the breach, compatible with each other,[356] and also with the prohibitions of the ASBO if the latter is to remain in force. Even where the threshold for a custodial sentence is crossed, a custodial sentence is not inevitable.[357]
9. An offender may be sentenced for more than one offence of breach, which occurred on different days. While consecutive sentences may be imposed in such cases, the overall sentence should reflect the totality principle.

Breach of an Anti-Social Behaviour Order

Crime and Disorder Act 1998 (section 1(10))

Maximum Penalty: 5 years imprisonment

Note: A conditional discharge is not available as a sentence for this offence

Nature of failure & harm	Starting point	Sentencing range
Serious harassment, alarm or distress has been caused or where such harm was intended	**26 weeks custody**	**Custody threshold—2 years custody**
Lesser degree of harassment, alarm or distress, where such harm was intended, or where it would have been likely if the offender had not been apprehended	**6 weeks custody**	**Community Order (MEDIUM)—26 weeks custody**
No harassment, alarm or distress was actually caused by the breach and none was intended by the offender	**Community Order (LOW)**	**Fine Band B—Community Order (MEDIUM)**

Aggravating factors	Mitigating factors
1. Offender has a history of disobedience to court orders. 2. Breach was committed immediately or shortly after the order was made. 3. Breach was committed subsequent to earlier breach proceedings arising from the same order. 4. Targeting of a person the order was made to protect or a witness in the original proceedings.	1. Breach occurred after a long period of compliance. 2. The prohibition(s) breached was not fully understood, especially where an interim order was made without notice.

E. Sentencing principles: Young Offenders SG-384

1. The approach to assessing the seriousness of a breach outlined above at paragraphs 7 to 25 applies equally to youths. A court must impose a community or custodial sentence only if such a sentence is warranted by the seriousness of the offence and no lesser sentence can be justified.
2. When sentencing a young offender, the normal approach is for the penalty to reflect both the reduction in culpability (for example, due to a lesser ability to foresee the consequences of actions) and the

[354] *Overarching Principles: Seriousness*, published 16 December 2004, www.sentencing-guidelines.gov.uk
[355] *Reduction in Sentence for a Guilty Plea*, published 20 July 2007, www.sentencing-guidelines.gov.uk
[356] *New Sentences: Criminal Justice Act 2003*, published 16 December 2004, www.sentencing-guidelines.gov.uk
[357] ibid.

more onerous effects of punishments on education and personal development in comparison with an adult offender.

3. The sentencing framework that applies to offenders aged under 18 is significantly different from that for adult offenders and key principles are set out in Annex C. The maximum penalty for this offence when committed by a young offender is a 24 month detention and training order (DTO). With the exception of a conditional discharge,[358] the full range of disposals of the youth court is available, and these are also outlined in Annex C.[359]
4. In most cases of breach by a young offender convicted after a trial, the appropriate sentence will be a community sentence.[360] Within the sentence(s) available, a range of requirements can be attached; the court will consider the seriousness of the breach, which requirement(s) will best prevent further offending and the individual circumstances of the offender.
5. The court must ensure that the requirements imposed are compatible both with each other and with the prohibitions of the ASBO if the latter is to remain in force, and that the combination of both is not so onerous as to make further breaches likely.
6. The particular stage of intellectual or emotional maturity of the individual (which may not correspond with actual age) will also influence sentence. A young offender is likely to perceive a particular time period as being longer in comparison with an adult, and this may be of relevance when considering how much time has elapsed between imposition and breach of the order.
7. The principles to be followed when sentencing a youth for breach of an ASBO are as follows:
   "First time offender"[361] pleading guilty: the court[362] must make a referral order unless it imposes an absolute discharge, a custodial sentence or a hospital order;

In all other cases:

(i) in some less serious cases, such as where the breach has not involved any harassment, alarm or distress, a fine may be appropriate if it will be paid by the offender, or otherwise a reparation order;
(ii) in most cases, the appropriate sentence will be a community sentence;
(iii) the custody threshold should be set at a significantly higher level than the threshold applicable to adult offenders;
(iv) the custody threshold usually will not be crossed unless the breach involved serious harassment, alarm or distress through either the use of violence, threats or intimidation or the targeting of individuals/groups in a manner that led to a fear of violence;
(v) exceptionally, the custody threshold may also be crossed where a youth is being sentenced for more than one offence of breach (committed on separate occasions within a short period) involving a lesser but substantial degree of harassment, alarm or distress;
(vi) even where the custody threshold is crossed, the court should normally impose a community sentence in preference to a DTO, as custody should be used only as a measure of last resort; and
(vii) where the court considers a custodial sentence to be unavoidable, the starting point for sentencing should be 4 months detention, with a range of up to 12 months. Where a youth is being sentenced for more than one breach involving serious harassment, alarm or distress, sentence may go beyond that range.

Aggravating and mitigating factors

8. As with adult offenders, factors that are likely to <u>aggravate</u> an offence of breach of an anti-social behaviour order are:
   - history of disobedience of court orders
   - the breach was committed immediately or shortly after the order was made
   - the breach was committed subsequent to earlier breach proceedings arising from the same order
   - targeting of a person the order was made to protect or of a witness in the original proceedings.
9. Factors that are likely to <u>mitigate</u> the seriousness of the breach are:
   - the breach occurred after a long period of compliance

[358] Crime and Disorder Act 1998, s.1(11) and s.1C(9)

[359] If the young offender has also been charged with a grave crime under s.91 Powers of Criminal Courts (Sentencing) Act 2000, the case may be committed to the Crown Court. Similarly, where the young offender is committed to the Crown Court for sentence under the dangerous offender provisions

[360] though see paragraph 7 below

[361] For the purpose of this requirement, a "first time offender" is an offender who has never been convicted by or before a court in the United Kingdom of any offence other than the offence and any connected offence, or been bound over in criminal proceedings; Powers of Criminal Court (Sentencing) Act 2000, s.17(1)(b) and (c)

[362] A referral order may be made by a youth court or other magistrates' court; Powers of Criminal Courts (Sentencing) Act 2000, s.16(1)

- the prohibition(s) breached was not fully understood, especially where an interim order was made without notice.

Personal mitigation

10. Offender mitigation is particularly relevant to breach of an ASBO as compliance with the order depends on the ability to understand its terms and make rational decisions in relation to these. Sentence may be mitigated where:
    - the offender has a lower level of understanding due to mental health issues or learning difficulties
    - the offender was acting under the influence of an older or more experienced offender; or
    - there has been compliance with an Individual Support Order or Intervention Order imposed when the ASBO was made.
11. Other offender mitigating factors that may be particularly relevant to young offenders include peer pressure and a lack of parental support.

PART 16 ATTEMPTED MURDER SG-385

. . . This guideline applies to the sentencing of offenders convicted of any of the offences dealt with herein who are sentenced on or after **27 July 2009**.

This guideline applies only to the sentencing of offenders aged 18 and older. The legislative provisions relating to the sentencing of youths are different; the younger the age, the greater the difference. A separate guideline setting out general principles relating to the sentencing of youths is planned.

. . .

Introduction SG-386

1. This guideline covers the single offence of attempted murder. The Council has published a separate definitive guideline for offences of assault which do not result in the death of the victim.[363]
2. There are critical differences between murder and attempted murder; not only is the intended result not achieved but also, for attempted murder, there must have been an intention to kill whereas a charge of murder may arise where the intention was to inflict grievous bodily harm. These differences are reflected in the approach set out below which supersedes previous guidance from the Court of Appeal in *Ford*[364] and other judgments.

A. Assessing seriousness SG-387

(i) Culpability and harm

3. The culpability of the offender is the initial factor in determining the seriousness of an offence. It is an essential element of the offence of attempted murder that the offender had an intention to kill; accordingly an offender convicted of this offence will have demonstrated a high level of culpability. Even so, the precise level of culpability will vary in line with the circumstances of the offence and whether the offence was planned or spontaneous. The use of a weapon may influence this assessment.
4. In common with all offences against the person, this offence has the potential to contain an imbalance between culpability and harm.[365]
5. Where the degree of harm actually caused to the victim of an attempted murder is negligible, it is inevitable that this will impact on the overall assessment of offence seriousness.
6. However, although the degree of (or lack of) physical or psychological harm suffered by a victim may generally influence sentence, the statutory definition of harm encompasses not only the harm actually caused by an offence but also any harm that the offence was intended to cause or might foreseeably have caused; since the offence can only be committed where there is an intention to kill, an offence of attempted murder will always involve, in principle, the most serious level of harm.

(ii) Aggravating and mitigating factors

7. The most serious offences of attempted murder will include those which encompass the factors set out in schedule 21 to the Criminal Justice Act 2003, paragraphs 4 and 5 that, had the offence been murder, would make the seriousness of the offence 'exceptionally high' or 'particularly high'. [See **E3.2**.]

[363] *Assault and other offences against the person*, published 20 February 2008, www.sentencing-guidelines.gov.uk
[364] [2005] EWCA Crim 1358
[365] see *Overarching Principles: Seriousness*, para. 1.17, published 16 December 2004, www.sentencing-guidelines.gov.uk

8. The particular facts of the offence will identify the appropriate level. In all cases, the aggravating and mitigating factors that will influence the identification of the provisional sentence within the range follow those set out in schedule 21 with suitable adjustments. These factors are included in the guideline [below].
9. The *Seriousness* guideline[366] sets out aggravating and mitigating factors that are applicable to a wide range of cases; [see **SG-21**]. Some are already reflected in the factors referred to above. Care needs to be taken to ensure that there is no double counting where an essential element of the offence charged might, in other circumstances, be an aggravating factor. An additional statutory aggravating factor has been introduced by the Counter-Terrorism Act 2008 for prescribed offences which include attempted murder.[367]
10. This guideline is not intended to provide for an offence found to be based on a genuine belief that the murder would have been an act of mercy. Whilst the approach to assessing the seriousness of the offence may be similar, there are likely to be other factors present (relating to the offence and the offender) that would have to be taken into account and reflected in the sentence.

SG-388 **B. Ancillary orders**

Compensation orders

11. A court must consider making a compensation order in respect of any personal injury, loss or damage occasioned. There is no limit to the amount of compensation that may be awarded in the Crown Court.

SG-389 **C. Sentencing ranges and starting points**

12. Typically, a guideline will apply to an offence that can be committed in a variety of circumstances with different levels of seriousness. The starting points and ranges are based upon an adult '*first time offender*' who has been **convicted after a trial**. Within the guidelines, a '*first time offender*' is a person who does not have a conviction which, by virtue of section 143(2) of the Criminal Justice Act 2003, must be treated as an aggravating factor.
13. As an aid to consistency of approach, the guideline describes a number of levels or types of activity which would fall within the broad definition of the offence.
14. The expected approach is for a court to identify the description that most nearly matches the particular facts of the offence for which sentence is being imposed. This will identify a **starting point** from which the sentencer can depart to reflect aggravating or mitigating factors affecting the seriousness of the offence (beyond those contained within the column describing the nature of the offence) to reach a **provisional sentence**.
15. The **sentencing range** is the bracket into which the provisional sentence will normally fall after having regard to factors which aggravate or mitigate the seriousness of the offence. The particular circumstances may, however, make it appropriate that the provisional sentence falls outside the range.
16. Where the offender has previous convictions which aggravate the seriousness of the current offence, that may take the provisional sentence beyond the range given particularly where there are significant other aggravating factors present.
17. Once the provisional sentence has been identified by reference to those factors affecting the seriousness of the offence, the court will take into account any relevant factors of personal mitigation, which may take the sentence below the range given.
18. Where there has been a guilty plea, any reduction attributable to that plea will be applied to the sentence at this stage. This reduction may take the sentence below the range provided.
19. A court must give its reasons for imposing a sentence of a different kind or outside the range provided in the guidelines.

SG-390 **D. Factors to take into consideration**

1. Attempted murder is a serious offence for the purposes of the provisions in the Criminal Justice Act 2003[368] for dealing with dangerous offenders. When sentencing an offender convicted of this offence, in many circumstances a court may need to consider imposing a discretionary life sentence or one of the sentences for public protection prescribed in the Act.
2. The starting points and ranges are based upon a first time adult offender convicted after a trial (see paragraphs 12–19 above). They will be relevant when imposing a determinate sentence and when

[366] *Overarching Principles: Seriousness*, paras. 1.20–1.27 published on 16 December 2004; www.sentencing-guidelines.gov.uk
[367] s. 30 and schedule 2. If a court determines that the offence has a terrorist connection, it must treat that as an aggravating factor, and state in open court that the offence was so aggravated.
[368] Sections 224–230 as amended

fixing any minimum term that may be necessary. When setting the minimum term to be served within an indeterminate sentence, in accordance with normal practice that term will usually be half the equivalent determinate sentence.[369]

3. Attempted murder requires an intention to kill. Accordingly, an offender convicted of this offence will have demonstrated a high level of culpability. Even so, the precise level of culpability will vary in line with the circumstances of the offence and whether the offence was planned or spontaneous. The use of a weapon may influence this assessment.
4. The level of injury or harm sustained by the victim as well as any harm that the offence was intended to cause or might foreseeably have caused, must be taken into account and reflected in the sentence imposed.
5. The degree of harm will vary greatly. Where there is low harm and high culpability, culpability is more significant.[370] Even in cases where a low level of injury (or no injury) has been caused, an offence of attempted murder will be extremely serious.
6. The most serious offences will include those which encompass the factors set out in schedule 21 to the Criminal Justice Act 2003, paragraphs 4 and 5 that, had the offence been murder, would make the seriousness of the offence 'exceptionally high' or 'particularly high': see [**E3.2**].
7. The particular facts of the offence will identify the appropriate level. In all cases, the aggravating and mitigating factors that will influence the identification of the provisional sentence within the range follow those set out in schedule 21 with suitable adjustments. This guideline is not intended to provide for an offence found to be based on a genuine belief that the murder would have been an act of mercy.
8. When assessing the seriousness of an offence, the court should also refer to the list of general aggravating and mitigating factors in the Council guideline on *Seriousness* (see [**SG-21**]). Care should be taken to ensure there is no double counting where an essential element of the offence charged might, in other circumstances, be an aggravating factor.

Attempted Murder **SG-391**

Criminal Attempts Act 1981 (section 1(1))

THIS IS A SERIOUS OFFENCE FOR THE PURPOSES OF SECTION 224 CRIMINAL JUSTICE ACT 2003

Maximum penalty: Life imprisonment

Nature of offence	Starting point	Sentencing range
Level 1 *The most serious offences including those which (if the charge had been murder) would come within para. 4 or para. 5 of schedule 21 to the Criminal Justice Act 2003*		
• Serious and long term physical or psychological harm	30 years custody	27–35 years custody
• Some physical or psychological harm	20 years custody	17–25 years custody
• Little or no physical or psychological harm	15 years custody	12–20 years custody
Level 2 *Other planned attempt to kill*		
• Serious and long term physical or psychological harm	20 years custody	17–25 years custody
• Some physical or psychological harm	15 years custody	12–20 years custody
• Little or no physical or psychological harm	10 years custody	7–15 years custody
Level 3 *Other spontaneous attempt to kill*		
• Serious and long term physical or psychological harm	15 years custody	12–20 years custody
• Some physical or psychological harm	12 years custody	9–17 years custody
• Little or no physical or psychological harm	9 years custody	6–14 years custody

369 *R v Szczerba* [2002] 2 Cr App R (S) 86
370 *Overarching Principles: Seriousness*, para. 1.19, published on 16 December 2004; www.sentencing.guidelines.gov.uk

Specific aggravating factors	Specific mitigating factors
(a) the fact that the victim was particularly vulnerable, for example, because of age or disability (b) mental or physical suffering inflicted on the victim (c) the abuse of a position of trust (d) the use of duress or threats against another person to facilitate the commission of the offence (e) the fact that the victim was providing a public service or performing a public duty	(a) the fact that the offender suffered from any mental disorder or mental disability which lowered his degree of culpability (b) the fact that the offender was provoked (for example, by prolonged stress) (c) the fact that the offender acted to any extent in self-defence (d) the age of the offender

The presence of one or more aggravating features will indicate a more severe sentence within the suggested range and, if the aggravating feature(s) are exceptionally serious, the case will move up to the next level.

SG-392 [Annex A is an extract from the CJA 2003, sch. 21. It is not reproduced here. For the relevant text, see E3.2.

Annex B reproduces the elements indicating higher culpability, a more than usually serious degree of harm and lower culpability and factors which may be relevant personal mitigation from the Council guideline *Overarching Principles: Seriousness*. See **SG-21** for the full guideline.]

SG-393 PART 17 SENTENCING FOR FRAUD—STATUTORY OFFENCES

. . . This guideline applies to the sentencing of offenders convicted of statutory offences of fraud who are sentenced on or after **26 October 2009**.

This guideline does not cover the common law offence of **cheating the public revenue**, or **conspiracy to defraud**. Judges should continue to refer to existing guidance from the Court of Appeal (Criminal Division) when sentencing these offences.

This guideline applies only to the sentencing of offenders aged 18 and over. The legislative provisions relating to the sentencing of youths are different; the younger the age, the greater the difference. A separate guideline setting out general principles relating to the sentencing of youths is planned.

. . .

SG-394 **A. Statutory provisions and Introduction**

1. Fraud offences involve offenders dishonestly intending to make a gain by exposing someone else to a risk of loss; the gain may be financial and/or involve other property. Fraud offences are diverse and there is an ever-increasing number of ways in which they can be committed.
2. This guideline applies to sentencing for statutory offences of fraud. This guideline does not cover the common law offence of **cheating the public revenue**, or **conspiracy to defraud.** The common law offence of cheating the public revenue is generally reserved for the most serious and unusual offences[371] and where a sentence 'in excess of the statutory maximum for other offences . . . would be . . . proper.'[372] As such cases are unusual, no proposals are made for sentencing offenders convicted of this offence. It would be open to a court to have regard to the principles expressed in the guideline for fraud against HMRC when sentencing an offender convicted of cheating the public revenue, but it should be used only as a point of reference as higher starting points are likely to be necessary. Sentencers should continue to refer to existing guidance from the Court of Appeal (Criminal Division) when sentencing these offences.
3. The statutory offences included in this guideline are set out in paragraph 5 (statutory definitions and maximum penalties are set out in Annex A). The generic fraud offence introduced by section 1 of the Fraud Act 2006 was designed to capture all forms of fraudulent activity committed by individual offenders, including minor offences. However, other offences will continue to be prosecuted, thus the proposed guidelines include related offences.
4. Since many of the offences are defined broadly (in order to encapsulate a wide range of behaviour), some types of fraudulent activity are capable of leading to conviction for more than one offence;

[371] *Mavji* (1987) 84 Cr App R 34
[372] *Ward* [2005] EWCA Crim 1926

accordingly, the guidelines focus on the type of fraud,[373] rather than the specific conviction offence, in order to establish appropriate sentence levels which take account of the interrelationship between the offences. The guideline aims to produce a coherent and consistent approach to sentencing all forms of fraudulent behaviour; it supersedes previous guideline (and other significant) cases which have been reviewed in the light of subsequent changes to the sentencing framework, particularly those in the Criminal Justice Act 2003.

5. In this guideline, the offences are grouped by type as follows:

- *Confidence fraud*

Fraud Act 2006, s. 1
Theft Act 1968, s. 17

- *Possessing, making or supplying articles for use in fraud*

Fraud Act 2006, ss. 1, 6 and 7

- *Banking and insurance fraud, and obtaining credit through fraud*

Fraud Act 2006, s. 1
Theft Act 1968, s. 17

- *Benefit fraud*

Fraud Act 2000, s. 1
Theft Act 1968, s. 17
Tax Credits Act 2002, s. 35
Social Security Administration Act 1992, ss. 111A(1), 111(1A), 111(1B), 111(1D) and 111(1E)

- *Revenue fraud (against HM Revenue and Customs)*

Fraud Act 2006, s. 1
Theft Act 1968, s. 17
Value Added Tax Act 1994, ss. 72(1), 72(3), and 72(8)
Finance Act 2000, s. 144
Customs and Excise Management Act 1979, ss. 170(1)(a)(i) and (ii), 170(1)(b), 170(2)(a), 170B, 50(1)(a), and 50(2)

6. The offence of **obtaining services dishonestly** (contrary to section 11 of the Fraud Act 2006) may be committed in circumstances that otherwise could be charged as an offence contrary to section 1 of the Act or may be more akin to *making off without payment*. For this reason, it has not been included specifically within any of these guidelines, and one of the following approaches should be used:
   - *where it involves conduct which can be characterised as a fraud offence (such as obtaining credit through fraud or payment card fraud), the court should apply the guideline for the relevant type of fraud; or*
   - *where the conduct could be characterised as making off without payment (that is, where an offender, knowing that payment on the spot for any goods supplied or service done is required or expected, dishonestly makes off without having paid and with intent to avoid payment),*[374] *the guideline for that offence*[375] *should be used.*

7. The primary consideration when sentencing fraud offences is the seriousness of the offending behaviour. Sentencers must also have regard to the five purposes of sentencing set out in section 142(1) of the Criminal Justice Act 2003; as a general principle, the approach to sentencing types of fraud offence should be the same, regardless of the context within which the offence was committed.

8. The approach to sentencing, starting points and ranges has taken account of the other sanctions and ancillary orders likely to be applied (some of which are mandatory and others discretionary), which may have a significant impact on an offender.

9. The guideline applies to the sentencing of adult offenders only; separate legislative provisions and sentencing principles apply to young offenders.

B. Assessing seriousness **SG-395**

10. When assessing offence seriousness, the court must consider the offender's culpability in committing the offence and any harm that the offence caused, was intended to cause, or might foreseeably

[373] The types of fraud are based on those used in *Current Sentencing Practice*, published by Sweet & Maxwell. However, the category 'mortgage fraud' has been expanded to include obtaining other forms of credit and is labelled 'obtaining credit through fraud'. Similarly, the category 'cheque fraud' has been expanded to include other forms of bank account and payment method fraud and is labelled 'payment card and bank account fraud'.

[374] Theft Act 1978, s. 3

[375] *Magistrates' Court Sentencing Guidelines*, page 79, www.sentencing-guidelines.gov.uk

have caused.[376] Key considerations are the degree of planning, the determination with which the offender carried out the offence and the value of the money or property involved.

(i) Culpability and harm

11. The Council guideline *Overarching Principles: Seriousness*[377] sets out four levels of culpability, the highest of which is an intention to cause harm. It is a general feature of fraud offences (with one exception)[378] that an offender intended to bring about a gain (whether for the offender or for another person) or to cause a loss, or risk of loss, to another. Generally, therefore, fraud offences involve the highest level of culpability. Within that level, culpability will vary according to the offender's motivation, whether the offence was planned or spontaneous and whether the offender was in a position of trust.[379]
12. Some of the forms of fraud covered by this guideline will, at times, involve offending by a number of people acting co-operatively. This will aggravate an offence of fraud because it will indicate planning or professional activity; it may also increase the degree of loss caused or intended. As a result, it is likely to cause an offence to be in a higher level of seriousness. The role of each offender will be important in determining movement above or below the starting point within the range applicable to that level (see aggravating and mitigating factors below).
13. Fraud is not a victimless crime. The monetary cost is significant, but fraud offences also cause considerable social and economic harm beyond their immediate financial impact. Fraud can be used to fund organised crime that may target vulnerable victims (drug and people trafficking, for example) and fraud offences that target individuals can ruin lives, close businesses or take life savings.
14. In assessing the harm caused by fraud offences, the primary consideration is the loss to the victim or to the community at large. In some fraud cases, the harm that results from an offence may be greater than the harm intended by the offender. In others, the offender may have intended more harm than actually results. In these situations, the harm caused by the offence should be judged in light of the offender's culpability.[380]
15. In general terms, the greater the loss, the more serious will be the offence. However, the financial value of the loss may not reflect the full extent of the harm caused by the offence. The court should also take into account:

(a) The impact of the offence on the victim

16. Whilst an offender who obtains a particular sum will benefit to the same extent regardless of the circumstances of the victim, the impact may vary considerably. Where the loss is significantly greater than the monetary value (for example, where, although relatively low in absolute terms, the value is high in proportion to the victim's financial circumstances or resources or the property has considerable sentimental value) the court should take into account the impact of the offence on the victim; this is likely to apply whether the victim is an individual, a small business or a large company.

(b) Harm to persons other than the direct victim

17. Some fraud offences will have a varying impact on different victims. For example, fraudulently using the credit or debit card details of another person will have a direct financial impact on the card issuer, who normally will be expected to absorb the loss, but it may also have an impact on the cardholder. The aggravation and stress of unscrambling the consequences of the offenders criminal activities often far outweighs the impact of the financial loss suffered by the card issuer.

(c) Erosion of public confidence

18. Frauds using credit and debit cards may undermine the integrity of those payment methods.

(d) Any physical harm or risk of physical harm to the direct victim or another person

19. As part of committing a fraud, a risk may be created of physical injury either to the victim or to some other person not directly involved. For example, where a person deliberately sets fire to premises owned by them or causes an innocent driver to crash into his or her vehicle, in order that an insurance claim may be made, the risk of injury and the impact on the innocent driver will increase the harm caused by the fraud on the insurance company.

[376] Criminal Justice Act 2003, s. 143(1)
[377] at para. 1.7, published 16 December 2004, www.sentencing-guidelines.gov.uk
[378] VAT fraud can be committed by recklessly making a statement that contains a false detail (Value Added Tax Act 1994, s. 72(3) (b))
[379] *Overarching Principles: Seriousness*, para. 1.17, published 16 December 2004, www.sentencing-guidelines.gov.uk
[380] ibid.

(e) Difference between loss intended and resulting

20. In the guidelines that follow, where the amount of money obtained is used as a determinant of seriousness, a court should take the starting point corresponding to the amount that the offender dishonestly intended to obtain and adjust the assessment of seriousness to reflect the degree of loss actually caused by the offence. Common situations include:
no loss intended: in obtaining credit through fraud, an offender may not intend to cause any loss but to repay any sums advanced or to keep the bank account in credit. Indeed, an application that was not fraudulent may have been successful. Whilst, in such a case, the offender does not intend to cause any harm, nonetheless a loss may result.

A court should use the starting point corresponding to no financial loss and, where a loss occurs, adjust the assessment of seriousness to reflect the degree of loss.

Gain intended but no actual loss results: in some insurance fraud cases, an offender may present a fraudulent claim to an insurer but the insurer, suspecting fraud, does not pay out any money. In these cases, although the insurer suffers no actual financial loss, it is possible to calculate the amount of money which the offender dishonestly intended to obtain.

In such cases a court should use the starting point corresponding to the amount which the offender intended to obtain and adjust the assessment of seriousness to reflect the fact that no loss has resulted.

(f) Legitimate entitlement to part or all of the amount obtained

21. In some cases an offender may be entitled honestly to all or part of the money that is obtained following the fraudulent activity. This is a feature of all exaggerated claims but may arise in other cases.

In such cases, the starting point should be based on the amount to which the offender was not legitimately entitled.

(ii) Aggravating factors

22. The Council guideline *Overarching Principles: Seriousness* sets out a number of factors that indicate a higher than usual level of culpability on the part of the offender or a greater than usual degree of harm to the victim.[381] The complete list is set out in Annex B [not reproduced here: see **SG-25**]. Those factors most likely to be present in offences of fraud are:

Factors indicating higher culpability
- Planning of an offence
- An intention to commit more serious harm than actually resulted from the offence (including any physical harm or risk of physical harm)
- Offenders operating in groups or gangs
- 'Professional offending'
- High level of profit from the offence
- An attempt to conceal or dispose of evidence
- Deliberate targeting of vulnerable victim(s)
- Abuse of a position of trust

Factors indicating a more than usually serious degree of harm
- Multiple victims
- Victim is particularly vulnerable
- High value (including sentimental value) of property to the victim, or substantial consequential loss

23. The Council has identified four factors that are particularly relevant to this type of offending behaviour:

(a) Number involved in the offence and role of offender

24. Where an offender was an organiser, planner or prime mover in a fraudulent enterprise carried out by a number of individuals acting together, this is likely to be an aggravating factor which will tend to move the sentence above the appropriate starting point.

(b) Offending carried out over a significant period of time

25. Where a fraud is committed by obtaining money or property on several occasions over a long period[382] (for example, in some benefit frauds where each payment is relatively low but the fraud continues over

[381] *Overarching Principles: Seriousness*, paras. 1.22 and 1.23, published 16 December 2004, www.sentencing-guidelines.gov.uk

[382] Due to changes in the rules governing indictments, frauds undertaken over a significant period of time may now be charged in one count where previously multiple counts were required: Criminal Procedure Rules 2005, r.14.2(2), inserted by the

a period), the seriousness of the offence will be assessed both on the amount of money or property involved and on the period of time over which it was obtained.

(c) Use of another person's identity

26. Use of another person's identity may increase the harm caused; this may vary depending on the origins of the stolen identity:
    - *using the identity of a living person is likely to cause emotional distress for that individual who will also have the practical and potentially stressful problem of untangling the financial consequences of the fraud;*
    - *using the identity of a deceased person is likely to indicate a higher degree of planning (as it can be an attempt to make the fraud more difficult to uncover) and is likely to cause considerable distress to the relatives of the deceased, especially if that person has only recently died.*

27. Using the identity of another person is an aggravating factor; the extent to which it aggravates an offence will be based on the degree of planning and the impact that the offence has had on the living victim or the relatives of the deceased. Accordingly, in itself, whether the identity belongs to a living or deceased person should be neutral for this purpose.

(d) Offence has a lasting effect on the victim

28. The lives of individual victims may be severely affected by fraud offences. Individual victims may lose most or all of their savings, be unable to make mortgage and loan repayments, or have to work beyond retirement age. Where the fraud was perpetrated by someone entrusted with the victim's financial affairs, the victim's ability to trust future advice may be permanently damaged. Such lasting impacts will aggravate an offence.

(iii) Mitigating factors

29. The Council guideline *Overarching Principles: Seriousness* sets out factors which indicate that an offender's culpability is unusually low or that the harm caused by an offence is less than usually serious.[383] These are set out in Annex B [not reproduced here: see **SG-25**]. Those factors most likely to be present in offences of fraud are:

    Factors indicating significantly lower culpability:
    - Mental illness or disability
    - Youth or age, where it affects the responsibility of the individual defendant
    - The fact that the offender played only a minor role in the offence.

30. The Council has identified three mitigating factors that are particularly relevant to this type of offending:

(a) Peripheral involvement

31. Where an offender played a minor or peripheral role in an offence of fraud or, rather than having planned to take part, became involved through the influence of others and not as an organiser or prime mover, this is likely to be a mitigating factor which will tend to move the sentence below the appropriate starting point.

(b) Behaviour not fraudulent from the outset

32. Where an offender originally had a legitimate entitlement to financial benefits but continued to claim following a change in circumstances that affected entitlement, the initial intention was not dishonest but it became so at the point when the changed circumstances were not disclosed to the financial authority and the offender made the decision to continue to claim.

33. In principle, continuing to claim monies to which there is no longer entitlement may in certain circumstances be less culpable than claiming monies to which there had never been a legitimate entitlement; therefore, this is likely to influence the assessment of the seriousness of the offence.

34. However, the degree to which this difference has an effect on the sentence imposed will depend on the circumstances that led to the failure to disclose, the effort that was involved in commencing or perpetuating the fraud, the length of time over which the sums were defrauded and the amount of money defrauded.

35. Where applicable, a guideline is based on an offence where the offender's initial intention is dishonest; accordingly, conduct that was not fraudulent from the outset is capable of being a mitigating factor. The degree of mitigation is likely to be greater where there is evidence that the customer service

Criminal Procedure (Amendment) Rules 2007. However, where multiple counts are charged and a trial of all those counts by jury would be impractical, a representative sample of counts can be tried by a jury with the remaining counts tried, if the defendant is convicted of the sample counts, by a judge sitting alone: Domestic Violence, Crime and Victims Act 2004, s. 17

[383] *Overarching Principles: Seriousness*, para. 1.25, published 16 December 2004, www.sentencing-guidelines.gov.uk

of the financial authority was inadequate and it proved difficult for the offender to understand the rules or to properly explain his or her position.

(c) Misleading or incomplete advice

36. Even where the behaviour was fraudulent from the outset, the fact that an offender can demonstrate that he or she was given misleading or incomplete advice may in certain circumstances be treated as a mitigating factor.

(iv) Personal mitigation

37. Having formed an initial assessment of the seriousness of an offence, the court should then take account of any offender mitigation. A number of factors may be present in relation to fraud offences and may influence the choice or severity of sentence in an individual case. These are considered below.

(a) Voluntary cessation of offending

38. In some cases, particularly those where a fraud has been carried out over a significant period of time, offenders may stop offending (or claim to have stopped offending) before they are apprehended. Where there is objective evidence to support such a claim, particularly where it is accompanied by a genuine expression of remorse,[384] this usually should be treated as offender mitigation.
39. The time that has elapsed since the commission of the last offence will be an important factor in determining whether the cessation of offending is genuine and was likely to have lasted even if the offending had not come to notice. In addition, the court will want to consider the reasons why an offender stopped offending; where that was because of a heightened fear of discovery or the fact that the additional funds were no longer needed, a court may conclude that the degree of mitigation is negligible or that this factor should not be taken into account at all.

(b) Complete and unprompted disclosure of the extent of the fraud

40. Some offenders voluntarily disclose offences of which the authorities were previously unaware. Others, when apprehended, make a complete and unprompted disclosure to the authorities of the extent of the fraud.
41. Where an offender admits to obtaining fraudulently a greater sum than that known to the authorities, this increases the likelihood that victims will be able to recover some of the money and ensures that the offender is sentenced for the complete extent of the fraud, rather than according to what would otherwise have been known to the prosecutor. This amounts to ready co-operation with the authorities, which the Council has recognised as offender mitigation.[385]
42. Where an offender provides information about other individuals who were involved in committing the fraud, the court will normally treat this as offender mitigation. In addition, the practice of reducing the sentence is now permitted by statute in some circumstances where the offender enters into a written agreement with a specified prosecutor.[386]
43. The point at which the disclosure is made, and the degree of assistance given to the authorities, should determine the amount of mitigation. In order to promote complete disclosure at the earliest possible time, generally the earlier the disclosure is given and the higher the degree of assistance, the greater the allowance for offender mitigation.

(c) Voluntary restitution

44. The point at which an offender voluntarily returns property or money obtained through fraud will be important and, in general, the earlier the property or money is returned the greater the degree of mitigation the offender should receive.[387] Providing an incentive to return property or money is particularly important as it may be difficult for a victim to recover his or her losses in any other way.[388] The timing of the voluntary restitution may be an indicator of the degree to which it reflects genuine remorse or is a calculated step designed to reduce the severity of the sentence that is likely to be imposed.

384 *Overarching Principles: Seriousness*, para. 1.27, published 16 December 2004, www.sentencing-guidelines.gov.uk
385 ibid., para. 1.29
386 Serious Organised Crime and Police Act 2005, s. 73
387 *Robbery*, page 7, published 25 July 2006, www.sentencing-guidelines.gov.uk
388 This is because the scope of restitution orders under the Powers of Criminal Courts (Sentencing) Act 2000 is tightly circumscribed and the courts traditionally have been reluctant to impose compensation orders in conjunction with custodial sentences.

45. If an offender has been temporarily or permanently prevented by circumstances beyond his or her control from returning defrauded items, the degree of mitigation should depend on the point in time at which, and the determination with which, the offender tried to return the items.

(d) Financial pressure

46. Whilst many fraud offences are motivated by greed or a desire to live beyond legitimate means, others may be motivated by financial pressure. In principle, financial pressure is a factor that neither increases nor diminishes an offender's culpability in relation to any type of dishonesty offence, including fraud. However, where financial pressure is *exceptional* and not of the offender's own making, it may in very rare circumstances constitute offender mitigation.

SG-396 **C. Other sentencing matters**

Combining custodial sentences and fines

47. The issue whether to impose a fine alongside a custodial sentence may arise when sentencing for fraud offences. If a fine is imposed, further issues arise concerning the impact of the fine on the length of the custodial sentence. Some guideline judgments relating to tax fraud[389] have indicated that a fine should be imposed alongside a custodial sentence and such an approach has been used as a means of confiscation.[390] However, these cases largely were decided before the creation of the extensive powers relating to confiscation and to seizure of assets or the proceeds of crime.
48. In the light of those additional powers and the general powers relating to compensation, forfeiture and confiscation, a court normally *should not* impose a fine alongside a custodial sentence. However, exceptionally, it may be appropriate to impose a fine in addition to a custodial sentence where:
    (i) a confiscation order is not being contemplated; **and**
    (ii) there is no obvious victim to whom compensation can be awarded; **and**
    (iii) the offender has, or will have, resources from which a fine can be paid.
49. A court must ensure that the overall sentence remains commensurate with the seriousness of the offence and that the size of the fine does not enable wealthier offenders to 'buy themselves out of custody'.

SG-397 **D. Ancillary and other orders**

50. Ancillary orders may aim to minimise the harm caused by the offender (either to the victim or, through the risk of re-offending, to society), may aim to achieve reparation or may aim to punish the offender.
51. Orders relating to property that either must be considered or are most likely to be imposed in relation to fraud offences are:

[Paragraphs 52 to 63 reproduce standard guidance on the use of (i) compensation orders, (ii) confiscation orders and (iii) deprivation orders, which mirrors in all but the most trivial ways the guidance found in the guidelines on theft (see **SG-371**)].

***(iv) Restitution order*[391]

64. A court may order that stolen goods be restored to the victim or that a sum not exceeding the value of the goods be paid to the victim from money taken out of the offender's possession at the time of apprehension. Further, on the application of the victim, the court may order that other goods representing the proceeds of disposal or realisation of the stolen goods be transferred to the victim. Where the stolen property cannot be traced or the offender is not in possession of sufficient money at the time of apprehension, a restitution order will not be available and a compensation order should be considered instead.
65. A restitution order should not normally impact on or influence the choice of sentence as the offender has no control over the making of the order.

[389] Ford (1981) 3 Cr App R (S) 15; *Attorney General's Reference Nos. 87 and 86 of 1999 (Webb and Simpson)* [2001] 1 Cr App R (S) 505
[390] See, for example, *Garner and others* (1985) 7 Cr App R (S) 285
[391] Powers of Criminal Courts (Sentencing) Act 2000, s. 148

66. Orders relating to the future conduct of the offender include:

(v) Disqualification from acting as a company director[392]

67. The general power to disqualify may be used where an offender is convicted of an indictable offence committed in connection with the management or general conduct of a company. The disqualification term may be for a maximum of 15 years if made by the Crown Court or 5 years if made by a magistrates' court.
68. A disqualification order should not normally impact on or influence the choice of sentence as its purpose is to protect the public from the risk of re-offending.

(vi) Disqualification from driving[393]

69. A court may disqualify any person convicted of an offence from driving for such period as it considers appropriate. This may be instead of or in addition to dealing with the offender in any other way.
70. Disqualification under this provision is a punitive sanction and should be taken into account in ensuring that the overall sentence is commensurate with the seriousness of the offence.

(vii) Financial reporting order[394]

71. Where there is a sufficiently high risk of the offender committing a further offence of fraud or dishonesty, an order may be made requiring a report of the offender's financial affairs to be made as directed, for a period of up to 15 years where the order is made in the Crown Court or 5 years if made by a magistrates' court.
72. As the purpose of the order is to minimise the risk of re-offending by those likely to commit financial crime, a financial reporting order should not be taken into account when deciding the appropriate sentence.

(viii) Serious crime prevention order[395]

73. On application by the Crown, where an offender is convicted by the Crown Court of a *serious offence* (or is committed to the Crown Court following conviction in a magistrates' court) an order may be made if the court has reasonable grounds to believe that it would protect the public by preventing, restricting or disrupting involvement by the person in serious crime. The order may contain such prohibitions, restrictions, requirements or terms as the court considers necessary to achieve the purpose of the order.
74. The order must be of a specified duration, not exceeding five years. Commencement of the order can be delayed, for example to commence upon the offender's release from custody.
75. A serious crime prevention order should not normally impact on or influence the choice of sentence as the purpose of the order is to provide protection to the public from future involvement of the offender in serious crime.

E. Sentencing ranges and starting points **SG-398**

1. Typically, a guideline will apply to an offence that can be committed in a variety of circumstances with different levels of seriousness. It will apply to a '*first time offender*' who has been **convicted after a trial**. Within the guidelines, a '*first time offender*' is a person who does not have a conviction which, by virtue of section 143(2) of the Criminal Justice Act 2003, must be treated as an aggravating factor.
2. As an aid to consistency of approach, the guidelines describe a number of types of conduct which would fall within the broad definition of the offences. These are set out in a column headed 'Nature of offence'. Additionally, the top row provides financial bands relating to the amount that the offender intended to obtain or was likely to be achieved from the fraudulent conduct.
3. The expected approach is for a court to identify the description and financial band that most nearly matches the particular facts of the offence for which sentence is being imposed. This will identify a **starting point** from which the sentencer can depart to reflect aggravating or mitigating factors affecting the seriousness of the offence (beyond those contained within the column describing the nature of the failure or of the harm) to reach a **provisional sentence**.

[392] Company Directors Disqualification Act 1986, s. 2
[393] Powers of Criminal Courts (Sentencing) Act 2000, ss. 146 and 147
[394] Serious Organised Crime and Police Act 2005, s. 76
[395] Serious Crime Act 2007, s. 1 and 19

4. The **sentencing range** is the bracket into which the provisional sentence will normally fall after having regard to factors which aggravate or mitigate the seriousness of the offence. The particular circumstances may, however, make it appropriate that the provisional sentence falls outside the range.
5. Where the offender has previous convictions which aggravate the seriousness of the current offence, that may take the provisional sentence beyond the range given particularly where there are significant other aggravating factors present.
6. Once the provisional sentence has been identified by reference to those factors affecting the seriousness of the offence, the court will take into account any relevant factors of personal mitigation, which may take the sentence below the range given.
7. Where there has been a guilty plea, any reduction attributable to that plea will be applied to the sentence at this stage. Again, this reduction may take the sentence below the range provided.
8. A court must give its reasons for imposing a sentence of a different kind or outside the range provided in the guidelines.[396]

The decision making process

[Sets out the standard sequential decision making process: identify starting point, consider aggravating factors, consider mitigating factors, apply reduction for guilty plea, consider ancillary orders, review in light of the totality principle and give reasons.]

SG-399 **F. Guidelines and approach to sentencing**

1. The guidelines are based on types of conduct reflecting common fraudulent behaviour. Confidence frauds are dealt with as a separate category as is the possession, making or supply of articles for use in fraud.
2. A further group includes those offences committed against an organisation in either the private or public sector; most commonly, in the public sector these will arise in relation to the tax and benefit system and, in the private sector, in relation to banking and insurance.
3. Although not intended to be exclusive, each guideline includes examples of the fraudulent activity likely to have taken place. In addition, the guideline refers to the offences under which the activity might be charged and the related legislative provisions.
4. The starting points and sentencing ranges for *banking and insurance fraud*, for *benefit fraud*, and for *fraud against HM Revenue and Customs (revenue fraud)* are the same since the seriousness of all offences of organisational fraud derives from the extent of the fraudulent activity (culpability) and the financial loss caused or likely to be caused (harm).
   (i) For ease of use, separate guidelines have been provided for banking, insurance and credit fraud, benefit fraud and revenue fraud, which has allowed greater detail of the types of activity and the aggravating or mitigating factors likely to be particularly relevant to be included.
   (ii) In relation to these types of fraud, the Council considers that there will be few cases where £100,000 or more is obtained in a single fraudulent transaction. Similarly, it is likely that there will be few cases where less than £20,000 is obtained in a professionally planned fraud carried out over a significant period of time or multiple professionally planned frauds. Accordingly, the Council has not proposed starting points and ranges for such frauds.

SG-400 **Confidence fraud**

Factors to take into consideration

1. The principal offences likely to be used to prosecute confidence frauds are **fraud under the Fraud Act 2006, section 1 and false accounting contrary to the Theft Act 1968, section 17**.
2. The following starting points and sentencing ranges are for a '*first time offender*' aged 18 or over who pleaded not guilty. They should be applied as set out [above].
3. This type of offending involves a victim transferring money and/or property as a result of being deceived or misled by the offender. An example of a simple confidence fraud is a person claiming to be collecting money for charity when, in fact, he or she intends to keep the money.[397] Other examples of common confidence frauds are:

   Advance fee frauds - Common advance fee frauds include *lottery/prize draw scams* where, in order to claim a 'prize', a processing or administration fee (or a customs levy in foreign lottery scams) must

[396] Criminal Justice Act 2003, s. 174(2)(a)

[397] See, for example, *Pippard and Harris* [2001] EWCA Crim 2925 and *Day and O'Leary* [2002] EWCA Crim 503

be paid and, after the fee is paid, the prize never materialises and *foreign money-making frauds* where persons claim to need assistance in transferring money overseas and offer a share of the money for help, or ask for money to be sent to cover customs levies, bribes and/or other fees.

Fraudulent sales of goods and services - These include goods that are never received by the purchaser or are worth less than the seller represents; services that are unnecessary, overpriced or not performed; and investments that are never obtained for the investor or are worth less than the seller represents.

4. A factor common to many confidence frauds, is that the offender targets a vulnerable victim; it is therefore a determinant of seriousness for this type of fraud. An offender is more culpable if he or she deliberately targets a victim who is vulnerable as a result of old age, youth or disability and there is a more than usually serious degree of harm where the victim is particularly vulnerable.[398]
5. Some victims of advance fee frauds may have personalities which make them 'vulnerable in a way and to a degree not typical of the general population'[399] because they fall for scams many times. It is a feature of some advance fee frauds that victims are targeted using 'sucker lists' of people who have previously fallen victim to scams. An offender who uses a 'sucker list' will have planned the offence and deliberately targeted vulnerable victims; therefore he or she has a higher level of culpability.[400]
6. As the determinants of seriousness include the 'value of property or consequential loss involved', the table provides both a fixed amount (on which the starting point is based) and a band (on which the sentencing range is based). Where the value is larger or smaller than the amount on which the starting point is based, this should lead to upward or downward movement as appropriate. Where the amount the offender intended to obtain cannot be established, the appropriate measure will be the amount that was likely to be achieved in all the circumstances.
7. A further determinant of seriousness is whether the fraud was a single fraudulent transaction or a multiple fraud. Most confidence frauds will by their nature involve many actual or potential victims and multiple transactions and should be regarded as multiple fraud.
8. When assessing the seriousness of an offence, a court must always have regard to the full list of aggravating and mitigating factors in the Council guideline *Overarching Principles: Seriousness* (reproduced in Annex B [not reproduced here: see **SG-25**]); those most likely to be present in offences of fraud are set out at paragraphs 22 and 29 above. Additional aggravating and mitigating factors likely to be particularly relevant to this type of fraud are considered at paragraphs 24–28 and 31–36 above.
9. The Council has identified matters of personal mitigation which may be relevant, which are set out in paragraphs 38 to 46 above.
10. In all cases sentencers should consider whether to make ancillary orders, particularly compensation, confiscation and/or deprivation (see paragraphs 50–75 above).

Confidence Fraud

Fraud: Fraud Act 2006 (section 1)
False accounting: Theft Act 1968 (section 17)

Maximum penalty: Fraud, 10 years custody
False accounting, 7 years custody

[398] *Overarching Principles: Seriousness*, paras. 1.17, 1.22 and 1.23, published 16 December 2004, www.sentencing-guidelines.gov.uk
[399] M. Levi, *Sentencing Frauds: A Review*, p. 58
[400] *Overarching Principles: Seriousness*, para. 1.22, published 16 December 2004, www.sentencing-guidelines.gov.uk

Value of property or consequential loss				
Nature of offence	**£500,000 or more** *Starting point based on: £750,000*	**£100,000 or more and less than £500,000** *Starting point based on: £300,000*	**£20,000 or more and less than £100,000** *Starting point based on: £60,000*	**Less than £20,000** *Starting point based on: £10,000*
Large scale advance fee fraud **or** other confidence fraud involving the deliberate targeting of a large number of vulnerable victims	**Starting point:** 6 years custody **Range:** 5–8 years custody	**Starting point:** 5 years custody **Range:** 4–7 years custody	**Starting point:** 4 years custody **Range:** 3–6 years custody	**Starting point:** 3 years custody **Range:** 2–5 years custody
Lower scale advance fee fraud **or** other confidence fraud characterised by a degree of planning and/or multiple transactions	**Starting point:** 5 years custody **Range:** 4–7 years custody	**Starting point:** 4 years custody **Range:** 3–6 years custody	**Starting point:** 3 years custody **Range:** 2–5 years custody	**Starting point:** 18 months custody **Range:** 26 weeks–3 years custody
Single fraudulent transaction confidence fraud involving targeting of a vulnerable victim			**Starting point:** 26 weeks custody **Range:** Community order (HIGH)–18 months custody	**Starting point:** 6 weeks custody **Range:** Community order (MEDIUM)–26 weeks custody
Single fraudulent transaction confidence fraud not targeting a vulnerable victim, and involving no or limited planning			**Starting point:** 12 weeks custody **Range:** Community order (MEDIUM)–36 weeks custody	**Starting point:** Community order (MEDIUM) **Range:** Fine–6 weeks custody

* Where the actual amount is greater or smaller than the figure on which the starting point is based, that is likely to be one of the factors that will move the sentence within the range (see paragraph 6 [above]).

Additional aggravating factors	Additional mitigating factors
1. Number involved in the offence and role of the offender 2. Offending carried out over a significant period of time 3. Use of another person's identity 4. Offence has a lasting effect on the victim	1. Peripheral involvement 2. Behaviour not fraudulent from the outset 3. Misleading or inaccurate advice

The presence of one or more aggravating factors may indicate a more severe sentence within the suggested range while the presence of one or more mitigating factors may indicate a less severe sentence within the suggested range.

The presence of aggravating or mitigating factors of exceptional significance may indicate that the case should move to a higher or lower level of seriousness.

SG-401 **Possessing, making or supplying articles for use in fraud**

Factors to take into consideration

1. The principal offences are contrary to the Fraud Act 2006 and are **possession of articles for use in frauds (section 6), making or supplying articles for use in frauds (section 7) and the general offence of fraud (section 1).**
2. The following starting points and sentencing ranges are for a '*first time offender*' aged 18 or over who pleaded not guilty. They should be applied as set out [above].

3. There are many ways in which offenders may commit this group of offences but, with the constant improvements in technology, computers have become a common and increasingly effective tool for both creating and disseminating *articles* for use in fraud. Thus, 'articles' will include any electronic programs or data stored electronically.[401] Examples of articles for use in frauds include false fronts for cash machines, computer programs for generating credit card numbers, lists of credit card or bank account details, 'sucker lists' and draft letters or emails for use in advance fee frauds.
4. As lists of credit card and bank account details constitute 'articles', the making of such lists through certain electronic programmes, which contravenes section 1 of the Fraud Act 2006, is also criminalised by section 7 of the same Act. The Council considers that carrying out the following activities should be treated as making articles for use in fraud and sentenced using this guideline, regardless of whether the offence is charged under section 1 or section 7:

   Phishing - where an offender sends an email purporting to come from a financial institution, which asks victims to follow a hyperlink to a (false) website and induces them to enter their card or account details (which may include their PIN);

   Vishing - where an offender uses an automated telephone system, purporting to be the telephone system of a financial institution, to induce victims to disclose their card or account details (which may include their PIN);

   Pharming - where victims intend to visit a financial institution's website but are redirected to the offender's website (which purports to be the financial institution's website) and induced to enter their card or account details (which may include their PIN); and

   Use of a 'Trojan' - where an offender installs a virus on victims' computers (often a 'keystroke logger', which captures all of the keystrokes entered into a computer keyboard) in order to gain access to their card or account details. Often the offender will send an email inducing victims to visit a website, where the virus is automatically downloaded onto their computers.
5. Making, adapting, supplying or offering to supply computer programmes, emails or websites for the above activities amounts to an offence under section 7 of the Fraud Act 2006.
6. Offenders who possess, make or supply articles for use in fraud intend their actions to lead to a fraud. Such offenders therefore have the highest level of culpability.[402] Whilst in many cases no financial harm will have been caused, in some cases, particularly where the 'article' is a list of credit card or bank account details, the victim(s) may have been inconvenienced despite not suffering any financial loss.[403]
7. There are three types of activity relating to articles for use in fraud: making or adapting, supplying or offering to supply and possession. The guideline does not distinguish between the first two categories; they carry the same maximum penalty and, depending on the sophistication and planning involved and the harm resulting from an offence, they may be equally serious.
8. The three offences in this group all involve an element of planning (whether by the offender or by another person); the planning of an offence has been identified by the Council as a factor indicating a higher level of culpability[404] and the proposed starting points incorporate this aggravating factor.
9. In relation to harm, the value of the fraud (either that intended by the offender where that can be ascertained, or that which was likely to be achieved) is not a determinant of seriousness for these offences in the way that it is for other offences of fraud. However, it is a factor that should be taken into account in determining the appropriate sentence within the sentencing range.
10. When assessing the seriousness of an offence, a court must always have regard to the full list of aggravating and mitigating factors in the Council guideline *Overarching Principles: Seriousness* (reproduced in Annex B [not reproduced here: see **SG-25**]); those most likely to be present in offences of fraud are set out at paragraphs 22 and 29 above. Additional aggravating and mitigating factors likely to be particularly relevant to this type of fraud are considered at paragraphs 24–28 and 31 above.

Sentencing Guidelines

[401] Fraud Act 2006, s. 8
[402] See *Overarching Principles: Seriousness*, para. 1.7, published 16 December 2004, www.sentencing-guidelines.gov.uk
[403] Where the article is a list of credit card or bank account details, the victims will need to cancel their cards and obtain new ones and/or change their bank accounts. See *Overarching Principles: Seriousness*, para. 1.17, published 16 December 2004, www.sentencing-guidelines.gov.uk
[404] ibid., para. 1.22

11. The Council has identified matters of personal mitigation which may be relevant, which are set out in paragraphs 38–46 above.
12. The sentencing range for the most serious category of offences is deliberately wide; most offences will be at the lower end of the range but there are likely to be some offences, possibly but not exclusively those with an international dimension, that will justify a sentence at the top end of the suggested range or even higher.
13. In all cases sentencers should consider whether to make ancillary orders, particularly compensation, confiscation and/or deprivation orders (see paragraphs 50–75 above).

Possessing, Making or Supplying Articles for use in Fraud

Possession of articles for use in frauds: Fraud Act 2006 (section 6)

Making or supplying articles for use in frauds: Fraud Act 2006 (section 7)

Fraud: Fraud Act 2006 (section 1)

Maximum penalty: Possession of articles for use in frauds, 5 years custody
For both other offences, 10 years custody

Nature of offence	**Type of offence**	
	Making or adapting (ss. 1 or 7) **or** Supplying or offering to supply (s. 7)	Possessing (s. 6)
Article(s) intended for use in an extensive and skilfully planned fraud	**Starting point:** 4 years custody **Range:** 2–7 years custody	**Starting point:** 36 weeks custody **Range:** 6 weeks–2 years custody
Article(s) intended for use in a less extensive and less skilfully planned fraud	**Starting point:** 26 weeks custody **Range:** Community order (HIGH)–2 years custody	**Starting point:** Community order (MEDIUM) **Range:** Community order (LOW)–26 weeks custody

Additional aggravating factors	**Additional mitigating factors**
1. Number involved in the offence and role of the offender 2. Offending carried out over a significant period of time 3. Use of another person's identity 4. Offence has a lasting effect on the victim	1. Peripheral involvement

The presence of one or more aggravating factors may indicate a more severe sentence within the suggested range while the presence of one or more mitigating factors may indicate a less severe sentence within the suggested range.

The presence of aggravating or mitigating factors of exceptional significance may indicate that the case should move to a higher or lower level of seriousness.

SG-402 **Banking and insurance fraud, and obtaining credit through fraud**

Factors to take into consideration

1. In relation to each of these types of fraud, the principal offences likely to be used to prosecute are **fraud under the Fraud Act 2006, section 1 and false accounting contrary to the Theft Act 1968, section 17**.
2. The following starting points and sentencing ranges are for a '*first time offender*' aged 18 or over who pleaded not guilty. They should be applied as set out [above].

3. Types of offending behaviour include:
Payment card and bank account fraud - Frauds involving the use of payment cards and bank accounts include use of another person's card, cloning another person's card, taking over or sending instructions relating to another person's bank or card account, and use of another person's cheque.
Insurance fraud - Fraudulent claims by or against the insurer (claims that are entirely fraudulent and those that are exaggerated through either claiming for injury, loss or damage that did not occur or increasing the value of a genuine claim for injury, loss or damage) and supplier fraud (whereby builders, motor repairers and other trades-people engaged by insurers to repair insured property charge for work that they have not done or inflate the cost of their work).
Obtaining credit through fraud - Obtaining credit through fraud includes the fraudulent obtaining of mortgages, loans, interest free credit, in-store credit, goods or services on a 'buy now pay later' basis, car finance, credit cards, store cards, and bank accounts (with overdrafts).
4. A payment card or bank account fraud is unlikely to be committed in circumstances where the offender's intention was not fraudulent from the outset.
5. As the determinants of seriousness include the 'value of property or consequential loss involved', the table provides both a fixed amount (on which the starting point is based) and a band (on which the sentencing range is based). Where the value is larger or smaller than the amount on which the starting point is based, this should lead to upward or downward movement as appropriate. Where the amount the offender intended to obtain cannot be established, the appropriate measure will be the amount that was likely to be achieved in all the circumstances.
6. A further determinant of seriousness is whether the fraud was a single fraudulent transaction or a multiple fraud. Where one false declaration or a failure to disclose a change in circumstances results in multiple payments, this should be regarded as multiple fraud.
7. The maximum penalty for most of the offences covered by this guideline is 7 years imprisonment. Where fraud under the 2006 Act is charged and the maximum penalty is 10 years, the proposed sentencing ranges leave headroom for offences involving the most serious frauds to be sentenced outside the range and up to the maximum.
8. When assessing the seriousness of an offence, a court must always have regard to the full list of aggravating and mitigating factors in the Council guideline *Overarching Principles: Seriousness* (reproduced in Annex B [not reproduced here: see **SG-25**]); those most likely to be present in offences of fraud are set out at paragraphs 22 and 29 above. Additional aggravating and mitigating factors likely to be particularly relevant to this type of fraud are considered at paragraphs 24 and 26–27, 31 and 36 above.
9. Use of another person's identity is an aggravating factor (see paragraphs 26–27 above). Whilst this factor may be present in any fraud, it is a feature of nearly all payment card and bank account frauds.[405] Courts should therefore depart from the suggested starting points in all cases of payment card and bank account fraud (and any other case in which it arises) to reflect the presence of this aggravating factor.
10. The Council has identified matters of personal mitigation which may be relevant, which are set out in paragraphs 38–46 above.
11. In all cases sentencers should consider whether to make ancillary orders, particularly confiscation and compensation (see paragraphs 50–75 above).

Banking and Insurance Fraud, and Obtaining Credit through Fraud

Maximum penalty: Fraud (prosecuted under the Fraud Act 2006), 10 years custody
For all other offences, 7 years custody

[405] In most cases the offender claims to be the account holder or a person authorised to deal with the account

Nature of offence	Amount obtained or intended to be obtained				
	£500,000 or more *Starting point based on: £750,000**	**£100,000 or more and less than £500,000** *Starting point based on: £300,000**	**£20,000 or more and less than £100,000** *Starting point based on: £60,000**	**£5,000 or more and less than £20,000** *Starting point based on: £12,500**	**Less than £5,000** *Starting point based on: £2,500**
Fraudulent from the outset, professionally planned **and either** fraud carried out over a significant period of time **or** multiple frauds	**Starting point:** 5 years custody **Range:** 4–7 years custody	**Starting point:** 4 years custody **Range:** 3–5 years custody	**Starting point:** 2 years custody **Range:** 18 months–3 years custody		
Fraudulent from the outset **and either** fraud carried out over a significant period of time **or** multiple frauds	**Starting point:** 4 years custody **Range:** 3–7 years custody	**Starting point:** 3 years custody **Range:** 2–4 years custody	**Starting point:** 15 months custody **Range:** 18 weeks–30 months custody	**Starting point:** 12 weeks custody **Range:** Community order (HIGH)–12 months custody	**Starting point:** Community order (HIGH) **Range:** Community order (LOW)–6 weeks custody
Not fraudulent from the outset **and either** fraud carried out over a significant period of time **or** multiple frauds	**Starting point:** 3 years custody **Range:** 2–6 years custody	**Starting point:** 2 years custody **Range:** 12 months–3 years custody	**Starting point:** 36 weeks custody **Range:** 12 weeks–18 months custody	**Starting point:** 6 weeks custody **Range:** Community order (MEDIUM)–26 weeks custody	**Starting point:** Community order (MEDIUM) **Range:** Fine–Community order (HIGH)
Single fraudulent transaction, fraudulent from the outset			**Starting point:** 26 weeks custody **Range:** 6 weeks–12 months custody	**Starting point:** Community order (HIGH) **Range:** Fine–18 weeks custody	**Starting point:** Community order (LOW) **Range:** Fine–Community order (MEDIUM)
Single fraudulent transaction, not fraudulent from the outset			**Starting point:** 12 weeks custody **Range:** Community order (MEDIUM)–36 weeks custody	**Starting point:** Community order (MEDIUM) **Range:** Fine–6 weeks custody	**Starting point:** Fine **Range:** Fine–Community order (LOW)

* Where the actual amount is greater or smaller than the figure on which the starting point is based, that is likely to be one of the factors that will move the sentence within the range (see paragraph 5 [above]).

Additional aggravating factors	Additional mitigating factors
1. Number involved in the offence and role of the offender 2. Use of another person's identity	1. Peripheral involvement 2. Misleading or incomplete advice

The presence of one or more aggravating factors may indicate a more severe sentence within the suggested range while the presence of one or more mitigating factors may indicate a less severe sentence within the suggested range.

The presence of aggravating or mitigating factors of exceptional significance may indicate that the case should move to a higher or lower level of seriousness.

Benefit fraud **SG-403**

Factors to take into consideration

The principal offences likely to be used to prosecute benefit frauds are:

- *Fraud (Fraud Act 2006, section 1)*
- *False accounting (Theft Act 1968, section 17)*
- *False representation to obtain benefit (Social Security Administration Act 1992, section 111A(1))*
- *Failing to disclose a change in circumstances (Social Security Administration Act 1992, section 111A(1A), (1B), (1D) or (1E))*
- *Tax credit fraud (Tax Credits Act 2002, section 35)*

1. The following starting points and sentencing ranges are for a '*first time offender*' aged 18 or over who pleaded not guilty. They should be applied as set out [above].
2. This guideline is based on an understanding that the prosecutor will generally seek summary trial for appropriate benefit fraud cases involving sums up to £35,000; the Council does not consider that the starting points proposed would interfere with that practice.
3. The Council's proposals are governed by bands based on amounts of money. The starting point defined at the top of each column relates to the midpoint of each financial band.
4. As the determinants of seriousness include the 'value of property or consequential loss involved', the table provides both a fixed amount (on which the starting point is based) and a band (on which the sentencing range is based). Where the value is larger or smaller than the amount on which the starting point is based, this should lead to upward or downward movement as appropriate. Where the amount the offender intended to obtain cannot be established, the appropriate measure will be the amount that was likely to be achieved in all the circumstances.
5. A further determinant of seriousness is whether the fraud was a single fraudulent transaction or a multiple fraud. Where one false declaration or a failure to disclose a change in circumstances results in multiple payments, this should be regarded as multiple fraud.
6. The Council considers it unlikely that more than £100,000 could be obtained in a benefit fraud, unless the offence was professionally planned and either carried out over a significant period of time or through multiple frauds. In addition, it is unlikely that more than £20,000 could be obtained in a single fraudulent transaction benefit fraud. Consequently, the guideline does not provide separately for such circumstances.
7. The maximum penalty for most of the offences covered by this guideline is 7 years imprisonment. Where fraud under the 2006 Act is charged and the maximum penalty is 10 years, the proposed sentencing ranges leave headroom for offences involving the largest scale frauds to be sentenced outside the range and up to the maximum.
8. When assessing the seriousness of an offence, a court must always have regard to the full list of aggravating and mitigating factors in the Council guideline *Overarching Principles: Seriousness* (reproduced in Annex B [not reproduced here: see **SG-25**); those most likely to be present in offences of fraud are set out at paragraphs 22 and 29 above. Additional aggravating and mitigating factors likely to be particularly relevant to this type of fraud are considered at paragraphs 24 and 26–27, 31 and 36 above.
9. The Council has identified matters of personal mitigation which may be relevant, which are set out in paragraphs 38–46 above. The court should have specific regard to personal and family circumstances of offenders which will vary greatly and may be particularly significant to sentencing for this type of fraud.
10. Generally, those who commit benefit fraud are asked to repay the sums defrauded, although the process of recovery may be spread over a significant period and may not be possible in every case. As recovery of defrauded benefits is not guaranteed and operates quite separately from civil or criminal sanctions, this has not been taken into account in the Council's proposals. The fact that defrauded sums may have been recovered is not relevant to the choice of the type of sentence to be imposed.

Benefit Fraud

Maximum penalty: Fraud (prosecuted under Fraud Act 2006), 10 years custody
For all other offences, 7 years custody

Nature of offence	Amount obtained or intended to be obtained				
	£500,000 or more *Starting point based on: £750,000**	**£100,000 or more and less than £500,000** *Starting point based on: £300,000**	**£20,000 or more and less than £100,000** *Starting point based on: £60,000**	**£5,000 or more and less than £20,000** *Starting point based on: £12,500**	**Less than £5,000** *Starting point based on: £2,500**
Fraudulent from the outset, professionally planned **and either** fraud carried out over a significant period of time **or** multiple frauds	**Starting point:** 5 years custody **Range:** 4–7 years custody	**Starting point:** 4 years custody **Range:** 3–5 years custody	**Starting point:** 2 years custody **Range:** 18 months–3 years custody		
Fraudulent from the outset **and either** fraud carried out over a significant period of time **or** multiple frauds	**Starting point:** 4 years custody **Range:** 3–7 years custody	**Starting point:** 3 years custody **Range:** 2–4 years custody	**Starting point:** 15 months custody **Range:** 18 weeks–30 months custody	**Starting point:** 12 weeks custody **Range:** Community order (HIGH)–12 months custody	**Starting point:** Community order (HIGH) **Range:** Community order (LOW)–6 weeks custody
Not fraudulent from the outset **and either** fraud carried out over a significant period of time **or** multiple frauds	**Starting point:** 3 years custody **Range:** 2–6 years custody	**Starting point:** 2 years custody **Range:** 12 months–3 years custody	**Starting point:** 36 weeks custody **Range:** 12 weeks–18 months custody	**Starting point:** 6 weeks custody **Range:** Community order (MEDIUM)–26 weeks custody	**Starting point:** Community order (MEDIUM) **Range:** Fine–Community order (HIGH)
Single fraudulent transaction, fraudulent from the outset			**Starting point:** 26 weeks custody **Range:** 6 weeks–12 months custody	**Starting point:** Community order (HIGH) **Range:** Fine–18 weeks custody	**Starting point:** Community order (LOW) **Range:** Fine–Community order (MEDIUM)
Single fraudulent transaction, not fraudulent from the outset			**Starting point:** 12 weeks custody **Range:** Community order (MEDIUM)–36 weeks custody	**Starting point:** Community order (MEDIUM) **Range:** Fine–6 weeks custody	**Starting point:** Fine **Range:** Fine–Community order (LOW)

* Where the actual amount is greater or smaller than the figure on which the starting point is based, that is likely to be one of the factors that will move the sentence within the range (see paragraph 4 [above]).

Additional aggravating factors	Additional mitigating factors
1. Number involved in the offence and role of the offender 2. Use of another person's identity	1. Peripheral involvement 2. Misleading or incomplete advice

The presence of one or more aggravating factors may indicate a more severe sentence within the suggested range while the presence of one or more mitigating factors may indicate a less severe sentence within the suggested range.

The presence of aggravating or mitigating factors of exceptional significance may indicate that the case should move to a higher or lower level of seriousness.

Revenue fraud (against HM Revenue and Customs (HMRC)) **SG-404**

Factors to take into consideration

The principal offences likely to be used to prosecute these frauds are:

- *Fraud (Fraud Act 2006, s. 1)*
- *False accounting (Theft Act 1968, s. 17)*
- *Fraudulent evasion of VAT (Value Added Tax Act 1994, s. 72(1))*
- *False statement for VAT purposes (Value Added Tax Act 1994, s. 72(3))*
- *Conduct amounting to an offence (Value Added Tax Act 1994, s. 72(8))*
- *Fraudulent evasion of income tax (Finance Act 2000, s. 144)*
- *Evasion of excise duty (Customs and Excise Management Act 1979, s. 170(1)(a)(i), (ii), (b))*
- *Fraudulent evasion of excise duty (Customs and Excise Management Act 1979, s. 170(2)(a), 170B)*
- *Improper importation of goods (Customs and Excise Management Act 1979, s. 50(1) (a), (2))*

1. The following starting points and sentencing ranges are for a '*first time offender*' aged 18 or over who pleaded not guilty. They should be applied as set out [above].
2. This type of offending may take many forms, including:
   Fraudulent evasion of VAT - this includes situations where a trader does not charge VAT to the customer, situations where a customer pays VAT to the trader but the trader does not pay it to HM Revenue and Customs (HMRC), and so-called 'Missing Trader Intra-Community Frauds' (MTIC Frauds) or 'Carousel Frauds'.
   MTIC Frauds involve traders importing goods from the European Union free from VAT, charging VAT when they sell the goods and then keeping the money rather than paying it to HMRC. *Carousel Frauds* are MTIC Frauds where the trader sells the goods to another trader who re-exports them and claims back the VAT paid to the first trader from HMRC. Usually the goods are passed along a chain of traders between the missing trader and the broker known as 'buffers', in order to disguise the fraudulent nature of the activity. Having been exported by the broker, the goods are typically re-imported by the missing trader and pass through the same circle of transactions again and again in rapid succession.
   Fraudulent evasion of income tax - this may be committed by failing to declare earnings in a tax return or by an employer keeping the tax collected from employees rather than paying it to HMRC.
   Fraudulent evasion of excise duty - this includes alcohol and tobacco smuggling and the laundering of 'red diesel' into diesel engine road fuel.[406]
3. For the purposes of this guideline the Council considers it unlikely that more than £20,000 could be obtained in a single fraudulent transaction against HMRC in circumstances where the offender's intention was not fraudulent from the outset or where the claim was exaggerated. In addition, it is unlikely that more than £100,000 could be obtained in a fraud against HMRC in circumstances where the offender's intention was not fraudulent from the outset.

[406] *Offences under the Customs and Excise Management Act 1979*, ss. 50 and 170 involving smuggling of prohibited weapons covered by minimum sentence provisions (carrying a maximum penalty of 10 years custody) are not covered by this guideline

Sentencing Guidelines

4. In most VAT frauds the offender intends to evade VAT. However, it is possible to commit the offence in section 72(3) of the VAT Act (and accordingly also the offence in section 72(8) of the same Act) by recklessly making a false statement for the purposes of VAT. The Council guideline *Overarching Principles: Seriousness*[407] states that an offender who acts recklessly is less culpable than an offender who acts intentionally. The proposals for the sentencing of frauds against HMRC take as a starting point an offender who acts intentionally. Where the offender has acted recklessly (relevant only to offences under the Value Added Tax Act 1994), courts should adjust the assessment of seriousness to take account of this lower level of culpability.
5. As in other types of fraud, the fact that the behaviour was not fraudulent from the outset may be a mitigating factor. Payments *to* HMRC may be evaded in order to increase the profitability of a legitimate business or the level of an individual's legitimate remuneration; payments may be fraudulently obtained *from* HMRC without any underlying legitimate activity at all as in a Carousel Fraud. Although the type of harm is the same since both result in a loss to HMRC, where payment is sought *from* HMRC in such circumstances, culpability is likely to be higher. Accordingly, such offences are likely to be regarded as more serious.
6. As the determinants of seriousness include the 'value of property or consequential loss involved', the table provides both a fixed amount (on which the starting point is based) and a band (on which the sentencing range is based). Where the value is larger or smaller than the amount on which the starting point is based, this should lead to upward or downward movement as appropriate. Where the amount the offender intended to obtain cannot be established, the appropriate measure will be the amount that was likely to be achieved in all the circumstances.
7. A further determinant of seriousness is whether the fraud was a single fraudulent transaction or a multiple fraud. Where one false declaration or a failure to disclose a change in circumstances results in multiple payments, this should be regarded as multiple fraud.
8. The maximum penalty for most of the offences covered by this guideline is 7 years imprisonment. Where fraud under the 2006 Act is charged and the maximum penalty is 10 years, the proposed sentencing ranges leave headroom for offences involving multi-million pound frauds to be sentenced outside the range and up to the maximum.
9. When assessing the seriousness of an offence, a court must always have regard to the full list of aggravating and mitigating factors in the Council guideline *Overarching Principles: Seriousness* (reproduced in Annex B [not reproduced here: see **SG-25**]); those most likely to be present in offences of fraud are set out at paragraphs 22 and 29 above. Additional aggravating and mitigating factors likely to be relevant generally to this type of fraud are considered at paragraphs 24, 26–27 and 31 and 36 above. Other additional aggravating factors specific to evasion of duty[408] are also included in the guideline.
10. The Council has identified matters of personal mitigation which may be relevant, which are set out in paragraphs 38–46 above.
11. In all cases sentencers should consider whether to make ancillary orders, particularly confiscation (see paragraphs 50–75 above).

Revenue Fraud (Against HM Revenue and Customs (HMRC))

Maximum penalty: Fraud (prosecuted under Fraud Act 2006), 10 years custody
For all other offences, 7 years custody

[407] *Overarching Principles: Seriousness*, para. 1.7, published 16 December 2004, www.sentencing-guidelines.gov.uk
[408] *Czyzewski* [2003] EWCA Crim 2139

Amount obtained or intended to be obtained					
Nature of offence	**£500,000 or more Starting point based on: £750,000***	**£100,000 or more and less than £500,000 Starting point based on: £300,000***	**£20,000 or more and less than £100,000 Starting point based on: £60,000***	**£5,000 or more and less than £20,000 Starting point based on: £12,500***	**Less than £5,000 Starting point based on: £2,500***
Fraudulent from the outset, professionally planned **and either** fraud carried out over a significant period of time **or** multiple frauds	**Starting point:** 5 years custody **Range:** 4–7 years custody	**Starting point:** 4 years custody **Range:** 3–5 years custody	**Starting point:** 2 years custody **Range:** 18 months–3 years custody		
Fraudulent from the outset **and either** fraud carried out over a significant period of time **or** multiple frauds	**Starting point:** 4 years custody **Range:** 3–7 years custody	**Starting point:** 3 years custody **Range:** 2–4 years custody	**Starting point:** 15 months custody **Range:** 18 weeks–30 months custody	**Starting point:** 12 weeks custody **Range:** Community order (HIGH)–12 months custody	**Starting point:** Community order (HIGH) **Range:** Community order (LOW)–6 weeks custody
Not fraudulent from the outset **and either** fraud carried out over a significant period of time **or** multiple frauds	**Starting point:** 3 years custody **Range:** 2–6 years custody	**Starting point:** 2 years custody **Range:** 12 months–3 years custody	**Starting point:** 36 weeks custody **Range:** 12 weeks–18 months custody	**Starting point:** 6 weeks custody **Range:** Community order (MEDIUM)–26 weeks custody	**Starting point:** Community order (MEDIUM) **Range:** Fine–Community order (HIGH)
Single fraudulent transaction, fraudulent from the outset			**Starting point:** 26 weeks custody **Range:** 6 weeks–12 months custody	**Starting point:** Community order (HIGH) **Range:** Fine–18 weeks custody	**Starting point:** Community order (LOW) **Range:** Fine–Community order (MEDIUM)
Single fraudulent transaction, not fraudulent from the outset			**Starting point:** 12 weeks custody **Range:** Community order (MEDIUM)–36 weeks custody	**Starting point:** Community order (MEDIUM) **Range:** Fine–6 weeks custody	**Starting point:** Fine **Range:** Fine–Community order (LOW)

* Where the actual amount is greater or smaller than the figure on which the starting point is based, that is likely to be one of the factors that will move the sentence within the range (see paragraph 6 [above]).

Additional aggravating factors	Additional mitigating factors
1. Number involved in the offence and role of the offender 2. Use of another person's identity 3. Making repeated importations, particularly in the face of warnings from the authorities 4. Dealing in goods with an additional health risk 5. Disposing of goods to under-aged purchasers	1. Peripheral involvement 2. Misleading or incomplete advice

The presence of one or more aggravating factors may indicate a more severe sentence within the suggested range while the presence of one or more mitigating factors may indicate a less severe sentence within the suggested range.

The presence of aggravating or mitigating factors of exceptional significance may indicate that the case should move to a higher or lower level of seriousness.

SG-405 ANNEX A: STATUTORY DEFINITIONS AND MAXIMUM PENALTIES FOR FRAUD OFFENCES INCLUDED IN THIS GUIDELINE

Offence	Statutory provision	Definition	Maximum custodial term in the Crown Court	Maximum custodial term in a Magistrates' Court	Financial reporting order available?
Fraud	Fraud Act 2006, s. 1	Dishonestly: – making a false representation; – failing to disclose information; or – abusing a position, – intending to make a gain for any person or cause a loss, or risk of loss, to another person.	10 years	6 months	Yes
Obtaining services dishonestly	Fraud Act 2006, s. 11	Dishonestly obtaining a service for any person by a dishonest act: – where the services are available on the basis that payment is made before, during or after receiving them, – knowing that the services are or might be being made available on that basis, – not paying in full, and – intending not to pay in full.	5 years	6 months	Yes
False accounting	Theft Act 1968, s. 17	Dishonestly: – destroying, defacing, concealing or falsifying any account, record or document made or required for any accounting purpose; or – when providing information for any purpose, producing or using any account, record or document made or required for any accounting purpose, knowing it is misleading, false or deceptive, with a view to creating a gain for oneself or another person or with intent to cause loss to another person.	7 years	6 months	Yes

Offence	Statutory provision	Definition	Maximum custodial term in the Crown Court	Maximum custodial term in a Magistrates' Court	Financial reporting order available?
Possession of articles for use in fraud	Fraud Act 2006, s. 6	Possessing or having under one's control any article for use in the course of or in connection with any fraud.	5 years	6 months	No
Making or supplying articles for use in frauds	Fraud Act 2006, s. 7	Making, adapting, supplying or offering to supply any article: – knowing that it is designed or adapted for use in the course of or in connection with any fraud; or – intending it to be used to commit, or assist in the commission of, fraud.	10 years	6 months	No
VAT evasion	Value Added Tax Act 1994, s. 72	Being knowingly concerned in or, in the taking of steps with a view to, the fraudulent evasion of VAT by any person. OR Producing, furnishing, sending or otherwise making use of any document which is false in a material particular for VAT purposes, or In furnishing any information for VAT purposes making any statement knowing it to be false in a material particular or making a statement that is false in a material particular. OR Where a person's conduct during any specified period must have involved the commission by him/her of one or more offences under this section.	7 years	6 months	Yes
Income tax evasion	Finance Act 2000, s. 144	Being knowingly concerned in the fraudulent evasion of income tax by any person.	7 years	6 months	Yes
Excise duty evasion	Customs and Excise Management Act 1979, s. 170	Knowingly acquiring possession of goods which have been unlawfully removed from a warehouse or Queen's warehouse or goods which are chargeable with a duty which has not been paid, or being in any way knowingly concerned in carrying, removing, depositing, harbouring, keeping or concealing or in any manner dealing with any such goods with intent to defraud Her Majesty of any duty payable on the goods. OR Being knowingly concerned in any fraudulent evasion or attempt at evasion of any duty chargeable on any goods.	7 years*	6 months	Yes

Offence	Statutory provision	Definition	Maximum custodial term in the Crown Court	Maximum custodial term in a Magistrates' Court	Financial reporting order available?
Taking preparatory steps for evasion of excise duty	Customs and Excise Management Act 1979, s. 170B	Being knowingly concerned in the taking of any steps with a view to the fraudulent evasion, by any person, of any duty of excise on any goods.	7 years	6 months	No
Improper importation of goods	Customs and Excise Management Act 1979, s. 50	With intent to defraud Her Majesty of any duty: – unshipping or landing in any port or unloading from any aircraft in the United Kingdom or from any vehicle in Northern Ireland any goods chargeable with a duty which has not been paid, or assisting or being otherwise concerned in such unshipping, landing or unloading; or – removing from their place of importation or from any approved wharf, examination station, transit shed or customs and excise station any goods chargeable with a duty which has not been paid, or assisting or being otherwise concerned in such removal.	7 years*	6 months	No
Benefit fraud offences	Social Security Administration Act 1992, s. 111A	Dishonestly making a false statement or representation or producing or furnishing or allowing to be produced or furnished any document or information which is false in a material particular with a view to obtaining any benefit or other payment or advantage for any person. OR Dishonestly failing to give a prompt notification or causing or allowing another person to fail to give a prompt notification of a change in circumstances affecting the entitlement of any person to any benefit or other payment or advantage, knowing that the change affects an entitlement to such a benefit or other payment or advantage. OR Where there has been a change of circumstances affecting any person's claim to any benefit or other payment or advantage under which the 'recipient' has a right to receive payments: – the recipient dishonestly fails to give prompt notification of the change in circumstances; or	7 years	6 months	No

Offence	Statutory provision	Definition	Maximum custodial term in the Crown Court	Maximum custodial term in a Magistrates' Court	Financial reporting order available?
		– causing or allowing the recipient to fail to give a prompt notification of the change in circumstances.			
Tax credit fraud	Tax Credits Act 2002, s. 35	Being knowingly concerned in any fraudulent activity undertaken with a view to obtaining payment of a tax credit by any person.	7 years	6 months	Yes

*10 years if goods are prohibited weapons covered by minimum sentence provisions (Criminal Justice Act 2003, s. 293) in relation to which this guideline does not apply.

PART 18 OVERARCHING PRINCIPLES—SENTENCING YOUTHS SG-406

Foreword

. . .This guideline applies to the sentencing of offenders on or after **30 November 2009**.

Generally, the Sentencing Guidelines Council has not produced offence specific guidelines for those under the age of 18 years. However, guidelines have been produced for those offences under the Sexual Offences Act 2003 which have a lower maximum penalty when committed by a person under 18 and for Robbery. These continue to provide the relevant starting points and ranges for all youths convicted of those offences and are not superseded by this guideline.

Overarching Principles—Sentencing Youths

General Approach SG-407

1. Statutory provisions

1.1 Offence seriousness is the starting point for sentencing. In considering the seriousness of any offence, the court must consider the offender's culpability in committing the offence and any harm which the offence caused, was intended to cause or might foreseeably have caused.[409] In imposing sentence, the restrictions on liberty must be commensurate with the seriousness of the offence.

1.2 When sentencing an offender aged under 18, a court must[410] have regard to:

a) the principal aim of the youth justice system (to prevent offending by children and young persons);[411] and

b) the welfare of the offender.[412]

1.3 In addition to the statutory provisions,[413] a court sentencing a young offender must be aware of obligations under a range of international conventions which emphasise the importance of avoiding 'criminalisation' of young people whilst ensuring that they are held responsible for their actions and, where possible, take part in repairing the damage that they have caused. This includes recognition of the damage caused to the victims and understanding by the young person that the deed was not acceptable. Within a system that provides for both the acknowledgement of guilt and sanctions which rehabilitate, the intention is to establish responsibility and, at the same time, to promote re-integration rather than to impose retribution.

---

409 Criminal Justice Act 2003, s.143(1)

410 This section does not apply when imposing a mandatory life sentence, when imposing a statutory minimum custodial sentence, when imposing detention for life under the dangerous offender provisions or when making certain orders under the Mental Health Act 1983

411 Crime and Disorder Act 1998, s. 37(1), see para. 2.6 below

412 Children and Young Persons Act 1933, s. 44(1), see para. 2.7

413 Criminal Justice and Immigration Act 2008, s. 9 (inserting s.142A into the Criminal Justice Act 2003) has not been brought into force

SG-408 **2. Sentencing principles**

2.1 **The approach to sentence will be individualistic.**

2.2 The youth of the offender is widely recognised as requiring a different approach from that which would be adopted in relation to an adult. Even within the category of 'youth', the response to an offence is likely to be very different depending on whether the offender is at the lower end of the age bracket, in the middle or towards the top end; in many instances, the maturity of the offender will be at least as important as the chronological age.

2.3 However, the sentence must remain proportionate to the seriousness of the present offence (except in the rare circumstances where the criteria for a sentence under the dangerous offender provisions are met) and should not impose greater restrictions on liberty than the seriousness of the offence justifies simply to deal with the risk of re-offending. Particular care will need to be taken where a young person has committed a relatively less serious offence but there is a high risk of re-offending.

2.4 Whilst a court is required to aggravate the seriousness of an offence where there are previous convictions (if the court considers that to be reasonable taking account both of the offence and the time that had elapsed since the previous conviction[414]), **a sentence that follows re-offending does not need to be more severe than the previous sentence solely because there had been a previous conviction.**

(i) Approach to determining sentence

2.5 When determining sentence, the court will:

(1) **Assess the culpability of the offender and the harm caused (or intended or foreseeable) taking into account aggravating and mitigating factors relating to the offence.**

The assessment of offence seriousness will fix the most severe penalty that can be imposed and will determine whether an offence has crossed the necessary threshold to enable the court to impose a community or custodial sentence.

Even where the custody threshold has been crossed, a court is not required to impose a custodial sentence; similarly with the community sentence threshold.[415]

Harm may be to individual victims or to the community or society at large. Of the four levels of culpability for sentencing purposes, intention is the highest followed by recklessness, knowledge and negligence. Even within those levels there will be gradations of seriousness.

Statutory aggravating factors (including previous convictions) will be relevant in assessing the seriousness of an offence.

(2) **Consider any mitigating factors that apply to the offender and any reduction for a guilty plea.**

When considering the maturity of the offender and its relevance to the sentence, it will only be in the most exceptional case that this will require more information than is available to the court through the representations of the advocates and any pre-sentence report.

(3) **Having taken account of all these factors, a court must then determine sentence including any relevant ancillary orders.**

The overall impact of the sentence and the ancillary orders must be considered to ensure that the restrictions on liberty are no more than is commensurate with the seriousness of the offence.

(ii) The principal aim of the youth justice system

2.6 By section 37 of the Crime and Disorder Act 1998, the principal aim of the youth justice system is to prevent offending by children and young people. For the offender, it incorporates the need to demonstrate that such conduct is not acceptable in a way that makes an impact on the offender whilst also identifying and seeking to address any other factors that make offending more likely. For any victim of the offence and society as a whole, it incorporates the need to demonstrate that the law is being effectively enforced and to sustain confidence in the rule of law.

(iii) The welfare of the offender

2.7 By section 44 of the Children and Young Persons Act 1933, 'Every court in dealing with a child or young person who is brought before it, either as an offender or otherwise, shall have regard to the *welfare* of the child or young person, and shall in a proper case take steps for removing him from undesirable surroundings, and for securing that proper provision is made for his education and training'.

[414] Criminal Justice Act 2003, s.174(2)
[415] ibid., s.148(5)

2.8 In other requirements or obligations, different terminology—*best interests, well-being* or *welfare*—may be used. Generally, although there are shades of difference between the meanings, it is unlikely that different decisions will arise solely from those differences.

2.9 Accordingly, since 'welfare' is the term used in the legislation applicable to England and Wales, that is the term used in this guideline. Welfare includes the obligation to secure proper provision for education and training,[416] where appropriate to remove from undesirable surroundings[417] and the need to choose the best option for the young person taking account of the circumstances of the offence.

In having regard to the 'welfare' of the young person, a court should ensure that it is alert to:

- **the high incidence of mental health problems amongst young people in the criminal justice system;**
- **the high incidence of those with learning difficulties or learning disabilities amongst young people in the criminal justice system;**
- **the effect that speech and language difficulties might have on the ability of the young person (or any adult with them) to communicate with the court, to understand the sanction imposed or to fulfil the obligations resulting from that sanction;**
- **the extent to which young people anticipate that they will be discriminated against by those in authority and the effect that it has on the way that they conduct themselves during court proceedings;**
- **the vulnerability of young people to self harm, particularly within a custodial environment;**
- **the extent to which changes taking place during adolescence can lead to experimentation;**
- **the effect on young people of experiences of loss or of abuse.**

2.10 In the light of the high incidence of these impairments amongst young people in custody or subject to a community sentence, and taking account of the fact that the principal aim of the youth justice system is preventing offending, a court should always seek to ensure that it has access to information about how best to identify and respond to those impairments and, where necessary, that a proper assessment has taken place in order to enable the most appropriate sentence to be imposed.

(iv) The purpose of sentencing

2.11 As set out in paragraph 1 above, a court sentencing a person under the age of 18 is obliged to have regard to the principal aim of the youth justice system (to prevent offending by children and young persons) and to the welfare of the offender. As the principal aim of the youth justice system[418] is the prevention of offending by children and young people, the emphasis should be on approaches that seem most likely to be effective with young people.

3. Effect on sentence of the offender being a young person SG-409

3.1 In addition to the distinctive range of penalties available for youths, there is an expectation that, generally, a young person will be dealt with less severely than an adult offender, although this distinction diminishes as the offender approaches age 18 (subject to an assessment of maturity and criminal sophistication). In part, this is because young people are unlikely to have the same experience and capacity as an adult to realise the effect of their actions on other people or to appreciate the pain and distress caused and because a young person is likely to be less able to resist temptation, especially where peer pressure is exerted.

3.2 Additionally, in most cases a young person is likely to benefit from being given greater opportunity to learn from mistakes without undue penalisation or stigma, especially as a court sanction might have a significant effect on the prospects and opportunities of the young person, and, therefore, on the likelihood of effective integration into society.

3.3 When sentencing a young offender whose offence involves sexual activity but there is no evidence of a coercive or abusive relationship or of anything other than consensual activity, a court will need to be aware that a desire to explore gender identity or sexual orientation may result in offending behaviour. Depending on the seriousness of the offending behaviour, offender mitigation may arise where that behaviour stems from sexual immaturity or confusion.[419]

[416] Children and Young Persons Act 1933, s. 44
[417] ibid.
[418] See para. 2.6 above
[419] the Sentencing Advisory Panel has previously stated that Crown Prosecutors and the court should take account of an offender's immaturity and normal juvenile experimentation: *Sexual Offences Act 2003 – the Panel's Advice to the Council* – page 4, para. 21, www.sentencing-guidelines.gov.uk

3.4 Individual sanctions are likely to have a greater impact on a youth than on an adult, especially lengths of time spent in a custodial establishment, not least because of the exposure to influences likely to entrench criminal conduct (to which a young person may be more susceptible than an adult) and the greater risk of self harm than exists in relation to an adult.

3.5 It is also important to consider whether the young offender lacks the maturity fully to appreciate the consequences of his conduct and the extent to which the offender has been acting on an impulsive basis and the offender's conduct has been affected by inexperience, emotional volatility or negative influences.

3.6 Factors regularly present in the background of those juveniles who commit offences include: low family income, poor housing, poor employment records, low educational attainment, early experience of offending by other family members or of violence or abuse (often accompanied by harsh and erratic discipline within the home) and the misuse of drugs.[420] There is also evidence that those young people who are 'looked after' have been more at risk of being drawn into the criminal justice system than other young people acting *in similar ways*.[421]

3.7 It is clear that these factors do not cause delinquency (since many who have experienced them do not commit crime); nonetheless, there is a strong association and any response to criminal activity amongst young people will need to recognise the presence of such factors if it is to be effective.

The following factors have led to a different approach to the sentencing of young people who offend (compared with the approach for adult offenders) and will affect the sentence imposed in an individual case:

- **offending by a young person is frequently a phase which passes fairly rapidly and therefore the reaction to it needs to be kept well balanced in order to avoid alienating the young person from society;**
- **a criminal conviction at this stage of a person's life may have a disproportionate impact on the ability of the young person to gain meaningful employment and play a worthwhile role in society;**
- **the impact of punishment is felt more heavily by young people in the sense that any sentence will seem to be far longer in comparison with their relative age compared with adult offenders;**
- **young people may be more receptive to changing the way they conduct themselves and be able to respond more quickly to interventions;**
- **young people should be given greater opportunity to learn from their mistakes;**
- **young people will be no less vulnerable than adults to the contaminating influences that can be expected within a custodial context and probably more so.**

SG-410 **4. The relevant considerations**

4.1 This guideline sets out a process that will enable the various obligations and requirements to be applied consistently. It is, however, only a framework and is intended to apply to the generality of cases.

In determining the sentence, the key elements are:

- **the age of the offender (chronological and emotional),**
- **the seriousness of the offence,**
- **the likelihood of further offences being committed, and**
- **the extent of harm likely to result from those further offences.**

The approach to sentence will be individualistic.

Proper regard should be had to the mental health and capability of the young person, and to any learning disability, learning difficulty, speech and language difficulty or other disorder, any of which is likely to affect the likelihood of those purposes being achieved.

4.2 The younger an offender (taking account of maturity and not just chronological age) the more likely it is that considering the welfare of the young person will be of greater significance. Since many young people 'grow out of' crime, the obligation to have regard to the welfare of a young person who has offended might in some circumstances be best manifested by protecting that person from the adverse effects of intervention in his or her life rather than by providing for some positive action.

[420] see, for example, the range of approaches in the *Youth Crime Action Plan 2008* Chapter 5: www.homeoffice.gov.uk

[421] see, for example, *Care experience and criminalisation* The Adolescent and Childcare Trust, September 2008 www.tactcare.org.uk *Sentencing Guidelines Council*

4.3 The requirement to have regard to the welfare of a young person is subject to the obligation to impose only those restrictions on liberty that are commensurate with the seriousness of the offence; accordingly, a court should not impose greater restrictions because of other factors in the young person's life.

4.4 In relation to custodial sentences, the reconviction rate is high and there are concerns about the effect on vulnerable young people of being in closed conditions. Risks commonly found are those of self harm and suicide and, in relation to female offenders, the additional impact on the offender herself and on the child if the offender is the primary carer of a child or is pregnant.[422] Since a court is obliged to have regard to the welfare of the young person, it must have regard to these issues when considering sentence.

4.5 Particular care should be taken where an offender has mental health problems, learning disabilities, learning difficulties or other disabilities. Research shows that there is a high incidence of these issues in young people in the youth justice system and, in particular, in custody.

4.6 These issues are not always able to be identified at an early stage in the proceedings leading to sentence. As a result, a court needs to be alert to the possibility that the conduct of the young person (and that of any adult accompanying them in court) might be affected by issues relating to mental health, learning or communication, or some other form of disability that has not previously been identified.

4.7 In such circumstances, care needs to be taken in ensuring that the young person is able to take a proper part in the court proceedings, is able to understand what the court requires as a result of the sentence imposed and that that sentence properly takes account of difficulties in compliance that may arise from those issues.

4.8 Some young people may attend court believing that they will be discriminated against or otherwise unfairly treated; this might be for any of a wide range of reasons including ethnicity and sexuality. However unjustified that belief is, a court will need to be alert to the fact that the young persons behaviour in court might be affected by it.

4.9 The obligations to treat the prevention of offending by children and young persons as the principal aim of sentencing and to have regard to their welfare both require a court to consider the impairments and life experiences noted above, not only in determining the sentence to be imposed, but also in determining the length or content of that sentence.

The proper approach for the Crown Court, a magistrates' court or a youth court when sentencing a young offender is for the court, within a sentence that is no more restrictive on liberty than is proportionate to the seriousness of the offence(s), to seek to impose a sentence that takes proper account of the matters to which the court must have regard (see paragraph 1 above) by:

- **confronting the young offender with the consequences of the offending and helping the young offender to develop a sense of personal responsibility—these consequences may be experienced by the offender himself or herself, by the family of the offender, by the victim(s) of the offence and/or by the community;**
- **tackling the particular factors (personal, family, social, educational or health) that put the young person at risk of offending;**
- **strengthening those factors that reduce the risk that the young person will continue to offend;**
- **encouraging reparation to victims;**
- **defining, agreeing and reinforcing the responsibilities of parents.**

5. Crossing a significant age threshold between commission of an offence and sentence SG-411

5.1 There will be occasions when an increase in the age of an offender[423] will result in the maximum sentence on the date of *conviction* being greater than that available on the date on which the offence was *committed*.

5.2 In such circumstances, the approach should be:

- where an offender crosses a relevant age threshold between the date on which the offence was committed and the date of conviction or sentence, a court should take as its starting point the sentence likely to have been imposed on the date on which the offence was committed;
- where an offender attains the age of 18 after committing the offence but before conviction, section 142 of the Criminal Justice Act 2003 applies (whilst section 37 of the 1998 Act and

[422] *The Corston Report – a review of women with particular vulnerabilities in the Criminal Justice System*, March 2007, www.homeoffice.gov.uk

[423] Primarily attaining the age of 12, 15 or 18

section 44 of the 1933 Act (see 2.6–2.10 above) apply to those aged under 18) and the sentencing disposal has to take account of the matters set out in that section;[424]

- it will be rare for a court to have to consider passing a sentence more severe than the maximum it would have had jurisdiction to pass at the time the offence was committed even where an offender has subsequently attained the age of 18;
- however, a sentence at or close to that maximum may be appropriate, especially where a serious offence was committed by an offender close to the age threshold.

SG-412 **6. Persistent offenders**

6.1 Certain sentences are available only where the offender is a 'persistent offender' – in particular, a youth rehabilitation order with intensive supervision and surveillance or with fostering in relation to an offender aged between 10 and 14[425] and a detention and training order in relation to an offender aged between 12 and 14.[426] This criterion does not have to be met before the Crown Court imposes long term detention (see paragraph 12 below) or detention for life.

6.2 Similarly, additional powers may be available to a court where a youth rehabilitation order has been breached 'wilfully and persistently'.

6.3 'Persistent offender' is not defined in legislation but has been considered by the Court of Appeal on a number of occasions. However, following the implementation of the 2008 Act, the sentencing framework is different from that when the definition was judicially developed, particularly the greater emphasis on the requirement to use a custodial sentence as 'a measure of last resort'.

6.4 A dictionary definition of 'persistent offender' is 'persisting or having a tendency to persist'; 'persist' is defined as 'to continue firmly or obstinately in a course of action in spite of difficulty or opposition'.

6.5 In determining whether an offender is a persistent offender for these purposes, a court should consider the simple test of whether the young person is one who persists in offending:

i) in most circumstances, the normal expectation is that the offender will have had some contact with authority in which the offending conduct was challenged before being classed as 'persistent'; a finding of persistence in offending may be derived from information about previous convictions but may also arise from orders which require an admission or finding of guilt – these include reprimands, final warnings, restorative justice disposals and conditional cautions; since they do not require such an admission, penalty notices for disorder are unlikely to be sufficiently reliable;

ii) a young offender is certainly likely to be found to be persistent (and, in relation to a custodial sentence, the test of being a measure of last resort is most likely to be satisfied) where the offender has been convicted of, or made subject to a pre-court disposal that involves an admission or finding of guilt in relation to, imprisonable offences on at least 3 occasions in the past 12 months.

6.6 Even where a young person is found to be a persistent offender, a court is not obliged to impose the custodial sentence or youth rehabilitation order with intensive supervision and surveillance or fostering that becomes available as a result of that finding. The other tests continue to apply and it is clear that Parliament expects custodial sentences to be imposed only rarely on those aged 14 or less.

SG-413 **7. Enforcing the responsibilities of parents and guardians**

7.1 A significant difference arising from the procedures for dealing with young people who commit criminal offences is the importance attached to the presence of a parent, carer or appropriate adult at key stages, especially when sentence is imposed. In addition, specific provisions exist to enable a court to reinforce the responsibilities of a parent or guardian.

7.2 The statutory framework clearly envisages the attendance of an adult with a degree of responsibility for the young person; this obligation reflects the principal aim of reducing offending, recognising that that is unlikely to be achieved by the young person alone. A court must be aware of a risk that a young person will seek to avoid this requirement either by urging the court to proceed in the absence of an adult or in arranging for a person to come to court who purports to have (but in reality does not have) the necessary degree of responsibility.

7.3 Insistence on attendance may produce a delay in the case before the court; however, it is important that this obligation is maintained and that it is widely recognised that a court will require such attendance, especially when imposing sentence. If a court proceeds in the absence of a responsible adult, it should ensure that the outcome of the hearing is properly communicated.

[424] Accordingly, when sentencing those convicted when aged 18 and above who have committed an offence whilst under that age, more general public policy considerations may play a greater part

[425] Criminal Justice and Immigration Act 2008, s.1(4)(c)

[426] Powers of Criminal Courts (Sentencing) Act 2000, s.100(2)

7.4 Where a person under the age of 18 is convicted of an offence, the court is under a duty to **bind over a parent or guardian** if satisfied that such a course of action would be desirable in the interest of preventing the commission of further offences.[427] Such an order may not be made where the court imposes a referral order. Similarly, the court has the power to make a **parenting order** where it would be desirable in the interest of preventing the commission of any further offence.[428] Where the offender is aged 16 or less and the court considers that a parenting order would be desirable, there is a presumption in favour of the order being made and reasons must be given if it is not made.[429] In most circumstances where an order is necessary, it is more likely that a parenting order will be appropriate.

7.5 When considering whether to impose a parenting order, the court should give careful consideration to the strength of the familial relationships and to any diversity issues that might impact on the achievement of the purposes of the order. Such factors and issues arising may be documented in a pre-sentence report.

7.6 Particular issues may arise in relation to an offender who is, or who runs the risk of, experiencing familial abuse or rejection on the grounds of sexual orientation. In considering such factors, which may be documented in a pre-sentence report the court must take care not to disclose facts about an offender's sexual orientation without his or her consent. Similar issues might arise in a family where racial tensions exist.

Sentences SG-414

8. Referral orders

8.1 Where an offender is being sentenced in a youth court or a magistrates' court, a referral order is a mandatory sentence in many circumstances in which a young person is to be sentenced for the first time and is discretionary in a wider range of situations. In particular, it is possible to make an order on a second conviction where a referral order was not made following the first conviction.

8.2 When an order is made, the court determines the length of the order (between 3 months and 12 months) but the action taken during that order is decided by a Youth Offender Panel consisting of members of the community supported by a member of a Youth Offending Team. Any victim of the offence may be invited to attend the meeting of the Panel at which the terms are agreed.

8.3 When determining the length of an order, although the needs of the offender are a factor, the primary consideration in most circumstances is the relative seriousness of the offence. Given the mandatory nature of the order in many circumstances, it is less likely that the needs of the offender will be considered in a pre-sentence report. This consideration is more likely to take place once the order has been made and in preparation for the Panel meeting since, within the period of the order, the Youth Offender Panel will agree what needs to be undertaken by the young person both in the light of the nature of the offence and of the young person's needs.

8.4 **A court should be prepared to use the whole range of periods allowed; in general, orders of 10–12 months should be made only for the more serious offences.**

8.5 Typically, the length of an order should be between 3–5 months for offences where the court assesses seriousness to be relatively low, between 5–7 months for an offence of medium level seriousness and between 7–9 months for an offence where the court considers seriousness to be relatively high. In determining which level applies, a court may find assistance in Section 2 of the Youth Court Bench Book issued by the Judicial Studies Board which provides indications of the level of seriousness of an average offence of the types described.[430]

9. Financial orders SG-415

9.1 A court may impose a fine for any offence. In accordance with statutory requirements, where financial orders are being considered, priority must be given to compensation orders and, where an order for costs is to be made alongside a fine, the amount of the costs must not exceed the amount of the fine.

9.2 In practice, many young people who offend have few financial resources. Where a young person is in receipt of the *Education Maintenance Allowance* or a similar provision which is related to the means of the offender or those with whom the offender lives, a court will need to consider the extent to which making a deduction from the allowance would prejudice the access of the young person to education or training.

[427] Powers of Criminal Courts (Sentencing) Act 2000, s.150
[428] Crime and Disorder Act 1998, s. 8(6)
[429] ibid., s. 9(1)
[430] www.jsboard.co.uk/downloads/ycbb/ycbb_section2.pdf

9.3 **As a general rule, it will rarely be appropriate to take the allowance into account as a resource from which a financial penalty may be paid, especially where the recipient is a young person who is living independently or as part of a household primarily dependent on state benefit.**

SG-416 **10. Youth Rehabilitation Orders**

10.1 The Criminal Justice and Immigration Act 2008 provides for a single community sentence (the youth rehabilitation order) within which a court may include one or more requirements variously designed to provide for punishment, for protection of the public, for reducing reoffending and for reparation.

10.2 A youth rehabilitation order with intensive supervision and surveillance or with fostering is also provided but may be imposed only where a custodial sentence otherwise would have been appropriate (see 10.23 below).[431]

(i) Threshold and availability

10.3 In order for a court to be able to impose a youth rehabilitation order, it must be satisfied that the offence is 'serious enough'.[432] Even where an offence crosses this threshold, a court is not obliged to make a youth rehabilitation order.[433]

10.4 In determining the content and length of an order, the guiding principles are proportionality and suitability since statute provides that the restrictions on liberty within such an order must be commensurate with the seriousness of the offence[434] and that, taken together, the requirements within the order are the most suitable for the offender.[435]

10.5 In contrast to the provisions relating to adult offenders, a court may impose a youth rehabilitation order (other than one with intensive supervision and surveillance or fostering[436]) for an offence that is not imprisonable.

10.6 A youth rehabilitation order is not an available sentence where the 'compulsory referral conditions' are found to exist; accordingly, the order will not be available in a youth court or other magistrates' court for a first time offender who has pleaded guilty to an imprisonable offence.

(ii) Effect of a guilty plea

10.7 Where a court is considering sentence for an offence for which a custodial sentence is justified, a guilty plea may be one of the factors that persuades a court that it can properly impose a youth rehabilitation order instead and no further adjustment to the sentence needs to be made to fulfil the obligation to give credit for that plea.

10.8 Where the provisional sentence is already a youth rehabilitation order, the necessary reduction for a guilty plea should apply to those requirements within the order that are primarily punitive rather than to those which are primarily rehabilitative.

(iii) Approach to determining nature and extent of requirements

10.9 In determining the nature and extent of requirements to be included within an order and the length of that order, the key factors are the assessment of the seriousness of the offence, the objective(s) the court wishes to achieve, the risk of re-offending, the ability of the offender to comply, and the availability of requirements in the local area.

10.10 Since a court must determine that the offence (or combination of offences) is 'serious enough' to justify such an order, a court will be able to determine the nature and extent of the requirements within the order primarily by reference to the likelihood of the young person re-offending and to the risk of the young person causing serious harm. This is in accordance with the principal aim of the youth justice system and the welfare principle.

10.11 Before making an order a court will consider a pre-sentence report. In preparing that report, (following national standards and practice guidance) the Youth Offending Team (YOT) will be seeking to identify an appropriate balance between the seriousness of the offence, the risk of harm in

[431] Criminal Justice and Immigration Act 2008, ss.1(3) and 1(4); Criminal Justice Act 2003, s.174(2)(ca) and (cb) as inserted by Criminal Justice and Immigration Act 2008, sched. 4, para. 80(2); however, it may be imposed in other circumstances following 'wilful and persistent' breach of a youth rehabilitation order: see para. 10.41 below

[432] Criminal Justice Act 2003, s.148(1)

[433] ibid., s.148(5)

[434] ibid., s.148(3)(b)

[435] ibid., s.148(3)(a)

[436] Such an order may be imposed following wilful and persistent failure to comply with a youth rehabilitation order imposed for a non-imprisonable offence: Criminal Justice and Immigration Act 2008, sched. 2, para. 6(13) and para. 8(12)

the future from any further offences the young person might commit and the needs of the young person.

10.12 In most cases, the assessment by the YOT will be undertaken by use of *Asset*[437] supported by professional judgement. An initial assessment will calculate the risk of re-offending; where necessary, an additional assessment will assess the risk of serious harm likely to be involved in further offending.

10.13 Those assessments will be reviewed by the YOT in the context of all other available information and the report will identify a level of intervention for the court to consider. There are three intervention levels:

- **Standard level** – for those who show a low likelihood of reoffending **and** a low risk of serious harm; in those circumstances, the order primarily will seek to repair the harm caused by the offence – typically, this will involve interventions to meet the requirements of the order and the engagement of parents in those interventions and/or in supporting the young person;
- **Enhanced level** – for those who show a medium likelihood of reoffending **or** a medium risk of serious harm; in those circumstances, the order will, in addition, seek to enable help or change as appropriate – typically, this will involve greater activity in motivating the young person and in addressing the reasons for non-compliance with the law and may involve external interventions;
- **Intensive level** – for those with a high likelihood of reoffending **or** a high or very high risk of serious harm; in those circumstances, the order will, in addition, seek to ensure control of the young person as necessary to minimise the risk of further offending or of serious harm—typically this will involve additional controls, restrictions and monitoring.[438]

10.14 For the broad generality of offences where a youth rehabilitation order is to be imposed, this approach will enable the writer of a pre-sentence report to make proposals that match the obligations on the court to balance the various statutory obligations that apply.

10.15 Where a young person is assessed as presenting a **high risk of re-offending or of causing serious harm** despite having committed a relatively less serious offence, the emphasis is likely to be on requirements that are primarily rehabilitative or for the protection of the public. Care will need to be taken to ensure both that the requirements are 'those most suitable for the offender' and that the restrictions on liberty are commensurate with the seriousness of the offence.

10.16 Where a young person is assessed as presenting a **low risk despite having committed a relatively high seriousness offence**, the emphasis is likely to be on requirements that are primarily punitive, again ensuring that restrictions on liberty are commensurate with the seriousness of the offence. In relation to young offenders, the primary purpose of punitive sanctions is to achieve acknowledgement by the young person of responsibility for his or her actions and, where possible, to take a proper part in repairing the damage caused.

(iv) Length of order

10.17 When imposing a youth rehabilitation order, the court must fix a period within which the requirements of the order are to be completed; this must not be more than 3 years from the date on which the order comes into effect.[439] Where the order contains two or more requirements, the order may specify an earlier date for any of those requirements.[440]

10.18 The period specified as the overall period for the order will normally commence on the day the order is made but, where the young person is already subject to a detention and training order, the court may specify that the youth rehabilitation order will take effect either on the day that supervision begins in relation to the detention and training order or on the expiry of the term of that order.[441]

10.19 It is not possible to make a youth rehabilitation order when the young person is already subject to another youth rehabilitation order or to a reparation order unless the court revokes those orders.[442]

10.20 The overall length of an order has three main consequences:

---

[437] A 'common, structured framework for the assessment of all young people involved in the criminal justice system' which is designed to 'identify a multitude of factors and circumstances . . . which may have contributed' to the offending behaviour: see www.yjb.gov.uk

[438] YOUTH JUSTICE: The Scaled Approach, YJB 2009 www.yjb.gov.uk/scaledapproach

[439] Criminal Justice and Immigration Act 2008, sched. 1, para. 32(1)

[440] ibid., para. 32(2)

[441] ibid., para. 30

[442] ibid., para. 30(4)

Sentencing Guidelines

- where a supervision requirement is included, the obligation to attend appointments as directed by the responsible officer continues for the whole period;
- where a young person is in breach of a youth rehabilitation order, one of the sanctions available to a court is to amend the order by including within it any requirement that it would have had power to include when the order was made;[443] however, that new requirement must be capable of being complied with before the expiry of the overall period;[444]
- a young person is liable to re-sentence for the offence(s) for which the order was made if convicted of another offence whilst the order is in force.[445]

10.21 In determining the length of an order, a court should allow sufficient time for the order as a whole to be complied with, recognising that the young person is at risk of further sanction throughout the whole of the period, but allowing sufficient flexibility should a sanction need to be imposed for breach of the order. Where appropriate, an application for early discharge may be made.

(v) Determining the requirements and the length of an order—summary

10.22 As set out in paragraph 2.1 above, the approach to the sentencing of a youth will be individualistic. Where a court is satisfied that an offence has crossed the community sentence threshold and that such a sentence is necessary or has crossed the custody threshold but is an offence for which a youth rehabilitation order is nonetheless considered to be appropriate, taking account of the assessment in the pre-sentence report, the consideration process that the court should follow is:

i) ***what requirements are most suitable for the offender?***
ii) ***what overall period is necessary to ensure that all requirements may be satisfactorily completed?***
iii) ***are the restrictions on liberty that result from those requirements commensurate with the seriousness of the offence?***

(vi) Orders with intensive supervision and surveillance or with fostering

10.23 Such orders may be made where:[446]

- the court is dealing with a young person for an offence punishable with imprisonment;
- that offence (or combination of offences) crosses the custody threshold; and
- custody would be an appropriate sentence.

If the offender was under 15 at the time of conviction, such an order may be imposed only where the offender is a 'persistent offender'.

10.24 When imposing such an order, the court must give its reasons for concluding that the offence(s) cross(es) the community sentence threshold and that the requirements set out above have been met.[447]

(a) With intensive supervision and surveillance

10.25 A youth rehabilitation order with intensive supervision and surveillance is an order that contains an 'extended activity requirement', that is, an activity requirement with a maximum of 180 days. As a result, there are further obligations to include a supervision requirement[448] and a curfew requirement.[449]

10.26 Where appropriate, a youth rehabilitation order with intensive supervision and surveillance may also include additional requirements, although the order as a whole must comply with the obligation that the requirements must be those most suitable for the offender and that any restrictions on liberty must be commensurate with the seriousness of the offence.

10.27 When imposing such an order, a court must ensure that the requirements are not so onerous as to make the likelihood of breach almost inevitable.

---

443 Criminal Justice and Immigration Act 2008, sched. 2, para. 6(2) (magistrates' court) and para. 8(2) (Crown Court)
444 ibid., para. 6(6) and para. 8(6)
445 ibid., para. 18 and para. 19
446 though see the additional powers where an offender has 'wilfully and persistently' failed to comply with a youth rehabilitation order; para. 10.41 below
447 Criminal Justice Act 2003, s.174(2)(ca) and (cb)
448 A requirement to attend appointments with the responsible officer (or any other person determined by the responsible officer): Criminal Justice and Immigration Act 2008, sched. 1, para. 9
449 A minimum of 2 hours and a maximum of 12 hours on any one day which must fall within the period of 6 months from the day on which the requirement first takes effect: ibid., para. 14; it is likely that this curfew will be electronically monitored: ibid., para. 3(4)(b) and para. 2

(b) With fostering

10.28 Where a fostering requirement is included within a youth rehabilitation order, it will require the offender to reside with a local authority foster parent for a specified period; that period must not exceed 12 months.[450] The court must be satisfied that a significant factor in the offence was the circumstances in which the young person was living and that the imposition of a fostering requirement would assist in the rehabilitation of the young person. It is likely that other rights will be engaged (such as those under Article 8 of the European Convention on Human Rights[451]) and any interference with such rights must be proportionate.

10.29 Before including this requirement, the court must consult both the young person's parent or guardian (unless impracticable) and the local authority; it cannot be included unless the offender was legally represented in court when the court was considering whether or not to impose the requirement or, having had the opportunity to be represented, the offender has not applied for representation or that right was withdrawn because of the offender's conduct.[452] This requirement may be included only where the court has been notified that arrangements are available in the area of the relevant local authority.

10.30 A fostering requirement cannot be included with intensive supervision and surveillance and it cannot be included in a youth rehabilitation order unless the higher criteria described above have been met. Where appropriate, a youth rehabilitation order with fostering may also include other requirements (and must include supervision) although the order as a whole must comply with the obligation that the requirements must be those most suitable for the offender and that any restrictions on liberty must be commensurate with the seriousness of the offence.

10.31 It is unlikely that the statutory criteria will be met in many cases; where they are met and the court is considering making an order, care should be taken to ensure that there is a well developed plan for the care and support of the young person throughout the period of the order and following conclusion of the order. A court will need to be provided with sufficient information, including proposals for education and training during the order and plans for the offender on completion of the order.

(vii) Breaches

10.32 Where a young person fails to comply with a youth rehabilitation order, the 'responsible officer' must consider whether there was a reasonable excuse. If the officer considers that there was no reasonable excuse and this is the first failure to comply with the order without reasonable excuse, the officer must issue a 'warning'.[453]

10.33 The warning will describe the circumstances of the failure to comply, a statement that the failure is not acceptable and a warning that a further failure to comply may lead to the order being referred back to the court. In most circumstances, two warnings will be permitted within a 12 month period before the matter is referred back to court.

10.34 There is a presumption in favour of referring the matter back to court after a third failure to comply and a discretionary power to do so after the second failure to comply.[454]

10.35 Breach of an order brought before a court may arise from a failure to keep an appointment or otherwise co-operate with the responsible officer or may arise from a failure to comply with one or more of the other requirements of the order.

10.36 Even where a breach has been proved, a court is not obliged to make any order but may allow the youth rehabilitation order to continue as imposed. In contrast with the powers in relation to an adult offender, there is no obligation on the court to make an order more onerous. Where a court determines that a sanction is necessary, it has the power to:

- impose a fine (in which case the order continues in its original form);
- amend the terms of the order; or
- revoke the order and re-sentence the offender.[455]

[450] Criminal Justice and Immigration Act 2008, sched. 1, para. 18
[451] Right to respect for family and private life
[452] Criminal Justice and Immigration Act 2008, sched. 1, para. 19
[453] Criminal Justice and Immigration Act 2008, sched. 2, para. 3
[454] ibid., para. 4; where a young person has attained the age of 18 since the order was made, except where the order was made in the Crown Court and no direction was made permitting breach proceedings to be dealt with in the youth court or a magistrates' court, breach proceedings will be dealt with in a magistrates' court other than a youth court: ibid., para. 5(3); however, the powers of a magistrates' court are the same as those of a youth court: ibid., para. 6
[455] ibid., para. 6 and para. 8

10.37 If amending the terms of the order, the court may impose any requirement that it could have imposed when making the order and this may be in addition to, or in substitution for, any requirements contained in the order. If the youth rehabilitation order did not contain an unpaid work requirement and the court includes such a requirement using this power, the minimum period of unpaid work is 20 hours; this will give greater flexibility when responding to less serious breaches or where there are significant other requirements to be complied with.[456]

10.38 A court may not amend the terms of a youth rehabilitation order that did not include an extended activity requirement or a fostering requirement by inserting them at this stage; should these requirements be considered appropriate following breach, the offender must be re-sentenced and the original youth rehabilitation order revoked.[457]

10.39 Before imposing a custodial sentence as a result of re-sentencing following breach, a court should be satisfied that the YOT and other local authority services have taken all steps necessary to ensure that the young person has been given appropriate opportunity and support necessary for compliance.[458]

10.40 Where the failure arises primarily from non-compliance with reporting or other similar obligations and a sanction is necessary, the most appropriate response is likely to be the inclusion of (or increase in) a primarily punitive requirement such as the curfew requirement, unpaid work, the exclusion requirement and the prohibited activity requirement or . . . the imposition of a fine. However, continuing failure to comply with the order is likely to lead to revocation of the order and re-sentencing for the original offence.

10.41 Where the offender has 'wilfully and persistently' failed to comply with the order, and the court proposes to sentence again for the offence(s) in respect of which the order was made, additional powers are available.[459] These additional powers include:

- the making of a youth rehabilitation order with intensive supervision and surveillance even though the offence is not imprisonable or a custodial sentence would not have been imposed if the order had not been available;
- even though the offence is not imprisonable, the imposition of a detention and training order for 4 months for breach of a youth rehabilitation order with intensive supervision and surveillance imposed following wilful and persistent breach of an order made for a non-imprisonable offence.

10.42 In considering whether the failure to comply is 'persistent', account should be taken of the principles set out in paragraph 6 above.

The primary objective when sentencing for breach of a youth rehabilitation order is to ensure that the young person completes the requirements imposed by the court.

Where the failure arises primarily from non-compliance with reporting or other similar obligations, where a sanction is necessary, the most appropriate is likely to be the inclusion of (or increase in) a primarily punitive requirement.

A court must ensure that it has sufficient information to enable it to understand why the order has been breached and that all steps have been taken by the YOT and other local authority services to give the young person appropriate opportunity and support. This will be particularly important if the court is considering imposing a custodial sentence as a result of the breach.

Where a court is determining whether the young person has 'wilfully and persistently breached an order, it should apply the same approach as when determining whether an offender is a 'persistent offender'. In particular, almost certainly a young person will have 'persistently breached a youth rehabilitation order where there have been three breaches (each resulting in an appearance before a court) demonstrating a lack of willingness to comply with the order.

SG-417 11. Custodial sentences

11.1 There is a statutory presumption that a person aged under 18 will be dealt with summarily, usually in a youth court; in such circumstances, the maximum custodial sentence will be a detention and training order of no more than 24 months. Such an order may be made only for the periods prescribed—4, 6, 8, 10, 12, 18 or 24 months.[460]

---

456 Criminal Justice and Immigration Act 2008, sched. 2, para. 6(7) and para. 8(7)
457 ibid., para. 6(8) and para. 8(8)
458 cp Education and Skills Act 2008, s.45(5)
459 In accordance with para. 6 and para. 8 of sched. 2 to the Criminal Justice and Immigration Act 2008
460 Although consecutive sentences may lead to different periods being imposed in total

11.2 The custodial sentences available in the Crown Court are:
- detention and training order of up to 24 months;
- long term detention—in relation to a young person convicted[461] in the Crown Court, under section 91 of the Powers of Criminal Courts (Sentencing) Act 2000;
- extended sentence of detention or detention for public protection – where a young person is sent for trial or committed for sentence to the Crown Court to be dealt with under the dangerous offender provisions; in each case, the minimum period to be spent in custody under the sentence must be two years;
- detention at Her Majesty's pleasure—for offences of murder.

11.3 A detention and training order may not be imposed on an offender aged 10 or 11 years at the time of conviction; an order may be imposed in relation to an offender aged between 12 and 14 at the time of conviction only if the offender is a 'persistent offender' (see paragraph 6 above).[462] However, the persistent offender criterion does not have to be met before the Crown Court imposes long term detention or detention for life in relation to offenders who are under 15 years of age.

11.4 A pre-sentence report must be considered before a custodial sentence is imposed.

(i) Threshold and approach

11.5 Under both domestic law and international convention, a custodial sentence must be imposed only as a 'measure of last resort'; statute provides that such a sentence may be imposed only where an offence is 'so serious that neither a community sentence nor a fine alone can be justified'.[463]

11.6 For a first time offender who has pleaded guilty to an imprisonable offence, in most circumstances a referral order will be the most appropriate sentence.

11.7 Since the minimum length of a custodial sentence in the youth court is 4 months (significantly in excess of the minimum available in relation to an adult offender) and since the term of a custodial sentence must be the shortest commensurate with the seriousness of the offence, it is inevitable that the custody threshold is higher in the case of a young person than in the case of an adult—any case that warrants a detention and training order of less than four months must result in a non-custodial sentence.

11.8 In relation to a person under the age of 18, in determining whether an offence has crossed the custody threshold a court will need to consider whether the offence has resulted (or could reasonably have resulted) in serious harm. In determining whether a custodial sentence is unavoidable, generally, a court will need to take account both of the seriousness of the offence (particularly the extent to which it caused (or was likely to cause) serious harm) and of the risk of serious harm in the future. A custodial sentence is most likely to be unavoidable where it is necessary to protect the public from serious harm.

11.9 In addition, a court must take account of:
i) the requirement to have regard to the principal aim of the youth justice system;[464]
ii) the requirement to have regard to the welfare of the offender and the evidence that the risks associated with young offenders in a custodial setting are high.[465]

11.10 Even where the threshold is crossed, a court is not required to impose a custodial sentence.

11.11 Before deciding to impose a custodial sentence on a young offender, the court must ensure that all the statutory tests are satisfied—namely:
i) that the offender cannot properly be dealt with by a fine alone or by a youth rehabilitation order,
ii) that a youth rehabilitation order with intensive supervision and surveillance or with fostering cannot be justified, and
iii) that custody is the last resort and in doing so should take account of the circumstances, age and maturity of the young offender.

11.12 When a custodial sentence is imposed, a court must state its reasons for being satisfied that the offence(s) is (are) so serious that no other sanction is appropriate and, in particular, why a youth rehabilitation order with intensive supervision and surveillance or with fostering cannot

[461] On the implementation of provisions contained in Criminal Justice Act 2003, sched. 3, this sentence is likely to be able to be imposed following conviction in a youth court also subsequent to an indication to plead guilty
[462] Powers of Criminal Courts (Sentencing) Act 2000, s.100(2)
[463] Criminal Justice Act 2003, s.152(2)
[464] The prevention of offending; see para. 2.6 above
[465] See para. 2 above

be justified.[466] This justification will need to be based on the principles set out in the statutory framework.

Where the offence(s) has crossed the custody threshold, the statutory tests are likely to be satisfied only where a custodial sentence will be more effective in preventing offending by children and young persons. The obligation to have regard to the welfare of the offender will require a court to take account of a wide range of issues including those relating to mental health, capability and maturity.

(ii) Length of sentence

11.13 A court imposing a custodial sentence is required to set the shortest term commensurate with the seriousness of the offence(s).[467] Offence specific guidelines do not generally provide starting points or ranges for offenders aged under 18 because of the wide range of issues that are likely to arise and the marked differences in the sentencing framework depending on the age of the offender. Where they are provided,[468] they are for offenders aged 17 with a provision that, for younger offenders, a court should consider whether a lower starting point is justified in recognition of the offender's age and maturity.

11.14 Any approach needs to take account of the general sentencing rules that apply where there is more than one offence or more than one defendant. Where the offence has been committed by offender(s) aged 18 or over and by offender(s) aged under 18, the court will need to consider the role of each offender and the number of offenders involved.

11.15 Where the primary offender is under the age of 18, a court is likely to determine sentence for that offender first giving proper weight to the offender's age and maturity; that will provide a framework within which sentence for the offender(s) over 18 can be determined. Where the primary offender is over 18, a court is likely to determine sentence for that offender first; that will provide a framework within which sentence for the offender(s) under 18 can be determined giving proper weight to age and maturity.

11.16 Where an offence crosses the custodial threshold **and** the court determines that a custodial sentence is unavoidable:

- **where the offender is aged 15, 16 or 17, the court will need to consider the maturity of the offender as well as chronological age. Where there is no offence specific guideline, it may be appropriate, depending on maturity, to consider a starting point from <u>half to three quarters of that which would have been identified for an adult offender</u>.**
  It will be particularly important to consider maturity when the court has to sentence more than one offender. When the offenders are of different ages, including when one or more is over 18, the court will also need to have proper regard to parity between their sentences.
  The closer an offender was to age 18 when the offence was committed and the greater the maturity of the offender or the sophistication of the offence, the closer the starting point is likely to be to that appropriate for an adult. Some offenders will be extremely mature, more so than some offenders who are over 18, whilst others will be significantly less mature.
  For younger offenders, greater flexibility will be required to reflect the potentially wide range of culpability.
  Where an offence shows considerable planning or sophistication, a court may need to adjust the approach upwards.
  Where the offender is particularly immature, the court may need to adjust the approach downwards.
- **where the offender is aged 14 or less**, sentence should normally be imposed in a youth court (except in cases of homicide or where the young person comes within the 'dangerous offender' criteria); the length of a custodial sentence will normally be shorter than for an offender aged 15–17 convicted of the same offence.
- **an offender aged 14 years or less** should be sentenced to long term detention[469] only where that is necessary for the protection of the public either because of the risk of serious harm from future offending or because of the persistence of offending behaviour; exceptionally, such a sentence may be appropriate where an offender aged 14 years or less has committed a very

[466] Criminal Justice Act 2003, s.174(4B) as inserted by Criminal Justice and Immigration Act 2008, sched. 4, para. 80(3)
[467] Criminal Justice Act 2003, s.153(2)
[468] Robbery pages 12–14; *Sexual Offences Act 2003* pages 133–139; *Breach of an Anti-Social Behaviour Order* pages 10–12: www.sentencing-guidelines.gov.uk
[469] Powers of Criminal Courts (Sentencing) Act 2000, s. 91

serious offence but is not a persistent offender and there is no risk of serious harm from future offending.

11.17 In determining the term of a detention and training order, the court must take account of any period for which the offender has been remanded in custody or on bail subject to a qualifying curfew condition and electronic monitoring.[470] As the available terms are specified, the proper approach in taking a remand period into account is to reduce, if possible, the sentence otherwise appropriate to reflect that period.[471] Where a short custodial sentence was being considered, the court might conclude that a non-custodial sentence was appropriate.

11.18 On the implementation of the relevant parts of schedule 3 to the Criminal Justice Act 2003, a 'plea before venue' procedure will be introduced for offenders under the age of 18 and will include a general power to commit for sentence where a court accepts jurisdiction following indication of a guilty plea. As with adult offenders, where a young person could have been dealt with in the Crown Court but the youth court has retained jurisdiction, where appropriate the maximum period of 24 months may be imposed following a guilty plea at the first reasonable opportunity where that plea was a factor in retaining a case for sentence in the youth court.

12. Trial and Sentencing of Cases in the Crown Court SG-418

12.1 There is a clear principle (established both in statute and in domestic and European case law) that cases involving young offenders should be tried and sentenced in the youth court wherever possible. This section summarises the relevant statutory provisions and case law.[472]

12.2 It has long been recognised that the Crown Court should be reserved for the most serious cases, noting the greater formality of the proceedings and the increased number of people likely to be present.[473] These factors present additional obstacles in ensuring that proceedings in the Crown Court involving young offenders are conducted in accordance with international obligations.[474]

12.3 Accordingly, it is rare for a young offender to be tried or sentenced in the Crown Court and for a sentence beyond the powers of the youth court to be imposed, except where that sentence is substantially beyond those powers.

12.4 A youth will appear in the Crown Court for trial and sentence only:

i) when charged with 'homicide';
ii) when subject to a minimum statutory sentence;
iii) when charged with a 'grave crime' and a youth court has determined that, if convicted, a sentence beyond its powers should be available; or
iv) when charged together with an adult offender who has been sent to the Crown Court and it has been determined that the cases should be kept together.

12.5 Where a sentence under the 'dangerous offender' provisions is likely to be needed the youth may be committed for trial or for sentence.

(i) Homicide

12.6 An exception to the presumption that a person aged under 18 should be tried summarily arises where the young person is charged with an offence of 'homicide'. For a case falling within this description, there is no discretion and it must be sent to the Crown Court for trial. The meaning of 'homicide' is not defined in statute.

(ii) Statutory minimum sentences

12.7 A further exception to the presumption in favour of summary trial arises where a young person is charged with an offence which has a statutory minimum custodial sentence and the criteria for that sentence would be likely to be satisfied if the young person were convicted.[475] A sentence of long term detention[476] may be imposed following committal where these mandatory sentence provisions apply; before there can be a departure from the minimum sentence prescribed, a court must find that there are 'exceptional circumstances'.

470 Powers of Criminal Courts (Sentencing) Act 2000, s.101(8) and (9); for these purpose, 'remanded in custody' includes periods held in police detention and certain remands or committals to local authority accommodation: ibid., s.101(11)

471 Such a period must be set against the part of the sentence that is to be served in custody, not the whole sentence: *Eagles* [2006] EWCA Crim 2368; *Joyce* [2007] EWCA Crim 3374

472 See in particular *R (H, A, and O) v Southampton Youth Court* [2004] EWHC 2912 (Admin)

473 ibid., [33]

474 See, for example, *S.C. v United Kingdom* (2005) 40 EHRR 10

475 Magistrates' Courts Act 1980, s. 24

476 Under Powers of Criminal Courts (Sentencing) Act 2000, s. 91

(iii) 'Grave crimes'

12.8 A further exception to the statutory presumption in favour of summary trial arises where a young person is charged with a 'grave crime' and a youth court has determined that, if convicted, a sentence beyond its powers should be available. In such circumstances, a young person may be sentenced by the Crown Court to long term detention under section 91 of the Powers of Criminal Courts (Sentencing) Act 2000. At present, such a sentence may be imposed only by the Crown Court and only where the offender was **convicted** in the Crown Court, and that court considers that neither a community order nor a detention and training order is suitable.

12.9 An offence comes within section 91 where:

- it is punishable with 14 years imprisonment or more for an adult (but is not a sentence fixed by law), or
- is an offence contrary to sections 3, 13, 25 or 26 of the Sexual Offences Act 2003,[477] or
- is one of a number of specified offences in relation to firearms, ammunition and weapons which are subject to a minimum term but in respect of which a court has found exceptional circumstances justifying a lesser sentence.

12.10 This general power should be used rarely since:

i) it is the general policy of Parliament that those under 18 should be tried in the youth court wherever possible;

ii) trial in the Crown Court under this provision should be reserved for the most serious cases, recognising the greater formality of the proceedings and the greatly increased number of people involved;

iii) offenders aged under 15 will rarely attract a period of detention under this provision and those under 12 even more rarely.[478]

12.11 Accordingly,

i) **a young person aged 10 or 11 (or aged 12–14 but not a persistent offender) should be committed to the Crown Court under this provision only where charged with an offence of such gravity that, despite the normal prohibition on a custodial sentence for a person of that age, a sentence exceeding two years is a realistic possibility**[479]

ii) **a young person aged 12–17 (for which a detention and training order could be imposed) should be committed to the Crown Court under this provision only where charged with an offence of such gravity that a sentence substantially beyond the 2 year maximum for a detention and training order is a realistic possibility**[480]

(iv) **Dangerous offenders**

12.12 There are rigorous statutory tests which must be satisfied before a court may conclude that a youth is a 'dangerous offender' and requires sentence under the dangerous offender provisions in the Criminal Justice Act 2003 (as amended).[481] Such a sentence may be imposed only where an equivalent determinate sentence of at least 4 years would have been imposed. Criteria relating to future offending and the risk of serious harm must be assessed in the light of the maturity of the offender, the possibility of change in a much shorter time than would apply for an adult and the wider circumstances of the young person.

12.13 At present, the provisions by which a potentially 'dangerous' young offender reaches the Crown Court are overlapping to some extent as a result of the only partial implementation of the provisions of the Criminal Justice Act 2003, which introduce a new section 51A to the Crime and Disorder Act 1998. This new section requires a young offender to be sent for trial where it appears that the criteria for imposition of a sentence under the dangerous offender provisions will be met on conviction. However, the power to commit for sentence following conviction in a youth court or magistrates' court is preserved.[482]

[477] Sexual assault, child sex offences committed by a child or young person, sexual activity with a child family member, inciting a child family member to engage in sexual activity

[478] See footnote [505]; those who meet the criteria for "dangerous offenders" will be dealt with under separate provisions: see below

[479] See *R(D) v Manchester City Youth Court* [2001] EWHC Admin 860

[480] See *C & D v Sheffield Youth Court* [2003] EWHC Admin 35 confirming the relevance of undisputed personal mitigation

[481] See the review of statutory provisions and case law authority in *Dangerous Offenders: A Guide for Sentencers and Practitioners* at p.18 www.sentencing-guidelines.gov.uk

[482] Powers of Criminal Courts (Sentencing) Act 2000, s.3C; where an offence falls within s. 91 (see para. 12.9) and, following committal under this section, the Crown Court does not impose a sentence under the dangerous offender provisions, it may impose a sentence of long term detention: ibid., s. 5A

12.14 The nature of the offence is likely to be very significant in determining both whether the offender meets the risk and harm criteria and, even if so, whether a sentence under the provisions is necessary (given that there is now wide discretion).

Since a young offender should normally be dealt with in a youth court, where a young person charged with a specified offence would not otherwise be committed or sent to the Crown Court for trial, generally it is preferable for the decision whether to commit under these provisions to be made after conviction.[483]

(v) Jointly charged with an adult

12.15 A further exception to the presumption in favour of summary trial arises where a young person is charged jointly with a person aged 18 or over; if the court considers it necessary to commit them both for trial it will have the power to commit the young person to the Crown Court for trial.[484]

12.16 Any presumption in favour of sending a youth to the Crown Court to be tried jointly with an adult must be balanced with the general presumption that young offenders should be dealt with in a youth court.

12.17 When deciding whether to separate the youth and adult defendants, a court must consider:

- the young age of the offender, particularly where the age gap between the adult and youth is substantial,
- the immaturity and intellect of the youth,
- the relative culpability of the youth compared with the adult and whether or not the role played by the youth was minor, and
- any lack of previous convictions on the part of the youth compared with the adult offender.

12.18 A very significant factor will be whether the trial of the adult and youth could be severed without inconvenience to witnesses or injustice to the case as a whole, including whether there are benefits in the same tribunal sentencing all offenders. In most circumstances, a single trial of all issues is likely to be most in the interests of justice.

(vi) Remittal from the Crown Court

12.19 Where a young person is convicted before the Crown Court of an offence other than homicide, there is an obligation to remit the young person to a youth court for sentence unless that is 'undesirable'.[485] In considering whether remittal is 'undesirable', a court should balance the need for expertise in the sentencing of young offenders with the benefits of sentence being imposed by the court which had determined guilt.

12.20 Particular attention should be given to the presumption where a young person appears before the Crown Court only because he or she is jointly charged with an adult offender. A referral order is not available in the Crown Court for a first-time offender and such orders may now be made following a second conviction in certain circumstances.

PART 19 CORPORATE MANSLAUGHTER AND HEALTH AND SAFETY OFFENCES CAUSING DEATH SG-419

Definitive Guideline

Foreword

. . .This guideline applies to the sentencing of organisations on or after **15 February 2010**.

This is the first offence guideline relating to sentencing organisations rather than individuals, and concerns sentencing for offences where the most serious form of harm was caused, the death of one or more persons.

The guideline takes a different form from that used for most other offences. It sets out the key principles relevant to assessing the seriousness of the range of offences covered which may involve a wide variation in culpability. Principles concerning the assessment of financial penalties are also provided and consideration is given to the additional powers available to a court imposing sentence for these offences.

[483] See, for example, the statement that there is a strong presumption against sending young offenders to the Crown Court unless clearly required: *R(W) v Southampton Youth Court* [2002] EWHC 1640 per Lord Woolf CJ

[484] The procedures around the transfer to the Crown Court of a young person charged with an offence will change on the implementation of the relevant provisions in the Criminal Justice Act 2003, sched. 3

[485] Powers of Criminal Courts (Sentencing) Act 2000, s. 8(2)

Corporate Manslaughter and Health and Safety Offences Causing Death

SG-420 **A. Elements of the offences**

1. Corporate manslaughter is created by the Corporate Manslaughter and Corporate Homicide Act 2007 (CMCHA). The offence:
   (a) can be committed only by organisations and not by individuals. The organisations which can commit the offence are exhaustively defined by section 1(2) and Schedule 1;
   (b) has as its root element *a breach of a duty of care* under the law of negligence (s. 2(1));
   (c) requires that the breach be a *gross* breach, that is to say one where the conduct falls *far below* what can reasonably be expected of the organisation (s.1(4));
   (d) further requires that a substantial element in the breach is the way in which the organisation's activities are managed or organised by its *senior management* (s.1(3));
   (e) is committed only where death is shown to have been caused by the gross breach of duty (s.1(1)(a)).

   An obligation is imposed upon the prosecution to prove each of these elements to the criminal standard.
2. Health and safety offences, typically (but not exclusively) those contrary to sections 2 and 3 of the Health and Safety at Work Act 1974 (HSWA):
   (a) can be committed by both organisations and individuals; **this guideline relates only to organisations;**
   (b) do not depend on the law of negligence; the root element is a breach of a duty to *ensure* the health and safety of other persons, or absence of risk to them, whether employees or members of the public affected by the activity of the defendant;
   (c) once an absence of safety, or at least a risk to the health or safety of others, is proved by the prosecution, involve a statutory reverse burden of proof placed upon the defendant to show that it was *not* reasonably practicable to do more than was done to comply with the duty;
   (d) do not involve the proof of any particular injury or consequence; whilst prosecutions will very often ensue where there has been injury or death, the offence does not require proof that that injury or death was caused by the breach; this may well be in dispute even if a breach is proved or admitted;
   (e) thus embrace a very wide spread of culpability from the minimal to the very grave.
3. Where death occurs, there may therefore be a significant overlap between the offences, and it is to be expected that some cases will be prosecuted in the alternative despite the increased complexity that that will entail for a jury.
4. However, there are considerable differences between the two offences:
   (a) because corporate manslaughter involves both a *gross* breach of duty of care and senior management failings as a substantial element in that breach, those cases will generally involve systemic failures; by contrast health and safety offences are committed whenever the defendant cannot show that it was not reasonably practicable to avoid a risk of injury or lack of safety; that may mean that the failing is at an operational rather than systemic level and can mean in some cases that there has been only a very limited falling below the standard of reasonable practicability;
   (b) in corporate manslaughter the burden of proof remains on the prosecution throughout; in particular this will ordinarily involve the prosecution identifying the acts or omissions which it relies upon as constituting the breach, and then proving them; by contrast, in a prosecution for a health and safety offence the prosecutor need only prove that there has been a failure to ensure safety or absence of risk, which it may often be able to do simply by pointing to the injury; once it has done so the burden of proof shifts to the defendant; the prosecution need not identify the precautions which it says ought to have been taken, nor need it prove how the accident happened;[486] usually however it will do so;
   (c) in corporate manslaughter the prosecution must prove that the breach was a significant (but not necessarily *the only*) cause of death; by contrast health and safety offences can be proved without demonstrating that any injury was caused by the failure to ensure safety; **this guideline is for cases where it is proved that the offence was a significant cause of death, not simply that death occurred.**

[486] *Chargot* [2008] UKHL 73 at paragraph 30, *Electric Gate Services Ltd* [2009] EWCA Crim 1942

B. Factors likely to affect seriousness SG-421

5. This guideline applies only to corporate manslaughter and to those health and safety offences where the offence is shown to have been a significant cause of the death. By definition, the harm involved is very serious.
6. Beyond that, the possible range of factors affecting the seriousness of the offence will be very wide indeed. Seriousness should ordinarily be assessed **first** by asking:
   (a) **How foreseeable was serious injury?**
   The more foreseeable it was, the graver usually will be the offence.
   (b) **How far short of the applicable standard did the defendant fall?**
   (c) **How common is this kind of breach in this organisation?**
   How widespread was the non-compliance? Was it isolated in extent or indicative of a systematic departure from good practice across the defendant's operations?
   (d) **How far up the organisation does the breach go?**
   Usually, the higher up the responsibility for the breach, the more serious the offence.[487]
7. In addition, other factors are likely, if present, to aggravate the offence (the list is not exhaustive):
   (a) **more than one death, or very grave personal injury in addition to death;**
   (b) **failure to heed warnings or advice, whether from officials such as the Inspectorate, or by employees (especially health and safety representatives) or other persons, or to respond appropriately to 'near misses' arising in similar circumstances;**
   (c) **cost-cutting at the expense of safety;**
   (d) **deliberate failure to obtain or comply with relevant licences, at least where the process of licensing involves some degree of control, assessment or observation by independent authorities with a health and safety responsibility;**
   (e) **injury to vulnerable persons.**
   In this context, vulnerable persons would include those whose personal circumstances make them susceptible to exploitation.
8. Conversely, the following factors, which are similarly non-exhaustive, are likely, if present, to afford mitigation:
   (a) **a prompt acceptance of responsibility;**
   (b) **a high level of co-operation with the investigation, beyond that which will always be expected;**
   (c) **genuine efforts to remedy the defect;**
   (d) **a good health and safety record;**
   (e) **a responsible attitude to health and safety, such as the commissioning of expert advice or the consultation of employees or others affected by the organisation's activities.**
9. Since corporate manslaughter requires proof of gross breach of duty and the substantial involvement of senior management, it is unlikely that the unauthorised act of an employee will significantly reduce the culpability of the defendant in that offence.
10. Commission of a health and safety offence may in some cases be established solely by the unauthorised act of an employee. In such a case the responsibility of the organisation must be assessed, for example for inadequate supervision or training. There may be some cases where there is very little culpability in the organisation itself.
11. It will generally be appropriate to require the prosecution to set out in writing the facts of the case relied upon and any aggravating or mitigating features which it identifies;[488] the defence may conveniently be required similarly to set out in writing any points on which it differs. If sentence is to proceed upon agreed facts, they should be set out in writing.[489]

C. Financial information; size and nature of organisation SG-422

12. The law must expect the same standard of behaviour from a large and a small organisation. Smallness does not by itself mitigate, and largeness does not by itself aggravate, these offences. Size may affect the approach to safety, whether because a small organisation is careless or because a large one is bureaucratic, but these considerations affect the seriousness of the offence via the assessment set out in paragraphs 6–8 above, rather than demonstrating a direct correlation between size and culpability.

[487] For corporate manslaughter the involvement of senior management is a necessary element in the offence

[488] In accordance with the Attorney General's guidelines on the acceptance of pleas and the prosecutor's role in the sentencing exercise, published November 2009

[489] see *Friskies Petcare (UK) Ltd* [2000] EWCA Crim 95; [2000] 2 Cr App Rep (S) 401

13. A large organisation may be more at risk of committing an offence than a small one simply because it conducts very many more operations. Some large corporate groups operate as a single company whereas others are structured as separate companies for separate operations. A large organisation may be operating upon a budget as tight (or tighter) than a small one because of the demands placed upon it—large local authorities, hospital trusts or police forces may be examples, but so might commercial companies with large turnover but small profit margins. However, in some instances, a large organisation may have less excuse for not dealing properly with matters affecting health and safety, since it may have greater access to expertise, advice and training resources, whether in-house or otherwise.
14. Size is, however, relevant. The means of any defendant are relevant to a fine, which is the principal available penalty for organisations. The court should require information about the financial circumstances of the defendant before it. The best practice will usually be to call for the relevant information for a three year period including the year of the offence, so as to avoid any risk of atypical figures in a single year.
15. **A fixed correlation between the fine and either turnover or profit is not appropriate.** The circumstances of defendant organisations and the financial consequences of the fine will vary too much; similar offences committed by companies structured in differing ways ought not to attract fines which are vastly different; a fixed correlation might provide a perverse incentive to manipulation of corporate structure.
16. The court should, however, look carefully at both turnover and profit, and also at assets, in order to gauge the resources of the defendant. When taking account of financial circumstances, statute[490] provides for that to either increase or decrease the amount of the fine and it is just that a wealthy defendant should pay a larger fine than a poor one; whilst a fine is intended to inflict painful punishment, it should be one which the defendant is capable of paying, if appropriate over a period which may be up to a number of years.
17. **Annex A** sets out the kind of financial information with which, in the ordinary way, a court should expect to be provided in relation to a defendant. The primary obligation to provide it lies on the defendant. As a matter of practice it would be helpful if the prosecution takes the preliminary step of calling upon the defendant to provide it to the court and prosecution and, if the defendant does not do so, of assembling what can be obtained from public records and furnishing that to the court. If a defendant fails to provide relevant information, the court is justified in making adverse assumptions as to its means, and may be obliged to do so.
18. It will not ordinarily be necessary for the prosecution to embark upon analysis of the figures, as distinct from ensuring that the raw material is available to the court, and it may not in any event normally have the expertise to do so. In a few complex cases of relevant dispute the prosecution can if genuinely necessary undertake such analysis either in-house or by the instruction of an accountant and if it can justify the expense as part of its necessary costs those costs will ordinarily be recoverable from the defendant.[491]
19. In assessing the financial consequences of a fine, the court should consider (inter alia) the following factors:
    (i) **the effect on the employment of the innocent may be relevant;**
    (ii) **any effect upon shareholders will, however, not normally be relevant; those who invest in and finance a company take the risk that its management will result in financial loss;**
    (iii) **the effect on directors will not, likewise, normally be relevant;**
    (iv) **nor would it ordinarily be relevant that the prices charged by the defendant might in consequence be raised, at least unless the defendant is a monopoly supplier of public services;**
    (v) **the effect upon the provision of services to the public will be relevant; although a public organisation such as a local authority, hospital trust or police force must be treated the same as a commercial company where the standards of behaviour to be expected are concerned, and must suffer a punitive fine for breach of them, a different approach to determining the level of fine may well be justified;**

    'The Judge has to consider how any financial penalty will be paid. If a very substantial financial penalty will inhibit the proper performance by a statutory body of the public function that it has been set up to perform, that is not something to be disregarded.'[492]

    The same considerations will be likely to apply to non-statutory bodies or charities if providing public services.

[490] Criminal Justice Act 2003, ss.164(1) and 164(4)
[491] Criminal Justice Act 2003, s.164(5)(b)(iii)
[492] *Milford Haven Port Authority* [2000] 2 Cr App R(S) 423 per Lord Bingham CJ at 433–4*Sentencing*

(vi) **the liability to pay civil compensation will ordinarily not be relevant; normally this will be provided by insurance or the resources of the defendant will be large enough to meet it from its own resources (for compensation generally see paragraphs 27–28 below);**
(vii) **the cost of meeting any remedial order will not ordinarily be relevant, except to the overall financial position of the defendant; such an order requires no more than should already have been done;**
(viii) **whether the fine will have the effect of putting the defendant out of business will be relevant; in some bad cases this may be an acceptable consequence.**

20. In the case of a large organisation the fine should be payable within twenty eight days. In the case of a smaller or financially stretched organisation, it is permissible to require payment to be spread over a much longer period. There is no limitation to payment within twelve months, but the first payment should be required within a short time of sentencing. An extended period for the payment of further instalments may be particularly appropriate for an organisation of limited means which has committed a serious offence, and where it is undesirable that the fine should cause it to be put out of business.
21. In some cases it may be apparent that a broadly quantifiable saving has been made by the defendant by committing the offence. In such cases it will normally be the proper approach to ensure that the fine removes the profit and imposes an appropriate additional penalty.

D. Level of fines SG-423

22. There will inevitably be a broad range of fines because of the range of seriousness involved and the differences in the circumstances of the defendants. Fines must be punitive and sufficient to have an impact on the defendant.
23. Fines cannot and do not attempt to value a human life in money. Civil compensation will be payable separately. The fine is designed to punish the defendant and is therefore tailored not only to what it has done but also to its individual circumstances.
24. The offence of corporate manslaughter, because it requires gross breach at a senior level, will ordinarily involve a level of seriousness significantly greater than a health and safety offence. The appropriate fine will seldom be less than **£500,000** and may be measured in **millions of pounds.**[493]
25. The range of seriousness involved in health and safety offences is greater than for corporate manslaughter. However, where the offence is shown to have caused death, the appropriate fine will seldom be **less than £100,000** and may be measured in **hundreds of thousands of pounds or more.**
26. A plea of guilty should be recognised by the appropriate reduction.

E. Compensation SG-424

27. The assessment of compensation in cases of death will usually be complex, will involve payment of sums well beyond the powers of a criminal court, and will ordinarily be covered by insurance.
28. In the great majority of cases the court should conclude that compensation should be dealt with in a civil court, and should say that no order is made for that reason.[494] There may be occasional cases, for example if the defendant is uninsured and payment may not otherwise be made, when consideration should be given to a compensation order in respect of bereavement and/or funeral expenses.[495]

F. Costs SG-425

29. The defendant ought ordinarily (subject to means) to be ordered to pay the properly incurred costs of the prosecution.

G. Publicity Orders SG-426

30. Publicity Orders are available in the case of corporate manslaughter only.[496] They may require publication in a specified manner of:
    (a) the fact of conviction;
    (b) specified particulars of the offence;
    (c) the amount of any fine;
    (d) the terms of any remedial order.
31. Such an order should ordinarily be imposed in a case of corporate manslaughter. The object is deterrence and punishment.

Sentencing Guidelines

[493] Observations in *Friskies Petcare (UK) Ltd* [2000] EWCA Crim 95; [2000] 2 Cr App Rep (S) 401 notwithstanding, it is no longer the case that fines of £500,000 are reserved for major public disasters
[494] Powers of Criminal Courts Act 2000, s.130(3)
[495] Under Powers of Criminal Courts Act 2000, s.130(9) and (10)
[496] Corporate Manslaughter and Corporate Homicide Act 2007, s. 10

(i) The order should specify with particularity the matters to be published in accordance with section 10(1). Especial care should be taken with the terms of the particulars of the offence committed.

(ii) The order should normally specify the place where public announcement is to be made, and consideration should be given to indicating the size of any notice or advertisement required. It should ordinarily contain a provision designed to ensure that the conviction becomes known to shareholders in the case of companies and local people in the case of public bodies. Consideration should be given to requiring a statement on the defendant's website. A newspaper announcement may be unnecessary if the proceedings are certain to receive news coverage in any event, but if an order requires publication in a newspaper it should specify the paper, the form of announcement to be made and the number of insertions required.

(iii) The prosecution should provide the court in advance of the sentencing hearing, and should serve on the defendant, a draft of the form of order suggested and the judge should personally endorse the final form of the order.

(iv) Consideration should be given to stipulating in the order that any comment placed by the defendant alongside the required announcement should be separated from it and clearly identified as such.

32. A publicity order is part of the penalty. Any exceptional cost of compliance should be considered in fixing the fine. It is not, however, necessary to fix the fine first and then deduct the cost of compliance.

SG-427 **H. Remedial Orders**

33. A remedial order is available both for corporate manslaughter[497] and HSWA offences.[498]

34. A defendant ought by the time of sentencing to have remedied any specific failings involved in the offence and if it has not will be deprived of significant mitigation.

35. If, however, it has not, a remedial order should be considered if it can be made sufficiently specific to be enforceable. The prosecution is required by section 9(2) CMCHA to give notice of the form of any such order sought, which can only be made on its application; although there is no equivalent stipulation in the HSWA it is good practice to require the same notice. The Judge should personally endorse the final form of such an order.

36. The cost of compliance with such an order should not ordinarily be taken into account in fixing the fine; the order requires only what should already have been done.

SG-428 **I. Summary of approach to sentence**

37. The normal approach to sentence should therefore be (in outline):

(1) consider the questions at paragraph 6;
(2) identify any particular aggravating or mitigating circumstances (paragraphs 7–11);
(3) consider the nature, financial organisation and resources of the defendant (paragraphs 12–18);
(4) consider the consequences of a fine (paragraphs 19–21);
(5) consider compensation (but see paragraphs 27–28);
(6) assess the fine in the light of the foregoing and all the circumstances of the case;
(7) reduce as appropriate for any plea of guilty;
(8) consider costs;
(9) consider publicity order;
(10) consider remedial order.

SG-429 **Annex A: Financial information expected to be provided to the court**

1. *For companies*: published audited accounts. Particular attention should be paid to (a) turnover, (b) profit before tax, (c) directors' remuneration, loan accounts and pension provision, (d) assets as disclosed by the balance sheet (note that they may be valued at cost of acquisition which may not be the same as current value). Most companies are required to lodge accounts at Companies House. Failure to produce relevant recent accounts on request may properly lead to the conclusion that the company can pay any appropriate fine.

2. *For partnerships*: annual audited accounts. Particular attention should be paid to (a) turnover, (b) profit before tax, (c) partner's drawings, loan accounts and pension provision, (d) assets as above. If accounts are not produced on request, see paragraph 1.

3. *For local authorities, police and fire authorities and similar public bodies*: the Annual Revenue Budget ('ARB') is the equivalent of turnover and the best indication of the size of the defendant organisation.

[497] Corporate Manslaughter and Corporate Homicide Act 2007, s. 9

[498] Health and Safety at Work Act 1974, s. 42

It is published on www.local.communities.gov.uk/finance/bellwin.HTM. It is unlikely to be necessary to analyse specific expenditure or reserves unless inappropriate or grandiose expenditure is suggested. Such authorities also have attributed to them a 'Bellwin factor' which represents the level of exceptional and unforeseen expenditure that they are expected by central Government to meet themselves in any one year without any claim to recourse to central funds. But since that is arithmetically related to the ARB (currently 0.2%) it will ordinarily add little of significance beyond an indication of budgetary discipline.

4. *For health trusts*: the independent regulator of NHS Foundation Trusts is Monitor. It publishes quarterly reports and annual figures for the financial strength and stability of trusts from which the annual income can be seen, available via www.monitor-nhsft.gov.uk/home/our-publications. Detailed analysis of expenditure or reserves is unlikely to be called for.
   Note that Monitor has significant regulatory powers including over membership of the boards of directors or governors.
5. *For 'third sector' organisations*: it will be appropriate to inspect annual audited accounts. Detailed analysis of expenditure or reserves is unlikely to be called for unless there is a suggestion of unusual or unnecessary expenditure.

Index